FISHER'S TECHNIQUES OF
CRIME SCENE
INVESTIGATION
FIRST INTERNATIONAL
EDITION

FISHER'S TECHNIQUES OF
CRIME SCENE INVESTIGATION
FIRST INTERNATIONAL EDITION

William J. Tilstone
Michael L. Hastrup
Camilla Hald

CRC Press
Taylor & Francis Group
Boca Raton   London   New York

CRC Press is an imprint of the
Taylor & Francis Group, an **informa** business

CRC Press
Taylor & Francis Group
6000 Broken Sound Parkway NW, Suite 300
Boca Raton, FL 33487-2742

Printed and bound in India by Replika Press Pvt. Ltd.
Version Date: 20120706

International Standard Book Number: 978-1-4398-1704-9 (Hardback)

Visit the Taylor & Francis Web site at
http://www.taylorandfrancis.com

and the CRC Press Web site at
http://www.crcpress.com

Table of Contents

Part I
THE FORENSIC PROCESS, PRINCIPLES, AND PRACTICE

3   The Forensic Process   39

4 Practical Scene Investigation 89

5 Practitioner Competency, Professionalism, and Codes of Conduct 111

Part II

FORMS OF EVIDENCE, IDENTIFICATION, AND RECOVERY

Part III

SCENE INVESTIGATION AND TYPE OF CRIME

13   Investigating Sexual Assault   **341**

14   Burglary Investigation   **357**

Prologue

Barry Fisher's *Techniques of Crime Scene Investigation* is used as a reference work by students of crime scene investigation, police investigators, crime scene technicians, attorneys, and even crime laboratory scientists. Its strengths lie in the broad experience of its author, who has had an illustrious career in forensic science spanning more than 40 years, and the data that he could draw on from time spent serving as Director of the Los Angeles County Sheriff's Department laboratory and from his network of friends and colleagues. Inevitably, given its current authorship, the work is focused on practices and approaches that are generally accepted within the United States. Barry and the publishers decided that it was time to prepare a companion work more attuned to non-US users and invited us to write what we came to refer to affectionately as "the rest of the world edition."

In accepting the invitation, we were to some extent looking backward to earlier times rather than forward to new horizons. The original *Techniques of Crime Scene Investigation* was a Swedish book first published in 1949, written by Chief Superintendent Arne Svensson and Superintendent Otto Wendell (see Figure P.1) from the Criminal Investigation Department of the Swedish police in Stockholm. An American edition was published in 1965, and Barry took over authorship with the third edition in 1981. It is most appropriate, then, that two of the authors of this new version work for a law enforcement department in Scandinavia, albeit in Copenhagen, Denmark, and not Stockholm, Sweden.

Writing a companion volume to any successful work is a challenge. Where to begin? Should we simply take the text of the revised 8th edition and write it in international English, replacing technical words such as "evidence" with the equivalent terms used in Europe and Australasia—"exhibits," in this instance—reversing the process used in 1965? Perhaps not.

Figure P.1 Arne Svensson (left) and Otto Wendell (right). (Photographs courtesy of the Swedish National Laboratory of Forensic Science, Linkoping.)

There is a saying, widely but incorrectly attributed to Winston Churchill or George Bernard Shaw, that "America and Britain are two nations divided by a common language." No written work of either author contains that quotation. The likely source dates back to 1882, when Oscar Wilde wrote in his short story "The Canterville Ghost": "We really have everything in common with America nowadays except, of course, language." However, attributing this quote to Churchill or Shaw makes a point of relevance as to why there should be a rest-of-the-world edition of Fisher's *Techniques of Crime Scene Investigation*. Not only can the same word have a different meaning in different countries, but the whole cultural framework of America also has differences from Britain that are hidden by a more or less common language and a degree of familiarisation through products of the entertainment industry.

In many ways, there is much more commonality between Britain and Europe, despite the significant language differences. The European Network of Forensic Science Institutes (ENFSI) has addressed the language issue with its Multilingua project, which provides a multi-language thesaurus of forensic terms (available online at http://www.ies.krakow.pl/multilingua/welcome/). The cultural divide between Europe and the United States is probably best illustrated by gun ownership and control. Guns are certainly used in criminal acts in Europe, but to a much smaller extent than in the United States, and European forensic science laboratories do not have the ubiquitous and large firearms sections found in the vast majority of American crime laboratories. And, of course, "crime laboratory" and "forensic science laboratory" provide another example of the language division. Forensic science in Australia and New Zealand falls somewhere in the middle of the spectrum. The language is more similar to that of Britain, but the federal structure of government in Australia lends some similarities to the US cultural environment.

Perhaps inevitably, we ended up concluding that a companion edition that was simply a translation of the parent would not work. This edition is therefore a little different from the American one, but we have tried to maintain direct links wherever we can. The similarities and differences are explained in the following section, which describes the book structure and goals.

Book Structure and Goals

As is the case with earlier US editions of *Techniques of Crime Scene Investigation*, this version is divided into three parts. Part I is entirely new and deals with the forensic process, principles, and practice. Part II (Forms of Evidence, Identification, and Recovery) and Part III (Scene Investigation and Type of Crime) share much of what can be found in the 8th edition, but they have been edited to be more appropriate outside of the United States.

There is no simple way to write about techniques of crime scene investigation because the crime scene is an intrinsically complex or even on occasion chaotic entity. The partition of the book into parts is a way to address the fact that crime scene investigation is an extremely contextually defined process. Addressing what happened, where it happened, who was involved, when it happened, how it happened, and—often overlooked but vital—why it happened shapes the investigation. These questions and their possible answers will determine the procedures used, the number and nature of specialisation of scene investigators, and the interactions with police investigators and lawyers. Their contextual answers create the difference between a simple "observe and collect" exercise, where a relatively untrained officer can complete the examination, and a highly complex one, requiring a considerable depth and breadth of knowledge of crime scene examination and cooperation with others in the investigation and analysis of forensic evidence.

The book structure emphasises the different dimensions of knowledge required by crime scene investigators to perform their job professionally. The broadness of these dimensions is also expressed in the span of the authors' educational and experiential backgrounds as we address the basic principles of science and the structure of inquiry. We do within the context of the investigation of crimes and scenes of crime, together with how technological advances have made it possible to identify new and more informative types of evidence, but always tempered by the practical knowledge and experience of the investigation of different types of scenes. The crime scene investigator, in turn, has to understand the principles and their applications to the practice of crime scene investigation and must be able to use professional judgements about how to address different forms of crime scenes. Just as importantly, the crime scene investigator must be able to adapt methods and procedures to the particular contexts presented within each new crime scene.

Another structuring principle that has determined the partition of this book into the three parts is the acknowledgement that there are many ways in which to logically describe and discuss the essentials of crime scene investigation. We therefore address scene investigation from three consecutive perspectives: from the perspective that scene investigation is a subdiscipline of forensic science which translates into the particular principles for practice, which is described in Part I; from the perspective that scene investigation is about identifying and recovering different forms of evidence, each with its own methods for identification, recovery, and analysis (Part II); and from the perspective that scene investigation is ultimately about describing the content, location, modus operandi, sequence of events, identity of persons involved, time frame, and motive or cause for different types of crime (Part III).

Part I departs the most from Fisher's 8th edition, not least by introducing a focus on the basic principles of forensic science and evidence rather than providing a narrative of illustrative examples. Chapter 1 gives a brief introduction to the philosophy of science, mainly so that the investigators understand the significance of the scientific method and where their work lies on the continuum from police investigator to highly specialised laboratory scientist. Chapter 1 then goes on to consider what is meant by evidence and how scene investigation applies the scientific method to the identification and interpretation of evidence. It closes with a brief introduction to using what we have termed the 6Ws—namely, WHAT, WHERE, HOW, WHO, WHEN, and WHY—to give an objective structure to the science of scene investigation.

Chapter 2 deals with the principles of the forensic process and introduces the *investigative star* as a tool for using the 6Ws throughout an investigation. The chapter shows how the star guides an iterative question-and-answer process, which leads to establishing identity and location, motive, the time frame of the incident, the sequence of events and modus operandi, and the content of the crime. Chapter 3 describes the forensic process in detail. It covers the activities from the first call notifying the police of an incident, the first response to the notification, and planning and conducting the scene examination to the interpretation and reporting of findings. Chapter 4 illustrates the forensic process and the investigative star in action, with a detailed account of a real case involving the investigation of a dead body found concealed in the woods. Part I closes with consideration of general codes of conduct, ethics, professionalism, and principles of best practice in Chapter 5.

Part II is intended to give some structure to dealing with the complexity and chaos of the scene by using the concepts of evidence as a guiding principle for the exposition of the techniques of scene investigation. As shown in Part I, scene investigation is essentially the first stage of a hunt for objective information that can be used as evidence in order to direct the investigation and any legal hearing that may result. Evidence can be defined and categorised in many ways, but much of it is directed to identification of people or objects. The chapters in Part II illustrate how crime scene investigation contributes to identification of people, through fingerprints and DNA, and of physical materials, including trace evidence, toolmarks, firearms, arson and explosive agents, and drugs and toxicology.

Part III takes up the baton from the concept of the investigative star and uses the 6Ws as an iterative process to identify, examine, and answer the critical questions introduced in Chapter 2 by addressing how different types of crime produce scenes and evidence in different ways. No two scenes are ever the same, and no two investigations pose the same requirements. There will always be contextual information and investigative demands that decide how a particular scene ought to be investigated; however, using the principles and procedures for practice presented in Part I requires that scene investigators have some knowledge of how different crimes produce different forms of evidence to be able to put the principles to proper use. Providing this knowledge is the goal of Part III.

In other words, Part III is concerned with different types of crime, the different forms of evidence that they typically produce, and how to identify them with respect to describing the content of the crime. An important aspect of the knowledge base of the scene investigator is experience with different forms of crime and the scenes they produce. The chapters in Part III deal with types of crime under the headings of sexual assault and domestic abuse, burglary, motor vehicles, and homicide. These are by no means the only crimes that a crime scene investigator will work on, but they represent the main types of volume crime and major crime that will typically be encountered.

An entirely new appendix addresses digital evidence. This is a very modern topic and one that will probably come to occupy a dominant role in forensic investigations due to the widespread applications of surveillance CCTV, the mushrooming of not only basic mobile phones but also their smartphone variants, and the widespread replacement of paper as a medium for making records and disseminating information and news. The actual recovery of digital information is a highly specialised field, and the role of the crime scene investigator in this area is one of identifying, preserving, and collecting, and not one of examination.

Finally, throughout the work we have tried not to let our attention be diverted from the most basic principle, that of the absolute need to protect the scene and the evidence in it, perhaps best captured in the words of Sherlock Holmes:

> Oh, how simple it would all have been had I been here before they came like a herd of buffalo and wallowed all over it.
>
> **—A. Conan Doyle ("The Boscombe Valley Mystery")**

Enjoy!

Acknowledgements

Preparing *Fisher's Techniques of Crime Scene Investigations First International Edition* presented us with many challenges and opportunities. Foremost was how to write something that was recognizable as an extension of Barry Fisher's original but yet had its own distinct identity. We believe that we have achieved that by taking a completely different approach to Part I of the book, Chapters 1 through 5, which sets the scene for what follows. Although much of the material is based on European and Australasian norms and perspectives, we hope that our colleagues in the United States will find it of interest, especially in dealing with challenges to whether crime scene examination and related forensic investigations have a basis in science, and in the use of the investigative star tool to guide the planning and execution of the investigation of a crime scene.

Part II, Chapters 6 through 12, deals with specific techniques, and Part III, Chapters 13 through 16, with their application in the investigation of various types of crime. The consistency of these with the originals should be obvious, but their presentation does reflect the many differences not only in language but also in approach that are found in non-American jurisdictions. Finally, we have dealt with the relatively modern but rapidly growing topic of digital evidence as an Appendix, emphasizing that the investigation itself is a highly specialised topic and the main role of the crime scene examiner is to identify and preserve potential evidence—but then, is that not always the case?

The cases presented in Parts II and III are very much those to be found in the 8th edition of the original text, and we join Barry and David in expressing our appreciation to the contributors, whose names are listed in no particular order:

S.C. Leung, former head of Forensic Science Division of the Government Laboratory, Hong Kong, China; Roger Kahn, PhD, Forensic Biology Director, Harris County Medical Examiner's Office, Houston, TX; Andrew Singer, Product Manager, Bode Technology, Lorton, VA; Michael Lyford, Sergeant, Washoe County Sheriff's Office, Forensic Science Division, Reno, NV; Christophe Champod, PhD, Professor, School of Criminal Sciences, Institute of Forensic Science, University of Lausanne, Switzerland; Staff Inspector Richard P. Nuzzo, Division Headquarters, New York State Police, Albany, NY; Mike Havstad, Supervising Photographer, Scientific Services Bureau, Los Angeles County Sheriff's Department; Frederic A. Tulleners, Director, Forensic Science Graduate Program, University of California, Davis, CA; Steve Nash, Manager of Business Development and Customer Relations, Cogent Systems, Petaluma, CA; Joseph Almog, PhD, Professor, The Hebrew University, Casali Institute of Applied Chemistry, Jerusalem, Israel; Antonio A. Cantu, PhD, forensic scientist (retired), US Secret Service, Washington, DC; Anna Barbaro, PhD, Chief of Forensic Genetics Department, Office of Medical and Forensic Investigations, Messina, Italy; Angela L. Williamson, PhD, Director of Forensic Casework and Assistant Vice President, Bode Technology, Lorton, VA; Senior Criminalists Manuel Munoz, David Vidal, and Deputy Dale Falicon (retired), Scientific Services Bureau, Los Angeles County Sheriff's Department; Lisa Jackson, Forensic Supervisor, Santa Monica

Police Department, Santa Monica, CA; Melissa Simons, Forensic Scientist, Oregon State Police, Central Point, OR; Jeffrey C. Kercheval, Supervising Forensic Scientist, Western Maryland Regional Crime Laboratory, Hagerstown Police Department, Hagertown, MD; Suzanne L. Noffsinger, Trace Evidence, Miami Valley Regional Crime Laboratory, Dayton, OH; Diana Faugno, Forensic Registered Nurse Consultant, San Diego, CA; Jay Jarvis, Alliance Forensics Laboratory, Inc., Ft. Worth, TX; General Jacques Hebrard and Yves Schuliar, MD, PhD, IRCGN (Institute of Criminal Research of the National Gendarmerie), France; William J. Bodziak, Bodziak Forensics, Palm Coast, FL; Tony Grissim, Public Safety & Forensic Account Manager, Leica Geosystems Inc.; Ray A. Wickenheiser, Laboratory Director, Montgomery County Crime Laboratory, Rockville, MD; Peter Diaczuk, John Jay College of Criminal Justice; Wendy van Hilst, Senior Forensic Investigator, Forensische Opsporing Amsterdam–Amstelland, Amsterdam, Holland; Dan Cheswick, Suffolk County Crime Laboratory, Suffolk County, NY; Lucian C. Haag, Forensic Science Services, Inc., Carefree, AZ; and C.M. Bowers, DDS, JD, Ventura, California.

We are especially grateful to the Copenhagen Police for permission to reproduce the photographs in Chapter 4.

We also wish to thank our editor Becky Masterman and project coordinator Jill Jurgensen, who were patient with us in making this edition a reality. We appreciate your kindness.

Our last but most important acknowledgement is to Barry and David Fisher, who encouraged the creation of this version of what is now known as Fisher's *Techniques of Crime Scene Investigation* and allowed us to use so much of the material that they prepared for the 8th edition of the book.

About the Authors

William (Bill) Tilstone has a BSc and PhD from the University of Glasgow. He spent seven years as a lecturer in the university's Department of Pathological Biochemistry, where his research on drug kinetics in overdose and on the biochemistry of the body's responses to major trauma led to his introduction to forensic science. He was a lecturer in forensic science at the University of Strathclyde, also in Glasgow, where he worked for 12 years and served as professor and head of the Forensic Science Unit for six years. While at Strathclyde, he was actively involved in casework, mainly in forensic biology for the public prosecutor and in toxicology for the defence.

Bill left his academic position to become the first director of the newly established Forensic Science Centre in South Australia, a position he held until 1996, when he accepted the position of executive director of the National Forensic Science Technology Center (NFSTC) in Florida. This history has given Bill a unique blend of experiences in forensic science, including practical casework, teaching, research, as well as executive management in academia, government, and private business, covering three different countries. Bill has contributed more than 100 papers and reviews to the literature and two books in addition to the present work.

Bill retired from the NFSTC in 2007 and now lives in rural Perthshire, Scotland, with his wife, Angela. They have a daughter, who is married and lives in Australia, and a son, who is married and lives in the United States, so they spend much of their time travelling. Although retired from permanent employment, Bill is the quality manager and assessor for an American forensic accrediting body and has also maintained his academic links in Scotland.

Michael Hastrup began his investigation career in 1984 when he was employed as a police officer with the Danish National Police. He has broad experience within police work, starting as a patrol officer followed by employment as a detective inspector before joining the National Centre of Forensic Services after nine years of service. He worked as a fingerprint examiner before moving to the Scene of Crime Section in Copenhagen, where he began his career as a crime scene investigator which continued until 2010. He now works in the Quality Management Section within the National Centre of Forensic Services.

Michael has an extensive history of training and field work in crime scene investigation. He has attended several training courses and programs, primarily in Denmark but also in Sweden and Norway. His crime scene investigation career encompasses hundreds of crime scenes covering homicide, suspicious death, suicide, rape, armed robbery, burglary, and property crime cases, not only in metropolitan Copenhagen and throughout Denmark but also in Greenland and the Faroe Islands. He has also conducted crime scene investigative work at major incidents such as train and airplane crashes, and he has taken part in disaster victim identification in relation to mass disasters scenarios such as the tsunami catastrophe in the Southeast Asia in 2004.

Michael represents Denmark within the European Network of Forensic Science Institutes (ENFSI), where he has been an active member of the Scene of Crime Working Group since 2005 and a member of its Steering Group since 2008. He also represents the Danish National Police in the ENFSI Quality and Competence Liaison Group (QCLG). Michael is the European CSI representative within the International Laboratory Accreditation Cooperation (ILAC) Working Group 10, which is tasked with producing a globally applicable guideline for implementation of accreditation standards in the field of crime scene examination.

Michael Hastrup is 48 years old and lives in the greater Copenhagen area, Denmark, with his wife and their twin sons, who are 14 years of age.

Camilla Hald received a MSc in social anthropology and subsidiary studies in rhetorics from the University of Copenhagen in 2002, and she received her PhD in anthropology from the University of Aarhus in 2011. Her dissertation was entitled "Web without a Weaver: On the Becoming of Knowledge. A Study of Criminal Investigation in the Danish Police." Camilla has acted as a consultant for the Danish National Police and has taught criminology at the Danish Police College since 2000. She has held a tenured position with the Danish National Police Knowledge and Research Centre since 2007 and is currently employed as chief advisor in the Research and Development Unit.

As part of her dissertation research, which was a philosophical anthropological study of the production of investigative knowledge, Camilla performed extensive fieldwork and worked side by side with expert investigators, scene investigators and forensic specialists in trying to develop a methodological understanding of how crime scene investigators work. During this research, she conceived of the model of the investigative star, which was further developed as an operational tool for the Danish National Police in close cooperation with Michael Hastrup from the National Forensic Division. Camilla is currently working primarily on epistemological and methodological issues related to crime investigation—scene investigation in particular—and is actively involved in the development of police science as a distinct discipline in Denmark and Europe. She is member of the European Police College (CEPOL) Research and Science Working Group, an expert group tasked with promoting the use and development of research and science in police practice and education within the European Union.

Camilla is 37 years old and lives with her husband and their 2-year-old daughter in the greater Copenhagen area, Denmark.

The Forensic Process, Principles, and Practice

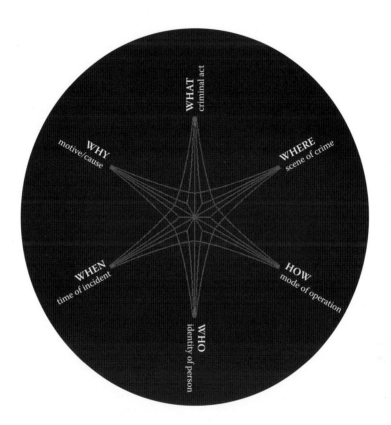

One should always look for a possible alternative and provide against it. It is the first rule of criminal investigation.

—A. Conan Doyle ("The Adventure of Black Peter")

Forensic Science and Evidence

1.1 Introduction

The American criminalist Paul Kirk's seminal monograph, *Crime Investigation*, contains this deceptively simple statement:

> All criminal investigation is concerned with people and with things. Only people commit crimes, but they invariably do so through the medium of things.

Those words are a perfect introduction to crime scene investigation, which is concerned with *things* and the stories they might tell of people, their actions, and relations. Crime scene investigation can be described as a series of activities in a process—what we here will term the *forensic process*—beginning with the detailed identification and examination of the scene of the incident and proceeding through the detection, recognition, collection, and interpretation of exhibits in order to convert the discovered things to stories and evidence.

As a discipline, crime scene investigation is part of the broader field of criminalistics, which belongs to the broader field of forensic science, which in turn is part of the much broader field of science. In this book, we are concerned with the use of forensic science in relation to criminal law, but it also applies to civil matters such as parentage testing, environmental damage, commercial and financial fraud, regulation of horse racing and gaming, authentication of art works, and other matters of fact under scrutiny by a legal or regulatory tribunal.

The term "forensic" is effectively synonymous with "of legal relevance" or "related to courts." The word originates from the Latin adjective *forensis*, meaning "of or before the forum." In Roman times, a criminal charge meant presenting the case before a group of public individuals in the forum. Both the person accused of the crime and the accuser would give speeches presenting their side of the story. The individual with the best argument and delivery would succeed. Today, the modern usage of the word *forensic* denotes a form of legal evidence (i.e., *forensic evidence*) and serves as a short representation of *forensic science*—that is, science related to and of relevance to courts (i.e., *forensics*).

Understanding what forensic science is, and how and where the activities associated with crime scene investigation fit into forensics and indeed into science, matters directly and indirectly to the scene investigator. It matters directly because, as we shall see, crime scene investigators are expected to understand often quite advanced technology in the performance of their tasks investigating the things at the scene, and they must apply the scientific method in developing a reliable story from them. Indirectly, it matters because significant controversy has arisen around whether forensics is, in fact, a science. The latter issue may seem an abstract and primarily philosophical question to the forensic practitioner, but derivative issues have led to increasingly critical scrutiny of the authority and competence of scene investigators and indeed of forensic scientists in general.

Although the concept of science may at first glance appear self-evident, it is in reality also an object of intense philosophical as well as professional debate. Scientists cannot agree what it is, and many crime scene investigators are highly critical of their colleagues in forensic science laboratories for not being attuned to the realities of investigation and being lost in a scientific dream world without any concept of the needs of investigations.

Understanding the role of science in crime scene investigation does matter, and this chapter is devoted to the discussion of forensic science, what it is, and what it can—and cannot—do in the investigation of crime. As we attempt to unravel the meaning of forensic science and its relation to scene investigation, we shall focus on two aspects: (1) an understanding of what is meant by *science*, and (2) an exploration of Kirk's things and the stories they tell by considering the processes involved and the purpose of the activity—namely, *evidence*.

1.2   Science

1.2.1   Science as a Process to Increase Our Knowledge

Not too long ago, the need to explain "science" would have seemed too academic and abstract for a book on crime scene investigation. That is certainly not so today. A relatively recently report (NRC, 2009) on forensic science in the United States was highly critical of forensic science, in general, and aspects of crime-scene-related criminalistics such as toolmarks and fingerprints, in particular, for not being well founded in science. The United Kingdom, too, has embraced basic scientific philosophy in the evaluation of forensic evidence; for example, proposed legislation on the admissibility of expert evidence requires that a trial judge may refuse to admit expert evidence based on a hypothesis that has not been subjected to scrutiny (including experimental or other testing) or has failed to stand up to scrutiny. These debates and developments of regulatory standards and frameworks make it necessary to dwell a little on the definition of science and its philosophical heritage.

1.2.1.1   *Development of the Scientific Method*

The root of the word "science" is the Latin *scire* ("to know") and hence *scientia* ("knowledge"). Over time, science became associated not with knowledge in general, but specifically with knowledge of the natural world in which we live. Unfortunately, what is regarded as knowledge can change over time. Until the early 16th century, for example, everyone knew that the Earth was at rest in the centre of the universe. This was a natural and inevitable conclusion arising from the essentially anthropocentric form of deductive logic that prevailed at the time—namely, that having accepted certain propositions we can increase our knowledge by using those to predict outcomes, and so new propositions come into being. Rather than accept the theoretical purity of the deductive models of the universe at that time (that is, drawing inferences from what were then widely accepted beliefs, deriving the particular from the general), Nicolaus Copernicus (1473–1543) (Figure 1.1) did something unusual in that he carried out observations on the heavenly bodies to see if they behaved as predicted. They did not, and the scientific method was born.

The next century saw the formalisation of the scientific method in inductive logic by Francis Bacon (1561–1626) (Figure 1.2). He proposed what is still regarded as the essence of the scientific method: the cycle of observations to determine facts, followed by application

Figure 1.1 Bust of Nicolaus Copernicus in Torun, Poland. (From http://commons.wikimedia.org/wiki/File:Pomnik_Miko%C5%82aja_Kopernika_w_Toruniu.JPG.)

Figure 1.2 Engraving of Francis Bacon. (From http://commons.wikimedia.org/wiki/File:Francis_Bacon.jpg#file.)

of inductive reasoning to formulate a hypothesis that explains the observations, followed by further experimentation to test the hypothesis, with the expectation that this will result in its refinement or rejection, and the cycle is repeated.

The understanding of the value of inductive reasoning, experimentation, and the formulation of hypotheses in science was fundamental to the flourishing of the era of scientific enlightenment that followed in the next three centuries. It also stimulated an interest in the philosophical basis of "science" as a subject and an awareness that neither deductive nor inductive reasoning provided an entirely secure foundation.

1.2.1.2 Significance of the Hypothesis

An important piece of the puzzle in describing what science (and, most importantly, forensic science) is can be found in the work of an American philosopher of science, Charles Sanders Peirce (1839–1914) (Figure 1.3). Peirce was the founding father of what is called the *pragmatist* approach to science and philosophy, and his work may be even more central to the understanding of the work of forensics than any other scientific discipline.

Peirce challenged the existing model of scientific inquiry as being either *inductive*—that is, inferring from an established body of experiential phenomena and observations of particular incidents to make predictions and propositions of a more general and universal character (also known as *empiricism*)—or *deductive*—that is, inferring from self-evident truths, using general laws to deduce necessary outcomes in the particular (also known as *rationalism*). He introduced a third concept of inference, *abduction*, which is inferring from a surprising event or occurrence to a probable explanation. This gives a new pathway into the scientific method.

The concept of formulating a hypothesis is essential to the scientific method and is central to Peirce's ideas about inference and abduction. In more practical terms, the hypothesis is the researcher's idea of the character of the phenomena he is about to investigate, or his qualified guess about what the end result of his research or experiment may be. Abduction is therefore the most fertile but least secure mode of inference. The hypothesis, being based on a "surprise event," is somewhat insecure and must have practical implications that can be tested.

Peirce laid the foundation for an integrated approach to the scientific method by insisting that abduction, deduction, and induction make incomplete sense in isolation from each other and that they ought to be seen as comprising a cycle understandable only as a whole, as they must be seen to collaborate to serve the inquiry's end. To use Peirce's own words: "Deduction proves that something must be; Induction shows that something actually is operative; Abduction merely suggests that something may be" (Peirce, 1934).

Figure 1.3 Charles Sanders Peirce. (From http://commons.wikimedia.org/wiki/File:Charles-Sanders-Peirce.jpg.)

We can see how induction, abduction, and deduction are essential elements of how Kirk's things are developed into a story during crime scene investigation. The crime, our "surprise event," leads to thinking about its probable cause and the formulation of an explanatory hypothesis; however, that one event does not constitute a sufficiently large set of particular observations from which to formulate a credible explanatory hypothesis. Traditional scientific method requires that the first step is induction, making observations, describing a sufficient body of facts and using these to formulate an explanation—the hypothesis. Induction is the opposite of deduction and takes us from the particular to the general. The possible explanation is then tested by reversing the process and using the hypothesis to predict something that must be true if the hypothesis is correct—the deduction. Abduction also leads us to postulate an explanation but is more imaginative. It is a "what if" process that enjoys exploring the unexpected and closely captures the intuitive actions of the crime scene investigator. Just as with the more linear, incremental process of induction, however, it is of no value unless it is shown to withstand rigorous testing.

1.2.1.3 *Critical Rationalism*

As should be clear, Peirce's philosophy of science translates well to the practical realities of searching for and developing hypotheses for the stories things may tell, but a problem remains: How do we evaluate a hypothesis with a view to establishing whether it is a matter of fact and not just a probable explanation?

The short answer is that science is not absolute, and we cannot prove any hypothesis to the exclusion of everything else. The longer answer is provided by the work of Karl Popper (1902–1994) (Figure 1.4). One of Popper's important contributions lay in realising that all observation is from a point of view. His point is therefore that any conclusion drawn from observations is coloured by our existing understanding, which means that conclusions

Figure 1.4 Karl Popper. (From http://upload. wikimedia.org/wikipedia/commons/6/6c/ Karl_Popper2.jpg.)

made from empirical observations of phenomena are coloured by our conscious or subconscious frame of reference. Again, as with Peirce and abduction, we find that the thoughts of a leader in the arcane subject matter of scientific philosophy have a direct impact on forensic science, as one of the areas subjected to the most severe criticism in the National Research Council report was that of conscious and unconscious bias on the part of the forensic specialist.

This point was controversial in the sense that the prevailing theory of science preceding Popper was one that relied on empirical observation as the basis of drawing scientific conclusions. If one could make direct observations in the world that supported one's theory, then the theory was believed to be verified and thus could be acknowledged as true.

To illustrate his point, Popper used the proposition that all swans are white, a proposition supported by centuries of observations, but all made in the Northern Hemisphere. The exploration of Australia by Europeans was accompanied by the discovery of black swans, thereby negating the proposition as expressed. Popper used this to illustrate the principle that using observation to verify your theory does not necessarily provide secure knowledge (the empirical truth). To meet this end, Popper made a suggestion regarding how one should work to produce knowledge in which we can trust—namely, that we should seek to falsify our theories, rather than to verify them.

One of the defining factors of Popper's critical rationalism is that he is critical of the unqualified use of inductive reasoning. He argues that, however compelling it may be to formulate a hypothesis and find repeatedly that conclusions based on it stand, the validity of the hypothesis and therefore its predictions are based entirely on our current knowledge and understanding. Put differently, we don't know what we don't know.

The swan metaphor has several implications for the theory of science, but two important and related ones are that in order to be tested a good theory must prohibit something so it can be *falsified by observation*, and that we cannot prove a hypothesis by finding examples that fit. We may not have looked in the right place or in the right way.

Falsification itself is not absolute and can itself be subject to falsification. Observations may produce information that apparently falsifies a hypothesis, but further testing may provide an explanation that maintains the integrity of the law. As an example, observations in 1846 showed that the orbit of the planet Uranus was not exactly as predicted by Newton's laws of gravity and motion. Rather than take this as evidence of falsification, scientists looked for an explanation and discovered a new planet, Neptune, with an orbit outside that of Uranus. Thus, the proposition that all swans are white is not unscientific in itself, as it is possible to falsify it simply by one observation of a swan in any other colour—for instance, black.

Falsification does not mean that findings in keeping with a hypothesis have no value. They do, but their value depends on how novel and unusual the hypothesis/prediction pairing is and how often the prediction has been confirmed. The value also depends on what we do with an apparent falsification; when it is used to redirect experimentation and explore new boundaries, it is arguably more valuable than even a sophisticated confirmation.

1.2.2   Science as the Work of Scientists

There is no constancy in the classification of the sciences part of forensic science for the simple reason that the courts, including the legal representatives of the parties in dispute, will call on any specialist when they believe that it will assist resolution

Figure 1.5 Thomas Kuhn. (From http://www.molwick.com/en/scientific-methods/041-scientific-methodology.html.)

of the matter before the tribunal. The mainstream elements of forensic science in criminal matters can however be conveniently grouped under the umbrella of *criminalistics*. The term was introduced in Europe in 1899, when Hans Gross (1847–1915) published his major work, *Handbuch fur Untersuchungsrichter als System der Kriminalistik*. Gross was an Austrian lawyer and the book was intended to be a guide to investigators as to what they could expect from the nascent field of forensic science. Today, *criminalistics* and the derivative *criminalist* are widely used in the United States to describe the work performed in a typical forensic science laboratory and those who do the work.

The idea that we can define science, or a branch of science, by reference to the characteristics of those working in it is a relatively modern concept in the philosophy of science and comes from the work of Thomas Kuhn (1922–1966) (Figure 1.5). Whereas Popper was concerned in the main with the logic of science, Kuhn explored how science progresses and specifically the idea that progress is incremental (little by little, experiment by experiment) by studying the history of science. Kuhn argued that scientists work within a conceptual paradigm that strongly influences the way in which they see data.

One of the stumbling blocks to truly new scientific discoveries is, according to Kuhn, the behaviour of scientists themselves. The paragons of the scientific community justifiably become accepted as authorities because of their research, but the authority discourages challenge and encourages only incremental advances on what has become the world view.

The worldview underlying the theories and methodology of a particular scientific subject Kuhn called a *paradigm*. Kuhn recognised that, because paradigms are a worldview, significant advances are not going to result from evolution, but from revolution. There will be resistance to change until the evidence for discarding the existing paradigm is overwhelming. Kuhn referred to this as *paradigm shift*. In conducting his research, Kuhn had to grapple with the essential question of what science is in order to be able to discuss how changes come about in scientific theories. He concluded that science is defined by communities of

Figure 1.6 Imre Lakatos. (From http://commons.wikimedia.org/wiki/Category:Imre_Lakatos.)

practitioners sharing properties related to the manner in which they conduct the exploration of knowledge about some aspect of the physical world. It is the existence of the communities that make the paradigm such a strong force defining the norms within the field and inevitably resulting in conservatism.

A degree of synthesis of the concepts of science as a process and science as the work of scientists was provided by the last of the scientific philosophers that we shall explore, Imre Lakatos (1922–1974) (Figure 1.6). Lakatos was concerned that a strict and unthinking interpretation of Popper's falsification concept meant a hypothesis would be rejected, but its core and usefulness might still be valid but lost. The apparent falsification should lead to further refinement and improvement of the apparently false hypothesis.

Thus, in the case of the swan metaphor, instead of falsification of the proposition that "all swans are white" by the empirical observation of black swans resulting in the discard of the whole theory of "what a swan is," falsifications are seen as steps in the (r)evolution of scientific theories. In this instance, the core properties that define a swan were revised and black swans accepted as a new species within the *Cygnus* genus. Note that this is very different from the apparent falsification issues discussed above in regard to the perturbation of the orbit of Uranus.

To remedy what he saw as a problem with Popper's theory, Lakatos introduced the concept of *research programmes* as a solution. A research programme is the aggregate of several theories that share a core and progress using a common set of methodologies. In Lakatos' approach, a scientist works within a research programme that corresponds roughly with Kuhn's paradigm. Whereas Popper rejected the use of *ad hoc* hypotheses as unscientific, Lakatos accepted their place in the development of new theories, as of course did Peirce.

1.2.3 Implications for the Crime Scene Investigator

The thoughts of Copernicus, Bacon, Peirce, Popper, Kuhn, and Lakatos are mirrored in the way that the crime scene investigator works to convert things into a story. The things are the objective facts that are the foundation for the hypothesis (Copernicus and Bacon). Peirce encourages us to deal with the unexpected—the crime scene—by being broad minded and imaginative in how we develop a hypothesis, or story, based on what limited information is available, but Peirce and Popper both counsel us that the story must be rigorously tested and not accepted just because it fits all the information known at the time. Popper further warns us to be aware of how the frame of reference for the development of the story is conditioned by our experiences, which may be incomplete.

Popper provides guidance as to how to validate our story—we must look for things that contradict it, not just things that support it. Kuhn reinforces Popper's caution that we are conditioned by our preexisting point of view and that this means that we will be influenced to some degree by the norms of the community to which the crime scene investigator belongs. Lakatos tells us not to fear rejection of a predicted event, but to be active in using new information to refine the story.

1.2.4   Science and Technology

Science and technology are inextricably linked. Advances in technology come from advances in science; for example, the solid-state electronics that make it possible for us to enjoy the benefits of computers and modern audiovisual entertainment systems are derived from the highly abstract concepts of quantum physics. On the other hand, it is technology's gifts that have permitted science to make new discoveries.

Indeed, most of the advances in forensic science have depended on advances in technology. The identification of drugs, especially at the very low levels encountered in toxicology, the power of DNA testing and databases, and the ability to render invisible residues of fingerprints visible are all significant advances in forensic science made possible by technology derived from other fields of scientific knowledge. However, this aspect of forensics has also been used to discredit its claim to legitimacy as science, the argument being that in fact forensic science is nothing but the use of technology developed by different fields of science to help detect, recover, collect, and analyse physical evidence. It would not be reasonable to expect the crime scene investigator to understand the detail and fundamental principles of the science and technology that underpin so many of the methods employed in scene investigation; however, the investigator must be sufficiently aware of the main elements in order to be able to know that the instruments and tests are functioning correctly, what to do to confirm this, and how to respond to malfunctions.

1.3   Evidence

Having explored the scientific method and, to an extent, how it can produce the knowledge inherent in forensic science, we shall turn to the purpose of this process, evidence. *Webster's Dictionary* defines "evidence" as something legally submitted to a competent tribunal as a means of ascertaining the truth of any alleged matter of fact under investigation before it. In forensic science in the United States, "evidence" is synonymous with "exhibit"; however, in legal terms, an "exhibit" is an object produced in a court as evidence. In this work, we will use the dictionary definition of evidence and the following definition of exhibit:

> An exhibit is an item or sample recovered as part of an investigation. This includes everything recovered from a crime scene, such as swabs, whole objects, and debris, and derived items, such as casts of footprints, and finger mark lifts.

Put differently, an "exhibit" is a thing presented before a court to serve as "evidence" to a proposition of matters of fact. Thus, any object, chemical or biochemical substance, mark or impression that can provide information about the incident under investigation can be an exhibit and result in evidence. In some respects, the root meaning of the word forensic is already inherent in the use of the word evidence (as something presented to a court). However, we will here make use of the term "forensic" in front of "evidence" in the meaning of "forensics," to emphasise the scientific nature of analysis that is decisive in converting Kirk's things to the story that they tell.

In the following, we shall therefore discuss forensic evidence in the context of the examination of exhibits with the aim of transforming them to evidence. An awareness of the different types of evidence that can result from the examinations and the principles governing their translation into elements of the story is essential to the knowledge base of the crime scene investigator. The awareness should go beyond the immediate specialisation of the individual crime scene investigator, as the final story could be the amalgamation of inputs from several experts, but nearly all will begin with the scene investigation.

1.3.1 Forensic Evidence and How It Can Be Used

We will begin the discussion of forensic evidence with an accepted legal characterisation, whereby evidence can be divided into two broad types: (1) testimonial evidence, and (2) real evidence based on the inspection or examination of exhibits. Because this book is about crime scene investigation and forensic science, we shall equate real evidence with forensic evidence.

Testimonial evidence is evidence given in the form of statements made under oath, usually in response to questioning, where someone relates what he or she has done or seen. Real (forensic) evidence arises from the examination of exhibits, which can be as large as a house, as small as a fibre, as fleeting as an odour, or as obvious as the scene of an explosion. In principle, forensic evidence has several advantages over testimonial evidence. It can contain information unknown to the lay observer, it can produce very compelling information, and compared to testimonial evidence it should be objective and reliable rather than subjective and sometimes unreliable.

The objectivity of forensic evidence versus testimonial evidence has been addressed in several studies on the reliability of eyewitness testimony, where factors such as context, prior knowledge of individuals, cognition, and memory changes with time have all been shown to be subjective and lacking in reliability. The Innocence Project in the United States has identified eyewitness misidentification as a leading factor in 75% of the wrongful conviction cases that it has successfully pursued.

Forensic evidence in turn can be classified according to the use to which it is put (see Table 1.1). It can be classified as inceptive, exclusionary, associative, or corroborative. *Inceptive evidence* can be used to prove that a crime has been committed. Examples include

Table 1.1   Types of Forensic Evidence

Type	Description	Example
Inceptive	Indicates a crime has been committed	Identification of a white powder as a controlled drug
Exclusionary	Eliminates something and so negates a hypothesis	DNA typing of semen showing it could not have come from the suspect
Associative	Uses exclusionary and corroborative to evaluate links between people and places	DNA, soil, fingerprints
Corroborative	Supports a hypothesis but could arise for other reasons	Fibres and other trace evidence

identification of the cause of a fire to differentiate between accident and arson, as well as identification of drugs in drug possession and trading cases. In the example of the cause of a fire, providing evidence for a cause due to arson could be established by recovery, collection, and identification of the presence of chemicals that could act as accelerants and that would not normally be present at the scene, such as oils, paint, alcohol, or the like. Evidence of accidental cause could be the finding that the source of the fire was a faulty electrical device. The drug examples range from identification of powders or tablets found in the possession of a suspect to the complex investigation of a drug laboratory. In the possession example, if the examination identifies a white powder containing cocaine, then that in itself shows that something not permitted by law has occurred. It may be necessary to quantify the amount of cocaine to differentiate between possession and trading.

Exclusionary evidence can be used to show that something did not occur and so exonerate the innocent. Exclusionary evidence is primarily evidence relating to the identity of a person, such as DNA profiling of semen in a rape case. If evidence in a case depends on identification of the source of semen recovered in a vaginal swab and testing shows that the DNA profile is different from that of the suspect, then the semen cannot be his, and to the extent that the case depends on identification of the source of the semen he is excluded as the perpetrator. Some of the most compelling examples of exclusionary evidence have come from the Innocence Project, which reports that as of March 2011 there had been 267 post-conviction exonerations in the United States arising from the application of DNA testing, the first being in 1989. The true suspects or perpetrators were identified in 117 of the cases. The example used to illustrate exclusionary evidence can be used to illustrate another important principle contained in the phrase "to the extent that the case depends on identification of the source of the semen he is excluded as the perpetrator." There are several situations where the absence of semen that could have come from the suspect would not be proof that he was not involved. He may have used a condom, or he may have not ejaculated, or the victim may have delayed reporting the incident during which time any semen deposited may have been lost. When interpreting the results of scene or laboratory investigations, we must only draw conclusions based on things that have been found and must avoid speculation on why something is not found.

Associative evidence is a somewhat different way of looking at corroborative evidence. It explores the relationship between things and therefore directly addresses the story that they may tell.

Much of traditional forensic science evidence falls into the category of *corroborative evidence*, where the findings are in keeping with the postulated events but other explanations are possible. An example would be finding fibres on the clothing of a suspect that

ABSENCE OF EVIDENCE IS NOT EVIDENCE OF ABSENCE

A good hypothesis prohibits something possessing a defined property. "Absence" is not a property, and there are many reasons why a presence may not be detected; however, we can make negative conclusions based on positive information. Perhaps the best illustration is in regard to DNA typing of semen in a rape case. Finding markers that do not match those of the accused man means that he cannot be the source of the semen, but what if that assailant wore a condom and the victim had had intercourse with someone else before the rape?

could have come from the clothing of the victim. If the two are strangers, this can be strong evidence of contact between them, but where there is nothing unique about the clothing, or where the victim and suspect are known to have had innocent contact with each other, its value is considerably reduced.

The creation of databases has been of considerable value in assessing the weight that may be given to corroborative evidence. Many countries now operate DNA databases populated with DNA profiles from known offenders and from unsolved crimes. The databases are used to identify possible perpetrators from the results of samples found at the scene and to link crimes. There are also databases for comparison of gun ammunition and for footwear. The ability of databases to assist in evaluating the weight that should be given to corroborative evidence lies not in the database itself but in the accompanying population frequency information. This point is important because several invalid applications of database information have been made in attempting to quantify the significance of information. Chief amongst these is the *prosecutor's fallacy*, in which the frequency (or rarity) of occurrence of the evidence such as a DNA profile is wrongly transcribed to become the likelihood of guilt or innocence.

1.3.2 Evidence, Identity, and Identification

The fundamental purpose of forensic science and the problem that it aims to resolve in aiding the legal process is that of *identity*. Everyday language uses identity and its derivative *identification* to indicate "uniqueness" and the act of "assigning a unique identity" to something or someone; however, this usage does not correspond to that in the natural sciences, and in forensic science in particular. Many textbooks on forensic science, including Fisher's original *Techniques of Crime Investigation*, introduce a related term, *individualisation*, and make the following distinction: *Identification* means that items share a common source or possess the same properties, and *individualisation* means coming from a unique source.

The Latin roots of the two concepts show the way to their difference in meaning. The root of identify (identification) is *idem,* which means "same," whereas the root of individualise is *individus*, meaning "not divisible." However, there are uncertainties in language and in nature regarding just when "same" becomes "unique." Given the confusion of the concepts, we will address the problem of identity from a slightly more pragmatic angle, using two questions central to the forensic process (which we will get into in more detail later in this chapter)—namely, the questions of WHAT and WHO. If we pose the question "WHAT is this?" together with the question of "WHO is this?" we can simplify the two terms into just one: identity. The answer to the WHAT question will be the correct identification of something as being *one of a specified group* of things, and the answer to the WHO question will be the correct identification of a *unique member* within that group.

This differentiation can be illustrated using the example of animal categorisation and returning to Popper and his swans. Setting aside the fact that there are seven known species within the swan genus, if we have sufficient agreed information to define what a swan is—the core properties—then we can test the hypothesis of whether or not something is a swan. Popper's example uses one property of "swan-ness"—colour. Note that Popper does not argue that all white birds are swans, but rather that one of the properties of being a swan is to possess white plumage. Let us therefore extend the proposition to be "a large waterbird with a long flexible neck, short legs, webbed feet, a broad bill, and all-white plumage." The finding of a bird with all but one of these would have three possible outcomes: The bird would be classified as other than a swan, the bird could be classified as a new species within the *Cygnus* genus, or the variant would be dismissed as an anomaly.

Having identified the core properties there will, however, be a myriad of variations within the organisms that we would classify as swans, but no two will be identical (birds generally do not have identical twins). In Fisher's language, we have identified "swan" from conformity with agreed defining core properties, and we may be able to individualise a specific swan from its non-core properties. In our terms, we are able to identify WHAT a swan is and WHO an individual swan is and so answer the questions "Is this a swan?" and "Which swan is it?"

The conclusions in our language are contextual and depend on the question being posed. If the question is "WHAT is this?" then we can identify it as a swan if it possesses the agreed core properties. If the question is akin to "WHO is this?" (i.e., which swan), then we need something other than the core properties to confirm its individual identity. How much more is one of the major issues in forensic science.

This approach makes it apparent that the question of identity is a matter of graduation on a scale from identification of class to unique individuation. Between these two points are an infinite number of degrees of identification.

Kirk was the primary exponent of the distinction and its importance in crime investigation and criminalistics. He also was the proponent of the paradigmatic definition of forensic science as being informed by the dictum that no two empirically existing things are completely alike, no matter our ability to measure it, and expressed it thus (Kirk, 1974):

> As a practical matter, the idea that two objects might have a totally identical set of properties is not realistic, and the criminalist will always have to accept the alternate concept that every object in the universe is in some meaningful or measurable manner different from every other object in the universe, regardless of the similarity between them. Different grains of sand from a beach are measurably different and leaves from the same tree are measurably different. Without this basic concept there would be very limited theoretical and philosophical background for the establishment of criminalistics as a science or as a discipline.

That view is entirely in keeping with the preceding discussion on identity as a gradation of sameness. If we accept Kirk's postulate, then the practical implications are

- No two things that happen by chance ever happen in exactly the same way.
- No two things are ever constructed in exactly the same way.
- No two things ever wear in exactly the same way.
- No two things ever break in exactly the same way.

The 2009 National Research Council report was critical of the first, third, and last of these implications, and it challenged the forensic community to conduct research to provide evidence to support the postulate on the basis of the results of well-designed experiments. We may challenge the second by reference to objects made from the same mould, since they will be very similar, so similar in fact that it may not be possible to differentiate between two that have been produced consecutively. However, that does not change the value of the postulates as providing an operational framework to forensic science. Based on this philosophy, Kirk distinguished three forms of evidence identity:

1. *Comparative identity*—The ascription of identity within a group based on their comparative properties
2. *Identity of source*—Identification of enough shared (individual) properties to identify a common source
3. *Causal identity*—Identifying enough common characteristics to confirm that two results were obtained from the same cause

These three forms of identity, Kirk argued, "are all that will be of concern to the investigator."

1.3.2.1 Class and Individualisation

The evidence categories of exclusionary and corroborative can be related to the goal of determining identity using forensic evidence, where the concepts of class and individualisation characteristics are important. Some investigators might believe that every item of physical evidence can be directly associated to a specific person, place, or thing and suppose that it is possible for a single strand of hair or a fibre to be linked to a unique source. This is generally not the case. Most physical evidence may only be associated with a class or group, as is the case with mass manufactured items.

An example would be tyre marks, where the general pattern can give information about the make of tyre and possibly the vehicle by combining data on wheel base and track width with tyre size; however, to individualise the track to a specific vehicle requires information unique to that tyre. This is generally accepted as being provided by marks produced by accidental damage or, to a lesser extent, wear. An example is shown in Figure 1.7.

At this point, we need to consider the definitions of sample and population. A *population* is all the members of a group that has been defined in some way (think "swans"). Statistically, a *sample* is a portion drawn from a population for the purpose of testing or analysis to determine the attributes of the whole or to represent those attributes. In forensic science, *sample* is sometimes used synonymously with *exhibit*, but we will not use it here in that sense.

Figure 1.7 A cast of a tyre impression (top) and a photograph of the same area of the tyre (bottom). The red arrows on the top point to the same defects as the white ones on the bottom. The general size and tread pattern allow identification of the make and model of the tyre but the defects are individual to that particular tyre.

Samples of a population will all share its class characteristics; reversing the thought process, class characteristics are the core attributes that define a population. Depending on the way that the attributes and population are defined, the group could be large and its members common, or it could be very small and membership very limited. This is illustrated in the box below.

Non-core attributes are features in addition to those of class and allow identification to the level of WHO to some extent, depending on their number and nature. Popper's concern about the limitations of inductive reasoning means that we can never be certain that our observed non-core properties show unique identity; again, we don't know what we don't know. However, people have their own concept of "beyond reasonable doubt" and would be prepared to accept individual identity at somewhere less than absolute certainty to the exclusion of everything else.

Two examples may make the distinction and the strengths and weaknesses of the concept clearer. The first is blood grouping. The frequency of the markers used in grouping human blood is well characterised, as are the factors that influence it. It is known, for example, that the frequency of markers depends on race and on social factors such as population

POPULATIONS LARGE AND SMALL

We know that the population of the world is large and growing as birth rates outstrip death rates. We know that the population of the EC is smaller than that of the world but has grown in the last 10 years as new countries are admitted to membership. We know that the population of Scotland is smaller than that of the EC and has been static for the last 10 years but are not sure why. I know that the population of the town in Scotland where I live is smaller than that of Scotland but has risen considerably in the last 10 years as people have chosen to leave cities and live in the country.

The assumption of "human-ness" is embedded in the concept of population in this example, and we can see a continuum of ever smaller populations that possess that core property. The world population consists of all members of the human species, a single and fixed property. The EC is a smaller and more specific population based on features such as citizenship, place of birth, and place of residence, in addition to the core property. Then, as we add the non-core property of the geographical area called "Scotland," the population definition increases in specificity and its size reduces further, and so on right down to the town, which is even more specific and the smallest of this set.

Taking the small town as an example, the properties that define the population have not changed in the 10 years, but its size has. Individuals have joined and left the population in that time, too.

The above are all populations in their own right, each defined by some boundary condition, and each of the smaller populations is a subset of the larger one that precedes it in the list, but are they samples of the larger ones? No, because although each is drawn from within the larger one, it is not wholly representative of it. The population of the EC is not racially, ethnically, and culturally identical to that of Asia, nor that of Scotland to Denmark, nor indeed that of the small rural community to the larger cities close by.

migration and inbreeding. Take the clinically important ABO blood typing system, and say we find a type B blood stain on an exhibit at a crime scene in Scotland. Approximately 12% of Scots are type B, so we have a class characteristic: type B blood, which while not unique (that is, will not allow identity to the WHO level) will reduce the possible source to about one tenth of the population. However, using the common battery of DNA markers used in forensic science laboratories today, the same stain may type as being a combination that is found in 1 in 4.5 million people. Is it still a class characteristic (defined by the attributes consisting of the selected DNA markers), or have we now answered the WHO question to the point of a single unique individual, the rarity of the DNA profile? By adding to the defining core attributes we have reduced the distinction between identification of a class and identification of an individual within that class.

The second example is rather different but typical of impression evidence. A tyre print is located in the snow at a scene in northern Denmark. A cast is made, and the size and general brand of the tyre are determined. The tread pattern shows uneven wear and an area of damage, probably a cut. Some months later, investigators identify a suspect whose car has tyres of the same make, one of which has similar wear and damage patterns. However, because of the amount of driving in the time interval and the problems of capturing fine detail in marks made in snow, there will be differences as well as areas of correspondence between the tyre and the print, and it will not be as clear as the example in Figure 1.7. It is therefore not always possible to conclude that the suspect car is the vehicle involved in the incident, but neither can it be concluded that it is not. This is an example of corroborative evidence. Finding sufficient detail to identify the make of tyre is a classic example of the application of class characteristics in this type of evidence. Wear and damage patterns are classic examples of potential individualisation characteristics.

The interpretation of the individualisation characteristics in the tyre example is limited by attributes that differ in this type of evidence from those that we illustrated in the blood and DNA example. First, the attributes that let us assign an ABO or DNA type to blood do not change in the source with time, and although they can degrade in shed blood the effect is usually to make typing not possible rather than to change the nature of the result. Second, we know enough about the nature of the population to be able to make a reliable assignment of the frequency of the entity that we test and so position where we are on the sliding scale from class to individualisation characteristic. Many of the common types of forensic evidence, such as toolmarks, fingerprints, and handwriting, are missing one or both of these characteristics (see Table 1.2).

The above discussion, together with the examples in Table 1.2, show that the characteristics of good forensic evidence are as follows:

- It should be stable and not change with time.
- It should have well-defined core attributes and known population statistics.
- The basis of variations in non-core attributes should be known and scientifically justifiable.

1.3.2.2   The Principle of Comparison

Up until this point we have dealt with the examination of exhibits in the context of the goal of identifying WHAT or WHO. Another framework that is widely used in practice and is essentially Kirk's first form of identity of evidence is the *Locard exchange principle*

Table 1.2 Constancy of Physical Evidence

Example	Changes with Time?	Population Characteristics
Toolmark	Yes, due to wear and accidental damage.	The number of a type of tool manufactured may be known but the number in the local population of relevance may not.
DNA	No.	Well defined.
Fingerprint	No, ignoring the effects of accidental injuries.	Not well defined, but there is a long history of observed uniqueness without a defined scientific basis relating this to random production of friction ridge characters.
Fibres	Basic fibres are stable but dyes may fade and transferred fibres may be lost and redistributed.	Not well defined.
Tyre and footwear impressions	Yes, due to wear and accidental damage.	Same as for toolmarks.
Paints	Same as for fibres.	Same as for toolmarks.
Bite mark	Yes, due to being unstable in most receiving media, such as skin and soft foodstuffs.	None, as analysis of dental records may provide information on dentition but this does not necessarily translate to bite marks.

and the use of comparison testing. Edmund Locard was born in France in 1877 and died there in 1966. He worked for some time with Alphonse Bertillon, the first person to realise the value of anthropometry in forensic science, and became interested in identification. Locard joined the police force in Lyon in 1910 and set up what became the official police laboratory in 1912. Locard recognised that dactyloscopy, or fingerprinting, was a better approach to identification than was anthropometry. He made several significant contributions to the new science of fingerprinting and first used it successfully in a case in 1910.

Locard can justifiably claim to be the first true forensic scientist. He was concerned about the scientific principles behind his work; thus, he was the first to set down rules for the application of Galton points and the detailed minutiae in a fingerprint in order to establish identity. He is credited with establishing the concepts of *poreoscopy* and *edge-oscopy*, which are the basis of what today's fingerprint examiners term *ridgeology* and are the basis of modern approaches to fingerprinting. His tripartite rule set three levels of interpretation: (1) more than 12 Galton points in a sharp and clear print is enough for identity; (2) the conclusion that can be drawn from a print with 8 to 12 depends on other factors; and (3) no reliable conclusion can be drawn from fewer than 8 points.

Locard is best known for the principle identified by his name: the Locard exchange principle. In summary, this principle states that every contact leaves a trace. Locard's principle is behind all trace evidence, which depends on comparing traces of materials found on a suspect with bulk material from the scene of the crime. The reasoning goes that the various contacts between the perpetrator and objects at the scene will result in a transfer of materials between the two on each contact. There are several things wrong with Locard's exchange principle. First and most practical is that it is not always possible to establish a reliable association between the two. Traces may be lost with time and movement of the perpetrator away from the scene. The materials exchanged may not be sufficiently unique, either alone or in combination to provide reliable evidence of contact, and the techniques used on the comparisons might not be capable of sufficient discrimination. The second problem is that Locard never said it. What he did say, in several ways in his publications, was that it is impossible for a criminal to perform an act of violent crime without leaving some trace of his presence. He also repeatedly asserted that the microscope was a powerful weapon to characterise the debris deposited on the clothing of people as they move through different environments. It is thus reasonable, then, that the concept is named after him.

Earlier we posed the question of how much information is required in regard to the move of identity from WHAT, or class, to WHO, or individualisation. The same issue of how much is enough applies to comparison testing. However, the fundamental aspect of individualisation is that we know the core properties that define "WHAT," and if they are not present then the person or thing is not a member of the class of interest. Comparison testing does not hinge around these core properties, and professional judgement has to be employed to decide if two items could have come from the same source.

1.3.3   Forensic Evidence: Purpose and Process

Science aims to produce secure knowledge about the natural world by observing empirical phenomena, developing explanatory hypotheses, and submitting these to objective experimental testing. The legal process starts out the same way, seeking to produce a reconstructive history of events through a process of inquiry in which hypotheses are formed and explored; however, the end phase differs, with the reconstruction being argued before a tribunal that will decide what is to be accepted as the truth of the matter under trial. Put differently, science and scientific inquiry are oriented toward establishing *what is*, whereas the legal process and investigative inquiry are oriented toward establishing *what has been which ought not*.

The decision-making process is not entirely different in the two. First, the legal process demands that any scientific evidence placed before it is secure and can be relied on, and therefore the rigour in scientific testing is carried into the legal arena. Second, when scientists conduct experiments to test their hypotheses, they usually employ some form of statistical evaluation that measures the probability that the observed results occurred by chance. By convention, results are discounted if that probability is greater than 5%, and the confidence in their validity rises as the probability of a chance result falls below 1% or less. Although subjective, the legal decision-making rule of "beyond reasonable doubt" is in essence the same idea.

The decision-making difference is further bridged in that forensic science, and scene investigation in particular, shares with law the goal and circumstances of the inquiry, with the purpose of forensics being to assist in establishing the material facts of a case ("story") through investigative inquiry into the circumstances of particular cases.

1.3.3.1   *Making Things Talk*

Forensic evidence plays a central role in the identification of the culprit and the essential aspects of the crime because of the scientific basis of its analysis and its ability to provide objective information. This role was stated quite eloquently by Kirk in his exposition of the core aspects of criminalistics (Kirk, 1974):

> Wherever he steps, whatever he touches, whatever he leaves, even unconsciously, will serve as silent witness against him. Not only his fingerprints or his footprints, but his hair, the fibres from his clothes, the glass he breaks, the toolmark he leaves, the paint he scratches, the blood or semen he deposits or collects. All of these and more bear mute witness against him.

This is evidence that does not forget. It is not confused by the excitement of the moment, it is not absent because human witnesses are. It is factual evidence. Physical evidence cannot be wrong, it cannot perjure itself, it cannot be wholly absent. Only human failure to find it, study it and understand it can diminish its value.

The purpose of forensics—making mute things give testimony—implies a process of adding informational value through analysis in order to move from the things as occurrences in and of themselves to things as evidence to propositions. This process mimics the scientific process of hypothesis production and testing, yet has the goal of answering questions relevant to the legal deliberation of case stories.

This is evident in the framework used for describing the goal of the forensic process, recognised worldwide, which consists of a model for questioning invented in the first century BC by the first advocates or "speakers before the forum." The model is comprised of a list of questions, each of which is predicated on an investigative word, such as what, where, when, who, how, and why.

National variants of the model differ, as some operate with four or five questions, and some have seven or eight; however, common to them all is the use of basic questions to provide guidelines for what circumstances are to be described to gain knowledge of a case to be presented before a court of law. In this book, we work with the 6 "W"s (which are actually five Ws and an H but are commonly known as the 6Ws), which is the model generally accepted within the European Network of Forensic Science Institutes (ENFSI).

In a forensic context, the 6Ws can be considered a mnemonic formula for getting the full story when investigating and presenting criminal cases:

- WHAT has happened?
- WHERE did it take place?
- HOW did it happen?
- WHO was involved?
- WHEN did it happen (at what time and in what sequence)?
- WHY did it happen?

The principle underlying the maxim is that each question should elicit a factual answer. What is important is that none of these questions can be answered with a simple "yes" or "no." They therefore present the incident as a problem to be solved. Solving the problem by providing factual answers to each dimension—each question—is the purpose of investigative inquiry. Figure 1.8 illustrates the two parallel, yet dependent, processes of inquiry through which evidence is made to tell their stories and the way in which science is applied in the service of law.

1.4   From Science to Scene

We have explored how forensic science in general and areas within it such as impression evidence and scene examination have been criticised for not being scientific, or even for being "junk science." Although there are differences between science and law—mainly in the way in which decisions are made—the differences are not all that great. To substantiate this claim it may be fruitful to go back to Peirce briefly.

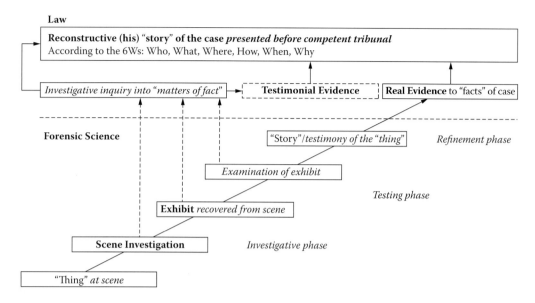

Figure 1.8 The processes of legal and scientific inquiry compared.

Peirce defined science as just part of a much broader understanding of inquiry or inquiry-driven processes to achieve knowledge, and he defined inquiry as the struggle to move from irritating, inhibitory doubt born of surprise, disagreement, and the like, to a state of *secure belief*, belief being that on which one is prepared to act. The goal of inquiry (and, as implied in his view, science) is not truth per se, but the resolution of doubt—whether about the nature of the world or resolving doubts about guilt or innocence. We will therefore end this chapter by comparing the forensic process at the crime scene with the basic scientific method.

1.4.1 Comparison between the Scientific Method and the Process of Crime Scene Investigation

No one but the perpetrator knows what happened at a scene, and there will be things that even he is not aware of. The investigator has to create possible answers and use the 6Ws to move it from a thought to a realistic possibility. The process that the investigator goes through mimics the scientific method, as it moves through the phases of abduction, induction, deduction—that is, hypothesis building, testing, and refinement. It is not an exact parallel, because of the control that the legal process imposes.

For example, in the formation of the initial hypothesis to explain the circumstances that created the crime scene the process has to be more imaginative (i.e., purely abductive) than the strictly inductive logic governing the formation of hypotheses in science. The process begins with nothing other than the observed circumstances of the scene (Peirce's "unexpected") rather than the considered and accumulated observations that form the first step in the scientific method (see Figure 1.9).

The scene investigator has to actively short-circuit the scientific method by considering alternative explanations from the very beginning, rather than waiting until the testing phase. This will help the investigator to keep an open mind and will assist the investigation by not closing off avenues that, while less obvious in the early stages, may well turn out to

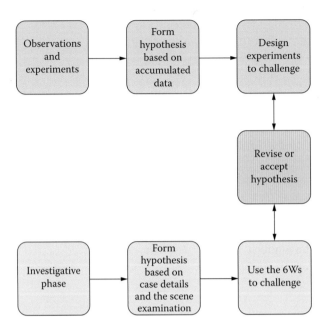

Figure 1.9 Comparison of scene investigation and application of the scientific method.

be correct. However, just as in the scientific method, continual refinement of the initial or revised hypotheses as more information becomes available should be an integral part of the process.

Scene investigation and the subsequent analysis of exhibits with the view to transform them into evidence iterates through these steps until the point where enough evidence has been tested that we can be secure in our belief that it corroborates the theory of the circumstances of the crime and can be presented before a court of law.

1.4.2   Confirmation Bias

One of the issues singled out in the NRC report is that of confirmation bias, essentially the conscious or unconscious actions and decision making that arise from approaching a problem by seeking data to verify it and that end up colouring the process and conclusions. This is why Popper's falsification concept and the scientific method of continually challenging hypotheses in an attempt to refine and improve are core to the correct application of the investigator to exploration of the scene.

1.5   Summary

"Science" is one of the features that characterise our current era, as the increasing knowledge of the natural world around us leads to new inventions that shape our lives. The contributions of forensic science to public safety have benefited from these advances in technology, but a review of the history of the development of science itself and a comparison with the process of scene investigation show that crime scene investigation can and should be regarded as a fundamental scientific activity.

Crime scene examination lies at the centre of the larger area of activity that we call *forensic science*. Some authorities have questioned to what extent, if at all, forensic science can be regarded as fundamentally a science, but comparison with the philosophies that define the scientific method rebut the question. The reasons for concluding that forensic science, and therefore the part of it described as "scene examination," is a fundamental scientific activity can be summarised in five points:

1. Forensic science is driven by the production and testing of hypotheses, through cycles of abduction, induction, deduction, and testing.
2. Forensic science is guided by a scientific approach to inquiry, recognising that the real is discoverable independent from particular opinion, but that inquiry may go wrong in and of itself, which is why the inquiry must continuously and purposefully be tested, criticised, corrected, and improved.
3. Forensic science is predicated upon an ethos of falsification in which practitioners continuously challenge their own findings and the premises of their analysis and conclusions.
4. Forensic science is empirical in that it adheres to the scientific philosophy that there is a real knowable world that operates according to fixed rules and that effects do not occur without causes.
5. Forensic science is open ended and amendable to amplification or to having its knowledge and errors corrected in the light of new evidence or new progressions of knowledge within the disciplines informing it.

Segmentation of forensic science from science in general arises from the purpose to which it is put—namely, producing evidence for courts or other legal tribunals by identifying what Kirk described as "things" and developing the story that they tell. The chapter closes by comparing and contrasting scientific decision making with decision making in a court of law. Forensic science has the purpose of using science in the service of legal (investigative) inquiries and of the legal deliberation of incidents under the scrutiny of law, aiding both in the investigative formation of hypotheses and in the establishment of "facts" before a competent tribunal in a legal hearing. While the process in the courts is more subjective—a direct evolution from the forums of Roman times—essentially, science and law are united by the principle of rejecting a hypothesis that is not proven beyond reasonable doubt.

The Investigative Star in Crime Scene Investigation

2.1 Introduction

Chapter 1 established that the goal of forensic science is to identify "things" at or associated with a crime scene and interpret them to provide evidence that will aid in the deliberation of cases before a court or other competent tribunal. Crime scene investigation is therefore a pivotal part of the forensic process (see Chapter 3 for a description of what is meant by the "forensic process"), because it is the actions at the crime scene that produce those things—physical entities, however small or nebulous—that can tell the story of what happened. Chapter 1 also introduced the concept that the development of the story, the reconstruction, involves a cycle of actions in which possible explanations, or hypotheses, are formulated, rigorously tested, and refined or rejected as more and more information is obtained. This cycle of actions is exactly that of the scientific process and therefore establishes crime scene investigation as a fundamentally scientific activity.

The integrity of the process is based on posing and answering the fundamental questions of WHAT, WHERE, HOW, WHO, WHEN, and WHY? These are the 6Ws, and in themselves and through their interrelationships they provide the strongest framework for the planning and conduct of the investigation of a crime scene. This chapter explores the principles that underpin the 6Ws concept and configure it as a tool, the *investigative star*, which is to be viewed and used as an operational device for accomplishing the goal of the forensic process.

2.2 The Investigative Star

The 6Ws are more than just a simple mnemonic for questions with very open-ended possibilities to assist in problem solving. The concept is well established in the discipline of rhetoric, dating back at least to Aristotle and his description of the *topoi* (literally, "place" and hence "topics"), which are the places—whether of a material or more abstract character—where one goes to look for the substance of argument. The translation of the Greek word *topoi* provides the English word "topic," which refers to the subject of learning, conversation, or discussion. Thus, a topic is not just a question but rather the *theme* or *subject area* to which it refers. The 6Ws are therefore subject areas, each of which has its own terms of analysis and possible special meanings. Those interested in pursuing the classical origins of the concept are referred to Cicero and Hermagoras, in addition to Aristotle.

The tool primarily serves as a framework for developing a more systematic approach to the planning of scene investigation and the process of production and evaluation of hypotheses and interpretations by the professional crime scene investigator. In a practical sense, the star is an operational tool for carrying out a systematic and thorough search for forensic evidence at the scene.

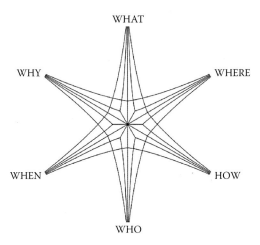

Figure 2.1 The investigative star.

The star has six points, or legs, each representing one of the 6Ws, or topics (Figure 2.1). An essential part of the representation is that the topics are not isolated, but each W has five lines that link it to each of the others. Each question can produce information that impacts on one or more of the others, and expressing the 6Ws in this form illustrates their mutual dependence and the necessity of visiting the different legs in the forensic process.

Starting at twelve o'clock in the star, one of the central purposes of forensic evidence (and the main task of the crime scene investigator) is to aid in the reconstruction of events—that is, to establish WHAT happened. The reconstruction is created by identifying and examining the scene or scenes where the incident took place—that is, WHERE things happened. To tell a meaningful story, the reconstruction will also address the question of HOW they happened, as well as the identity of the suspect and the victim—that is, to establish WHO was involved in the incident and WHO was culpable for the acts carried out. There will be occasions when being able to provide answers to the question of WHEN something occurred, at what time or in what sequence, will provide important corroborative or exculpatory evidence. Finally, the question of responsibility or culpability involves trying to answer the question of WHY something occurred and often raises several other questions and leads to problems of facts that have to be established. It implies, for instance, that a criminal content can be established, which again often rests on the proper description of the sequence or course of events, as well of the causality between them—that is, WHAT happened, HOW did it happen, and WHY did it happen?

Culpability is just one example of how the questions are intimately connected. Consider for instance the circumstances related to the WHO leg in the star. Without this important question being answered, it is not possible to produce a case and a suspect to be presented with a criminal charge—because knowing WHAT happened and WHERE and HOW does not produce a suspect to be apprehended and charged. However, establishing the identity of the suspect and victim does not make a case, either. If, for instance, criminal content or culpability cannot be established—that is, WHAT happened and WHY in the sense of causality and/or motivational reasons—then there will not be substantial ground for the prosecution of a crime. Similarly, without knowing WHERE a crime took place it is very difficult to produce factual information and physical evidence to establish criminal content or culpability of specific individuals related to the WHAT and WHO dimensions of the star.

What may seem an obvious point is made here, to underline the complex, versatile, and diverse role of forensic evidence in the forensic process and to highlight how each question of circumstances is essential not only in producing factual knowledge and in reconstructing a coherent case narrative, but also in actually making possible the material processing of the case. Each leg in the star and the principal questions it addresses are thus to be seen as essential to the making of a case (this is illustrated in Chapter 4).

The star model represents a sort of box-in-box system where each leg or topic can beneficially be investigated with reference to and by using the other legs (or topics). It is a tool that is both *general*, in that it has general application to the investigation of cases in a thorough and full way, and *particular*, in the sense that each object, layout, scene, and concrete investigative action can be addressed using the questions in the star.

The particular aspect of the star includes recognising that each leg, or topic, may involve its own norms in regard to the search for related evidence and its analysis. Thus, the WHO question tends today to be highly focused on DNA and fingerprint techniques, but WHEN is entirely open ended, and WHY even more so. The star formalises and organises this implied knowledge and application of sound professional judgement (which has often become a tacit knowledge of the experienced crime scene investigator) according to the different topics, so it can be put into practice in concrete investigations. The crime scene investigator (CSI) must be careful not to let the norms distract from other valuable avenues; for example, the widespread use of closed-circuit television (CCTV) to monitor public places was invaluable in identifying suspects in the investigation of the July 2007 London Transport terrorism attack.

2.3 Tactical Use of the Star

With respect to crime scene investigation, each of the 6Ws translates into particular facts that must be identified or established. Although the six topics represented in the investigative star are interconnected and to a large extent synergistic, two are axiomatically more important in the context of crime scene investigation. These are the WHO and the WHAT. Unless we can identify a suspect and unless we can derive from the reconstruction of what happened that indeed a crime has taken place, then there can be no closure to the investigation.

2.3.1 The Topics of the Star

To make the best use of the topics of the star, it is important to have a good understanding of their meanings in the context of the model.

2.3.1.1 WHAT Happened?

The topic WHAT is about establishing a criminal content or *corpus delicti*. It is also about ensuring that the incident is reconstructed and described in the greatest detail possible (using not least the remaining five legs in the star) by the discovery of as many exhibits as possible to permit the most complete and reliable reconstruction of the actions and circumstances pertaining to the crime. This topic is the leg in the model most directly related to the search for inceptive evidence—that is, evidence that may help establish criminal content (or exculpate the incident from criminal content). For an incident to be processed as a crime in a court of law, proof that a criminal act has been committed or taken place must be produced. The topic is a primary and overarching one, not only because of its legal importance but also in the sense that covering it involves making good and proper use of the rest of the topics in the investigative star.

Establishing WHAT happened, with a view to establishing whether the incident has any criminal content or not, involves applying the question WHAT to the remaining topics of the star in order to form a sum total, from which as full a reconstruction of the incident as possible can be made. In order to do that one must seek out evidence that provides answers to WHAT was the sequence of events that occurred during the commission of the act, WHAT was the possible motive, WHAT was the modus operandi of the persons involved, WHAT inanimate objects (e.g., tools, vehicles, weapons) were involved in the act or incident, WHAT was placed or left at the scene during and/or as a result of the incident, and WHAT was removed from the scene during and/or as a result of the incident? However, on a particular level, to the crime scene investigator the topic WHAT also entails a focus on the description and documentation of all of those things at the scene that could produce potential evidence. It is only through detailed documentation of all the WHATs (from large objects to latent traces) that evidence can be found at the scene and that the final reconstruction may be performed and properly supported by evidence.

2.3.1.2   *WHERE Did It Take Place?*

The topic WHERE is about identifying and describing the scene of crime and thus the place or places that may reveal potential evidence about the incident and the identity of the people involved. To the crime scene investigator, the importance of the crime scene may be self-evident, and it may seem unnecessary to go into detail about this topic. However, as experienced CSIs well know, it is by no means always self-evident where the crime has actually transpired (see, for example, Chapter 4). Establishing this as well as how wide a space to search for potential exhibits related to the crime can be not only a tremendous task but also sometimes quite a challenge. The topic is also significantly about contributing to the establishment of the origin of the potential evidence. For the CSI this implies asking questions with regard to WHERE a particular object or trace originates from (e.g., piece of broken glass, fibres, marks). Thus, the topic of WHERE is intimately related to working toward establishing the identity (WHO) of physical evidence as outlined briefly in Chapter 1. Furthermore, one can add two subtopics to this leg of the star which relate to mobility between locations of people and objects as well as possible evidence to this mobility. These subtopics are WHERE FROM and WHERE TO. In this respect, WHERE is also a topic that addresses the potential of evidence to link places and persons.

The topic WHERE is the one that relates most directly to the responsibility and territory of the CSI. The topic is quite a bit broader than it may appear. It is not only the identification of places of crime—scenes of crime—but also the location of things within it. Furthermore, the topic WHERE includes the search for all the possible locations or loci related to a criminal event and the discovery and location of these. Possible loci to be discovered include any place or object related to the incident, such as the victim's body, the suspect's body, the location in which the body was found, the location in which the crime was carried out, locations in which the victim has been held, vehicles used to transport any of the involved, and the residence or workplace of the suspect and those of the victim.

2.3.1.3 HOW Did It Happen?

The topic HOW concerns the mode, form, and development of the incident and the mode of operating of the perpetrator also known as the modus operandi. Modus traces are a category of their own in investigative vocabulary, but to the CSI the focus on modus must be broadened to include all aspects of the incident and all evidence that may help reconstruct the history of the event in terms of HOW it unfolded. To the CSI, the topic also concerns the course of events of inanimate objects and traces at the scene. HOW did a particular object participate in the course of events, HOW did a particular piece of trace or situational evidence come into existence, and HOW did a concealed body get to where it was found? These questions reinforce the interdependence of the topics, as their answers can provide information as to WHEN, WHO, and WHY.

2.3.1.4 WHO Is Involved?

The topic WHO is the question of identifying which individuals were involved in the incident and of establishing identities, whether of the victims, suspects, or witnesses. WHO was the victim? WHO was the perpetrator? WHO witnessed the crime? To the CSI, this topic addresses the search for classical forms of imprint evidence such as fingerprints, as well as blood, semen, and saliva. A successful identification of the persons involved is, as outlined earlier, of vital significance to the completion of the case; however, the topic may also involve the identification of evidence that provides more interpretive forms of information—that is, evidence that may possess some sort of intelligence value to the case investigation. There may be evidence that points to the possible identity of someone but is less direct than body fluids or fingerprints. The cascade of evidence as to WHO diminishes in this sequence: immutable and unique characteristic of the person, such as a full DNA profile or fingerprint; characteristic of the person that may not be unique or immutable, such as a partial DNA profile, dentition, or tattoo; characteristics that require subjective interpretation, such as photographs, voice, or signatures; and things associated with the person, such as footwear, personal belongings, and clothing. There is an intelligence value for all of these, and even the more tenuous examples can help to link evidence, scene, and person and may lead to identity.

2.3.1.5 WHEN Did It Take Place?

The topic WHEN directs the investigation toward establishing the time of the (criminal) incident and any other issues of the determination of time relevant to an investigation. These issues could include the time of death in a homicide investigation or the time when drugs were transferred in a narcotics investigation, for example. To the CSI, WHEN is about establishing as precisely as possible relevant time issues, the most important one being the time of the criminal incident, but there are many smaller problems of time related to the establishment of HOW the crime was carried out. Having identified the events that occurred at the scene, being able to identify the sequence in which they happened and as far as possible the actual time can assist in reconstructing the crime scene. WHEN, in other words, is a topic that both covers the search for exact points in time when something happened and addresses the chronological relation between objects, events, and people—such as establishing what happened before, after, or simultaneously with what.

2.3.1.6 WHY Did It Happen?

The topic WHY relates, on a general level, to the disclosure of motive or, to be more specific, to evidence that may provide information as to possible criminal intent involved in the incident. Motive is a multivalent term here, designating motivations as well as opportunity, possibility, and reasons for participating in the incident under investigation. The topic WHY is intimately connected to the disclosure of criminal content and assignment of responsibility for the crime (or *culpability*, in legal terms) by relating the acts to the common experience of rational human agents and the calculated consequences of particular acts. To the CSI, however, the topic is more intimately related to questions of causality and less to the question of human motivation and reason. The topic WHY is often closely related to WHAT, in regard to the evaluation of inceptive evidence. It has a broader value, in that looking for relations of causality—WHAT caused what to happen, WHY does something appear the way it does—WHY can interact with the other legs of the star and lead to other questions and lines of investigation.

2.3.2 The Investigative Star in Practice

The legs of the star are presented as representations of each of the 6Ws, but it is useful to explore the model with some illustrations as to the outcomes of its application with reference to the expanded descriptions of the topics shown in Figure 2.2.

2.3.2.1 Establishing Criminal Content (Corpus Delicti)

Was a crime committed or not, and, if so, was it planned or accidental? The answers may be obvious, such as in counterfeiting cases where the counterfeit banknote, the falsified documents, or the false signature can serve as evidence of criminal content. When considering the

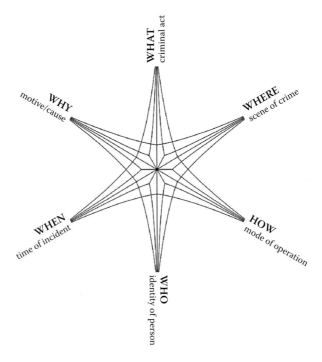

Figure 2.2 Expanded investigative star.

CRIMINAL INTENT

Theft and burglary are two of the most straightforward examples of how the WHAT question directly impinges on criminal intent. Others can be more complex—for example, when an apparent murder may be the result of an accident with no intent to kill or in the case of concealment of the corpse of an accidental death, as described in one of the cases in Chapter 12.

LOCATION, LOCATION, LOCATION

Forensic science is being used more and more in circumstances beyond those of conventional crimes, such as human trafficking. The immediate scene presented to the CSI may be a brothel where trafficked women are being forced to work as prostitutes, but the case investigation should include many other WHEREs, which will be identified by posing the HOW and WHEN questions. HOW did the women get from their own country? HOW do they get from where they are kept to where they have to work? HOW long have they been sex slaves? HOW does the person in charge obtain the money paid by the clients? Questions such as these will lead to the examination of vehicle and building scenes, paper and computer records, and a network of locations that could lead to the key of identifying WHO the women are and WHO is behind the trafficking.

WHAT topic in the investigative star, the CSI should continually refer to and from the other legs, particularly WHO, HOW, and WHY. Dealing correctly with this topic emphasises that scene investigation and the application of the investigative star should be an iterative process.

2.3.2.2 Establishing Location (Scene of Crime)

Knowledge of WHERE the incident took place is essential in any investigation. It is also necessary to create the boundary of the area where the incident took place and thereby the physical frame of the crime scene in which the other Ws must be addressed. The question WHERE, like the other elements of the 6Ws, contains multiple layers and dimensions. WHERE was the crime planned? WHERE was the perpetrator before the crime was committed, and what route did he take to the crime scene and to leave it? WHERE was the crime committed? WHERE did the incident occur—are one or more other scenes connected to the incident under investigation? Generally, an indoor crime scene is easier to deal with in regard to the question of WHERE than are outdoor ones where the boundaries of the scene can be difficult to define.

2.3.2.3 Establishing Mode of Operation (Modus Operandi)

Forensic evidence can often provide information about HOW a crime was carried out. The strength of the information will depend on the case circumstances and the nature of the evidence. For example, there may be indications of association between the suspect and the tools used in the crime, such as footwear marks or DNA on a knife handle, but if the thing providing the associative link is common, then the evidence is not compelling. Examples that establish evidence on the modus operandi include the following:

- Toolmarks showing that a locking device was broken open
- The location of a spent cartridge case showing the relationship between where a gun was fired and where the projectile was found
- Reconstruction of a detonated bomb, to determine the modus operandi in regard to its design and construction

In some cases, it may be impossible to determine HOW; for example, a fire scene may be so damaged and burned that it is not possible to conduct reliable investigations into all possible causes. The electrical wiring may be burned and melted into a state where it is not possible to determine its integrity, the extent and intensity of the fire may have consumed all traces of accelerants, or flammable liquids may have been stored at the location, making it impossible to identify the source of any residues detected.

2.3.2.4 Establishing Identity (Victim, Perpetrator, and Others Relevant to the Investigation)

An obvious and crucial part of any investigation is to establish the identity of the persons involved—victims, perpetrators, witnesses—and several types of evidence can contribute to this topic. The discussion of the WHO topic immediately above presented the idea of a cascade of possibilities for establishing WHO. Fingerprints and DNA are the most powerful tools (see Chapter 6), particularly when coupled with databases. Generally, the closer the evidence material is to being part of the body, the greater the value of the identity inferred. The search for evidence to establish the identity of the perpetrator should be conducted wherever he or she could have left evidence in relation to identity. Where the perpetrator entered, moved around, stepped, touched, made changes to conditions, and left the scene must all be examined. In addition to these main areas, the structured search for evidence to establish identity will often include other locations such as the route to and away from the scene, other locations where actions in relation to the crime could have been performed by the perpetrator, and vehicles that may have been used by the perpetrator.

THE ANGEL OF DEATH

Authorities became concerned about a sudden sequence of unexplained deaths of residents in an aged-care home. Although they were elderly and frail, the medical history of each deceased contained no suggestion of imminent death. Autopsy revealed no obvious cause of death, and routine toxicology screening was negative. When the bodies were reexamined even more closely, petechial haemorrhages were noted in the mucous membranes. Although not diagnostic, these lesions can be associated with hypoglycaemia and led the pathologist to think about the administration of insulin as the cause of death. Very close examination of the arms revealed pin-prick needle marks. The tissues around these were excised and sent for insulin analysis, which was positive. None of the deceased was a diabetic. Further inquiry led to the arrest of a recently employed nurse who denied the charge but was tried and found guilty. No motive was ever proved but it was suspected that she regarded herself as an "angel of death," helping to end what she regarded as the pointless lives of the residents.

ADOPT THE IDENTITY

Establishing identity can vary from physical recognition of the person to biochemical analysis of infinitesimally small traces. It is crucial for the CSI to become a *doppelgänger* of the perpetrator and thereby try to reconstruct what may have been the perpetrator's actions and what kind of identity evidence might have been left behind. One way to achieve this is to literally follow in the footsteps of the perpetrator, starting at the point of entry and ending the search where the person likely left the scene. Suppose the point of entry was through a window; after smashing the window glass, the perpetrator reached in to unlock and open the window, climbed in, and entered the living room. In this situation, the CSI must ask the following questions: In order to enter through the window, where did the perpetrator put his hands, his feet, his shoes? Was he out of breath, possibly leaving saliva on the window ledge or on the internal window sill? Did he step on the pieces of broken window glass? Did he leave shoe marks in the ground outside the window, on the outside of the wall, on the window ledge, or on the internal window sill? Did he cut himself on the edges of the broken window glass? Did he leave fibres from his clothing on the window components? Could paint, soil, or any other substance have been transmitted to his clothing? Did he by coincidence lose any personal belongings while entering the house, such as a lighter or papers?

2.3.2.5 *Establishing Time of Incident and Sequence of Events*

Traditional forensic evidence can sometimes prove WHEN a crime took place, but far from all cases. The existence of a fingerprint on a bottle does not reveal when it was deposited, only from whom it originated. A wet bloodstain will be recent—depending on how much blood, perhaps less than an hour; a dry but red stain will be a few days old; and a dark

WHEN DID HE DIE?

Although the time of the incident and the sequence of events are both examples of WHEN, they are different in their demands on the CSI. Of the two, establishing the time of the incident can be the more important (as it may exclude a suspect from consideration) and the more difficult to establish. The toxicology case provided in Chapter 12 and referred to above is an example of lateral thinking in establishing WHEN. The known rate of decay of two drugs in blood was used to estimate the time of death of the deceased relative to the time that he was known to have consumed them and excluded the allegation that he had been murdered by his wife imprisoning him without access to food or water. This is also an example of how the answer to one W question (WHEN) can lead to answering another (WHAT). In regard to the sequence of events, the physical nature of the scene may reveal valuable information. An obvious example is homicide by beating, where bloody footprints leading away from the body will have arisen by someone stepping in the blood after seepage from the body at the place where it was lying. Bloody footprints leading toward the body tell a different tale and will lead the CSI to explore other places where the assault may have taken place, a case of WHEN leading to WHERE.

HELL HATH NO FURY ...

A body of a young man was found at the entrance to a park, just before dawn on a Sunday. His head had been beaten in with a large rock. His possessions were untouched despite there being a considerable sum of money in his wallet. There were no obvious reasons for the killing, and police were inclined to regard it as a random, motiveless event. Interviews with friends of the deceased revealed that a neighbour in the apartment building where he lived had made homosexual advances to him which had been rebuffed. This man was now a suspect, and a search of his apartment found clothing with blood spatters that could have come from the deceased and traces of moss and soil that matched those on the rock. The suspect confessed that he was angered not only by being rebuffed but also by the manner in which it was done, so he followed the victim and attacked him.

brown one will be much older. It is therefore often essential that information regarding the time of an incident be judged in the context of the case. WHEN a crime has taken place can be a great forensic challenge. Establishing evidence of WHEN a crime was committed can be important for judging whether the suspect has been able to carry out the crime.

2.3.2.6 *Establishing Motive/Criminal Intent and Cause*

It is rare that forensic evidence in and of itself is able to produce factual information related to human motivations and intent. However, there may very well be indicators of these aspects at the scene, not least when coupled with the information and knowledge gained through police investigations. A homicide scene where the body exhibits an excessive amount of stab wounds may become evidence in support of a hypothesis that the killing was committed during a state of rage with intent to harm or obtain revenge, which could direct the investigation toward a particular suspect, or it could be evidence that could support an argument by the defence that the defendant was momentarily insane when committing the crime with no prior intent. This aspect of scene and evidence interpretation runs the risk of giving in to speculation if not performed professionally and with a keen awareness of the limits of the evidence. It is especially important to be rigorous in looking for alternative explanations and to try to falsify the hypothesis by considering as much different evidence as possible. However, the question WHY must not be overlooked or discounted when applying the tool to scene investigation. WHY is related to issues of causality, and addressing it can lead to answers to WHAT and WHO. It is also a topic that can involve very close interaction between police investigators and the CSI and other forensic personnel.

2.4 Strategic Use of the Star

The forensic process begins with the making of tactical and strategic decisions with regard to what is of interest to the scene examination and the overall investigation and how the processes are to proceed. It is therefore important to make strategic use of the star from the moment a notification has been made until the time that the case is presented in court (for a detailed description of the practical aspects and procedures of the different phases of the process, see Chapter 3; for a description of this process in relation to a real case investigation, see Chapter 4). We close this chapter by showing how the star is to be used at a strategic level and as a tool for developing a strategy and communicating about the examination and investigation of the scene and evidence recovered from it, across the different phases. The topics, or legs of the star, should therefore be considered in all of the following activities:

- In preparing scene of crime attendance in response to the information conveyed by the notifier
- In the initial assessment of the scene by the first officer attending
- In developing a scene of crime investigation strategy by the CSI scene manager
- In undertaking scene of crime investigation by the CSI team and specialists
- In the assessment of scene of crime findings
- In considering the need and potential for further examination
- In interpreting the scene in the light of evidence gathered
- In the assessment of the intelligence value of evidence obtained from the scene
- In the communication between all personnel involved in the case
- In planning the laboratory examinations
- In interpreting the results of examinations and tests

The general topics of the star apply also to the following activities of the forensic process:

- In maintaining the integrity of evidence collected at the scene
- In documenting the scene investigation
- In preparing reports and statements
- In the final presentation of evidence in court

2.4.1   Strategies for Investigation and Analysis

The investigative strategy is the development and implementation of a plan that describes what is to be done, where and how it is to be done, by whom, and when. These elements, and why they are being performed, are the same as the topics of the investigative star—the 6Ws. The strategy may be simple and almost reflex or may require considerable discussion between the interested parties. Either way, the star provides a framework for the full and appropriate development of the strategy and formalises the process, in some way analogous to the pre-take-off checks that are a constant and essential action on the part of a pilot, no matter how experienced.

In major crimes and crimes where the scene plays a central part in establishing the criminal content, the strategy is often made by the police investigators and the scene investigators working together on the basis of their communication related to the initial assessment and examination of the scene. It is good practice to properly explicate and communicate the strategies across the different roles and phases of the forensic process, and between the different parties involved, even in volume crime cases or cases involving only a few people working the case and the crime scene.

In dealing with more complex investigations and major crimes the investigative strategies of the different parties must be explicated, communicated, and aligned. This applies not only among members of a team working a scene, but also between the scene investigators and police investigators and between scene investigators and forensic analysts.

Using the topics of the star as a common model may help this alignment and provides a shared methodological tool to systematise and streamline the communication process. Each participant in the forensic process can thus contribute to the strategy and investigation on the basis of their particular field of expertise and the types of evidence and information recovered. Any strategy made at any level of the investigation and the forensic process can and should be adapted as the work proceeds. Any such revisions, however, should be based on clear communication between the police investigators and the CSI or the forensic analyst to ensure that there is proper coordination and that the forensic evidence is put to the best use in the investigation and processing of the case. The topics delineated in the star are the common denominator, which cuts across the differences in methods, processes, tasks, and roles occupied by different parties in the forensic process.

2.4.2   Strategy and Planning of the Scene Examination

Having produced an initial assessment of the scene and the possible content of the incident under investigation, a clear strategy for the full examination of the crime scene and the subsequent analysis of evidence can be formed and the 6Ws directed toward assigning the proper people and resources. The strategy will involve forming an initial hypothesis of possible causes for the current state and layout of the scene and what forms of evidence may be present. It will help in prioritising the search and tasks—for example, which sectors to identify and search and in which order, as well as what forms of evidence to search for first and why.

Because the initial hypothesis is an informed guess based on a combination of the first available information and the experience of the investigators and CSI, accompanied by a sensible tendency to begin by posing the worst-case scenario, formulating a hypothesis may be thought of by some as introducing bias to the process right from the start. This, however, is a misunderstanding of the basics of scientific inquiry, a cornerstone of which is that the process is transparent and that experiments can be reproduced based on the description made by the scientist. Its applicability to scene investigation will be sound provided that the CSI has the discipline to continually challenge the current hypothesis or hypotheses developed to explain events—for example, by seeking to falsify them.

The strategy of crime scene investigation and examination is exactly like the basic scientific method and can be likened to the design of an experiment or experiments to test a hypothesis within the sciences, by testing one premise at the time through experimentation. As a consequence, more perspectives and points of view in the process are developed, and it becomes possible to critically assess whether all the possible forms of evidence and findings that may challenge it have been searched for. The same goes for the rhetorical foundation of how to use the topics when producing proofs for arguments; here, the rhetor must consciously try to imagine all the arguments that can be posed against his own argument (hypothesis) and seek to refute them by means of visiting all the topics from as many perspectives as possible (possible explanations) to be sure he has actively sought the truth of the matter.

Using the star to form a strategy for examination in cooperation with the police investigators involves posing a great number of questions, the answers to which can guide the decisions to be made on the use of personnel, technical equipment, and specialist assistance, as well as deciding on which exhibits to secure and submit for analysis and in which order (for an example of this, see Chapter 4). According to the star, it is necessary to determine the following: WHAT needs to be done to initiate the investigation? WHERE is it deemed most beneficial to search for evidence and where is the scene (or scenes)? WHEN should the agreed forms of investigations and analysis be initiated and in what order? WHO should conduct the examinations, with which competencies or specialist knowledge? HOW should evidence be searched for; that is, how should the immediate scene investigations proceed and with what techniques or procedures? And, just as importantly, WHY should the investigation proceed; that is, what are the circumstances that led to a suspicion of criminal content of the incident under investigation?

Several questions must be considered in the development of the strategy: What type of crime is the investigation most likely dealing with? Are there any suspects at present, or is it a high priority to produce evidence that may give indicators to the identity of the perpetrator on which the investigation can move forward? Can a criminal content be clearly established, or should the examination of the scene pay specific attention to producing inceptive evidence in order to decide the contents of the incident or case?

Forming a strategy involves posing a host of sub-questions, which are also covered by the star but which are more specific with regard to the topics and the routes for searching for information, as well as the disciplines or roles of individual participants in the process. The topics and the routes inherent in addressing them are different for the police investigator, the crime scene investigator, and the forensic analyst at the laboratory.

2.4.3 Systematic Documentation

We have given many examples of the importance of the forensic process as a source of objective and informative evidence for investigators and courts; however, a key part of any methodology is to make it transparent and reproducible. This is why it is vital that the CSI be able to demonstrate every single step undertaken, in order to ensure the traceability and integrity of the exhibits from the scene of the crime to the court room. The value of even the most carefully recovered and telling evidence may be lost if the chain of custody of the exhibit that provides it is not maintained. The questions in the star may also serve as a reminder when it comes to ensuring that a proper log is kept of the scene investigation, in addition to providing a framework for the final report and for further analysis of exhibits. There are different formats for logging and documentation in different national contexts, and more detailed descriptions of common procedures are treated in more depth in Chapter 3, but, generally, remembering the 6Ws as a mnemonic tool will ensure that all the necessary procedures are followed and documented and assist in the production of a logical and informative report.

2.4.4 Evaluation of Efforts

The production of objective evidence, on which to deliberate cases, is the goal of the forensic process. One of the principal methods in this regard involves keeping a continuous evaluative awareness of the evidence and frequently pausing to evaluate process, evidence, and methods. The star diagram and the questions it poses may be used for this purpose, or even as a means to get on with an investigation that has become stuck or has run out of obvious places and means of looking for or finding potential evidence. Using the star for evaluation purposes is, at the simplest level, a question of checking whether all the legs in the star are covered and that enough evidence is recovered that one can legitimately produce an interpretation of the scene and its evidence.

One should also continuously use the star as a means of pointing the examination or investigation in new directions, possibly leading to the location of new and different forms of evidence to achieve as many perspectives of the evidence as possible. It can also be used to find ways to challenge and test different hypotheses held in relation to each of the questions, and thus challenge the internal coherence and robustness of the evidence in relation to the interpretations (hypotheses) made. The principles behind the use of the star for evaluation purposes are to keep asking questions and search for evidence to solve those questions until the possible explanations are exhausted. This questioning can be applied to consideration of the evidential value of specific exhibits or to the level of developing perhaps more complex alternatives to the starting hypotheses about WHAT has happened, WHERE it happened, HOW the scene was created, WHO was involved, WHEN the events occurred (time or sequence), and WHY.

The final but most important principle in evaluation, and one that we have emphasised repeatedly in this work, is that the best way to maintain the essential scientific and rhetorical integrity of the process is to consciously look for evidence to the contrary of what one expects. Thus, if everything seems to point to the fact that the crime has only transpired in the living room, the CSI should not disregard the involvement of other loci and should just as diligently look for evidence to the contrary—keeping an open mind with regard to what might prove to be wrong when investigating the bedroom, the kitchen, the bathroom, and the exterior of the house.

2.5 Summary

The investigative star can serve as a means of structuring or evaluating the whole investigation of a crime scene, from the very first step of developing an investigative strategy in response to the circumstances contained in the notification of an incident to the very last step of writing the report for the court. The questions contained in the six legs of the star may seem simple and intuitive and hardly worth a mention; however, they have a long and august heritage going back to the Hellenic rhetoricians, and the topics add a formalised objectivity to each step in which they are applied. The application of the investigative star to the planning and execution of crime scene investigation should now be clear and is illustrated with a specific case in Chapter 4. However, beyond those direct and obvious applications, the CSI must always be aware that making evaluations is a continuous part of the crime scene investigation. The objectivity endowed on the evaluation by using the star is a safeguard against lack of systematisation and objectivity and provides a way to make sure that one does not get stuck or too attached to a specific hypothesis, thereby becoming subject to confirmation bias.

The Forensic Process
Performance, Practice, and Procedures of Scene Investigation

3.1 The Forensic Process

The involvement of science in the investigation and resolution of criminal offences begins at the scene of incident—the crime scene. Without the correct identification of the scenes and their correct examination, all the tools of forensic science are useless. The authoritative international document published by the International Laboratory Accreditation Cooperation (ILAC), *Guidelines for Forensic Science Laboratories* (referred to as ILAC G19), defines *crime scene* as a "scene of incident prior to establishing whether a criminal or illegal action has taken place or not." The crime scene is not restricted to the location of the incident (primary crime scene), but also includes areas where relevant acts were carried out before or after the crime (secondary crime scenes). The crime scene is also relevant to incidents such as accident investigation, suspicious fires, terrorist attacks, and disaster victim identification, in addition to conventional criminal offences.

Correct examination of the scene is the precondition for forensic science to be able to provide reliable, impartial, scientifically rigorous, and informative evidence about a given incident that may not be possible to obtain by any other means. The crime scene investigator (CSI) is at the frontline of the process of discovering and providing objective information, and the activities of the scene investigator at all points in the process can be decisive in determining the outcome of this process.

The task of the scene investigator, whether conducting the overall examination of the scene or in the role of specialised examiner of particular forms of evidence, is a complex and demanding one for several reasons:

- Errors made may never be corrected or may be impossible to correct and have the potential to jeopardise the entire process and ultimately the resolution of the case.
- Crime scenes are dynamic and can be rapidly changing environments. Ensuring the optimal conditions for the identification, containment, and preservation of evidence may therefore be a complex and challenging task.
- Every scene presents its own unique circumstances and holds its own unique story to be told; each scene has its own unique combination of possibilities and constraints on the examination, analysis, and interpretation of exhibits. Decisions must be made at each new scene according to its specific demands with regard to the skills, competences, procedures, methods, and equipment required to establish sufficient knowledge and evidence of the crime for the case to be processed.
- Continuous developments within forensic science present new and increasingly challenging possibilities and constraints on the task of the scene investigator, not only in terms of what they can reveal but also because of the accompanying need for still more detailed and complex procedures to avoid the dangers of degeneration,

INTERNATIONAL GUIDELINES

ILAC Guide 19 defines contamination as "the undesirable introduction of substances or trace materials to exhibits at any point within the forensic process." Contamination and its opposite, the loss or degradation of evidential materials, are the constant enemies of forensic scientists, whether working as a scene investigator or as a laboratory analyst. The whole value of their work is based on the assured integrity of the materials identified, analysed, and interpreted. This is why so much emphasis is rightly placed on preservation of the scene, from access control to the manner in which recovered items are packaged, labelled, and stored.

contamination, and cross-contamination of evidence. A good example is the widespread use of the polymerase chain reaction (PCR) technique within DNA analysis, which has set new standards in the amount of biological materiel required to be able to obtain a full DNA profile (see Chapter 8 for a detailed description). However, this exquisite sensitivity means that CSI personnel must wear extensive protective clothing to prevent contamination from their breath, skin, and hair. Similar improvements are being made in other fields of forensic analysis, such as fingerprints on human skin, identification of debris and accelerants related to arson and explosives, and profiling of narcotics to identify the origin of the drug. These advances are constantly setting new standards and unfolding new possibilities for the outcome of investigations. These developments, therefore, are making it possible to obtain more and better information in an investigation, but also increase the complexity within the activities of the forensic process.

- Documentation and records of the exhibit chain of custody, examinations of the scene, and protocols and results of testing are coming under increasing scrutiny by the courts in the course of a trial and are a vital part of the process of ensuring the continued trust of the public in the facts produced by the forensic process. The rigorous documentation and recording of these and all activities at the scene are not pointless bureaucratic distractions from the "real work" but are an essential part of the process.

Add to these points the fact that the scene is an uncontrolled environment, unlike the laboratory, and it becomes clear that the task of the frontline personnel—the scene investigator—is extremely challenging. The expectations of the public and investigative personnel regarding the ability of scene investigators and forensic scientists to disclose the secrets held by the crime scene and the truth about it, quickly and in full, are high, sometimes unrealistically so. The job is one of minute procedure, which demands patience, pertinence, and perseverance, where progress is often drawn out and small in scale in comparison to the efforts necessary in bringing it about.

Creativity and innovative thinking are central to the job of the scene investigator in discovering potential evidence, in directing and focusing the search, and in putting together the small dots of factual information into a coherent case narrative that can be properly supported. By contrast, there is an increasing focus on problems of conscious and unconscious bias, resulting in still more procedures, controls, and assessment schemes being put in place in an effort to control and constrain the individual investigator's subjective faculties.

The above responsibilities properly lie on the shoulders of every CSI, but the individual scene investigator is often just one of a number of people involved, and one without complete control and sometimes only little influence on the final outcomes of his efforts in terms of the final success or failure of the investigation and resolution of the case. The job of the crime scene investigator is a job with many inherent tensions and contradictory demands on its practitioners, all of which add to the complexity and challenging character of the job. These tensions—the ever-changing methodology and technology environment, the need for communication and teamwork covering the variety and numbers of personnel that may be involved, and the need to conform to formal standards of technical and procedural operation—can be expressed as three fields of practice in which any forensic science practitioner must excel: *discipline*, *discretion*, and *documentation*, referred to as the 3Ds.

3.1.1   The 3Ds of Forensic Science Practitioners

3.1.1.1   Discipline

Discipline reminds the practitioner that there are certain standards of procedure and modes of action associated with each step in the forensic process that must become second nature to scene investigators in order to be able to release their creativity in relation to solving the task without falling prey to errors that may compromise the integrity of the scene or the evidence. Scene investigators must be disciplined in their actions, in following proper procedures of analysis, and in the sense of being rigorous in applying method and methodology, as well as documenting practices—thereby creating the proper level of transparency and repeatability of analysis that can withstand any scrutiny of results and professional judgements.

3.1.1.2   Discretion

Discretion requires the investigator to always exercise professional judgement in order to adapt to the situation and chooses and performs the proper procedures and techniques relevant to the particular scene and situation. The scene investigator must always act with discretion in every aspect of the case and in interpretation of the scene and exhibits that will serve as evidence. Discretion is the vital link between the need for the CSI to be imaginative and ready to think laterally in posing questions about the scene, but yet be objective and rigorous in the execution of its examination and the drawing of conclusions from the findings. Exercising discretion means that the CSI will always keep an open and critical mind, with regard not only to the scene and circumstances but also to his own actions and decisions. The investigator must be able to juxtapose the different goals of the investigative and the scientific inquiry and always stay within the bounds of what the evidence allows, not giving in to speculation where speculation is not called for, yet at the same time assisting to the best of his ability in the search for evidence. The investigative star is a valuable tool to resolve the contradictions in being thorough, imaginative, and open minded in the search for evidence regarding what happened at the scene. Discretion is intimately linked to the other two Ds. Scene investigators must possess the discipline to accept whatever evidence and signs they encounter, uninfluenced by personal feelings, and should be willing to question and investigate all of their findings, whether they like them or not. A degree of scepticism, then, should be a characteristic of the process of scene examination so the investigator may distinguish truth from the opinion or inclination of both self and others.

The proof of the successful application of discretion in the investigation lies in its documentation, and the act of documentation can at times be a stimulus for the CSI to perform some degree of critical self-appraisal.

3.1.1.3 *Documentation*

An informal rule of quality systems is "If it isn't written, it didn't happen," and forensic science is no different with regard to documentation. It is *the* key factor in investigative practices that binds the different parts of the process together and makes the production of knowledge possible across time and space. Without proper documentation, there is no reliable knowledge that will stand up to scrutiny at the time of the investigation and trial and no knowledge to pass on for any retrospective analysis or reconstruction. It is the quality of documentation that makes possible the transformation of mere information to knowledge based on evidence by bringing together the web of mutually supporting facts, thus making an interpretation sound and solid. Documentation is part of the way that we deal with changing technology, and the records in case notes and results should be good enough so that the case can be reopened 25 years later. The aim of documentation of the scene is to produce a permanent record of it, of the physical items at the scene, and of any changes taking place at the scene. Documentation of the scene therefore is the starting point of the chain of evidence (chain of custody), so the value of meticulous note-taking cannot be overemphasised. The processing of a crime scene from the first response to the identification and recovery of evidence is a complex and sometimes stressful endeavour. All officers, from first responders to scene investigators and specialists, have many jobs to perform right from the start of an investigation, and information is at serious risk of being lost in the process if it is not effectively recorded. Thorough, detailed, and contemporaneous note-taking must be undertaken in the form of writing, photography, or voice recording. The recording should be thorough, and value judgements as to things being insignificant or mundane should be avoided.

3.1.2 Performance-Based Standards of the Activities in the Forensic Process

Within almost every profession a certain structure is established and implemented for dealing with the activities involved. In an attempt to contribute to the development of the discipline and the professionalism of forensic science practitioners, best practice manuals (BPMs), standard operational procedures (SOPs), and similar quality-enhancing devices have been implemented throughout the world. The contents of these are often quite similar in phrasing, as the practice of forensic science investigation has been built on international cooperation and the exchange of experiences and sharing of knowledge across borders and jurisdictions. Worldwide, networks and communities of police, forensic, and other authorities and organisations develop and make available forensic BPMs, SOPs, and guidelines.

This chapter is structured around European Network of Forensic Science Institutes (ENFSI) standards and definitions of the forensic process. They may not be identical to those in other regions, but they have a core that is applicable in crime scene investigations in any jurisdiction. The ENFSI standards deal with the following procedures:

1. Undertake initial actions at the scene of incident.
2. Develop a scene investigation strategy.
3. Undertake scene investigation.
4. Assess scene findings and consider further examination.

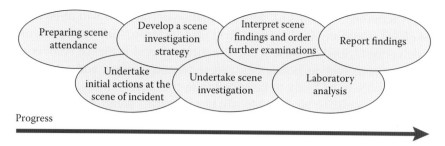

Figure 3.1 Summary of the forensic process, based on ENFSI standards.

5. Interpret and report findings from the scene of crime.
6. Carry out laboratory examination, testing, and presumptive testing.
7. Interpret findings.
8. Report findings.

The standards are not prescriptive in the sense that they detail how a given activity is to be performed; instead, they recognise that there may be more than one acceptable way of carrying out a task and are written in terms of outcomes rather than procedures of practice. The activities may seem to define a chronology or specific timeline; however, this is not necessarily the case, and the order in which they are performed depends on several factors, ranging from national legislation and the manner in which provision of services within the forensic community is structured to the impact of case specificities and the iterative processes inherent in investigative methodology.

They do, however, capture the main elements of a process that has a central flow from the time that an incident is reported, through its investigation, to presentation of the findings of the scene examination and their interpretation in a formal report and possibly at a trial.

The forensic process is illustrated in Figure 3.1. Note that each activity is depicted as overlapping with those around it; this is to emphasise that they are not discrete but inter-act. Note also that the figure condenses some of the discrete steps of the ENFSI standards, again emphasising their overlapping nature. Indeed, in some circumstances they will jump to a non-neighbouring activity; for example, results from the DNA laboratory or anthropology laboratory may indicate that the discovered remains of a dead body are not those of the person suspected and the process will jump back to the first stages. The flow can be turbulent and change direction several times in response to the increasing knowledge resulting from the scene examinations. Overall, however, the process has three distinct phases:

1. Activities undertaken before the scene examination begins
2. Activities at the scene
3. Activities after the scene examination is completed

Finally, the forensic process, as its name implies, covers the whole gamut of forensic science activities, but only those directly impinging on the CSI are considered here.

3.1.3   The Scene Investigator

The scene investigator is not a single person or narrowly defined role. Who will carry out the function of scene investigation varies according to both national and jurisdictional legislation and policies, as well as the severity of the incident. In cases of volume crime (e.g., robbery, auto theft, vandalism), the examination of the scene will often be completed by the first officer attending (FOA) or by other personnel from the local police jurisdiction, such as a detective trained in basic scene examination and evidence recovery. In major crime cases, however, such as homicides, rapes, assaults, arsons, and robberies, CSIs or forensic scientists are most likely to be assigned to the scene examination from the very beginning of the process. To be clear, we will use the term "scene investigator" in the following to describe anyone and any role or task, however small, related to the part of the forensic process taking place at or in direct relation to the scene of incident.

Although different law enforcement personnel may process the crime scene, the rules are the same in all cases. Crime scenes contain potential information that, if sought in a systematic, legal, and scientific way, can help the investigator apply the 6Ws to the forensic process in regard to the scene examination: what happened, who was involved, in what way, and so on. Personnel involved in criminal investigations must be able to derive the maximum possible reliable information from the crime scene, and this task defines the role and work of the scene investigator.

3.1.4   Roles within a Crime Scene Unit

Table 3.1 lists the roles most common to most crime scene units, although titles or descriptions may vary, as will the extent of the activities conducted. For example, the investigation of the scene of a volume crime requires no more than basic competencies in latent print development and identification, along with competency in the preservation and collection

Table 3.1   Roles at a Crime Scene

Role	Expertise/Responsibilities
Case management	Manage interface between investigation needs and crime scene activities
Crime scene coordinator	Technical scene management (CSI)
General crime scene examination	Crime scene examination (CSI)
Volume crime scene examination	Crime scene examination (police)
Specialised CSI roles	
Blood pattern analysis	Blood pattern analysis
Marks examination	Footwear marks, toolmarks, etc.
Firearms examination	Examination of guns, trajectory determinations
Vehicle accident examination	Vehicle accident examination
Latent print examination	Fingerprint enhancement and comparison
Other specialist roles	
Forensic pathology	Body examination, autopsy
Forensic odontology	Teeth examination and comparison
Forensic chemistry	Chemical, biological, radiological, and nuclear (CBRN) agents, drug laboratories
Forensic biology	Search, recover, and analyse blood, semen, etc.
Fire scene examination	Chemical, electrical, and other causes of fire
Explosives and bomb examination	Render safe, identify
Anthropology	Examine human remains
Entomology	Estimate time of death from infestation of corpse

of evidence such as blood or body fluid stains. The investigation of the scene of a major crime or a scene such as a bomb or major fire will involve personnel with more highly developed and sometimes even subcontracted specialised competencies. To some extent, the differentiation of roles between CSI and non-CSI personnel is artificial as different jurisdictions assign roles in different ways, and what follows may have to be modified to fit with individual administrative arrangements; however, the technical roles are more or less constant in all investigations, and it is only the administrative aspects that vary. Handwriting analysis, for example, may be conducted by personnel in a crime scene unit, in a public forensic laboratory, or by subcontractors from a private company.

3.2   The Forensic Process Prior to Scene Examination

Activities 1 and 2 of the ENFSI standards listed in Section 3.1.2 apply to what takes place before the formal examination of the scene, but they do not include the vital step of preparing for scene attendance, which takes place from the time that notification of the incident is made until the initial actions at the scene are implemented. The forensic process prior to examination of the scene by the CSI or CSI team is shown in Figure 3.2, starting with the preparations for attendance and ending with development of the scene investigation strategy. The arrows linking the three activities for this part of the overall process describe the outcomes of the activity that feed into the one that follows, so the outcomes from "develop a scene investigation strategy" are the inputs to the first activity in the "activities at the scene."

As already mentioned, activities may overlap or even jump activity modules, depending on circumstances. In regard to the forensic process prior to scene examination, the procedure "undertaking preservation and control" will be carried out to some degree by the investigator who was the first officer attending and may jump directly to the development of a scene investigation strategy if it is determined that there is no need to call out a CSI unit. The FOA may even need to process part of the scene as a means of securing fragile evidence before it is destroyed or may have to first of all attend to an injured person. The most extreme example of overlap or jumping, and which applies to the activities in all three phases of the forensic process, is where a volume crime scene is processed by the investigative officer. For that reason, the discussion on the forensic process will be centred on major crimes, but the basic principles also apply to volume crime.

Jumping and overlapping can and will occur throughout the planning, execution, and reporting of a scene investigation. Questions arising at the reporting stage may result in identification of another possible scene and jump back to the beginning of the process, or the planned sequence of examination of a scene may be changed because there is either an unforeseen need to expedite part of it (e.g., finding a blood trail) or a need to pause (e.g.,

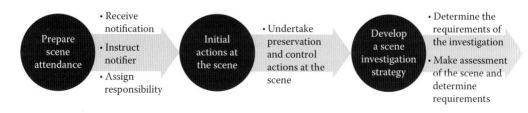

Figure 3.2 The forensic process prior to scene examination.

finding a computer that appears to contain files relevant to the examination but is processing data and requires the urgent attention of a digital evidence expert). The rule throughout the process is to behave in a professional manner but to be flexible and use common sense.

3.2.1   Prepare Scene Attendance

3.2.1.1   Receive Notification

The response of law enforcement to the scene of incident can be initiated in a number of ways: The police may receive a notification from a citizen, they may be alerted by an alarm from a bank being robbed, a police patrol unit may be called on while patrolling or observe and intervene in an apparent criminal incident, or the police may be dispatched from the dispatch desk handling alarm calls to the authorities. The individual receiving the call from the notifier, or the person responsible for implementing the initial response, must obtain all relevant and available information regarding the situation and the circumstances of the incident. Relevant information could include the following:

- Name and location of the notifier
- Number from which the notifier is calling
- A clear description of the incident
- Whether there are dangers to the lives or safety of individuals at the scene
- Whether there is need for medical attention
- What the conditions are at the scene
- A description of the injuries and state of potential victims
- A description of a potential suspect
- The number of people present at the scene

Whoever is responsible for responding to the notification must assess the nature of the response required and notify the proper authorities and dispatch the appropriate personnel. The response will be based on the information provided by the notifier and through initial questioning designed to elicit relevant information. Actions performed at this point may decisively influence the further progress of the investigation. Not only information and potential evidence but also lives may depend on the task being addressed professionally and speedily. If possible, the questions asked to elicit information should be based on the 6Ws of the investigative star.

3.2.1.2   Instruct Notifier

In cases where there are any indications that the incident may be of a criminal nature and thus the object of investigation, the notifier will need to be given instructions in order to protect and preserve the scene until the FOA arrives. The responder who takes the call will not be a CSI but should be able and competent to provide sufficient guidance to the notifier about preservation of the scene, even if only the simple instruction to ensure that the scene is kept as close to the *status quo* as possible, untouched, and if possible without any disturbance until the police unit arrives.

Actions after the criminal event but before the arrival of the FOA can have a significant effect on the scene. People at the scene—the notifier or witnesses—can be in a state of anger, shock, or devastation, which can lead to undesirable, yet understandable, changes in the crime scene. Victims of sexual abuse may feel an urgent need to wash themselves and their clothing; victims of arson might attempt to find and save items of monetary or personal value to them such as jewellery, photographs of their family and relatives, and keepsakes; or victims or witnesses may begin to conduct their own search of the premises to gain an overview of the situation, to determine whether or not the scene is safe, to assure themselves that their pets are safe, or for any one of a number of reasons that seem sensible to them in a moment of stress and distress.

As a result, significant changes may be made to the circumstances and layout of the scene, and important evidence may be destroyed, contaminated, or diminished in value; for example, a witness may destroy or blur footwear marks present in blood or in dust or move items around, seriously changing the circumstances (i.e., original condition) of the scene in a way that compromises its interpretation if such actions are not discovered and recorded.

More detailed instructions than a simple "don't touch" may therefore include:

- Provide life support if necessary.
- Keep witnesses separated and away from the scene.
- Keep a keen eye on the situation in order to be able to relate to the police unit what has happened at the scene until their arrival.
- Take note of any changes made to the scene.
- Make contact with the police unit on arrival.
- Give an accurate and logical statement to the police.
- Give a description of possible suspects or central witnesses.

3.2.1.3 Assign Responsibility

If possible, the responder should stay in contact with the notifier until the police arrive and can assume responsibility for the situation and the scene; however, it is important that communication is established between the responding police unit and the notifier at the scene. This may be done by instructing the notifier to look out for and establish immediate contact with the dispatched patrol officers or by instructing the police patrol on how to locate the notifier and to affirm when contact with the notifier is established, before terminating the dispatch role.

Depending on the size or seriousness of the incident, the appropriate personnel must be notified and all the available information communicated to them. It is also at this point that the first assignment of responsibility of the case is made and therefore why it is important that the person receiving the notification obtains enough of the right kind of information to ensure that a qualified judgement can be made as to what the situation requires. The critical questions at this stage are what kind of police and medical response units may be required and for what purpose. The receiver of the call should be competent enough to pay attention to details and to assign responsibility for immediate attendance at the scene to a patrol officer, to an on-call CSI, or to a more senior CSI or CSI team. The sooner an incident that may be a matter of a serious crime is classified and the proper personnel notified, the better.

The person responding to the notification should also be familiar enough with the key questions of the forensic process (the investigative star) to be able to ask them from the earliest moment, in addition to listening attentively for significant information indicating criminal content, the identity of any victims or suspects, time of the incident, sequence of events, and mode of operation. An example of such attentiveness could relate to the calling in of the finding of a dead person hanging. Here it is important to get a clear picture of the situation and the appearance of the scene and situation, so investigators are alerted to signs of foul play. These may be many and diverse, and anything from the type of knot to the position of the body may give reason for a heightened state of alert in relation to assigning responsibility and the response of the proper personnel. The receiver of the notification should:

- Identify the contact person (i.e., person in charge or deputy for the person in charge) for each unit required for the response.
- Communicate the information given by the notifier to the responders, as well as the information received through questioning, with regard to the number of people present, the conditions of the scene, the nature of the incident, injuries, possible suspects, etc.
- Communicate if any dangers to health and safety might be expected and whether other authorities have been or will have to be notified.
- Make sure the names, phone numbers, and other contact details for the members of each unit are exchanged and noted by all involved.
- Be sure that contact is made with other authorities and communicate with them about what type of service is required in relation to the incident, at what time and in what sequence, and advise them on where to go and whom to contact in the responsible unit at the scene.
- Decide and communicate a contact point at the scene for all units involved.

3.2.2   Undertake Initial Preservation and Control Actions at the Scene

3.2.2.1   The Role of the First Officer Attending

The first officer attending the scene is entering an unknown scenario, and the primary role of the FOA is to convert the unknown to a known with sufficient certainty to direct the correct subsequent actions. The spectrum of demands of the scene can range from none (i.e., it is clear that there has been no crime committed) to considerable (e.g., a multiple homicide by shooting involving several suspects, many victims, and more than one location). The competencies of the FOA will depend on the individual's training and experience, which can also cover a wide spectrum. The steps that follow are intended to cover the range of possibilities for the incident and for the individual officer. The core content can be summed up in two words: *protect* and *inform*. The FOA must protect lives, protect the scene, protect evidence, and inform whoever is responsible for coordinating the response to the notification of the incident as to the actual circumstances. The FOA must then inform the CSI or other personnel who follow as to what he has found and done. Inevitably, there is overlap with the work of the CSI, but that has to be treated not as duplication, but as the FOA establishing a secure foundation for the scene examination phase.

3.2.2.1.1 Protecting Lives of Victims and Suspects   In general, the first officer attending has the overriding obligation to take control of the situation, protect the lives and safety of people at the scene, and protect the scene itself in order to preserve its evidential value. This will include carrying out an initial assessment of the scene and its surroundings to get an impression of what one is dealing with, in order to make an appropriate response and call for relevant assistance. Saving lives is the first priority and takes precedence over all other considerations. The nature and sequence of other activities will reflect the particular situation and events as they unfold. On arrival, one of the first tasks of the FOA is therefore to check for survivors and undertake rescue actions if need be.

If an injured person is on the scene, first aid should be administered immediately even if it means risking the loss or destruction of valuable evidence; however, it is possible to deal with emergencies and deliver effective first aid while minimising the impact of this action on the value of physical evidence present. To achieve this, the FOA should note factors surrounding the person being treated, such as

- The original position (e.g., lying; sitting; position of arms, hands, or legs)
- The condition of the clothes and expressions or state of mind of the victim, including any utterances made by the injured person
- The original direction of flow of any blood or other fluids present
- The location, condition, and spatial orientation of any objects that must be or have been moved in order to administer first aid and rescuing actions
- The presence of any objects or material (e.g., textiles, fibres, hairs) in the hands or foreign material (e.g., skin, dirt, blood) under the fingernails of the injured person, in which case the FOA should either collect these or take steps to ensure that they are not lost (e.g., bagging the hands if later sampling for gunshot residues may be undertaken, an example where the material is inferred from circumstances rather than direct observation)

It may be necessary to make these notes mentally initially, due to circumstances, but they should be recorded in writing, by photography, or (when relevant) in sketches as soon as the situation is under control.

When paramedics or emergency medical personnel arrive, the officer should, without interfering in their work, instruct them how to enter the scene without disturbing it unnecessarily. The FOA may assist the forensic process significantly by observing the movements of medical personnel and take proper notes of their actions, movements, and any objects moved as described above.

By the time emergency personnel are ready to transport any injured persons to a hospital facility it is highly unlikely that the FOA will be the only police officer at the scene. If there are any indications that the injuries are due to a criminal action, the victim must also be considered part of the scene and a potential source of evidence to be preserved and protected. A police officer should therefore accompany any injured person taken from the scene. This officer will be able to carry out protective and preserving measures regarding the victim and potential evidence, such as

- Listen to and take note of anything said by the injured person that might have a bearing on the case (e.g., names of people involved in the incident or of the assailant, utterances about the incident itself that may be key information in the investigation).
- Protect the victim from further attack, if necessary (including approaches from the media).
- Detain the injured person if he or she is a suspect.
- Advise medical personnel in the ambulance and at the hospital about how best to collect evidence from the patient, consistent with best medical practice.
- Receive into custody any physical evidence taken from the injured person.

It is important that the officer accompanying the victim is a trained police officer. An alert investigator may hear an important word or accusation or what might be equivalent to a dying declaration that might be the key to the entire case but which may be lost on civilian emergency medical personnel, who do not have the training nor necessarily the time to pay attention to such details while attending to their task of providing medical care. It is also preferable, but perhaps not everywhere and not always possible, for the accompanying police officer to be present during treatment of the victim. Either way, the officer should arrange for proper removal and custody of the victim's clothing and other personal belongings that may be of evidential value. In carrying out this task, proper procedures for recovery, preservation, documentation, packaging, and transport should be followed to prevent risks of cross-contamination or degeneration of evidence (see Section 3.3.1 for more details).

3.2.2.1.2 Personal Safety   The first thing an officer should do when entering a scene is to render the scene safe. The officer should always remember that his own safety is of paramount importance. The risks to health may be many—and include the possibility that the suspect may still be in the location. When rendering the scene safe, the FOA can encounter several challenges simultaneously, such as being confronted with an ongoing crime, apprehending a suspect still at the scene, delivering first aid or life-support aid, evacuating people from a burning building, and so on. These activities all include possible risks to the health and safety of both the FOA and others who might follow: A building could collapse as a result of a fire or explosion; hazardous smoke, gases, or fluids may be present; hypodermic needles or body fluids could be contaminated with HIV or hepatitis C virus; airborne traces of potent narcotics or psychotic drugs could be present; or the building may contain asbestos or industrial chemicals such as acid. The FOA who perceives threatening health risks or dangers to health and life at the scene should take appropriate safety precautions, report these conditions to his supervisors, and arrange for the proper authorities and experts to be called.

3.2.2.1.3 Dead Bodies   Having dealt with the living, the attention of the FOA can turn to any apparently dead persons at the scene. If the officer is able to establish certain signs of death, such as lesions that are incompatible to life (e.g., head separated from the body, a shotgun blast to the chest), clear rigor mortis, odour, lividity, the beginning of decomposition, and so forth, then the body is not to be touched or removed until a detailed

---

SECURE TELECOMMUNICATIONS AT THE SCENE

It is not uncommon for police radios to be monitored by the press or members of the public with special interest in radios or the police, a fact that should be taken into consideration when communicating about a scene of incident of a serious crime. The FOA might consider using a mobile phone for this purpose rather than the police radio—or whatever means of communication is accessible locally—and in accordance with local policies (e.g., safe frequencies). Any landline or other phone that is part of the scene must *not* be used.

examination can be made. When the FOA has established that the victim is dead and has made a cursory inspection of the crime scene, superiors must be notified regarding the nature of the case via safe lines of communication.

Whether the coroner or equivalent agency should be contacted at this point of the investigation is often a matter of local custom. Some agencies, by agreement with the coroner, first wait for the investigating officers to arrive and begin their investigation. Notification of a death may be made at this time, with an estimate of when the coroner or pathologist will arrive. This can save time by not having to wait needlessly at the scene until a common approach path has been identified and examined for traces and exhibits before being cleared for use. Policies should be arranged with the coroner's office on such callout matters. The CSI scene coordinator with responsibility for scene management must know the jurisdictional requirements regarding the agency and office within it that has legal responsibility for the control of a scene where there is a dead person. The body must not be moved or searched without the consent of that office.

On rare occasions (e.g., where there is a risk of fire spreading from another part of a building to the place where the dead body has been found), the first officer may be forced to take immediate steps to remove the body from the scene. In these situations, the officer must ensure that the body is placed on the stretcher in the same position in which it was discovered, if circumstances permit. Limbs rigidly fixed in a certain position should not be straightened. If the victim is found face down, the body should remain in that position because lividity may change position and appearance, and trickles of blood may change direction.

If the rigidity or rigor mortis must be broken in order to transport the body, the officer must make note of it, preferably with sketches or photographs showing the original position. Before the body is moved, its position should be documented by making markings on the floor, measuring, and sketching or photographing the body. It is important to document the position of the head, arms, hands, knees, and feet and to show these on a sketch. The officer should also note the condition of the clothes and bloody tracks that may be present. This can be extremely important in answering the question of whether the body had previously been moved. Blood may run while the body is being removed. A question may later arise about the source of this secondary flow of blood.

POSTMORTEM CHANGES

Rigor mortis is a stiffening of the limbs of a corpse that begins about 3 hours after death and progresses through a maximum at about 12 hours, then diminishing until no longer evident at about 72 hours. It is caused by postmortem biochemical changes in the muscles and gives some indication of the time that has passed since death. Postmortem lividity, or livor mortis, results from the pull of gravity drawing blood and fluids to the lower portion of the body, causing a purplish red discolouration of the skin. Contact with the ground or another object impedes the settling, and these areas will not become discoloured. The pattern of livor mortis can therefore be used to determine whether or not a body has been moved; for example, if the body is found lying face down but livor mortis is present on the back, then the body was originally positioned face up.

Case 1

A woman was found dead on the floor in her bedroom. The first officer at the scene made a superficial examination of the scene. Some of the deceased's relatives stated that the woman had been very ill. Concluding that she had died of natural causes, the officer had the body removed from the scene without examining it further. After the deceased was moved, it became apparent that she had died of strangulation. A scarf had been tightly wound around the neck three times and knotted at the throat. A trickle of blood had run over one cheek from the mouth in an upward direction in relation to the position of the head at the time of the brief examination. Not discovering these important facts at the scene before moving the body could have compromised the investigation of the case. For example, determining whether the blood was there when the body was at the scene or was a consequence of actions during removal was made impossible because of the officer's premature decision to allow the body to be removed. It never could be established whether the blood flowed during or before transportation.

3.2.2.2 Actions Required of the FOA

3.2.2.1 Determine Basic Facts   One of the first actions at the scene is to determine whether or not the incident is a criminal matter and whether or not the investigation should be continued. This preliminary judgement rests on an initial assessment of the scene and the testimonies of victims or possible witnesses. Upon arrival, the FOA should therefore try to establish and document the basic facts. A factual account of what happened is of great assistance to the CSIs when they arrive because it helps them decide on the next move; however, the officer should never undertake lengthy and detailed interrogations that may compromise later questioning or give rise to misleading suggestions in the statements of witnesses. Furthermore, taking control of the situation and preserving and protecting the scene take priority over any investigative actions, and the officer cannot properly guard the scene if occupied with interrogations.

When making an initial assessment or judgement of the situation, the FOA should take into account any prior information or knowledge gained from the responder answering the call or during transport to the scene. The most straightforward way to begin assessing the situation is to informally interview the notifier. This will enable the FOA to obtain first-hand information about the nature of the incident, the possible order of events, and key timings. It is important, just as with the CSIs who will follow, for the FOA to keep an open and inquiring mind and to make and document his own observations. Information provided during what may be chaotic and stressful moments may be fragmentary, confusing, and possibly misleading—sometimes even wilfully so.

During the initial assessment of the scene the FOA should pay particular attention to any inceptive evidence associated with different forms of criminal content that may shed some light on the incident. In many instances, in order to make a proper judgement of the situation and the need for assistance, the FOA may have to enter the scene. This must be done with great caution and with due regard to the health and safety of both the officer concerned and anyone present and the avoidance of any unnecessary damage to potential evidence. The 3Ds of discipline, discretion, and documentation that apply to the actions of the CSI also apply to those of the FOA. The first officer has to decide how far it is necessary to engage with the scene in order to protect it and anyone present. The FOA must exercise considerable self-discipline and keep physical interventions to the minimum—the more serious the offence, the greater the need for discipline. The FOA must, of course, also exercise a degree of discretion in regard to positive actions to preserve life or evidence, such as dealing with a small fire or perhaps turning off running water in a bath containing a dead body. Whatever direction discretion leads, the actions and reasons must be documented.

Many scenes have natural physical barriers through which anyone entering the site needs to pass to gain access to the scene of incident; these should be considered in the sequence in which they would be encountered in moving from the perimeter or approach to the centre of the scene. The probability of finding forensic evidence at the points of entry and exit of such barriers is particularly high. The FOA should therefore attempt to discover, from direct observations or from witnesses, the most likely locations of these points and attempt to avoid them when entering and exiting the scene. If there is no alternative, the FOA should enter the scene with great caution to avoid contamination or degradation of evidence. The same caution should be exhibited in relation to any activities at the scene. The FOA should also pay due attention to avoiding focal points of the event and activities leading up to it (e.g., light switches, floors, visible traces and exhibits). While moving through the scene, the FOA should avoid unnecessary disturbance of any part of it, and take care not to damage any preexisting marks and impressions that might be present (e.g., fingerprints, footwear marks, impression marks) or leave his own fingerprints at the scene. If a door must be opened to enter the scene, its original state must be noted and the officer should attempt to identify possible imprints, while himself taking precautions to handle the door accordingly (e.g., do not use the doorknob or edges of the door but instead place one's fingertips on the top of the door to move it—see Figure 3.3).

Figure 3.3 CSI opening door by placing fingertips of gloved hand on the top edge.

KEY ISSUES FOR THE FOA ENTERING
BEYOND THE SCENE PERIMETER

When entering a crime scene, the FOA should:

- *Avoid obvious natural routes* when entering the scene; for example, enter along the wall instead of walking in the middle of the hallway.
- *Stay clear of wet substances* and other exhibits such as blood, visible shoe-prints, soil, or objects which, due to their position of character, may be of potential interest to the investigation.
- *Avoid touching* anything unless it is absolute necessary.
- *Avoid using any of the facilities at the scene* (e.g., toilets, sinks, towels, phone).
- *Avoid leaving any marks or imprints* on the scene of potential exhibits; for example, use disposable latex gloves, and if it becomes necessary to handle objects touch them in unusual places.
- *Use a light*, even in daylight conditions, to light the floor or surface to be stepped on so footwear marks and other trace evidence may be recognised and not destroyed.
- *If possible take photographs* during the inspection; these may be used as documentation and during the briefing of those next in line in the forensic process.

An effort must be made to observe details, particularly those that are fleeting, and to take written notes as soon as possible on such points as

- *Doors*—Open, closed, or locked? On which side was the key?
- *Windows*—Open or closed? Were they locked?
- *Lights*—On or off? Which lights were on? Remember to look for this even if it is daylight when you attend the scene.
- *Shades, shutters, or blinds*—Open or closed?
- *Odours*—Cigarette smoke, gas, gun powder, perfume, decomposition, sweat, spices?
- *Signs of activity*—Meal preparation, dishes in the sink, house clean or dirty, etc?
- *Signs of changes from normal or natural situation*—Everything is in good order but a blanket is lying on the floor or a cabinet with open doors appears to have been searched, etc.
- *Date and time indicators*—Mail, newspapers, dates on milk cartons, stopped clocks, spoiled foods, items that should have been hot or cold but were at room temperature.

A useful rule for the CSI is to examine the scene by literally following in the likely footsteps of the perpetrator, but this is exactly what the first officer attending must *not* do, and alternative approaches must be sought that either will leave no traces or can be solely ascribed to the actions of the FOA.

The first officer attending may or may not be familiar with the type of case encountered but should be sufficiently experienced to be able to identify matters of relevance and make specific notes that will assist the subsequent investigation.

DEALING WITH CLEAN-UP ACTIVITIES

On occasion, the victim or a relative may attempt to clean up the scene, perhaps to put everything in proper order when the police arrive or to try to conceal something. Occasionally, cleaning serves a psychological need to put everything back in its proper place. If a clean-up is in progress when the officer arrives, it should be stopped. If a clean-up has been completed or the officer suspects one has been performed, a detailed inquiry should be made to determine the original condition of the scene. It may be possible to recover material or undamaged items that were thrown out or discarded (e.g., blood or illicit drugs in the U-bend traps in the plumbing system, garbage recovered from adjacent public containers).

3.2.2.2.2 Scene Integrity and Control Nothing at the crime scene should be moved by the FOA unless absolutely necessary. The crime scene should remain as close as possible to its original condition for the investigating officers to see when they arrive. If it becomes necessary to remove any object because others may disturb it, the officer should consider the possibility that the item may have fingerprints present and act accordingly. Before any object is moved, its location should be noted. The exact position of an object at a scene may become important later in the case. Its position should be noted in the report, outlined in chalk, sketched, photographed, or videotaped. The details of all persons present at the scene and information obtained about the nature of the incident and the initial actions of the FOA and others present at the scene during this stage of the process should be recorded with a view to brief the investigative officer and as foundation for any further investigation.

Scene control is critical to the integrity of the scene and the evidence within it and is considered in detail in Section 3.3.1. A single FOA, or even a team of two, will find it difficult to control a large scene, which makes it all the more important to implement actions to protect the integrity of evidence within it. There may be limited options for exercising control, but identification of the main access points and either creating a barrier with scene tape or maintaining them under direct surveillance should be deployed to the fullest extent possible. The FOA can secure smaller scenes, such as an apartment, by scene tape, locking it up, or standing guard. At the scene of a volume crime such as a domestic burglary, the exclusion of unauthorised people might be achieved by careful instructions to the householder concerning what may and may not be touched before arrival of the personnel who will process the scene.

DON'T TOUCH!

Don't touch items or anything that would naturally be touched by people at the scene or that could be expected to be touched by the perpetrator or by any persons involved in the case. Before touching items or exhibits, make a visual inspection to determine where you can put your hands to avoid touching other possible evidence. If it is necessary to move a chair, for example, look underneath the seat to see if anything is present there; if not, then place your hands underneath the chair to lift it to its new position.

The initial assessment made by the FOA should include consideration of the environmental conditions at the scene, and the officer should take measures to secure fragile evidence. For evidence such as footwear marks or a small weapon, suitable protection may be afforded by, for example, placing a clean cardboard box over it or redirecting any overland flow of water away from it. Large objects that are easily moved may be placed in a sheltered area (e.g., a shed or garage) to protect them from the weather. Before doing this, the position and orientation of the object should be recorded in notes, sketches, and possibly photographs, as appropriate.

3.2.2.2.3 Dealing with Witnesses, Suspects, and the Public   A less obvious, but equally important, aspect of preserving the integrity of the scene and evidence is the actions of the FOA with regard to witnesses and suspects. The FOA should:

- *Keep the suspect and witnesses separated wherever possible.* Allowing the suspect and witnesses to talk may interfere with later questioning. Family members may be left in the care of neighbours when necessary, taking care that no alcoholic drinks or sedatives are administered. Remember that the dramatically grieving relative may be the prime suspect.
- *Instruct witnesses not to discuss the events.* This can prevent distortion by suggestion. If possible, the principal witnesses should be separated. In relating events to one another, witnesses may distort each other's impressions to the point where they believe that they saw things that they really did not see or that never happened.
- *Avoid discussing the crime with witnesses or bystanders.* This is also intended to prevent suggestion and distortion. Furthermore, circulating details of the crime may hinder the investigation.
- *Listen attentively but unobtrusively.* An alert officer can often pick up information of vital importance to the investigation simply by being a good listener.
- *Protect evidence that is in danger of being destroyed.* During inclement weather, take the steps described above to protect evidence. If the crowd of onlookers becomes large, it may become necessary to expand the protective measures at a given location to prevent trampling of the evidence.

The FOA may need to arrest or detain a suspect. In such cases, the most important duties should be done first. The police officer must use common sense in taking whatever measures are necessary in order to protect the scene. If it is not possible to hold the suspect at the scene or in the police vehicle, and a back-up officer is unavailable, a possible alternative is to find a reliable person to protect the scene until other officers arrive. The first officer must instruct such persons on how to guard the premises because the task is likely to be unusual for them.

The first officer should also be aware that the longer the suspect remains at the crime scene, the greater the possibility that the suspect could change or contaminate it. The suspect could, for example, remove evidence, leave new evidence, or even gain information from the opportunity of observing the scene in detail. Thus, the suspect should be searched and removed from the location as quickly as possible.

The FOA needs to communicate effectively with members of the public present at the scene. This includes handling any media present. News reporters sometimes arrive at the scene before investigators. The first officers on the scene should not, under any

MEDIA COOPERATION

The following fictitious scenario illustrates how there can be a positive interaction with the media: A fire broke out at night in a commercial warehouse near the local television station. The blaze was intense and dramatic, and a crew from the television station, the first on the scene, captured the size and spread of the fire on video. The media team interviewed people at the scene, including the night guard who had discovered the incident and reported it. CSI and fire investigators were able to use the tapes to assist in their reconstruction and to prove inconsistencies in the guard's account given to the police, which led to his arrest for arson.

circumstances, give information about the case to reporters. To inform the press is the responsibility of the police chief or designated public relations officers. In dealing with reporters, officers should be neither curt nor nonchalant, but they should be firm, even when reporters are persistent. When handling the media, the officer should remember that reporters often give invaluable assistance in the investigation of major crimes and should act with discretion and tact in order to sustain good working relations. However, when it comes to access to the crime scene there is no such thing as a "press pass"!

3.2.2.2.4 Transition to the Next Phase of the Forensic Process   The FOA has the immediate responsibility of initiating the discussion as to whether the forensic process should progress to "undertake scene investigation" (ENFSI Activity C). This decision must be made in line with any national or local policies, procedures, and priorities of the force concerned—for example, with regard to at what point and in what manner items are submitted to the forensic laboratory for searching rather than it being carried out at the scene by the CSIs. The policies and procedures should describe the communication and chain-of-command steps that the FOA must now take. The factors to take into account when making decisions regarding moving to the next activity and, if so, whether it is performed by the FOA directly or by CSI units or more specialised personnel include:

- The seriousness of the crime
- The competencies of the FOA
- The likelihood of recovering evidence (here, it is important for the FOA not to draw conclusions too hastily, as specialised personnel may well be able to discover and collect evidence not directly visible or apparent to the FOA)
- The disruption of the business of the public that evidence collection will cause
- The fragility of potential evidence

In many European countries, it is highly likely that further assistance may appear within a few minutes of arrival of the first officer attending. The FOA must brief arriving law enforcement personnel as soon as practicable to convey his initial assessment of the scene and all the actions carried out so far. On arrival, the CSI unit will take responsibility of the control and preservation of the scene, as well as for the collection and protection of evidence.

The tasks of the FOA are many, varied, and unpredictable, depending as they do on the actual circumstances encountered at the scene. They can range from nothing (a situation where it is clear that no crime has been committed) to a very substantial demand on the

Table 3.2   Main Tasks of the First Officer Attending

Do	Don't
Limit access to the crime scene by using tape or other boundary control, and log entry and exit to the scene.	Permit unnecessary personnel to enter the crime scene.
Attempt to identify possible routes used by the suspect.	Use routes possibly used by the suspect.
Note original conditions at the crime scene.	Assume others will note original conditions, etc.
Record changes in conditions, especially in regard to your activities or those of others at the scene.	Fail to document any changes or contamination at the scene.
Protect evidence from adverse environmental conditions.	Allow evidence to be compromised by nature.
Conduct all administrative duties outside the tape (drinking coffee, smoking, using the toilet).	Eat or use any facilities or the phone within the crime scene.
When protection of evidence requires that items must be moved or removed from the scene, record their location first, and make sure that clean and adequate packaging materials are used.	Move or collect anything without documentation, preferably including photographs, and never place items together in one container.
Keep an open mind as to what might be evidence.	Ignore items that appear out of place or are difficult to explain.
Be aware that you are a potential source of evidence and contamination.	Touch anything unnecessarily.
Take photographs of items at 90° with and without L-scales.	Photograph items without scales.
Call expert personnel to crime scenes for detailed or difficult collection or documentation.	Assume that the expert can always answer the questions from non-expert collection or documentation.

Source: Originally developed by Ronald Linhart and Elizabeth Devine, Los Angeles County Sheriff's Crime Laboratory, Los Angeles, CA.

officer's ingenuity, judgement, and organisational skills, such as any scene with large and indistinct boundaries, with many people present, or with a need for emergency action to protect lives and evidence. Most importantly, the success of the transition to the next phase of the forensic process can depend on the actions of the FOA. The main tasks, common to most incidents where there has been a crime, are summarised in Table 3.2.

3.2.3   Develop Scene Investigation Strategy

Moving to the activity of planning the scene investigation by developing a scene investigation strategy, a note of caution is called for. A crime scene investigation should not be started by general law enforcement personnel if there is even the remotest possibility that specialised personnel (CSI or other) will be needed at any point in the investigation. If CSI personnel or others are to perform the examination of the scene, which is most often the case in relation to serious crime, they should be put in charge of the intact crime scene after being fully briefed by the investigator in charge of the investigation. As discussed in Chapter 2, a scene investigation strategy consists of a strategically formed and aligned investigative strategy defining the core purpose and focus of the investigation with relation to the 6Ws, as well as a more practical plan of action—a plan for the actual scene examination—that relates to planning the specific tasks and order of examination and analysis of the scene.

Precise roles and definitions vary among and even within countries, but we shall use the following here:

- *Tactical investigation* is the investigation of the case by the police.
- *Case manager* is the police officer in charge of the overall tactical investigation, and whose duties include management of information about and obtained from the scene in relation to the needs of the investigation.
- *Technical investigation* is the examination of the scene, including interpretation of findings.
- *Crime scene coordinator* is the senior CSI in charge of the technical examination and responsible for liaison with the crime scene manager and specialist forensic personnel, including laboratory scientists.

In cases of major crime, the responsibility for the scene will most likely be transferred from the case manager to the scene coordinator at this point, as it marks the start of the technical investigation. The first task of the CSI coordinator will be to develop a strategy for the scene investigation, based on the requirements of the tactical investigation communicated by the case manager, his own assessments of the scene, and the information provided by the FOA. A well-developed strategy will result in a clear understanding of the needs of the investigation and provide the operational framework for the scene examination. The strategy should take account of the legal, scientific, and practical requirements for the examination, recording, and collection of evidence. The derived action plan should detail the systematic examination of the scene, including which steps must be performed before others. It is, of course, impossible to anticipate every detail in a crime scene investigation; however, the strategy should direct tactical and technical investigators to a common goal.

3.2.3.1 Align Tactical and Technical Investigations

Communication between personnel in the tactical investigation and those in the technical investigation is central to proper cooperation and to ensure the efficiency and effectiveness of the scene investigation in addressing the requirements of the tactical investigation. It is also important in terms of providing the CSI coordinator with a foundation on which to form hypotheses, discover evidence, prioritise efforts and examinations, and provide information that helps ensure the objectivity of the investigation by establishing matters of fact that may either challenge or support the hypotheses being considered. As always, due caution is required, and the decisions regarding the development of a scene investigation strategy should not be made too hastily. Communication between the CSI coordinator and the scene manager should be maintained during the duration of the processing of the scene with respect to ensuring that the requirements of the investigation are met and that new evidence is incorporated into the investigation and used to review the investigative theory (hypothesis) as soon as it is unearthed.

3.2.3.2 Initial Survey by the CSI Coordinator

With regard to the details of the three elements available when first developing the strategy—the needs of the case manager, the report of the FOA, and the initial observations of the CSI coordinator—the first step is that the scene coordinator should (if possible without risking compromising possible evidence) make a complete and systematic survey of the scene and its immediate surroundings, both indoors and outdoors. If the FOA has documented the scene in photographs, these can be used as the basis for an assessment of the scene by the scene coordinator. Circumstances must be considered when deciding for or against a full survey of the scene by entering it. If a visual survey is to be performed, caution should be taken so as not to disturb or destroy evidence, and proper measures against contamination should be taken (see Chapter 4 for an example). This initial assessment or survey of the scene and surroundings has three overall purposes:

1. Review the initial actions and dispositions of the FOA and investigators and make adjustments.
2. Decide what resources and equipment will be needed for the scene examination.
3. Form a plan of action for the examination, based on the communication about the requirements of the investigation and the needs of the investigative process informed by the 6Ws (aligning investigative strategies).

A review of the scene and the steps taken to control it and preserve evidence should be performed prior to establishing a plan of how to conduct the overall scene examination. The steps to be taken are shown in the box below.

Scene coordinators should keep a record of their initial actions as well as the communications made and decisions taken with regard to the technical strategy and the plan for examination. Thus, if the CSI receives copies of the police reports or other material during the initial communication, this should also be documented. The record should be kept throughout the examination and should include all relevant data pertaining to the intended investigation, recorded accurately and at the time of the examination. Specific practical matters to be incorporated into the strategy include the following.

SCENE REVIEW BY THE CSI COORDINATOR

- Evaluate the actions of the first responders and what was done prior to CSI attendance (e.g., setting preliminary cordons).
- Assess scene security, adjust cordons if necessary and ensure that access is controlled and logged.
- Assess the scene for any health and safety risks and implement appropriate strategies for dealing with identified and potential risks.
- Assess type and range of evidence types to be searched for.
- Assess the competencies needed from internal and external sources.
- Discuss the sequence of evidence collection—that is, the order in which these should be searched for and collected (depends on evidence type, scene and evidence conditions, type of equipment needed).
- Consider what must be documented and which media, methods, and order are most appropriate.
- Take photographs and possibly draw sketches to use when briefing the CSI team and any forensic specialists involved in the examination.

- Making an assessment of what is technically possible and what is worthwhile in order to meet the needs of the investigation:
  - Ensuring the health and safety of personnel performing the examination
  - Physical risks, including building collapse; possible unexploded devices; chemical, biological, radiological, or even nuclear hazards; sharp edges; syringes; diseases; poisons; gases; smoke; carbon monoxide; flammable fluids; booby traps
  - Basic needs, such as accommodations, food and water, and toilet facilities, depending on how long the examination will last (some scenes can be dealt with within a few hours, others require days or even weeks)
- Storage and transportation of evidence and exhibits during the examination:
  - Temporary cold storage of bodies and remains in the case of a mass disaster (e.g., obtaining refrigerated transportation vehicles)
  - Air-lifting time-critical evidence items from a remote location to a laboratory for DNA profiling, for example, or special latent fingerprint development in connection with the detention of suspects
- Special resources and equipment required for the scene investigation:
  - Specialist personnel in addition to any special equipment that must be brought to the scene, either from the CSI unit or from an external agency
  - Special equipment beyond the technology necessary for the detection and collection of evidence, such as equipment that may help preserve or control the scene (e.g., tents, light poles, mobile fences to maintain privacy)

During the survey of the scene, the scene coordinator should consider where possible sources of evidence are located and try to visually identify and locate potential evidential material, guided by the investigative star:

- WHAT occurred at the scene?
- WHERE did it occur?
- HOW did it occur?
- WHO was present at the scene at the time?
- WHEN did it occur?
- WHY did it occur?

The CSI should be conscious that key evidence may not always be found in the primary scene area. The coordinator must therefore be attentive to the possibility of secondary or linked crime scenes to ensure that all relevant avenues of investigation will be followed and included in the investigative strategy and in the plan for examination and analysis of evidence.

For investigative purposes, the area of a crime scene is always larger than the actual site or room where the crime occurred; therefore, both the primary and secondary areas of the scene must be identified and isolated (see box on next page). If a body was found indoors, for example, the primary area of the crime scene is the room where the body was found. The secondary crime scene perimeter is the remainder of the house or building, along with all the doors, windows, and corridors that give access to the primary area, including front and back yards. The secondary areas may contain important evidence of a fight, footwear prints, fingerprints, broken windows or doors, tyre prints, bloodstains, etc. In cases when a highly probable suspect is known, the suspect's house or car may also be

PRIMARY, SECONDARY, AND LINKED SCENES

The fire unit arrived at a burning house after an alert from a neighbour. The first floor of the house was almost completely burnt out by the time the fire was extinguished. An elderly woman was found lying dead in what was left of the bedroom on the first floor, which therefore became the primary area of the crime scene, but everything was completely burnt out and no kind of evidence was found in that area. The autopsy revealed that the woman had been stabbed with a knife or similar weapon, and the case became one of murder. No kind of evidence was found on the two entrance doors to the house, which were both unlocked when the firefighters arrived at the house.

The ground floor of the building, the rear of which bordered the garden, was not disturbed by the fire. The windows were still intact, and the rooms inside showed no signs of disturbance in relation to the case, so this was assessed as a secondary area of the crime scene. A toolmark found on one of rear ground-floor windows was collected as possible evidence, even though the attempt to force the window open had been unsuccessful. One and a half weeks earlier, a break-in had occurred at a house on the same road, during which the burglar had entered by forcing a window. Toolmarks left on that window matched the toolmark in the murder case. In addition to the toolmarks left when he broke that window open, the burglar has also cut himself, and blood was found on the edge of the window. The DNA profile matched a known burglar, who was apprehended and charged for both the case of burglary and the murder.

He confessed to both cases. With regard to the murder case, he explained that he had tried to break the ground-floor window open but was not able to. He gave up, but before leaving to find another house he tried the handle of the back door and was surprised to find it open. When he searched the house for items of value he at some point arrived in the bedroom on the first floor. The elderly homeowner would not tell him where she kept her valuables, and she started fighting. The burglar panicked and stabbed her.

treated as a secondary or linked crime scene, even if it is not located in the proximity of where the crime was committed. All physical evidence identified in both areas may help in the reconstruction of the chain of events of the criminal act.

The CSI coordinator conducts an initial assessment primarily to form an impression of the scene and possible evidence to aid in developing a good investigative strategy around a reasonable preliminary hypothesis. Communication of the initial assessment with the case manager may provide new and different views on the scene and result in a reevaluation of the initial assessments performed by the FOA or the police investigator.

Performing the assessment as the basis for developing a scene investigation strategy and plan of examination, the scene investigator should adopt an air of curiosity about everything concerning the crime scene. Distractions should not be allowed to interfere with the investigator's initial reconstruction of the case. Quiet deliberation is essential to planning the course of the investigation intelligently and getting the most information out of the scene. One of the most essential qualities of the professional scene investigator is a clear head that does not give in to stressors or external pressures but keeps an open, inquiring, and critical mind throughout the entire process.

3.2.3.3 *Plan the Scene Examination*

The final stage in developing a scene investigation strategy is to take all of the above—considerations made in the initial review, communication with the case manager and FOA, and the preliminary scene assessment conducted by the CSI coordinator—and incorporate them into a plan for conducting the scene examination that considers:

- The areas within the scene that require examination
- Whether specialist advice or specialist attendance will be required
- What examinations are to be conducted at the site and in what order
- Whether any additional specialist examination equipment is required
- What may have to be collected

THINK THE WORST

Right from the beginning of the process, the safe rule is always to consider as a default the worst-case scenario. Treat an unexplained death as suspicious and a suspicious death as murder. That way, the plan and actual examination will not overlook vital information. The following case example illustrates this point.

A husband called and seemed pretty shocked. His wife had fallen from the fourth-floor window. Ambulance and police were dispatched to the scene and found her lying dead on the footpath. She was wearing underwear, pants, sweater, socks, and rubber gloves of the type normally used for household cleaning activities. On the sidewalk beside her lay one clog. A pathologist confirmed her to be dead. She had several injuries that could have been due the fall from the window. Blood was found present on her hands, *inside* the rubber gloves; therefore, she must have had blood on her hands before the rubber gloves were put on, which indicated a suspicious death. Her husband, who was present in the apartment, was arrested and the scene was guarded until CSI unit arrival.

The forensic examination found that the bathroom window facing the footpath was open, and her other clog was on the sill. There was an overturned chair by the window. Walls and ceilings in the bathroom were wet as if due to washing or showering, and there were no visible traces of blood on the ceiling, floor, and walls. Examination with luminol, however, showed several bloodstains on these surfaces. There was visible blood in the floor drain, and a few bloodstains in several places down the facade under the bathroom window.

The cause of death was determined at autopsy to be blunt violence—the victim had been dead before she hit the footpath. Inquiries among neighbours revealed that several had heard a quarrel, with the wife shouting and screaming, a few minutes before her husband reported the incident. DNA profile analysis of blood traces in the bathroom, on the facade of the house, and on her hands (under the rubber gloves) matched the blood of the victim. Her husband then acknowledged having been violent and causing her death, and that he had tried to conceal the crime by making it look as though she had fallen out of the window while cleaning the bathroom. He had put rubber gloves on her hands before he lifted her up and out of the window.

- The specific requirements for collection of items:
  - Resource requirements
  - Detection and collection methods for the identified types of material
  - Other practitioners and experts
- Any specific health and safety hazards associated with the scene or material and the level of personal protective equipment to be used during the examinations to prevent contamination of the scene as well as to protect the examiner

In making the plan, consideration should be given to prioritising the following:

- Collection or protection of any material that is in danger of being destroyed (e.g., by wind, rain, vehicles, tides)
- The collection of any material that will enable safe access to any deceased remains or any other critical area of a crime scene along entry and exit paths
- Any critical crime scene areas that may render the most relevant material or, once processed, enable removal of any deceased remains
- Any area that may give an early indication as to the identity of the offender(s)
- Any material that will allow earlier release of guards and other resources

The plan should be reassessed as the scene examination proceeds and may need to take into consideration such things as new facts emerging, changes in the weather, and new material located at the scene.

3.2.4   Summary of Activities in the First Stage of the Forensic Process

The first stage of the forensic process, "activities undertaken before the scene examination begins," involves responding to notification of the incident, conducting an initial evaluation by the first officer attending, and developing a scene investigation strategy. Responding to the notification requires that the person receiving the notification is able to elicit relevant information from the notifier and identify the appropriate first responder. The receiver must also be able to instruct the notifier on actions to preserve lives and protect the scene. The first officer attending can have the simplest or most difficult job of all the people involved in the forensic process, depending on what is found at the scene of the reported incident. The primary functions of the FOA are to protect and inform. The final step in this phase of the forensic process is to develop a scene investigation strategy, or action plan. The strategy will take into account the needs of the tactical investigation and the circumstances of the scene, as they both appear at that time; however, things can and almost certainly will change as the results of the actual scene examination become available.

3.3   The Forensic Process at the Scene

3.3.1   Undertake Scene Investigation

The elements of the forensic process in the "activities at the scene" phase are shown in Figure 3.4. For convenience, the "laboratory examinations" element is included, as this is an example of "order further examinations" and is fed by the findings from the scene investigation, but it will not be considered further. The elements relevant to the CSI are those associated with undertaking the scene examination and interpretation of scene findings.

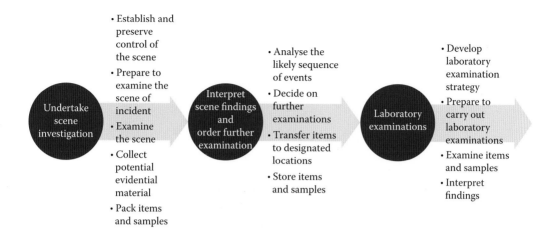

Figure 3.4 The forensic process at the scene.

3.3.1.1 *Control of the Crime Scene*

The requirements for the control, preservation, and recording of a scene apply throughout the life of its examination and end only when the scene investigation process is completed and the scene is released. Delineation of the area to be protected is a complex activity, and the boundaries of the scene may change as the investigation unfolds. What appears to have been an obvious placement of a cordon at the outset may have to be reevaluated due to new information or new findings or observations at the scene. One of the key responsibilities of the scene investigator at the point of transferral of responsibility of the scene is to see to it that the activities of the first officers attending have been completed in a proper way and to make any corrections or adjustments deemed necessary.

The strategy developed should ensure that the scene coordinator has sufficient resources to secure the scene. The first step after completing the initial assessment should be to review the adequacy of boundary definition and control made by the FOA and modify as required. An access log should be opened and responsibility for its maintenance assigned. Access routes should be cleared and defined.

In general, indoor crime scenes are more easily secured than outdoor ones, as it is easier to ascertain the routes of access and the extent of the area in which the incident has transpired than is the case outdoors. Also, an outdoor scene may be more prone to unauthorised access by curious people who do not respect the cordon, thereby placing greater resource demands on restricting access to the scene. Outdoor scenes must be protected against environmental degradation, such as wind or precipitation. Figure 3.5 shows CSIs at an outdoor scene where they have erected a canopy to protect it from rain.

Whether outdoors or indoors, many scenes will require a physical barrier (cordon) around their perimeter along with a posted guard in order to restrict access. In some cases, a suitable barrier may already be present, such as a fence or gates that surround a house; however, in many cases—not least for outdoor scenes—natural barriers may be absent or do not fully encompass the scene. In such cases, a barrier must be made with plastic tape and overseen by a police officer to ensure that only authorised personnel enter. In situations where the scene relates to a major criminal investigation, the scene should be secured and access logged. Access to any scene should be via a single access point to minimise

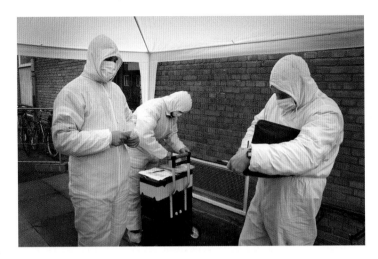

Figure 3.5 Crime scene investigators completing their notes after examining a scene protected from rain by an overhead canopy.

scene disturbance. Figure 3.6 shows the scene coordinator being briefed by CSIs after they have left the scene. Their protective clothing will be discarded at this point. Note the use of crime scene tape to mark out the approach route to the scene.

In cases of serious crime, it is crucial to police the cordon around the perimeter of the scene at all times, from the moment it is established until the processing of the scene is complete. The officer in charge of the cordon must vigilantly exclude all people, including senior

Figure 3.6 Three crime scene investigators briefing the scene coordinator. Note the protective clothing, the tape delineating the approach path to the scene, and the paper bag for discarding trash and worn clothing.

members of the police, who do not have a pressing and legitimate operational need to be at the scene. When it has been determined who should have legitimate access to the scene, a record—the crime scene log—should be kept of all who enter it, along with a description of their reasons and actions at the scene. Everyone entering the scene should wear relevant protective clothing such as shoe covers, disposable overalls, hairnets, and gloves.

3.3.1.2 *Prepare to Examine the Scene*

Preservation is an important issue throughout the examination of the scene, but so is preventing contamination. Examiners must be continually aware that, just like the perpetrator, they too will bring materials to and leave materials at the scene. This means, for example, that they must not lean against walls or door frames while reflecting on particular occurrences or exhibits, nor should they move or remove anything without documenting it. They should also avoid leaving new traces or damaging existing ones on objects by being careful in how they handle them. If a table must be moved, for example, it should be done by placing the fingertips on the underside of the table top some distance from the edges, after checking that there is nothing on the underneath surface, rather than by lifting it by grabbing the edges of the table top as would normally be done. If there are objects on the table, consider whether these should be collected before moving the table and the implications of that action on the strategy for collecting evidence.

Guidance should be given toward ensuring that nothing is done by anybody attending the scene of an incident or by others responsible for taking samples from the victim or suspect that may lead to adventitious links being established between suspects and the scene, victims and suspects, or suspects with suspects through the mishandling of materials whilst in their possession. For example, the examination and collection of exhibits from the victim should be done at a different time and place from that of the suspect, and personnel should wear disposable protective clothing that is discarded and replaced between the examinations.

Consideration of appropriate precautions against contamination should be based not only on precautions necessary for the examinations under discussion but also on all evidence types that may potentially be available. If these include materials that may be required for subsequent DNA analysis, extreme caution should be taken because of the sensitivity of current DNA techniques. Precautions include the wearing of appropriate barrier clothing, including gloves and face masks. Figure 3.7 shows a CSI team suiting up outside their incident response vehicle, ready to begin their search. Note the gloves, face masks, shoe covers, and disposable overalls.

A good precaution against contamination is establishing an "entrance sluice" to the crime scene, the place where one changes into protective clothing before going in and where one leaves used protective clothing when going out. The sluice should contain clean equipment, such as disposable coveralls, masks, shoe covers, hairnets, and gloves, as well as a receptacle for used equipment (see Figure 3.5). Technical equipment that will be used in the examination and protective equipment such as gloves should be laid out on a clean surface and must be kept strictly separated from used gloves, test strips, packaging, tweezers, and so on. The latter items can be put directly into a receptacle in the sluice area.

Gloves must be changed every time an exhibit has been handled. Packed equipment must be clean before it is brought into the scene, but also be very conscious and careful while handling the equipment within the scene. It is desirable, for example, to have set routines for handling CSI cameras or lamps. A reliable method is to make it a habit to only

Figure 3.7 A CSI team donning protective clothing outside their response vehicle.

operate the camera without gloves, thereby preventing transfers from scene to glove to camera to glove to scene. The sequence is as follows: remove gloves, take photograph, place camera on a clean surface, put on a pair of clean gloves, and continue the investigation.

Recovered material should be handled as little as possible, and control or reference materials must be kept strictly separate from any surfaces, items, clothing, or people with whom it might subsequently be significant to establish contact. No one who has attended the scene should be involved in examining suspects or victims for the recovery of trace evidence, or in the packaging of such evidence, unless they have thoroughly decontaminated themselves (e.g., by showering and changing their clothing). Where multiple suspects are involved, in addition to the necessity for keeping material from the victims separate, material from each suspect should be recovered and kept separate from each other and from that of the victims.

At the very start of the investigation, investigators should designate a particular area as a trash pile where things may be put that should not be lying about the scene. A certain amount of waste normally accumulates from used swabs, blood-testing materials, gloves, disposable suits, etc. The trash collection point should be located as far away as practical from the central crime scene. Spreading a newspaper or using a paper trash bag and marking it accordingly is enough to establish the trash pile. Large evidence collection bags can also be used as trash bags. A work area can also be designated for filling out evidence tags, developing fingerprints on small objects, handling casting material, and so on.

3.3.1.3 Recording the Crime Scene
The crime scene can be regarded as a snapshot of what occurred from the very first to the very last moments of the crime, provided that it has not been subject to any material changes. In that respect, the scene provides a significant starting point for the investigation (i.e., for the inquiry to determine the circumstances of the case by providing answers to the 6Ws). The recording of the scene can be performed initially using written notes or it can be orally recorded and transcribed later. Whatever the initial format adopted, notes should be completed in written form and in full as soon as practicable in order to minimise loss of information and to secure as accurate an account as possible. The record of the scene should

include all relevant physical conditions, such as accessibility to the area, security conditions, general observations, any obvious odours (e.g., accelerants, chemicals, gun powder residue, perfume, cigarette smoke), and environmental data such as temperatures inside and outside and weather conditions. Recording and documenting the scene serve the purposes of

- Providing a permanent record of the crime scene in the state in which it was found, for use during the investigation and in court should the case culminate in a trial
- Providing an account of the steps taken during processing of the crime scene
- Providing a record of fragile physical evidence before it is recovered in case it is destroyed during the recovery process

Photographs constitute a significant part of the recording of the scene. Better than any other medium, photographic images produce a permanent record of its appearance prior to the removal of any evidence. Ideally, this record should be made while the scene is in exactly the condition it was in when the first officer arrived. Thus, there is good reason for the FOA to make a photographic record of the undisturbed scene during his initial assessment, particularly if he has to enter it to perform emergency actions such as rendering first aid.

Irrespective of the actions of the FOA, substantive examination of the scene by the CSI should begin with making a photographic record of its initial condition. The record will begin at the perimeter and progress to what is at the time regarded as the primary scene. As far as possible it will show the scene as it was left by the perpetrator, or as it was after any emergency actions undertaken by the FOA, or emergency personnel. There may be reasons to disturb objects—for example, a computer at risk of damage from water. In these instances, the initial disposition of the objects should be photographed, the location marked, the object photographed, and the object returned to its original location so the overall sense of the scene is preserved. The scrupulous recording of the initial condition is important in order to prevent a subsequent error in interpretation caused by incorrect understanding of the relative location and condition of the objects.

Case 2

Police are notified by a man that his wife has drowned in the bath. Upon their arrival, he tells the police that he became alarmed when she seemed to be taking too long to return to the living room. He went to the bathroom, found her apparently dead, drained the water, and tried to resuscitate her, but without success. The CSI noted that the bath was empty but there was water trapped in the crook of her elbows where they were positioned against her torso and where her upper legs bent from the waist. This water would have been disturbed if the husband's story was true. Photographs of the trapped water before removing the body for autopsy gave a critical record of a significant element in reconstructing what had happened.

Photographs of the scene may serve many purposes in the investigation. Their prime function is to document the scene, but they are also used when presenting evidence and for briefings, for refreshing memory, for reassessing the scene once it has been released, or even to corroborate or refute statements made by suspects or witnesses. Photographs may also serve to preserve fragile evidence that might be damaged during its recovery (e.g., fingerprints, footwear or tyre marks). In some instances, photographs may be used not just as documentation of evidence at the scene but also as substitutes for something that could not be successfully recovered from the scene or could not be presented in court. A dead body is an obvious example, as are photographs of bloodstains rendered visible by luminol treatment.

A proper photographic record from a scene examination should include:

- *Still photographs that show the environment* of the scene in all directions—Walls, doors, windows, streets, gardens, facades, footpaths, alleyways, sometimes even aerial photos to show the extent of the scene and its broader environment.
- *Still photographs that show the overview or general appearance of the scene*—Paths through the scene likely to have been used; 360° views from focal points of the scene; overlapping photographs from focal points to produce panoramas of the scene; all interior walls, ceilings, and doors.
- *Still photographs of exhibits in situ* before they are recovered—With and without size scales, with and without the use of different forms of enhancement, at long and medium range in addition to close-up.

The record may also be made by videorecording; however, this record should not replace still photographs of the scene completely, and photographs of the exhibits *in situ* before their recovery must be made in still photography. The scene should be photographed from eye height and from a number of different angles, using both long- and medium-range shots. Such measures will help maximise the accuracy of the impression of the appearance of the scene, for both investigators and potential witnesses.

3.3.1.4   *The Examination of the Scene*

The search for evidence should proceed according to a structured procedure decided during the planning of the examination (e.g., grid, wheel, lane). The search pattern that is chosen should be documented in the written report of the scene investigation. Examples of search patterns are shown in Figure 3.8. Some texts include spiral as a pattern, but those shown in Figure 3.8 are more straightforward and effective in implementation. Figures 3.9 to 3.11 show how an actual search was planned and its pattern recorded. The scene was a house, the front approach to which consisted of a grassy area and a paved driveway to the garage. These and the ground floor rooms are shown in the plan drawing in Figure 3.9.

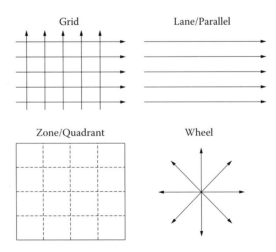

Figure 3.8 Examples of scene examination patterns.

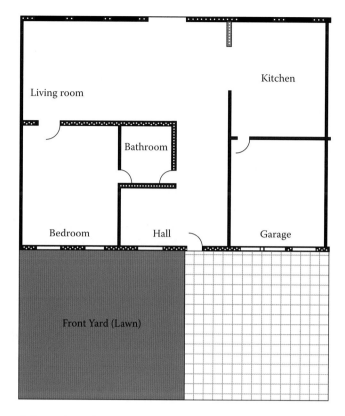

Figure 3.9 Ground-floor plan of house and front outside area.

The living room was searched using a wheel pattern, starting at the entry from the front hall and moving around the area in a clockwise direction. Each object of interest was searched as it was encountered—first the storage unit against the bathroom/bedroom wall, then the entry to the bedroom, followed by the seating and table in the corner, and finally the remaining seating (Figure 3.10).

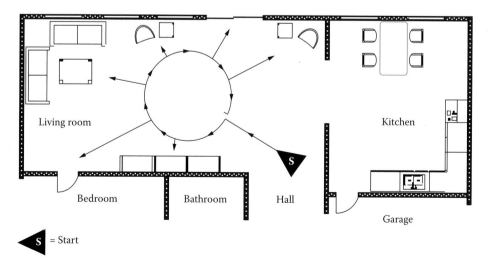

Figure 3.10 Wheel search pattern used to examine the living room.

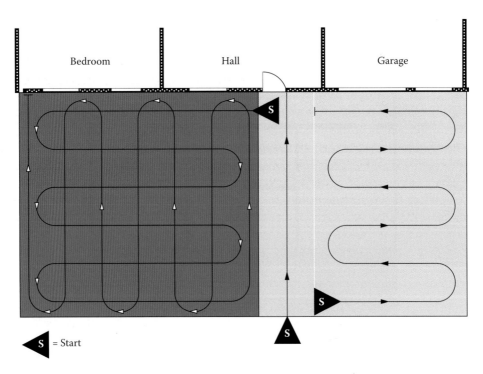

Figure 3.11 Grid (left) and lane (right) patterns used to search the outside of the house at the front.

The outside of the house at the front (the grassy yard and the driveway to the garage) was searched using a grid or lanes. The grass area was searched as a grid in two dimensions, first from right to left (as viewed in the figure) and then from top to bottom. Note that the entry point was a corner, and that when making the transition in direction the CSI returned to the entry point by searching along the right-hand perimeter, thereby minimising the chance of any cross-contamination. The paved driveway was searched in lanes and in only one dimension; however, the start and end points were set to be in the corners to avoid contamination during the search process. The patterns are shown in Figure 3.11. Notice also the cleared pathway from the perimeter to the door of the house.

When searching a scene, special attention should be paid to the following areas:

- *Point of entry*—In many instances, force will have been used, yielding latent fingerprints, toolmarks, or other forms of damage. The chance of finding fingerprints and footwear marks in this area is high.
- *Route through a crime scene*—Areas that may afford marks should be examined, including dirty floor areas and garage floors, or when moving from a wet area to a dry area.
- *Point of exit*—The same process should be applied with the exit as for the entry.
- *Areas of interest*—These will include areas where a significant event related to the crime being investigated has occurred.
- *Exterior areas*—These will include areas in the vicinity of the entry and exit points. Outside areas that could provide marks include dirt, sand, or muddy areas over which the suspect has walked or driven.

An indoor crime scene can be searched beginning with the criminal's suspected point of entry, followed by the area adjacent to the criminal event, and finishing with the rest of the room and suspected point of departure if it is different from the point of entry. However, these may not be known or may not be relevant; for example, the scene illustrated earlier did not have an obvious point of entry and was searched according to the identified areas of interest.

Crime scene investigators should attempt to work according to an established routine that does not vary greatly from case to case. This helps to reduce the risk of overlooking a seemingly insignificant article of trace evidence or a larger object that the perpetrator may have left behind or accidentally dropped. Basing the search on an established routine will permit the use of a checklist, perhaps included in the SOPs or less formal; however, to keep a broad perspective, progress should be reviewed in the context of the principles embedded in the investigative star tool.

The search can be carried out by a single investigator or by CSI teams consisting, for example, of two or three people. When a team is used, one member should be designated as being responsible for the investigation team and for the examination performed. A single crime scene investigator can do an effective job of searching for and collecting physical evidence, but two are better. Two persons working together are able to observe much more than a single person can. Whatever one of the investigators discovers should immediately be reported to the partner. They also should discuss the various possibilities of how a certain clue might have been left at the scene and how the criminal proceeded. An idea that might not occur to one person may well occur to a second. It will not always be practical to use a team, for example, in some emergency circumstances and small, limited crime scenes.

Scene investigators should be used to working on crime scenes in teams and should be able to cooperate. One way to divide the work is for one investigator to do the actual examination while the other keeps notes and assists by making personal observations, making measurements, and helping to examine a particular area. A CSI team consisting of three persons is often ideal because the responsible person can record the progress and findings,

APPLYING THE SEARCH PATTERNS

Figure 3.10 shows the wheel search pattern, in which everything is collected in one round; however, the wheel can be repeated in sequences within the scene. The repeats may be by location (e.g., in searching the floor surfaces, the furniture, walls, and ceiling surfaces) or by task (e.g., fingerprinting, blood spatter analysis, or ballistics trajectory analysis). Figure 3.11 shows the lane and grid patterns applied to relatively small areas; however, both search patterns can also be applied to large areas, as in the Lockerbie case or other mass disasters. The decision on the pattern to use should be made at the initial strategy meeting and will depend on the nature of the scene, the experience of the CSI team members, and the nature of the potential evidence. The wheel, for example, is more suitable to one or two CSIs searching a living room because of its size and furnishings and because the purpose is to search for any associative evidence. Searching for a specific physical object in a large outdoor area is probably better conducted by teams using lanes.

while the other two on the team perform the examination. One of these two would serve as the principal examiner and the other as co-examiner, mainly acting as photographer in addition to preparing evidence bags, packaging evidence, and writing labels, but also available for assistance in the hands-on examinations if needed. The team approach is beneficial when examining surfaces using scene lamps; they can stand on each side of the actual surface to observe the surface in and against the light, which often increases the success of discovering traces on surfaces.

The search for evidence will very often start with a survey of the floors, not only because these can yield valuable evidence but also to clear access to other parts of the scene. Where for special reasons it is decided to examine the floors later (e.g., if it is decided to examine another room first where a victim was found), stepping plates can be laid out on the floor to protect them as personnel access other rooms or areas of the scene.

After the evidence search and examination of the floors, the investigation can continue in an adequate and systematic manner to the surfaces of the furniture, walls, and ceiling. During this process, overview and detailed photography of findings and evidence should be performed.

It should by now be clear that the processing of the scene with regard to the discovery and collection of evidence must be thorough and systematic to be fully effective, but not everything is obvious and there are side issues that the scene investigator must deal with to ensure success. The most important is time. There are a number of pressures and risks due to time restraints and conditions that impinge on the process of collecting evidential materials. Long periods spent at the scene with monotonous work and few results may cause investigators to become stressed, tired, or bored, posing a risk that evidence may be overlooked or contaminated. Expectations to deliver results quickly must not cause scene investigators to jump to conclusions and provide police investigators with information that has not been properly substantiated. They must not rush their examination of the scene and risk missing important evidential material or making wrong judgements about the significance of findings or the deployment of methods. Another potential threat adding to the pressure placed on scene investigators, and one that we illustrated earlier and address further in Chapter 4, is the possibility of deteriorating weather conditions that may pose a danger to evidence if it is not protected or collected rapidly.

Crime scene investigators and the crime scene coordinator should be aware of these risks and manage the investigation in a manner that will avoid or minimise them. Mistakes and omissions made during the collection of evidence cannot be rectified at a later time or during laboratory examination of the recovered materials and exhibits. Most often it will not be possible to return to a scene after it has been processed. Even if it is possible to return to the scene and an item is still present, it may not be possible to be sure that the item has not been altered or perhaps was placed at the scene after its initial closure and release.

The importance of keeping GIFT ("Get It First Time") in mind during the processing of the scene cannot be overemphasized; it is extremely important to spend the necessary time processing the scene and collecting evidence, not giving in to pressures of any sort. GIFT also emphasises the fact that it is better to secure too large a collection of exhibits and samples than risk missing important evidential material. This does not mean that proper judgement should not be exercised when securing the efficiency and effectiveness of an investigation, nor that a strategy for the collection of evidence should not be made and constantly revised in the light of findings at the scene.

3.3.2 Collect and Package Items

Different forms of evidence material have different packaging requirements. Irrespective of the seriousness of the crime being investigated, it is imperative that items are appropriately packaged once recovered from the scene. The packaging must be made in separate, clean, unused bags and containers to avoid the risk of cross-contamination between items. When forensic evidence is collected, adequate control samples should also be secured. The collection of control samples primarily serves two purposes:

1. Enable evidentially valuable information to be distinguished from the background of legitimate and naturally existing materials at the scene (e.g., a blanket used by a paramedic to cover a fatally injured victim just before death should be taken as a control sample so that any fibres found on the body matching these may be eliminated from the investigation and not confused with fibres that might possess evidential value).

2. Facilitate comparisons between known control samples and questioned samples taken elsewhere (e.g., a sample of the carpet at the crime scene could be used as a control sample in comparison with fibres found on a suspect, linking him to the scene of crime).

Sampling can also refer to taking representative parts from units that are too large to submit for laboratory testing—for example, swabbing bloodstains from a wall. In both senses, great care must be taken to ensure that the sample taken is indeed representative of the host material. In order to identify the samples that should be taken and the sequence of performing different sampling or tests, a sampling strategy, sampling plan, and sampling procedures are required. Sampling must take account of the following:

- The background information available
- Prioritising the questions that need to be answered
- The type of forensic analysis that is relevant
- The need to employ statistical sampling
- Any special considerations that must be taken into account, such as weather, health and safety considerations, location of exhibit, possibility of contamination, possibility of exhibit being tampered with, interference with other exhibits, or lack of homogeneity of the sample
- The sequence in which the sampling must take place (e.g., for a fingerprint in blood, the fingerprint examiner must examine the print prior to the blood being removed for DNA profiling)
- Consulting all relevant experts and personnel
- Establishing a strategy to ensure that appropriate samples are taken
- Legal requirements
- Policies of the organisation
- The accuracy and precision required in any subsequent laboratory testing

Table 3.3 shows examples of evidential items, where they may be found, and how they should be packaged, and Figure 3.12 shows a breathable evidence bag of the type that can be used for biological materials; the figure also illustrates a bar code used to provide unique identification of the item and so ensure the integrity of the chain of custody, as well as the evidence tape seal at the top of the bag.

Table 3.3   Packaging of Items Commonly Encountered at Crime Scenes

Item	Remarks	Packaging (Must Be Sealed)
Blood	Bloodstained garments or items	Paper bags or breathable evidence bags
	Bloodstains from items that cannot conveniently be taken to laboratory	Lift with cellophane tape or scrape onto paper or on cotton swabs, to be placed in swab containers, paper bags, or breathable evidence bags
	Soaking and dripping bloody clothing, etc.	Plastic bags at scene for transfer to drying facility; after drying, repackaged in paper bags or breathable evidence bags
Cartridges	Loose, collected from weapon, etc.	Paper bags, cardboard bags, or plastic containers
DNA	Swabs from scene	Swab containers, paper bags, or breathable evidence bags
	Cotton swabs from scene	Vials
	Clothes	Paper bags
	Items from scenes	Paper bags
Drugs	All powder, tablets, or suspected resin	Plastic envelopes
	Plant material	Paper bags
	Items thought to have drug traces	Plastic bags
Explosives	Bulk samples	Nylon bags
	Garments worn by suspect	Nylon bags
Fibres	Items likely to shed or pick up fibres	Paper bags
	Seat covers, bedclothes, etc.	Paper bags
	If items cannot be brought to the laboratory:	
	Cellophane tape lifts of area of contact for transferred fibres	Plastic envelopes
	Tufts of fibres or pieces of cut material as samples of the source of fibres	Secured on cellophane tape in plastic envelopes
Fingerprints	Items and exhibits	Fixed in cardboard box to avoid friction with the surface of the item or exhibit
	Fingerprints collected on gelatine plates	Envelopes or paper bags
Fire accelerants	Debris from seat of fire	Nylon arson bags or metal arson cans
	Liquids for identification	Screw-cap glass jars or metal arson cans
	Clothing or shoes thought to carry traces of accelerants	Nylon arson bags or metal arson cans
Firearms	Hand guns, rifles, etc.	Fixed in cardboard boxes to avoid movement and friction causing damage to fingerprints
Footwear and tyre marks	Item bearing the mark	Pack to avoid damaging
	Gel lift or photograph of mark to scale (two rulers at right angles)	Cardboard box
	Cast of marks/print	Cardboard bags or plastic containers
	Cast of three-dimensional mark	Casting kit
	Shoes of suspect(s)	Paper bags
Glass	Items likely to pick up broken glass, such as clothes or tools	Paper bags
	Control samples of all sources of broken glass	In folded paper in plastic bags or envelopes

Table 3.3 (cont.)   Packaging of Items Commonly Encountered at Crime Scenes

Item	Remarks	Packaging (Must Be Sealed)
Gunshot residues	Kits used to examine hands and face of person thought to have fired gun	Gunshot residue kit bags
	Garments worn at time	Paper bags
Hair	Hair collected from items, exhibits, surfaces	Fixed on acrylic plate with hair set underneath the protective plastic cover, then placed in envelopes or folded papers
	Control head hair combing of suspect	Hair combing kit
	Items onto which hair might shed, such as caps or jackets	Paper bag
Indented writing	Questioned document	Paper bag or plastic charteque
Knives, etc.	Knives and shorter sharp instruments	Adjustable evidence tubes (PVC) or cardboard boxes
Locks and keys	Items to be examined for toolmarks	Small paper bags, cardboard bags, or plastic containers
Liquids	Water, acids, fuel, oil, paint, etc.	Screw-cap glass jar or metal arson cans
Paint	Flakes of paint	Paper bags, cardboard bags, or plastic containers
	Swabs from wet paint	Screw-cap glass jars, nylon bags, or metal arson cans
	Liquid paint	Screw-cap glass jars or metal arson cans
	Control samples/dry, very near the damaged area	Paper bags
	Items likely to pick up paint, such as clothes or tools	Paper bags
Semen	Swabs from sexual offence examination kits	Sexual offence examination kits
	Garments or bed clothes that might be stained with semen	Paper bags or breathable evidence bags
Soil	Samples of surface soil from near area of contact	Clear evidence jars, paper bags, or plastic bags
	Soil-stained items (e.g., shoes)	Paper bags
Toolmarks, etc.	Item bearing mark or cast of mark	Small plastic containers
	Cast of toolmarks	Small cardboard bags or plastic containers

ASSOCIATIVE EVIDENCE

Consider a case in which a murder suspect during an interview emphatically denied ever having been in contact with the victim. Forensic examination of his clothing revealed a hair that was shown by DNA profiling to have belonged to the victim. In addition, several fibres that matched fibres taken from the victim's clothing were found on the clothing of the suspect. Under normal circumstances, these findings would constitute strong associative evidence with respect to linking the suspect to the victim and would challenge his statement that he had never been in contact with the deceased. If, however, it could be shown that the forensic examiner participating in the scene investigation was the one who examined and packaged the suspect's clothes, then the associative potential of the evidence would be severely diminished.

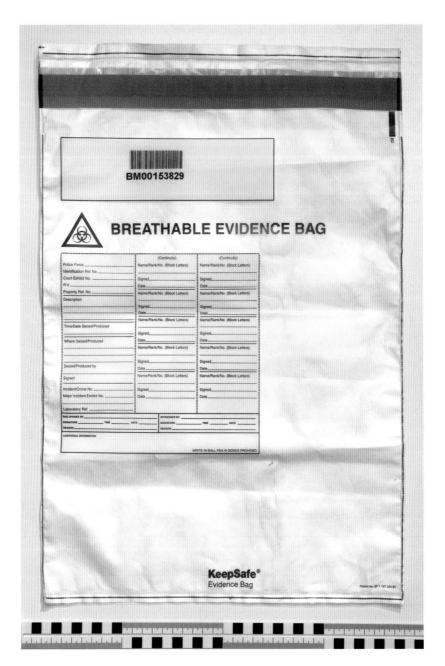

Figure 3.12 Breathable evidence bag.

Items must be stored in secure facilities at all times and under conditions that minimise their deterioration and prevent contamination. Different types of evidence material present different requirements to the storage facility and storage conditions. In general, however, dry exhibits and samples sealed in paper bags or cardboard boxes can be stored in cool and dry conditions. Biological evidence items, such as bloodstained clothing or wet vegetation, must not be stored wet (Chapter 8 gives advice on drying and the general handling of wet biologicals). Very-long-term storage of reference bloods is best achieved by making a stain, drying it, and keeping at –70°C or less, but this is the responsibility of the forensic biology laboratory. The primary protection discussed so far is that of packaging, but environmental factors such as temperature and humidity should be controlled and recorded. Where the material consists of trace quantities, such as hairs and fibres, they should not be stored near the bulk samples, and that includes making sure that contamination through the flow of air in the air conditioning system is not possible.

3.3.3   Interpret Scene Findings and Order Further Examination

The final aspect of the activities at the scene that we shall consider is that of interpreting scene findings and ordering further examinations. Interpretation at this stage means the continuous evaluation of the findings, feeding into the loop of hypothesis testing and modification regarding scene investigation and reconstruction, in addition to reviewing the resources required at the scene and determining whether or not to engage further technical experts. Activities related to examinations in the forensic laboratory are part of this phase of the forensic process but are not considered here.

3.3.3.1   *Interpret Scene Findings*

Using the information received from the scene during the examination, the CSI should attempt to form a mental reconstruction of the actions of the criminal by constantly asking WHAT, WHERE, WHEN, WHO, HOW, and WHY: WHY did the criminal do this? WHY is the layout of the scene like this? WHY is this item placed in that position? HOW could this item have ended up in that position or location? WHEN was it placed in this position? WHAT would account for the presence of this exhibit here? HOW was the building entered? HOW was this mark made? WHERE did this item come from? WHERE did the perpetrator enter the premises? WHERE did he exit? WHERE are the focal points of the incident? WHO or WHAT could be the cause for this mark or layout?

Interpreting the scene requires that scene investigators take time to think through, discuss, and mentally recreate the incident. One way to proceed is to produce and eliminate scenarios while reasoning for the contrary; for example: "If it happened this way, then this should also be present." "If it could not have been done this way, then how might it have happened?" "If this is not here, then what could account for its absence?" "Assuming this is what happened, what could speak to the contrary?"

As discussed in Chapter 2, interpretation of findings is an activity with certain internal tensions. The CSI must be ready to be imaginative and broad-minded when considering possible explanations but must be rigorous and firm in accepting or rejecting options. The rigour comes from demanding that there is clear and objective evidence on which to base the decision, and the carefully documented observations of the scene are a valuable resource for such information.

The relationship between findings and interpretation is two way. Having developed a credible and evidence-based interpretation, the CSI will go on to consider what other tests could be conducted to challenge the hypothesis, whether further examination is necessary and possible to perform, or whether further examination is regarded as impossible or irrelevant. At this stage, the CSI coordinator will discuss with the case manager whether samples need to be sent to a forensic laboratory for further analysis and examination. The discussion can also include involved subcontractors or other organisations (e.g., the coroner).

The review of the findings achieved from the scene examination is in fact performed continuously throughout the scene examination activities, as the relevance of each item discovered is assessed. It is one of the most essential activities within the forensic process, which is why it is treated separately in the standards of performance. The results of the continuing assessment (i.e., interpretation of findings) are also fed back into the forensic process at a higher level, where the coordinator will use them to cycle through the strategy–examination–review sequence and update until the aim of the strategy is estimated to have been achieved—or the possibilities for further examinations at the scene are regarded as impossible or irrelevant. The continuous review of findings must include what has been found, what has not, and anything that appears to be an abnormality or irregularity. The interpretation of what has been found can lead to one of two conclusions: (1) the aim of the strategy has been fulfilled, or (2) a revised strategy must be made.

Abnormalities and irregularities are findings and observations that do not fit into the general expectation about the scene in the context of the supposed crime—for example, finding a body in the boot of a car being examined as a case of theft of a motor vehicle. Irregularities include anything that would cast doubt on the suitability or integrity of the exhibit, such as inadequate sealing. Abnormalities or irregularities found by the investigation team should be recorded and clarified before the investigation itself commences. These could influence the subsequent direction of the investigation or require modification of procedures. It may be necessary to consult with the case manager about whether and how the available resources should be used.

3.3.3.2 *Order Further Examination*

It can seem that everything in crime scene examination is in a cycle of do–evaluate–refine, and that applies at the end of the examination as much as it did before and during it. The evaluation of what the scene findings tell can lead to identification of further testing that may either add to the confidence in the correctness of the working hypothesis or offer the opportunity to falsify it. Some of these tests will be within the scope of the resources and competencies of the crime scene unit, but some will require that external resources are requested to assist. The essential elements of what is required under "order further examinations" are that the CSI unit is able to be outward looking and understand that being able to identify the need to engage external resources is a strength, not a weakness, and that in selecting the resources the CSI unit makes sure that the provider is as open-minded and thorough in application of the forensic process as it has been.

3.3.4 Summary of Activities in the Second Stage of the Forensic Process

The second stage, "the forensic process at the scene," involves establishing, preserving, and controlling the scene; preparing for and conducting the examination; and collecting and preserving items that may provide evidence. Effective control is vital to preserve the integrity of the scene and potential evidence contained within it. Necessary steps include procedures to prevent contamination (e.g., footwear marks and DNA originating from the CSIs) and procedures to prevent the alteration of the scene and its contents. The examination itself should be logical, thorough, and appropriate to the circumstances. Finally, it is necessary to ensure the integrity of documentation of what took place and of the physical samples collected and removed for possible further examination.

Figure 3.13 The forensic process after the scene examination is completed.

3.4   The Forensic Process after the Scene Examination Is Completed

Chapter 1 of this book showed how crime scene examination is a scientific activity, the objective of which is to provide evidence to assist a court or similar tribunal in its deliberations. The last phase of the forensic process deals with communicating the results of the scene examination and, as we discussed in that chapter, to discover the story that is told by the things found at the scene. To do this, the crime scene examiner, like the other participants in the forensic process, has to interpret the examination findings in the context of the information that they contain regarding the incident and produce a report that details what was done, where it was done, when it was done, who did it, how it was done, what was found, and what it means. The final phase is shown in Figure 3.13.

3.4.1   Interpret Findings

The main difference between "interpret scene findings" and "interpret findings" is the purpose of the interpretation. At the scene, the object of the interpretation is to inform the case manager and any other forensic professionals about the scene and to feed back into the scene coordinator's own evaluation and updating of status and validity of the scene examination strategy. After the scene examination is completed, the interpretation is directed to the needs of the users: investigators and those involved in the court process. There is an overlap, however, in that at some point all of the findings in the scientific investigation are collated to explore how they support or otherwise further the development of a consensus reconstruction of events at the scene.

This is a much more complex procedure than that of interpreting scene findings. The first issue is the difference in interpreting for investigators and interpreting for prosecuting lawyers and lay jurors. Here, by agreement, the level of certainty as to the interpretation for the investigator may be closer to the civil law one of a balance of probabilities than to the criminal law's beyond reasonable doubt; the customer requirement is information that will help decide whether or not to devote resources to a line of enquiry.

The interpretation for prosecuting lawyers must meet formal rules of admissibility and discovery. In general, across most jurisdictions in Europe, North America, and Australasia, there is agreement that there is an onus on the witness to declare any limitations on the interpretations, to reveal all evidence that may be exculpatory, and to limit interpretations to what can be supported by the results of the examinations conducted. The interpretation for the lay juror demands that the test methods, the results, and the meaning of the results are expressed in everyday language. This is not always easy; for example, at present there is still some debate and disagreement about using the word "match" to describe the alignment of properties in a comparative or direct analysis. At one end is the view that if the test results are the same then it is correct to say that they match, but at the other is the view that many people will interpret "match" to mean that the items are identical, when in fact they may not be. The question of how much information from tests or observations is needed to conclude identity is discussed in Chapter 1.

3.4.2   Produce Report

The forensic practitioners responsible for the scene investigation and the analysis of evidential material during an investigation must write up the findings in the form of a report or statement, depending on the material and analysis in question. The report of the scene examination or any forms of analysis following from this should meet the above requirements for interpretation of findings.

3.4.2.1   *Report Format*

The forensic report represents the culmination of all the work carried out during the forensic process. The form and content of forensic reports may vary nationally, organisationally, and in relation to area of expertise, and many countries have no prescribed formats for the forensic report; however, some forms of information are customarily included in the report:

- Full name, work address, and qualifications of the examiner responsible for compiling the report
- A statement of truth verifying the report that is signed and dated
- Background details for the case to make the reader understand the context of the various tests and procedures
- A catalogue of the exhibits received or secured for forensic examination, including information on the transfer of these items
- Explanations of relevant technical issues
- A description of the examination or analysis conducted, the reasons for the performance of them, and a summary of their result
- A forensic examination record detailing the names and qualifications of any assistants charged with carrying out the examinations and tests
- An interpretation of the results of the examination conducted (if more than one is feasible, all should be presented along with the examiner's opinion as to which is the most probable under the circumstances of the case)
- A summary of the conclusions reached

The example below illustrates how a CSI report can be structured. For practical reasons, the exemplar is provided with numbering of the sections. The table of contents will vary depending on the type of case to be reported.

Example CSI Report Format

Table of Contents
- 1.0   General Case Information
- 2.0   Background Details
- 3.0   Crime Scene Conditions
- 4.0   Crime Scene Description
- 5.0   Crime Scene Examination

6.0   Evidence and Exhibits
7.0   Summary
8.0   Conclusions
9.0   Evaluation and Interpretation
10.0   References

1.0   General Case Information

General Case Information can include the following sections:

1.1   *Notifier/client*—Name, rank, and agency (e.g., police unit and division); date and time when the notification was received.

1.2   *Crime Scene*—Location/address, type of crime.

1.3   *Involved Persons*—Names of the victim, suspect, etc.

1.4   *Scene response*—Who responded from the unit; their names, rank, and time of arrival.

1.5   *Subcontractors*—List of authorities involved (e.g., special forensic units, pathologist).

1.6   *Appendices*—List appendices to the report (e.g., photograph albums, sketches, lists of exhibits).

1.7   *Definitions*—Definitions of relevance to the case (e.g., pertaining to blood-stains and bloodstain patterns).

2.0   Background Details

Background Details can include the following sections:

2.1   *Received Background Information*—What was received either orally or in writing (e.g., reports, statements) from the notifier, FOA, police unit, etc. (clear reference must be made to police reports received).

2.2   *Contract and Scope*—What was agreed among the CSI, forensic service, and notifier with regard to the scope of the examination (e.g., which areas or locations were to be examined, the purpose of the examination, the scope of the examination). The writer can note such a contract agreement in the report by referring to a written contract form, an electronically based and received contract, or a transcribed oral agreement made at the scene in the report. Any changes to the contract made or agreed upon during the scene examination should be stated in writing in the report.

3.0   Crime Scene Conditions

Crime Scene Conditions can include the following sections:

3.1   *Scene assessment*—Description of the environmental conditions at the crime scene, including immediate health and safety risks, proper cordoning of the scene, evacuation of the scene, what actions that had already been taken at the scene by police and rescue units, etc.

3.2   *Initial actions*—Description of initial actions performed by the CSI team, such as instructions given to the FOA, police, notifier, etc., and what might have been initiated by the examiner upon arrival (e.g., extending the cordoned-off area, contact with special units required to assist on the scene).

4.0   Crime Scene Description

Crime Scene Description can include the following sections:

4.1   *Type of Crime Scene*—Field, beach, factory, farm, cottage, terrace house, flat, vehicle, boat; description of construction materials (e.g., type of construction, type and colour of the walls and roof, type and colour of the doors and windows); description of any vehicles (e.g., brand, type, colour, registration number, type of tyres).

4.2   *Location*—Remote community, country village, industrial zone, parking house, city centre, apartment building on the sixth floor, etc.

4.3   *Physical Nature*

Outdoor scene—Trees, vegetation, type of ground, type of road (e.g., asphalt), forest trail, walking paths, wilderness, distances to roads or other fixed points.

Indoor scene—Type and number of rooms on each floor; descriptions of the interior of these specific rooms (e.g., location of tables, chairs, beds, cabinets); descriptions of the types of doors and windows (e.g., open out or in, type of locks).

4.4   *Scene Access*—How the scene could be accessed; normal outdoor and indoor pathways to and from the scene; access between separate rooms, storeys, etc.

Sketches or maps can be inserted in Crime Scene Description to support the text.

5.0   Crime Scene Examination

Crime Scene Examination can include the following sections:

5.1   *Responsibility*—Who was in charge of the examination, who conducted the examination, and who assisted on the team (include names, qualifications, and other relevant information for everyone involved).

5.2   *Examination Period*—When the examination was conducted (e.g., date and start and ending times).

5.3   *Scene Examination*—A detailed (floor by floor, room by room) description of the examination performed. The text should be supported by photographs (sketches and maps, if relevant) and should include the unique numbering of the exhibits collected. This section could also include a description of the CSI methods and equipment used, as well as documentation regarding pretesting and calibration of the CSI equipment used.

Inside areas—Basement, first floor, second floor; front hall, living room, sleeping room, kitchen, bathroom, etc.

Outside areas—Roads outside the building, neighbouring grounds, front yard, back yard, separate building in the yard, facade of the building, etc.

When the examination of dead persons found at the scene is to be included in the crime scene report, the Crime Scene Examination could include a section for this purpose:

5.4   *Examination of dead persons*

5.4.1   *For CSI unit examinations*—Depending on legislation that governs such investigations, this section should describe and illustrate the examination and evidence collection performed by the CSI unit in relation to the body and its immediate surroundings, such as how the body was prepared for transport to the morgue, when the body was transported from the scene, examination of the surface underneath the body.

5.4.2   *For coroner or medical examinations*—Name, rank, and agency (e.g., police unit and division).

5.4.3   *Autopsy*—When and where the autopsy was conducted.

6.0   Exhibits

Exhibits can include the following sections:

6.1   *Exhibit List*—All of the exhibits collected during Scene Examination (5.3) must be documented in the report, but it is also advisable to have a section in the report where all the exhibits are listed. This listing can be set up in a table format that is included in the report, or they can be listed in a separate document and referred to in the report.

6.2   *Examination of Exhibits*—This section describes which exhibits were sent where and for what purpose. If the exhibits were further examined by the writer of the report, that person can either summarize the examinations done and their results in this section or refer to a separate report for these examinations.

7.0   Summary

A Summary can often be useful for readers when the report is very extensive. The Summary should be a relevant and concise account of the objective findings taken from the extensive description in Crime Scene Examination (5.0) and from the results of Examination of Exhibits (6.2). The Summary must be objective, and no subjective considerations of any kind should be included in it.

8.0   Conclusions

Conclusions should be based on objective findings in the examination and written with reference to approved conclusion scales. In arson cases, the Conclusions can be further divided into the following sections:

8.1   *Point of Origin*—Description and conclusions

8.2   *Cause of Fire*—Description and conclusions

8.3   *Other Findings*—Other relevant conclusions (e.g., signs of "breaking and entering")

9.0   Evaluation and Interpretation

It is very important to keep the description of the objective findings separate from the account of the interpretations or professional judgements drawn from them. This can be done by writing each in a separate, appropriately identified section of the report. The evaluation and interpretation may address one or several subtopics within the 6Ws, but examiners must keep their evaluations within the limitations of the results of knowledge obtained during the scene examination and within the limitations of the CSI boundaries. As an example, the CSI could conduct a blood pattern analysis from which the possible actions causing the blood pattern can be deduced. The CSI should report *only* on the pattern and its meaning and should not attempt to associate his findings with a specific individual; the source of the blood will be provided from the laboratory analysis of the DNA profile of the blood. The content of this section must be based on documented findings from the scene examination, as described in Crime Scene Examination (5.0) and Examination of Exhibits (6.2). If a CSI is asked by the police or a person involved in the case (e.g., victim, suspect) to address a specific question or statement, documentation of the request must be clearly noted in the report. When an interpretation of scene findings is made, the writer should make a point of discussing the opposite question, describing what supports his professional judgement on the hypothesis, and indicating what could contradict or lead to rejection of this hypothesis.

10.0   References

This section lists relevant references to standards, working manuals, procedures, etc.

3.4.2.2   *Wording in CSI Reports*

The wording used in CSI and forensic reports should always be accurate, precise, and as objective as possible, but the writer should also keep in mind that the report must be readable and understandable to every user and reader of the report. Where exact technical or professional terms are necessary, these should be accompanied by explanatory text to assist the lay reader's understanding.

3.4.2.3   *Definitions*

Definitions used in the report must be approved by the unit, and the wording of these must not be changed.

3.5   Summary

Crime scene examination is not an isolated, discrete activity, in which there is a standard operating procedure that can detail the actions to be taken at every scene or even at every scene of a specific type. No two scenes are identical, and nobody, with the possible exception of the perpetrator, knows what happened. Rather, it is a process, and the one that lies at the centre of the series of interlinking elements that make up the forensic process. Scene examination is a problem-solving activity that mirrors the scientific method by continually cycling through the steps of using observations to formulate a possible explanation that accounts for the crime scene, testing it from the results of the scene examination, and rejecting, refining, or supporting the explanation as appropriate.

The process begins before the scene is even seen, with preparation for attendance, instructing the first officer attending, and developing a scene investigation strategy to respond to the requirements of the investigation. The FOA will probably not be a trained CSI but will have to attend to some of the main tasks associated with the scene investigation, such as security and control of the scene and the evidence within it. What the FOA does can have a major impact on the investigation, the strategy, and the work of the CSI team and is discussed in some detail.

The forensic process at the scene is mainly about undertaking the investigation, from establishing control, through preparations, and on to examination, in addition to the collection and packaging of evidence items. Following this, the CSI has to pause and consider the scene findings and decide on what further actions if any are required. Further actions could be a complete revision of the initial strategy, the identification and examination of another scene, or the transfer of items to the forensic laboratory or other specialist for examination.

The final phase of the forensic process is what happens after all of the examinations have been completed. Here, the parties involved communicate and collate their results. One or more reports are prepared and issued, and the overall interpretation of the forensic investigations is communicated to the investigating police and lawyers. The reports are the basis of the evidence arising from the forensic process that will be part of the decision on whether to prosecute and part of the information to be considered by the court or tribunal. Great care has to be taken with the thoroughness of the report and the manner in which the work conducted, the findings, and their interpretation are expressed to non-technical users.

Practical Scene Investigation
The Body in the Woods

4.1 Introduction

Having described the derivation and theoretical applications of the investigative star in the previous chapter, we will now work through an example of the practical use of the 6Ws in a concrete case. The exposition will not be exhaustive, as a large-scale forensic investigation entails a large number of activities, exhibits, and observations, which continuously rely on and contribute to the production of hypotheses and part-hypotheses to support them, and to describe them all would neither be possible nor productive here. Rather, this chapter serves as a heuristic to show the logic of the investigative star in practical reasoning at the scene of crime, by using it to formulate and seek answers to the six questions (or "topics") that it represents.

The positive emphasis on the seeking of answers to the questions should be associated with a note of caution, however, so as not to fall prey to the pitfalls of confirmation bias. Whenever a question is raised—such as "Where did it happen?"—it is essential to address the opposite question—"Where did it *not* happen?"—to ensure that one keeps an open mind and looks for evidence that may falsify the hypothesis. It is important to look for evidence that would help prove the opposite question, such as evidence indicating that the incident did not happen there. Maintaining an open and inquiring mind is the best way to secure one's position, and this attitude must be kept throughout the investigation.

Before we turn to the case story, a few remarks on the roles and forensic organisation that applied to the investigation are necessary, as they reflect how the forensic process is organised in Denmark and may not be the same as the forensic organisation in other countries. In Denmark, the investigation is divided into the tactical investigation (i.e., the ordinary police investigation) and the technical investigation (i.e., the forensic investigation, or scene investigation and criminalistics analysis). Personnel from the Danish National Police, National Centre of Forensic Services, perform virtually all the work at the scene, and it is rare that staff from the forensic laboratory secure exhibits and samples at crime scenes. The objects, exhibits, and samples that the crime scene investigation (CSI) personnel secure from the scene (e.g., fingerprints, surface marks, documents, ballistics, firearms) are examined in the department's own laboratories, while the analysis of biological residues and fibres, as well as chemical analyses, are sent for examination and analysis to various forensic laboratories, which in Denmark are part of the state university system. The National Centre of Forensic Services personnel are responsible for conducting the preliminary examination of items such as bedding and clothing collected from the scene and suspect.

It is a general principle that autopsies are required in deaths that are deemed suspicious continuously throughout the process, from the arrival of the first officer attending (FOA) to completion of the initial medical examination. In Denmark, the autopsy is conducted according to requirements for cooperation between the National Coroner's Office, at the Forensic Medicine University Institute, and the National Centre of Forensic Services. The purpose of the autopsy is to determine the cause and manner of death, and samples for further forensic examination are taken during the forensic examination of the body. The samples include organ tissues for microscopy, blood samples for drug and alcohol analysis and DNA typing, as well as swabs from genitalia and body cavities. The crime scene technician assists the coroner during the autopsy process, takes photographs for documentation purposes, and manages the process of identifying and transferring exhibits that are to be investigated by the National Centre of Forensic Services. This usually consists of searching for and securing such forensic evidence as fingerprints, fibres, gunshot residues, and photographic evidence of possible impression evidence such as from blunt weapons or footwear marks on the deceased's body. The technician is also responsible for collecting the clothing for further examination in the forensic department. All the photographs are shared with the coroner for use in his report.

Responsibility for the technical investigation is assigned to a crime scene coordinator, who is in charge of the scene investigation, the work performed in the National Centre of Forensic Services' laboratories, and coordination with external forensic laboratories and experts, including police dog units. Examination of large outdoor areas is done by sectioning into smaller delimited sectors, whereby the scene is examined on several fronts simultaneously, to increase and optimise the identification and collection of evidence.

4.2   Discovery of the Body in the Woods

One Wednesday morning in mid-January, a man drove his car into a small forest near his home to walk his dog. The landscape was still wintery and the ground covered with snow. The forest is located in a suburb of Copenhagen and is widely used by people for walking, jogging, and dog walking. From the main road, this man turned into the forest car park, parked the car, and let his dog out. The dog was not on a leash, and on the forest trail at the parking lot it immediately showed a strong interest in a reddish coloration in the snow (Figure 4.1). The man got the impression it could be blood. There appeared to be a track associated with the colouring, as if someone had dragged something bloody along the trail. He decided to follow the reddish trail, which extended along the path for approximately 500 metres deeper into the forest. At that point, the track became less visible but could be seen to continue into a dense stand of fir trees. On the ground inside the stand, 25 metres from the forest path, was a pile of heaped-up snow, on top of which some broken-off branches from trees were spread out (Figure 4.2). He decided to examine the pile, removed some of the branches, lifted some of the snow away, and found a sleeping bag underneath. The purple sleeping bag was completely zipped up and tied with ropes and wires. He felt the bag and could clearly discern that there was a person inside. He shook the bag, but there was no response. The man was in no doubt that the concealed body was the result of a serious crime, and he immediately alerted the police.

4.2.1   First Officers Attending

The police arrived at the scene some minutes later and met the man at the parking lot. Because saving lives is always the highest priority, the officers, acting with the utmost caution, decided to examine the body. In the bag, they found a man with a severe and open

Figure 4.1 The red trail in the snow. (Photograph courtesy of the Copenhagen Police.)

cranial wound to his head (Figure 4.3), and they were able to ascertain that he was not alive. The first officers attending then proceeded to secure the scene and reported back to begin the investigation and to get reinforcements to cordon off, secure, and protect the scene. They also initiated the process of taking care of and questioning the notifier. The investigation of a homicide had now begun.

Figure 4.2 The mound of snow covered with branches, with the purple sleeping bag partly visible. (Photograph courtesy of the Copenhagen Police.)

Figure 4.3 The victim. (Photograph courtesy of the Copenhagen Police.)

4.2.2   Contact with the CSI Unit and Other Forensic Services

The police district called and requested assistance from the CSI unit of the National Centre of Forensic Services in Copenhagen to lead and be in charge of the CSI examinations to be performed at the scene. The CSI unit immediately appointed a coordinator, who established contact with the police district for more information on the conditions at the scene, as well as information about the observations and actions made so far by the police with respect to the crime scene.

This is where planning of the scene investigation begins; it involves deciding on how the CSI team should be put together, what competencies and specialists are required, what equipment is needed, and which external specialists should be called on, such as a pathologist and marks and prints (sole and finger) specialists. These personnel are then contacted and briefed. The CSI coordinator also interacts with the police to determine what further actions need to be taken at the scene before the arrival of the CSI unit. Because in this case they were dealing with an outdoor scene, considerations were made with regard to the weather and possible changes that might influence conditions at the scene. A point of contact was also agreed upon.

At this early point in the tactical investigation, the police have received notification of the incident and classified it as a possible murder. It is now up to the technical investigation to develop its own approach, one that will address the elements of the investigative star, beginning with WHAT. There is no doubt that it is a suspicious death, but what are the possible themes? Murder? Perhaps the death was an accident or suicide or due to natural causes, and the body was concealed for reasons not known at this point. All possible themes should be considered and addressed during the investigation, and these can be broken up into sub-themes or elements relative to the other elements of the 6Ws. In this context, it is exceedingly important to frame actions by the worst-case principle until a final conclusion can be made. Every suspicious death or possible murder must begin with that hypothesis until proven otherwise. In any case, even in circumstances as apparently obvious as those described so far, it is absolutely crucial to obtain adequate knowledge of whether or not a crime has occurred and, if one has, what type of crime has been committed and where.

Even in cases where the cause of death appears to be probably due to an accident, such as when a cyclist has been run down by a motorist who fled the site and currently is unknown, one must ask, "Was this a deliberate and premeditated act? Is this actually a case of murder and was the vehicle used as the weapon?"

4.3   The Scene

When the CSI team arrived at the agreed point of contact, the CSI coordinator met the designated case manager of the police district and was briefed on the information that so far had been gathered on the case. The police district officers were still working to complete the cordoning off and guarding of the crime scene, which included the forest park and a large part of the forest for quite a long way from the spot where the body was found. Guarding all points of entry to the forest was established by the police district.

Even this basic and essential task can be enlightened by application of the 6Ws: WHAT (e.g., how far away from the immediate scene where the body was found should areas be blocked off); WHO (e.g., police or CSI personnel); WHERE (e.g., possible access points from which unauthorised persons could enter and compromise the scene); HOW (e.g., closing access roads and pedestrian pathways); WHEN (e.g., all of it immediately or carried out in stages, with critical areas being identified and cordoned off first); and WHY, with the objective of securing the integrity of the scene. In this way, basic physical control over the crime scene is established, and the task becomes one of establishing and exercising strategic control and management over the crime scene investigation, guided by the 6Ws.

The CSI coordinator made a reconnaissance by walking in the intact layer of snow along the forest trail from the parking lot to the location in the forest where the body was found. By doing this, we know that any footprints there are those of the CSI and not related to the incident. During this reconnaissance and preliminary scene assessment, he made observations similar to what had been observed by the notifier and the arriving police. He also noticed the reddish trail in the frosty snow on the forest trail which, from his experience, he was sure was blood. Here and there along the track of what was assumed to be blood he noticed faint impressions of two pairs of footwear marks, one pair on each side of this track. During his walk, the CSI coordinator took pictures so he could brief his CSI staff and could include these photographs in the scene assessment and discussion of strategy for the examination.

It was obvious that the forest and the forest tracks were regularly used by the public, as many more or less blurred footwear marks and tyre marks from bicycles were present in the frosty snow on the forest trail. The snow on the ground along both sides of the forest trail was almost undisturbed and, apart from a few smaller marks from four-legged animals (probably dogs or deer), the snow was untouched, indicating that no one had been walking off-track, or outside the forest trail, after snowfall.

While performing his reconnaissance, the CSI coordinator had to consider a wide range of questions: What is the limitation or boundary of the scene? How and when did the perpetrators arrive? Did they arrive by car, and did they arrive at the parking lot or at another of the entrances to the forest? After placing the body where it was found in the forest, did they then leave using the same path as used when entering? Did they return to the parking lot or did any one or all of them continue into the forest? If so, did they continue using this trail to the other side of the forest or could they have walked off-track? Did they discard or leave any items in the forest? If so, what distance from the forest trail could an item have been thrown? Did one or more other people wait in the transporting vehicle while the body was placed in the forest? Could a possible third or fourth person have acted as a lookout? If so, could this person have been walking around at or near the parking lot, on the forest trail, or even outside and away from the forest on the pavement and street? Will it start to snow, or could the temperature rise to above zero and thereby melt and destroy footwear marks? Should any safety precautions be taken? Which ones? Has the scene been properly cordoned off and at an adequate distance from where the body was found to be sure that the entire scene is under control and protected?

Addressing these questions directed the CSI coordinator's search and helped him develop a strategy for examination of the scene, while at the same time he was able to assesses the surroundings to decide what evidence may be important and should be protected and secured due to risks of deterioration, destruction, or contamination. The reconnaissance and observation made by the CSI coordinator provided him with information and documentation to be used for performing various initial actions at the scene, to prepare and form a strategy for the scene examination, and thereby to address any questions arising from his reconnaissance.

Throughout the world there might be different opinions on whether the CSI coordinator should perform a reconnaissance or not. Could his approach disturb or contaminate the scene? Should the scene be left as untouched as possible? Could the strategy for the examination be built on the observations and information given by the notifier and the first officer attending? It would be very easy to reply that this depends on the circumstances of the case and every case is different. The general position and policy in Denmark are that initial reconnaissance should be performed in every case where possible and thereby provide a stronger overview and more knowledge from which to build the investigative strategy and scene examination.

At this point, and during preparation of a plan for the CSI examination, the general and obvious questions raised by the 6Ws should be included in the strategy. An example would be the question of establishing the content of the case. Has any observation made by the CSI coordinator brought more knowledge to be added regarding WHAT happened at this particular scene? At this point the answer must be *no*; it is still a completely open question as to what actually happened here and if this is a case of homicide or anything else. When considering the perspective of WHAT, the question must be addressed within the context of the worst-case scenario for this situation; that is, it must be treated as a case of murder, and it should be examined as such until collected and gathered knowledge contradicts and proves this hypothesis to be wrong.

After he had performed his reconnaissance and scene assessment, the CSI coordinator returned to the CSI team. He decided to divide the scene into two sectors, each to be examined by a CSI team consisting of three crime scene investigators. The CSI coordinator gave first priority to examination of the sector with the dead body, the sector of the parking lot, and the sector of the forest trail between these locations. He gave second priority to the areas of the forest outside these prioritised scene sectors, and they were to be searched with police dogs. The reason for using police dogs was to try to establish if anybody had been recently walking off-track or on other forest trails in the forest, or if any items had been thrown or left behind.

The coordinator decided that the scene sectors must be examined for all types of possible evidence, and that taking impressions of shoe prints and tyre prints in the frosted snow was one of the top priorities because of the risk that the temperature could rise and this evidence would melt away. Fibres, DNA, gunshot residues, and fingerprints were also given top priority. Access to the sectors was to be made by alternative approach trails where the snow was intact and undisturbed. The approach trails themselves would be carefully examined and marked with cordon lines along both sides of the trail.

Each CSI team consisted of two general CSI examiners and one who was a marks specialist. The team examining the sector with the dead body included a forensic pathologist and an assistant pathologist from the Department of Forensic Medicine at the University of Copenhagen. One of the three CSIs in each team was appointed as team leader and each team conducted a full examination within their scene sector. Mobile phones were used to conduct briefings between the coordinator and teams every 90 minutes and for the teams to report if they found anything of possible significance.

As an example of this, the team conducting the examination of the sector with the victim discovered impressions of two different pairs of shoes in snow underneath blocks of snow that were used to cover the body. The CSI team immediately reported this information and provided a description of the size and sole pattern to the CSI coordinator and the other team to alert them to be on the lookout for the same impressions elsewhere on the crime scene. Particular attention was given to the parking lot, as this could provide an association with a possible vehicle, and perhaps they would be able to find and collect impression of tyre marks from it. If such tyre marks were present, this information and pictures of the impressions would be provided to the police investigation as soon as possible, in order to contribute to their investigation and assist in determining possible further actions to be taken in relation to the potential evidence.

The crime scene investigation was now underway and progressing through three elements of CSI activities—strategy, examination, and interpretation—which would continue in a loop throughout the crime scene examination. The CSI team briefings allowed them to share and discuss every action, observation, and detail of what had been found and collected within each scene sector. Based on the observations and findings, the original hypothesis and strategy were reviewed before continuing the examination of the scene sectors.

4.3.1   The Victim

In the sector of the crime scene where the body was found, the CSI team completed the examination of the broader sector before examining the body and its near surroundings. These were then examined in cooperation with the forensic pathologist and his assistant. When blocks of snow were lifted away from the pile covering the body, two pairs of shoe prints were found in the snow underneath. The sleeping bag with the body was partially open as a result of the actions of the first officers attending. The victim was a man, possibly 20 to 30 years of age, with dark hair and facial characteristics typical of the Middle East or Balkan region. He was dressed in normal clothes on his upper body. The body was apparently wrapped in plastic as well as in blankets, pillows, and quilts. The sleeping bag was tied on the outside with ropes and wires.

The pathologist could determine that a shot had gone through the victim's head, with the bullet entering in the area of the right temple and leaving through the left temple. Based on the corpse's core temperature, the conditions in relation to clothing worn, the insulating effect from the packaging, and the temperature of the surroundings, the pathologist estimated that the time of death was probably between 10 and 16 hours before the body of the victim was found in the forest. The sleeping bag and the victim were not further examined in the forest, as it was decided to perform these examinations at the Department of Forensic Medicine at the University of Copenhagen. The sleeping bag with the body was carefully wrapped and transported there, and examination of the sleeping bag and the body as well as the autopsy of the body were conducted that very same day.

The examination of the sector was fully completed, but nothing other than the shoe prints could immediately contribute to knowledge and evidence regarding the identity of the perpetrators. Various exhibits and types of further possible evidence were collected from the sector, such as the branches that had laid on top of the pile of snow, to be examined for the possible presence of DNA from the perpetrators; the tree trunks and the lower branches were taped for the possibility of finding fibres.

4.3.2   The Items Collected

It took two days of extensive work to complete the crime scene examination. It was soon quite apparent that the victim had not been killed there. This was a secondary scene, and the primary crime scene (where the victim had been shot) had yet not been found. During the examination of the crime scene in the forest many items were collected, which are listed in Tables 4.1A–D. The observations and findings obtained thus far would become the basis for the next phase of the examination strategy, including the iterative process of

Table 4.1A   Observations and Exhibits Collected from the Crime Scene Sector Where the Body Was Found

Observations and Exhibits	Remarks
A sleeping bag holding the body of the victim inside	Blood leaked from the body to the underside of the sleeping bag. Examination and collection of evidence were conducted later during the autopsy, so the results are not available at this point.
Blood	There was a smaller trail of blood on the snowy forest ground between the sleeping bag and the forest trail.
Four different pairs of footwear marks in the snow	Two of the four pairs of footwear marks were found at several places in the snow on the ground of the sector, as well as in the snow underneath the blocks of snow that covered the body. One of the four pairs of footwear marks matched the shoes of the notifier, and one of the four pairs of footwear marks matched the shoes of the first officer attending. Two pairs of footwear marks thus remained unidentified at this point.
Broken branches from the tree next to the sleeping bag	No DNA or gunshot residues were found on the branches. Textile fibres were found on three of the branches. The woody surface and structure excluded the possibility for fingerprints on the branches.
Snow and the upper layer of the forest ground from this sector	These were brought to the CSI unit and examined. Nothing was found in this material.

Table 4.1B Observations and Exhibits Collected from the Crime Scene Sector between the Forest Parking Lot and Where the Body Was Found

Observations and Exhibits	Remarks
Considerable amount of impressions: footwear marks, some amounts of footprints from four-legged animals, and a few impressions of bicycle tyre marks	All were blurred and not of sufficient quality to be compared and identified.
A track of blood	Detectable and visible 20 metres from the forest parking lot into the sector with the victim. The DNA profile from the blood matched the DNA profile of the victim (this result was provided 4 days after the scene examination).
Two different pairs of footwear marks, one on each side of the track of blood and very close to this	The two pairs of footwear marks matched the unidentified two pairs of footwear marks in the sector with the victim. The prints led from the parking lot to the victim and had a stride length of approximately 40 cm.
Two different pairs of footwear marks	The two pairs of footwear marks matched the unidentified two pairs of footwear marks in the sector with the victim and the footwear marks along the track of blood. The prints led toward the parking lot. There were only a few of these, and it was not possible to determine the stride length.
A considerable amount of waste paper from a cigarette package, candy, several cigarette butts, pieces of chewing gum, etc.	These were found here and there on the forest trail. Some of these appeared to be recently left at the scene, but some were obviously in a condition such that they had been lying there for a long time.

Table 4.1C Observations and Exhibits Collected from the Forest Parking Lot Sector

Observations and Exhibits	Remarks
Considerable amount of impressions: footwear marks, some amounts of footprints from four-legged animals, and a few impressions of bicycle tyre marks	All were blurred and not of sufficient quality to be compared and identified.
A few impressions of tyre marks	The different types of tyre marks were suitable for comparison and identification, but these were never identified.
A few impressions of footwear marks	The different types of footwear marks were suitable for comparison and identification, but these were never identified.
A considerable amount of waste paper from a cigarette package, candy, several cigarette butts, pieces of chewing gum, etc.	These were found here and there on the forest trail. Some of these appeared to be recently left at the scene, but some were obviously in a condition such that they had been lying there for a long time.
A baby shoe	The shoe was very dirty and appeared to have been lying on the ground for a long time.
A woman's brown leather boot and a small leather bag (child's size)	These were very dirty and appeared to have been lying on the ground for a long time.
A parking ticket for Copenhagen City	The ticket was dated December (2 months earlier).
No blood	
No intact or ejected cartridges	

Table 4.1D   Observations and Exhibits Collected from the Forest Outside the Crime Scene Sectors

Observations and Exhibits	Remarks
Considerable amount of impressions footwear marks, some amount of footprints from four-legged animals, and a few impressions of bicycle tyre marks on several other forest trails	These were mostly blurred and not of sufficient quality to be compared and identified.
No scent or appearance of recent walking tracks in the off-track areas of the forest	The police dogs did not indicate any signs or indications of such in these areas.
No exhibits or items	The police dogs did not find or react to any exhibits or items on the forest ground.
No blood	No blood was found anywhere in the forest outside the scene sectors.
Some amount of different kinds of paper, plastic bags, and waste paper from candy, several cigarette butts, pieces of chewing gum, etc.	In general, these appeared to have been lying there for a long time because of their condition.
Nearest house 800 metres away	Nearest house was in an area with family houses and multiple-storey buildings with flats.
Public transportation	The nearest bus stop was 200 metres away, and the nearest train station was 1100 metres away.

forming and testing hypotheses and sub-hypotheses to account for the findings and reconstruct the probable conduct of the crime. We will now explore the operational and practical application of the 6Ws to this phase, including the interdependence and relationships between some of the star themes:

- *WHERE did the crime take place, and which areas are involved?* The information obtained thus far supports the hypothesis that the sector with the victim and the path leading to it are part of the crime scene. It is not possible to say whether or not the parking lot or any other parts of the forest are part of the crime scene. Everything points to the forest scene being where the body was dumped, with nothing to indicate it is where the man was killed. It appears more likely that death did not occur in the forest but somewhere else, another place that would be described as the primary crime scene and is currently unknown.
- *HOW did it happen?* The observations support the hypothesis that two people pulled the sleeping bag with the victim along the forest path and into the final location in the woods. Because the shoe prints were also present beneath the blocks of snow, and no other footwear marks were present there, this supports the hypothesis that the same two people had covered the sleeping bag with snow and branches from the trees. Because there were no tyre marks or other types of wheel marks found along the blood trail or by the footwear marks on the forest path, this does not support a hypothesis that some form of transporting of the body using a wheeled carrier had taken place, but only that the bag containing the body had been dragged along the forest path to the spot where it was concealed. No objective findings at this point could support or reject the use of a vehicle to transport the corpse from another location to the forest. If a possible vehicle was identified, it could be searched for evidence associating it with the sleeping bag, the body, and the parking lot.

- *WHEN did it happen?* The forensic pathologist's estimation of the presumed time of death indicates the approximate time period when the death, and thus the possible time when the killing, may have occurred. Information from the Danish Metrological Institute regarding temperatures and precipitation in the area allowed an estimate that the latest time that footwear marks could have been made in the snow was 02:00h the previous evening.
- *WHO is involved?* Summarising what is known and can be inferred from the examination up to this point:
  - The victim is a man, approximately 20 to 30 years old, possibly of Middle Eastern or Balkan ethnicity, but his identity is still unknown.
  - The footwear marks indicate that at least two people were involved in placing the victim in the woods, but their identities are still unknown.
  - There are no objective findings to confirm or disprove whether additional offenders may have participated in placement of the body in the woods.

The results of the examination so far have addressed four of the 6Ws: WHERE, HOW, WHEN, and WHO. They have also shown how interactions between elements of the investigative star involve correlations; for example, there is a strong interaction between the WHERE, WHO, and HOW provided by the footwear marks, but these depend on the WHEN because of the role of the weather in the formation and preservation of the impressions.

4.4   The Autopsy

Before beginning, the CSI coordinator and the forensic pathologist discussed the case and developed an examination strategy. The autopsy process began with the forensic technicians photographing the sleeping-bag-wrapped body before it was removed from the bag. The photographic records included overviews and close-ups. The photographs were directed toward showing how the bag was wrapped with wires and cords and how the individual knots were made. One of the assessments considered here was where it would be most likely that someone would have grabbed hold of the sleeping bag or wrappings to pull the bag along the path. These are areas where DNA could be present and therefore could associate or dissociate someone with placement of the body.

The outside of the sleeping bag was taped to collect any fibres present. The bag was then opened and the unpacking began. The sleeping bag itself was packaged securely for subsequent examination that would focus on DNA evidence from the zipper mechanism and from places where it probably would be natural or necessary for a person to hold the bag to carry or drag it with the body inside. Likewise, the wires and cords from around the sleeping bag were wrapped and carefully packaged separately for further forensic investigation, including DNA. The sleeping bag did not appear to be very new, as it had some wear and soiling on various surfaces both inside and out.

The body, once removed from the bag, was undressed layer by layer, with continuous assessment of the types of evidence to be searched for and collected and in what order. The process continued until the body was completely stripped and the various possible types of evidence and clothing had been examined, collected, and safely packed to be further examined in the laboratory. Thorough and comprehensive documentation, including photography, was made throughout. The preliminary observations made in the autopsy process were as follows:

- The body was wrapped in the sleeping bag, which was tied with cords and wires.
- Inside the sleeping bag, the corpse was wrapped with three black plastic bags, and there were black plastic bags around his head and feet.
- Under the plastic bags, the corpse was wrapped in a red and yellow plaid blanket.
- Laying partly underneath the corpse's head was a striped pillow, and along the left side of the head and left side of the upper body lay a blue towel.

The examination of the body revealed the following:

- The victim was wearing a pair of black socks marked "Lloyd," a pair of black pin-striped trousers marked "Yves Saint Laurent" and closed with a leather belt marked "Hugo Boss," a pair of briefs marked "Bjorn Borg," a black T-shirt marked "Rocky," and a black turtleneck sweater marked "Luciaono Soprani."
- The clothing on the upper body was wet and damp with blood and fluid exudate, primarily on the underside, dorsal side of the body and the front of the chest on the sweater.
- There were many small bloodstains on the front of the sweater.
- The clothing on the lower body was dry, with the exception of the area at the top of the left knee, where there was large bloody area with runners of blood extending down toward the edge of the trousers leg.
- The clothing was not in abnormal position or disorder.
- The zipper in the trouser fly was closed and the pockets were empty.
- The victim had no tattoos, and he wore no jewellery or rings.

At the bottom of the bag at his feet lay a Tokarev pistol, 7.62 mm × 25 mm, engraved with "CCCP." The gun was empty and there were no cartridges in the chamber or in the magazine. Upon completion of the medicolegal autopsy, the pathologist's conclusions were as follows:

- The body was that of an unidentified 20- to 30-year-old, normal-weight male. There were signs of violence in the form of a gunshot wound in the head with an entry wound opening in the right temporal region and outgoing wound in the left temporal region. There were bruises in the soft tissues of the cranial dome and fracture of the skull corresponding to both temporal bones, as well as lacerations, mainly of the right brain hemisphere, but also involving the left brain hemisphere.
- The observed lesions were fresh and made while the person was alive. There was a near-contact gunshot discharge pattern.
- There were no other signs of violence on the deceased person. On the upper side of the fingers on his right hand was a small amount of bloodstaining, most of which had a diameter less than 3 mm, and the majority consisted of spots with a diameter of approximately 1 to 1.5 mm.
- There were no signs of illness.
- The cause of death was brain trauma from the gun shot.

- X-ray of the whole body in connection with the autopsy found no foreign objects and no fractures, apart from those described in the skull.
- In addition to the autopsy, samples were taken of nail scrapings, material was collected for DNA profile analysis, hair samples were taken, testing for acid phosphatase (semen) was performed, alcohol levels were measured, and forensic screening and microscopic examinations were performed.
- When the outcome of these became available, an additional statement would be sent.

These conclusions were signed by the coroner and the national deputy coroner.

The bloodstains found on the upper side of the fingers on his right hand were examined by a crime scene technician specialising in blood pattern analysis. There were too few to permit a full analysis but it was concluded that, because of their small size, they had been deposited as the result of a high-energy impact such as that from a bullet injury. The stains were sampled for DNA profiling. A CSI fingerprint technician took prints from the corpse's fingers and palms, as well as footprints, for possible identification of the victim. The prints could also serve as a reference for subsequent comparisons with prints from locations and objects that may be located elsewhere. The crime scene technician took photographs of the deceased's face for police interrogation and for possible entries and inquiries from the press and other media. Finally, the forensic odontologist conducted an examination and documented the corpse's teeth for possible identification from dental records.

The autopsy was now complete. Crime technicians brought the collected exhibits and possible evidence to the National Centre of Forensic Services' laboratories, where further examination and analysis would be performed. The victim's clothing would be examined for several types of evidence. The gun would first be examined for evidence such as DNA and fingerprints and then undergo a ballistic and weapon examination, including test shooting so the firing marks could be entered into the Interagency Border Inspection System (IBIS) database to determine whether the gun was a match with other crime scenes in the database. Consideration had to be given to whether a request should be sent to other countries to search their databases. One of the primary, urgent tasks was still identifying the victim, which was crucial for the investigation. Table 4.2 provides a summary of the observations, items, exhibits, and trace evidence collected during the autopsy.

Table 4.2 Summary of Observations and Exhibits Collected at the Time of the Autopsy

Observations and Exhibits	Remarks
Sleeping bag, cords, wires	These could be examined for different types of evidence, such as DNA, fibres, hair, gunshot residues, particles, soil, plant pollen.
Black plastic bags, red and yellow plaid blanket, pillow, towel	These could be examined for different types of evidence, such as DNA, fibres, hair, gunshot residues, particles, soil, plant pollen. Foreign DNA from several persons was found on these exhibits. No identifiable fingerprints were found on the plastic bags.
Sweater, T-shirt, trousers with belt, pants, a pair of socks.	These were found with blood here and there, as described earlier in this chapter.
Handgun (Tokarev)	No cartridges or shells were found in either the chamber or in the magazine. DNA or fingerprints were not found on the gun.
Possible evidence on the body beside the already mentioned bloodstains, such as hair, fibres, DNA, gunshot residues	The results of examination of this possible evidence are provided in the text.

We will now discuss how the 6W model can be applied to the above in further developing the investigation:

- *HOW did it happen?* The autopsy supported the hypothesis that the victim died as a result of a shot through the head, very probably a contact or near contact shot where the projectile had a trajectory through the right temporal region and out through the left temporal region. There was nothing in the related forensic examinations that contradicted this conclusion. There were fine blood spatters on the upper side of the victim's fingers on his right hand, which could indicate that the arm and the hand may have been in the vicinity of the head when the shot was fired. There were no bloodstains on the victim's left hand, which is possibly an indication that this hand was not in the immediate vicinity of the head (and thus the outgoing lesion in the left temple) when the shot was fired. The blood traces on the top of the left knee of the trousers and blood runners down the trouser leg may support a hypothesis that the victim was sitting down when the shot was fired. He may have then fallen forward and down to the left, so the blood from the head wound spread on to the upper side of the knee region.
- *WHERE did it happen?* The victim was wearing indoor clothing, which was dry except for blood from the wound and postmortem exudates. The blood distribution on the victim indicated that the victim was sitting when the shot was fired. These findings support the hypothesis that the primary crime scene was indoors rather than outdoors. Again reflected here is the correlation between the elements of the 6Ws. The findings on the clothing address not only HOW the victim was killed (shot in the head) but also WHERE (inside while seated). The findings also touch on the question of WHO. They do not tell us the identity of the victim, but do open avenues of inquiry that may provide the answer. It may, for example, be possible to trace who purchased the clothing from shop sales or credit card records.

4.5 Identification of the Victim

The identity photographs taken at the autopsy were passed to the tactical investigators who in turn sent them out to all of the country's police forces, asking whether the victim could be recognised by anyone. Only an hour later a response was received from the police station in an asylum refugee centre north of Copenhagen. A police officer believed he recognised the victim from the photograph and had traced his address from data in the police register of registered asylum seekers. In Denmark, anyone applying for asylum is registered, is given a personal applicant identification number, and has a record made with photograph and fingerprints. The fingerprints are kept in the asylum register in the national fingerprint database, separately from those in the register of convicted persons. The Fingerprint Section within the National Forensic Services Division was then requested to make a comparison between the prints taken from the deceased and those from the person mentioned by the police officer. They matched, and the victim was identified as a 21-year-old man from Armenia, who had been denied asylum in Denmark 3 months previously. He had not been present at court when the asylum decision was announced, and a police search was in vain. He was declared a wanted person to be deported from Denmark.

Knowing WHO the victim was brought the investigation closer to a solution. The investigating police now had a new and quite specific direction to investigate: Was he alone or with other persons when in the asylum centre, did he have any visitors while he was there, and, if so, what was the identity of such persons? Did they live in Denmark? Where in Denmark? These specific issues could now be addressed and investigated.

Five days later, the investigation led the police to an apartment building in the north-eastern part of Copenhagen, where it was suspected that the victim could have lived. The police interviewed the residents of the apartment building, one of whom thought that he recognised the victim from the photograph of the victim's face taken during the autopsy. He indicated that "the man in the photo" until recently had lived in apartment 26, ground floor to the right. The investigating police notified the National Centre of Forensic Services that a suspected flat had been found and that a forensic crime scene examination of this particular apartment might be required. The CSI forensic coordinator from the National Centre of Forensic Services and the police district were now in communication with each other, and in the same manner as for the investigation of the crime scene in the forest began planning their investigation of the probable primary crime scene.

During the 5 days since the forensic examination of the crime scene in the forest had been performed, the National Centre of Forensic Services had examined several vehicles to determine whether these possibly could be related to the case. Similarly, the police collected and sent a large number of objects from various locations to be examined in the National Centre of Forensic Services, including, for example, the contents from rubbish bins from bus stops and a subway station near the crime scene. So far, these examinations had not produced significant or conclusive findings. No blood or relevant fibres were found in any of the vehicles examined, and they were all excluded and exempt from suspicion, which of course is just as important in the forensic investigation as being able to confirm or prove associations.

4.6   The Primary Crime Scene

Police and the CSI team arrived at apartment 26, ground floor to the right, and rang the bell, but there were no signs of life and no response from the apartment. No one opened the front door. A locksmith was called. He opened the front door, and the police cautiously entered the apartment. Everyone was aware that a perpetrator could be present and armed and thereby dangerous. Police safety is of great importance at such a stage, but acting with utmost caution when entering the scene also minimises any disturbance of the potential crime scene. The police found the apartment abandoned and no person was present.

The CSI forensic coordinator and the team of crime scene technicians set out a strategy for the examination. It was decided to conduct the examination of the staircase and external areas close around the apartment before they investigated the apartment itself. This was because of the weather forecast of possible snow, which would hide any tyre marks that could be compared to those at the parking lot at the scene in the woods. Shortly after the scene examination had begun, a bullet hole was found in the window of the apartment's living room, and close to one curb on the partially iced lane in front of the apartment a slightly deformed projectile was found. After the external examination was completed, the examination of the apartment itself was begun. The apartment consisted of an entrance hall, kitchen, bathroom with toilet, living room with exit to the balcony, a bedroom, and an office. The examination started from the doorstep in the hallway and then progressed step by step further into the apartment. A large variety of types of evidence were constantly sought, including, of course, footwear or footwear marks that could be compared to those from the scene at the woods.

When the CSI team came to the living room they discovered numerous blood trails in the area of a sofa, coffee table, and chairs. More specifically, numerous bloodstains were present on the sofa and on the wall above it. There was a larger quantity of bloodstaining on the right of the sofa, running from the front of the seat downward and onto the floor. Bloodstains were also found on the north wall in the living room.

When the curtains were closed, a bullet hole was found that lined up with the one in the window and a position on the sofa. There was no indication that other shots had been fired in the apartment. The pattern of the bloodstains on the wall and on the area by the front right of the sofa, in conjunction with reconstruction of the bullet trajectory line, supported the hypothesis that someone could have been sitting on the couch while being shot in the head (see Figures 4.4 to 4.6). This examination, documentation, reconstruction, and interpretation of the findings led to a professional observation and reconsideration of the murder hypothesis by the CSI team.

One of the first things that had to be determined in this case was what happened—what kind of crime are we facing here? Considering the available information—the concealed body of a man killed by a close-range shot to the head—and following the principle of begin with the worst-case scenario until it is proven otherwise, it was concluded that it was more probable that this was a case of homicide rather than one due to any other cause of death. As we have repeatedly emphasised in theory and now in practice, this hypothesis, like all others, must be subject to continuous review and reassessment as more information becomes available.

The examination results, observations, and discoveries in the apartment raised the following issues:

- If the blood is related to the victim, then the perpetrator should have been standing at the same spot where the CSI examiner is holding the bullet trajectory cord in Figure 4.5.

Figure 4.4 Reconstruction showing a CSI sitting on the sofa in the position where the victim may have been shot. The red cord shows the trajectory of the bullet. (Photograph courtesy of the Copenhagen Police.)

Figure 4.5 Reconstruction showing the bullet trajectory as viewed from the direction from the victim toward the window. (Photograph courtesy of the Copenhagen Police.)

Figure 4.6 Part of the northern wall, showing the location of the blood spatters. (Photograph courtesy of the Copenhagen Police.)

- The evidence from the bloodstain pattern on the northern wall seen behind the CSI holding the bullet trajectory reconstruction line (shown in Figure 4.6) poses a serious challenge to this explanation. If the perpetrator were in fact positioned there when firing the shot that killed the victim, then the bloodstains would very likely have landed on him and not been spread out on the wall in the pattern shown, since his body would have acted as a shield.

In an effort to explain this apparent contradiction, the crime scene investigators tried out different possible explanatory scenarios to see if any of them might provide an answer. Could a perpetrator have been standing somewhat sideways and so let bloodstains spray onto the wall? Every reasonable consideration of this scenario, however, led to the answer of not very likely. Could the perpetrator have been sitting down or kneeling down when he released the shot, then? This hypothesis does not seem very likely, either. Could there have been a struggle before the shot was fired, resulting in the perpetrator being out of the trajectory line for the blood spatter—that is, out of the line between the contact point and the wall? Again, the same professional answer would be not very likely. The evidence found seemed to contradict rather than support the working theory that this was a case of murder.

The problem of investigating WHAT happened and WHO was involved, having established WHERE it happened by identifying the deceased and then the living room of the apartment as the primary crime scene, has seriously challenged the initial hypothesis made at the scene where the body was found and recovered. The initial interpretation of the evidence at the first scene—that it was probably a homicide carried out somewhere else and then the body was moved to hide the evidence, was shown not to be correct, and new investigative questions, actions, and lines of inquiry were needed to solve this inherent tension between the different hypotheses and the evidence supporting each. The CSI examination of the flat continued, ending with a fingerprint examination. To establish WHAT happened, HOW it happened, and WHO was involved, based on the crime scene investigation (WHERE), the CSI team then turned to the examination of the many different exhibits recovered from the scene and the body. Listed in Table 4.3 are some of the observations, items, exhibits, and trace evidence collected during the CSI examination of the flat.

WHERE did the crime take place, and HOW did it happen? The findings from the examination of the apartment supported and reinforced the hypothesis that it was the primary crime scene. The bloodstains on the wall, the pool of blood by the sofa, the trajectory of the projectile and its relation to the Tokarev gun, the evidence indicating this was where the body was wrapped (e.g., a matching pillow case and a roll of plastic bags, even though these are common and may be found in many homes in Denmark) all added up to compelling information that led the CSI team to conclude that the shooting that resulted in the death of the victim took place in the apartment and to revise the initial hypothesis. The bloodstain evidence contributed not only to answering WHERE the crime was committed (generally, the apartment; specifically, the living room), but also HOW it happened, and again highlights the mutual relation between activity and legs in the 6Ws.

The examination of the flat supported the conclusion of the pathologist after the autopsy, that the victim could well have been sitting down normally on a chair or sofa when the gunshot was fired and then fell down to the left, which is completely consistent with the factual findings and observations in the apartment. Knowing WHO was involved may also contribute to determining WHAT, WHERE, and WHY. It is difficult to reconstruct

Table 4.3   Observations and Exhibits Collected from the Primary Scene

Observations and Exhibits	Remarks
Footwear marks	No identifiable footwear marks were found in the apartment. The floors were generally partly covered with rugs of different kinds.
Footwear	No footwear matching the footwear marks in the woods was found in the apartment.
Bloodstains and other traces of blood	The point of origin of the spatters on the wall was approximately head height for a person of the same size and height as the victim if seated on the sofa. On the carpet in front of the couch was a dried pool of blood corresponding to a bleeding person falling down to the left toward the floor. The DNA profile of bloodstains and the pool of blood in the apartment matched the victim. No blood was found on any clothing in the apartment.
Bullet hole in the curtain, continuing through the window	The bullet trajectory line ran from the point of origin of the bloodstains on the wall, through the hole in the curtain, and then out the window and into the street.
A roll of black plastic bags	These were identical to the black plastic bags in the sleeping bag. No identifiable fingerprints or DNA were found on the roll of plastic bags in the apartment. Only three plastic bags remained in the roll.
A pillow case	In appearance and pattern, this pillow case was identical to the pillow case found with the corpse in the sleeping bag.
A large amount of fingerprints	These were collected from various surfaces and objects in the apartment and could contribute to knowledge about who has lived and moved about in the apartment.
A fired projectile, found on the street next to apartment's living room window	Marks on the projectile showed, by comparison, that it had been fired from the Tokarev gun in the case.
Several exhibits for further examination and analysis	Various other items that could contribute to knowledge of the persons who could be related to the apartment were collected.

the scene with someone firing the fatal shot other than the deceased while he was seated on the sofa. Although there may not have been others involved or present when the shot was fired, there certainly were others involved in removal and concealment of the body.

4.7   Examination of Exhibits

The clothing from the victim was closely examined. Many bloodstains were found on the sweater that he wore. Some were found in the area of the right shoulder and chest, and on the right arm many were located on the upper side of the underarm. This pattern and the blood-stains found earlier on the victim's fingers indicated that the victim had been holding his arm in this position (see Figures 4.7 and 4.8) when the shot was fired. The analysis of gun-shot residues found a large number on the outer side on the fingers of the victim's right hand. As mentioned in the section on the autopsy, fine blood spatters were found on the right hand of the deceased, but not on the left (Figure 4.9). The possible explanation for these findings that was suggested earlier was not correct; instead, the blood spatters came from blow-back of the fine mist of blood caused by the high-energy impact of the bullet to the head.

Figure 4.7 Reconstruction of the position of the gun when the deceased fired the shot. (Photograph courtesy of the Copenhagen Police.)

Figure 4.8 As for Figure 4.7, but a closer view showing the blood spatters on the sweater. (Photograph courtesy of the Copenhagen Police.)

4.8   Continuing the Investigation by Other Means

The police continued the investigation and managed to identify, apprehend, and interrogate three persons who had been living in the apartment at the same time as the victim. They turned out to be illegal immigrants, also with relations to Armenia. They explained that they had returned to the apartment on Tuesday evening and found the victim lying dead in front of the sofa in the living room. He had shot himself with the gun. The victim

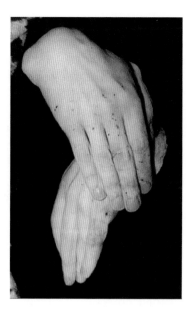

Figure 4.9 Blood spatters on the right hand of the deceased. (Photograph courtesy of the Copenhagen Police.)

had been quite depressed for some time because of his situation. He was a refugee from his own country who had applied for asylum in Denmark and been denied. During the past month he had become more and more depressed.

The persons living in the flat were aware that if the police were notified and came to conduct an investigation then their illegal existence would be revealed and they would be arrested and deported. For this reason, they decided to move the body. They wrapped and packed it using items present in the flat, placed it in the trunk of their car, and drove away to find a suitable place for concealment. They were familiar with the forest and placed the body there around midnight on Tuesday night. After that they decided to stay away from the apartment for awhile, at least until they found out whether or not the body had been found.

The vehicle that they said they had used to transport the body was examined. No blood was found in it, but fibres from the trunk matched fibres found on the outside of the sleeping bag. The footwear of two of those arrested matched the footwear marks found in the woods, the marks along the track, and in the snow in the sector where the body was found. There were no bloodstains found on the clothes they were wearing.

The output from all the CSI and forensic examinations were provided to the police district and as a result the police attorney decided to bring charges against two of the arrested persons for illegal concealment of a dead body. They pled guilty and were again expelled from Denmark.

4.9 Summary

What appeared to be an obvious case of homicide was subsequently found *not* to be a murder, but instead a case of suicide in combination with illegal handling of a dead body by concealing it in the forest. The results of the police investigation, the CSI examinations, and the forensic analysis all contributed to addressing WHAT, WHERE, HOW, WHO, WHEN, and WHY—not by contributing absolute scientific answers and knowledge but by being sufficiently objective to allow reasonable and legally acceptable conclusions to be drawn. The question of WHY (the motive) was not extensively addressed in this case example, and the investigators had only the word of the associates of the deceased that he was depressed. But, within forensic investigations the WHY must always be included equally with the other elements of the 6Ws. It is very often the fact that CSI and forensic investigations can lead to observations, findings, and analysis results that could support or reject a hypothesis about the motive for the case in question. An example would be the death of a woman where the investigation reveals semen on her thighs, indicating a sexual motive behind the murder. It must be borne in mind, however, that forensic examinations are not intended to produce a profile of the offender; rather, their intent is to interpret the crime scene and collect as much knowledge as possible about the total circumstances of the crime.

In the reviewed case, the detainees stated that the victim's motive for suicide was depression caused by the victim's life situation. The two detained persons gave very precise and detailed descriptions about their observations, their actions, and movements in the flat and in the forest, which could be and was tested and confirmed by the CSI team and forensic investigations. The consistency between the statements of the detained persons and the findings in the case supported the credibility of their statements.

From the very beginning of an investigation, the elements of WHAT, WHERE, HOW, WHO, WHEN, and WHY are included in the actions of the police investigator, by the CSI team, and by the forensic laboratories. Often, these elements will be intuitive, but formalising the elements by applying the investigative star ensures that valuable data is not overlooked; in a way, it is the CSI equivalent of a pilot's pre-take-off checklist.

This "Body in the Woods" case illustrated how these elements should be assessed and evaluated continuously during any investigation, examination, and analysis process. The police investigation and crime scene examination will continually produce new information. The ongoing production of knowledge will continuously contribute to evaluation and reconsideration of earlier findings and related hypotheses, as well as the unfolding of new strategies, leading to new examinations and findings. It is not a hard and absolute process, but rather one of making, in a continuous loop, new hypotheses and sub-hypotheses to be addressed within the case investigation.

The actions that happen at crime scenes will produce things, physical entities however small or nebulous, that can tell the story of what happened. The development of the story, the reconstruction, involves answering the fundamental questions of WHAT, WHERE, HOW, WHO, WHEN, and WHY? These are the 6Ws of the investigative star that in themselves and through their interrelationships provide the strongest tool for planning and conducting investigations of crime scenes. Their value, however, rests on the integrity and diligence of the investigator in rigorously testing each reconstructive option and revising the story that is told as evidence unfolds.

Practitioner Competency, Professionalism, and Codes of Conduct

5.1 Introduction

Chapters 1 through 3 laid out the theoretical background and principles that underpin the work of the crime scene examiner, and Chapter 4 showed them in action. Chapter 6 and those that follow it deal with the practical aspects of scene investigation. This chapter provides a bridge between theory and practice and is a reminder that the theories and principles presented so far are only a framework, the effectiveness of which depends on the personal and professional values and conduct of all the practitioners involved in the process.

5.2 Education, Training, and Competency

5.2.1 Education

Education, the process of receiving or giving systematic instruction, is usually differentiated from training, in that while both are about giving instruction training is directed toward imparting a specific skill. Over the years, there has been some debate about the role of education in forensic science. In brief, the negatives are usually presented as the following:

- In the laboratory, the things that matter are the basic knowledge of the analyst in chemistry, molecular biology, or physics and engineering. A forensic science degree cannot teach these to the required depth and also deal with forensic topics, and it can only deal with the forensic issues in an abstract or theoretical manner. In contrast, the place of employment can deal effectively with the forensic aspects during its training programs, adding these to the chemistry or other education that the new employee has received.
- At the scene, practical forensic skills are vital and require experience and practice to learn and understand. Field conditions cannot be adequately replicated in an educational environment.
- It has been argued that no identifiable research programme in forensic science exists, an argument most recently found in the US National Research Council of the National Academy of Science report published in 2009. There is certainly very little fundamental research in forensic science and very little funding, apart from that with a military purpose.

The other side of the debate agrees that there are shortcomings in education in forensic science, that there is indeed an absence of an identifiable research programme, that there should be far more involvement of practitioners in forensic education, and that the level of funding for university courses and research without constraints on the academic freedom of the researchers is inadequate. Those of this view would point to the many cases of

Table 5.1   Science and Forensic Content of Canberra Institute of Technology Bachelor of Forensic Science in Crime Scene Programme

Science	Forensics
General chemistry	Principles of forensic science
Organic and analytical chemistry	Principles of forensic investigation
Biochemistry	Communication in forensic science
Math and physics for forensic science	Crime scene investigation (major crime, volume crime)
Anatomy and physiology for forensic science	Comparative analysis
Statistics for forensic science	Criminalistics
	Principles of ridgeology and fingerprint comparisons
	Principles of ballistics and firearm identification
	Principles of vehicle examination
	Principles of forensic document examination
	Bloodstain pattern analysis
	Fire scene examination
	Professional practices in forensic science

failures of forensic science from Australia, to Canada, to the United Kingdom, and most of all in the United States, and argue that it is the lack of appreciation and support for education and research that is the root cause.

There has been progress. In the United States, the American Academy of Forensic Sciences has established its Forensic Science Education Programs Accreditation Commission (FEPAC). The object of the commission is to maintain and to enhance the quality of forensic science education through a formal evaluation and recognition of college-level academic programs. The primary function of the Commission is to develop and maintain standards and to administer an accreditation program that recognises and distinguishes high-quality undergraduate and graduate forensic science programs. The standards include a requirement for a significant practical content in courses. In Australia, the Australian Federal Police, Canberra Institute of Technology, and the University of Canberra have come together to establish the National Centre for Forensic Studies (NCFS), offering a range of programmes, including a Bachelor of Forensic Science in Crime Scene, the curriculum for which is summarised in Table 5.1.

Both FEPAC and NCFS are recent initiatives, but Europe has a long-standing history of forensic science in its universities. Bragging rights for the first university department of forensic science probably belong to the University of Lausanne in Switzerland. The forensic program in the School of Forensic Science and Criminology can trace its history back to 1902 and Professor Rudolphe Archibald Reiss. Reiss, who was born in Lausanne in 1876 and died in Belgrade in 1929, was yet another of the pioneers of forensic science who had worked with Bertillon (see Chapter 1). He established a forensic photography course at the university around the turn of the century and developed it into a full forensic science program in 1909. Today, hundreds of courses have the word "forensic" in their title.

One of the most well established of the modern courses (modern relative to Lausanne, that is) is the Master of Science program at the University of Strathclyde, which began in 1966. This program is well established and addresses the negative points presented above with a mix of core forensic material and advanced study in aspects of chemistry or molecular biology. The Centre for Forensic Science at the university is part of the Department of Chemistry and offers a joint degree in analytical chemistry and forensic science, another approach to the science + forensic issue.

5.2.2 Training

Although education can be regarded as the province of universities, professional bodies and vocational institutions have much to offer through training programmes. Frequently, the shift in emphasis from education to training is accompanied by curricula that are modelled on the core competencies required by the course. An example is the Professional Postgraduate Diploma in Crime Scene Investigation offered by the Forensic Science Society in the United Kingdom. The essential elements of the course relating to crime scene investigation are summarised in Table 5.2. The diploma curriculum includes competencies in the specific technical tasks of photography, fingerprints, and physical evidence. Assessment consists of written, oral, and practical examinations.

Table 5.2 Core Course Elements of the Professional Postgraduate Diploma in Crime Scene Investigation Offered by the Forensic Science Society in the United Kingdom

Competencies	Content
Be able to describe the purpose of crime scene examination and investigation.	Know the roles of the first officer attending, investigator, crime scene examiner, scientists, pathologists, and other specialists.
Know how to prepare for an investigation.	Determine the examination requirements. Identify sources of information and the means of recording the information obtained. Determine the types of examination to use.
Be able to plan the scene examination.	Establish priorities and the structure and sequence of examination types. Identify preservation requirements and resources and equipment requirements; establish consent and authority. Establish a common approach path. Understand the use of personal protective equipment. Be familiar with pre-cordon and pre-preservation person examination.
Conduct an examination.	Allocate responsibilities and limitations of personnel. Review scene boundaries, approach paths, cordons, and maintenance of cordon logs; communicate information and intelligence. Control scenes without loss, damage, degradation, or contamination of potential evidence. Be familiar with search and examination methods. Conduct examination plan reviews. Record examination findings. Understand equipment usage and the use of screening and presumptive tests. Recover materials of potential evidential value without loss, damage, degradation, or contamination. Recover control and reference samples. Evaluate evidential materials during recovery. Consider health and safety issues.
Review the examination.	Review the examination and investigation. Consider the potential for additional examinations by other specialists. Communicate with the investigator. Consider the information requirements of other specialists.

5.2.3 Competency

The examples provided in Tables 5.1 and 5.2 and the related text are adapted from education and training programme curricula. The issue of competency has been addressed at the practitioner level by ENFSI, with publication in 2002 of its extensive *Performance-Based Standards for Forensic Science Practitioners*, which provided the framework for Chapter 3.

5.3   Professions

Webster's Dictionary has defined *profession* as a calling or vocation "requiring specialised knowledge and often long and intensive preparation including instruction in skills and methods as well as in the scientific, historical, or scholarly principles underlying such skills and methods, maintaining by force of organisation or concerted opinion high standards of achievement and conduct, and committing its members to continued study and to a kind of work which has for its prime purpose the rendering of a public service." Law, medicine, accountancy, and architecture are examples of vocations that would be regarded as professions and that embody the "long and intensive preparation" part of the definition. To become a practitioner in the profession requires successful completion of a defined academic course of study together with induction training, usually in the form of some kind of residency training.

These examples of professions share some other features: The services delivered by the practitioners require exercise of judgement; entry to the profession is regulated, usually with a significant element of self-regulation and requiring successful completion of the induction training and continuing professional development (CPD); and they have codes of ethics that must be complied with to maintain membership. Conformity to the professional requirements is linked to the granting of some form of license to practice by the state.

Like science in general, forensic science shares the professional characteristics of requiring specialised knowledge and lengthy study, having a prime purpose of rendering public service, and requiring the exercising of judgement in delivering the service. Unlike law, medicine, and most other recognised professions, however, forensic science does not have regulated entry, does not have a requirement for a licence to practice, and does not have a requirement to abide by a code of ethics to maintain one's professional status (see Table 5.3).

The requirement of a licence to practice is a political matter, imposed by governments at a local or national level, but the professions link the granting of a licence with their education, training, and CPD requirements as a way of maintaining standards. The absence of a linkage to a licence to practice does not mean that forensic science ignores induction training, codes of ethics, or continuing professional development. Numerous university courses provide education in the basic and applied sciences that will provide the required knowledge base in the various disciplines within forensic science, and today these are more or less globally followed by significant in-service induction training built around the competencies required for technical proficiency.

Table 5.3 Comparison of Education, Training, and Regulatory Requirements in Law, Medicine, and Forensic Science

Profession	Education	Training	Regulated Profession with Code of Ethics?	License to Practice Required?
Law	Degree[a]	Certificate of practice required before being licensed	Yes	Yes
Medicine	Degree[b]	Residency and discipline-specific postgraduation training	Yes	Yes
Forensic science				
DNA analyst	Degree[c]	Induction training on gaining employment	No[d]	No
Crime scene examiner	Degree and/or several years of in-service training[e]	Induction training on gaining employment	No[d]	No

[a] Required to practice; in some countries, law is a postgraduate degree.

[b] Required to practice; in some countries, medicine is a postgraduate degree.

[c] A *de facto* requirement for employment in the area. The degree syllabus, induction training, and in-service training required for a DNA analyst in the United States are tightly specified in federal government regulations, and technical leaders are required to have a postgraduate degree.

[d] Many professional associations in forensic science include a binding code of ethics for members, but membership is not required to practice in the discipline.

[e] Some form of degree and/or verified training is a *de facto* requirement for employment. There are several certificate programmes with high academic standards for crime scene examiners, such as those offered by the International Association for Identification in the United States and by the Forensic Science Society in the United Kingdom.

There are other definitions and usages of *profession* and *professional*, one of which is the concept of a professional society, where the members are engaged in an activity requiring special skills but are not required to have membership in a profession as described in the definition above. There are many professional organisations in the forensic sciences, such as the American Academy of Forensic Sciences, Australian and New Zealand Forensic Science Society, European Network of Forensic Science Institutes, Forensic Science Society, International Association for Identification, and Association of World Police Medical Officers. Professional societies such as these have addressed ethics and conduct in their membership requirements.

5.4 Controlling Codes

5.4.1 Codes of Conduct

Although there is no licence-to-practice requirement for forensic science, governments are beginning to display some interest in regulation. The 2009 National Research Council report in the United States has already been mentioned, and there is a degree of state involvement in forensic science in the United Kingdom through the office of the Forensic

Science Regulator, which is a public appointee whose function is to ensure that the provision of forensic science services across the criminal justice system is subject to an appropriate regime of scientific quality standards. The activities of the Regulator include the following:

- Identifying the requirement for new and improved quality standards
- Leading on the development of new standards where necessary
- Providing advice and guidance so service providers will be able to demonstrate compliance with common standards (e.g., in procurement and in the courts)
- Ensuring that satisfactory arrangements exist to provide assurance and monitoring of the standards

Practical examples of the work of the Regulator include the introduction of accreditation and the publication of an extensive code of conduct linked to the quality requirements of the agreed standard used in the accreditation programme.

5.4.1.1   The UK Code of Conduct

The draft "Codes of Practice and Conduct for Forensic Science Providers and Practitioners in the Criminal Justice System" was published by the office of the Forensic Science Regulator in 2011. It is a lengthy document that primarily links conduct specifically to clauses in the accreditation standard (ISO/IEC 17025) that the Regulator is using to give objective evidence of the competency of the laboratories. Note that the Code was in draft and under discussion at the time of this writing; however, even the draft content is a relevant example of how a forensic scientist should behave. The introduction to the draft states that it is intended to set "out for all practitioners ... the values and ideals the profession stands for," and it requires the following of practitioners:

- Your overriding duty is to the court and to the administration of justice.
- Act with honesty, integrity, objectivity, impartiality and declare at the earliest opportunity any personal interest that could be perceived as a conflict of interest.
- Provide expert advice and evidence only within the limits of your professional competence.
- Take all reasonable steps to maintain and develop your professional competence, taking account of material research and developments within the relevant field.
- Establish the integrity and continuity of items as they come into your possession and ensure they are maintained whilst in your possession.
- Seek access to exhibits/information that may have a significant impact on your findings.
- Conduct casework using methods of demonstrable validity.
- Be prepared to review any casework if any new information or developments are identified that would significantly impact on your findings.
- Inform a suitable person within your organisation if you have good grounds for believing there is a situation which may result in a miscarriage of justice.
- Preserve confidentiality unless the law obliges, a court/tribunal orders, or a customer explicitly authorises disclosure.

5.4.1.2   The ENFSI Code of Conduct

Although ENFSI is a professional organisation and not a governmental agency, in 2009 the European Commission granted it the monopoly position to provide advice or information on forensics when needed by the Commission. The work of ENFSI thus carries significant weight in Europe and includes a code of conduct covering the following:

1. *Behaviour*
   - Act with honesty, integrity, and objectivity.
   - Do not discriminate on grounds of race, beliefs, gender, language, sexual orientation, social status, age, lifestyle, or political persuasion.
   - Recognise that your overriding duty is to justice.
   - Declare to your client and employer any prior involvement or personal interest that may give rise to a conflict of interest, real or perceived, and act in such cases only with the client's explicit written consent.
   - Declare to your employer any pressure to influence the result of an examination.
2. *Competence*
   - Know the limits of your competence and provide expert advice and evidence only within those limits.
   - Decline to undertake work if you are not competent to carry it out or do not have access to the necessary facilities or equipment.
3. *Casework*
   - Take all reasonable steps to ensure that you have the information necessary to carry out the work required.
   - Take all reasonable steps to gain access to all relevant available evidential materials necessary to reach a meaningful conclusion.
   - Establish, as far as is reasonably practicable, whether any evidential materials may have been compromised before coming into your possession.
   - Ensure that, except when it is necessary to conduct destructive tests, that the integrity and security of evidential materials are maintained whilst in your possession, and the integrity and security of any information derived from all evidential material are also maintained.
   - Carry out all your work in accordance with the established principles of your profession, using validated methods, wherever possible, and appropriate equipment and materials.
   - Accept full responsibility for all work done under your direction.
   - Conduct all your professional activities in a manner that protects the health and safety of yourself, your colleagues, and the public.
4. *Reporting*
   - Present your advice and evidence, whether written or oral, in a balanced and impartial manner.
   - Be prepared to reconsider and, if necessary, change your advice, conclusions, or opinion in the light of new information or new developments in the relevant field, and to take the initiative in informing your client and employer promptly of any such changes made.
   - Take appropriate action if you have good grounds for believing there is a situation that could result in a miscarriage of justice.

- Preserve client confidentiality unless: (a) explicitly authorised by the client or mandator to disclose specified information; (b) ordered by a court or tribunal to disclose specified information; (c) required by the law to disclose specified information available to a designated person; or (d) there is an overriding duty to the court and the justice system for disclosure.

5. *Continual professional competence*
  - Take all reasonable steps to maintain professional competence, taking account of material research and developments within the relevant field.

5.4.2 Codes of Ethics

Ethics generally refers to the moral principles that govern behaviour, with the proviso that the behaviours are not selfish but are ones that embody respect and benefit to society. Professional ethics are somewhat more specific. The general concept blurs the boundary between ethics and morals and relates to generally agreed behaviours, but, in regard to professions, ethics is a more specific concept that refers to a set of guiding beliefs, standards, or ideals that define the group. They are situational and are codified; that is, they vary from place to place but exist as a formal or informal code for the organisation. Professional codes are written, monitored, and enforced on a peer level. A professional code is

- Regulative of the conduct of members
- Protective of the public interest
- Specific and honest in its content
- Enforceable and enforced

A good example of a code of ethics, from outside of the forensic sciences, is that of the American Engineers' Council for Professional Development (ECPD), shown in the box on the next page.

5.4.3 Dealing with Breaches

There is considerable overlap in the content of the examples of codes of conduct and codes of ethics, since codes of ethics are about behaviour and the codes of conduct include behavioural issues. Whatever term is used to describe the code, the characteristic required to make it effectual is that it must be enforceable and enforced. Because codes are written sets of rules, any suspected breaches of the code must be able to be described in the language of one or more of the clauses in the code. If you cannot express the behaviour or act in that way, then it is not a breach no matter how much you disapprove. Conversely, anything that can be so described is a breach no matter how trivial. The degree becomes a factor in deciding how to deal with the breach, not whether there has been one. The linkage between the Forensic Science Regulator's proposed code of conduct and the Regulator's promulgation of ISO/IEC 17025 accreditation introduces a degree of objectivity and enforceability into the code. The main difference between the codes of ethics and the codes of conduct is that the latter include requirements relating to practice, as is clear from the ENFSI code. Inclusion of practice leads us to consider the concepts of *best practice* and *accreditation*.

CODE OF ETHICS OF THE AMERICAN ENGINEERS' COUNCIL FOR PROFESSIONAL DEVELOPMENT

Fundamental Principles

Engineers uphold and advance the integrity, honor and dignity of the engineering profession by:

I. Using their knowledge and skill for the enhancement of human welfare;
II. Being honest and impartial, and serving with fidelity the public, their employers and clients;
III. Striving to increase the competence and prestige of the engineering profession; and
IV. Supporting the professional and technical societies of their disciplines.

ECPD Canons

1. Engineers shall hold paramount the safety, health, and welfare of the public in the performance of their professional duties.
2. Engineers shall perform services only in the areas of their competence.
3. Engineers shall issue public statements only in an objective and truthful manner.
4. Engineers shall act in professional matters for each employer or client as faithful agents or trustees and shall avoid conflicts of interest.
5. Engineers shall build their professional reputation on the merits of their services and shall not complete unfairly with others.
6. Engineers shall act in such a manner as to uphold and enhance the honor integrity and dignity of the profession.
7. Engineers shall continue their professional development throughout their careers and shall provide opportunities for the professional development of those engineers under their supervision.

5.5 Best Practice

Best practice is not a concept that is well understood or embraced within all parts of forensic science. The most usual objections are that it is business school jargon irrelevant to the real world of forensics, and that every case is different so how can there be such a thing as best practice for forensic investigations? Best practice is certainly not an absolute, but rather, as the ENSFI guidance document for best practice manuals states, it can best be described as the means by which the optimal outcome can be achieved for a particular requirement under a given set of circumstances. It follows from this that the best approach to use for any given forensic examination could differ according to the circumstances of the offence, the questions being asked, the intended use of the output, and the legal systems of the country.

As we have seen from Chapters 1 and 2, however, and from our exploration of profession above, there is a constant theme of universal basic principles of forensic practice. Knowing and understanding these will result in the right people doing the right thing in the right way to answer the 6Ws and so provide evidence to matters being considered by tribunals.

The approach taken by ENFSI in providing a guidance document that agencies can use as a template to write their own jurisdiction and discipline-specific guidelines and standard operating procures manuals recognises the common core and operational variations. The guidelines cover the whole forensic process, from the crime scene to presentation of evidence, and are written in chronological order. The sequence relevant to the work of the crime scene examiner is shown in Table 5.4, and some parts are further discussed below. The ENFSI manual also gives guidance on the topics of examinations in the laboratory, prioritisation and sequence of examinations, the actual laboratory examination process, evaluation and interpretation, presentation of evidence, and health and safety.

5.5.1 Assessment and Procedures at the Scene

There is normally only one opportunity to carry out an examination and recover relevant material from the scene of an offence or incident. It is vitally important that all the possible evidential avenues at the scene are considered before any practical work commences. The guide recommends that all relevant available information about the incident should be obtained before starting any examinations and an agreement should be reached with the customer as to what is required to be ascertained. This is in contrast to the views of some nonscientific commentators who feel that all work should be carried out without any knowledge of what may have happened, as they believe that this may result in unconscious bias in the work and conclusions. The best way to address this objection is the recommendation that all possible hypotheses, from all sources, should be considered as part of this process.

Table 5.4 Summary of ENFSI Best Practice Guidelines for the Crime Scene Element of the Forensic Process

Sequential Step	Specific Actions
Customer requirements	Define purpose of examination.
	Have protocols in place for prioritisation, communications, change in direction of investigation, change in scene status.
Case assessment	Review the approach to take; develop a matrix of what is technically possible and what is best to answer the customer's requirements.
	Review the information available and required.
	Review all possible hypotheses pertaining to the customer's request.
	Consider all possible hypotheses, from all sources, as part of this process, as well as alternative explanations; assess the impact of actions on the integrity of items.
Examination of scene, victims, and suspects	Have procedures in place for securing the integrity of the scene.
	Have procedures in place for the recovery, preservation, and recording of items and for avoiding contamination of items, including possible subsequent analyses.
	Have procedures in place for search, recovery, sampling, preservation, and packaging of items.
	Maintain the chain of custody.
	Transport recovered materials.

The scene examiner expert (the CSI coordinator, in the language used in Chapter 3) should consult with the crime scene manager and any other experts and agree with them what examinations should take place, and in what order, so as to maximise the information that can be obtained from the scene. It is best if the scene can be preserved until all the experts are available. Where this is not possible or practicable, all scene examiners should ensure that adequate records are made of the scene prior to any disturbance of the scene on their part and during their subsequent examinations.

Particular emphasis should be given in the manual on the procedures for the avoidance of contamination and advice given to assist individuals to manage the specific risks associated with the analysis. The guidance should be directed toward ensuring that nothing is done by anybody attending the scene of an incident, or by others responsible for taking samples from the victims or suspects, that may lead to adventitious links being established between suspects and the scene, victims and suspects, or suspects with suspects through the mishandling of materials whilst in their possession.

Consideration of appropriate precautions against contamination should be based not only on those for the examinations under discussion but also on all evidence types that may be potentially available. If these include materials that may be required for subsequent DNA analysis, extreme caution should be taken because of the sensitivity of current DNA techniques, including the wearing of appropriate barrier clothing, such as gloves and face masks (refer to Chapters 3 and 8).

Guidance covering search and recovery of evidence should be given. All scenes (e.g., indoor, outdoor, vehicles) should be protected at the earliest opportunity to reduce the risk of the loss of any material or post-incident movement or contamination. Scenes should be searched systematically and thoroughly for the relevant materials, targeting and prioritising areas that, in the context of what has been alleged, are most likely to yield significant material of evidential value. Recovered material should be handled as little as possible, and control or reference materials must be kept strictly separate from any surfaces, items, clothing, or people with whom it might subsequently be significant to establish contact. No one who has attended the scene should be involved in examining suspects or victims for the recovery of trace evidence, or in the packaging of such evidence, unless they have thoroughly decontaminated themselves (e.g., by showering and changing their clothing). Where multiple suspects are involved, in addition to the necessity for keeping material from the victims separate, material from each suspect should be recovered and kept separate from each other and from that of the victims.

The manual should recommend the most appropriate packaging materials for given applications and the preservatives of choice where appropriate. All items should be packaged and sealed as soon as they are taken, using bags or containers of an appropriate size and material composition to avoid the packaging being damaged or the seals being broken. Packages should be sealed in such a way that all gaps are covered and secure (e.g., folded bags should be sealed with adhesive tape along all open edges). Once sealed, packages should not be reopened outside of the laboratory environment. If under exceptional circumstances they are reopened, then comprehensive documentation detailing the conditions under which they were opened must be made.

For legal purposes, in order to maintain the chain of custody, it is essential to be able to prove who has handled which item and what that person did with it. The manual should describe how items and evidential material recovered from an incident should be logged and labelled at the time of seizure, where appropriate. A record should be made, at the time of seizure of items from the scene or from the suspects or victims, describing the exact locations from where the items were recovered. It is also helpful to mark this location on a sketch or plan of the scene or person. Labels should be attached to each package at the time of packaging. If for any reason labels are not available, then relevant information and individual numbering should be made on the package.

5.6   Accreditation

Accreditation is a means of determining the competence of the forensic unit to show that it is performing its work correctly and to appropriate standards, and it provides a benchmark for maintaining that competence. It is a two-part process: the adoption of relevant standards and an independent audit of conformity to them conducted by an accrediting body. Globally, the top-level body setting standards is the International Organisation for Standardisation (ISO), and the audit process is formalised by the accrediting bodies, themselves being audited for conformity to an ISO standard, "Conformity Assessment—General Requirements for Accreditation Bodies Accrediting Conformity Assessment Bodies" (ISO/IEC 17011). The auditing is conducted globally on a regional basis by accreditation cooperations, including the National Association of Testing Authorities, Australia (NATA), and the European Co-operation for Accreditation (EA).

Two ISO standards have been applied to accreditation of crime scene units, "General Criteria for the Operation of Various Types of Bodies Performing Inspection" (ISO/IEC 17020) and "General Requirements for the Competence of Testing and Calibration Laboratories" (ISO/IEC 17025). The latter is the standard that is the basis of forensic science laboratory accreditation and was the first to be applied to crime scene examination for units that are administratively part of a laboratory.

Having accreditations conducted by recognised accrediting bodies using ISO standards results in uniformity and comparability of the standards, no matter where the accredited work is performed. ENFSI approached the EA for cooperation in establishing confidence and comparability in crime scene investigation work throughout Europe. Professional judgement is a core performance criterion that has to be applied in the investigation of crime scenes; for example, when deciding on the limits of the crime scene, the investigators have to use professional judgement based not only on the observations made at the scene but also on previous experiences. This type of decision making continues throughout the process.

The ENFSI/EA working group recognised that the importance of professional judgement in the crime scene process made it very appropriate to use ISO/IEC 17020, "General Criteria for the Operation of Various Types of Bodies Performing Inspection," as the base standard for crime scene investigations, rather than ISO/IEC 17025. ISO/IEC 17020 is a generic standard for inspections, and its clauses reflect best practice in setting up and following quality management systems. The main clause headings are shown in Table 5.3. To make the standard relevant and specific to crime scene investigation, the ENFSI/EA working group wrote a companion guidance document, "Guidance for the Implementation of ISO/IEC 17020 in the Field of Crime Scene Investigation" (EA-5/03). The brief description of content in Table 5.5 is based on the EA-5/03 guidance. Note that the content is *not* a comprehensive account of the requirements of each clause.

Table 5.5 Summary of Clauses of ISO/IEC 17020 and Main Elements of the EA-5/03 Guidance

Clause	Content
Scope	Summarises the forensic process at the crime scene ("assess, plan, do, review") and differentiates between screening testing at the scene and application of analytical techniques for analysis of exhibits.
Administrative requirements	Places the work of the crime scene investigation within the relevant laws, regulations, and rules of the jurisdiction. Requires unit to defines its scope of competence.
Independence, impartiality, and integrity	Requires the unit to put in place processes that ensure the integrity of its impartiality, irrespective of its administrative structure.
Quality system (described in a quality manual with supporting documentation such as standard operating procedures)	Must be available at all relevant locations and to all relevant staff; manuals may be in electronic form. Quality audits should include planned audits of crime scene procedures.
Personnel	Defines roles and responsibilities. Requirement for "relevant knowledge of the technology" refers to an understanding of the technology behind the crime (e.g., firearms) and the technology used to investigate the crime (e.g., fingerprints, DNA, bloodstain pattern analysis). Requirement for understanding the "significance of deviations" refers to crime scene investigation personnel recognising the significance of the unusual at a crime scene (e.g., staged burglary). Extensive guidance on training and induction programmes.
Facilities and equipment	Defines these terms and requires monitoring of environmental conditions where these can influence reliability. Provides guidance on calibration and reference materials. Sets out requirements for records.
Inspection methods and procedures	Defines and describes use of standard and non-standard methods. Describes assignment review requirement and review procedures. Provides health and safety requirements.
Handling of inspection samples (exhibits)	Describes documentation and recording requirements. Describes how to deal with unexpected findings. Provides a sequence of events and requirements for preservation of evidence.
Records	Documents processes to record and recover information in technical records and notes.
Investigative team reports	Contains all the results of examinations and observations, including visual evidence, as well as the findings and, where appropriate and admissible, conclusions arrived at from these results. Should be complete and should contain the information on which an interpretation might be made.
Subcontracting	Describes when and how outside resources can be used in the investigations.
Complaints and appeals	Describes how to deal with these, including responding to successful challenges to court decisions.
Cooperation	Encourages cooperation with similar organisations.

There is considerable overlap in the requirements of ISO/IEC 17020 and ISO/IEC 17025, and which one is appropriate to any crime scene unit will depend on its specific circumstances. The main difference between the two standards is the content that governs technical procedures involving calibration. ISO/IEC 17020 is in no way a lesser accreditation, and the EA-5/03 incorporates steps to ensure the technical reliability of any screening tests conducted during the examination of a crime scene.

5.7   Summary

It is fitting that the text in this chapter ends by citing ISO/IEC 17020, because the core of this standard is the exercising of professional judgement, and it is that activity that makes crime scene examination a core contributor to the scientific investigation of crime. "Scientific investigation of crime" is not a synonym for "forensic science" but is the application of the scientific method to investigations. That is embodied in the way in which the CSI approaches scene investigation, from the initial strategy formulation to the final report and testimony, by a continual cycle of formulation, testing, and modification of hypotheses to explain the scene. Scene investigation is indeed a scientific process, but wherever judgement is involved, the practitioner must beware of the introduction of conscious or unconscious bias. That is why the combination of the characteristics of a profession described above with the objectivity that comes from application of the 6Ws and the investigative star described in earlier chapters is so important to the crime scene examiner.

Forms of Evidence, Identification, and Recovery

II

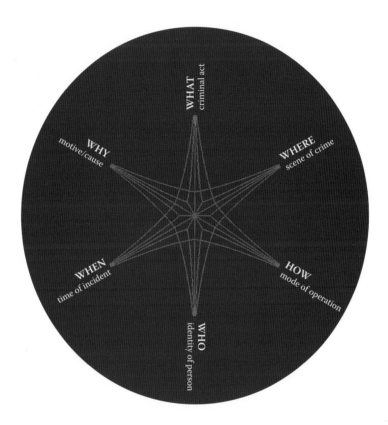

You know my methods, Watson. There was not one of them which I did not apply to the inquiry. And it ended by my discovering traces, but very different ones from those which I had expected.

—**A. Conan Doyle** (*The Memoirs of Sherlock Holmes*)

Establishing Personal Identity

6.1 Introduction

The concept of "identity" was discussed in Chapters 1 and 2 in the context of the investigative star and what are generally known as class and individualising characteristics. As we explored identity we saw that the answer is contextual and depends on the question posed in the hypothesis. We also have seen that the investigative hypothesis has to be refined as possible explanations are either eliminated or find increasing support and that new information will provide entry points to other arms of the star.

As an illustration, excavations in the centre of the English city of Norwich in 2004, during the construction of a shopping centre, uncovered a pile of bones in what had been a well. If these had been of non-human origin, then no further enquiry would have been required. However, reconstruction by an anthropologist showed that the bones were from 17 human skeletons, 11 of them being children between the ages of 2 and 15. The location and nature of the bones gave an age range for the remains of around the 12th to 13th century. The investigation began by attempting to identify what the bones were—human or animal—but changed direction once it was known that they were indeed human. The focus was now on determining how and why 6 adults and 11 children, all related, ended up at the bottom of a well and, if possible, who the individuals were and how they died. Among the hypotheses explored were that they were victims of plague (which was eliminated because there were no known outbreaks of plague at the time of death and even plague victims were buried with a degree of respect and formality) or were victims of some other disease (leprosy and tuberculosis were not uncommon but there were no tell-tale signs of damage to the bones). There were no signs of injuries from stabbing or bludgeoning, but the adult skeletons showed evidence of injuries that could have been caused by the bodies being thrown down the well. The skeletons of the children were at the top of the pile and bore no marks of trauma, perhaps because their fall was cushioned by the bodies underneath. DNA typing showed that the remains were from related people of Jewish descent, and historical records showed that there had been active persecution of Jewish people around Norwich at that time. The investigators concluded that this was an instance of brutal ethnic cleansing with a large family being thrown head-first down the well.

The case illustrates the broader aspects of establishing personal identity, but one of the more immediate purposes of physical evidence obtained from the crime scene is to establish the identity of the suspect or victim. This identification is possible through a variety of methods discussed in this chapter. Fingerprints are usually thought of first when considering methods of identifying individuals; however, techniques such as handwriting examination, forensic anthropology, and forensic odontology are also important and will be discussed. DNA typing is also widely used in establishing identity and will be covered in its own chapter (Chapter 8.)

The material presented in this chapter is intended to assist the crime scene investigator when questions of personal identity arise, and it covers a wide range of situations. Some, such as fingerprints, are quite likely to involve the investigator directly in the examination and interpretation of results. Others, such as handwriting, are presented as background, as investigators most likely will not be involved directly in such examinations and interpretation, but they do need to be aware that the evidence can contribute to the investigation and should know what to do (or not do) at the scene.

6.2   Fingerprints and Palm Prints

Some of the most valuable clues at the crime scene are fingerprints and palm prints (bare footprints are sometimes discovered and may also identify a person, provided there are known exemplars). Prints can be conclusive evidence. An expert's report will generally state one of three possible findings:

- The subject made the print.
- The subject could not have made the print.
- The print had insufficient detail to be evaluated.

Some examiners, though, include another finding, "The print had sufficient details to be evaluated," but do not draw a conclusion. The value of fingerprints is greatly enhanced by the possibility of identifying a criminal by searching a database of reference prints.

In this section, the term fingerprints includes all types of prints of friction ridge skin. Prints of the palms or soles of the foot are made under the same conditions as fingerprints and are preserved in the same manner. It is sometimes difficult to decide whether a print has been left by a finger, the palm, or the sole of a foot. For this reason, in ordinary speech, the term fingerprint has come to include prints of the palms or feet also.

6.2.1   How Does Fingerprint Evidence Occur?

Touching something with bare fingers will usually leave a print. The prerequisites for depositing fingerprints are the environmental temperature, the condition of the fingers, and their ability to secrete sweat or sebum, as well as the structure of the surface of the object involved. Very cold temperatures can often reduce the production of sweat or sebum from a person which can in turn reduce the person's ability to leave prints. High temperatures could have the opposite result, but high temperatures can result in a print drying out, thus making it impossible to enhance. The structure of the surface is also important, as a rough surface will make it less possible to leave prints and a smooth surface will make it more likely to leave prints.

When criminals work, they will often leave clues in the form of fingerprints unless they wear gloves or some other form of protection. Prints may be produced when criminals take hold of an object or support themselves with their hands. Prints may also be formed when fingers are contaminated with a foreign material, such as dirt, blood, or grease, or when the fingers are pressed against a plastic material and produce a negative impression of the pattern of the friction ridges.

6.2.2   Where to Look for Fingerprints

In burglary investigations, the perpetrator's point of entry should be the place at which to start a search for prints. It may be possible at that point to determine if the burglar worked with gloves or uncovered hands. If a door was broken open, prints (including shoe prints) may be located on the lock, the immediate surroundings, or other places on the door where the entry had been forced. With broken windows, particular attention should be given to searching for pieces of broken glass, which are useful for standards and may contain prints or blood. The common method used to break a window is to knock a small hole in a windowpane. A burglar can then break away pieces of glass with his fingers until he has succeeded in making an opening large enough to be able to reach the window latch. Often, fingerprints or glove prints are found on broken pieces of glass. Broken glass does not always lie just inside the window because burglars sometimes dispose of the broken glass shards to conceal the entry. Fingerprints may be left on the inside of the windowsill, the window frame, and jamb when the burglar climbs through the window and grips these parts of the window frame.

Searches for fingerprints also should be made in areas where the burglar is suspected to have eaten or had a drink. Prints on glass or china are generally of good quality. Criminals are very aware of the advances in crime scene examination and usually take care not to leave fingerprints; however, they sometimes make mistakes because of negligence or even due to intoxication. Gloves may be removed because they were getting in the way, and prints may be left on glasses or china or on bottles that were moved and examined by the thief.

Case 1

The perpetrator entered a convenience store in Kodiak, Alaska, where he robbed the clerk, hit her in the head with a gun, and forced her into a back room, where he tied her up with an electrical extension cord and attempted to rape her. The police developed a credible suspect, but the clerk was unable to identify him. Inked finger and palm prints were submitted, and identification was made from the latent prints developed on the plug of the extension cord (see Figure 6.1).

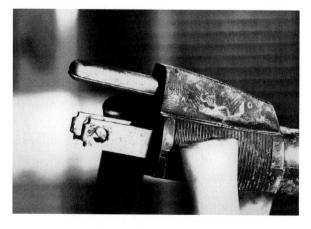

Figure 6.1 Finger and palm prints found on the electrical plug. (Photograph courtesy of Scientific Crime Detection Laboratory, Alaska Department of Public Safety, Anchorage.)

Burglars who wear gloves might remove them during the crime and leave fingerprints at the scene. Light switches, circuit breakers, and fuses should always be examined, as well as any light bulbs that were loosened or removed. If the criminal wore gloves, special care should be taken at places where the activity was of a type where gloves would have been a hindrance. For example, opening a case of drawers with difficult locks or searching in the drawers of a bureau may be difficult with gloves. Also, if the thief used the toilet, he might have removed his gloves. Prints should be searched for on the toilet tank lever, on the door lock, and on any paper that may have been used.

Burglars sometimes bring tools or other objects to the scene and leave them behind. Fingerprints may be detected on papers used to wrap tools, on flashlights (do not forget to examine the batteries), and on other items such as the inside of latex gloves. All smooth surfaces on which prints could have been left should be examined. Good prints are often found on glass; china; polished, painted, or other smooth surfaces; and smooth cardboard cartons or paper. In some cases, prints have been recovered on rough surfaces, starched collars, cuffs, and newspapers. When examining furniture, do not omit places the criminal may have touched when pulling out drawers or moving the furniture. Even if the thief worked with gloved hands, prints may have been left when a heavy piece of furniture was moved because the gloves may have slipped and a part of the wrist or palm left a print.

Fingerprint powder is the most common means used at a crime scene to visualise latent prints on most nonporous surfaces. The technique is easy to use and inexpensive but can be messy. Using a ductless fume hood is an effective way to reduce the amount of fingerprint powder in the workplace. This is illustrated in Figure 6.2.

A flashlight is a good tool for searching for latent prints. Fingerprints can be observed by holding the flashlight at low angles so the surface is observed under oblique lighting; however, flashlights may not work on all surfaces. If prints are expected in a particular place and they are not discovered, the area must be examined by special methods described below.

6.2.3   Different Types of Fingerprints

Fingerprints can be divided into three main groups: (1) plastic fingerprints, (2) prints of fingers contaminated with some foreign matter or "visible prints," and (3) latent fingerprints.

- *Plastic fingerprints* occur when a finger touches or presses against plastic material and creates a negative impression of its friction ridge pattern, as shown in Figure 6.3. These prints are found on such materials as fresh paint, substances that melt easily or soften when held in the hand (e.g., chocolate), adhesive tape, thick layers of dust, plastic explosives, putty that has not hardened, candle wax, sealing wax, fats, flour, soap, thick and sticky oily films, grease, pitch, tar, resin, and clay, to name a few.
- *Prints from fingers contaminated with foreign matter* are common. Dust prints occur when a finger is pressed in a thin layer of dust and some of the dust sticks on the friction ridges. When the finger is then placed on a clean surface, a fingerprint results. In some cases, a dust print may be fully identifiable and may be clear enough to search in a single fingerprint file. Prints can be left when fingers are contaminated with other substances such as pigments, ink, soot, flour, face powder, oils, safe insulation, or blood.

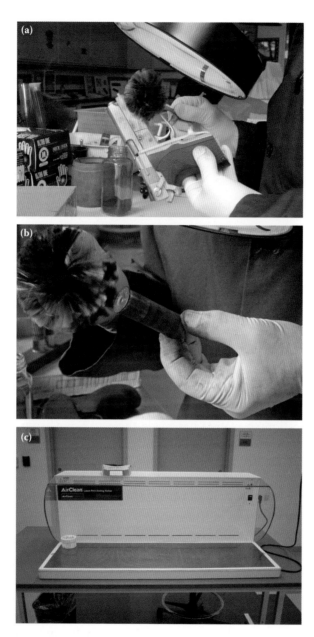

Figure 6.2 (a, b) Items that have been treated with powder to reveal latent prints. It is clear that the technique is somewhat messy. (c) A ductless hood, which draws air from below the examination platform (front, bottom of the illustration). (Photographs (a) and (b) courtesy of the Los Angeles County Sheriff's Department, Los Angeles, CA; photograph (c) courtesy of Parish Sheriff's Office laboratory, Harvey, LA.)

- *Latent fingerprints* result from small amounts of natural oils, sweat, and dirt deposited on a surface. Skin on the hands and soles of the feet have no oil glands. Grease found on fingers comes from other parts of the body that the hands have touched. Secretion from friction skin contains 98.5 to 99.5% water; the balance is organic and inorganic components. If the hands are cold, practically no liquid is secreted; when they become warm, secretion returns to normal. Latent prints are

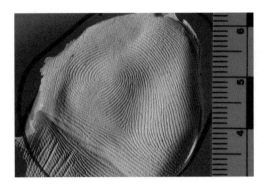

Figure 6.3 Negative impression left by a finger touching soft putty, an example of a plastic fingerprint.

most often found on objects with polished or smooth surfaces and on paper; however, under some conditions they may also be detected on rough surfaces, and even on smooth fabrics. Latent prints include those invisible to the unaided eye plus all others that are visible but only properly examined after development.

6.2.4   Fingerprint Developing Techniques

Significant advances in techniques for visualising fingerprints are occurring continually. Most of these involve chemical reagents that react with materials present in the components that make up the print or contaminants. Collaboration between forensic scientists and forensic identification specialists has made these techniques possible and continued effort is to be encouraged. Development of latent prints at the scene has benefited markedly from these advances and much can be done by appropriately trained and equipped personnel within crime scene units or in specialised sections within a crime scene unit. Many of the techniques used require specialised equipment and chemicals and are best conducted in laboratories. Ideally, forensic scientists and crime scene specialists will work together to develop and use these more complex chemical-based fingerprint visualisation techniques.

Many procedures are available to develop latent fingerprints. Those listed in the next sections are some of the standard procedures in use; however, new ones are developed regularly. *It is important to understand that practical experience with these procedures is needed to use them effectively.* Certain methods work better than others for different materials. The sequence of using them is also important because it is possible to use multiple procedures, one following the other, to search for prints. Some procedures have an adverse effect on other types of evidence; for example, certain solvents can cause inks to run on documents or render biological evidence unsuitable for DNA typing. Latent fingerprint examiners are cautioned that they should know which of these techniques might adversely interact with other classes of evidence before trying them on casework.

Latent print examiners should work closely with forensic scientists to develop procedures for using chemical developing methods with safeguards to avoid destruction of other types of physical evidence. Latent print examiners should consider forming regional user groups to help keep up with rapidly changing technology. Such groups are made up of local practitioners who meet quarterly and share technical experiences with other practitioners. These regional groups are especially helpful in small identification sections with only one or two examiners, who may be unable to attend technical conferences.

6.2.4.1 *Development with Powders*

Brushing fingerprint powder over a latent print makes it visible. The choice of powder depends partly on the kind of surface on which the print is found and partly on how it is to be preserved. If the latent print is of high quality, the choice of powder for development is not especially important. Several types of fingerprint powders are commercially available: black, white, coloured, aluminium, copper, fluorescent, and magnetic. The type used is determined by the colour of the background and the nature of the surface. Material Safety Data Sheets (MSDSs) for fingerprint powders are available from suppliers and online. Common sense suggests that long-term exposure to fine particulate matter may cause respiratory problems over time. Persons who routinely use fingerprint powders can wear dust masks or use specially designed fingerprint hoods to minimise the amount of powder breathed.

Fibreglass, animal hair, and synthetic or natural fibre brushes may be used to apply the powders. If the brush is damp or oily, it is useless. The brush is first lightly dipped in the powder and then tapped with the finger so that only a small amount of the powder is left on the brush. The object is then lightly brushed in curved strokes. Powder particles will adhere to places where there is grease or dirt. Any fingerprints present on the object will show up more or less clearly. Procedures should be in place to avoid the brushes being a source of contamination of items in between, especially regarding DNA.

Powder should not be sprinkled over or tapped onto the object while brushing. Prints from sweaty or dirty fingers or produced by a firm grip may cause the friction ridges to spread out, filling up the spaces between the ridges. Too much powder can destroy these prints. If too much powder is used, it can be removed by pressing a fingerprint lifter against the print. The lifter will remove the excess and the spaces between the ridges may be nearly free of powder. If necessary, the latent print can be reprocessed to get usable results. Some fingerprint examiners use black fingerprint powder as a universal developer on smooth nonporous surfaces. On dark surfaces, such as furniture and firearms, aluminium or copper powders give good results. These powders are useful if the print is to be photographed before being lifted. Remember that aluminium-powdered lifts appear reversed from prints developed with black powder.

Perspiration and grease from fingerprints absorb into porous surfaces such as paper and cardboard and do not usually give results with powdering methods. On porous items, another method should be used, such as iodine, ninhydrin, or silver nitrate treatment (Figure 6.4). Another aid to fingerprint development is the Magna Brush, which uses

Figure 6.4 Combining visualisation techniques enhances the final image quality. (Photographs courtesy of Forensic Science Department, Zurich Cantonal Police, Zurich, Switzerland.)

Figure 6.5 Magnetic fingerprint powders work well on some items. Only the magnetic powder comes in contact with the surface. (Photograph courtesy of the Los Angeles County Sheriff's Department, Los Angeles, CA.)

magnetic powders and a magnetic applicator. Streamers of magnetised powder are brought in contact with the suspected surface, as can be seen in Figure 6.5. Powder adheres to the latent print, while the magnet removes the excess. This method has the advantage of not leaving excess powder on the object and the surrounding area. Because of the nature of the process, it can be used effectively only on nonmagnetic surfaces.

Fluorescent powders are yet another type that may be used in some special cases. Available in powder and aerosol forms, they are technically not fingerprint powders because they are used prior to the prints being deposited or to enhance developed prints, as shown in Figure 6.6. They are used to dust paper currency and documents and are sprayed in areas where recurring thefts take place. After the suspect has handled the money or touched the dusted area, the area is examined with ultraviolet light. The latent fingerprint is easily visualised by ultraviolet light and may be photographed.

6.2.4.2 *Chemical Reagents*

- *Amido Black*—This stain turns proteins present in blood blue–black. It does not react with any of the normal components of fingerprints and should be used in conjunction with other developing techniques. Other more sensitive stains such as Coomassie blue, a general protein stain used in forensic biology, may be considered. Fingerprint specialists should always consult forensic biologists before using any protein stains on bloody fingerprints because some stains may cause difficulties in DNA testing.
- *DFO (1,8-diazafluoren-9-one)*—DFO is a ninhydrin-like analogue that reacts with proteins to give a highly fluorescent, red-coloured product that is more sensitive than ninhydrin. Although some prints developed using DFO will be visible to the naked eye, illumination with high-intensity light improves the sensitivity; however, interference may become a problem from certain coloured inks and papers that fluoresce. Longer wavelength light sources, such as mercury vapour lamps at 546 nm, lessen the interference. Ninhydrin may be used in conjunction with DFO; however, DFO must be used first.

- *Gentian violet*—This dye, also known as crystal violet or methyl violet, stains the fatty components of latent prints purple and is especially effective when used on the sticky side of adhesive tape. The material is toxic, and appropriate laboratory precautions must be taken. Using a laser increases the sensitivity of the procedure. A yellow–orange light source yields the best results (e.g., a copper vapour laser at the 578-nm line). An alternative dye, basic fuchsin, yields good results with green excitation and has an absorption maximum at about 500 nm.

- *Iodine*—Iodine is one of the oldest methods of visualising latent prints on porous and nonporous substrates. The technique is simple to use; however, iodine vapours are toxic and corrosive, and the reaction is not permanent. Methods have been introduced for fixing prints developed by iodine fuming (e.g., 7,8-benzoflavone), which also increases sensitivity.

- *Ninhydrin solution*—Ninhydrin is another technique for use with porous surfaces (e.g., paper, cardboard, wallboard, raw wood). Ninhydrin reacts with amino acids to form a purple-coloured compound called *Ruhemann's purple*. The reaction is speeded up by means of humidity and elevated temperatures (see Figure 6.7). Treating with zinc chloride solution and viewing with a laser improve the sensitivity of the techniques. Background fluorescence may be overcome by using a cadmium nitrate solution cooled to liquid nitrogen temperatures and viewed with a laser. Modifications to the chemical structure of ninhydrin have been synthesised and show usefulness under certain conditions. The importance of these analogues is that they fluoresce at different wavelengths and provide a way to overcome background interference from certain substrates.

- *Physical developer (PD)*—Also called *stabilised physical developer* (SPD), PD is a silver-based solution used as a substitute for the conventional latent print silver nitrate procedure. PD is useful in detecting latent prints on porous surfaces that are wet or have been wet (e.g., paper, cardboard, raw wood). The technique may be used following ninhydrin. PD reacts with components of sweat and appears in shades from grey to almost black. PD-developed prints are preserved by photography.

- *Silver nitrate*—Silver nitrate solution reacts with chlorides in prints, but with the advent of PD it is not in widespread use today. It may have some application on raw wood; however, the background staining of the substrate may cause problems in photography.

- *Small particle reagent (SPR)*—This is a wet process for developing latent prints on wet surfaces. The reagent is a suspension of molybdenum disulphide particles prepared in a detergent solution. Molybdenum adheres to lipids found in prints as a grey deposit. The process works well on nonporous surfaces (e.g., plastic bags, wax paper, glass, painted surfaces) and may be used effectively on water-soaked firearms. Visible prints may be lifted and photographed.

- *Sudan black*—This process is used on nonporous articles (e.g., glass, plastics, metal). Usually less sensitive than SPR, Sudan black may be the method of choice if the substrate is oily or greasy. Sudan black reacts with the lipid components of prints and stains them blue–black. It is messy to use and not effective on dark-coloured objects.

- *Super glue or cyanoacrylate fuming*—Super glue is used on nonporous surfaces to produce visible prints that are white. The visible prints may be dusted with powder, photographed, and lifted, or washed with laser-sensitive dyes such as Rhodamine

Figure 6.6 Super glue fuming in a humidity chamber, followed by high-intensity dye staining and examination of the evidence under high-intensity light, followed by computer-enhanced examination of the prints. Although these techniques may be time consuming, they can lead to outstanding results. (Photograph courtesy of the Los Angeles County Sheriff's Department, Los Angeles, CA.)

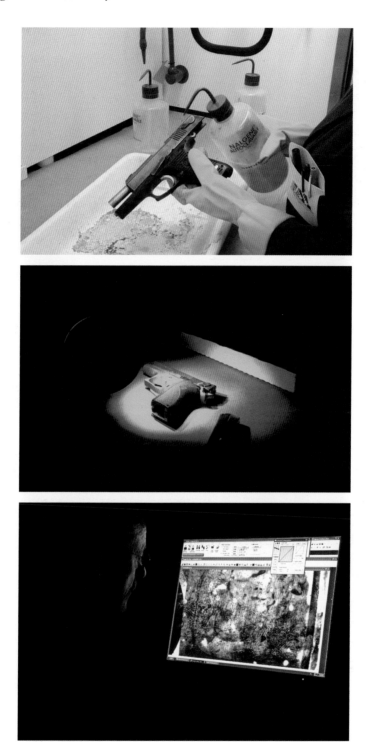

Figure 6.6 (cont.) Super glue fuming in a humidity chamber, followed by high-intensity dye staining and examination of the evidence under high-intensity light, followed by computer-enhanced examination of the prints. Although these techniques may be time consuming, they can lead to outstanding results. (Photograph courtesy of the Los Angeles County Sheriff's Department, Los Angeles, CA.)

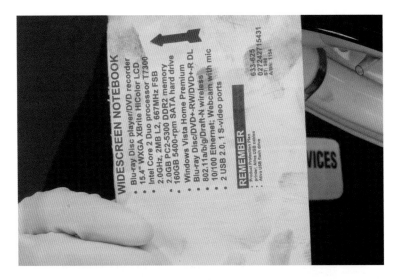

Figure 6.7 The characteristic Ruhemann's purple caused by the reaction of ninhydrin on proteins left on paper products. (Photograph courtesy of the Los Angeles County Sheriff's Department, Los Angeles, CA.)

Figure 6.8 A super glue fuming cabinet suitable for examination of large items. (Photograph courtesy of Jefferson Parish Sheriff's Office laboratory, Harvey, LA.)

Figure 6.9 Vacuum metal deposition (VMD) places a thin film of gold followed by a film of zinc on latent prints left on smooth surfaces such as plastic bags. VMD is a very sensitive technique for fingerprint development on nonporous and semiporous surfaces. (Photograph courtesy of the Los Angeles County Sheriff's Department, Los Angeles, CA.)

6G and others, and viewed with lasers or alternative light sources (see Figures 6.6 and 6.8). Super glue is one of the easier procedures to use; however, in some instances, other latent print visualisation techniques may yield superior results.

- *Vacuum metal deposition (VMD)*—Vacuum metal deposition is an effective technique for most smooth, nonporous surfaces (e.g., plastic bags, plastic packaging material). The major drawback to VMD is that the equipment is expensive and the sample chamber of the vacuum coater is not very large. The procedure evaporates gold or zinc in a vacuum chamber, and a very thin film of the metal is deposited onto the latent print, making it visible (see Figure 6.9).

6.2.4.3 Other Techniques

6.2.4.3.1 Fluorescence Examination   Using lasers, alternative light sources, or ultraviolet lamps on untreated surfaces may yield prints. Various naturally occurring chemicals and contaminants present in latent prints fluoresce without treatment with laser-sensitive dyes. Although the chance of finding autofluorescent latent prints is limited, the ease of the procedure suggests its use.

6.2.4.3.2 Lasers and Alternative Light Sources   The word *laser* is an acronym for "light amplification by stimulated emission of radiation." Lasers and other alternative light sources have been found to be quite effective in locating and visualising latent prints, as well as other types of physical evidence such as fibres and certain types of biological evidence at the crime scene and in the laboratory. No single wavelength of light will work best in all forensic applications, and several types of alternative light sources are in current use. Several factors need to be considered in choosing the most suitable type of high-intensity light, including cost, colour of light or wavelengths available, light intensity or power output, portability, voltage requirements, safety, available service on an emergency basis, and the ability to use the unit in other forensic applications. Technology has moved light sources along greatly, and a wide variety of units is available; some are very portable and look like handheld flashlights.

Figure 6.10(a) shows a workstation that combines an alternative light source, digital camera, and computer hardware and software to achieve good results using chemical processing techniques with latent fingerprints. Figure 6.10(b) shows the work station of the Los Angeles County Sheriff's Department Cogent Automated Palm and Fingerprint Identification System (CAPFIS), but many automated fingerprint identification systems are available globally. Naturally, the more sophisticated the unit, the more cost becomes a factor. Some units used in laboratory settings may require special setups and workspace remodelling, such as darkened work areas to take photographs, laboratory sinks and fume hoods to handle light-sensitive dyes, specific power requirements, plumbed-in water to cool the unit or additional units to recirculate coolant to the laser, liquid nitrogen for use in certain laser procedures—the list can be formidable and must be considered when budgeting for certain units. Other costs include the purchase and maintenance of component parts that must be replaced from time to time.

Safety is a concern with high-intensity light sources. The intensity of the light can cause eye fatigue and eye damage. Persons working with these tools should be required to wear appropriate eye protection to minimise any damage.

6.2.4.3.3 Image Processing   New developments in computer technology are being used to enhance latent prints that heretofore were of insufficient quality to be used. Image processing costs have lowered to such a degree that most forensic laboratories can afford the hardware and software. Latent prints are examined by means of a high-resolution digital camera whose output is fed into a computer. Unlike the human eye, the computer is capable of distinguishing among the hundreds of shades of grey that show up as varying degrees of density captured in the image. The computer in turn can process the digital image in several ways. The image can be shown in reverse (equivalent to a photographic reversal or negative) or in colour. This is particularly advantageous if the print is on a textured surface that makes it difficult to examine because of the background pattern interfering with the ridge detail of the print. Various light sources—visible, infrared, ultraviolet, high-intensity, laser, filtered, and unfiltered—give considerable range to latent print identification. Digitising images along with readily available computer software gives excellent results.

6.2.5 Automated Fingerprint Identification Systems

The Automated Fingerprint Identification System (AFIS) is one of the greatest advances in fingerprint identification technology in recent years. The AFIS allows comparison of a latent fingerprint discovered at a crime scene with those in a criminal fingerprint database. The amount of human effort to conduct a manual search for a latent print against several million inked prints is astronomical and prior to AFIS was simply out of the question.

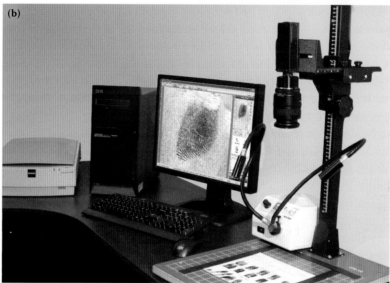

Figures 6.10 (a) Workstation combining an alternative light source, digital camera, and computer hardware and software to achieve good results with chemical processing techniques for latent fingerprints. (Photograph courtesy of Los Angeles County Sheriff's Department, Los Angeles, CA.) (b) Los Angeles County Sheriff's Department Cogent Automated Palm and Fingerprint Identification System (CAPFIS). (Photographs courtesy of 3M Cogent, Pasadena, CA.)

Cold searches, or searching a database of several million prints for a single latent found at a crime scene, are a daily occurrence. Even more staggering, the search of prints on file in an AFIS database takes only about 10 minutes. AFIS has revolutionised the way police departments search latent prints for matches. At one time, it was not uncommon for some crime scene investigators to dust low-property-value crime scenes to placate crime victims who wanted the police to do something. The effort put into dusting a scene seemed to give victims a feeling that the police were doing something. In only a small percentage of cases would latent prints be matched to those of a criminal. Some police administrators even questioned the value of going through the effort of trying to locate fingerprints in low-property-value, residential burglaries and automobile burglaries. AFIS, however, has completely changed that way of thinking. Simply stated, the more high-quality latent prints collected at crime scenes and searched against AFIS, the greater the chance of identifying criminals.

The quality of the inked fingerprint cards used to create the AFIS database is critical. Poorly taken fingerprint cards uploaded into the AFIS database eliminate the possibility of making a correct identification when conducting a latent print search. Because a surprisingly high number of crimes may be associated to one perpetrator, the quality of the inked fingerprints and the AFIS data entry process becomes very important.

An alternative to taking inked prints is an electronic technique known as Live Scan. Live Scan technology produces high-quality print cards without the need to take inked prints. Each finger is inserted into a reader and its fingerprint is captured. At the end of the process, a standard print card is produced. The next step of the process is to input the print card into the AFIS database. A shortcoming of the system is that AFIS systems are proprietary, and Live Scan systems cannot transfer electronic data directly into AFIS.

Several AFIS technologies can be found throughout the world, most of which provide effective database storage and interrogation. Integrating AFIS systems over differing jurisdictions and incorporating other personal identification factors are more challenging. The Australian CrimTrac system is one of the more successful examples, as it integrates DNA and friction ridge data over all six states and the two administrative territories in the country. CrimTrac is populated with data from more than 100 Live Scan units and includes the world's largest palm print library.

Data can be shared in several ways, even when there are operational differences among AFIS systems. INTERPOL maintains an AFIS database that member countries can upload to. Records are saved and exchanged in the format set by the National Institute of Standards and Technology (NIST) and are available for interrogation at all times. Similarly, the European Union has an agreement whereby each member country will search its national database for matches to prints submitted by any other member country. The Eurodac fingerprint database, which collects the fingerprints of asylum seekers and some illegal entrants, is a single database used by the European Union to monitor and prevent illegal entry to EU countries.

6.2.6   Preservation of Fingerprints

6.2.6.1   *Photography*

Fingerprints found at the scene of a crime should be preserved by photography when possible. This procedure has many advantages. Photography leaves the objects intact so that further photos can be taken if the first are unusable. It also makes it easier to show the evidence in court because the object on which the latents were discovered can be seen in the picture. The photography of fingerprints and other evidence differs from ordinary picture taking. The photographer must be skilled in photographic techniques and understand how to obtain a reproduction of a fingerprint that is as accurate and true to the original as possible. Additionally, knowledge of the principles of fingerprint comparison is helpful to appreciate what the person making the print identification requires. The finished photograph should be white on a black background or black on a white background. It should be 1:1, the actual size, and a ruler should be included in the photograph to allow for the printing to be 1:1. The person taking the photograph should advise the person making the fingerprint comparison whether the print is a direct or mirror image or a positive or negative image. If the print is visible without fingerprint powder development, it should be photographed as found, in view of the possibility that any measures taken for development might destroy it. This can generally be done by a suitable arrangement of lighting. An attempt can then be made to make the print clearer—for example, by treatment with powders, after which more photographs are taken. Fingerprints should be photographed with a scale in the picture.

6.2.6.2 Preservation of Plastic Fingerprints

When a fingerprint has been left in material that has hardened or is able to withstand transport and when it is on a small, easily transportable object, it may be sent directly to the crime laboratory. If removing the plastic print poses some special problem, it should be photographed using oblique light to bring out as much detail as possible. An appropriate casting material may then preserve the fingerprint impression.

Frequently, curved surfaces with latent fingerprints present, such as doorknobs, are difficult to photograph or do not lend themselves to the use of cellophane lifting tape. For such surfaces, elastic or rubber material works well. Rubber lifters are commercially available items made of a thin, rubbery material coated with an adhesive. A transparent celluloid material removed prior to use and replaced after use protects the adhesive. The colour of the lifter is either black or white for use with different fingerprint powders.

To use this technique, the latent fingerprint is first dusted with an appropriately coloured fingerprint powder. The protective covering of the lifter is pulled away, and the sticky surface is pressed against the print and then pulled away. Part of the powder sticks to the lifter and gives the mirror image of the print. After the print is collected, the protective covering is carefully replaced on the lifter.

The lifter comes in different sizes and can be cut for a specific use. It is useful for picking up footprints in the dust as well as fingerprints. The lifting method is simple and easy to master. It requires no knowledge of photography and no photographic equipment. Its use, however, requires greater accuracy in specifying the position of the print. Carelessness in this respect can have disastrous results.

6.2.6.3 Preservation with Fingerprint-Lifting Tape

One way to collect latent fingerprint evidence is to use special transparent cellophane tape. The material is supplied in rolls and is usually 0.5 to 1 cm wide. After the surface is dusted with fingerprint powder, the tape is placed over the print. Care must be taken to prevent any air pockets. The tape is smoothed down over the print with the aid of a finger and then drawn off. Particles of fingerprint powder adhere to the sticky surface of the tape and thereby transfer the fingerprint pattern. The tape is finally placed on a card whose colour contrasts with the colour of the powder used. If insufficient ridge detail is present for any useful comparison, the epithelial cells on the tape can be used for DNA typing. Alternatively, the print may be lifted with a gel lifter.

6.2.7   How Long Does a Fingerprint Remain on an Object?

Plastic prints can remain for any length of time provided that the objects on which they are left or the substances in which they are formed are stable. In investigations, it sometimes happens that police officers find fingerprints that give the impression of having been made in dust, but upon closer examination these are found to be dust-filled plastic prints in oil paint made years earlier. Prints that have resulted from contamination of the fingers with soot, flour, face powder, or safe filings are soon destroyed. Prints of fingers contaminated with blood, pigments, ink, and oil are more resistant and can be kept for a long time under favourable conditions. Latent prints on glass, china, and other smooth objects can remain for years if they are in a well-protected location. On objects in the open air, a print can be developed several months after it is made. Fingerprints on paper are very stable and will last for years, provided that the paper does not become wet and deteriorate.

6.2.8   The Effect of Temperature Conditions on the Possibility of Developing Fingerprints

When objects that may contain fingerprints are found outdoors in ice or snow, they must be thawed slowly and placed so that the thawed water does not run over and destroy the prints. A suitable method of treatment is to scrape away as much snow and ice as possible, with the greatest care, before the object is brought to a warm place. Only when the object is dry should the print be developed. When plastic fingerprints are present in oil or grease, the thawing must be allowed to proceed slowly and under close scrutiny because the print may easily be destroyed by heat. Such prints should be photographed when they appear. Damp objects should be dried indoors at ordinary room temperature. As a general rule, never examine cold objects, especially metal, until they have been kept for at least some hours at room temperature. In indoor investigations in a cold house, the rooms should first be heated. The heating should be done slowly so that water from thawing does not run off frosted objects or places.

6.2.9   Examination of Developed Fingerprints

The officer who investigates the crime scene should only search for, develop, and preserve the fingerprints. Unless specially qualified by training and experience in the identification of fingerprints, the officer cannot be expected to carry out the continued examination of the developed prints. A detailed account of fingerprint identification is not included here, partly because it lies outside the scope of crime scene investigation and partly because it is a vast and specialised subject. Several comprehensive works on this subject are available, however.

The officer examining the scene should preserve all developed fingerprints. Even small, fragmentary prints that might seem insignificant to a non-specialist may turn out to be very valuable when examined by an expert. Large fingerprints are not necessarily more valuable than small ones. It happens frequently that the larger print is usable only for comparison with a suspect's fingerprints; it is useless for searching in a single fingerprint file. The smaller print, however, may be usable for both purposes.

6.2.10   Related Marks

The crime scene investigator should be aware of other marks related to fingerprints that may be found at the scene. These are marks from skin surfaces other than fingers and marks from gloves or other items used to cover the hands and prevent the deposition of fingerprints.

6.2.10.1   Palm Prints

Patterns of friction skin are on the inside of the hand just as they are on the fingers and they are of equal value as evidence. When part of a palm print is found, the area involved can often be deduced from the position of the print or from other parts of the hand and possibly fingers having left marks in the form of smears or portions of print. If the position of the hand represented by the fragment can be estimated, a simple sketch of the inside of a hand greatly facilitates the expert's work.

6.2.10.2   Prints from the Sole of the Foot

Friction ridges on the soles of the feet have the same evidentiary value as fingerprints and are developed and preserved in the same way as other prints. Cases sometimes occur in which burglars lacking gloves for their hands have taken off their socks and put them on their hands to avoid leaving fingerprints. The thought of leaving footprints never entered their minds!

6.2.10.3   Ear, Lip, and Other Prints

Occasionally, ear and lip prints are found at a crime scene. A suspect might have put his ear to a door or wall to listen to what was going on on the other side. Lip prints have also been found in lipstick on letters or envelopes placed by female suspects. Another method used by criminals is to hold an object between the index and middle fingers like a scissors to prevent leaving fingerprints. The sides of the fingers, lips, and ears, however, all have markings that can be used for useful comparisons, but the results need to be evaluated with care because these have not been subjected to the same validation as fingerprints.

Caution: The reliability of these marks has not been demonstrated and, depending on the jurisdiction, they may not be admissible.

6.2.10.4   Prints from Gloves

The general knowledge of the value of fingerprint evidence has resulted in criminals using gloves as the most usual protective measure. In many cases, when an investigator is looking for fingerprints, glove smears are found and, all too often, little attention is paid to them. The search is concentrated at places where it may be expected that the individual would have preferred to work with bare hands and used a good deal of force so that his gloves would slip and the wrist, or a part of the palm near the wrist, would be exposed, leaving an imprint. Prints of gloves, however, may be just as valuable as fingerprints so it is advisable always to examine and preserve them for closer investigation as long as they are not typical smears formed by the glove-covered hand slipping against a surface (see Figure 6.11). The leather of a glove shows a surface pattern that is often of a very characteristic appearance. It may show furrows in a more or less definite pattern or may be perforated in a fairly regular manner. It is much the same with fabric gloves. The surface pattern varies according to the method of manufacture and the yarn or material used. It is the wrinkled or textured surface pattern of leather gloves that can make identification possible.

 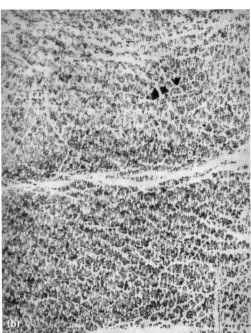

Figures 6.11 Animal hide is friction ridged and smooth like human skin. It is individual in its minute characteristics and can be conclusively identified. The latent glove print (a) was compared with test print (b) on the basis of the size, shape, orientation, and interrelationship of plateau areas delineated by tension lines in the leather. Three areas have been darkened to serve as a starting point in the comparison. (Photographs courtesy of Contra Costa County Sheriff's Department, Criminalistics Laboratory, Martinez, CA.)

In contrast, the surface pattern of fabric gloves is regular for each type so, in general, identification cannot be based merely on this. Characteristic and, from the point of view of identification, very valuable formations in the seams may be present, especially at the tips of the fingers. After they have been worn for some time, leather or fabric gloves become shaped to the hands, and typical wrinkle formations often are produced in the leather of the fingers, at the seams, or at places where the gloves do not fit the fingers properly. These wrinkle formations and injuries in the form of tears or holes or, in the case of leather gloves, cracks in the surface of the skin generally show in the print and are most valuable. In rare cases, it is even possible to find fragments of a fingerprint within a glove print. This can occur when the gloves have such large holes that some part of a finger is exposed and leaves a print at the same time as that of the glove.

If prints of gloves and friction ridges appear together, it may be difficult to distinguish the difference without closer examination. At first glance, the print gives the impression of being blurred or composed of two glove prints within each other. On closer examination, however, its regular lines, which lack the detailed pattern of the friction ridges, distinguish the glove print. Glove prints are always formed best on smooth surfaces. Their development requires great care because the prints are not as strong as fingerprints and therefore are easily destroyed if too much powder is used. To ensure not destroying any such prints that may be present at the scene of the crime, the area should not be painted vaguely. A systematic search may be made with the aid of a lamp and then cautious brushing. On the other hand, there is the prospect of finding glove prints at conspicuous and easily accessible places because, in most cases, the criminals abandon all caution and believe that they are fully protected by their gloves and so use their hands freely.

In developing prints, white or black powder may be used. A fingerprint lifter can lift the developed print, but it is better to take possession of the object on which the print is found so that it can be compared directly with prints from the gloves of a suspect. Leather or fabric gloves can produce a print. With the former, the leather contains some fat, while both leather and fabric gloves become contaminated with dirt, skin grease, and the like after being in use for some time. In addition, the warm and moist secretion from the skin of the hands plays an important part, at least with fabric gloves.

Comparison prints from the gloves of a suspect are best made on glass, which is generally most convenient even when the original prints are on furniture. In certain cases, however, it may be necessary to form a print on the same kind of material as that at the scene of the crime. Where possible, such material should be packaged separately when a print and gloves from a suspect are sent for examination. Comparison prints should be made in a manner similar to that used for the original ones. For example, if it is possible to decide how the hand of the suspect gripped the object, this information should be communicated to the expert so the same grip can be applied for the comparison print. Consideration must also be given to the degree of pressure that may have been used in forming the original print, and this should be noted. It is important that neither too much nor too little pressure is used when making the comparison prints because the appearance is greatly affected by pressure. It is often difficult to make clear prints with a glove, but breathing slightly on the finger of the glove may assist the operation. In certain instances, it may be treated with powder, fat, or the like; however, this technique risks destroying any characteristic details.

6.2.10.5 *Prints from Other Coverings*

Instead of gloves, other items such as socks, towels, and handkerchiefs are sometimes used as protection for the hands. It has also happened that individuals have protected the insides of their hands with adhesive tape to prevent the formation of fingerprints. In most cases, when using the above-mentioned objects, prints are left only if the material is thin, dirty, or somewhat damp. If, however, it is thick, dry, or relatively clean, it leaves no prints. Prints of such hand coverings rarely have any value from the point of view of identification. Identification is possible only in cases in which the material used has a characteristic surface pattern and shows typical injuries, unusual seams, or characteristic crease formations that are reproduced in the print. In such a case, the investigation is tedious because the extent of the edges of the protective medium is not definitely fixed as it would be in the case of a glove; therefore, it must be searched for before a direct comparison can be undertaken. Although the possibility of identification of hand coverings in such cases is not great, the print should still be given some attention because the method of operation may be typical for a particular individual or gang who has perhaps carried out other crimes in the same or another area.

6.2.11 Packing Objects on Which Prints Are Found

The crime scene investigator must decide the best way to transport objects that are to be examined for fingerprints. Wrapping such items directly in paper, cloth, or plastic bags should be avoided because prints may be destroyed. If possible, the object should be wedged firmly in a strong box so the packing does not touch the surface. Because a rigid suspension can cause breakage or other damage to an object in transit, the box must be wrapped in a sufficient quantity of soft material such as cotton, corrugated paper, crumpled newspaper, etc. If nails are used to fix the object in the box or for the lid, they should not be hammered completely in; the heads should be left free so they can be pulled out without using much force.

6.2.12   Taking Fingerprints for Elimination

As a rule, persons who have legitimate access to the premises leave the majority of the fingerprints found and developed at the crime scene; thus, it is important to eliminate these fingerprints so the continuing examination may concentrate on the remaining prints, presumably those of the perpetrator. The investigating officer should, therefore, always take elimination prints of all persons on the premises. These should be submitted to the fingerprint examiner together with the crime scene prints. Because the identification of legitimate fingerprints is as critical as identification of the criminal's prints, the elimination prints should be as clear as a criminal's prints recorded for filing purposes. Elimination prints should therefore be taken by printer's ink or by specially prepared ink pads. It is not required, however, that they be recorded on standard fingerprint forms as long as they are clearly marked as being for elimination purposes. A large proportion of latent prints developed at a crime scene are palm prints; therefore, elimination palm prints should also be taken. Inked palm prints require special care to ensure that they are useful for comparison purposes. The palm should be inked with a roller to ensure that all parts of the palm are inked. The prints should be made on a sheet of white paper. Place the inked palm flat on the paper and press on the centre of the top of the hand.

6.2.13   Latent Fingerprints on Human Skin

Several techniques have been reported for developing latent prints on human skin. These show some value, but success has been limited. One technique used in the United States is the Kromekote® lift technique. The equipment required includes a fibreglass filament brush, fingerprint powder, and Kromekote cards, which are approximately 14 by 18 cm, high-gloss, "80-lb" paper similar in appearance to photographic paper. Kromekote is generally available from local paper suppliers or online. The Kromekote card is used to lift the print from the skin surface by placing the card over the skin in the suspected area and applying pressure for about 3 seconds. The card is carefully removed and then dusted with black fingerprint powder to develop the print transferred onto the card. The fingerprint obtained is the mirror image of a normal print and can be reversed photographically (see Figure 6.12). In Europe, the most common approach is to use black magnetic powder, but in the United States, success is somewhat limited.

After the Kromekote technique is used, fingerprint powder can be applied directly to the skin to develop prints. The literature reports that the Magna Brush gives results superior to a fibreglass filament brush. If a print is developed by this method, it must be photographed and then may be lifted using cellophane lifting tape. Fingerprints on skin surfaces appear to last about 1.5 hours on living victims. Deceased victims should be examined for latent prints on the skin as soon as possible. The technique is still somewhat experimental, but the method's simplicity and ease of use will result in greater use on the part of experienced investigators.

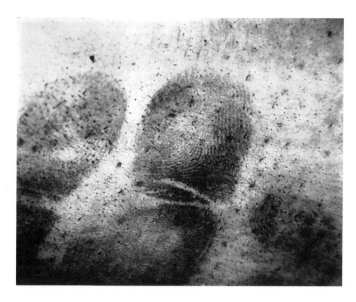

Figure 6.12 Prints developed from a body by dusting the surface using the Magna Brush and photography. (Photograph courtesy of Office of Medical Examiner, Metropolitan Dade County, Miami, FL.)

6.3 Handwriting Examination

Handwriting is a somewhat different aspect of personal identity. It is not part of the body but is very much a part of the make-up of the individual and is imparted onto physical objects by that person. Like fingerprints, it offers the investigator the ability to establish the identity of an individual with some degree of relative certainty.

6.3.1 Handwriting

Handwriting characteristics are of two types: *style* and *personal*. Style characteristics are the general type to which cursive writing belongs. This general type is learned in school and used by almost everyone. Personal characteristics are changes made in the general style characteristics both intentionally and unconsciously by the writer. Personal characteristics are the ones used to establish the identity of the writer. Handwriting examination is mostly used to determine if a signature or document is a forgery or whether two writings were made by the same person. The document examiner makes a careful examination of the questioned writing and known exemplar writings. Factors such as the relative size of letters, their slope and spacing, the way in which they are formed, and other personal characteristics are used to make a determination.

Written documents occur widely, even in today's electronic society. Daily business transactions include the use of cheques, credit card receipts, money orders, purchase receipts, sticky notes, and so forth. Writings may occur on paper as letters and notes, but they also may be found on desks, table tops, walls, floors, doors, and even on dead bodies. Wherever they occur, they should not be overlooked. Once a document is discovered, it must be properly handled and preserved. Failure to do so may result in its inadmissibility as evidence. Indeed, treatment of the document itself can be a significant part of the process, as seen in Figure 6.13, which shows the reconstruction of a shredded document before its subsequent examination.

Excessive handling may damage the document and smudge or obscure important writing characteristics, which may preclude any possibility of identification and eliminate latent fingerprints. The document should be preserved in the same condition in which it is found. Generally, this is best accomplished by placing it into a clear plastic envelope or

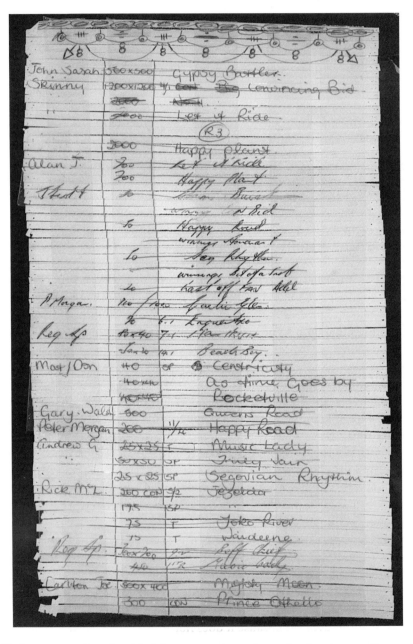

Figure 6.13 Reconstructing shredded documents in an investigation is very time consuming, but it was an integral part of the prosecution's evidence in this case. (Photograph courtesy of State Forensic Science Laboratory, Melbourne, Australia.)

sheet protector that keeps the document clean, preserves fingerprints, and prevents damage or destruction of minute identifying details. If the document is wet or soaked with blood, it should first be allowed to air-dry at room temperature and be placed in a cardboard box for delivery to the laboratory. Documents should be handled with forceps so as not to leave prints or DNA that may confuse subsequent tests.

Documents should not be altered in any way and should not be folded or creased. If the document is damaged or torn, no attempt should be made to repair it. The investigator should not write on the document to identify it. Documents should not be stapled together or to reports. If the original document is stapled, the staple should be removed slowly and carefully so as not to tear the paper. A staple remover should not be used. Do not use a paper punch on a document. Documents should not be left under paper on which the investigator may be writing because indentations may damage the identifying characteristics on the questioned writing. The side of a lead pencil should not be rubbed across the document in order to observe indented writing. Stickers or gummed labels should not be affixed to the document.

The document bearing the writing can be processed for fingerprints and DNA; it should be handled as little as possible and never by the suspect during the course of the investigation. Non-destructive testing should always take precedence over destructive testing, whether the purpose is examination of the paper or ink, the development of fingerprints, or removing surface sweat residues for DNA analysis. The first step should always be to make an accurate record of the document by photographing it with a document scale present and making a photocopy. The physical examination of the document (e.g., in the case of indented writings) should then be completed. Chemical testing is the last procedure to be conducted. After the chemical processing is completed, the paper should not come into contact with other papers because the stain can transfer. Paper should not be handled because additional fingerprints and smudges can easily be deposited onto it. Chemically processed documents should be kept in clear plastic envelopes or sheet protectors.

Documents damaged by fire could contain information valuable to the investigation. Arson has long been used in insurance fraud or to conceal another crime. If possible, burned documents should be left in their container and handled as gently as possible. (Refer to Chapter 7 for a more detailed discussion of preserving burned documents.)

If questioned writings are found on a wall or body in a homicide case, it is advisable to contact a document examiner for possible assistance at the crime scene. If this is not possible, photographs should be taken of the area. Writings on walls, desktops, mirrors, and other surfaces should be photographed with a scale present. If possible, the item containing the writing should be removed and submitted to the laboratory. If the writing is confined to a relatively small area, such as a wall, and circumstances justify it, the section should be cut out and taken to the laboratory.

It is necessary to mark documents that later may be entered into evidence during presentation of the court case. The best place to mark a document is usually on the back. The investigator's initials and the date should be added as inconspicuously and as far away from other writings as possible. In the event this is not possible, the best solution is to use a pen with a different colour ink so the marking cannot be confused with the questioned writing. Red ink should be avoided because it does not survive well when ninhydrin is used to develop latent fingerprints. Extraneous markings and writings should never be placed on the document. If additional information beyond the investigator's initials and the date is necessary, it should be recorded in the officer's notes.

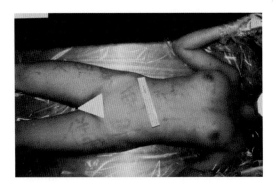

Figure 6.14 Not all handwriting cases involve traditional writings. In this case, a deceased woman was found with Chinese writing in lipstick on her body. The Hong Kong forensic laboratory conducted chemical comparisons on the lipstick as well as writing comparisons in an effort to solve the case. (Photograph courtesy of S.C. Leung, former head of the government laboratory in Hong Kong, China.)

It is generally necessary to store documents for varying lengths of time, sometimes several years, pending final disposition of the case. The documents can be stored in protective plastic envelopes or sheet protectors and filed in folders or envelopes large enough to keep them flat. In this way, they will remain in good condition for long periods of time. Photographs can be kept in flat folders or envelopes. Documents processed for fingerprints with ninhydrin or other chemicals must be enclosed in clear plastic envelopes or sheet protectors. Documents should be stored in an area with a relatively cool, dry temperature and away from excessive heat or direct sunlight. Not all handwriting cases involve traditional writings. Figure 6.14 shows the writing examined in the case of a deceased woman found with Chinese writing in lipstick on her body. The Hong Kong forensic laboratory conducted chemical comparisons on the lipstick as well as writing comparisons to solve the case.

When the questioned documents have been discovered and received as evidence and have been properly handled and marked for identification, exemplar writings must be obtained. Exemplar writings are known specimens from the suspect or victim. They are extremely important and necessary to connect the suspect or victim to the document. Like the questioned document, exemplars must be properly identified and cared for. They should not be stapled, folded, rolled up, torn, punched, smeared with fingerprints, or otherwise damaged if they are to be acceptable as evidence. The purpose of exemplars is to give the examiner of the document in question a known specimen of the subject's writing, thus providing a source of the writer's individual writing habits and personal style characteristics.

There are two general types of handwriting exemplars: *informal* and *formal*. Informal exemplars are also referred to as *non-request writing*. These include the routine, normal course of business writings such as letters, application forms, business records, cheques, etc. These documents are sometimes difficult to admit as evidence because their authenticity may be in question; however, they are the best examples of normal or natural handwriting. The subject prepares formal or "request writing" exemplars, usually at the request of the investigator. The format generally used is a handwriting exemplar card designated for that purpose. In addition to an exemplar card, fingerprint cards, booking slips, and, at times, tablet paper may also be used to obtain miscellaneous or specific exemplar writing samples. The investigating officer will witness these writings.

The investigator should keep several helpful suggestions in mind when obtaining request exemplars. It is useful to study and become familiar with the questioned document, paying close attention to names, specific words, spellings, and other unusual features of the document. The writing instrument should be in good working order. It is preferable to use a ballpoint pen with blue or black ink. Felt-tip pens and pencils should be avoided unless they are the type of writing instrument used in the questioned writing.

The writer should be provided with a comfortable writing area. Generally, exemplars written in the back seat of a police car en route to the station are worthless. The investigator should be present to observe the writing because he or she will be called upon in court to testify to this fact. Only like materials can be compared; that is, cursive writing must be compared with cursive, printing with printing, and block letters with block letters. Figure 6.15 illustrates this with reference to handwriting examinations made in the case of Ivan "John" Demjanjuk, where the question of identity was proven by forensic document examination. Know as "Ivan the Terrible," Demjanjuk was a prison guard at German concentration camps during World War II. Through a series of legal proceedings in the United States, Israel, and Germany, Demjanjuk, age 91, was ultimately convicted in 2011 in Germany of war crimes and of complicity in the murder of over 28,000 Jews while serving at Sobibor. The court, however, ordered him released pending appeal. In addition to handwriting, the question of Demjanjuk's identity was resolved using the following techniques: the chemistry of photographic paper and emulsion, the chemistry of the writing inks, the chemistry of paper and stamp pad ink, the alignment of stamp impressions, and comparisons with ink and paper from known documents of the alleged period from the National Archives and German and Russian archives.

Specific writing specimens should be requested in addition to the exemplar card, including material contained in the questioned document. The wording of this questioned document should be dictated to the subject; the actual document should not be placed before the writer from which to copy. The writing instrument should be similar to the one used on the questioned document, and the paper should be similar with respect to size, weight, and style (e.g., plain or ruled). Several specimens should be obtained as long as the subject is willing to cooperate. If the writer is trying to disguise the writing, it is best to interrupt the periods of writing with conversation and fresh paper from time to

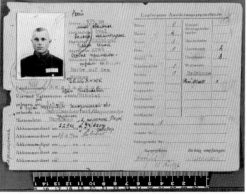

Figure 6.15 In the Ivan "John" Demjanjuk case, the question of identity was proven by forensic document examination, including the handwriting on these official documents. (Photographs courtesy of Anthony Cantu, PhD, formerly with the US Secret Service Laboratory.)

time. This procedure makes it difficult for the subject to maintain a consistent alteration of natural writing habits. In the event of wide variation or difference in the questioned writing and the exemplar, it may be useful to have the writer provide additional exemplars with the other hand. Handwriting reflects the effects of age, illness, injuries, and mental state. Because narcotic addicts may show writing that varies from time to time, it may be necessary to obtain writing exemplars at various time intervals, sometimes several days apart. It is sometimes necessary for the investigator to obtain additional exemplars of the individual's writing by obtaining informal exemplars.

6.3.2 Signatures

Signatures are a specialised form of handwriting and are unique for most people. They are written many times as a personal identification, and each writer develops his or her own special stylised version that is nearly impossible to reproduce and sometimes difficult to decipher. The signature becomes a reflex, almost automated, piece of writing. Because it acts as proof of identity for authorisation for credit cards, contracts, securities, and so on, signatures are often subjected to attempts at falsification. They present an additional challenge in that the amount of material for examination is restricted to the few letters in the name or style adopted by the signatory.

Forged signatures are usually made either by tracing over an original or by what is in effect making a drawing of the original. As a result, there are several things that a hand-writing expert will look for and assess in trying to reach a conclusion on a given specimen signature. These may include:

- Tremors in the trace
- Unnatural pen lifts
- Pen strokes with blunt ends
- Tracks on patches
- Differences in size
- Incorrect proportioning of letters
- Unnaturally large similarities

Tremors in the trace that can be seen under the microscope will often occur when a forger concentrates on precisely copying the genuine signature by slowly tracing or drawing, thus losing the fluid movement that characterises normal writing. Similarly, unnatural pen lifts are made as the counterfeiter pauses to check the work. Blunt ends of the trace or the stroke indicate that they have been made slowly and deliberately and not fluently. The proportions and scales of the signature also help to detect fraud, in contrasting ways. The forger may not replicate the natural style, size, and proportionality that the signature owner naturally has in his writing, or, in contrast, the forger may make such a good copy that it is identical in all respects to an example of an authentic signature, when in fact no two signatures are exactly the same.

The location of the writing on a document in relation to the line or box in which it is made, while not proving forgery, can also suggest that the writing is not the natural signature of the supposed author. Tracing and drawing will both leave clues in the formation of the writing as described above, but tracing will produce other evidence. The act of tracing can result in unnatural pressure in the writing which can be detected through examination for indented writings, as described below.

Case 2

The importance of exemplar writing samples, and the need to be careful in drawing conclusions from handwriting, is illustrated by the Hitler diaries case. In April 1983, the German magazine *Die Stern* paid almost 10 million marks for a 62-volume collection that claimed to be the diaries of Adolph Hitler. Linguistic and historical experts vouched that the content was authentic, and document examiners vouched that the diaries matched an example of Hitler's handwriting that they were given. The historians were wrong. More extensive examination showed the material to contain errors, and indeed the errors pointed to the source of the fake content. The handwriting experts were right, though—the various samples had indeed been written by the same person, just not Adolph Hitler. In fact, the diaries were forgeries and the so-called authentic sample of Hitler's writing was itself a fake. The failure of the handwriting experts to identify that the writing was forged was because all the writings were in the natural hand of the same author. Further testing showed that the materials were anachronistic. The paper contained additives that were not introduced until 1954, and the ink was less than a year old and was of a type not available at the supposed time the diaries were written.

6.3.3   Indented Writing

Indented writing is the result of a writing tool being pressed down against the surface during the writing, leaving a relief of the writing in the surface of the layer or layers of paper beneath the paper being written on. Indented writing can be found several sheets down, but the depth of the impression decreases the farther down the paper is from the top. The indentations will vary depending on the pressure of the original writing, the nature of the paper, environmental conditions (particularly humidity), and storage of the document.

Examination for the possible presence of indented writing on paper and similar exhibits can be performed by shining light obliquely onto the document and looking for shadows in the indentations. Today, the best method is to use an electrostatic detection apparatus (ESDA). The document or paper is placed on a porous bronze plate on the apparatus, and a thin plastic film is then pulled over the plate and the document. This thin plastic film is then pulled down on the document on the plate by a vacuum air pump. A high-voltage electrostatic source is then held about 2 inches above the document and moved back and forth over the paper. Where there is indented writing on the document the process will result in an area of opposite polarisation. Toner powder applied on the thin plastic film on top of the document will be attracted to the indentation by the induced electrostatic force. The detected indented writing is preserved by bonding a transparent plastic sheet on top of the thin plastic film.

As mentioned above, indented writings are used in examinations of signatures for forgery by tracing. It is also a valuable tool for showing that writing has been added to a multiple-page document at a different time from the original, as there should be an exact agreement between indentations (or their absence) in lower pages with the writing on the top page. ESDA examination can also be used for examination for other types of latents marks on a document, such as shoe prints or other latent marks that may be present on the document.

Caution: The ability to detect indented writings means that investigators should not lean on any documents at the scene when making notes, as the indentations from their writings may destroy valuable evidence on the original.

6.4   Identification of Human Remains

As with living persons and intact corpses, DNA and fingerprinting are the best methods of identifying human remains, with the qualification that modern DNA typing, especially mtDNA (see Chapter 8), is now probably the method of choice even for skeletal or fragmentary remains.

6.4.1   Anthropology, Dentistry, and DNA

The traditional fields of forensic anthropology and forensic odontology (dentistry) have made major contributions over the past decades in the identification of human remains, especially in the area of mass casualty incidents. An in-depth examination is beyond the scope of this book; however, it is worthwhile for the investigator to be aware of some of the information that can be gleaned from semi-skeletal remains. Forensic anthropology and odontology techniques are useful in cases where normal methods of identification, such as facial photographs, fingerprints, physical description, and markings on the body, are not available for use. Such cases may involve major disasters, as well as the discovery of buried bodies, badly burned bodies, or skeletal remains.

It is often possible to determine two types of information from remains. The first is physical characteristics such as sex, ethnicity, approximate age, stature, certain disease states, and old injuries. The second type, which is far more important for forensic purposes, is the actual identification of the individual. To accomplish this identification, adequate records indicating the deceased's physical characteristics must be available as a basis for comparison with data collected from the examination.

Case 3

Skeletal remains were discovered in an unused cistern near the Omaha, Nebraska, airport and were positively identified through comparison of antemortem and postmortem dental x-rays. Although nearly 9 years had elapsed between the death and discovery, the bones and teeth revealed evidence of the application of a corrosive substance at or around the time of death (see Figure 6.16).

Personal identification is one of the most important functions of an investigation. The identity of a living person at a crime scene establishes a strong link between the suspect and the crime. Likewise, the identity, or non-identity, of a dead person sets the investigation in motion. Because relatives or acquaintances kill the majority of murder victims, knowing the identity of the victim provides a starting point. From the identity, the character of the victim suggests possible suspects. Although not a responsibility of criminal investigations, the identity of innocent decedents enables the deceased person's relatives to collect insurance, settle estates, and provide for the welfare of dependents.

When police are called to a death investigation, relatives or acquaintances of the dead person or documents or possessions found on the body generally help to establish its identity. Caution should always be exercised in making a determination of identity merely because documents concerning a certain person are found on the body, as such documents may be stolen, false, or "planted." Furthermore, the body itself may be planted to permit someone to disappear. Substitute bodies have been discovered when the dead person's measurements did not agree with those of the alleged victim.

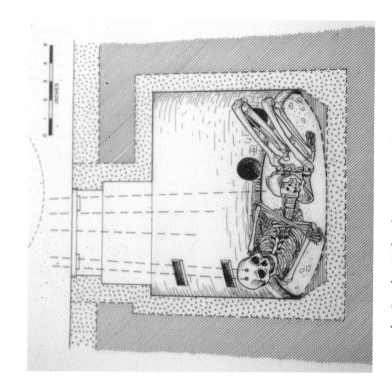

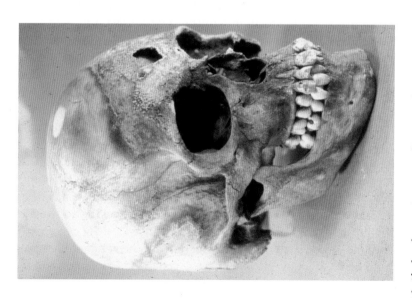

Figure 6.16 Skeletal remains were discovered in an unused cistern near the Omaha, Nebraska, airport and were positively identified through comparison of antemortem and postmortem dental x-rays. Although nearly 9 years had elapsed between the death and discovery of the body, the bones and teeth revealed evidence of the application of a corrosive substance at or around the time of death. (Photographs courtesy of Douglas H. Ubelaker, PhD, Curator of Anthropology, Smithsonian Institution, Washington, DC; Norman Sperber, DDS, Chief Forensic Dentist for San Diego and Imperial Counties, San Diego, CA.)

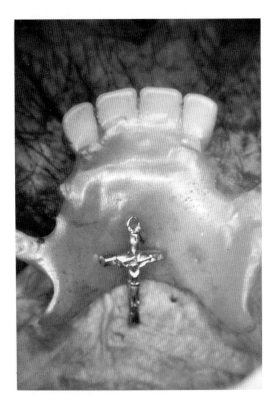

Figure 6.17 A gold crucifix found attached to the dentures of an unknown person could provide useful identifying information. (Photographs courtesy of George E. Burgman, DDS, forensic odontologist, Niagara Falls, Ontario, Canada.)

It cannot always be assumed that a relative or acquaintance is competent to identify the body. Instances have occurred in which, due to the state of the body, even a spouse has made a mistake as to identity. It is necessary, therefore, to be careful in establishing a body's identity even though it can be determined with a fair degree of probability. These precautions consist of taking the fingerprints, photographing the body, noting the description (including the dental data), and examining and describing in detail the clothing and objects found on the body. This is illustrated in Figure 6.17, where a gold crucifix found attached to the dentures of an unknown person provided useful identifying information.

Sometimes, when the body of an unknown person is found, it is better to postpone a definite conclusion for a few days until the discovery has become generally known through publicity in local papers or the national press. Relatives or acquaintances of missing persons who read or hear of the discovery and communicate with the police identify most unknown bodies. The examination by the pathologist at the autopsy of the body will assist greatly in its description, particularly if the body is in an advanced state of decomposition. The pathologist will be able to give such details as apparent age, height, build, weight, and scars (including surgical scars). If all of this information, general examination, and publicity fail to establish the identity of the dead person, and the body must be buried as that of an unknown individual, it is most important that everything that may be a guide to later identification be preserved for possible future use. DNA and dental data should be recorded.

In the identification of an unknown body, the police officer may need to work with bodies in varying states of decomposition. The most frequent case is that of a body found in water. These cases are considered the most repugnant and difficult; in warm weather, the body will swell up and the skin will become almost black only a few days after death. More rarely, a mummified or petrified body is under inquiry. A dead body may become mummified when it lies in a dry place exposed to sun and air; the tissues do not putrefy but gradually dry up. Under certain conditions, a body can become petrified; the external parts are as if they are calcified due to formation of adipocere (also known as grave wax or mortuary fat) and the body resembles a marble statue. Formation of adipocere occurs chiefly in bodies that lie in a very damp place. It also may be necessary to identify a greatly changed or mutilated body or one of which only the skeleton or certain portions remain.

When a body that is found is obviously from someone who had been dead for several days or even weeks, the time of death can help in determining its identity. The body may have decomposed and become infested with flies and insects. An entomologist can provide an estimate of how long the body has been at the locus from the type of infestation and the stage in the life-cycle of the flies or larvae present.

Because the deceased may be a murder victim, the investigation should be carefully planned before attempting to identify the person. It must be decided how much of a search of pockets and other articles for identifying documents can be permitted without destroying other important evidence. It may be necessary to move the body or other form of remains to a mortuary where a careful examination can be conducted.

Generally, the first procedure is a preliminary investigation of the pockets of the clothes. If any documents or other material that can be a guide to identification are found, careful note should be taken. If this does not lead to any result, the work of identification is continued by taking photographs and fingerprints, preparing an accurate description, and making a detailed investigation and description of clothes and belongings, after which the discovery of the body may be published in a police bulletin for distribution to other agencies and the general press. A form of identification work that requires exceptionally careful organisation is the identification of victims of a catastrophe. The procedure for this type of identification is described later in this chapter.

Modern advances in DNA typing, particularly mtDNA, have revolutionised the identification of human remains. The main problem with the technique is that it is time consuming and costly, a combination that favours the more traditional methods being used first. However, mtDNA has two outstanding advantages: the nature of the chemical and the nature of its inheritance. This form of DNA, found in mitochondria rather than the cell nucleus, is stable and found in relatively high quantities, even in tissues such as bone and hair that are resistant to degradation. It is inherited differently than nuclear DNA, being passed solely from the mother. That means that direct comparisons can be made with samples from any family member with a direct female line of descent. Today, most countries maintain databases of the DNA of their armed forces' service members. This can be a useful resource.

DNA typing is discussed in greater detail in the section on forensic biology in Chapter 8. *Note:* If the victim received a transfusion prior to death, that information should be made known to the forensic biologist performing the DNA typing.

6.4.2   Taking Fingerprints

Even if an individual is not on record in the fingerprint file, there is a possibility of identifying the body through fingerprints. In many cases, there is reason to assume that a body is that of a certain missing person but even near relatives are unable to identify it because it has altered so much. Under these conditions, fingerprints are taken in order to compare them with latent prints in the home of the individual or at the place of employment. This type of investigation often gives a positive result.

There is no special difficulty in taking fingerprints from a body after the rigidity has relaxed or when rigidity has only developed to a small extent and the body has not undergone any considerable change. If fingers are rigid, the joints should be bent several times until they are sufficiently flexible. The tips of the fingers are then inked, using a rubber roller and printing ink or commercially available inking materials, and the prints are taken on small pieces of thin card that are pressed against the papillary pattern on the tip of the finger. The finger should not be rolled against the card because the print will inevitably suffer from slipping. With some practice, the card may instead be rolled around the fingertip for satisfactory results.

A number of prints of the same finger are taken so the best results can be selected. When a sufficient number of prints have been taken from one finger, each piece of card is marked to show to which finger it corresponds. When prints have been taken from all the fingers, the best are selected from each and stuck onto the respective sections of a fingerprint card. It is important to be careful not to get the fingers mixed up when sticking on the prints; if prints of two fingers do happen to get interchanged, then a search in the register will probably be fruitless. It is best to make up two cards, one to be sent to the state or federal file and the other filed with the records. If suitable thin cards cannot be obtained, ordinary glazed writing paper can be used. In such a case, using a piece of wood or sheet metal cut to a form fitting the finger facilitates taking the prints. The pieces of paper are placed on this and fixed or held fast on it when the prints are taken.

Once the rigidity of the body is complete it is difficult to take fingerprints because the fingers are bent toward the palm of the hand and are so stiff that they cannot be straightened. There is no point in attempting to extend such a finger. In this case, it may be necessary to cut certain tendons in the fingers so that they can be straightened. Certainly, this method is quite effective, but it is not necessary to go to this extreme. It is simpler to bend the hand backward at the wrist to a right or acute angle to the forearm, whereby the fingers will be straightened. It is then possible to hold a finger firmly and lift it up to make the print, with the bend at the wrist becoming slightly reduced. If this method is difficult, then the wrist is bent down again and the required finger is pressed down toward the palm, which makes it accessible from below.

Difficulty is often experienced when the body is considerably decomposed. The changes in the fingers consist either of their drying up and becoming hard or of the tissues becoming loose and filled with liquid and the epidermis becoming fragile and puckered ("dishpan hands"). The first generally occurs when the body has been in a dry place and the second when it has been in water.

When the fingers have shrivelled and dried up, fingerprints cannot be taken by the methods just described. Other methods must be employed. The prints may be read directly from the fingers and classified without taking impressions. It is necessary to be very careful and, if possible, perform ridge counting and ridge tracing also on those fingers not required for the classification formulae. A selection is then made of the finger or fingers most suitable for recording with printing ink. When this has been done, a search can be made. Only persons with considerable experience in fingerprint classification can use this method. When reading a pattern directly from a finger it must be remembered that the print is seen reversed, as in a mirror.

Another way to record fingerprints from deceased persons is by photography. This method is rather tedious and difficult to carry out. If the fingers are stiff and bent, it is necessary to photograph each finger separately.

Frequently, fingertips are so dried out and wrinkled that the friction ridge pattern cannot be read because important parts are concealed in hard folds of the skin. The pattern may be read by removing the fingers from the hand and softening the skin; however, the pathologist should have an opportunity to view the deceased before this step is taken. The fingers should be cut at the second or middle joint and placed in individual labelled bottles, each bottle noting the hand and finger. Only the pathologist or other competent person should perform this operation. The investigator should be present to verify that the fingers do not get mixed up.

One method for softening dried fingers is to let them soak in a solution of diluted liquid fabric softener for 1 or 2 days, after which they are carefully kneaded until they are sufficiently soft for a print to be taken with the aid of printing ink. If difficulties are still encountered, the fingers must be photographed. Another useful techniques, used in the identification of bodies after the tsunami disaster in Asia in December 2004, is to place the hand in very hot water, 60 to 90°C, which will distend the skin on the hand and fingers.

Taking fingerprints from a corpse removed from water is difficult because of changes in the body. In general, changes may be divided into three stages: (1) the epidermis of the fingertips becomes loose and coarsely ridged, (2) the epidermis is loose everywhere and can be removed, and (3) the epidermis is completely missing. In the first stage, the fingertips must be washed and dried, preferably with cotton or a soft towel. This operation must be done with care and without rubbing so the skin is not torn off. Fingerprints are then taken in the usual way.

When the skin is wrinkled and granulated, water must first be injected into the upper joint of the finger so that the creases and granulations are smoothed out. For this purpose, a 10-mL hypodermic syringe with a fine needle is used. The needle is inserted approximately at the centre of the inside of the middle joint and brought close to the bone in the upper joint, after which water is injected until the skin appears hard and tense. The needle must not be allowed to come too near the skin because the pressure might be sufficient to break the skin, nor should it be put in or too near the outer joint—the return path would be so short that the water would run out again. After the needle has been removed, the print is taken in the usual way. In earlier technical literature, an injection of glycerin, paraffin, or even melted tallow was recommended; however, a properly performed injection with water gives better results and is easier to perform.

In the second stage, when the epidermis has loosened, it is easier to take fingerprints. The loose skin (finger stalls) of the tip is pulled or cut off from the fingertips; the skin from each finger is placed in a labelled test tube filled with water. The finger stalls should not be put in an envelope or other paper wrapping because after a time they will dry up and stick to the paper. When they have been removed this way, the finger stalls may be sent to the fingerprint unit for examination.

For easier handling and photographing, the best procedure is to place the skin from each finger separately between two glass slides. To do this, the fingerprint pattern is cut out of the finger stalls. Because the cutout pieces of skin are then convex, they easily split when flattened between the glass slides. This splitting is unavoidable; therefore, it is necessary to make cuts in the edges so that the splits do not occur in parts of the fingerprint pattern needed for the purpose of classification. When placing them between the glass slides, a small piece of paper or card with the name of the finger is placed near the top of the sample to indicate that the print is being viewed from the correct side. There is not much risk of any such piece of skin being the wrong side because the inside is lighter, smoother, and glossier than the outside. If, however, in a particular case some doubt exists as to which is the inside, taking the piece of skin out and viewing it can determine which side is concave. The glass slides should be taped together. The fingerprint patterns should be photographed by transmitted light; the lines will show up very distinctly.

Prints may also be taken with the aid of printing ink. After careful cleaning and drying, the pattern area is coated with printing ink in the usual way and pressed against a piece of paper. This method is difficult to carry out because the skin is generally so fragile that the print can be destroyed by the slightest carelessness. Occasionally, the finger stalls are so strong that they can be picked up on a finger and the print can be taken as it would be from a living person. However, only in rare cases is the skin on all 10 digits in such good condition that this method can be used.

It often happens that large portions of the epidermis become loose, but small parts remain so firmly attached that the finger stalls cannot be removed whole. Careful scraping of the attached tissues may loosen the tips in a comparatively whole condition. If this is impossible, the part of the underlying tissues to which the finger stalls are attached is cut off, and the whole piece is mounted on a piece of plasticine. The fingerprint can then be taken with printing ink or photographed.

It is far more difficult to take a fingerprint from a dead person when the epidermis of the fingers has fallen away and cannot be found. This occurs generally with bodies that have been in water for a long period of time. Sometimes it is possible to make out the fingerprint pattern in the remaining under-skin. Only rarely is it possible to take these fingerprints with printing ink, due to very low ridges in the pattern. The only possible method is to photograph the pattern. In general, however, it can be assumed that the fingerprint pattern will have disappeared entirely because of loosening of the skin.

It is difficult to take a palm print from a dead body, even in a case where the body has undergone little or no change. There is hardly any hope of taking a complete palm print and it is therefore necessary to take portions of the print on small pieces of paper or card. To simplify the identification of these prints, each piece of paper should have outlined on it a hand on which the part corresponding to the palm print is marked. In taking finger and palm prints from bodies, printing ink is the best medium because the impressions can be mounted directly onto a fingerprint card or other suitable form. These forms can later be filed with other cards. An alternative method that may be used employs black fingerprint powder. In some cases, the results of this method may be superior to those with printing ink. The finger or palm is lightly coated with the black powder, using a brush. The impression is obtained by lifting transparent fingerprint tape. The pieces of tape are then mounted directly onto a fingerprint card or on paper cut up into squares for attachment to the card. In the case of palms, the pieces of tape should be laid lengthwise over the whole palm area and removed one at a time before being mounted onto a card or paper. This method is somewhat more difficult than the inking method, but it is superior in that a full impression is obtained. A condition for successful lifting is that two persons are available: one to hold the hand and one to manipulate the tape.

6.4.3 Photographing

In photographing an unknown body, full-face and right-profile face photographs are always taken. If necessary, further pictures should be taken, including a whole view, left profile (especially with a view to identification from the ears), and detailed photographs of scars, injuries, teeth, tattoos, clothes, etc. It is good practice to ensure that an unidentified body is not buried before it is photographed; however, it is important to photograph the body before putrefaction sets in and swells or discolours the features. With regard to a body that has undergone some degree of change, although a photograph of the face may be considered quite meaningless, it should still be done. It should also be remembered that the individual may be identified after burial and that the relatives may ask to see the photograph of the face. For a full-face picture, the body should be laid on its back with the face turned upward.

When the body is in a mortuary, a wooden rack or other structure that is generally placed under the head should be removed for the photograph. The lower jaw has a tendency to drop, causing the mouth to open, so it is recommended to prop the chin up with a peg or other object that will not be too conspicuous in the photograph. The camera is placed vertically above the face. The colour of background material should be chosen so that the outer contour of the head is well defined against it. Often the simplest way is to spread a towel under the head. When profile portraits are taken, the body should be raised so the camera can be placed at the side of the head. A suitable background is also required for this exposure so the profile shows up distinctly. The head should not be turned to one side to make it easier to photograph because this might cause considerable alteration in appearance due to the position of the camera.

When photographing whole-face pictures, the camera is placed high above the body. If this is not possible because of a low roof, then the body can be turned a little to one side, but the procedure must be well thought out to avoid the possibility of blood running down or other conditions of the body being altered. Under no circumstances should the body be tied or suspended in a leaning position. In photographing scars, injuries, tattoos, and details of clothing, a measuring tape or scale should always be placed on or by the side of the object to provide scale. A ring flash should also be used.

Photographs are best taken in colour; however, in certain instances when tattoos or other marks present on the body are poorly contrasted, appropriate filters or black-and-white photography may be helpful. Tattoos may help identify victims as well as suspects. In one case, a detective was looking through tattoos of gang members when one caught his eye. The tattoo depicted an unsolved murder crime scene he had investigated. It seems the gang member tattooed a depiction of the crime on his chest (see Figure 6.18).

Even at such an early stage when the changes in the body are limited to rigidity and lividity stains, it may be difficult to distinguish scars, strawberry marks, and birthmarks from livid stains, discolourations of the skin, and wrinkles. The further the deterioration has proceeded, the greater the difficulties. Blue tattooing can be barely perceptible when the skin becomes dark coloured and blistered. Under such conditions, the police officer must not rely on personal judgement, but must consult the pathologist. Any special characteristics are described in essentially the same way as for living persons, except in one

Figure 6.18 Tattoos may help identify victims as well as suspects. A detective was looking through tattoos of gang members when one caught his eye. The tattoo depicted an unsolved murder crime scene he had investigated. It seems the gang member tattooed a depiction of the crime on his chest. (Photograph courtesy of the Los Angeles County Sheriff's Department, Los Angeles, CA.)

respect. In the case of a description of a living person with a large number of tattoos, only those that are characteristic or unusual (e.g., names, dates, emblems) are described.* With unknown bodies, however, all tattoos should be described, including the most common types. It is very important that these and other special characteristics be described accurately in a recognised manner with respect to kind, form, size, and position.

Ultraviolet (UV) photography and ultraviolet video imaging techniques are useful methods for studying and recording injuries on human skin, such as bite marks and ligature marks, using fluorescent UV photography, reflective long-wavelength UV photography, and short-wavelength UV photography. Taking UV photographs is a cumbersome procedure in that it is difficult to focus UV images because they cannot be seen. One procedure involves using an ultraviolet image intensifier. One unit marketed by Hamamatsu has the appearance of an infrared night scope and can be used coupled to a camera or video unit or by viewing through an eyepiece in the unit. It allows for quick and easy viewing of trauma and even some latent fingerprints on surfaces using ultraviolet lighting.

Many people are x-rayed for the purpose of diagnosing medical conditions or for detecting dental cavities. These films are often retained in medical files for many years. Before an unknown body is autopsied or buried, dental and body x-rays should be taken. They not only provide a means of definite identification, but might also provide information as to the cause of death.

6.4.4   Marks of Trades or Occupations

Although less common today than in the past, marks and calluses on the hands associated with specific trades may be instructive. When examining victims and suspects, consider the following characteristics of various tradespeople:

- *Clerk, draftsman*—Hardening of the last joint of the right middle finger at the point where the pen rests when writing or drawing; for draftsman, hardening on the part or the ball of the right little finger that lies nearest the wrist
- *Baker*—Hardening on thumb and index fingers of both hands from handling the edges of hot pans and plates

---

* Gang members often have elaborate tattooing. Such tattooing may suggest specific gang membership.

- *Engraver, jeweller*—Wear on nail of right thumb
- *Tailor, dressmaker*—Marks and scars of needle punctures in tip of left index finger
- *Shoemaker, upholsterer*—Round hollows in front teeth from biting the thread; for shoemaker, wear on left thumbnail
- *Glazier*—Hardening between middle and index fingers, arising from handle of diamond being held between these fingers
- *Dyer, photographer, chemist*—Nails dry, brittle, and often discoloured
- *Butcher*—Calluses and hardening on inner joints of fingers and on neighbouring parts of palm of the hand that holds knives
- *Bricklayer, stonemason*—Hardening of right hand from grip around trowel or hammer; skin of left hand worn very thin from holding bricks or stone
- *Carpenter, joiner*—Hardening in ball of thumb of right hand from grip on plane; unusual number of injuries and scars on left index finger
- *Painter*—Calluses and hardening between right index and middle fingers from grip on handle of brush

If evidence of repetitive operations is observed, it should be noted, sketched, and photographed. It may take imagination, ingenuity, and some practical research in order to connect these calluses to a specific occupation, hobby, or sport.

6.4.5 Description of the Body

Making a satisfactory description of a dead body takes time and is often difficult, especially if the body has begun to decompose. In compiling descriptions, it is therefore best to avoid using too definite an expression when describing details for which there is some doubt as to the most suitable choice of words. In case of difficulty, the pathologist should be consulted. The body may conveniently be described in the following order: estimated age, length, build, shape of face, neck, hair, beard or moustache, forehead, eyes, eyebrows, nose, base of nose, mouth, teeth, chin, ears, hands, feet, and any outstanding characteristics.

If the body has undergone a certain amount of change, it is often nearly impossible to decide the age; even a trained pathologist will often avoid making any definite statement. In many cases, the age can be determined only by postmortem examination. The length of the body is measured with the body stretched out on its back. The measurement is taken from the heel to the crown of the head. It is often difficult to describe the build. In the case of a swollen body that has been submerged, there may be the temptation to write "well nourished" or "stocky" in the notes, which may be an error. The facial appearance can be described to some degree, but a complete description of the face cannot be specified when a body has undergone considerable change. The colour of the hair also may change some time after death. When a body has been in dry earth or in a hot, dry location, the hair may become reddish; however, with a submerged body, hair colour may not appreciably change.

In describing the hair, note if it has been well cared for, how it is parted, etc. Hair samples should be taken from bodies that cannot be identified. DNA typing may be possible after comparison with hairs found in the home or workplace of a missing person. In describing facial hair, avoid using a term such as "unshaven." That description may be inaccurate as the stubble on the face arises from the hair roots on the face. Hair roots, which lie at an angle to the skin, straighten up after death because of drying and shrinking of the skin—hence, the myth that hair and beards grow after death.

It is often difficult to judge the eye colour of a dead person because the eyes undergo considerable change after death. Attention should also be given to artificial eyes. The forehead is not likely to change much with respect to form. It is difficult to judge the form and size of the nose because it may swell considerably. On a body that has not undergone any considerable changes, the profile of the nose may be altered considerably due to shrinking of the tissues in the tip of the nose. As a result, a living person's nose that is concave may become straight after death, and a straight nose may become convex. It is usually impossible to decide the size of the mouth because the lips undergo great changes in the very early stages of decomposition. The size and form of the ears may undergo only minor changes. In cases where the face and body become completely unrecognisable, the ears may look relatively normal. When examining the hands, note the condition of the fingernails. If applicable, take nail scrapings. Debris under the nails sometimes yields pertinent information. When an unknown body is found without shoes, measure the foot length and width to estimate the approximate shoe size.

The pathologist should take a blood sample from the body. Comparisons with blood found at the crime scene or on the perpetrator may be important. In missing person cases, it may be possible to do reverse paternity typing to demonstrate that the victim was related to someone. A genetic profile may lead to a family connection or to excluding possible identities. Typing of putrefied blood or tissue may be difficult, but breakthroughs in forensic biology are improving the chances of identifying missing persons through more sensitive techniques.

6.4.6   The Deceased's Clothing

The outer clothing is described first, including accurate indications of the type of material, quality, colour, buttons, damage and, if possible, how the damage is thought to have occurred, stains of dust and dirt, etc. A preliminary examination is made of the pockets and other areas of the clothing (e.g., between the outer layer and the lining where objects may be found) that can be a guide for identification. Garments should be removed one at a time, placed on clean paper, and allowed to air-dry at room temperature. If at all possible, the clothing should not be removed by cutting or tearing but should be carefully removed in the usual manner. The person undressing the corpse should be aware that microscopic trace evidence may be present on the clothing, and appropriate care should be exercised so that no useful evidence is lost. If the clothing must be cut from the body, care must be taken to avoid cutting through areas with bullet holes or knife cuts because these areas will be examined in depth later.

After the garment has been removed and air-dried, it should be packaged and sent to the crime laboratory for examination for debris, trace evidence, and marks of identification such as laundry marks, monograms, manufacturer's markings, and dry cleaning tags. Garments should not be laundered until after the clothing has been carefully examined for trace material and photographed. After these procedures, the garments can be laundered so that clear identification photographs can be made of the clothing and laundry marks may become visible. Articles of clothing should be repackaged following examination at the laboratory and retained until after adjudication of the case. Under no circumstance should these or any other evidence be destroyed until after all legal proceedings have been completed. This allows the investigator to reexamine the clothing at a later time if new questions arise.

Shoe size, colour, make, and style should be noted. If the size cannot be determined, it is possible to approximate the shoe size by the length of the shoe. Repairs, degree of wear, defects, etc. may also be used as a possible means of identification. Shoes should be submitted to the laboratory for examination for the presence of soil, debris, and other trace evidence that may be helpful in determining identity.

6.4.7 Laundry Marks

In searching for laundry marks on clothing, it should be noted that they may be invisible. Many large laundries now stamp all incoming laundry with a colourless dye imperceptible to the unaided eye but which fluoresces strongly in ultraviolet light. The mark usually comprises the identification mark of the laundry and the number given to the customer. The identification mark sometimes consists of the first letters of the firm's name. The number of the customer is registered with the laundry. The marks are quite durable and remain even after many washings. When the laundry marks the garment, a search is first made for old laundry marks, which are crossed out with invisible ink before the new mark is put on. In this way, a garment may have several laundry marks, which greatly facilitates identification. It is also common practice in the cleaning and laundry industries to identify garments with a paper tag clipped to the article. Unless this tag is attached in an obscure place, the customer usually removes it before wearing the garment.

A good lead for identification can be obtained from monograms, manufacturer's marks, firm's marks, stamp numbers, embroidered initials, and markings made with marking ink. In the case of more valuable garments such as fur coats, overcoats, and suits, it is important to look for marks or alterations often placed on parts turned toward the inside with the idea that the garment may be stolen and that the thief would remove the usual marks. Such identification marks may consist of seams sewn with a different thread, small cuts or pieces cut out of the cloth or lining, threads sewn in, etc.

6.4.8 Watchmaker's Marks

If a watch is found on an unknown dead body, it should be examined for any marks or figures that might aid in the identification. Usually the serial number of a watch is stamped inside the case. Certain watchmakers mark their watches with letters or symbols that indicate their watchmaker's society, together with their membership number. When a sale is made, it may be recommended to the customer to take out insurance on the watch, in which case the purchaser's name and the serial number on the watch are registered by the watchmaker. Some watchmakers mark the date of sale on the inside of the case. When a watch is taken in for repair, it is customary for the watchmaker to scratch the inside of the case with certain letters or marks and figures that are partly special marks of the individual watchmaker and partly a repair number. The latter is recorded together with the serial number of the watch, name of the owner, and type of repair. The watchmaker's own mark generally consists of one or more initials but may also be a monogram, Greek letters or other characters, shorthand signs, punctuation marks, private marks, lines, figures, or mathematical signs. Investigators should seek assistance from a professional watchmaker.

6.4.9   Jewellery

Finger rings usually remain on a body even when it has decomposed to a considerable extent; therefore, they can be a means of identification. Inscriptions may often be found inside engagement, wedding, and other commemorative rings, while signet rings may carry initials, insignia, seals, crests, or other distinctive markings. In a number of countries, graduates of universities wear special rings. Orders, societies, and associations may use rings as marks of membership. Systems are available for the identification of precious gems. These systems are based on macroscopic and microscopic imperfections in any gemstone that are not likely to be found in their entire combination in any similar gem. Investigators should seek assistance from a professional jewellery expert. All jewellery should be photographed.

6.4.10   Eyeglasses

Eyeglasses discovered on or near a dead body may provide a means of identification. If the name of the optometrist is on the eyeglass case, it may be possible to determine the victim's name from the doctor's records. Even if the identity of an individual cannot be determined from a prescription, eyeglasses may be useful. Friends or relatives of the victim may be able to identify the eyeglasses as similar to those worn by the victim.

6.4.11   Teeth

Information of special value for identification can be obtained from investigating the teeth of a dead person because they are often characteristic in many respects. This applies not only to the appearance of the dead person who has not altered to any appreciable extent but also to greatly decomposed corpses, badly mutilated victims of airplane accidents, explosions and catastrophes, and burned bodies. The teeth are very resistant to the normal changes of decomposition as well as to fire and chemicals due to their enamel.

When the teeth are examined, attention is always directed to the changes or injuries in the face of the dead person that may possibly interfere with the subsequent postmortem examination or identification. If a body is altered considerably, the tissues of the face may be missing or may fall apart if the lower jaw is moved out of its position. In such a case, photographing and examining the body should be done first. If for any reason a police officer must examine the teeth of a body before the arrival of the odontologist, he should do so in such a way that no marks of the flow of blood or injuries on the face are aggravated or changed; particularly, the position of any object in the mouth should not be changed.

The first note to make in connection with the teeth is how many are present. A note should be made as to which teeth are missing in the upper and the lower jaws. This may be done by making a sketch of the teeth of each jaw. Special forms and computer programs, sometimes used for this purpose, greatly facilitate the work. These sketches or forms are marked with the position and size of any visible damage resulting from decay and pieces broken away, cracks, missing fillings, jackets and other crowns, bridge work, implants, root canals, etc. The material used in crowns, fillings, and the like is also noted. Sometimes entire gold crowns melt when teeth are exposed to high temperatures from fire. This is apparent from the amalgam filling running out and around the mouth.

Complete or partial dentures should be kept because the material used in them may possibly be a guide for identification. Dentures may have some identification inscribed on or attached to them. It may be the inmate number, service serial number, doctor's identification, or patient's name. A study of the style of the inscription will give some indication of the probable source. All characteristics of the teeth should be carefully noted. Teeth can be very light (white) or dark (brown); the teeth of the upper or lower jaw may be directed inward or outward and the teeth may be widely spaced, close together, or wedged in against one another. Exceptionally large spaces may be found between the middle front teeth (central incisors), the central teeth in the upper jaw may be exceptionally powerful (wide), and the front teeth in the upper or lower jaw may have noticeably smooth, uneven, or inclined cutting surfaces. Attention should also be given to the bite—that is, the relation between the teeth of the upper and lower jaw when they come together. In a normal bite, the lower edge of the front teeth of the upper jaw fits outside the front teeth of the lower jaw, and the outer chewing surfaces of the upper molars bite hit somewhat outside the corresponding teeth in the lower jaw. This is called normal occlusion. However, the bite may be such that the front teeth of the upper jaw are quite appreciably outside or inside the front teeth of the lower jaw, or that the front and canine teeth in the upper jaw are alternately in front of and behind the corresponding teeth of the lower jaw, resulting in an overbite or underbite.

When examining teeth, the assistance of a dentist should be obtained if possible. This is especially important for root fillings and other work that may be difficult for the untrained individual to detect. A small mirror is valuable help in the examination. If dental work is apparent, identification is possible through the dentist who treated the patient. Dentists keep records of the work on their patients. In an important case, an x-ray examination should be made. Any roots, root fillings, or the like remaining in the jawbones may have a characteristic appearance; an x-ray photograph may agree exactly with one that a dentist has kept.

If teeth are entirely or partially missing from the body, there is reason to suspect that the individual used a full or partial denture. The latter may be found at the house of a missing person or with relatives, and it can then be fitted in the mouth of the dead person, whereby identity or non-identity can be proved.

In addition to identification of a victim by means of x-rays of teeth compared with dental records, other useful information can be developed through dental examination. These data are useful in identifying the remains of a decomposed or skeletal body. Age can be determined through dental examination. The ages for eruption of deciduous (baby) teeth and permanent teeth are fairly well established. X-rays of the jaw and examination of the mouth allow the forensic odontologist to make an age determination of the deceased. Habits or occupation may also be deduced through a dental examination. For example, a pipe smoker may have stained and worn surfaces on the teeth, and a tailor may have a groove on the surface of two opposing teeth caused by biting thread. Such characteristics, like those discussed earlier with regard to skin calluses on hands, may prove useful in certain cases.

The arrangement of teeth in the mouth can be useful for identification. Thus, crooked or buckteeth of a deceased may be used as a means of elimination or identification of a particular person. Similarly, disease states, missing teeth, chipped or broken teeth, etc. are helpful for identification. A tooth found by itself at a crime scene may also yield information. The tooth can be cut open and the pulp can be extracted for DNA typing at the crime lab.

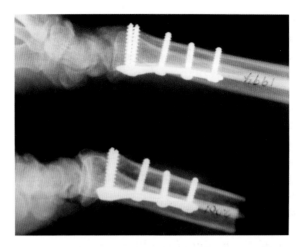

Figure 6.19 Radiograph of the forearm from a missing person compared to clinical records. (Photograph courtesy of C. Michael Bowers, DDS, JD, Ventura, CA.)

Case 4

Police investigators obtained medical records of a person reported missing. The records indicated the person had been treated for a fractured forearm. A stainless steel fixation device was placed with screws and remained in place. Autopsy radiographs determined the presence of a similar device in the same forearm of the human remains. The concordance of shape and materials of this device is obvious in the radiographs shown in Figure 6.19.

6.4.12   Medical Devices

Permanently installed medical devices, surgical implants, and prosthetics with recorded serial numbers offer another way to identify victims of crimes or natural disasters. There is a considerable number of such medical devices; a few of the more usual ones include hip and knee replacements and breast implants. In addition to dental x-rays, x-rays of the entire body may be useful.

6.4.13   Facial Reconstruction

Occasionally, the police investigator will want to obtain a photograph of the reconstructed face of a mutilated victim. In instances where parts of the face are missing, it is possible to reconstruct the area with various types of mortuary supply materials and cosmetics to a point where a reasonable likeness of the deceased can be made. The procedure requires a fair amount of skill and workmanship but is possible in instances where a reconstruction for identification is needed.

6.4.14   Determination of Gender

For the determination of gender, the skeletal characteristics are as follows:

- *Pelvis*—Size and form are different for men and women. The preauricular notch and pubic curve are especially significant, and even small fragments can make a determination of gender possible.
- *Cranium*—The walls of the cranium are normally thinner in men than in women. The angle of the root of the nose where it comes out from the forehead (frontal nose angle) is more pronounced in a man. The curve of the eyebrows is generally more rounded in a man than in a woman.
- *Head of joint of upper arm*—This is generally larger in a man than in a woman; the size of the head of the joint shrinks only slightly under the action of fire.
- *Breastbone, thighbone, and shinbones*—Both size and form are significant for determination of gender.
- *Skeleton*—The entire female skeleton, with the exception of the pelvis, is in general more lightly constructed than that of a male.
- *Teeth*—In the case of the remains of a child, an important point for the determination of gender is the uninjured crown of the first permanent incisor of the upper jaw. In certain cases, these can show the gender according to whether their width is especially great (boy) or small (girl).
- *Organs*—The uterus or the prostate gland will indicate gender; however, a uterus exposed to decay can become very fragile, so great care should be taken.

6.4.15   Determination of Age

Teeth are especially significant in the determination of age, which is possible even when only one tooth is available; however, it is necessary to allow for a certain percentage of error in this case (according to some authorities, about 15 to 20%). If a number of teeth are found, the reliability of the determination is increased. The determination of age from teeth is based on the changes the teeth undergo with ageing. These changes are listed below:

1. Wearing down of chewing surfaces (abrasions)
2. Loosening (paradentosis), which is detected from changes in the attachment of the roots
3. Formation of secondary dentin inside the pulp cavities (can also be formed as reaction to disease of the teeth)
4. Deposition of cement on and around points of the roots
5. Degree of transparency of lowest parts of roots (root transparency)
6. Corrosion of root points (root resorption)
7. Closing of root openings, which is of special importance for young individuals because until the teeth are completely formed the size of the root openings is in direct relation to the age

If the body has been completely burned, the crowns of grown-out teeth break up but the roots often remain whole. If the teeth of a child or young person have not erupted, they do not get broken up. The discovery of teeth that have not erupted or of remains of deciduous teeth thus gives a direct indication of age. When more than one tooth is found, it is important to determine whether the remains come from one or more individuals. DNA can be used for this purpose.

The roof of the cranium gives information that is especially valuable for the determination of the age of an individual; the sutures (ossification lines) are extremely significant. With newborn babies and children up to 3 years of age, the sutures are straight or slightly curved. After this, they begin to become saw-edged in form, growing slowly into the forms typical of the adult. With increasing age, the sutures grow together more and more, finally disappearing entirely; those of a woman, however, join up considerably later than those of a man. The appearance and degree of fusion give an opportunity of estimating an age up to 50 years old.

If the cranium is exposed to great heat, the sutures split up, but if they have grown together completely, the cracks resulting from the heat may take a new path. To some extent, this circumstance makes possible an estimation of age even from small portions of the roof of a cranium. The thickness of the roof of the cranium and also the character of the outside and inside parts of the walls and the intermediate parts give information that may be used as a guide for determination of the age of an individual.

The form of the wedge bone part of the inner ear differs in children and adults. This part is already formed at the fifth month after conception. The epiphyses at the ends of the long bones fuse with the diaphyses at fixed stages in the development of the skeleton. This occurs when the increase in length of the particular limb is complete; therefore, it is important for the determination of age to note whether this calcification has occurred and to what extent.

6.4.16   Length of Body

The approximate body length of an individual may be determined from the skeleton or a part of it, assuming that some of the longer bones of the limbs (femur, fibula, tibia, humerus, radius, and ulna) are found. The length of some of these is measured, after which the body length is calculated with the aid of formulae and tables developed by anthropologists. The values given by the tables represent the length of the skeleton and should be increased by an inch or so to allow for other tissues and to give approximately correct value for body height.

6.4.17   Hair Colour

Hair is very resistant to change providing it has not been exposed to fire, but it may often be difficult to find at the scene of a discovery when the body has changed greatly. Generally, only the hair of the head—more rarely hair from other parts of the body—can be used as a basis for estimating hair colour as required for a description. Great caution should be exercised, however. Surprising changes in the colour of hair may have taken place after even a comparatively short time, depending on the character of the soil and other such factors.

6.5   Identification in Mass Disasters

In occurrences of a catastrophic nature in which a large number of people are killed, such as terrorist incidents, rail and airplane accidents, major fires and explosions, the collapse of a building, accidents at sea, or other natural disasters, the work of identification must be organised as quickly as possible and carried out in such a way that there is no danger of faulty identification of the human remains. It is not only for sentimental considerations that accurate identification is essential. Legal requirements for proof of death must be satisfied. Issues concerning pension rights, the payment of insurance, and estate matters depend on the correct identification of the dead. In addition, consideration of religious beliefs and the psychological health of victims' families is a major consideration in mass casualty situations.

If available, it is important to obtain a list showing all persons who may have been killed. In some commercial transportation accidents, this can be obtained from the passenger manifest list. When that information is available, the task of identification is relatively easy as long as the victims are not badly mutilated or burned or the bodies have not undergone any considerable amount of decomposition. When that information is not available, such as in mass fatality incidents such as 9/11, the task becomes much more difficult.

There is wide variation in the way in which countries deal with the management of mass disasters and mass disaster victim identification, but in general primary responses operate at a local level, with national and regional involvement often being restricted to coordination and assistance. Most countries today have prepared for mass disaster scenarios, developed procedural manuals, defined responsibilities, and stockpiled supplies for such an event. Those who are faced with a major event for the first time would do well to call for assistance because the task may be enormous and beyond smaller agencies' resources and readiness.

INTERPOL publishes a *Disaster Victim Identification Guide,* which is available to member countries and contains excellent assistance in the form of a guide to the investigation and a set of forms to use in recording findings. The guide covers the very practical aspects of scene management, recovery and evidence collection, methods of identification, data collection from living relatives, and evidence collection from the deceased.

The basic principles of scene investigation apply to mass disaster scenes, beginning with ensuring the safety and protection of people by taking measures to prevent or reduce further danger, the provision of first-aid to victims, and implementation of personal security measures. These steps are followed by procedures to secure the physical scene, before proceeding to its investigation. The overall response will take account of the nature of the mass disaster, and victim identification will run alongside cause and perpetrator investigations in situations such as aircraft crashes and terrorist bomb attacks.

When disaster response forces have arrived at the disaster site, the first step is to obtain an overview of the scope of the disaster. An official organisation or agency must assume command of the operation as a whole in order to ensure effective coordination of personnel and material resources. The agency may be local, supported by national and international resources, or it may be national, supported by local and other resources. In most cases of disaster, it will be a police agency that assumes command responsibility for the operation as a whole. An exception is in the case of national emergencies in which responsibility may be assumed by a government ministry or a terror attack when military or national defence agencies have overall responsibility.

Scene evaluation will include:

- The area and extent of the scene
- State of the corpses
- Evaluation of the likely duration of the investigation

- Medicolegal institute able to respond, including its proximity and whether there is a need for special equipment at the scene
- Methodology to remove the bodies (composition and number of teams)
- Transportation of corpses
- Storage

The work of identification should preferably be done by groups, which generally consist of teams made up of a pathologist, dentist, fingerprint examiner, DNA analyst, and law enforcement representative with experience in the identification of dead bodies. The group also needs assistants varying in number for each particular case. The identification group should be present when the first measures of rescue and clearance are started at the scene of the catastrophe and, as bodies are found, they should take charge of them. If the group cannot be organised or does not reach the scene in time, a suitable police officer should be assigned to take the first steps in securing the bodies.

As with any possible crime scene, documentation of the site and the scene must be done. When possible, all items should be photographed. Those present at a major scene should expect a degree of chaos until adequate resources can be assembled. Maintaining the health, safety, and psychological well-being of personnel who staff a major disaster is an important consideration for those charged with coordination of the investigation and recovery efforts.

The record is made during the course of the work. When the body of a victim is found, it is given a number that is written on a card affixed to the body. Any objects found beside the body are collected in a bag that is also numbered, but the contents should not necessarily be presumed to be personal effects belonging to the deceased. When possible, each victim and object should be provided with a label giving more detailed information, such as who found it, the time of discovery, and a statement of the nature of the location, preferably in the form of a simple sketch. The objects are entered in the record in succession in such a way that others can easily refer to them, and the position of the object in relation to the body is recorded. Photographing should be done thoroughly. The photographing and sketching must be considered a precaution that may possibly be of use in the work of identification. The numbered places of discovery are also marked on the sketches. If parts of bodies are found, they are given new numbers and placed in bags. As victims are found and the proper measures are taken, the bodies are wrapped in sheets or placed into body bags so that loose objects cannot fall out and get lost. The bodies are then taken to a suitable place where the work of identification is to be done.

When the scene of a catastrophe is so large that the bodies can neither be collected by the identification group alone nor protected by police personnel working under the group, then the victims must first be brought to the identification point by suitable means. There, each body or, more likely, portion of a body is given a number and labelled with an accurate statement of the position where it was discovered, time of handing over, and name of the person who found and transported it. If possible, the stretcher bearers who collect the bodies should be given instructions as to their activities so as to avoid any mistakes.

Under all conditions, the scene of the catastrophe should be cordoned off as quickly as possible, and the authority in charge should see that unauthorised persons do not take part in the rescue work. Stretcher-bearer patrols should be under the command of a specially selected supervisor, preferably a police officer. Relatives of deceased persons should not be allowed to take part in this work because they may choose an unidentified body that they think they recognise but is possibly a different individual. The INTERPOL guide includes advice on establishing family support centres.

When the scene has been thoroughly searched, all bodies and remains have been found, and all objects assumed to belong to victims have been collected, the work of identification can start. The record made during the first stage should be written up in a clean copy or transferred to an electronic database, and the photographs should be arranged in order as quickly as possible so they will be available for reference together with the sketches.

During the time taken for the rescue and clearing up, and before the actual identification is started, the police authorities should obtain information on the number of persons involved and a listing of their names, occupations, and dates of birth. If it is anticipated that the identification will be difficult, then statements that can assist the identification must supplement the list of names. These are obtained from the relatives of the deceased or from persons who know them sufficiently well. In an especially difficult case, the following information should be obtained:

1. Description, preferably in the form normally used by the police
2. Any illnesses, operations, or bone fractures (possibly x-ray photographs)
3. Fingerprints, if they have previously been taken for any reason
4. Photographs (simple amateur pictures are better than retouched studio portraits)
5. Dental history
6. Description of garments and shoes (if possible, samples of cloth and place of purchase, make, size, markings, repairs, etc.)
7. Description of personal belongings that might be presumed to be the deceased's clothes, together with rings, jewellery, and watch; also, as necessary, a statement about what would have been near the deceased (e.g., briefcase, handbag, travelling case)
8. Known DNA exemplars

Thus, when the work of identification begins, all bodies, portions of bodies, and objects have been numbered in sequence. This numbering is preliminary and should be employed only as an aid to identification.

Identification begins with the least injured bodies or with those that offer the best possibilities of quick and satisfactory identification. One of the police officers in the identification group keeps the record. In the work of identification, the bodies should lie on a suitable table or bench. All loose objects in or on the clothing or on the body are recorded and then placed in bags.

If any identifying documents such as a passport, visitor's card, driver's license, identification card, or other similar items are found on a body, and they agree with statements obtained regarding a person supposed to have been killed, then the identification may be considered complete. However, in some cases identifying documents have been found on a body belonging to another person killed at the same time; when the bodies were thrown against one another, the documents were transferred from the owner to another person. If information regarding the dead person has been obtained, it must be compared with the body to confirm the identification. The first body examined is given the number one, after which numbers are given to the bodies in succession as subsequent measures of identification are taken. The bags containing the belongings are given the same numbers as the bodies to which they belong, and clothes are bundled together and given corresponding numbers. Statements regarding injuries and assumed cause of death are made in the usual manner. The pathologist decides whether these statements should be made in a separate report or included in the report of the identification.

As the bodies are identified, they are put to one side. Clothes and belongings are placed next to the bodies. It is safest not to allow a body to be removed before all the others have been identified so that any mistakes can be rectified in time. When the deceased are placed in coffins, the work should be supervised and controlled by at least two members of the identification group. The coffins are marked with number and name.

The work of identification then proceeds to the more difficult cases and the identification group must rely more on and refer to statements that have been obtained. In due course, it can become easier to work on the principle of elimination; however, this method cannot be employed except in cases where information on the number of victims and their names is absolutely reliable and the statements obtained are detailed and reliable. For the most difficult cases, the group must work according to the methods described in the preceding sections of this chapter. An effective disaster management system, such as that described in the INTERPOL guide, is a must.

In cases of a large number of victims, the police or other authorities should not allow the body of any victim to be removed before the identification group has been organised and arrives at the scene. Even if, at an early stage, a particular body can be identified with absolute certainty, its removal should not be permitted. The identification group has the responsibility of identifying all the victims. If this group deals only with the difficult cases, it could be under the suspicion that the bodies released earlier might have been wrongly identified, which could eliminate the possibility of certain identification of the last, more difficult cases.

6.6 Summary

By definition, "Personal Identity" addresses the question WHO in the investigative star. Implying as it does the investigation of a dead human being, personal identity is potentially one of the most impactful situations that the CSI will encounter. All of the techniques described in this book can be brought to bear, with results that will vary from confirmed and unique identification of the individual, to information in keeping with the assignment of an identity but not conclusive, to being unable to identify the body.

Trace Evidence and Miscellaneous Materials

7.1 Introduction

Most crime scene examiners are aware of the Locard exchange principle, usually captured in the phrase, "Every contact leaves a trace." Setting aside the fact that Locard never actually said that, although it is implied in his writings, the principle has had negative as well as positive consequences in forensic science. On the positive side, it is a reminder that the purpose of much of forensic science is to investigate associations between people and places and people with other people, as part of testing the hypotheses formulated around events at the scene. On the negative side, issues of loss, redistribution, contamination, and lack of reference statistical databases, as well as many questions regarding the integrity of conclusions based on comparison of often limited and ill-defined properties of materials rather than on showing their identity, have led to less and less reliance being placed on the time-consuming and subjective examination of traditional forms of trace evidence.

Over the years, the development of trace evidence focused on the two different meanings of *trace*: (1) a mark, object, or other indication of the existence or passing of something, or, increasingly, (2) a very small quantity, especially one too small to be accurately measured. Sometimes the second meaning seemed more important than the first, as it was difficult for a criminal to be aware of all the traces that could be picked up or transferred and to take actions to eliminate them.

Today, more and more crime scene units and forensic science laboratories have moved away from the traditional areas and concentrated on DNA and fingerprints because of the exquisite sensitivity of detection, the availability of searchable databases that incorporate statistical information, and the fact that the tests themselves point directly to identity. Add to this that in an era of resource restrictions the cost–benefit value of traditional trace evidence is seen to be limited, and in the space of less than 20 years what was the peak of criminalistics evidence is now used less and less.

Despite this trend, awareness of the traditional areas of trace evidence examination is important as they still can provide valuable associative evidence. The main examples are described in this chapter, in many cases with an account of the steps that should be followed in collection, preservation, and analysis. Procedures will vary depending on the practices of the jurisdiction, as well as the availability of equipment and trained and knowledgeable personnel.

When an individual comes into contact with a person or location, certain small and seemingly insignificant exchanges occur. Small items such as fibres, hairs, and assorted microscopic debris may be left by the person or picked up from contact with the environment or another individual. In short, it is a general rule that when someone comes in contact with an environment they will change it in some small way by adding to it or taking something away from it. This broader concept of transfer is why the Locard exchange principle is the basis for trace evidence in criminalistics. The importance of the exchange evidence is that it links suspects to victims or locations. It is physical evidence of contact and, although microscopic, can become a significant part of an investigation.

Case 1

The body of an 18-year-old female was found on the side of a road near Porvoo (a small town about 50 km northeast of Helsinki, Finland). The deceased was completely naked from the waist down, and the upper part of her body was clothed normally. The victim's jeans, stockings, and underwear were bundled on her chest. The technical research team took the clothing of the deceased, fingernail scrapings, head hair and pubic hair combings, and known hair samples. Fibre evidence was found in the victim's hair.

The autopsy determined that the cause of death was strangulation and that the victim had been raped. Semen was found in vaginal and rectal samples collected during the autopsy. The ABO blood group was determined to be A (note that this case occurred prior to the use of DNA typing). The hope of solving the case centred on the fibre evidence, and an hypothesis was made that the fibres must have had something to do with the crime. Eleven brown, uniform, and multicoloured acrylic fibres were found from the combed hair samples. Similar fibres were collected from tape-lift samples taken from the victim's clothes, and about 200 fibres were found on the clothes. With the help of reference samples, it was deduced that these fibres most probably originated from the seat cover of a car. The police were advised that the laboratory was especially interested in brown automobile seat covers made from pile-type material, and that while searching cars they should give special attention to red textiles (Figure 7.1).

From the samples combed from the victim's head hair and pubic hair, two and three viscous fibres were found, respectively, that were unusual in their colour and dying. The victim's clothes yielded 28 similar fibres. In the combed samples, an orange-red woollen fibre was found that was about 3 cm long, and 13 similar fibres were found on the clothes. Because of the number of red-coloured fibres found, it was possible to consider primary transfer. It was assumed that the origin of the fibres must have been from a textile other than clothes worn by the suspect because neither of the fibre types belonged to typical cloth textile fibres (Figure 7.2).

The technical research team examined 12 cars over a 2-month period. They collected seat covers that were a possible match to the fibres on the body, picked hairs and fibres and tape lifts from the seats, and searched for the victim's fingerprints. The extraneous fibre samples taken from the victim did not match the samples taken from these cars. In regard to transfers in the opposite direction, the victim's clothes were white and light blue and made mainly of cotton; therefore, it was pointless to try to collect these types of fibre.

The 13th car to be examined belonged to a person who, 9 years earlier, had been charged with rape but released due to insufficient evidence. The suspect was also a type A secretor. The seat cover material in his car matched the acrylic fibres from the hair and the clothes of the victim. Also, the samples taken from the seat covers contained red-coloured viscous and woollen fibres similar to those found on the samples

Figure 7.1 Discovery of the body at the roadside near Porvoo (top) and close-up of the victim (bottom).

Figure 7.2 The suspect's car.

Figure 7.3 The suspect's home as originally found (top) and after the examination had been completed (bottom). The bottom figure shows the red blanket.

taken from the victim. Thirty-nine samples were taken from the interior textiles in the suspect's residence and also from his clothes. The red viscous fibres proved to be the same as the pillowcase cloth fibres found on the sofa in the living room of the suspect's residence. The red woollen fibres were the same as fibres from a blanket found on the sofa (Figure 7.3).

The samples taken from the victim's hair, pubic hair, fingernail scrapings, and clothes were compared with the fibre samples taken from textile material from the furnishings in the suspect's residence and from his clothes. The victim's hair yielded 13 dark-blue cotton fibre samples; one of the same type was found in the fingernail scrapings. These fibres could not be differentiated from the fibres taken from the suspect's blue trousers. In the clothes of the victim, three thick yellowish-brown V-shaped viscose fibres were found. Their colour, quality, thickness, shape, and size were the same as plush fibres found in a velvet sofa cover in the suspect's residence. The sixth fibre similarity between the samples taken from the victim and samples taken from the suspect's residence was pink acrylic fibre, of which three found in the victim's clothes were similar to fibres on a sweater in the suspect's residence. All the different types of fibres were found in the suspect's car seat cover and clothing.

During the investigation, it was concluded that the victim had not been to the suspect's residence but the suspect's untidy habits transferred the fibres from his residence to his car, which resulted in a secondary transfer. None of these fibres that associated the victim to the suspect were found at the victim's residence, at her mother's home, or on her clothing other than that worn by her at the time that she was attacked.

Polarising light microscopy, fluorescence microscopy, and microspectrophotometry were used in the fibre identification. Fourier transform infrared (FTIR) spectroscopy was used to investigate the brown acrylic fibres. The accused did not confess to the crime but admitted only that the victim had been in his car. He was convicted and sentenced to 10 years on the basis of the evidence produced by the fibre identification.

7.2 Sources of Trace Evidence

7.2.1 Clothing

Clothing is an excellent source of trace evidence. Microscopic and macroscopic substances may cling to clothing by static electricity or become caught in the fabric. Transferred items are not always retained permanently at the point of contact. They can be redistributed from there to other areas of the clothing, some can be lost, and others may be redistributed to other surfaces right from the time of contact. In general, larger items are lost first and the smallest, microscopic ones are retained longest.

After the suspect is apprehended, his or her clothes should be cursorily inspected for obvious physical evidence connected with the crime. If evidence is observed, its location and description should be noted. If possible, the subject should be made to undress while standing on clean wrapping paper. The paper will catch any trace evidence that might fall from the clothing. The clothing should then be collected, tagged, or marked for chain of evidence purposes and packaged in paper bags or other type of breathable evidence bag. Plastic bags should be avoided when packaging clothing because the clothes may mildew. Care should be taken when placing the garments into paper bags; they should never be shaken because that might loosen or dislodge trace evidence. If the clothes are wet or bloodstained, they should first be allowed to air-dry prior to packaging or securely wrapped and immediately taken to a drying facility as described later in this section.

Protective clothing should be worn during the undressing procedure in order to avoid contamination. The protective gloves must be replaced after handling and collecting every single item of clothing. It is especially important to keep the suspect's clothing away from any sources of trace evidence located at the scene. If known samples from the scene have been collected as exemplars, they should never be packaged with the clothing. Similarly, a subject should not be brought to the crime scene while clothed in the same garments worn during the crime. This will stop the argument that any trace evidence found on the clothes was from the visit to the scene while in the custody of the police.

Case 2

Police were called to the scene of a warehouse burglary. The suspects gained entrance by chopping a hole through the roof. Officers at the scene collected samples of roofing tar, wood, and plaster to be used as exemplars for any trace evidence that might be found on the suspects. The suspects were subsequently arrested a short distance from the scene of the crime. They were taken to the police station, and their clothes were examined. Some building materials and tar-like material adhering to their pants in the knee area were noted. The clothes were packaged in paper bags along with known debris specimens collected from the crime scene. When the evidence arrived at the forensic laboratory and was opened, it was discovered that the known material had been thrown into the paper bag along with the clothes. Although building material was found on the pant legs of the suspect's clothing, it was impossible to determine whether the debris came from the crime scene or the exemplars submitted in the paper bag.

When clothing has been collected and packaged in paper bags, it should be submitted to the forensic laboratory for careful examination. When considering traditional types of trace evidence on clothing, we generally think in terms of hairs, fibres, and other debris; however, in light of advances in more sophisticated forensic biology techniques and procedures, investigators should also consider the possibility of detecting small quantities of DNA from clothing and other types of evidence at the crime scene. This is illustrated in a case of aggravated robbery committed at a jewellery store. During the crime, one suspect grabbed the complainant's shirt in the shoulder/neck area. A mixture of DNA including the complainant's DNA profile and an unknown male DNA profile was obtained from the right shoulder of the complainant's shirt (Figure 7.4). The unknown male DNA profile subtracted from the mixture on the shoulder of this shirt hit to a convicted offender in the national US DNA database.

Although some agencies may have equipment to vacuum the garments and send the sweepings to the laboratory, it is preferable to allow the laboratory to conduct the search. In instances in which extremely small items of evidence such as a single hair or fibre might be lost, evidence should be carefully packaged in a test tube, pillbox, or other appropriate container. Naturally, the location of this evidence should be noted and the items appropriately marked for identification.

Figure 7.4 DNA from contact between the perpetrator and victim. (Photograph courtesy of Harris County, Texas, Medical Examiner's Office DNA Laboratory.)

Clothes from murder and assault victims pose other problems for consideration. Trace evidence may be present on the victim's clothes in addition to those of the suspect. These garments, however, may have been removed by other than law enforcement personnel who usually are not knowledgeable about proper collection and preservation of evidence. Problems invariably arise when paramedics or hospital personnel remove clothing during life-threatening emergencies. It is not uncommon for clothing to be cut off the victim with the aim of initiating emergency procedures. Often this results in cutting through bullet holes, tears caused by stabbing, and the like. Frequently, wet, bloodstained garments are rolled up and packaged in a large plastic bag and tightly sealed. In these instances, police and forensic science agencies can do little more than attempt to educate those groups and hope that the potential value of the evidence was not too badly diminished; however, we must always honour the principle that the first priority is the well-being of the injured. Forensic science laboratory personnel should be advised that the victim's clothing was cut off so they can effectively interpret the information in their attempt to reconstruct the crime.

Clothing on deceased victims requires further considerations. Before the victim is undressed, the body should be carefully examined for trace evidence by the investigator, scientist, or pathologist. The clothing should be carefully removed and placed onto clean wrapping paper. In most instances of violent death, the clothes will be wet from blood. The garments should be air-dried prior to packaging. In some situations, a temporary exception to the "do not wrap in plastic" rule may be helpful. Clothing that is totally or partially soaked with blood can be wrapped in plastic for transport to the drying facility. The item should be placed on top of a sheet of plastic, then another sheet placed on top, and the item and its wrappings rolled. This will minimise the spread of blood and prevent contamination of other areas of the clothing.

Caution: This is advisable only when the items are being taken to be dried out and must not be used if they will be left for more than a few hours.

Another exception to the "no plastic" rule is where clothing will be submitted for detection of accelerant traces. Here it must be contained in a non-breathable bag or sealed can to prevent evaporation of the accelerant.

7.2.2 Footwear

Shoes and other footwear are valuable items of evidence. They may have dust, soil, debris, vegetation, bloodstains, or other types of trace evidence on them. In addition to the presence of trace evidence, shoes and other footwear are useful in shoe impression evidence comparison. Figure 7.5 shows the sole of a shoe with a wear defect (left) and the impression left in soil by it (right). Shoes should be individually packaged to avoid cross-contamination. Particular care must be taken when packaging footwear evidence containing clumps of dried soil. Careful examination of the soil might lead to determination of the path that a suspect took. This possibility would be greatly lessened if the soil became dislodged and pulverised in transit to the laboratory.

7.2.3 Evidence from the Body

Useful trace evidence may be discovered by a careful examination of the suspect or victim's body. Injuries caused by a struggle between the victim and suspect may be noted. Microscopic particles of gunshot residue are often present on the hands, face, or hair of a shooter following discharge of a firearm. Hair is sometimes found on the victim's body

Figure 7.5 The sole of a shoe (left) with a defect shown by the arrow, and the impression left by it in soil (right). (Photographs courtesy of the Forensic Laboratory Services, Royal Canadian Mounted Police.)

in rape cases. Bloodstains on a victim or suspect's body are not uncommon in assault and murder cases. A close examination of the head, ears, fingernail scrapings, and hands may yield traces of debris from a burglary, assault, or other crime in which there was contact between the subject and another person or the crime scene.

7.2.4 Trace Evidence from Guns

7.2.4.1 Trace Metal Detection

The trace metal detection test (TMDT) has been used with varied results. The solution is sprayed on the subject's hands and observed under ultraviolet light. The presence of dark areas indicates the location of metal. Different metals give somewhat different colours. The TMDT is commonly used to test whether a subject recently held a metal object, such as a weapon. In the case of a handgun, it is sometimes possible to see the location of the trigger on the index finger and the location of the strap, the metal frame that touches the palm. The drawback with the test is that results are not always consistent or predictable. We live in a highly technological society and come into contact with metal objects every day, so some amount of background trace metals will always be present on our hands. In addition, tests with the method have shown that holding a handgun with a metal frame and test firing it does not always produce a positive trace metal detection test results. Apparently, the amount of perspiration on an individual's hands may change the results of the test. Also, if a suspect is in an environment in which there is metal, grasping an object may also result in a positive test. Washing or any kind of mechanical motion of the hands naturally lowers the likelihood of a positive result.

7.2.4.2 Gunshot Residue Analysis

If the investigator's purpose in using the TMDT is to determine whether a suspect recently fired a weapon, other test procedures are available. Gunshot residue (GSR) analysis may be considered, although the TMDT may still provide investigatory leads.

7.2.5   Other Objects as Sources of Trace Evidence

Trace evidence may be present on tools and weapons, as well as other objects. When possible, the items should be carefully wrapped to protect the material on them. This may be done best by placing a paper bag secured by cellophane tape over smaller objects. If the instrument bears larger particles that may be lost, the particles should be carefully removed and placed in appropriately labelled containers. Tools used in burglaries may contain traces of building material, metal shavings, paint, and so forth. These items may be used to establish a connection between the tool and the location and corroborate the results of the toolmark comparison. Similarly, a weapon such as a knife may have paint, hairs, or fibres present that may prove to be useful evidence. Figure 7.6 illustrates this from the examination of a screwdriver used in a burglary case, where a streak of paint was transferred from the scene to the blade of the screwdriver. Larger items may be fruitful sources of trace evidence—for example, a vehicle from a hit-and-run accident. Naturally, objects of this size may not be routinely brought to the laboratory; however, a careful examination in the field can recover items such as hairs, fibres, skin, and blood.

Microscopic evidence presents more of a challenge than a problem to modern crime laboratories. Use of low-power and high-power light microscopes and sophisticated instruments, such as scanning electron microscopes and various types of spectrographic tools, makes the examination and characterisation of minute items of evidence commonplace. A far greater problem than size is quantity of material. Particles and material collected from

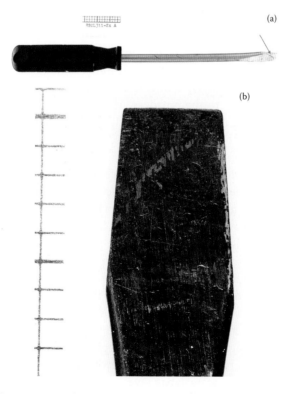

Figure 7.6 (a) Screwdriver seized from a suspect in a burglary case. (b) Close-up of the blade of the screwdriver showing the presence of a small amount of red paint, which matched the paint and the breaking and entering location. (Photographs courtesy of the Forensic Laboratory Services, Royal Canadian Mounted Police.)

vacuum sweepings and careful searches of evidence can yield thousands of microscopic items to be examined. Only patience and the examiner's expertise can ultimately determine the nature and utility of these collected items, as the following case shows.

Case 3*

On 27 March, 2003, in rural Darke County, Ohio, a married couple was shot to death execution-style while asleep in their bed. The only other occupant in the house at the time was their 4-year-old great-grandson, who discovered the bodies. The boy attempted to call emergency services; however, the phone lines had been cut. Knowing that he needed help, he ran nearly a mile to a church where he attended preschool. He told the teacher that his grandparents were "melting." The victims had been shot at point-blank range with a 12-gauge shotgun.

It appeared to the investigators that the murderer had intended the crime scene to look like a robbery; however, a deposit bag containing a large amount of cash remained undisturbed in the kitchen, and no jewellery or other valuables appeared to be missing. A basement window had been forced open and partial footwear impressions were casted from adjacent soil. Recovered from the head of the bed was a makeshift silencer composed of a quilting material. This material was wrapped in a cone-shaped fashion and exhibited masking tape on one end and black powder on the other.

Over the course of the following week, investigators eliminated a number of suspects and began to focus on the son/stepson of the victims. The suspect's girlfriend informed investigators that the suspect had left for work exceptionally early the day of the murders. An acquaintance of the suspect had also come forward and claimed that the suspect had contacted him shortly before the murders about acquiring an unregistered firearm. Investigators compared the suspect's mobile phone records with local ads listing firearms for sale. They located a man who claimed to have sold a 12-gauge shotgun to the suspect just days prior to the murders. This man still had the firearm box that included the shotgun serial number, but investigators did not have a murder weapon for comparison. Subsequent interviews and a search of the suspect's house failed to reveal a shotgun or any probative evidence.

Five days after the murders, an extensive search of nearly 30 miles of roads, bridges, and waterways between the crime scene and the suspect's place of employment was conducted. The search was unsuccessful until, on a hunch, one investigator and a Darke County sheriff's deputy drove to a bridge over the Stillwater River. In the shallow water right off the side of the bridge, they recovered a 12-gauge shotgun with a piece of masking tape on the barrel. About a mile downstream, a large black trash bag was found snagged on a tree branch and was recovered. The shotgun and trash bag were taken to the Miami Valley Regional Crime Laboratory for examination. Among the items recovered from the bag were two spent shotgun shells, a roll of masking tape, a pair of black athletic shoes, latex gloves, a package of quilting material, and clothing items.

Trace evidence examination of masking tape pieces recovered from the makeshift silencer at the scene, the barrel of the shotgun recovered from the river and the roll of masking tape recovered from the trash bag revealed numerous fracture matches connecting the first 9 feet of tape off a new roll, shown in Figure 7.7(a) and (b). It was concluded

---

* This case is courtesy of Suzanne Noffsinger, Trace Evidence Examiner, Miami Valley Regional Crime Laboratory, Dayton, Ohio.

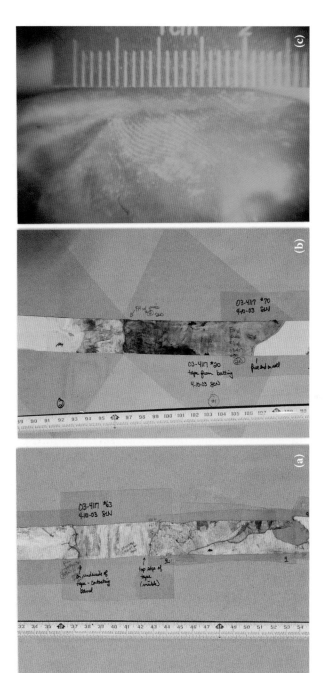

Figure 7.7 Trace evidence in the Darke County murder. (a) Masking tape from a roll found in the trash bag; (b) tape from the silencer on the shotgun, showing matching tear patterns; and (c) initial photograph of the partial latent print on the latex glove found in the trash bag, as observed with a reflected ultraviolet imaging system (RUVIS) prior to processing.

that the tape from the silencer and the shotgun barrel originated from the roll of tape in the trash bag. Also, the quilting material recovered from the bag was the same composition as that used in the makeshift silencer. The shotgun was processed by the Firearms and Toolmark Section in an attempt to restore the obliterated serial number. Five of the eight digits in the serial number were successfully raised. These digits matched the corresponding numbers on the box obtained from the seller. Additionally, the spent shell casings from the bag were found to be the same brand as those recovered from the victims at autopsy. The athletic shoes recovered from the trash bag were compared to the partial footwear impressions recovered from the scene and were found to be the same tread design. It was noted that these shoes were approximately two sizes smaller than those worn by the suspect.

At this point, many of the items from the bag could be linked back to the crime scene but nothing could be directly linked to the suspect. That changed upon examination of the latex gloves by a latent print examiner. Remarkably, one of the gloves revealed a partial fingerprint under ultraviolet light. This partial print was intact despite immersion of the evidence in water for nearly a week. This anomaly was likely due to the deposition of an oily residue on the suspect's hands prior to donning the glove. Comparison of this partial latent print revealed it matched a portion of the suspect's right index finger, his trigger finger (Figure 7.7(c)).

The motive in this case was determined to be financial. The suspect was losing his home to foreclosure and he stood to inherit his father's property if his father and stepmother were deceased. The suspect, age 25, was convicted on all charges and was sentenced to life in prison without parole.

7.3 Collection and Preservation of Trace Evidence

As with all evidence, the investigator or crime scene technician must be concerned with various legal and scientific aspects of collection and preservation of trace materials. In addition to best practice procedures, such as are described in the European Network of Forensic Science Institutes (ENFSI) guidance document for best practice manuals, crime scene examiners will need to follow any legal requirements regarding issues of chain of custody and admissibility of evidence that they collect. Although generally similar, legislations will have some variations between jurisdictions, and examiners must know those that apply to their situation. Scientific requirements depend upon the nature of the evidence collected and the proximity of the laboratory conducting the examinations. It is obvious that if evidence needs to be mailed or sent by a parcel carrier, extraordinary care must be taken to preserve fragile substances properly.

A question sometimes asked is "Is it better to remove an item of trace material from a larger item or leave it alone?" The answer is "It depends!" If a hair, fibre, loose paint chip, or other very small and easily lost item of evidence can reasonably be expected to become dislodged or lost from the item to which it is attached, that smaller item should be removed. On the other hand, if in the investigator's opinion the smaller substance will not be lost, then it should not be handled. It is preferable to submit the entire item with trace evidence attached to it to the laboratory for an examination. Of course, in those instances in which the item is too large or inconvenient to transport, the trace material should be carefully removed, packaged, and sent to the laboratory for examination.

Small items of evidence should always be double packaged. Double packaging means that the evidence should be first placed into an appropriate container and secured. The first container should then be inserted into a larger container. Both containers should be appropriately marked to uniquely identify the item; to indicate the person performing the packaging, the date and time, and the case number; and to provide a very brief description of the item. If the inner container should inadvertently open, the outer one will contain the evidence. As an example of double packaging, consider a hypothetical case. Suppose an investigator has observed a small fibre on the bumper of a car suspected in a hit-and-run accident. Bringing the car to the laboratory or a location where it could be placed on a lift and raised for a thorough examination of the underside of the vehicle would in theory be the best way to conduct an examination. Assume, though, that this is not possible. The detective still wants to collect the fibre for comparison with the victim's clothing. The fibre should be carefully removed and placed in a test tube, small envelope, pillbox, paper bundle, or any other appropriate package. The inner package would be marked with the item's unique identification mark or number, the officer's initials, date, time, case number, and so on and would then be placed into a second, or outer, package. This outer package would also be appropriately marked.

Control or known samples should be collected wherever possible. The investigator should make every attempt to collect a sufficient quantity of known material to be submitted with the items in question. The known exemplars must never be packaged with the questioned samples. This separation is necessary to avoid cross-contamination of unknown specimens by known specimens.

Almost all types of trace evidence can be placed in a class or group (i.e., identified). Only in rare cases is trace evidence of the type discussed in this chapter capable of conclusively indicating a specific source or origin. A single fibre cannot be shown to have come from a unique garment, nor a clump of dirt from a specific location. Does this mean that trace evidence is of no value? On the contrary, because of its usefulness as circumstantial evidence, trace evidence may often be the sole means of corroborating testimonial evidence in a case.

7.4 Examples of Trace Evidence

7.4.1 Building Materials

Building materials of a wide variety may be encountered in burglary cases. Materials such as stucco, cement, brick, mortar, plaster, plasterboard, window glass, wood, and paint constitute evidence generally considered as building materials. This type of evidence could be found on the clothing of burglary suspects, in their cuffs, pockets, and shoes. Another possible location for this type of debris is on tools used to break into a location. How far to go in identifying and collecting such evidence will have to be considered at the point of developing a scene examination strategy. For example, items suspected of containing building material debris could be carefully packaged and submitted along with appropriate exemplars to the forensic science laboratory, but it may be that better evidence is available from fingerprints or DNA.

The investigator should carefully examine the crime scene to ascertain the nature of the trace evidence that may be worth collecting and analysing. In breaking-and-entering cases, the point of entry or any other location indicating damage should be examined for fingerprints and blood. If none is found, exemplars of building material could be collected. If toolmarks are present at the point of entry, samples of building materials should not be collected from the area of the toolmark, but rather adjacent to the mark, if at all. Furthermore, if an area is to be cut out, particular care must be taken not to cut through the toolmark.

In cases of building material that shows indications of tampering at several locations, it is necessary to collect known specimens of the material in question from each of the damaged areas. This is important because the composition of the building material may vary from site to site. It is very important to package each item of evidence separately, properly marking the package and noting the location where the specimen was collected.

Tools may be useful sources of building material evidence. Bits of paint, plaster, wood, and even glass may become attached to the tool. In addition to the debris they may contain, tools are useful for toolmark comparisons and for physically matching broken pieces of the tool. If building material is noticed at the end of a tool, the area should be carefully wrapped so as not to dislodge the evidence. If the item is too large to be transported, the trace material can be carefully removed from it by scraping with a clean tool such as a scalpel blade onto a clean sheet of paper. The paper is then folded and placed in an envelope. Both paper and envelope should be properly marked.

The interior or the boot of a suspect's vehicle should be searched for the presence of building materials. Vacuum sweepings may be taken for a later search of debris. Clothing is an especially good place to find building materials. The clothes should be collected from the suspect as promptly as possible to minimise any loss of evidence.

Physical, chemical, and microscopic means can characterise building materials. In most cases, building material evidence can only demonstrate class characteristics and cannot be shown to be unique to a specific source. As with other evidence of this type, it has some value as corroborative evidence.

7.4.2 Safe Insulation and Asbestos

Although asbestos is no longer permitted for use as insulation, it may be present in older buildings and some safes. It can be identified microscopically. Various types of materials are used in fire-resistant safes to prevent the contents from burning. Some common materials used are diatomaceous earth, vermiculite, and cement. These materials may readily become deposited on a safe burglar in the course of opening the safe. Examination of a suspect's clothing, shoes, and tools may yield safe insulation, which can be identified microscopically and chemically. Expertise in recognising the types of insulation used by various manufacturers may allow the analyst to make an educated guess, useful for an investigative lead.

7.4.3 Paint

Paint evidence is frequently recovered in hit-and-run accidents, burglaries, and forced-entry cases. In some cases, it is possible to show conclusively that the paint came from a specific location if the chips are large enough and the edges can be fitted together in jigsaw puzzle fashion. In most instances, however, only class characteristics can be demonstrated. Paint and other protective coatings such as lacquer, enamel, and varnish can be identified by physical and chemical properties. Physical characteristics such as colour, layering, weathering, and texture are useful in characterising this evidence. Chemical properties such as solubility and composition can indicate the type of paint and identify the pigmentation and fillers used in the manufacturing process.

Even if a vehicle cannot be identified as to manufacturer, known and questioned specimens can be compared by examining chemical and physical properties. The best that can be stated is that the paints from the control and questioned sources are consistent; that is, they could have come from the vehicle in question or any similarly painted vehicle. In some instances, vehicles and residences that have been painted and repainted many times may have so many layers of paint that upon examination the probability is very high that the two specimens share a common source. This, however, will depend on the specific case as well as the expertise of the analyst.

When standard specimens of paint are taken from automobiles or a door or window in a forced-entry case is collected, the specimen should be taken as close to the area of damage as possible to lessen the possibility that an area further away from the location of interest was painted differently. In burglary cases, it is particularly important not to collect a standard or control paint sample from the pry area. The specific area of the jemmy or pry will contain a toolmark that may be compared with a pry bar or other tool found at a later time. (See Chapter 9 for a discussion of toolmarks.)

When collecting paint samples in a hit-and-run investigation involving two vehicles, a total of four paint samples should be collected and separately packaged. From vehicle A, collect a sample from the point of impact that contains a paint transfer from vehicle B. Also, collect a standard paint sample that shows no damage but is adjacent to the damaged area. Similarly, two samples should be collected from vehicle B, one from the damaged area and a second from the undamaged area to be used as a standard.

If dislodged paint chips are present in the damaged area of the vehicle, they should be carefully collected and packaged to avoid breaking. They may be able to be fitted with other, larger paint chips collected from the scene of the accident or the second vehicle.

To collect a known paint sample from a vehicle, hold a folded piece of paper and tap the side of the vehicle with a pocketknife or similar device. This will dislodge some paint and allow it to fall into the paper. Care should be taken not to separate the outer layer of paint from the undercoating. Avoid using cellophane tape to collect the paint samples. It is best to place the paint sample into folded paper or a small box with a good seal. Small envelopes are not advised for this type of evidence because the seams of the envelope located in the bottom corners are generally not sealed. Paint chips placed in envelopes usually fall out through the small, unsealed space. Small plastic bags should also be avoided because they have a static electric charge that makes it extremely difficult to remove the chips once the evidence is received at the laboratory. Paint on tools should not be removed. It is preferable to wrap the end of the tool carefully so as not to dislodge the paint and submit the tool to the laboratory with the paint intact.

Case 4

A hit-and-run vehicle had apparently struck a parked car. The police, however, suspected that the complainant had struck a steel pole. Paint chips from the vehicle and base of the pole were examined. Not only did the paint from the pole match the transfer to the car, but also a physical match was made of the chip (Figure 7.8, left) from the pole and the chip (Figure 7.8, right) from the car.

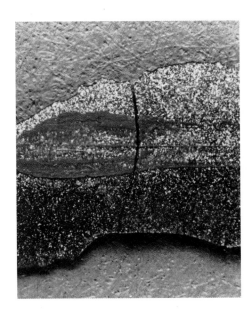

Figure 7.8 Comparison of paint in a hit-and-run between a car and a steel pole. A physical match was made of the chip from the pole (left) and the chip from the car (right). (Photograph courtesy of Centre of Forensic Sciences, Toronto, Canada.)

7.4.4 Metals and Rust

Filings, shavings, and other metal particles can easily be identified chemically or spectrographically. It is possible to make a comparative analysis of a known and questioned metal sample that can show class characteristics. Metal filings located in the jaws of pipe wrenches are fairly common sources of this type of evidence. The wrench is used as a burglary tool by placing it onto a doorknob. Metal filings present in the teeth can be compared to those from the doorknob. Rust stains may sometimes be confused with bloodstains; however, rust will not give a positive response to the various presumptive tests available for screening for blood.

Case 5

In the case of an alleged jailbreak attempt, the investigator wanted to know whether the inmate had used a hacksaw blade on his leg chains (Figure 7.9). When the crime was reenacted, a magnet was able to pick up numerous metal particles from the clothing of the investigator, whose hand was also slightly injured from using the blade. None of this evidence was found on the inmate, calling into question the hypothesis that he had tried to escape on his own.

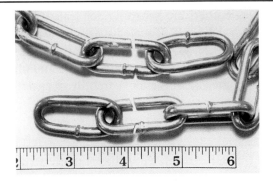

Figure 7.9 Links in the leg chains showing hacksaw cuts. (Photograph courtesy of Los Angeles County Sheriff's Department, Los Angeles, CA.)

The following more extensive case example illustrates an unusual instance where detection of metals produced vital evidence.

Case 6

A 13-year-old boy, evidently quite bright, decided to poison his mother slowly with mercury. He collected enough mercury by breaking into a number of homes in the neighbourhood with a 17-year-old friend and removing the mercury in their thermostat switches. He may have read that mercury salts are highly toxic and mistook this to mean that elemental mercury and table salt together are highly toxic. Whatever the reason, he placed the mercury in a glass salt shaker along with table salt, shook the contents to break the mercury into fine droplets and left the shaker to be used by his mother (Figure 7.10, left). The forensic science laboratory was requested to show that the shaker had been used to dispense the mercury. The lid of the shaker was examined using a scanning electron microscope (SEM) with an energy-dispersive x-ray spectroscopy (EDX) detector. This combination allowed the operator to magnify an image of the object and determine its elemental composition. The lid of the salt shaker was made of plastic coated with nickel and chromium to give it a shiny appearance. The area around the holes in the shaker's lid was examined for traces of mercury (Figure 7.10, right). Using SEM, one fine droplet of elemental mercury, clinging to the nickel plating at one of the holes, was found and identified as mercury by the EDX detector.

Figure. 7.10 A glass salt shaker used by a boy in an attempt to poison his mother (left). One of the holes of the shaker was photographed using scanning electron microscopy (top right). The magnification clearly shows the droplet of mercury (bottom right). (Photographs courtesy of Centre of Forensic Sciences, Toronto, Canada.)

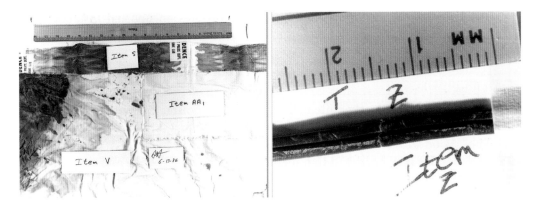

Figure 7.11 The match between the strips of cloth from the scene and the sheet from the house of the suspect (left) and that between the speaker wires (right). (Photographs courtesy of the Crime Laboratory Section of the Detroit Police Department, Detroit, MI.)

Case 7

The bodies of two teenage girls were discovered with multiple gunshot wounds. One of the girls had been bound with electrical speaker wire and gagged and covered with bedding. The bedding was a sheet with several strips of cloth missing. When a search of the suspect's house was conducted, several strips of cloth were found that matched the sheet from the scene. Pieces of speaker wire from the house matched the wire from the scene (see Figure 7.11).

7.4.5 Textiles and Fibres

Fragments of cloth may become evidence in a wide variety of cases. Torn fabrics have been examined in murder cases in which the victim was tied and gagged with torn fabric, in burglary cases in which a suspect left a small torn piece of clothing caught at the point of entry, and in hit-and-run cases in which torn clothing was left on the undercarriage of the suspect's vehicle. Fragments of textile evidence may yield class as well as individual characteristics. A portion of fabric may be physically fitted into another piece of fabric, thereby proving a common source. A number of physical, chemical, and microscopic characteristics of textiles can be used for comparison purposes. Properties such as colour, type of cloth, dye, direction of fibre twist, and thread count are useful in characterising the evidence.

When a fragment of fabric is found during the course of a crime scene search, its location should be noted, indicated in a crime scene diagram, and photographed. As with other items of trace evidence, it is preferable not to remove the fabric from the object to which it is attached. If this is not possible, the fabric should be packaged in a clean container properly labelled with the appropriate chain-of-custody information. Fragments of fabric found at a point of entry may be useful as investigative leads. They may suggest looking for damaged clothing of a particular type.

Investigators may overlook fibre evidence because of its extremely small size compared to fabric evidence. Five types of textile fibres can be encountered as evidence: animal fibres, such as wool; vegetable fibres, such as cotton; synthetic fibres, such as polyester, nylon, rayon, etc.; mineral fibres, such as glass wool; and blends of synthetic and natural fibres, the most common of which are polyester and cotton. Fibre evidence may be transferred by one person's clothing coming into contact with another's or from articles such as blankets, carpet, upholstery, and so forth. Fibres may be located on clothing, in fingernail scrapings, on hit-and-run vehicles, at point of entry, and on hair covered by knit hats.

Transferred fibres collected from the clothing, bodies, or objects associated with the victim or scene should be carefully labelled and kept, as the fabrics from which they originated will not change over time, apart from possible fading of dyes.

Case 8

In a 4-month period between October 1977 and February 1978, the nude bodies of 10 girls and young women between the ages of 12 and 21 were found dumped on hillsides in Los Angeles. All had been raped, tortured, and strangled. One of the victims found lying at the side of a road had a small tuft of fibre on her left wrist. Fibres were subsequently collected from a chair found in the suspect's home almost 2 years after the murders and compared. The suspects—Angelo Buono, a 48-year-old auto upholsterer, and his cousin, a 32-year-old former security guard named Kenneth Bianchi—posed as police officers and "arrested" young women, who were then raped and sodomised and sometimes tortured before being slowly strangled to death. Fibres from one of the murders linked the victim to the assailants' home. A Monsanto Cadon fibre made only between 1968 and 1974 and a second, rare modified "Y" fibre produced by Rohm and Haas for a short period of time were important evidence in the trial. The defendants were found guilty of nine counts of murder and sentenced to life imprisonment without the possibility of parole (see Figures 7.12, 7.13, and 7.14).

Figure 7.12 The body of one of the victims, found at the roadside. (Photograph courtesy of Los Angeles Police Department, Los Angeles, CA.)

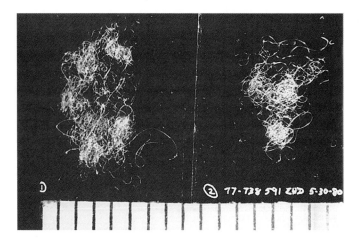

Figure 7.13 Tuft of fibres found on the left wrist of the victim. (Photograph courtesy of Los Angeles Police Department, Los Angeles, CA.)

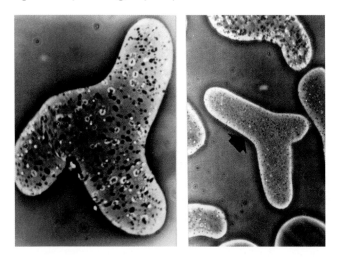

Figure 7.14 Monsanto Cadon fibre (left) and "Y" fibre produced by Rohm and Haas (right) that were present in the scene and suspect's home samples. (Photographs courtesy of Los Angeles Police Department, Los Angeles, CA.)

Removal of fibres from other objects is best done at the forensic laboratory. If this is not possible, fibre evidence can be removed by using forceps or cellophane tape, or by vacuum sweeping. Of the three procedures, the tape method is probably the best. A length of tape about 10 cm long is held between the thumb and forefinger of each hand and dabbed over the surface to be sampled. Alternatively, the length of tape is joined end-to-end, forming a circle with the sticky side of the tape on the outside. The hand is inserted into the centre of the tape circle and the sticky side of the tape is pressed on the item of interest. After sampling, the tape is placed sticky side down on a microscope slide for submission to the laboratory. The procedure has its advantage in that it only collects surface material, whereas vacuum sweeping collects huge quantities of debris and forceps may miss many items of trace evidence.

The laboratory can determine the type of fibre and whether or not it is similar to the control fibre specimen. It is not possible, with fibre evidence, to state with complete certainty that it came from one and only one source because most garments and textiles used today are mass produced. It is usually not possible to determine if a specific sample came from the garment in question or from another garment of similar manufacture.

7.4.6 Buttons

Buttons come in a very wide range of sizes and patterns; only in exceptional cases is it possible to match a button with the buttons of a particular garment. When a button is torn off, generally the thread and sometimes a piece of fabric may be present. If exemplars of the sewing thread and the garment are available for comparison, a more definitive conclusion about the source of the button may be made. If a piece of broken button is discovered, it is possible to match the broken piece physically with another portion of the button. This type of evidence can lead to a conclusive statement about the source of the evidence. Figure 7.15 shows a button found at a burglary scene (left) compared with one found on the suspect's jacket (centre). A photomicrograph (right) shows manufacturing marks on each indicating common class characteristics.

7.4.7 Cordage and Rope

Pieces of string or rope are sometimes found at crime scenes. If they were used to tie up a victim, the knots should not be untied; rather, the rope should be cut and tied back together with string. The knots present in the rope may provide useful evidence. Tied knots must be carefully examined and documented, as these can bring substantial knowledge to the case. The fibres of the rope and string may provide evidence such as DNA and extraneous fibres, and the variety of types of knots themselves are many and very different and may tell us something about the person who made them. Knots have been developed over centuries in different settings of work and recreation, such as sailing, scouting, and transport. There are differences in the way that the same type of knot is formed in different countries, or even within a country, due to factors such as whether or not the person lives close to the sea. So, when a knot is found that appears to be very rare, practices in other parts of the country (or even in the world) or in any particular professions have to be considered, as they may provide a natural and logical explanation for the way the knot has been tied.

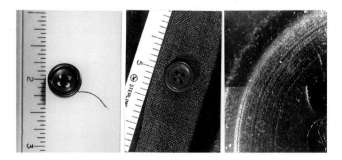

Figure 7.15 A button found at a burglary scene (left) compared with one found on the suspect's jacket (centre). A photomicrograph (right) shows manufacturing marks indicating common class characteristics. (Photographs courtesy of Orange County Sheriff–Coroner, Santa Ana, CA.)

Rope and cordage evidence can be compared with exemplars for similarities. Properties that can be examined include the material from which the cordage is manufactured, the number of strands, direction of the twist in the rope, colour, diameter, and weight per unit of length. All of these properties taken together will allow the examiner to determine whether the material is of a similar manufacture. Only in very rare cases in which a microscopic examination indicates that a cut rope came from a specific exemplar can a conclusive statement of source be made. In some cases, rope and cordage evidence may have other trace evidence attached to it. In cases of strangulation it may be possible to identify epithelial (skin) cells attached to the cordage.

7.4.8   Cigarettes and Tobacco

Cigarettes, cigarette ends, tobacco, and ash are sometimes found at crime scenes and may be overlooked as potentially useful evidence. From the point of view of forensic science, very little work has been done in the identification of various types of tobacco; however, this does not lessen the possible use of this type of evidence. Some laboratories maintain cigarette libraries from which they can often identify the brand from a cigarette end. In some cases, information about the brand a subject smokes may be useful to the investigation. Similarly, the appearance of ash left at a location may indicate that a suspect smoked a pipe or cigar, which is useful in describing the habits of that individual. Cigarette ends may be a useful source of other physical evidence. In some cases, latent fingerprints have been developed from cigarette ends by the ninhydrin process. It is often possible to determine the smoker's DNA from the saliva left on the end. Empty cigarette packages may also be found along with cigarettes. Besides the brand and the possibility of determining fingerprints, it is sometimes possible to determine the general location of the sale of the cigarettes by the numbers on the package. The ability to determine the area of sale depends on whether or not the distributor kept records of these numbers. Sometimes seemingly insignificant items left at the scene are important. The cellophane wrapping from a pack of Marlboro cigarettes was shown to have come from a pack of cigarettes found on a suspect (see Figure 7.16).

7.4.9   Matches

Matches may be wood or paper. The type of wood, microscopic appearance of the cardboard, colour, dimension, and shape are useful in comparing a burned match with some exemplars associated with the suspect. If the matches are made from paper or cardboard, it may be possible to show a connection between the cardboard left in the matchbook and that of the match. In some instances, it is possible to fit the match into the book by the appearance of the torn end of the match and the remaining end in the book. The match, whether paper or wood, may retain DNA from the user. Matches are sometimes used as toothpicks. If the end of the match appears to be chewed, it may be possible to determine the DNA of the chewer from the saliva.

7.4.10   Burned Paper

Burned papers and charred documents are sometimes found in arson investigations or in instances in which an attempt was made to destroy records by fire. Burned documents can be deciphered, provided they are reasonably intact. If the paper has been reduced to ashes

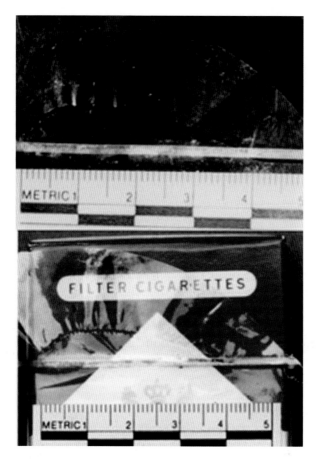

Figure 7.16 Cellophane wrapping from a pack of Marlboro cigarettes found at the scene. Top figure shows a close-up of the torn piece to the wrapping, and the bottom figure shows the fit of the recovered piece to the wrapping in place on the pack. (Photographs courtesy of Los Angeles County Sheriff's Department, Los Angeles, CA.)

it is not possible to determine any writing. For this reason, it is particularly important to exercise extreme care when collecting, preserving, and transporting this type of evidence. If burned paper is found in a metal file box, it should not be removed from the box; rather, it should be transported in the container in which it was found. If the documents are found in the open, or if the files they are in cannot be taken to the laboratory, the paper should be carefully placed into rigid cardboard boxes. Charred papers can be picked up by gently sliding a flat piece of cardboard under them. Once picked up from the scene, they can gently be placed in boxes. It is preferable to hand carry boxes to the laboratory because of the fragile nature of this evidence. If this is not possible, the paper must be packaged so that it will not break up in transit. Cotton or any other similar material that will preserve the evidence can be layered in the cardboard boxes. If the burned material consists of a book, folded papers, or currency, no attempt should be made to separate the layers of paper. The debris should be kept together and submitted to the laboratory in that state. Chemical treatment, photography, and examination under ultraviolet and infrared light often make the writing legible in charred documents; however, the documents must arrive intact in order for such examinations to be conducted.

7.4.11 Ash

The composition of ash will vary greatly depending upon the source. It can sometimes be identified microscopically, chemically, or by means of spectroscopy; however, the source of the ash may prove difficult to determine.

7.4.12 Soil

Soil evidence may be encountered in a wide variety of criminal investigations. It may be found on shoes, clothing, digging tools, or the underside of motor vehicles and is useful in tying the suspect or victim to a location. A tyre or footwear impression in soil makes it possible to associate the object with the scene (see Chapter 9 for a discussion of impression evidence). Soil is a mixture of decaying and weathered rock and decomposed organic material known as humus. It contains a wide variety of minerals such as quartz, feldspar, and mica, as well as partially decomposed leaves, pine needles, pollen grains, and other plant fragments. Thus, it is easy to differentiate soils from various locations by microscopic examination of various components. Known soil specimens from the crime scene are required for an analysis of the evidence sample. Samples should be collected from various regions at the specific location in question and several feet away from it, as well as at other locations, such as the subject's home and work, for elimination purposes (see box below).

Known samples can be placed in individual small glass jars or metal cans. Small screw-top glass jars are useful for this purpose. Two or three tablespoons of topsoil are all that is usually required for known specimens. It is important not to dig deeper than an inch or so when collecting these specimens. The subsoil may have a significantly different composition from the topsoil and lead to confusing results. Again, the containers should be appropriately labelled and the location of each sample noted. Soil specimens on shoes and other objects should be carefully handled. In certain instances, in the lab it may be possible to remove successive layers a little at a time and reconstruct the activities of the subject based upon the different types of soil present.

HOW FOOTWEAR IMPRESSIONS CAN PROVIDE ASSOCIATIVE EVIDENCE

A murder victim's home was entered through a bedroom window. Beneath the window was a somewhat muddy planting area. A poorly defined footprint, believed to be the suspect's, was found in the planting area. A suspect was arrested a short time later, and the police confiscated his muddy shoes. The suspect maintained that the mud was due to some gardening work he was doing at his home. Soil specimens were submitted to the laboratory from several locations at the crime scene, the suspect's home, and two other locations where the suspect claimed to have been that day. The examination of the evidence indicated that the soil on one shoe did not come from the suspect's home or either of the two other locations. The soil was consistent with that from the crime scene. The other shoe contained two different soils, one consistent with the suspect's home and the second consistent with the crime scene. (Adapted from the Innocence Project, http://www.innocenceproject.org/understand/Unreliable-Limited-Science.php.)

7.4.13 Wood

As evidence, wood may be present as sawdust, splinters, chips, large pieces used as assault weapons, etc. Evidence may be present at the crime scene, on a suspect's clothing, or in a wound. Wood may also have toolmarks. Because of the wide variety of wood types and its use in building, furniture, and hand tools, this type of evidence is most valuable. It is possible to identify, compare, and match sources of wood evidence. Wood may be divided into two types: hardwoods and softwoods. It is possible to determine the type of wood and often the type of tree from pieces the size of sawdust particles. The examination of wood is done microscopically.

If the question is to decide whether two pieces of stem from a tree originally belonged together, the original external contour of the stem is a good guide, if it is in good condition. Cracks in the bark, structures and formations on the surface of the bark, and the position of the sawed surface in relation to the longitudinal axis of the trunk, together with the placing and general appearance of any felling cut, have their own significance for the task of identification, which is simply a matter of seeing how the different pieces fit together. By matching them against one another it is frequently possible to determine the correspondence between two pieces of wood separated from each other in the longitudinal direction of the tree.

The annual rings of a tree are very characteristic. By making a transverse section of an object under investigation it is often possible to obtain a picture characteristic of the tree but within a limited region of the stem. Bruises and decay in the wood are often characteristic in position and extent and may assist in identification.

If an object under investigation is made from wood that has been worked in some way with tools (knife, plane, saw) or has been painted or its surface treated in any other way, the possibility of identification is increased. Imperfections in the edge of the knife or plane blade (including planing machines) leave characteristic marks that can possibly be found on both pieces of wood.

Wood that has not been planed, when sawed in the direction of the grain, often shows marks of varying width and depth from the saw used. In the case of frame-sawed lumber, these marks arise during the upward and downward movements of the frame saw. The variations are caused by inequalities in the setting of the teeth and by variations in the pressure on the wood under the saw. The same conditions hold for wood cut with a circular saw; the marks are more or less curved, depending on the diameter of the saw, and differ from the marks of a frame saw, which are straight but may be more or less oblique with reference to the grain of the wood. These saw marks have special significance in the identification of pieces of wood separated from one another in the direction of the grain.

It can be more difficult to determine, solely with the aid of marks from the saw used, whether two cut-off pieces originally belonged together. If the cutting was done with a hand saw, identification is sometimes possible because the marks of such a saw are often irregular and show characteristic formations. This is connected with the fact that changes in the position of the saw, in relation to the piece of wood, always occur on the forward and backward strokes of the sawing arm. Also, after a pause in sawing, the saw never takes up exactly the same position again when restarted. Machine saw marks are generally regular and meaningless and therefore usually cannot be used for identification. A transverse section of wood has a poorer power of reproducing marks from a saw than a longitudinal section, due to the difference in the structure.

If pieces of wood have been painted or surface-treated in any way, shades of colour may be useful for identification, and the pigment can be chemically and spectrographically examined to confirm the agreement or difference between the constituents. There may be several coats of paint, and agreement or difference in this respect may be noted.

Any knots or cracks in pieces of wood, as well as drill holes, nail holes, or screw holes, are significant when it is necessary to decide whether or not pieces of wood originally were a unit. Based on nail or screw holes or remaining nails or screws, it is sometimes possible to determine whether a certain piece of wood was previously combined with another piece or formed part of a floor or wall.

If pieces of wood are separated from one another by a break running in the direction of the grain, identity can be determined by fitting the pieces to one another. Certain difficulties are associated with a break going across the grain because the broken surfaces are often badly splintered and a number of fibres may have fallen away and been lost.

7.4.13.1 *Chips and Splinters of Wood*

Considerable quantities of chips or splinters may be found at the scene of a forced entry. These chips and splinters are usually examined in order to find traces of paint or marks from the tool that was used to gain entry. Chips of wood can also be valuable in the identification of the tool in another way. Mixed in with chips from the forced door or window may be chips that have broken off the handle of a chisel, hammer, or other tool. These pieces of a broken tool handle may be compared later with a tool recovered in the perpetrator's possession. Pieces of wood from the tool may be painted in the same way as the handle of the tool or the pieces may make a physical match with the tool in jigsaw-puzzle fashion.

7.4.13.2 *Sawdust, Wood Meal, or Other Particles of Finely Powdered Wood*

Particles of wood can sometimes be found in the pant cuffs, pockets, hat, or gloves or may be detected on tape lifts of the suspect's clothes. Clues consisting of these particles may also be left behind at the scene if the clothes of the criminal were contaminated with them and the trace material brought to the scene. In some cases, the species of tree can be determined simply by microscopic examination, and the occurrence of any foreign bodies on or together with the particles can be confirmed. Wood anatomy and identification is a narrow specialty not found in many forensic laboratories. University experts are available for assistance in such cases.

7.4.14 Plant Material

A wide variety of materials of plant origin may serve as useful sources of physical evidence. Leaves, seeds, bark, twigs, and pollen are sometimes collected as evidence, in addition to wood. These types of plant material may be attached to clothing, found in a vehicle, or present on a weapon. Fragments of plant material generally require a high degree of expertise to identify. Botanists employed at natural history museums or at a local arboretum may be willing to lend their expertise in the identification of such material. Pollen is a useful material for determining whether a subject was present in an area where flowering plants are located. Vacuum sweepings of a suspect's clothing may yield microscopic pollen grains whose species can be microscopically identified.

Figure 7.17 Galls of eriophyid mites (left) and pollen (right). (Photographs courtesy of Los Angeles County Sheriff's Department, Los Angeles, CA.)

Case 9

A small, fresh fragment of *Adenostoma fasciculata* containing growths on its leaves, which were found to be galls of eriophyid mites, was recovered from a suspect's vehicle. This unusual plant specimen was also present at the location where the victim's body had been dumped. This particular plant only exists at certain elevations on east-facing slopes and only near disturbed environments such as a road. Other plant materials (e.g., pollens) are sometimes encountered as trace evidence. (See Figure 7.17.)

7.4.15 Glass

Glass may be useful evidence in a wide variety of cases. Hit-and-run cases often have headlamp glass or windshield glass present, burglaries frequently involve window glass, and bottle glass is sometimes found in assault cases. Broken glass may yield information about the direction and speed of a projectile and, in the case of multiple projectiles, the sequence of events.

7.4.15.1 *Broken Panes of Glass*

The police investigator often must decide whether a pane of glass was broken from the outside or the inside or if it was struck by a bullet or by a rock. Pieces from the broken pane or the hole often show marks characteristic of the type of injury and the direction of the force. If correctly interpreted, these indications give useful information. Anyone who examines the edge of a piece of broken glass will note a series of rib-shaped lines or ridges that form right angles with one side of the pane and curve tangentially with the other side. These fracture lines are a result of force applied to the glass pane and are referred to as *Wallner fractures*; they are concave in the direction from which the crack propagated.

When an object has been thrown through a glass pane, two types of fractures that form a pattern resembling a spider's web will be seen. These fractures are called *radial* and *concentric* fractures (see Figure 7.18). Radial fractures are cracks that start at the centre or point from which the object struck the glass and run radially outward or in a somewhat star-shaped pattern from the point at which the break starts. Concentric fractures form concentric circular cracks in the glass around the point of impact.

Figure 7.18 Radial and concentric fractures in glass (vehicle windshield). (Photograph courtesy of Connecticut State Police.)

Determining the direction of force becomes a simple matter of examining conchoidal fractures along the edges of radial or concentric fractures. Before drawing any conclusions about the direction of force, the examiner must be certain whether a radial or a concentric fracture is being examined. It is also worthwhile to mark the pane of glass to clearly show the inside and outside.

The determination of the direction of force is accomplished as follows: Carefully remove a piece of broken glass, locate an edge that corresponds to a radial fracture, and examine it edgewise, noting the presence and configuration of the Wallner lines. Observe with which surface of the glass the conchoidal fractures make a right angle, because that side of the glass is not the side from which the force came; instead, the force came from the opposite side. The 4R rule is a convenient means of remembering the directionality of glass fracture markings for radial and concentric cracks: Ridges on Radial cracks appear at a Right angle to the Rear. More simply, the 4R becomes the 3R rule: Radial cracks make Right angles to the Reverse side (Figure 7.19).

The results of concentric fractures are opposite those of radial fractures. In examining the edge of a concentric fracture, the side of the glass forming the right angle with the ridges is the side from which the force came. Because of this obvious chance of confusion,

Figure 7.19 Wallner lines on the broken edge of a sheet of glass.

it is very important to be able to distinguish between radial and concentric fractures and not to get the sides mixed up. It is advisable to collect all the pieces of glass and fit them together so a complete picture is obtained of the broken pane where the force acted. In the case of windowpanes, a useful indication can be obtained from the layer of dirt often present on the outside of the glass.

Definite conclusions should be drawn from the curved lines of the edge surfaces only in the case of fractures that lie nearest to the point of attack. Solely with these closest fractures can one be sure that the conchoidal fractures resulted from the break in question. Fractures at a greater distance from the point of attack may have been produced, for example, when the object used for breaking the glass was brought back, or by projecting and interfering points of glass being broken off by hand.

When glass is transported to the laboratory for examination, the pieces should be carefully marked and individually wrapped in paper. The wrapped evidence may then be placed together into a box for easier transportation. Packaging should be done to minimise breakage.

7.4.15.2 *Glass Perforated by a Bullet*

If a bullet perforates a pane of glass, the hole is expanded in a crater on the side where the bullet exited the pane. The location at which the cone-shaped crater is narrowest indicates the direction from which the bullet was fired (see Figure 7.20). The appearance of the hole can indicate the velocity of the projectile. High-velocity bullets leave an almost circular hole in a pane of glass without noticeable cracking or with cracks merely starting. Lower velocity ammunition leaves an almost regular polygon with radial cracks running outward.

A shot at very close range more or less completely shatters the glass from the pressure of the muzzle gases; the extent depends on the power of the cartridge and the thickness of the glass. In such cases, it is impossible to obtain a clear idea of the appearance of the shot hole unless the shattered splinters of glass can be pieced together. In most cases, this is not possible because the splinters from the parts nearest the actual hole are too small. In a very favourable case, indications of the metal of the bullet on the edges around the hole may be detected spectrographically. A reliable indication that the glass was shattered by a shot at close range is the presence of gunshot residue particles on the glass.

It is sometimes difficult to determine whether a hole in a pane of glass was caused by a bullet or by a stone that was thrown. A small stone thrown at relatively high speed (such as one flung by the action of a tire of a passing car) can produce a hole very similar to that

Figure 7.20 Bullet hole in a glass pane, showing the cratering from the entry to exit points.

caused by a bullet; however, the crater-like expansion of a hole caused by a small stone may not show the same uniform, conchoidal fracture in the glass as a bullet hole would. Furthermore, holes caused by small stones generally do not show the same geometrical regularity in the radial and concentric cracks in the glass around the hole as that usually shown by a bullet hole. On the other hand, a large stone can shatter a pane of glass in a manner that nearly resembles the results of a close-range shot. Thus, a careful search for the projectile is necessary to determine the cause of the break.

If the pane of glass has a number of breaks, it is sometimes possible to determine the order of events producing the holes. Radial cracks produced by the first incident stop by themselves or run to the edges of the glass. On the other hand, cracks from subsequent incidents stop when they meet a crack already present in the glass as a result of earlier fractures. Even when the damage is extensive and large portions of glass have fallen away, the order of the damage can often be established by fitting the pieces together.

7.4.15.3   Cracked or Burst Panes of Glass

If a pane of glass has been cracked by the action of heat, it shows characteristic long wavy fractures. Pieces that have fallen out are generally found in the same direction as the source of heat. If a limited area of the glass has been exposed to a direct flame, a piece of glass corresponding to that area often breaks off. Automobile safety glass breaks completely or partially into pieces or small rods of a regular form when subjected to a violent blow or shock. Automobile manufacturers use tempered glass intentionally because it lessens the chance of being cut by flying glass.

A pane of tempered glass shattered by a bullet may still remain hanging in position on the vehicle. In a typical crackle pattern, the crack formation extends over the entire pane, but close around the point of fracture a large number of small pieces of glass usually come loose and fall away; thus, a study of the crater formation in the glass is possible only in rare cases. If pieces that have fallen out are found, however, in favourable cases they can be pieced back together near the point of impact and the appearance of the fracture can be reconstructed.

If a few small pieces believed to be tempered glass are found at the scene of an accident, a simple test can determine whether the glass is in fact tempered. Interference patterns caused by strain in the glass are easily observed by examining the glass with polarised light. A specimen of glass is placed over a light source with a polarising filter. The glass is viewed with a second polarising filter and a characteristic pattern is observed, indicating tempered glass.

7.4.15.4   Glass Splinters

At a scene where the criminal has obtained entry by breaking a window or glazed door, the investigating officer should always remember to collect pieces of glass for comparison purposes. If a suspect is found at a later time, a careful examination of the clothing may show splinters of glass. Glass splinters may also be found in the handle of a tool used to force entry into a building. A burglar may be linked to a window he smashed by the tiny fragments of glass that fly backward onto his person and clothing (Figure 7.21). When such splinters of glass are found on a suspect's clothing or tools from a burglary investigation, they will usually be too small to make a direct physical comparison against the pane of glass from which they possibly came. However, a number of other comparisons

Figure 7.21 Breaking window showing fragments flying inward onto the person and outward away from him in the direction of the blow. (Photograph courtesy of Centre of Forensic Sciences, Toronto, Canada.)

can be made to show a common source between the exemplar and questioned glass specimens. Glass evidence may be examined for a number of physical and chemical properties. Density, refractive index, colour, thickness, and chemical composition are some of the common characteristics examined to differentiate glass. These tests are conducted in the forensic laboratory (Figure 7.22) and will not result in a definite identification because glass is a mass-produced material with wide use. Lack of identity, however, can be proved, and this may be useful information. When known samples of glass evidence are collected as exemplars, several samples should be taken from different parts of the same pane of glass and packaged separately because there may be variation in glass properties in the same pane.

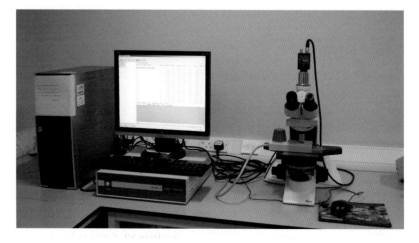

Figure 7.22 GRIM apparatus used to measure the refractive index of glass fragments. (Access to instrument courtesy of University of Strathclyde, Glasgow, Scotland.)

7.4.16   Objects Left at the Crime Scene

Criminals sometimes leave items behind at the crime scene that they believe have no further use. Items may be lost or forgotten by the suspect. The criminal may have been surprised during the act and forced to leave abruptly without picking up personal effects. Items left behind can be extremely valuable to investigators; they may help connect the suspect to the crime in other ways or indicate the suspect's identity if fingerprints are present. Examples of lost items that can be found at a scene include jewellery, wallets, mobile phones, eyeglasses, and credit cards.

7.4.17   Paper

Paper, such as newspaper, wrapping paper, or paper bags, is sometimes left at a crime scene. Besides trace evidence, handwriting and latent fingerprints may be present. If the paper at the scene is torn or cut, a search of the suspect's home or car may turn up a matching piece of paper that can be fitted together with the evidence. In some cases, watermarks or stains on a piece of paper may be used to show a connection to paper located at another site.

7.4.18   Articles of Clothing

Manufacturer's markings on clothing are occasionally of value. The presence of a foreign label in clothing may indicate the nationality of the wearer; however, because a large number of clothes are imported, any conclusion is open to question. Size and laundry marks may be valuable. Size gives an indication of the physical characteristics of the subject, and laundry marks may identify the suspect. Other marks such as initials and even names are sometimes found and, of course, are valuable evidence. Hair should always be searched for, as well as other trace evidence. If secretions or dried blood are found on an article of clothing left at a crime scene, the subject's DNA type may be determined. Pockets should be searched as a matter of course; in some cases, useful evidence will be found. Torn pieces of clothing are valuable. If a matching piece of clothing can be found in the suspect's home or car it can easily tie the suspect to the location. Testing for DNA around the neck and sleeves of a shirt or sweater, or the waistband or pockets of trousers or jeans, could provide information about the identity of the wearer.

7.4.19   Product Markings

Many commercial products bear manufacturer's marks on the label, package, or container. The markings are used to designate the date, lot number, location of manufacture, and other such details as a control to assist the manufacturer in checking on distribution and sales of the product. The markings may also assist the investigator in determining the origin of products found at crime scenes. Because the markings are usually in code form, the manufacturer or distributor must be contacted to determine the meaning of the information. In a highly unusual case, two revolvers each had the same serial number from the factory stamp (Figure 7.23). When one of the guns was submitted to the laboratory as part of a criminal investigation, a record check showed that the weapon belonged to an individual residing in northern California. The owner was contacted and advised that his revolver had been recovered. To the investigator's surprise, the owner reported that he had the gun in his possession. The firearms investigator obtained the second gun to photograph this unusual occurrence. The lesson here is never assume anything is as it seems. You could be surprised!

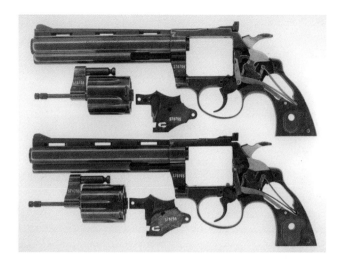

Figure 7.23 Two different guns with the same serial number. (Photograph courtesy of Los Angeles County Sheriff's Department, Los Angeles, CA.)

7.4.20 Foodstuffs

Foodstuffs in the form of stains or debris are sometimes found as evidence and may be useful in determining the type of work in which a subject is engaged. For example, if vacuum sweepings are examined and a quantity of wheat starch is found, it could indicate that the suspect had been baking. Through careful examination, it is possible to determine the nature of very small samples of foodstuffs through microscopic and microchemical means.

7.4.21 Cosmetics

Cosmetics such as lipstick, nail polish, and various creams and lotions may sometimes be collected as evidence in cases. If exemplars are available, a laboratory can make a chemical comparison to determine whether the known and questioned specimens share a common source. Cosmetics firms are constantly reformulating their products, so if the brand of the cosmetic can be determined it may be possible to determine the approximate time a given specimen was on the market. Starch, which has a highly characteristic appearance under polarising light, is sometimes used in cosmetics in place of talc (Figure 7.24).

7.4.22 Hair

Hair evidence is generally associated with crimes involving physical contact such as murder, rape, assault, and traffic accidents. Hair may be found at the crime scene, on the victim or suspect, or attached to a weapon, tool, vehicle, or article of clothing. Because of its small size, hair may be difficult to find. Care and patience are required to conduct a thorough search for this evidence. The microscopic features of hair vary from person to person, and the differences have been used to assign the source of hairs recovered at a crime scene to an individual. It is becoming increasingly clear, however, that this may be a less reliable method of identification than has been claimed. Recovered hairs may include adherent roots with nuclei and therefore are amenable to DNA typing. Even if they do not, the hair shafts contain mitochondrial DNA (mtDNA) which can be typed. These provide a much more reliable and discriminating approach to exploring the source of hairs.

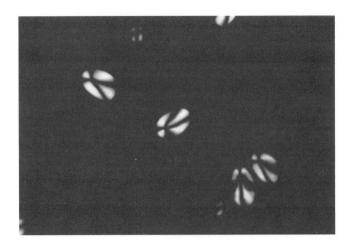

Figure 7.24 Starch has a highly characteristic appearance under polarising light microscopy which is sometimes referred to as a "Maltese cross." This photomicrograph is of potato starch. (Photograph courtesy of Los Angeles County Sheriff's Department, Los Angeles, CA.)

Determining if hairs come from a similar source is a controversial subject, and the Innocence Project has uncovered cases in which the interpretation of hair examinations has been in conflict with the DNA test results. Reports stating that the known and exemplar hair specimens are "similar and may have come from the same person or a person with similar hair characteristics" only beg the question. A forensic examiner is not able to provide the degree of certainty to a statement of similarity, and laypersons may incorrectly conclude that the term "similar hair characteristics" is more specific than it actually is.

The remainder of this section concerns microscopic and morphological examination of hair. Although such examinations can exclude a suspect hair, they cannot positively prove that a sample came from one and only one person. If the hair strands found at a crime scene and those of a subject show similar characteristics, the strongest statement that can be made is that the subject could not be excluded as the donor of the hair. The hairs could have come from that subject or any other individual with similar characteristics. A statement about probabilities of a given hair coming from a specific person is not appropriate at the present state of the art of hair examination in criminal cases.

Even though it is not possible to determine the person from whom a strand of hair came, there is probative value in hair examination due to the information to be gained, such as species, location of growth on the body, hair treatment, and hair disease. It is also possible to exclude someone as a source of a hair, the obvious example being the exclusion of someone of negroid race as the source of a long blond hair.

When conducting a hair examination, the first step is to determine whether the material is of animal or synthetic origin. Microscopic examination quickly determines whether the evidence is animal, synthetic, or simply a plant fibre. Furthermore, it is possible to determine whether the hair is human or animal in origin and, if animal, the species of the animal. Domestic animals such as dogs, cats, cows, and horses are somewhat common. Hairs from wild animals are sometimes collected at crime scenes (e.g., at the scene of skeletal remains). It is not possible to determine whether two hair specimens come from a specific animal. Although differentiating between human and animal hair is not difficult, determining the species of animal requires a greater degree of expertise from a hair examiner. The ability to ascertain this is determined by the experience of the individual performing the analysis.

In addition to determining whether or not a specimen of hair is human, it is usually also possible to determine whether the hair is from the head or another part of the body. At one time it was possible to infer the gender of an individual based on the length of a hair strand. Current hairstyles no longer make that deduction valid.

Examination of hair may indicate that it was chemically treated. Hairs that have been bleached, dyed, straightened, or otherwise treated can be compared with specimens from a subject to determine whether the subject's hair has been treated in the same way. Sometimes, hair shows the presence of lice or fleas, which can be useful as a means of comparison. Microscopic examination of the hair root may suggest that the hair was forcibly pulled out as opposed to falling out naturally. Such information may be used to indicate a struggle; however, some naturally shed hairs have roots and some pulled hairs have no roots, so this is not strong evidence to support violence.

Searching for hair at the crime scene is a tedious process. Subjecting the floor, furniture, and other objects to a very thorough examination is necessary; a flashlight and pair of forceps are suggested for this purpose. Hair found on an object or in a certain location may be folded in a clean sheet of paper and placed in a properly labelled envelope. Detailed notes should be made to indicate the date, time, and location of the hair. A sketch or photograph of the area should be made. When a number of hair samples are collected from the same location at the crime scene, sorting the specimens is not recommended. They should be submitted to the crime laboratory for careful and expert examination. If several hairs from different locations are collected, it is important not to package them together. Confusion will arise if the hairs are different and in the same package.

Hair evidence is frequently found on the body of a victim. Pulled-out strands of hair may be found clutched in the hands or under the fingernails of a murder victim. A rape victim sometimes has her assailant's pubic hair present on her body or the bed or location where she was lying. Pubic hair combings in rape and rape–murder cases are a routine way of collecting hair evidence. It is advisable to collect hair as well as other types of evidence associated with these cases as soon as possible. Trace evidence such as hair is quickly lost unless gathered promptly. Clothing belonging to the victim of a murder, rape, or assault victim should be examined for hair evidence. Hairs may become entangled among threads of the fabric. Generally, a very careful examination of the clothing is necessary to locate hairs.

If microscopy is to be attempted, the crime scene examiner will need to ensure that appropriate reference samples are collected. At least 10 and preferably 25 hairs from the body region of interest should be collected by combing or pulling out, not cutting. Because pulling out is considered assault in some jurisdictions, the examiner responsible for making the collection or assisting medical personnel in doing so must be aware of any legal restrictions.

7.4.23 Feathers

In rare instances, feathers may be collected as evidence in an investigation. Most crime laboratories have very little or no expertise in analysing this type of material. Feathers should be collected if discovered and may be identified by experts at museums or academic institutions.

Figure 7.25 An example of the physical fit of two pieces of wire demonstrating that they were once a single piece. (Photograph courtesy of Los Angeles County Sheriff's Department, Los Angeles, CA.)

7.4.24   Electrical Wire

Insulated electrical wire is sometimes collected as evidence. Wire may have been used to tie up a victim of a crime, or perhaps it was attached to a car stereo, CD player, or MP3 player stolen from a vehicle. In both cases, it may be possible to show that one end of the wire was once part of another end. Figure 7.25 shows an exact fit between two wire ends showing that they were once a single piece. Generally, electrical wire that has many strands does not lend itself to toolmark examination. The wires are so fine that sufficient markings are not imparted onto the wire from the tool. If the wire is of a thicker gauge, it may be possible to examine extrusion marks on both ends to determine if each of the pieces has the same class characteristics. Extrusion marks will also be present on the wire insulation. Because the insulation has a greater surface area, it is easier to work with that portion of the evidence. The extrusion markings along with the cut edge, which sometimes can be made to fit the other piece of wire evidence, can lead to the conclusion that the wires were once from the same continuous piece. If a positive fit cannot be made, physical characteristics such as the number of strands of wire, the gauge, the appearance of the break, and the colour and markings on the insulation may be used at least to show that the wire was of a similar manufacture. Whatever type of examination is made, it is always necessary to have an exemplar to compare with the evidence wire in order to make a conclusion.

7.4.25   Broken Tools

Broken tools are frequently discovered at burglaries of safes and breaking-and-entering cases. Broken ends from screwdrivers, wrecking bars, and metal punches are important types of physical evidence. Their usefulness lies in the fact that, if the remaining part of the tool is discovered, a positive statement can be made that the piece found at the scene and the tool were once intact. Figure 7.26 shows a broken knife and pieces recovered from a crime scene. Broken knives are a kind of tool often found at crime scenes. A piece of knife blade may be discovered at the scene of an assault or murder or may be present in the wound of a victim. If the other part of the knife can be recovered, the two parts can be physically fitted together. In addition to the fit, a microscopic examination of the knife and the broken piece of blade usually shows fine scratches caused by wear and use on the flat surface of the blade. These markings run continuously through the area of the break and can conclusively show that the broken piece and the blade were once a continuous piece.

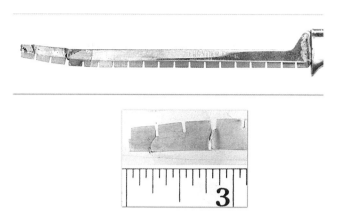

Figure 7.26 A broken knife blade (top) is shown with pieces recovered from a crime scene (bottom). (Photographs courtesy of Los Angeles County Sheriff's Department, Los Angeles, CA.)

7.4.26 Tape

Electrical, adhesive, masking, and cellophane tape are sometimes recovered at crime scenes. The tape may have been used to bind a victim or to tape two objects together. If a roll of tape is located in the suspect's belongings, it may be possible to piece together the portion of tape from the scene and that found in the suspect's possession. If the tear at the end of the tape is ragged enough, a conclusive statement about a common source may be made. If the cut on the tape is very sharp, such as that made by scissors, only a statement about class characteristics can be made. Figure 7.27 shows a jigsaw fit between the end of tape from a roll and a piece from the scene.

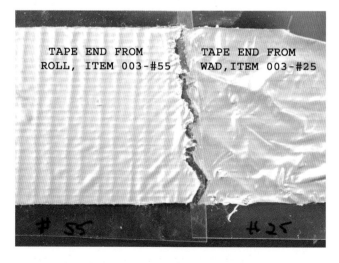

Figure 7.27 Jigsaw fit in tape from the scene and a possible source. (Photograph courtesy of Frederic A. Tulleners, Director, Forensic Science Graduate Program, University of California, Davis, CA.)

7.4.27 Headlamps

Headlamps from automobiles and other motor vehicles can be submitted to crime laboratories in traffic accident investigations. A careful examination of the headlamp filament may help determine whether the lamp was on or off at the time of the accident, because a hot filament will deform on impact but a cold filament will break. The traffic investigator should be aware of this possibility and collect any pieces of broken headlamp, tail lamp, or other debris present at the scene of the accident.

7.5 Summary

"Trace evidence" consists of a miscellany of materials that share the property of providing associative evidence. Trace evidence therefore covers mainly the WHAT, WHERE, and WHO of the investigative star, but may on occasions address HOW, WHEN, and WHY. The chapter describes the more common examples and how to collect and preserve them. The diversity of potential associations that can be provided by trace evidence must be tempered by an understanding of its often limited strength, with most examples being restricted to corroborative evidence rather than identity.

Forensic Biology

8.1 Introduction

Forensic biology deals with the identification of blood and other body tissues left at a scene. It has a particular value because, although its primary purpose is to answer the question WHO, its very presence out of the body of the donor carries with it information about WHAT took place (see box below). A bloodstain on broken glass at the point of entry of a break-in creates a nexus between the offence and the person who committed it. Semen in a vaginal swab creates a nexus between the act of intercourse and the male involved. Even without the results of typing tests, as we saw in Chapter 4, the physical pattern of blood-stains can yield information about the manner in which they were deposited. A force-ful event, such as running through a pool of shed blood, beating with a club, or a bullet entry, will produce spatters, the size of which becomes smaller as the energy of the event increases. Such spatters contrast with the smears produced by rubbing against shed blood.

Case 1

Police responded to a call from a husband who said he came home after a night of play-ing cards with friends and discovered his wife on the floor covered in blood and his house ransacked. When questioned by police about the blood on his clothes he said that he got the bloodstains on his shirt and trousers when he leaned over his wife's body to administer CPR. After examining his clothes, investigators determined that the majority of blood on the suspect's clothes was from a spatter-producing event and were not transfer stains. After being presented with this evidence, the suspect con-fessed to beating his wife with a baseball bat and turning his house upside down to make it look like a break-in.

DIFFERENTIATE WHO FROM WHAT

DNA typing of bloodstains alone does not necessarily solve a case. A suspect who claims he was acting in self-defence is not disputing the fact that he caused the vic-tim to bleed. DNA typing showing that blood at the scene and on the suspect's cloth-ing came from the victim would not be very helpful in proving or disproving the suspect's claim. Bloodstains showing upward directionality and clustered on a wall close to the floor, however, indicate that it was highly likely that the victim was lying on the floor when the suspect stomped and kicked him and would disprove the self-defence claim.

It is the question of WHO, however, that dominates forensic biology, and we shall deal with that aspect first. The ability to answer that question was revolutionised in the mid-1980s with the introduction of DNA analysis. Forensic DNA tests have provided a tool that permits what is in effect identification and that requires only very small amounts of sample. Blood and semen are by far the most common body tissues examined. Semen and saliva are addressed in Chapter 13 (Investigating Sexual Assault and Domestic Abuse), and hair and traces of sweat or skin cells were dealt with in Chapter 7 (Trace Evidence and Miscellaneous Material). We deal mainly with blood in this chapter.

8.1.1   Is It Blood, and Where Did It Come From?

The core approach to blood evidence consists of this sequence:

1. *A screening procedure*, usually a chemical test. Screening procedures are sometimes called *presumptive tests*, and they provide an indication of whether or not something could be blood. They are best regarded as a way to eliminate samples. Samples that test positive are subjected to further testing and those that do not are not.
2. *A confirmatory test*, to identify the material and so confirm or falsify the hypothesis that the material is indeed blood. For example, stains from chocolate milk and tomato ketchup may have the appearance of blood and give a positive presumptive test, but they would be eliminated by a negative confirmatory test.
3. *A species test*, to confirm that the blood is of human origin. It is a test to determine the species of animal from which a blood sample came and depends on the principle that proteins in blood have structural differences in different animals. These differences can be used to make an antiserum containing specific antibodies to the blood from the target species. An antiserum to human blood will react with human blood but not that from non-primate animals, an antiserum to dog blood will react only with blood from a dog, and so on. The amount of blood required for this test is very small; however, it is important to have a control specimen to rule out the possibility of false-positive tests due to contamination or cross-reactions in the reagents, which depend on a reaction of components in the blood with species-specific antibodies to them. Sheep and goats, for example, are closely related species, and many reagents will not distinguish between the two. Species determination is useful in animal poaching cases. Approximately two dozen different animal antisera are commercially available for use in the species origin test. For criminal cases, the most often used antisera are human and domestic animal antisera such as dog, cat, cow, horse, and deer.
4. *Genetic analysis* of some form that can type the body fluid or tissue by identifying genetically determined markers in the sample. Historically, the clinically important ABO blood typing system was used, along with several other biochemicals found in blood. Today, all forensic laboratories use tests that identify variable regions in the DNA present in blood. Most use procedures that target between 10 and 20 of these regions to create a DNA profile. The most common example is the form of DNA analysis known as short tandem repeat (STR), which is the basis of nearly all databases. The usual STR analyses include markers that are human

specific, and some laboratories do not conduct step 2 or 3 in their examinations. In these cases, reports must indicate that the screening revealed material that could be blood, not that it was blood and not that it was human blood. The report can then go on to say that DNA testing showed the stain was of human origin, together with a comment on whether or not it could have come from someone in the case.

5. *Evaluation of results*, by direct comparison with reference samples or with samples in a database, followed by statistical comparisons with the known frequencies of the selected markers in the population. As discussed in Chapter 1, the results may be exclusionary and so help exonerate the innocent, or they may be corroborative and so rare that they approach the level of identification of the person from whom the blood or tissues came.

The first step in the sequence is often the only one directly employed by crime scene investigators, with steps 2 to 5 being conducted in the forensic laboratory. Blood screening kits that are specific for human blood are available, such as the ABAcard® HemaTrace® test strips manufactured by Abacus Diagnostics, Inc. Awareness of the whole process provides useful background for the crime scene investigator by providing context for decisions on screening and collecting exhibits from the scene.

Case 2

A suspect physically assaulted the victim and slashed him several times on his body. The suspect fled the scene prior to the arrival of the police and later admitted to washing off the knife that was used in the attack. The knife was submitted to the lab and examined for the presence of blood. Although the suspect admitted to washing the knife, a small amount of reddish-brown staining was noted around a screw on the handle of the knife as well as on the edge of a clip attached to the opposite side of the handle of the knife. A positive result for a presumptive test for blood was obtained from the staining in each of these areas. The DNA profile obtained from the blood around the screw of the knife handle was a mixture with the major DNA profile matching the victim. In addition, the DNA profile obtained from the blood on the edge of the clip of the knife handle matched the victim. Figure 8.1 shows the location of the screw on the handle of the knife where the reddish-brown staining was located and the reddish-brown staining around the screw on the handle of the knife taken at 12.5× magnification with a stereo binocular microscope.

8.1.2 Before You Begin—Safety First!

Before discussing any testing procedures concerning blood and other biological fluids, some remarks are appropriate about the dangers of bloodborne diseases, such as hepatitis B, hepatitis C, and human immunodeficiency virus (HIV). Individuals working around wet or dried blood at crime scenes or autopsies and in crime laboratories where whole blood or other biological specimens are present are advised to use universal precautions. These include wearing personal protective equipment (PPE), such as, Tyvek™ suits, lab

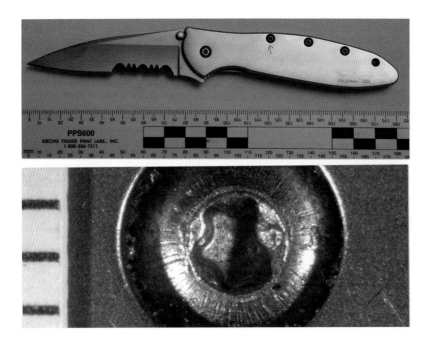

Figure 8.1 Knife (top) and screw with spot of blood (bottom).

coats, gloves, and goggles or face shields. The important thing to remember is that the type of barrier protection should be appropriate for the type of exposure anticipated. Persons who routinely work with blood and blood products should consider receiving hepatitis vaccinations.

Surgical gloves should be worn when working with any biological products (e.g., blood, saliva, semen). Nitrile gloves are available for those with latex allergies. Cut-resistant gloves should also be worn when scraping an item for DNA evidence with a razor blade. Smoking, eating, or drinking in areas that contain these items is not to be permitted. When specific questions arise about proper handling of biological evidence, crime laboratory forensic biology personnel are good resources. Working around biological samples of unknown sources has a potential risk; however, with appropriate care and caution those risks can be minimised.

Guidelines for handling biological materials should be posted and discussed with personnel who must handle these materials. Periodic briefing and refresher training to remind personnel how to handle this type of evidence is important. Appropriate procedures must be taken for disposal of biological evidence as well. Commercial disposal companies that specialise in biohazard disposal should be used to destroy such materials.

8.2   Contamination

Contamination is a major concern when it comes to DNA and biological evidence. The techniques used are able to type such minute amounts of DNA that, when collecting evidence or processing a crime scene, it is critical to eliminate, or at least, minimise the accidental transfer of DNA as much as possible. Contamination can occur between items of evidence; it is for this reason that collected items of evidence should be packaged separately.

Commingled items that are packaged together run the risk of biological material being transferred from one item to the other. Known and questioned samples must *never* be packaged together. One should ensure that any tools or equipment used to collect or process evidence do not become a source of contamination, as well. If disposables cannot be used, tools can be cleaned by various methods, such as being wiped down with a 10% bleach solution followed by 70% ethanol. See Table 8.1 for the recommendations reported by an international advisory group to INTERPOL in 2009.

Contamination can also occur when investigators or crime scene technicians inadvertently deposit their own DNA on items of evidence. This can occur by coughing, sneezing, or talking at a crime scene (or in the lab) without a mask. Handling or touching an item without gloves can also leave behind trace amounts of epithelial (skin) cells that could contaminate any DNA profiles that are subsequently developed (see Chapter 3 for more information). The same personal protection equipment used to prevent infection also serves to prevent contamination.

Table 8.1 Anticontamination Guidelines Recommended by INTERPOL DNA Monitoring Expert Group

Due to the sensitivity of current DNA techniques, extreme caution, including wearing a face mask, must be taken if the person undertaking the crime stain sampling has a medical condition that causes the shedding of body fluids or particles (e.g., colds, coughs, influenza). Other conditions such as eczema or severe dandruff may require wearing additional barrier clothing.

All containers used for transportation (e.g., coolers, crates, boxes) should be cleaned before and after use, or, if possible, not reused.

The work areas of crime scene officers should be cleaned regularly with wipes containing chlorohexadine.

Wherever possible, sterile, disposable sampling materials should be used.

Disposable gloves must always be worn over cuffs and should be changed after handling individual items/objects. Barrier clothing should also be used as often as possible.

For serious offences, disposable face masks, overshoes, and hooded suits should be worn.

Handle items as little as possible; items should not be reopened even for interview purposes. Use paper bags with transparent panels.

Always handle only one item at a time.

It may be necessary to change gloves between handling different items.

Where possible, take the container to the evidence and not the evidence to the container.

Contact between victim and suspect samples should be avoided at all times.

Ensure that any person attending a crime scene has no contact with a suspect or the suspect's clothing.

Multiple suspects, the victim, and their clothing must be kept apart at all times and should not be allowed to come into contact with the same objects (e.g., police car, interview room, custody suite).

Each item should be packaged, sealed, and labelled as soon as it is taken.

Never pack several items or objects together.

Use bags of a suitable size or shape; do not force items into packaging that is too small, as bags may tear or lids may be forced off.

Seal all packaging securely; use adhesive tape on all edges, and sign and date over seals.

Never use staples or pins to seal packages.

Never reuse packaging.

If an item will not fit or packaging is used in error, do not use it for a different item. The packaging must be discarded.

Never eat, drink, or smoke when recovering evidential samples.

Unless they are already included in the database, any individual entering a crime scene (including police officers, no matter how high their rank) should submit their own DNA samples to the testing laboratory for quality assurance measures. Elimination samples such as these can be used directly by the laboratory for comparisons of results with investigative personnel and witnesses involved. Some jurisdictions maintain a separate database of police and crime scene investigator DNA; for example, the United Kingdom maintains a national Police Elimination Database with fingerprint and DNA data from police officers.

8.3   Searching for Bloodstains

A dried, but relatively fresh, bloodstain is generally reddish-brown in colour and glossy, in contrast to, for example, rust stains. In a very thin layer, the colour may be greyish green. The gloss slowly disappears under the action of sunlight and heat, wind, and weather or as the result of an attempt to wash it away. Bloodstains can assume other colours from red to brown or black, or they may appear green, blue, or greyish white. The colour and the time required for the change depend on the underlying material; the change is quicker on metal surfaces and slower on textiles. With some types of cloth the blood soaks into the threads; with others, it lies on the pile. The surface gloss is often less marked on fabric. Bloodstains on wallpaper may show surprising colours because of the blood taking up colour from the paper. Certain other stains, composed of pigment, rust, tobacco, snuff, urine, faeces, coffee, and other substances, can easily be confused with bloodstains. In searching for bloodstains, marks should not be classified according to colour and character because a stain that appears to deviate from the normal character of a bloodstain may be composed of blood, whereas one that resembles blood may be composed of some other substance.

When searching for stains it is convenient to allow the light from a flashlight to fall obliquely against the surface under examination and view with and against the direction of the light. Sometimes a stain shows up better against a surface when it is illuminated with coloured light. Red, green, and ordinary white light have been used successfully. When the presence of blood is suspected but there are no visible stains, consideration has to be given to how to record the position and physical nature of the stain, and infrared photography may be useful. Figure 8.2 shows a pair of dark-coloured trousers that showed no obvious bloodstains in normal light but which gave a positive presumptive test in several areas. The image on the left is a normal exposure photograph of the trousers and that on the right is of the same trousers when illuminated and photographed to show reflected light in the infrared region. The bloodstained areas are clearly seen.

Occasionally, the assailant will clean up the scene. Furniture is straightened, damage is concealed, and blood is washed off—all for the purpose of concealing the crime, delaying its discovery, or destroying evidence. The search of the scene should therefore also be extended to places that are not in direct view. A criminal with bloody fingers may, for example, have opened a drawer, leafed through papers, or grasped a doorknob or a handrail. Washbasins, waste bins, and similar items should be given close attention. Drain traps should also be examined because blood may be in the trap if the criminal washed his hands there. Towels, curtains, and other fabrics that may have served to wipe off blood should also be examined. If a floor has been washed in order to remove bloodstains, blood may possibly be found in cracks, in joints between tiles, under the edges of linoleum, behind floorboards and electric socket plates, and in similar other places. An item that is absent

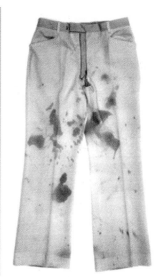

Figure 8.2 A pair of dark-coloured trousers with bloodstains photographed under normal light (left) and using infrared photography (right).

of blood that is believed to have been touched or handled by a perpetrator can be swabbed and submitted for high-sensitivity DNA testing (also known as low copy number, or LCN, DNA testing.) Car steering wheels are an example.

The search for blood on clothes must be carried out carefully and systematically. Even if blood has been washed off the more conspicuous parts, stains may still be found on the seams, on the lining, inside the sleeves, in pockets, and so forth (Figure 8.3). Stains that have been diffused by washing may still be detected at the scene and successfully typed in the laboratory. Suspects may have bloodstains not only on their clothes but also on their body. Clothing can also be swabbed to recover sweat and skin epithelial cells that can be DNA typed to determine who might have been wearing a particular garment.

An item that is absent of blood that is believed to have the perpetrator's saliva can also be swabbed or collected. Figure 8.4 shows the mouth of a beverage container being swabbed for subsequent saliva and DNA testing. According to the owner, the container was full when she left in the morning for work. During the commission of a burglary, the thief became thirsty and left the empty container on the counter.

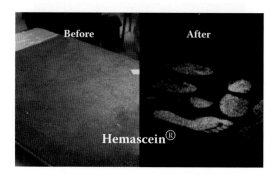

Figure 8.3 Visualisation of washed bloody footwear marks using the proprietary reagent Hemascein®. (Photographs courtesy of Abacus Diagnostics, West Hills, CA.)

Figure 8.4 Mouth of a beverage container being swabbed for subsequent saliva and DNA testing. (Photograph courtesy of New York City Office of Chief Medical Examiner.)

In the open air, the search for bloodstains is often more difficult. Rain, snow, sun, and wind may have obliterated the marks more or less completely. The blood mark may have changed its colour in a very short time because of the character of the ground. If the ground gives an impression of dampness in certain areas, these parts should be given special attention, as should blades of grass, leaves, and branches of trees.

Objects on which the presence of bloodstains is suspected should be examined very carefully in areas such as cracks and joints, because bloodstains can sometimes be found in such places even after the object has been washed or cleaned. It should also be remembered that it does not follow that blood must be found on a knife or similar object that has been used in a murder or assault. The edges of the wound may wipe the blood off the blade as it is drawn out.

If blood has run through bedclothes on a bed it is necessary to consider whether it has run through all the bedclothes or has remained in the mattress, for example. This is very important in estimating the total quantity of blood and sometimes in enabling the pathologist to decide on the time that has elapsed since death.

Clothing with no visible blood can also be sampled for sweat or epithelial cells and DNA typed to determine who might have been wearing it. Figure 8.5 shows a sterile razor blade being used to scrape an article of clothing.

Figure 8.5 Clothing being scraped for skin cells to determine who might have been wearing it. (Photograph courtesy of New York City Office of Chief Medical Examiner.)

8.3.1 Screening Tests for Blood

Historically, several chemicals have been used as presumptive tests to determine the presence of blood, including leucomalachite green, phenolphthalein, *ortho*-tolidine, and tetramethylbenzidine. Another presumptive test, luminol, is described later. Apart from luminol, these presumptive tests work on the same principle—the peroxidase activity of haemoglobin converts a colourless chemical into a coloured one. They are extremely sensitive and can easily detect very small quantities of blood. The test methods are easy to perform and lend themselves to use at the scene. Interpretation of test results is critical because other materials can give false-positive results. A variety of plant materials exhibit peroxidase activity. Chemical kits used for presumptive tests are available through various specialist supply companies, or bulk chemicals may be purchased at considerable savings from chemical supply houses. Of the foregoing tests, *ortho*-tolidine and tetramethylbenzidine are considered to be the most sensitive. Generally, however, the phenolphthalein or Kastle–Mayer test (Figure 8.6) is a good overall choice, with more than adequate sensitivity and fewer safety issues (*ortho*-tolidine and tetramethylbenzidine are related to chemicals known to be carcinogenic, and *ortho*-tolidine is classified as being "possibly carcinogenic to humans").

Testing is best conducted by swabbing or wiping the suspect area with filter paper or cotton-tipped swabs. A drop of the phenolphthalein reagent is added followed by a drop of hydrogen peroxide solution. A positive is shown by the rapid development of a pink colour. Colour development after adding the phenolphthalein or more than 30 seconds after adding the peroxide are false positives and not used. Performing the test directly on the evidence should be avoided.

The luminol test is very useful for searching large areas for blood, particularly if the area has been cleaned. The chemical, luminol, exhibits chemiluminescence when exposed to an oxidising agent and a catalyst. The reagent mixture contains hydrogen peroxide as the oxidiser, and the iron-containing chemical haem present in haemoglobin is the catalyst. A drawback of the test is that the room must be dark because the chemiluminescence is faint and will be masked by sunlight. It is also short lived and lasts only about 30 seconds.

The test works best on older stains. In some instances, outlines of shoes and even marks caused by mopping or wiping up an area can be clearly visualized by means of this test. Experience in interpreting this test is required. At times, pinpoint glowing is observed that is not the result of bloodstains; with a positive test, whole areas are seen glowing. Luminol

Figure 8.6 Kastle–Mayer test showing a positive presumptive test for blood. (Photograph courtesy of Los Angeles County Sheriff's Department, Los Angeles, CA.)

Figure 8.7 The application of Bluestar® reagent to latent blood indicates that the bathtub was cleaned up. (Photographs courtesy of Bluestar, Monte Carlo, Monaco; http://www.bluestar-forensic.com/.)

is susceptible to false positives from copper and some bleaches which limits its usefulness in scenes that have been cleaned with bleach. The advantage of sensitivity can also be a disadvantage, and false positives have been found with urine and faeces stains.

The commercial product Bluestar® is based on luminol but is presented as a proprietary reagent with a formulation that increases its effectiveness, including reducing any deleterious effect on DNA in the sample. Figure 8.7 shows a bathtub that had been washed clean to the naked eye but revealed blood traces after application of Bluestar.

8.3.2   Description and Recording of Bloodstains

A description should be made of the form, colour, size, and position of any bloodstains, as well as the direction of any splash or similar features. The best way to preserve the appearance of bloodstains is through photography. Photographs depicting overall, medium-range, and close-up views should be made. A scale should be included for the close-up photographs. Infrared photography will record the image by detecting infrared radiation reflected from the surface of the item. The amount reflected will vary depending on the character and nature of the surface. The photograph is taken by directing incandescent lamps toward the item and capturing the reflected radiation with a camera or video set to allow only the infrared wavelengths to be recorded. This method is illustrated in Figure 8.5 and has the advantage of being non-destructive and will not interfere with the physical pattern or the DNA in the stain.

Caution: It is very important to be aware that the infrared exposure is not specific for finding blood; it only records the presence of a stained area because of differences in the intensity of the reflected infrared light.

In addition to photography, a rough sketch is useful to show the general appearance of the stains as well as their position relative to other areas of the crime scene. The sketch should contain the location and direction of the stains—for example, "A drop of blood located 25 cm from the floor and 16 cm east of the doorway on the north kitchen wall and with a shape indicating a downward direction."

8.4   Collection and Preservation of Bloodstains

Blood is an enigma with regard to its stability and preservation at a scene. The biochemicals in shed blood degrade, some of them very rapidly. In all cases, the stability of blood is situational and must be included in considerations regarding the testing to be carried out and environmental conditions. The stability and utility of bloodstains will vary from a day or so to months or even years. Wet blood packaged in a plastic bag will degrade rapidly, but a small smear that has air-dried quickly but been protected from sunlight can be stable for years. An advantage of DNA typing using STRs is that these are amongst the most robust of techniques. Once blood evidence has been found it must be collected and preserved in a manner that will achieve maximum benefit. All too often improper collection and preservation of this type of evidence make the forensic laboratory's work difficult and sometimes impossible.

8.4.1 Preservation

Correct preservation procedures improve the chances of success in laboratory testing. It is a certainty that wet or damp bloodstains packaged in airtight containers, such as plastic bags, will be useless as evidence in a relatively short period of time. Any type of packaging technique that hastens putrefaction should be avoided. Thus, storing bloodstains that are still damp in airtight containers or in warm environments will accelerate deterioration of the specimen. Conversely, an air-dried sample stored in a paper bag at room temperature will retain its evidentiary usefulness for a significantly longer period of time. The differences can range from as short as a few days to many years and are of practical importance not only in the active collection and preservation of blood but also in the success of reprocessing old cases. Many cold case investigations have been solved by DNA typing of small samples.

The idea of avoiding plastic packaging may seem counterintuitive to a new crime scene examiner who is used to the concept that plastic, airtight containers prevent loss and deleterious change (think of food in the refrigerator or freezer) and is aware that the wet blood transferred from a stain to the paper bag could be violating the principle of avoiding contamination. The key to understanding is that wet = putrefaction = degradation, and dry = preservation = no or minimal change. Whenever possible, wet samples should be gently air dried first, but paper allows them to breathe and dry. Alternatively, as described in Chapter 3, breathable evidence bags are available, and packaging in plastic is advised when wet clothing has to be transported to a drying facility. Figure 8.8 shows a laboratory drying cabinet used for small samples such as swabs. Other steps such as physical separation

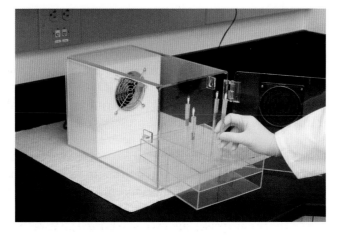

Figure 8.8 Laboratory drying cabinet used for small samples such as swabs. (Photograph courtesy of Los Angeles County Sheriff's Department, Los Angeles, CA.)

should be employed to prevent contamination. Preservation of blood and other biological evidence may require special handling in jurisdictions with case law dealing with preservation of such evidence.

8.4.2   Collection

Blood may be present in a liquid, damp, or completely dry state. Depending on the circumstance, different procedures may be used. The easiest method of collection of wet blood is to place an absorbent piece of material into the still liquid pool of blood. Materials such as filter paper, cotton-tipped applicators, and cotton gauze may be used. A good procedure is to use sterile cotton-tipped applicators, which can be used in the collection of wet and dried bloodstains. The cotton swab is placed in the liquid blood and allowed to become saturated. The swab can then be left to air-dry and then placed in an envelope or other receptacle. The envelopes should be marked to clearly indicate where the specimen came from and who collected it. This is especially important when several blood samples are collected.

8.4.3   Bloodstained Objects

If wet or damp bloodstained items cannot be air-dried, they should be packaged separately in wrapping paper or paper bags. They should not be tightly rolled or bundled up because this accelerates putrefaction of the stains. Whether wet or dry, newspaper should not be used. When items of clothing are collected, a useful habit to develop is to initial the items as soon as the evidence is received. Develop a routine of always marking the item in the same location, such as on the inside collar of a shirt or the back inside waistband of trousers. Often it is not feasible to submit an entire large item of bloodstained evidence (e.g., a bloodstained carpet or mattress) to the laboratory. There are two ways to collect blood in such instances. The first is to follow the already outlined procedure of using the moistened cotton swab. The second is simply to cut out a portion of the item containing the bloodstain. The cutting is then placed in an appropriate package and marked.

8.4.4   Semen-Stained Objects

One of the most probative pieces of evidence in dealing with a sexual assault case is the presence of semen. It is usually found on bedding, clothing, tissues, towels, condoms, and the like. An alternate light source is often used to locate semen stains due to the fluorescent properties of semen under certain wavelengths of light (Figure 8.9). Once a possible semen stain is located, a presumptive test is performed to determine if the stain is presumptively positive for semen. This is done by looking for the presence of an enzyme, acid phosphatase (AP), which is found in large quantities in semen. The presumptive test is a colour spot test that changes from clear to reddish-purple (Figure 8.10). Once an AP-positive presumptive test is established, a confirmatory test is required. This is done either by a microscopic visualization of sperm or the detection of prostate-specific antigen (PSA), or p30. Although PSA is found in low levels of other body tissues in both men and women, high levels of the protein are indicative of the presence of semen (Figure 8.11). The PSA test can demonstrate the presence of semen even in the absence of spermatozoa, such as aspermic men who have had a vasectomy.

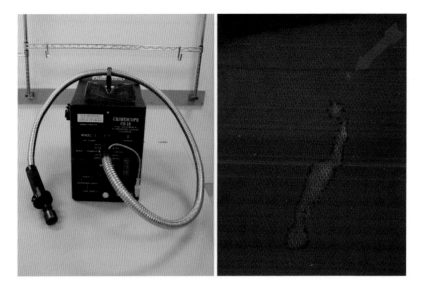

Figure 8.9 Example of an alternative light source (left) and a semen stain visualised with it (right). The stain could not be seen under normal light. (Photographs courtesy of Los Angeles County Sheriff's Department, Los Angeles, CA.)

8.5 DNA Typing

DNA typing is capable of eliminating suspects as well as incriminating them; however, to give meaning to biological stains collected at a crime scene, DNA samples from victims and suspects must be routinely submitted to the forensic laboratory along with the evidence. Elimination samples from consensual partners, people with legitimate access to a crime scene, crime scene investigators, ambulance and emergency services personnel, and other individuals whose DNA might be present at a crime scene should also be submitted

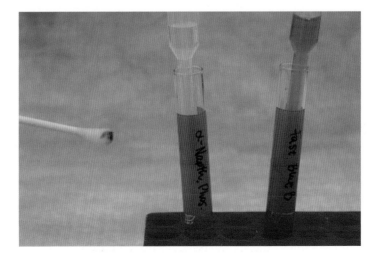

Figure 8.10 A positive presumptive test for the presence of acid phosphatase, an enzyme found in large quantities in semen. (Photograph courtesy of Los Angeles County Sheriff's Department, Los Angeles, CA.)

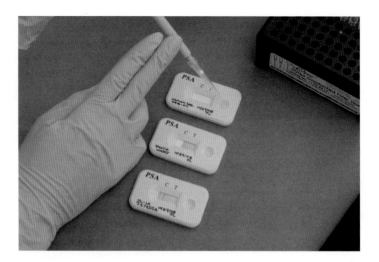

Figure 8.11 The PSA test can demonstrate the presence of semen even in the absence of spermatozoa, such as aspermic men who have had a vasectomy. Here, the unknown sample is run alongside a positive and negative control. (Photograph courtesy of Los Angeles County Sheriff's Department, Los Angeles, CA.)

to the laboratory for testing. As already noted, some jurisdictions have regulations regarding reference databases, and in these the log of personnel accessing the crime scene has an added significance should contamination be suspected.

8.5.1   Collection of Known Specimens

It is important to collect DNA specimens in an appropriate way. It is especially important to use the proper collection container. Buccal swabs, or swabs from the inside cheek, are an excellent alternative to collecting blood samples. Commercial kits are available for this purpose.

8.5.2   Forensic DNA Typing

DNA typing is based on our genetic makeup. Anyone who has attended a sporting event or been in a large crowd of people recognises the obvious: People look different. Differences are manifested by gender, race, stature, hair colour, eye colour, and shape of facial features, to name a few of the common features. The fact is that people can easily recognise others through some subjective mental process.

We also recognise family traits among brothers and sisters, parents and children, and sometimes even more distant familial relationships. How often have people commented that a son looks just like his father or mother, or "I can see Grandmother's eyes in yours"? These family characteristics can be seen over and over in family lineage.

An individual's physical appearance and family traits are a manifestation of the biochemical blueprint and building blocks that make people unique. The notion of differences and similarities in individuals has its scientific basis in the study of genetics. The roots of genetics go back to the mid-1800s, when Gregor Mendel elucidated the laws of inheritance and described what we now call a "gene," although the name itself was not used by him.

Over the next century, major strides were made in the study of genetics, culminating in the discovery by Watson and Crick in 1953 that it was the chemical structure of deoxyribonucleic acid (DNA) in chromosomes that determined the genetic code.

DNA is the biochemical key to differentiating uniqueness among individuals (with the exception of identical twins). It has been called the *chemical messenger* in that it conveys genetic information that is the basis of the way individual living things take shape, grow, and reproduce. DNA is found in the nucleus of the cell, folded into microscopic bundles called *chromosomes*, and it exists in identical form in all cells of the body that contain nuclei. DNA is not present in red blood cells because these cells have no nuclei; other cells present in blood do contain DNA, however. DNA is present in blood, seminal fluid, tissues, bone marrow, hair roots, saliva, urine, and tooth pulp. Each of these samples has the potential to yield DNA typing results.

The DNA molecule resembles a twisted ladder or double helix. The steps within the ladder consist of four chemical subunits or bases: guanine (G), adenine (A), thymine (T), and cytosine (C). These bases pair in predictable ways (A always with T, and G always with C) and form the steps or rungs of the double-stranded DNA helix. The combinations of A–T and G–C are referred to as *base pairs*. Human DNA contains over 3 billion base pairs, and the entirety of the DNA is called the *genome*.

Genes makes up less than 2% of the total human genome, the remainder being noncoding DNA. Forensic DNA tests depend on identification of inherited variations in parts of the noncoding DNA. The areas of interest are the short tandem repeats (STRs) referred to earlier, because they consist of sequences of 2 to 50 bases repeated head-to-tail, and the genetic variation is in the number of repeat sequences in the STR. More than 10,000 STRs have been identified, with around 20 being of forensic interest.

The amount of DNA in even a very large bloodstain is far too small to permit direct analysis of the STRs in it. The process therefore begins with targeting a specific STR in the DNA molecule and using a technique called the polymerase chain reaction (PCR) to multiply the amount by more than a million times.

8.5.3 Polymerase Chain Reaction

The polymerase chain reaction copies short segments of DNA millions of times in a process that resembles the way in which DNA duplicates itself naturally in the body. It works best for small sequences of DNA, such as those in STRs, and becomes more prone to errors as the length of the DNA targeted increases; thus, the science fiction notion of reviving a dinosaur from its DNA remains science fiction!

Apart from being necessary to provide sufficient DNA for the STRs to be characterised, PCR is a powerful technology to use in combination with STRs in forensic science because it can be applied to any tissue specimen, is resistant to degradation and ageing, and is relatively fast, requiring only a few hours to complete the process. The amplification process itself is so effective that it takes us from where the amount of DNA in the sample is impossibly small to study to where the STR type can be identified from a single hair with its root, dried saliva on the back of a letter or postage stamp, microscopic samples that have been stored for years from old cases (cold cases), or a swab from the steering wheel of a car. This extreme sensitivity is why it is so important to prevent contamination at the scene.

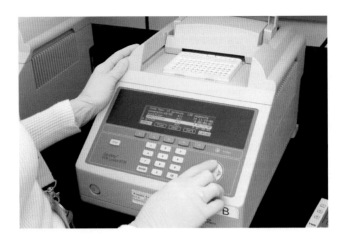

Figure 8.12 A thermocycler heats and cools a sample for predefined set amounts of time, allowing the polymerase chain reaction (PCR) process to proceed. Each cycle roughly doubles the amount of DNA. (Photograph courtesy of Los Angeles County Sheriff's Department, Los Angeles, CA.)

The PCR process is performed in an instrument known as a *thermocycler*. It consists of initially separating the DNA double helix into two strands by heating the sample (Figure 8.12). A PCR reaction mixture is then added. It consists of a pair of DNA primers (short segments of DNA that are added to locate the target segment of DNA to be copied), DNA polymerase (an enzyme that catalyses the reaction), and the four nucleotide bases, A, C, T, and G. This mixture contains all the ingredients necessary to copy both of the original DNA strands that were separated and therefore double the amount of DNA. The doubling procedure is repeated, usually 28 times, which multiplies the amount of DNA nearly 270 million fold. After the PCR process, the mixture of DNA fragments is separated according to their size, using a process called *capillary electrophoresis*. A laser then reads the DNA samples, and software converts this electronic data into an electropherogram (Figure 8.13).

8.5.4   High-Sensitivity DNA Testing (Touch DNA)

High-sensitivity DNA testing is used to recover and detect small amounts of DNA (generally this refers to amounts less than 100 picograms). The technique is also referred to as low template DNA, low copy number (LCN) DNA, or touch DNA. The methods and instruments employed are the same as traditional DNA typing, except for a few modifications to increase sensitivity, principally using increased cycle numbers for the PCR process. Examples of items that are candidates for high-sensitivity testing include car swabs, handles of weapons or tools, keys, pens, air bags, objects used for binding, door handles, touched clothing, and degraded or old samples. Figure 8.14 shows the specialised swab used by the New York City Office of the Chief Medical Examiner's DNA unit for touch DNA sampling.

8.5.5   Short Tandem Repeats and DNA Profiles

The repeated units in forensic STRs are mainly four or five bases long, and their forensic value lies in the genetically determined variations in the number of repeat sequences in the STR. The different forms of each STR are called *alleles*, and each STR has around 20 allelic

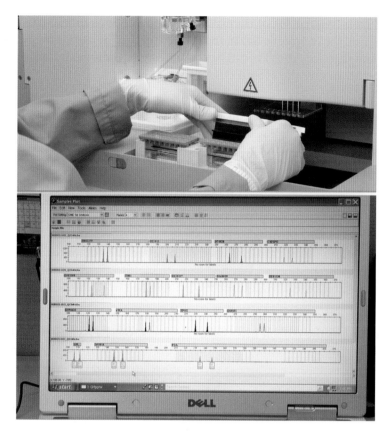

Figure 8.13 Separating the PCR products by capillary electrophoresis (top) and the resultant electropherogram (bottom). (Photographs courtesy of Los Angeles County Sheriff's Department, Los Angeles, CA.)

Figure 8.14 The New York City Office of Chief Medical Examiner uses its own patent-pending, specialised, high-sensitivity swab to maximise the amount of DNA collected from an item. (Photograph courtesy of the New York City Office of Chief Medical Examiner.)

forms with known frequencies of occurrence in populations representative of the main races. The power of the technique lies in the fact that each STR used is found on a different chromosome and therefore the data can be combined. The individual allele frequencies are multiplied together to give the overall DNA profile frequency.

8.5.6 Some Illustrative DNA Cases

Case 3

Two women were raped in separate attacks. A suspect was arrested and identified by both victims. Meanwhile, two more women were raped under similar circumstances. A second suspect was arrested for those rapes. DNA typing was performed on semen from the victims' vaginal swabs from the second set of rapes and compared to the second suspect. The DNA testing identified him. Because of the similarity of circumstances, the vaginal samples from the first two rapes were also tested and compared to both suspects. The first suspect who had been identified by both victims in court and held to answer was excluded, whereas the second suspect was identified in all four rapes.

Case 3 shows the value of the objective scientific test of DNA typing compared to what lay people assume is the reliable identification of someone by a witness.

Case 4

A comatose teenage female was discovered to be pregnant. A juvenile friend of the victim's brother was the suspect. The foetus was aborted and submitted along with blood from the victim and the suspect for paternity testing. DNA samples from the victim's father and brother were also submitted for elimination. The juvenile suspect was excluded from having fathered the foetus. Unexpectedly, the brother was identified as the father.

Case 4 illustrates how DNA can be used to ascertain parentage, and, once more, the power of DNA to provide exclusionary and corroborative evidence.

Case 5

Three males allegedly gang-raped two women. No semen was found in the vaginal samples; however, three used condoms were recovered from a trash can at the scene. Three suspects were arrested and identified by the victims as having participated in the rapes. One of the suspects was adamant that, although he was there, he did not participate in the rape. DNA testing was performed on the semen found inside each of the three condoms. The exterior surfaces of the condoms were tested for the victims' DNA. It was determined that one of the suspects had raped one of the victims and a second suspect had raped both of the victims. Contrary to the victims' statements, the suspect who was adamant about not participating in the rapes did not contribute the semen found in any of the condoms.

Case 5 could be taken as an example similar to Case 3, but it could also be an example of the principle that "absence of evidence is not evidence of absence," which we described in Chapter 1; for example, what if the third suspect had disposed of his condom differently from the others? Complete interpretation is difficult without knowing the circumstances of the search, but there is certainly a caution to the crime scene investigator here to be thorough and set the boundaries of the scene wide rather than narrow, as we emphasised in Chapter 3.

Case 6

An adult female was found murdered and left in a position suggesting a sexual assault. Three suspects were generated by the investigation, with no investigative means to determine the true assailant from among them. Fingernail scrapings collected by the coroner's office contained a trace quantity of blood. DNA typing showed the blood was not the victim's. The results were compared to blood samples collected from the three suspects. One was included and the others were eliminated. No other methods available could have yielded a result on such a trace quantity of blood evidence.

Case 6 is an excellent illustration of how the ability of DNA testing to provide results on the tiniest of samples can assist an investigation ... and an example of good practice by the crime scene investigators.

Case 7

Police conducting surveillance on an unrelated case discovered decomposing parts of a dismembered human body. The remains included the victim's head. A suspect was developed, and blood drops were recovered in a search of his residence. The dismembered remains were too decomposed to provide a reference for genetic typing using conventional methods. Hair was removed from the victim's head and provided sufficient DNA for comparison to the blood drops recovered from the suspect's residence. The blood drops matched the victim and murder charges were filed.

Case 7 illustrates two aspects of DNA typing: (1) its ability to give results even in degraded samples, and (2) that it can produce typing from tissues other than blood.

Case 8

In the early 1980s, a young college student was raped and murdered while jogging in a park close to the campus. A suspect was identified and arrested soon after. He was unable to provide an alibi during the time of the murder. Throughout his trial, the man accused of the brutal rape and murder was adamant that he was innocent of the charges against him. A witness, who originally was not able to identify the defendant, identified him as the murderer at a trial that led to the man's conviction. He continued to maintain his innocence during his prison term and was able to get his state's Innocence Project to take his case. Recent legislation in the United States allowed him to secure post-conviction DNA testing on the victim's underwear, which was located after a long search of the police department property warehouse. It had never been tested for DNA. The results of the DNA testing excluded him as the semen donor found on the victim's underwear. The profile that was developed matched the database profile of a convicted offender already in prison for another rape.

Case 8 is an example of how DNA methods can produce results even on traces of old evidence items.

Case 9

An executive in a major southern California business firm received threat letters. A suspect was identified who was an employee of the firm and had had an affair with the executive's wife; however, evidence was insufficient for an arrest or a search warrant. Subsequently, the chief of the investigating agency received a mail bomb and a threat letter. The saliva residues on the threat letter envelopes sent to the executive and the Chief of Police were subjected to DNA typing. The results were also compared to saliva residue from love letters sent by the suspect to the executive's wife during their affair. The DNA types matched. This provided sufficient evidence for a search warrant for a sample of the suspect's DNA. The DNA sample also matched the saliva residues on the letters, and the suspect was charged with attempted murder. The case was adjudicated by a plea bargain because of the strength of the identification of the suspect using DNA typing.

Case 9 shows not only how DNA can produce valuable evidence (e.g., from analysis of saliva traces on envelopes) but also how it can give crime scene investigators a tool to assist in their investigations.

8.6   DNA Databases

8.6.1   History

The attributes of forensic DNA testing described above lend themselves to using a database of DNA profiles to associate profiles found in DNA at a crime scene with those from other scenes or from known offenders. A DNA database can contribute to the criminal justice system in the following ways:

- Different crime scenes can be linked and old cases solved when there are matches between crimes.
- Matches enable investigators to identify serial offenders and perpetrators, coordinate investigations, and even share leads across jurisdictions.
- It ensures early identification and arrest of serial offenders and prevents criminal activities.
- DNA can provide important investigative leads to help resolve issues of human identification.
- Cold hits from other laboratories or even other countries may link with a suspect from a completely different type of crime, years later.
- Crime prevention is the ultimate goal achieved through the deterrence effect of database sampling (i.e., "Do not commit a crime because we have your DNA profile, and we'll catch you!").
- Familial searches on the DNA database can result in identification of the offender through links generated with the offender's close biological relatives.
- Police can spend more time on investigative work and focus on one or more individuals, whilst still performing a complete investigation in less time.
- The combination of DNA data and other forensic evidence can be invaluable in investigations—for example, when an unknown DNA profile is linked to the fingerprints of a known suspect.
- The use of an international DNA database extends the scope of an enquiry and thereby facilitates criminal investigations.

In general, the databases all use STRs and all have exacting standards that must be met before profiles can be entered. The rules for what kind of samples are entered and how long they are retained vary. Some examples of the variety are given below; however, most profiles that are entered consist of between 10 and 20 STRs, and there is sufficient overlap to make country to country searches worthwhile.

The first operational DNA database was the National DNA Database (NDNAD), established in the United Kingdom in 1995. Australia, France, Germany, New Zealand, Norway, Portugal, Sweden, and the United States are just some of the countries that now have fully functioning national DNA databases. According to INTERPOL, 120 countries were known to use DNA profiling in their police investigations in 2008, and 54 countries were known to have a national DNA database.

The original NDNAD reference database consisted of profiles from suspects in investigations by police in England, Northern Ireland, Scotland, and Wales. Profiles from any person arrested on suspicion of a recordable offence in England, Northern Ireland, and Wales were retained permanently, irrespective of the outcome. Scots law differed and required the profiles of persons subsequently acquitted to be removed. Retention procedures in the other three UK countries have now been brought into line with those in Scotland. Germany, Norway, and Sweden require court orders and restrict the circumstances under which records can be stored, and a court order is required in Germany and Norway. Australia has had a national DNA database since 2001, consisting of profiles from samples collected at crime scenes, from convicted offenders, suspects, and unidentified bodies. During investigations, whether or not samples can be taken from suspects or from charged persons varies according to state laws.

8.6.2   DNA Databases in Investigations and Unsolved Cases

The use of DNA typing in forensic laboratories has changed the way forensic laboratories prioritise their casework, including rape cases lacking a suspect. Prior to DNA typing, most laboratories did not perform blood typing on evidence in sexual assault cases in which there was no known suspect. The reasoning was simple: Typing results could not be compared with a suspect, and because resources are always limited such cases were not typed. DNA databases have reversed this policy by making it possible to identify unknown suspects based on their DNA type. Serial crimes such as rapes and murders will have a better likelihood of being solved because DNA typing results can be compared with DNA typing records collected from convicted offenders. Two things must happen, however: (1) the convicted person's specimen must be collected and typed, and (2) the laboratory must routinely examine its non-suspect sexual assault cases.

8.6.3   Partial Matches and Familial Searching

Occasionally a partial match between a forensic profile and an offender profile is observed during a routine database search. A partial match occurs when there is a similarity in profiles between a forensic unknown and a known exemplar. A partial match is not an exact match of the two profiles, but when it meets a particular statistical threshold, it is indicative that a close biological relative of the offender may be the source of the forensic unknown. Further DNA testing should be done in such cases (such as Y-STR testing to determine if the two profiles are of the same paternal relative). A known DNA sample from the biological relative should also be obtained for direct comparison. Familial searching is an intentional or deliberate search of the database conducted after a routine search for the purpose of potentially identifying close biological relatives of the unknown forensic sample associated with the crime scene profile.

8.7   Development of Forensic DNA Techniques and Standards

Methods used in forensic testing must be reliable. Reliability is ensured by various quality control methods, but the power of DNA testing, its dependence on modern advances in molecular biology, and most of all the potential impact of errors in profiles held on databases make quality in DNA analysis paramount. Database applications also make it desirable if not essential to have harmonisation of practices over larger regional areas. For these reasons, there has been a tendency for quality assurance standards, validation and introduction of new typing systems, and technical and legislative aspects of database management to be coordinated by working groups.

In Europe, the coordination is mainly achieved through the European Network of Forensic Science Institutes (ENFSI), which operates a DNA Working Group that has issued reports on DNA database management, DNA legislation, contamination prevention, validation of methods, and staff training. ENFSI has a strong working relationship with the European DNA Profiling (EDNAP) Working Group within the International Society for Haemogenetics. The main objective of the EDNAP Working Group is harmonisation of DNA typing technology for crime investigations. It has been addressed by organising a number of collaborative inter-comparison exercises and by discussing the results at the regular meetings of the group. Australia and New Zealand have a similar coordination, managed through the Australia New Zealand Policing Advisory Agency and the CrimTrac DNA database. The Federal Bureau of Investigation (FBI)-supported Scientific Working Group on DNA Analysis Methods (SWGDAM) performs a similar role in the United States.

The significance of these groups for the crime scene examiner is that the whole field of forensic DNA is constantly changing globally. There is significant national, regional, and international cooperation between the scientists involved, but crime scene examiners need to be sure that they keep abreast of changes and are able to input their needs and respond to changes in work practices.

8.8   Other DNA Typing Systems

Although STRs are the engine of forensic DNA typing and database applications, they are not the only systems used in forensic science that are DNA based. We will very briefly consider three other systems:

- SNPs
- Y-STRs
- Mitochondrial DNA

8.8.1 SNPs

The acronym for single nucleotide polymorphism is SNP. *Nucleotide* is the generic name for the CATG building blocks that make DNA, and *polymorphism* means "many forms." SNPs, therefore, are places in the DNA molecule where one of the nucleotides has been replaced by its complementary one; for example, the sequence AATCGGTACC might have a variant form of AATCGCTACC. SNPs are the most common type of variant in DNA but are of limited practical value in characterising nuclear DNA.

8.8.2 Y-STRs

Short tandem repeats found on Y-chromosomes are referred to as Y-STRs. Y-chromosomes are only found in males and are passed from father to son. They are of value because they permit direct typing of DNA of male origin.

8.8.3 Mitochondrial DNA

Mitochondrial DNA (mtDNA) is a completely different form of DNA from that found in nuclei. Mitochondria are small physical units found in the cell that are responsible for energy metabolism. They contain their own DNA in the form of a double-stranded loop, consisting of 16,569 bases. Mitochondrial DNA is passed from the mother to her children, both boys and girls. It is particularly valuable in identifying skeletal or putrefied remains, because there are hundreds of copies of mtDNA in each cell, compared to only two copies of nuclear DNA. Mitochondria are also very robust. A third advantage when identifying remains is that the mtDNA will match that of any female relative, making tracing much easier.

8.9 Bloodstain Pattern Analysis (BPA)

Bloodstain pattern analysis (BPA) is a field in and of itself, and an in-depth discussion of it is beyond the scope of this book. BPA requires much experience and training in order to correctly make interpretations about bloodstain patterns. Beginning and advanced bloodstain pattern interpretation courses are available and it is highly recommended that such courses of study be taken prior to performing crime scene reconstruction on actual cases. Continuing education and experience will allow the investigator to draw the most accurate conclusions. Crime scene reconstruction through the use of bloodstain pattern interpretation is a useful technique but only for those who are properly trained. All too often, unfortunately, investigators overstate their conclusions based on a limited understanding of bloodstain pattern analysis and crime scene reconstruction.

Case 10

An elderly female was assaulted by her daughter with an oxygen tank and a wine bottle while in the living room of her apartment. The woman lived for a period of time but eventually died due to injuries she sustained from the assault. Figure 8.15 depicts various bloodstain patterns on the entryway floor of the apartment. Eight pressurized oxygen cylinders were also on the entryway floor near the entry door.

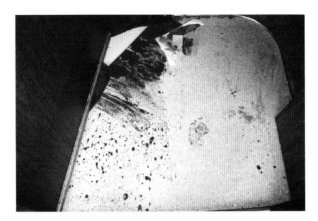

Figure 8.15 Bloodstain patterns on the entryway floor of the apartment.

Impact spatter was noted on seven of the cylinders, while one of the cylinders was heavily bloodstained with apparent hair adhering to it. A ring of blood was also seen on the floor beneath this heavily bloodstained cylinder. In addition, impact spatter was seen on the wall behind this cylinder, indicating that the cylinder was not in this position when the spatter was deposited. Voids were visible on the wall behind the other seven cylinders indicating that these cylinders were in their current positions when the assault occurred. A *void* is a term used to describe an area within a generally continuous bloodstain pattern that lacks bloodstains. Based on the significant amount of blood and apparent hair attached to the one cylinder, as well as the presence of impact spatter on the wall behind the cylinder and the ring of blood on the floor beneath the cylinder, the heavily bloodstained cylinder was likely used as a weapon to assault the victim. Figure 8.16 shows the locations of the oxygen cylinders, the impact spatter on the wall behind the heavily bloodstained cylinder, the ring of blood on the floor where this cylinder was positioned, and the lack of impact spatter behind the remaining cylinders.

Bloodstain pattern evidence is often present at the scene of crimes of violence. Because shed blood obeys the laws of physics that apply to the behaviour of fluids, the shape, grouping, and distribution of bloodstains can assist the investigator in reconstructing what took place at the crime scene. In addition to determining to whom the blood belongs through DNA, it is often necessary to determine the movement and direction of persons, the sequence of events, the area of origin of a pattern, the number of impacts during an incident, and the object used to create a specific pattern. These determinations can be used to corroborate or contradict statements made by victims, suspects, and witnesses.

Basically, there are two general categories of bloodstains: (1) spatter, caused by blood travelling through the air; and (2) transfer stains, which result from contact with a bloody surface. Determining whether a stain was made by a transfer or by a spatter-producing event can be a critical piece of information. Directionality can be determined from the shape of the bloodstains. The pointed or tail end of the bloodstain indicates the direction of travel. The angle of impact can be determined by using the formula:

$$\theta \text{ (angle of impact)} = \arcsin (\text{width of ellipse/length of ellipse})$$

Figure 8.16 Locations of the oxygen cylinders, impact spatter on the wall behind the heavily bloodstained cylinder, ring of blood on the floor where the cylinder was positioned, and the lack of impact spatter behind the remaining cylinders. (Photographs courtesy of Melissa Simons, Oregon State Police Central Point Forensic Laboratory.)

Figure 8.17 Blood drops that have hit a surface at an angle (left) compared to contact smears (right). The tail end of the bloodstain indicates the direction of travel.

and is illustrated in Figure 8.17, which shows blood drops that have hit a surface at an angle (left) in contrast to contact smears (right). The tail end of the bloodstain indicates the direction of travel.

The degree of spatter of a single passive blood drop depends on the smoothness of the target surface more than the distance the drop falls. The coarser the surface, the more likely the drop will be ruptured and spatter. A rough surface, for example, will cause a drop to spatter to a considerable extent from a relatively short height, whereas a drop falling over 100 feet will not spatter at all if it lands on glass or on another smooth surface.

When describing blood marks at a crime scene, some of the terms generally used include bloodstain, swipe, wipe, spatter, drip stain, expired blood resulting from blood forced by airflow out of the nose or mouth, parent stain, satellite stain, and insect stain.

8.10   Summary

The story of forensic biology today is the story of DNA. All body tissues contain DNA, either in their nuclei or mitochondria. Advances in technology allow profiles to be developed in samples too tiny to be seen by the naked eye, the so-called "touch DNA." Add its resistance to degradation, ability to produce profiles with population frequencies that are near individual in non-twins, and the growth of databases, and we can see that it is a powerful tool for scene investigators exploring the question of WHO. It is important, however, not to overlook the value of other aspects of forensic biology, such as blood pattern analysis. These can provide information on WHERE, WHAT, HOW, and perhaps also WHY and WHEN. The crime scene investigator must know where to look for biological evidence, and collect and preserve it for the laboratory analysis. And, as some of the illustrative DNA cases show, the work of the scene investigator can be critical in providing the framework required for interpretation of the laboratory tests.

Impression Evidence

9.1 Introduction

Impression evidence is an example of associative evidence. This simple title spans a wide range of sources, reliability, and evidential strength. Its essential basis is the identification, recording, and comparison of marks, and its value lies in Kirk's postulates discussed in Chapter 1:

- No two things that happen by chance ever happen in exactly the same way.
- No two things are ever constructed in exactly the same way.
- No two things ever wear in exactly the same way.
- No two things ever break in exactly the same way.

Although the National Research Council report challenged the absolute nature of some of these elements, there is no doubt that impression evidence is a valid tool in the forensic process. Note that the everyday use of the word implies a mark made by pressing something onto a softer surface, so that its outline is reproduced in three dimensions. Here, we also use "impression" to refer to two-dimensional marks, such as a bloody footprint, and will generally distinguish these by referring to them as "prints."

Case 1

Charlie Richardson, a 30-year-old student, was completing his final year in medical school. Maria Richardson was his wife of several years. Their relationship appeared normal to those who knew them. On the morning of 30 December, 1988, Charlie drove Maria to her workplace, a laboratory located in El Cajon, California. Later in the morning, one of Maria's co-workers found her dead in the laboratory. The police arrived and began an investigation. Meanwhile, Charlie purchased items at several locations in the San Diego area, including roses for his wife. At noon, he returned to the laboratory saying he had come to have lunch with Maria. He wondered why he was not allowed to see his wife and why detectives were around the lab. Charlie was told of Maria's death and was then asked for background information about her. Charlie related his actions of the morning, explained how he left his wife at work and then went to the library to study. He told investigators that he planned to meet Maria for lunch and produced time-stamped receipts from various locations.

The victim had ligature marks around her neck and chin. Several items that could have been used as the ligature were collected, including a long telephone cord attached to a wall phone. During the investigation, a small crescent-shaped abrasion was noted on the edge of Charlie's right pinkie finger. Charlie was now a suspect and was cautioned. He explained the abrasion as a burn received while he was cooking; however, he was unable to explain a very small, less visible matching abrasion along the edge of his left pinkie finger. Charlie Richardson was arrested for the murder of his wife, Maria.

Casts and photographs of the suspect's fingers and of the ligature marks on the victim's neck were taken and compared with the wall telephone cord from the scene. In this case, the cord became critical evidence. A search of the suspect's home yielded evidence of disharmony in the marriage; investigators also found writings by Maria in which she said she was afraid of Charlie. The trial ended with the defence agreeing to plead to a charge of involuntary manslaughter. (See Figures 9.1 to 9.6.)

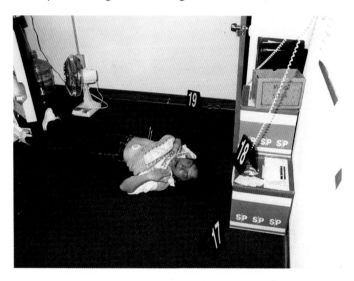

Figure 9.1 The victim found at the scene of her murder. Note the proximity of the telephone cord to her head. (Photograph courtesy of Norman Sperber, DDS, Chief Forensic Dentist for San Diego and Imperial Counties, San Diego, CA; El Cajon Police Department, El Cajon, CA.)

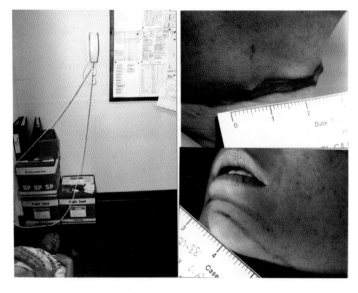

Figure 9.2 The wall telephone and cord (left) and the ligature marks on the victim's neck (top right) and chin (bottom right) that were compared to the telephone cord. The marks are of a size and nature consistent with strangulation with the telephone cord. (Photographs courtesy of Norman Sperber, DDS, Chief Forensic Dentist for San Diego and Imperial Counties, San Diego, CA; El Cajon Police Department, El Cajon, CA.)

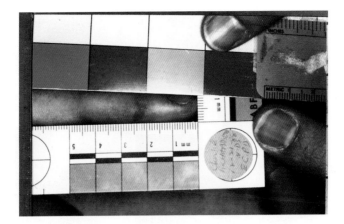

Figure 9.3 The abrasion on Charlie Richardson's right pinkie finger, which the defendant explained was due to a burn received while he was cooking. He was unable to explain another less visible one on his left pinkie finger. (Photograph courtesy of Norman Sperber, DDS, Chief Forensic Dentist for San Diego and Imperial Counties, San Diego, CA; El Cajon Police Department, El Cajon, CA.)

Figure 9.4 Dr. Norman Sperber making castings of the defendant's left and right little fingers. (Photograph courtesy of Norman Sperber, DDS, Chief Forensic Dentist for San Diego and Imperial Counties, San Diego, CA; El Cajon Police Department, El Cajon, CA.)

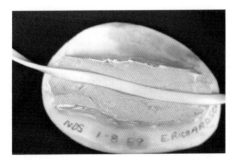

Figure 9.5 The telephone cord fitted into a casting of the ligature mark on the victim's neck. Although generally featureless, the findings do not falsify the hypothesis that the cord was responsible for the ligature marks on the neck of the victim. (Photograph courtesy of Norman Sperber, DDS, Chief Forensic Dentist for San Diego and Imperial Counties, San Diego, CA; El Cajon Police Department, El Cajon, CA.)

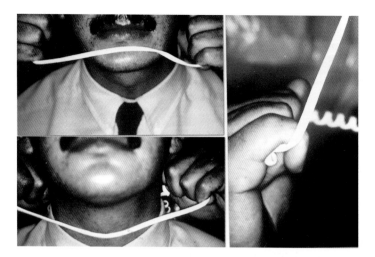

Figure 9.6 Reconstructions showing how the markings on the defendant's pinkies and on the victim's chin might have occurred. (Photographs courtesy of Norman Sperber, DDS, Chief Forensic Dentist for San Diego and Imperial Counties, San Diego, CA; El Cajon Police Department, El Cajon, CA.)

9.2   The Nature of Impression Marks

Minute imperfections on a large variety of objects such as tools, footwear, tyres, and so on produce markings in their normal (and sometimes unusual) usage. These markings are often characteristic of the type of tool or object used. In many instances, very small and sometimes microscopically unique markings are left that can be traced directly to the object or instrument in question. Such marks caused by a tool are of two general types: *compression marks* and *scraping marks*. Compression marks are those left when an instrument is in some way pushed or forced into a material capable of picking up an impression of the tool. Examples include shoe impressions, tyre impressions, bite mark impressions, fabric impressions, marks left by a hammer hitting a piece of wood, marks of a screwdriver used to jemmy a window, breech mark impressions on shell casings, typewriter marks, and so on.

Scraping or striated marks are produced by a combination of pressure and sliding contact by the tool and result in microscopic striations imparted to the surface onto which the tool was worked. Examples of scraping marks are those found on fired bullets, left by a cutting tool such as a bolt cutter, from a wrench used on a doorknob, from an axe used to cut wood, from a screwdriver blade dragged over a surface, and teeth marks used to bite through a soft material capable of picking up an impression. In order for compression or scraping marks to be observed, the tool must be made of a harder material than the object on which it is used.

The random nature and microscopic imperfections found on tools are a result of their manufacture and usage. Casting, grinding, and polishing metal instruments, as well as using them, result in small but observable differences from one tool to the next. Such differences have even been demonstrated in consecutively manufactured items. Comparative examination is the method by which impression-type evidence is studied. The marks left at the crime scene (or castings of the mark) are compared with test markings made by the tool or object in question. Through careful but often tedious examination of the known and questioned evidence, a determination can be made as to whether or not a particular item was responsible for a specific mark.

9.3 Footwear Marks

Footwear marks are a common type of impression evidence found at or near crime scenes. In favourable situations, such evidence may provide an association between the footwear and, by inference the person wearing the item and the scene of the crime. Although this discussion concerns footwear impressions, the investigator should be aware of other types of evidence such as DNA that might later be discovered on a suspect's shoes. When a cast is made of a footwear mark in soft ground, one would expect to obtain a faithful reproduction of the heel and sole of the shoe that made the print. As a rule, however, the result of casting is actually quite different—the cast can very often have an arched form. The back of the heel and the point of the toe are considerably lower than the other parts of the cast because, in normal walking, the back of the heel is placed on the ground first. After that, each part of the heel and sole is pressed down on the ground in succession until the foot is lifted, with a final strong pressure of the point of the toe against the earth. The pressure that regulates the depth of the impression is the greatest at the back of the heel and at the point of the toe. When the person is running, the footwear marks are less distinct, partly due to slipping of the foot and partly to sand and earth thrown into the print. The form of the print depends on the individual's style of running; many people run on their toes, others set both heel and toe hard in the ground, and others set the whole foot down in the earth at once. In deciding whether an individual walked or ran, the length of the step is the only certain guide.

9.3.1 Value of Footwear Marks

Individual footwear marks are generally preserved only if they contain details of value for identification. The most valuable details are signs of wear, characteristic fittings or marks of fittings that have come off, injuries, marks of nails and pegs (especially when these are irregularly placed), and repair marks. If they are particularly characteristic or occur in sufficient numbers, such details may form decisive evidence. In the interest of thoroughness, footwear marks should be preserved even if they do not show any details. Although the size and shape of the shoe or a pattern in the heel or sole are of lesser evidential value, a representative print should nonetheless be preserved for its value as an investigative lead, including the possibility to exclude someone as a suspect.

If footwear impressions are found in snow that has a frozen crust, it is a waste of time to attempt to take a cast of them. When the foot breaks through the hard surface of the snow, the surface snow goes with it and forms a hard bottom to the mark. The coarse grains of ice in the surface layer do not reproduce any details of the shoe—not even such large defects as a hole through the sole—and it is not possible to obtain any useful information of the size by measuring the impression because the hard snow is broken and pressed down at points considerably outside the outer contour of the shoe.

Figure 9.7 Plaster cast from shoe impression in snow. (Photograph courtesy of Forensic Science Department, Zurich Cantonal Police, Switzerland.)

A footwear print may be a three-dimensional impression or a two-dimensional print. Footwear impressions occur when the foot treads in some mouldable material such as earth, sand, clay, or snow. Two-dimensional prints are formed on a hard base when the foot or the sole and heel of a shoe are contaminated with some foreign matter such as road dirt, dust, flour, blood, or moisture. Prints are also left when the footwear makes contact with an intact layer of dust or similar material, and the sole of the shoe lifts the dust, leaving an imprint of the sole but usually without any comparable details. Footprints may also be latent when naked or stocking-covered feet on a smooth surface have formed them. Figure 9.7 is a plaster cast from a shoe impression that was made in snow and shows good detail of the shoe sole pattern. The cast surface was coloured with silver spray to enhance the detail for photography. Footwear impression evidence and information from the gait pattern may indicate that the subject was walking or running, had sustained an injury or walked with a limp, was possibly intoxicated, had a tendency to walk toe-in or toe-out, or was carrying a heavy object.

9.3.2 Preservation and Collection of Footwear and Tyre Impressions

Although the focus here is on footwear, much of what follows concerning preserving and collecting this type of evidence applies equally well to tyre impression evidence. Foot impressions are generally found outdoors; the first precautionary measure is therefore to protect the impression from alteration or destruction, preferably by covering it with a box or cordoning off the area. Impressions in thawing snow are especially troublesome, so a box covered with snow to prevent thawing should be used to protect them. If a foot impression is in such a position that it is possible for it to gradually fill up or be damaged by running water, it must be surrounded by a wall of earth, sand, or snow; alternatively, a hole may be dug close to the impression and the water drained toward the hole. These protective measures are only stopgaps, however, and the actual preservation should be undertaken as soon as possible. Interior locations often have footwear marks present, especially on surfaces such as tiled floors, items such as newspapers lying on the floor, glass, desktops, counter tops, window sills, and chair seats. A simple procedure to locate these indoor prints is to turn off all the interior lights and, by means of a high-intensity flashlight, search the surfaces by shining the light at a low angle. Often these impressions are dust prints and very easily destroyed. Once detected, care must be taken to make certain they are preserved.

When a shoeprint is detected it is important to document the exact location where it has been located and determine the direction in which the step has been made. If the shoeprint is not sufficiently clear to permit drawing a conclusion in relation to direction, the orientation of the print must be indicated, such as by drawing an arrow indicating north on the backside of the special black lifter sheet, the photographic paper, electrostatic dust lifter foil, or whatever was used to make the lift. The direction of the shoeprint can be vitally important for possible reconstruction and establishing the events of the crime scene.

9.3.3 Preservation Techniques

Documentation and preservation of this type of evidence should be done first by photographing any observed marks, followed where appropriate by techniques such as casting impressions, lifting dust prints, or chemical processing, such as in the case of faint or latent prints made by transferred blood. Faint or latent prints should be photographed before and after developing by a chemical process. Visible footwear prints will not always be found but may be developed using processes such as electrostatic lifting (Figure 9.8). Following detection and preservation on the dust lift foil, these prints can and must be photographed.

9.3.3.1 Photography
Overall, taking quality photographs is relatively simple, but it requires practice. The basic rules to be followed to make good-quality photographs of footwear and tyre impressions and prints at a crime scene include the following:

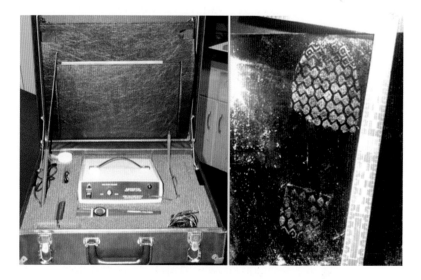

Figure 9.8 An electrostatic dust print lifter (left) and a dust print (right) lifted by this technique. (Photographs courtesy of Forensic Services Section, Department of Police, Montgomery County, Maryland.)

- Use a tripod to support the camera.
- Shoot perpendicular to the impression.
- Use a scale or ruler in the photograph.
- Use oblique lighting.

The camera should be placed vertically above the impression on a tripod with a scale placed next to the impression. The film plane should be parallel to the impression so as not to cause distortion of perspective in the photograph. For the same reason, it is best to use a normal focal length lens and to set the aperture to $f16$ or $f22$. The impression should be lit from at least two sides and preferably include photographs made with oblique lighting and taken from different angles. It is good practice to place two scales in the photograph at right angles to each other. One rule can be placed adjacent to the long axis of the foot impression and a second perpendicular to the first, in the region adjacent to the heel.

Case 2

In 1992, a young woman was murdered in a retail store in Manhattan. The victim was bound and gagged in the rear office and stabbed multiple times with a screwdriver. At the scene, New York Police Department detectives noted bloody shoeprints on the cement floor. Bloody shoeprints were found on a portion of the concrete floor. That portion of floor was stained by the examiner to make the prints more visible. The soles of the suspect's shoes and a print of the shoes were compared, and the examiner concluded that the suspect had made the prints on the cement floor. (See Figures 9.9 to 9.11.)

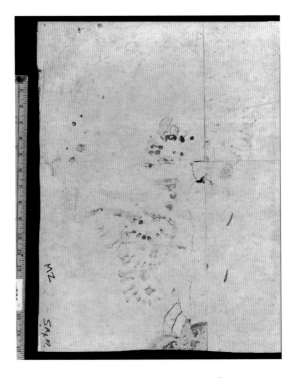

Figure 9.9 Bloody shoeprints on a portion of the concrete floor.

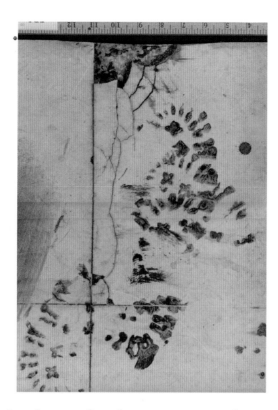

Figure 9.10 The portion of cement floor shown in Figure 9.11 that was stained to make the prints more visible. (Photograph courtesy of William J. Bodziak, Bodziak Forensics, Palm Coast, FL, and formerly with the FBI Laboratory.)

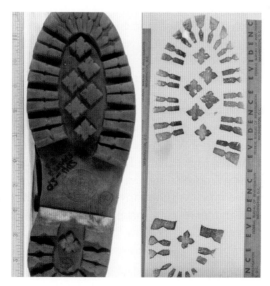

Figure 9.11 The soles of the suspect's shoes (left) and a print of the shoes (right) were compared and the examiner concluded that the suspect made the prints on the cement floor. (Photographs courtesy of William J. Bodziak, Bodziak Forensics, Palm Coast, FL, and formerly with the FBI Laboratory.)

Although large-format cameras (e.g., 4 × 5 or 2-inch formats) allow for larger negatives, 35-mm cameras have become more widely used for crime scene work and produce acceptable results. High-resolution images are required for footwear and tyre impressions to adequately capture the fine details. Professional-level digital cameras can now approach the resolution of film; however, some examiners may prefer traditional photographic prints to digital ones. Other factors to be considered in camera choice are cost and convenience. Some agencies have changed to digital because of the easier sharing and storage of images and the savings gained from not having to process the film.

If the bottom of the impression is appreciably deeper than the surface of the ground or snow, the scale should be brought down to the same level. Before photographing, any material that may have fallen into the impression after it was formed should be cleaned away. For this purpose, it is convenient to use forceps or a piece of paper onto which lumps of earth are rolled (or other such objects that cannot be picked up by the forceps). If it is not possible to carry out this cleaning without injuring details of the impression, it should be omitted. Materials trampled into the impression, such as leaves or grass, should not be removed because they form part of the impression and no details will be found under them. Careless removal of a trampled blade of grass can destroy large parts of the impression. Any water that may be present should be carefully removed by a hypodermic syringe or small pump. If the impression has been made in snow, it may be difficult to get a clear picture of it. Hard snow may be dusted with aluminium powder or red fingerprint powder, which gives a clearer picture. With loose snow, the powder can be dusted into the mark by tapping the brush.

Because the details in foot impressions are three dimensional, the photograph should be made under illumination that will bring out those details to the best advantage. Direct sunlight enhances the details by creating highlights and shadows. When the sky is cloudy and the daylight diffuse and practically without shadow, artificial light must be used; photoflood or flash illumination is suitable. These considerations, of course, also apply to situations in which it is imperative that the pictures be taken at night. The important point to remember about the illumination is that the light must not be held at too low of an angle because too much shadow will obscure rather than emphasise detail.

9.3.3.2 Casting with Dental Stone

Dental stone is a type of gypsum or calcium sulphate that can be used to cast shoe and tyre impressions. At one time, plaster of Paris was more widely used for this purpose; however, dental stone is superior and readily available from dental supply companies. Dental stone can be used for casting most impressions, even in snow. Foot impressions in loose, dry sand and earth can often be taken without any special preparation. Some literature suggests removing loose twigs and leaves, but this practice can damage the impression and is discouraged. Also, using fixatives such as spray lacquers or talc, practices generally recommended for use with plaster of Paris, is not necessary with dental stone.

9.3.3.3 Casting Water-Filled Impressions

Dental stone lends itself quite well to casting water-filled impressions. If an impression is very muddy or filled with water, no attempt should be made to remove the water because this may damage the impression. A retaining wall or frame should be placed around the impression. The retainer should allow for a cast at least 5 cm in thickness. Dental stone is lightly sprinkled or sifted directly into the water-filled impression to about an inch thickness, followed by normally prepared dental stone that has been prepared with a little less water and is slightly thicker. The cast should be poured to about 5 cm thick and allowed to set in place for an hour. To cast a footwear impression in the ground, about 1.2 kg of dental stone in about 500 mL of water is used. A clean rubber bowl can be used for mixing. Water should first be added to the bowl followed by sifting in the dental stone. The mixture should be stirred to remove any lumps and air bubbles. The final mix should be the consistency of pancake batter. An alternative method is to use a zippered plastic bag to carry the dental stone and to mix the material right in the bag. This procedure is reported to be very convenient to use. (Note that when dental stone is mixed with water the solution heats up. This heating causes difficulties when casting impressions in snow. For this reason, a small amount of snow or ice should be added to the mixture to keep the temperature down, and the mixture should be made slightly more viscous than pancake-batter consistency.)

After the material is mixed it should be gently poured onto an area adjacent to the impression and allowed to flow onto the impression. If it is necessary to pour the material into the impression, a baffle such as a flat stick or spoon can be used to lessen the impact of the material. Great care needs to be taken that the dental stone does not destroy any of the fine material in the impression. Before the cast hardens it should be marked using a twig, scribe, or other sharp instrument; the information should include the date, investigator's name or initials, case number, and location of the impression. The material will harden sufficiently for removal in about 30 minutes. Clumps of soil and rocks clinging to the cast should not be disturbed, and the cast should be allowed to air-dry thoroughly for about 48 hours. If the impression is deep and firmly seated it should be carefully excavated so that it finally lies on a pillar that may then be cut off.

9.3.3.4 *Casting Impressions in Snow*

Several techniques are available for casting footprints in snow. One simple one is to use Snow Print Wax™. The impression is prepared first by spraying a thin layer of Snow Print Wax and allowing it to dry. The print should be photographed a second time after application of the Snow Print Wax spray. After the applications of spray have dried, dental stone is carefully poured into the impression. The stone is prepared with cold water and snow and should be made slightly thicker than normal. The material should be allowed to set for at least an hour before marking and removal and should be allowed to dry for about 48 hours (see Figure 9.12).

Sulphur casting is another procedure used by some for snow prints. About 2 kg of powdered sulphur is needed for a print. The sulphur is melted in a 1-litre aluminium pot and poured into the print, using a channel to direct the flow of the molten sulphur. The trick to using sulphur is not to heat the material too much. Sulphur melts at 115°C, but, if heated to 170°C, it changes characteristics and cannot be used. For best results, it should be heated slowly and continuously stirred. The molten sulphur must be poured quickly because it will solidify as soon as it comes into contact with the snow. The cast should remain in place for about an hour. Because it will be very fragile, extreme care must be taken when handling it.

9.3.4 Recovery of Footwear Prints

After photographing the mark, one of the following methods should be used to recover the actual mark, or a facsimile of it. Obviously, the casting techniques described above for preserving impressions will serve the same purpose.

Figure 9.12 Casting a footwear impression in snow using Snow Print Wax™. A thin layer of Snow Print Wax is sprayed on to the impression and allowed to dry (top left); dental stone is then carefully poured in and allowed to set (top right), and an identification mark is applied to the top of the cast (bottom left). Finally, the cast can be removed after it is completely set (bottom right). (Photographs courtesy of BAE Systems, London.)

9.3.4.1   Recover the Object on Which the Mark Has Been Made

Footwear prints are often found on objects stepped on by the criminal (entering in the dark through a window, for example). If the window is broken, all fragments of glass should be examined. This type of print is usually best detected by low-angle illumination from one side. Rubber heels and soles leave exceptionally good prints on glass. Detailed prints are often also found on paper or cardboard that may be strewn about the room during a safe burglary. All such loose objects bearing prints should be carefully preserved for transport to the laboratory. When the seriousness of the crime warrants it, and when the print consists of a dried liquid such as blood or ink, it may be advisable to remove a portion of the linoleum or floor tile that bears a clear impression.

9.3.4.2   Lifting by a Special Lifter

This method is preferred whenever dust or a dust-like substance holds the print from the shoe. The lifter is a sheet of black rubber with a slightly sticky surface that is pressed against the print, picking up a faithful replica of the whole print. Oblique light photography under laboratory conditions will bring out a dust print to a contrast often better than that observed in the original print. If a sufficiently large fingerprint lifter is available, it may be used instead of the special lifter. Care must be taken not to stretch the rubber lifter because the dust image may become distorted.

9.3.4.3   Lifting by Photographic Paper

When special lifters are not available, photographic paper can be used as a substitute. Black (exposed, developed, fixed, and washed) or white (fixed and washed) photographic paper is used, as determined by the colour of the material in the print. The paper is dampened with water or dilute ammonia, laid emulsion side down over the print, and beaten against the print with a stiff brush or clapped with the palm. When the whole surface has been thoroughly beaten, the paper is removed and laid out to dry.

9.3.4.4 Electrostatic Lifts
Electrostatic lifts are very effective (see Figure 9.8). Companies selling evidence collection equipment also sell electrostatic dust print lifter field kits, which are used to pick up dust prints onto Mylar®-coated foil by means of static electricity. This procedure has applications in certain situations in which suspects have walked on tile floors.

9.3.5 Chemical Processing and Development of Footwear Marks in Blood

The development of faint footwear prints in blood can be performed by chemical processing. There are many different methods in use throughout the world, and the most commonly used are described below. Reference should also be made to Chapter 8 for information on detection of blood. As in the general examination of footwear marks, the specific location of the mark should always be documented, as well as the direction of the step where possible. When examining bloody footwear marks it is important to ask, "Was the print made *by* blood or *in* blood?" In other words, did the step transfer or leave the blood on the surface or did someone step in blood that was already there? Answering this question is important in relation to establishing a sequence of events:

- If the print only shows the bloody pattern of the sole, this strongly indicates that the print was made by blood transfer.
- When the blood is also found in the intervals of the sole pattern, this indicates that the step and print were made in wet blood.
- If the boundary of the blood present at the scene continues outside of the boundary of the footwear mark, this strongly indicates that the step and print were made in wet blood.
- If the step has removed blood, leaving a clean imprint of the sole pattern in the shed blood, this proves that the step and the print were made in wet blood.

It is often best that the chemical processing of prints in blood be performed in the laboratory; however, there are situations when processing at the scene is preferred, such as enhancement of bloody prints as part of the examination and recording of the scene. Also, there is the advantage that larger areas at the scene can be examined quickly.

The type of method to be used for the purpose of enhancement of faint prints in blood depends on the type of material, porous or nonporous, and the colour of the surface (light or dark). Leucocrystal Violet (LCV) and Amido black are among the more widely used reagents, but treatment with them is not always optimal if the colour of the surface is dark or black, as the enhancement might not be visible on such types of surfaces. On the other hand, luminol will work well on dark surfaces and has the added advantage of high sensitivity; however, marks developed with luminol may be difficult to record because of the nature of the light and may lose detail because the reagent is sprayed on. Chemical processing by the use of LCV, Hungarian Red, or Amido Black is often more convenient and versatile than using luminol because they can be applied and the results documented in existing ambient light.

Caution: Whenever working with chemicals, always follow the safety instructions given in the method, such as the use of goggles, gloves, and respirators with sufficient filtering capacity.

9.3.5.1 *Leucocrystal Violet*

Leucocrystal Violet (LCV), known as Gentian violet in some countries, can be used to enhance and develop latent prints of blood on light porous and nonporous surfaces such as clothing, carpets, furniture, floors, and human skin. It is used not only for footwear prints in blood but also for the development of latent fingerprints. LCV is a reduced and colourless form of crystal violet. When LCV comes in contact with haemoglobin, a catalytic reaction occurs (see Chapter 8), turning the solution somewhat violet or dark purple. Biological material is not destroyed when treated with LCV, and DNA profiling can be performed afterward.

The use of LCV provides the examiner with an uncomplicated method for the enhancement and detection of faint prints of blood. This is one of the reasons why LCV is now more commonly used than Amido Black, Hungarian Red, diaminobenzidine (DAB), or luminol. It is easy to use when examining large areas, it is easy to mix and handle, and it does not require the same safety precautions as the other products mentioned do, particularly luminol and DAB. The LCV solution can be applied directly to the examined surface in one step, because the 5-sulphosalicylic acid in it fixes the blood. An examination with LCV can be followed up by an examination with Hungarian Red or Amido Black, but not with DAB.

The choice of method should always consider the specific circumstances of the scene, item, surface to be examined, and the aim and purpose for the examination. For example, if the purpose is to try to detect footwear prints in blood with the purpose of obtaining the best possible result for comparison of the print, then luminol would not always be the best choice because of the risk that the print could become too wet when sprayed, leading to details in the print becoming blurred or washed out.

The area or surface should be photographed before chemical processing. The reagent must be tested on a known positive and a known negative sample before use. The reagent is then sprayed gently onto the surface to be examined. Alternatively, it may be poured onto the surface to immerse it in reagent; the 5-sulphosalicylic acid will fix the blood and prevent it from being diffused or washed out. The LCV will react rapidly when it comes into contact with haemoglobin. When carefully spraying the reagent on to the surface, watch to see if the blood reacts by foaming up, which can occur when the volume of blood is high.

Developed prints should be either photographed on the scene or cut out to be brought to the laboratory for further examination and documentation. Enhanced prints can be further developed by processing with Hungarian Red or Amido Black (see later on in this chapter). Figure 9.13 shows a faint bloody shoeprint before and after LCV treatment.

9.3.5.2 *Hungarian Red*

Development of footwear marks in blood can be performed using Hungarian Red, which is a chemical dye solution in a water/acetic acid mixture. It can be used, and works very well, on non-absorbent material and surfaces such as flooring made of linoleum or similar painted surfaces, as well as glass. Hungarian Red is not the best choice when working with absorbent surfaces such as carpets, clothing, or paper. Enhanced prints will become dark red or dark brown. It must be considered if DNA should be collected from the print before processing, as the surface will be washed and dried during the process. Because Hungarian

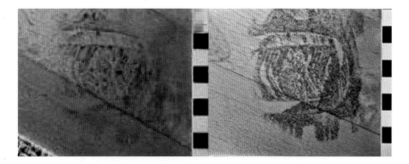

Figure 9.13 Photographs of faint footwear prints in blood on a wooden floor before (left) and after (right) treatment with Leucocrystal Violet (LCV).

Red is an aqueous solution, prints in blood should be fixed before developing to prevent the loss of details due to the print being diluted. Unless the surface to be examined has undergone previous treatment with LCV reagent, a solution of 2% 5-sulphosalicylic acid in water must first be applied for fixation.

After fixation, the surface is then stained or sprayed with Hungarian Red, and the chemical should be left in contact with the surface for about one minute before carefully washing the surface with water to remove non-exposed chemical from the surface. When washing the surface with water, it is very important not to rub or make any kind of scratches in the print. To dry the surface, use a fan or paper towels, or similar soft, absorbent tissue.

Developed prints in blood should be lifted by the use of white gelatine lifters, which will produce a suitable background colour for photographing the print. It is important for the gelatine lifter to be fully in contact with the surface and that no air bubbles occur, as these can lead to the loss of details in the print when it is transferred to the gelatine lifter. The gelatine lifter should stay in contact with the enhanced print for a period of 15 to 30 minutes before lifting. The developed prints can be further examined with green light (515 to 560 nm), which will excite the fluorescence in the Hungarian Red in the lifted print. This may increase the observable detail and can be recorded by photography using a red or orange lens filter. Photographing the developed print, either by normal or fluorescence photography, should be done within a few hours after the print has been developed because the solution will slowly diffuse and blur the enhanced print. An example of the use of Hungarian Red is shown in Figure 9.14.

9.3.5.3   Amido Black

Amido Black reacts with proteins, including those found in blood and in other substances, and is therefore not a presumptive or conclusive test for blood. Amido Black reagent is a dye solution that will react to contact with blood by turning dark blue or almost black. This method is suitable for use on nonporous surfaces, but it is important to be aware that it is a corrosive solution and it will cause corrosion to metal if it is not properly washed away after processing. Amido Black should not be sprayed on the surface. A paper towel dampened with reagent should be layered onto the surface and left for 2 to 3 minutes for the colour to develop. The paper can then be removed and the surface rinsed with distilled water. During this process it is very important not to rub or make any kind of scratches in the surface. To dry the surface, use a fan, paper towels or similar. If the chemical processing produces a somewhat weak or faint impression, the process can be repeated to provide

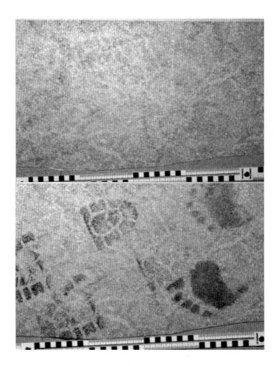

Figure 9.14 Faint marks on linoleum before (top) and after (bottom) treatment with Hungarian Red.

a better result, but the risk of overdevelopment must be kept in mind. Developed prints should not be a problem to document by photography unless the background colour is dark. In such cases, it is advisable to perform a fluorescence examination to enhance possible photographic contrast. The use of a forensic light source (set between 550 and 600 nm) is recommended; the examiner must wear red goggles and apply a dark red filter on the camera lens in order to be able to take a photograph of the print.

9.3.5.4 *Luminol*

As we have already seen, luminol is a versatile chemical that emits blue light when it comes in contact with haemoglobin (see Chapter 8) or other substances that are active oxidants. Luminol is therefore presumptive but not conclusive in relation to blood. Luminol is useful when the amount of blood present is so small that it will not react to LCV, Hungarian Red, Amido Black, or similar chemicals. To perform luminol processing, the scene must be completely darkened and no light allowed in. The solution is sprayed on the surface, and if blood is present it will emit a blue glow lasting for approximately 10 to 30 seconds, depending on the amount of blood present or the amount of luminol added to the surface. When searching for latent bloody footwear marks it is important to spray as little luminol as possible; otherwise, there is a risk that the details will be blurred or washed out. Enhanced prints can be photographed using a normal camera and a long exposure time. If traditional film is used, the following settings will usually produce acceptable results: film, 800 ISO colour negative; aperture, *f*2.8; exposure, 5 to 7 minutes; and film speeded 2.5 steps during the developing process. Figure 9.15 shows a wooden surface that has been cleaned and has no visible staining, before (left) and after (right) luminol treatment.

Figure 9.15 A wooden surface that has been cleaned and has no visible staining, before (left) and after (right) luminol treatment.

9.3.5.5 *Alginate and LCV*

An alternative method for enhancement and preservation of a latent footwear print in blood on a porous surface, such as carpets or clothing, is the combined use of alginate and LCV. Alginate is not at all hazardous and does not require any special safety precautions. The product is especially suited for taking quick and highly detailed moulds from almost any material and has been used for years by dentists, sculptors, and various industries. It is a very useful material for crime scene investigation and forensic science purposes when it is necessary to lift a print in blood from a porous surface. After the print has been located (e.g., by the use of luminol), the alginate is mixed at room temperature by adding water in the correct amount according to the recipe for the product. The mixture is poured out on the surface until it covers the print. The layer of alginate flattens out to a thickness of 3 to 5 mm and hardens within a few minutes. The cast can then be carefully pulled away from the surface. The latent print can then be developed by spraying LCV onto the surface of the cast. If a print is developed it must be photographed shortly thereafter, as the cast can shrink when drying out. If chemical processing with LCV does not develop a print as expected, this may be because the amount of blood is very low, and enhancement with luminol should be attempted. The process is illustrated in Figure 9.16.

9.3.6 Taking Comparison Footwear Prints

Prints from the scene have to be compared to prints made from the possible source footwear. Before doing this, the items should be examined for any other evidence that may be relevant to the case. When making comparison prints, the examiner should try to replicate the force that would be exerted by the original wearer, either by inserting his hands into the footwear and pressing down hard or by wearing them. When the original prints are from covered feet (e.g., shoes), the examiner making the comparison prints should wear the shoes.

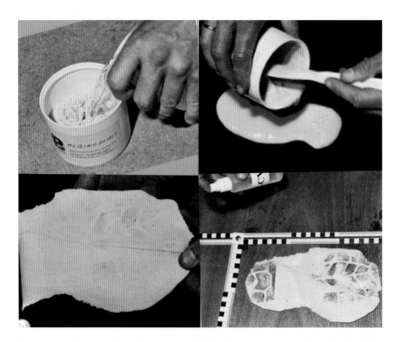

Figure 9.16 Alginate and LCV development of bloody prints. Preparing the alginate (top left), pouring the alginate on to a print on a jacket (top right), pulling the cast away (bottom left), and the resultant print after development with Leucocrystal Violet (LCV) (bottom right).

There are many variations on the procedure used to transfer the sole pattern to a reference print. Examples include inking and dusting. The first of these involves coating the soles with water-based ink using a large ink pad. The inked shoes are then carefully placed on a sheet of tracing paper or acetate sheet. In the second, the soles are dusted with aluminium powder; the excess is tapped off by carefully knocking the shoes against each other before making the comparison print on a medium such as special black lifter foil. Yet another method for obtaining known footwear exemplars involves using talcum powder and black carbon paper. A thin coating of talc is spread on a sheet of newspaper placed talc side up on about 10 more sheets of newspaper that act as a cushion. The shoe is placed on a foot and walked onto the talc-covered newspaper. The talc-covered shoe is then impressed onto black carbon paper, carbon side up. The carbon paper is similarly cushioned with about 10 sheets of newspaper. The resulting print is photographed 1:1 using high-contrast copy film. The developed negative will show a positive reproduction of the impression that can be superimposed over a negative from the crime scene.

When taking prints of bare feet, the feet are blackened by pressing them against a thin layer of printing ink. In order to get a true picture of the formation of the sole of the foot in different positions, four different prints are taken: normal standing position, standing position with pressure against the outside of the foot and then with pressure against the inside, and finally when walking. This also applies to stocking feet.

9.3.7   Comparison of Footwear Prints

Comparison between prints found at the scene of a crime and those of a suspect should be made by an expert, but this does not prevent a police investigator from undertaking a preliminary examination. Figure 9.17 shows the lifting of a footwear mark in the laboratory that will

Figure 9.17 Comparison of a shoeprint found at a scene and that of suspect shoe. (Photograph courtesy of Los Angeles County Sheriff's Department, Los Angeles, CA.)

be examined and reported by a marks expert, but the evidence began when the crime scene investigator saw and understood the importance of the mark at the scene. Prints or impressions of shoe-covered feet are seldom the same size as the shoes, as slipping and the movement of walking can alter the prints. The mark of a naked foot in movement can be as much as 300 mm longer than the mark of the same foot in the standing position. A foot impression in wet earth can become appreciably smaller when the earth dries; in clay, the length can decrease by up to 20 mm. Thus, in establishing identity, too much significance should not be attached to dimensions. When examining the mark of a shoe-covered foot, the circumference characteristics should be checked. If the marks from the scene of the crime and from the suspect are similar in form, it is less important that they may differ somewhat in size.

Associating a crime scene print or impression with an item of footwear is based mainly on comparison of characteristic marks on the sole or heel. To be accepted as characteristic, the marks must be other than those made during manufacture and have some specific and identifiable feature. Marks caused by general wear would not be sufficient.

The examination is best done by comparison of the preserved footmark from the scene of the crime with the footwear item. The scene mark could be in the form of a photograph, cast, or print. Scene marks are compared to the original or exemplar prints taken from it, and comparison points are identified and recorded. When it is a question of prints of bare feet, an examination is made first to see if there are any identifiable friction skin patterns and, if this is the case, the investigation is carried out as for finger and palm prints.

In examining the foot covering of a suspect, dust, dirt, and earth should be kept and, if necessary, compared with similar materials at the scene of the crime. If the perpetrator has left overshoes at the scene, they may be compared with a suspect's shoes. Characteristic marks on the shoes, particularly on the soles, may be reproduced inside the overshoes; for this examination, the overshoes must be cut open. If a shoe is found at the crime scene, it may contain characteristic marks of wear from the owner's foot. Such marks can then be compared with the markings inside shoes and in some cases may be shown to have been worn by the suspect. When performing an examination to identify the owner or user of the footwear, other types of evidence should, of course, also be kept in mind, such as DNA and fibres.

Footwear examination can also be used for intelligence purposes, to link crime scenes. In relation to serious and major crime, such as homicide, robbery, and rape, the perpetrator may dispose of clothing, including footwear, worn at the time. Recovered footwear may yield DNA that can be searched in the database, and marks can be recorded and compared. Because of this, when developing the strategy for searching the home of a suspect, the scene examiner should search for footwear marks as well as the obvious step of examining the actual shoes, sneakers, or boots.

9.4 Marks on Clothing, Possessions, and Parts of the Body

If clothing is pressed against a smooth surface, a latent print of the fabric may be produced. Such a print is developed in the same way as a fingerprint or glove print. Clothing contaminated with a foreign material such as blood can also form a print. When clothing comes into contact with a plastic substance (e.g., clay), an identifiable plastic impression may be formed in it. When a mark from clothing is to be recorded, it must be photographed with the camera placed vertically above or centrally in front of the mark. A scale must be placed at the side of the mark. If the mark is sufficiently large, the scale may be placed in the centre of it. In such cases, a number of pictures should be exposed and the scale should be moved to either side for each exposure so that details are not concealed. Marks of clothes are identified with the aid of the structure of the fabric, faults in the fabric, seams, patches and other repairs, damage, and the like.

Case 3

A man picked up a prostitute and, while in her room, produced an Australian Federal Police badge, hoping to get some free "service." The prostitute retaliated and was assaulted. The suspect discarded the badge, which was a facsimile he carried in a clear plastic wallet. The badge was subsequently located by police, and the plastic wallet was found in the possession of the suspect. An examination of the wallet revealed the outlines of a badge of similar size and shape to the one found at the scene (Figure 9.18).

Figure 9.18 Australian Federal Police badge (left) and outlines of a badge on the wallet (right). (Photographs courtesy of State Forensic Science Laboratory, Melbourne, Australia.)

Sometimes a whole section of the body forms impression marks from a body print or impression. In one case, a burglar fell from a water spout onto the damp earth below, making an impression that showed clearly the face with a characteristic nose and both hands, one holding a crowbar and the other a pistol. When a hand has made a print or impression on a plastic medium, one should look for identifiable friction skin patterns. Other marks may also be found, such as those of rings, injuries, characteristic skin wrinkles, hand coverings, and so on. The preservation of marks of parts of the body is done in the same way as for footwear prints.

9.5   Tooth Marks

Tooth marks may leave compression or scraping marks and can occur in butter, cheese, fruit, chocolate, and the like. Bite marks may also occur on the skin of victims of rape or sexual murder, or on a criminal. Cases have occurred in which the criminal has become involved in a hand-to-hand fight and a tooth has been knocked out or a dental plate broken, and parts of the tooth or the dental plate have been found. Bite marks can, at times, be so characteristic that they may indicate the identity of a suspect. The relative positions of the teeth, their width, and the distance between them, together with ridges on the edges of the teeth and grooves on the back or front, vary for different individuals and may show in the bite mark.

Caution: Although dentition can possess quite specific characteristics, whether or not these will be result in useful bite mark evidence will depend to a large extent on the medium. In particular, bite marks on skin are best dealt with by DNA analysis and not by physical mark comparisons.

Deformations resulting from injuries or illness in the form of portions broken away, characteristic wear of the teeth, fillings and other dental work, and the loss of certain teeth are noted in the bite (Figure 9.19). In a homicide case involving two suspects, a wad of used chewing gum was discovered at the crime scene. Dental impressions of the victim and suspects were made and compared with the gum. An unusual feature of the gum's

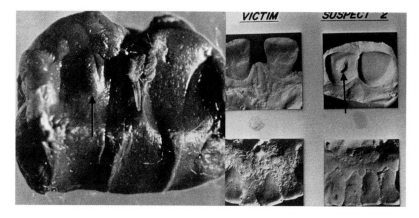

Figure 9.19 Bite marks on the wad of used chewing gum (left) and dental impressions of the victim and suspects (right). (Photographs courtesy of Norman Sperber, DDS, Chief Forensic Dentist for San Diego and Imperial Counties, San Diego, CA.)

impression was a defect corresponding to an opening drilled in the back of one suspect's upper incisor during root canal therapy. In a further comparison, blood typing revealed a blood type that was the same as that of the suspect. Generally, tooth marks come from front teeth in the upper and lower jaws. With children and young people, the edges of the front teeth usually have three ridges (at times more) that are distinguished by shallow incisions, sometimes in the form of furrows, continued on the front and back sides of the teeth. With increasing age, these ridges and furrows usually disappear so that by age 30 the front teeth are generally smooth.

9.5.1   Preservation of Bite Marks

As with other physical impression mark evidence, bite marks should be carefully preserved by photographing and casting. They are generally formed in material that cannot be sent away or kept for a long time without the mark changing in appearance due to drying or decomposition of the material. Marks made in fruit can be preserved in 0.5% formalin solution, which prevents changes resulting from drying, decay, and so forth; however, it is not advisable to leave the fruit in solution for shipment by mail to an expert because it may be broken up and mixed with the solution as the result of shaking. An apple showing a bite mark that is to be sent for examination should instead be fixed by soaking in the solution for several hours, and then wrapped in tissue paper moistened with formalin solution. The whole package is then packed in a carton or box. For photography, oblique lighting is used so that details appear most clearly. It should be noted that there is a risk that butter or soft cheese, for example, might melt under the heat from a photographic lamp. All bite marks should be photographed before casting because the casting may go wrong and bite marks are generally altered in such a way that a fresh cast cannot be taken.

9.5.2   Casting Material for Bite Mark Evidence

The casting material must be chosen with regard to the properties of the material in which the bite has been made. If the material contains water-soluble substances (e.g., chocolate and certain types of cheese), then the bite mark should be isolated from the casting mass by spraying it with a thin layer of collodion or the like.

9.5.2.1   Bite Marks in Human Skin

Bite marks in human skin should be photographed, but for reliable evidence they are best processed as DNA evidence and not as marks.

9.5.2.2   Foods

Bite mark impressions may be left in cheese, butter, sandwich meats, fruit, chocolate, chewing gum, and other such foods. If the food is water soluble, dental impression creams, such as polysulphide rubber-based impression materials, may be used. Other materials such as plaster and molten sulphur (provided that the material is not heat sensitive) have applicability. If dental stone is used, the surface should first be lightly sprayed with lacquer or similar material if the item to be cast contains water.

9.6 Toolmarks

Marks of tools or of objects that have been used as tools are often found at the scene of a crime, especially in cases of burglary. Marks may have been left in wood, metal, putty, or paint. Among the tools that leave identifiable marks are axes, knives, screwdrivers, chisels, crowbars, pliers, cutters, and drill bits. Some of these tools may be homemade. These marks are essentially of two types: those in which only the general form and size of the tool are apparent and those in which injuries, irregularities, and other peculiar characteristics are reproduced in the form of striations or indentations. Marks of the first type may not make a definite identification of the tool possible but do serve as a guide when it is necessary to decide whether the tool of a suspect could have produced the marks. Toolmarks that show striations, indentations, or similar details resulting from damage or other irregularities in the tool are the most valuable as evidence.

9.6.1 Preservation of Toolmarks

Whenever possible, toolmarks should be kept in their original condition. This may be done by recovering the whole object or part of the object on which the marks appear. Sometimes, it can be arranged that the marks remain untouched at the scene of the crime but can be recovered later if this is required. This is only permissible, however, when the marks are in such a position that they are completely protected—for example, a small mark on the inside of a door or window frame. If a mark in metal is not immediately recovered, it should be covered with a thin film of oil to prevent oxidation. When recovering the mark, it is important that it be protected against dirt, moisture, and scratching during transport. Tissue or other soft paper should be placed over the toolmark in packaging.

Case 4

A stolen outboard motor was identified by comparison of the toolmarks made when the rubber fuel lines between the portable tank and motor were cut (Figure 9.20).

Figure 9.20 Cut end of the fuel lines. (Photograph courtesy of Centre of Forensic Science, Toronto, Canada.)

Case 5

The victim and his friend had been on a night out and were walking through the pedestrian zone in the centre of the city. It was early in the morning of January 5, just a few minutes before 6 a.m., and was bitterly cold. The streets were generally quiet. At some point, a group of three young men approached the victim and his friend. One of the youngsters demanded the hat that the victim was wearing, but he refused to give it away. The youngster continued his aggressive approach and was now physically attacking the victim, trying to take his hat. The victim fought back. The two other youngsters also started attacking the victim, and the victim's friend tried to come to his aid. Suddenly the situation had changed into a violent fight and attack that would end the life of the victim.

During the attack, two of the youngsters drew folding knives, and the victim was stabbed three times in the right thigh and received one lethal stab wound to the chest. In addition to being stabbed, the victim, along with his friend, was punched and kicked. The victim collapsed and fell down on the pavement. The attack was noticed by other nearby pedestrians, some of whom started to run toward the scene, shouting for the attack to be stopped. The three attackers stopped and ran off.

A witness called the emergency services, and an ambulance and the police arrived at the scene within a few minutes. The ambulance took the victim, who was now not wearing his hat, to the hospital for emergency treatment. Witnesses were able to give the police descriptions of the attackers, and a suspect (suspect A) was apprehended by police officers only a few hundred metres from the scene. When the scene and surroundings were searched, a folding knife was found on the pavement near the scene. The folding knife had what appeared to be blood on the handle and the blade. The crime scene was cordoned off, and the crime scene investigation department was contacted and requested to conduct the crime scene examination.

The part of the pedestrian zone where the crime took place was monitored by surveillance cameras. The recordings showed that the attack happened as described by the witnesses, but the recordings were not of such quality that the perpetrators could be identified. Furthermore, the recordings did not show with certainty if the victim was stabbed by one or both of the perpetrators.

The victim died after arriving at the trauma centre. The stab to his chest had gone into his heart. The autopsy showed that the direction of the stab to the chest was almost perpendicular and then curved when the stab went through the rib bone and entered the heart. A number of samples were taken during the autopsy. The cut edges of the rib bone were examined in order to try to find useful evidence and information regarding the knife used. Casts of the cut edges of the rib bone were made by using an Isomark™ cast material (a two-component cast material similar to Micro-Sil™) in order to collect marks from the blade edge of the knife (see Figure 9.21). After the autopsy, the samples, the cast from the rib bone, and various other items were brought to the CSI unit and to the forensic laboratory for further examination. The cast made from the cut edge of the victim's rib bone showed striation marks due to minor damage on the edge of the knife blade (Figure 9.22).

The apprehended suspect denied having anything to do with the crime. The surveillance recordings from the crime scene were released to the public, asking for help to identify the perpetrators. Twelve hours later, two young men entered a police station

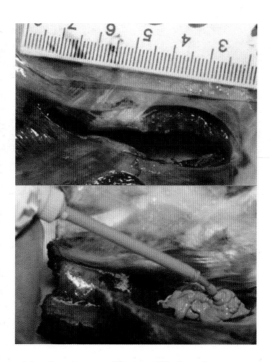

Figure 9.21 Stab wound (top) and wound being filled with casting material (bottom).

and gave themselves up (suspect B and suspect C). They were arrested, but both of them denied having stabbed the victim. When the police searched the apartment where suspect B lived, a folding knife was discovered and collected for further examination.

The two knives found in the case—one near the crime scene (knife 1) and the other that was found in the apartment (knife 2)—were now examined and compared to the marks on the cut edge of the victim's rib bone. Both knifes had very similar dimensions,

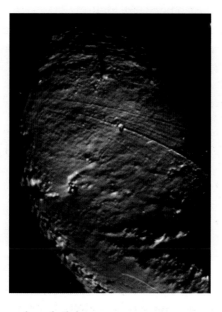

Figure 9.22 Cast from cut edge of rib bone.

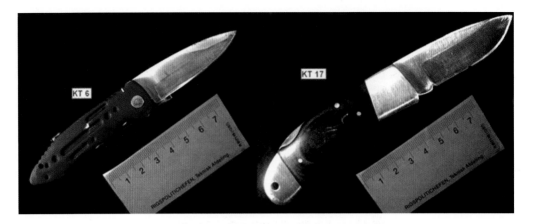

Figure 9.23 Knife 1 (left) and knife 2 (right).

such as length and thickness of the blade (Figure 9.23). Blood was found on the handle of knife 1, but no blood was found on knife 2. This knife had been found more than 12 hours after the crime had been committed, so the question was asked: "Could knife 2 have been washed and cleaned, since no blood was found on it"? Examination of knife 2 showed that it was completely dry, it showed no signs of rust from having been wet, and examination with luminol was negative.

Comparison cutting and stabbing marks were made from the blades of knife 1 and knife 2. The marks were made in blocks of Isomark™ and included a number of comparison marks made from "low curving" to "step curving." The comparison showed that the marks from the knife found near the crime scene (knife 1) matched the marks preserved from the cut edge of the victim's rib bone. The comparison marks from the knife found in the suspect's apartment showed that it could be eliminated as being the murder weapon, as the details in the striation marks from this knife did not match the marks in the cut edge of the rib bone (see Figure 9.24).

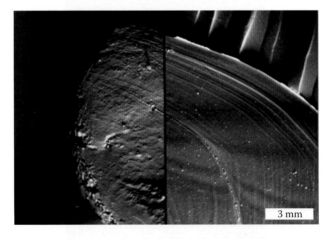

Figure 9.24 Comparison of striations in rib bone cast (left) and striations on the blade of knife 1.

The DNA result from the forensic laboratory added further information to the case. The blood on knife 1 matched the DNA profile of the victim, and DNA was found on the handle and the blade of the knife that matched that of the suspect apprehended near the crime scene. There was no indication of blood being present on knife 2, and any DNA found on this knife matched the DNA profile of the suspect living in the apartment.

When the case came to court, suspect A was sentenced to 12 years in prison for the murder of the victim. Suspects B and C were convicted of serious assault and assisting and robbery and given lesser sentences.

9.6.1.1 Casting Toolmarks

Casting or other methods of taking impressions of a toolmark should be used only as a last resort. No matter how good a cast is, it can never be equal to the original. This applies especially to marks made in soft materials such as wood, putty, and paint; many of the casting media most suited for these materials are unable to reproduce all the finer details important for identification. Experiments have shown that an impression or a cast cannot reproduce scratches in paint caused by extremely small irregularities in the edge of a tool; consequently, a microscopic comparison of the cast with a mark made from the suspected tool may not lead to any positive results. If, however, the original mark is compared with one made directly by the tool, then a positive identification may be possible.

Case 6

Consecutive manufacture comparison marks of plastic trash bags in a murder case proved to be important evidence. Figure 9.25 depicts a single layer of two plastic bags placed edge to edge. Characteristic die line and homogeneous mixing in the original plastic sheet are continuous between individual bags. These bags were used to link a box of trash bags from a residence and bags from the alleged crime vehicle with two bags found at the murder scene.

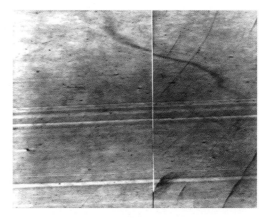

Figure 9.25 Two plastic bags placed edge to edge. Characteristic "die line" and homogeneous mixing in the original plastic sheet are continuous between individual bags. (Photograph courtesy of Oklahoma State Bureau of Investigation.)

In the casting of marks, however, very satisfactory results may be obtained with dental impression materials, silicone rubber, or similar products, and the completed cast will show fine detail. Difficulties and some expense may be involved in taking possession of the original toolmark; therefore, it should be subjected to a close examination with the aid of a magnifier to make sure that it shows typical details from the tool before any further steps are taken. In each particular case, consideration must also be given to the type of crime, value of the object, whether or not a tool from a suspect is available, the probability that such a tool may be found, etc. Whether the actual mark is recovered or a cast is made, the toolmark should be photographed whenever practical. The picture should show clearly the location of the mark in relation to the rest of the object. Close-up photographs are generally taken in cases in which the mark may be destroyed in the casting process or during removal. The photographs must be made with the film plane parallel to the mark and should include a scale. Oblique lighting is used to enhance details in the mark. Close-up photographs should be in actual size, if possible, or, in the case of smaller marks, enlarged. It is generally not possible to identify the tool used from photographs.

9.6.2   Trace Evidence on Tools

In connection with all toolmarks and suspected tools, it should be remembered that the tool might also have deposited traces in the form of paint, oil, or other contamination. In turn, clues in the form of wood fragments and paint from the object may be found on the tool. These traces are sometimes just as valuable as the toolmark. Samples should therefore always be taken from the area of the toolmark whenever the actual mark is not recovered. Valuable toolmarks are also sometimes found on splinters of wood, loosened flakes of paint, and chunks of safe insulation.

Case 7

Two men and a woman were arrested following a long-term drug investigation and charged with conspiracy to supply and import heroin. Part of a plastic bag with brown powder was recovered from the woman. A plastic bag with brown powder was recovered from one of the men, and five plastic bags and some condoms with brown powder were recovered from the other man. The brown powder was analysed and found to be heroin; the condoms were found to have epithelial cells present on the outside. It was believed that the female smuggled the heroin secreted in her vagina and handed it over to the second man for the purpose of supply. The plastic bags were examined by transmitted polarising light and observed through a rotating polarising filter. A pattern of interference bands was observed; this property originates in the manufacturing process. In some makes of bags, the interference pattern is continuous through several bags, while in others the pattern tapers out within the length of one bag. When applied to the bags, the technique showed that three of the batch of five bags were similar to each other, and one was found to be the same as the single bag recovered from the first man (Figure 9.26). The evidence was able to link all three defendants. During the examination of the crime scene, the possibility should always be kept in mind that any toolmark found might be compared with marks from previous crimes. It happens frequently that identity is established among toolmarks from different burglaries long before the criminal is apprehended or the actual tool is found.

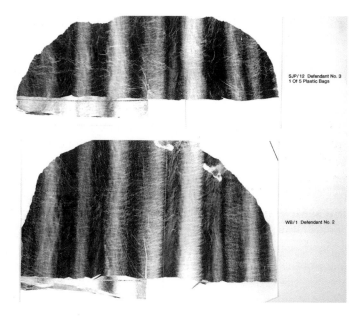

Figure 9.26 Two of the plastic bags photographed under polarising light showing the same banding pattern. (Photograph courtesy of Forensic Science Service, London.)

Case 8

A young girl was found stabbed to death on her bed. A search of the crime scene uncovered a broken fingernail in the vicinity of the bed. Fingernail clippings were collected and a comparison was made on silicone rubber castings of the underside of each nail, using reflected, oblique lighting (Figure 9.27). The examination established that the broken nail came from the victim, not from the unknown perpetrator.

Figure 9.27 Side-by-side comparison of fingernail clippings, showing alignment of the striations. (Photograph courtesy of New York State Police.)

The investigating officer should always endeavour to imagine being in a position similar to that of the criminal when the toolmarks were made to consider how the criminal held the tool, stood, or was supported when breaking in or prying open. A burglary may be faked with the goal of concealing embezzlement or of defrauding an insurance company; therefore, the investigator should always examine the opposite part of a mark (e.g., in a doorframe). The fake burglar often overlooks the fact that this other part of the mark must be present.

Moreover, it is essential for the expert who is to carry out the comparative examination of the tool and the toolmarks to understand how the criminal held the tool when making the marks. In most cases, if the examination is to have any prospect of leading to the identification of the tool, the expert must make a comparison mark in exactly the same way as the criminal has done. This applies especially to those toolmarks that show scratches resulting from damage or other irregularities in the tool. The distance between the scratches varies according to whether a knife, for example, is held at right angles to its direction of movement or is held askew; the appearance of the scratches depends on the angle taken by the knife in relation to the plane of the cut. It is best if the position of a fixed mark and the conditions at the place are shown to the expert in a sketch or a comprehensive photograph. A statement that the suspect is right or left handed should be added if this is possible to ascertain.

In some countries, it is required to make a comparison mark in the same material as the mark, but in other countries it is common and accepted to make a comparison mark in a different material such as lead. If possible, it is best that the comparison mark be made in the same material as the mark at the scene of the crime (with the same paint or surface treatment, of the same degree of moisture, etc.) because the clarity of definition of the microscopic scratches varies with different materials. Thus, a quantity of material for use in producing comparison marks should be sent with the tool and toolmark; it may be necessary to make ten or more such marks with the suspected tool.

The police officer should not attempt to fit the tool into the mark or make a comparison mark with a suspected tool. In most cases, the officer does not have access to an instrument suitable for closer examination of the character of a toolmark, which may be necessary in order to decide how the comparison mark is to be made. Also, traces of paint or foreign metal on the tool, only observable with a microscope or powerful magnifying glass, may be lost or the tool may be damaged.

Casts or impressions of toolmarks should be packed in such a way that they cannot be altered or destroyed during transport. Positive casts should never be made because this may cause fine details to become obscured. If the negative cast of the mark might be destroyed in transmission, it is best to make two and to keep one in reserve.

Regarding boring marks, only wood bits and certain spiral bits generally leave identifiable marks. The bottom of the boring, if there is one, and boring chips are important. With other types of bits, identification is possible only in the most favourable cases and then as a rule only when the bottom of the boring is present.

Occasionally the question arises from which side of a window frame (outside or inside) a hole has been bored. In most cases, this can be seen from the more or less loose wood fibres around the entrance and exit holes of the bit, but with some bits it may actually be difficult to decide the direction of boring. Reliable information is obtained by cutting through the surrounding wood in the longitudinal direction of the hole—by first sawing through the wood around the hole from each side up to about 1/2 inch from the hole and then breaking the wood apart. It will then be found that the wood fibres are directed upward from the hole in one edge of each half and downward in the other edges. The wood fibres around the boring are displaced in the direction of rotation of the drill, so cutting the boring into two parts in this manner reveals clearly the direction of boring. The degree of orientation of the wood fibres varies for different types of bits, and it is possible to obtain an idea of the type of bit used by carrying out test borings with different bits.

Saw marks usually do not offer any possibility of identifying the saw used. In a few cases, some idea may be obtained by noting the degree of set and possibly also the number of teeth per inch of the saw used, but this can be done only if sawing was stopped before the wood was sawn through. In some cases, it is possible to find, in the base of the saw cut, impressions of the teeth of the saw made when the saw was at rest for an instant before it was withdrawn. It is also possible to obtain from the base of the saw cut a measure of the width of cut and therefore of the approximate amount of set.

Hacksaw marks offer little possibility of identification. For blades with different numbers of teeth per inch, however, if the blade did not go through the piece of metal then it may be possible to examine the bottom of the cut and observe the impression of the teeth to obtain an idea of the number of teeth per inch. This may also be observed at the sides of the actual cut where the saw jumped and left shallow marks of the teeth in the surface of the metal, especially when first started.

9.6.3   Preserving a Tool

When the tool has been found, care should be taken to preserve its evidentiary value. It should be carefully marked or tagged. The tool should be preserved in its original condition. Do not mark it, and always package it in a way that will protect any possible DNA or fingerprint evidence. Similarly, minute items of trace evidence should be carefully preserved. The tool should be carefully packaged for transportation to the laboratory. Toolmarks made by cutting tools generally present little difficulty when the object cut is large enough to collect sufficient characteristics, such as the shackle of a padlock. Smaller items such as wire cable and multistrand wire show identifiable markings only in exceptional cases. If the wire has plastic insulation as a covering, a physical match may be made by an examination of the extrusion markings on the cable as well as the microscopic jagged cut on the ends of the insulation. Generally, striations on the fine wire will be insufficient. Manufacturing marks such as casting, extruding, grinding, and so on are important when attempting to match items together physically. These markings and random breaks that occur when tools or other materials break or tear are important means of identification.

Impression or casting media must be chosen for each particular case, taking into consideration the type of material in which the mark is formed and its orientation (i.e., on the horizontal or vertical). Some impression materials such as plaster and plasticine have a tendency to shrink or expand after setting; they should not be used for casting. Dental impression creams have been found useful as casting materials. They generally come packaged in individual tubes, with one being the catalyst and the other the setting agent, which are simply mixed and are easy to apply. Other materials such as moulage, polysulphide rubber-based material, and silicone rubber are also useful.

A retaining wall should be built around the impression. Modelling clay or putty may be used for this purpose. The casting material should be thoroughly mixed according to the manufacturer's instructions and applied to the impression by means of a spatula. A tag with string attached may be used for identification purposes. The string may be inserted just below the surface of the casting material.

9.6.4 Fragments of Tools

At crime scenes where doors, windows, or locked drawers show signs of forcible entry, the investigating officer must remember to examine the floor immediately adjacent to the point of entry carefully before examining the actual toolmarks. It is not uncommon for burglary tools to break during forced entry; therefore, large or small fragments of the tool may be found at the scene and prove to be very valuable as evidence. Broken pieces of a tool might also be found inside a lock on which picking or prying has been attempted. In many cases, it is possible to establish that such broken fragments originally were parts of tools found in the possession of a suspect. The physical matching of two or more pieces that originally were one piece—a so-called fracture match—is a most convincing and easily demonstrable type of proof against an offender. The reverse situation should also be kept in mind. A broken tool left by the burglar at the crime scene can be matched with fragments of that tool that may be found in the suspect's clothing, home, or place of business.

Pieces may also have been left at the scene of another burglary. The search for such tool fragments is best done with a flashlight, the beam of which is directed over the search area at a very low angle. When the light strikes a metallic fragment, it will give off bright reflections that make the particles easy to find. Any suspected fragment should be recovered and placed in a vial, envelope, or pillbox that can be labelled as to the time and place of recovery. A magnet can also be used to search for tool fragments. If a deliberate effort to look for such pieces of broken tools is not made, there is the risk of trampling them into the ground, embedding them in the officer's shoes, or kicking them aside while engaging in other routines of crime scene search.

9.6.5 Comparison and Identification of Toolmarks

In Chapter 1, we discussed the concepts of identity and identification, from the perspective of scientific principles. We also discussed the importance of formulating hypotheses regarding examination of the crime scene and the need to continually revise and update as information becomes available. Crime scene examiners face these issues in a very practical way when drawing conclusions on the identification of toolmarks. The European Network of Forensic Science Institutes (ENFSI) Marks Working Group has addressed the question by considering the language that could be used to express results in the context of the hypothesis that the questioned tool caused the mark (proposition A) and the alternative that it did not (proposition NotA). The Working Group report includes an illustrated table that relates six levels of conclusions (from identification to elimination) to the evidence available. Table 9.1 shows the Working Group conclusions, together with added illustrations courtesy of the Danish National Police, National Centre of Forensic Science. The table considers two statistical approaches, the likelihood ratio and the unconditional probability. The likelihood ratio is the ratio of the probability of proposition A to that of proposition NotA. The unconditional probability can be derived from the full Bayes' theorem or by classical statistical estimations.

Caution: The Working Group emphasises that ultimately the interpretation of evidence is a legal matter and will depend on statutes and case law in the applicable country.

Table 9.1   ENFSI Guidelines for Mark Identification

	Likelihood Ratio (Partial Bayes' Rule)	Probability (Full Bayes' Rule)	A	B
1	Identification	Identification		
2	Very strong support for proposition A Strong support for proposition A	Very probably		
3	Moderately strong support for proposition A Moderate support for proposition A	Probably		
4	Inconclusive	Inconclusive		
5	Limited support for proposition NotA Moderate support for proposition NotA Moderately strong support for proposition NotA Strong support for proposition NotA Very strong support for proposition NotA	Likely not		
6	Elimination	Elimination		

9.7   Typed Documents

Marks from typewriters and check protectors are rarely encountered today but are a special class of toolmarks. As with other toolmarkings, these impressions may show specific and unique characteristics that may aid in the identification of a class or specific model of the instrument used. Documents found at a crime scene may be typed or have some typing present. The investigator would like to determine the make, model, and specific typewriter or instrument used. In some instances this is possible; however, with the use of electric typewriters and interchangeable type balls, this may be difficult. The best results are obtained in instances when the suspect typewriter has a functional defect or a damaged typeface. With electric typewriters, factors such as keystroke pressure may not be a factor in identification.

It is preferable to bring the suspect typewriter to the questioned document examiner for comparison with the typewritten material in question. If this is not possible, the investigator should obtain ample specimens at the scene. These specimens should include several exemplars of all typefaces, both uppercase and lowercase, and several prepared portions of the text should be copied from the document. The investigator's initials, date, and the make, model, serial number, and location of the machine must properly identify these exemplars. If the location is in an office, the area should be thoroughly searched (including wastepaper baskets) for discarded typewriter ribbons and interchangeable type balls. Care must be taken when handling typewriters not to inflict additional damage on a machine.

Check protectors are used by financial institutions and many businesses. They are frequently used to imprint the amount on stolen or forged checks and money orders. Often checks are taken in burglaries and imprinted on machines located in the offices of the victim prior to the suspect's leaving the scene. Generally, the make of the machine can be determined without too much difficulty by an experienced document examiner; however, the machine should be taken to the examiner for inspection and comparison with impressions on the questioned document. If the machine cannot be moved, extensive exemplars must be made in the field. Several exemplars of the questioned amounts should be prepared, preferably on specimen checks or money orders similar to the questioned documents. Additionally, specimens of all numerals and characters on the check protector should also be prepared on plain sheets of paper. All of these exemplars must contain proper identification, including the investigator's initials, the date, and the machine's make, model, and serial number.

9.8   Summary

Impression evidence is often encountered at crime scenes, in the form of two- or three-dimensional imprints of objects on a recipient surface. It is an example of what Kirk described as "comparative identity" and directly addresses WHAT and WHO in the investigative star. Consideration of all the elements in the scene investigation and the possible explanatory hypotheses allows us to extend the use of the star to use impression evidence to make inferences on WHERE, HOW, and WHEN. The chapter has explored the various types of impression evidence and described how to preserve and collect them for comparative analysis. Submitting that evidence to the laboratory along with the suspected tool frequently results in an identification.

Firearms Examination  10

10.1 Introduction

Crimes involving the use of firearms represent a significant area of police investigation. Firearms evidence may be present in crimes such as murder, attempted murder, suicide, assault, and rape. A number of questions may be answered by proper use of firearms evidence: What kind of weapon was used? Was the weapon in proper working order? How far away was the weapon fired? In what direction was the weapon fired? Did a specific weapon fire a bullet? Did a particular person fire the weapon?

Because of the importance of reconstructing the circumstances of the crime and corroborating accounts of the crime by witnesses, suspects, and victims, firearms evidence is particularly important. This chapter deals with the major areas of firearms examination as they relate to crimes of violence. The field of firearms identification is sometimes referred to as *forensic ballistics* or simply *ballistics*. This is an improper use of terminology. Ballistics generally refers to the trajectory taken by a projectile and requires an understanding of physics. Firearms identification, on the other hand, refers to the study of firearms and includes the operation of firearms, cartridges, gunshot residue analysis, bullet and cartridge case comparisons, powder pattern determination, and the like.

Many date the beginnings of modern forensic firearms identification to the Saint Valentine's Day massacre on 14 February, 1929, in Chicago. With the aid of a newly developed comparison microscope, Col. Calvin Goddard was able to identify the two Thompson submachine guns used in the infamous crime (Figure 10.1). The first recorded case of a

Figure 10.1 A modern comparison microscope used to compare two bullets allegedly fired from the same gun. (Photograph courtesy of Los Angeles County Sheriff's Department, Los Angeles, CA.)

successful investigation of a murder involving firearms was much earlier, in 1835, and also involved someone by the name of Goddard. Henry Goddard, a Bow Street Runner (an early London police officer), solved a murder by identification of the source of the fatal projectile by applying the very scientific processes of careful observation, rational thinking, and awareness of surrounding circumstances. There are no clear accounts of the circumstances, but the most likely reconstruction is that a servant shot and killed his employer. Goddard was able to identify the source of the projectile (a ball shot) by matching an imperfection on it to one on the mould that the servant used to make his shot. Goddard also was able to trace paper wadding involved in the shooting to paper in possession of the servant.

10.2   Characteristics of Firearms

10.2.1   General Characteristics

Today, there are literally thousands of types of firearms. They can be classified broadly into two groups: (1) long arms such as rifles and shotguns, and (2) handguns such as revolvers and pistols or automatic and semiautomatic pistols. (Bipod, tripod, and other exotic weapons are also sometimes encountered.) Of interest to law enforcement, handguns represent the firearm used most often in crimes; shoulder arms are used less frequently. Obsolete weapons such as muskets, unusual firearms such as those disguised to appear as something other than a handgun, and homemade weapons such as zip guns are used with even less frequency (Figure 10.2).

Firearms may also be characterised by whether they have smoothbore or rifled barrels, the former being used in shotguns and the latter in most other firearms. Rifling found in gun barrels is spiral grooves cut into the barrel in order to impart a rotation motion to the bullet as it leaves the barrel, resulting in more stable flight. Muskets are another type of smoothbore (and sometimes partially rifled) firearm.

Firearms may be single shot, revolver, automatic, or semiautomatic. The single-shot firearm is loaded manually, fired once, and unloaded manually. The revolver differs from the single-shot pistol in that it has a rotating cylinder holding from 4 to 24 cartridges. Each time a cartridge is fired, the cylinder revolves by means of cocking the hammer or pulling the

Figure 10.2 An operational firearm made to appear like an ordinary object, in this case a mobile phone. (From http://www.geeky-gadgets.com/wp-content/uploads/2008/11/cellphone-gun1.jpg.)

Figure 10.3 The inside of a shotgun shell showing the gunpowder and shot. This type of cartridge is used for trap shooting. (Photograph courtesy of Lucian C. Haag, Forensic Science Services, Inc., Carefree, AZ.)

trigger, which places the cartridge into position to be fired. The automatic firearm generally found in military weapons is a repeating type. Cartridges are fired in succession as long as the trigger is pressed and until the ammunition supply is exhausted. The semiautomatic pistol (often improperly referred to as an "automatic") functions similarly to the automatic, but fires only one shot each time the trigger is pulled. In single-shot and revolver types of firearms, the cartridge casing generally remains in the weapon after firing, although single-shot weapons have been made that eject cases automatically. With automatic and semiautomatic firearms, the cartridge case is ejected from the weapon automatically.

Shotguns differ in two major ways from other firearms: Shotgun barrels are usually not rifled but are smoothbore, and they fire a different type of ammunition consisting of many lead pellets, rifled slugs, sabots, or shot (Figure 10.3). There are also some who load shot shells with various other materials such as rock salt, flechettes, lead balls, piano wire, or less lethal materials such as beanbags or rubber bullets. Shotguns are of the single- or double-barrelled break action for reloading, pump action, semiautomatic, or bolt action types.

The calibre designation of a firearm, a somewhat complicated topic, is a measure of the bore of the barrel and is measured in 1/100 or 1/1000 of an inch or in millimetres (Figure 10.4). The calibre of a rifled weapon is generally determined from the diameter of the bore, measured between two opposite lands, although there are some exceptions to this rule. Shotgun bores are measured in gauges; the smaller the number is, the larger the diameter. Thus, a 12-gauge shotgun has a larger diameter bore than a 20-gauge shotgun. The term *gauge* was originally the number of lead balls of that size weighing 1 pound. This system does not hold for the .410 "gauge," which in actuality is a calibre.

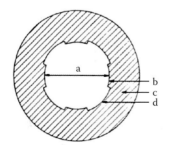

The caliber of a rifled weapon is generally determined from the diameter of the bore, measured between two opposite lands. There are, however, exceptions to this rule.

(a) caliber, (b) land, (c) barrel, (d) groove

Figure 10.4 The anatomy of a gun barrel: (a) calibre, (b) land, (c) barrel, and (d) groove. Note the lands and grooves. (Illustration courtesy of Lucian C. Haag, Forensic Science Services, Inc., Carefree, AZ.)

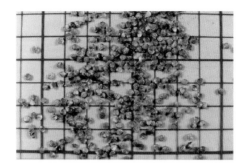

Figure 10.5 A photomicrograph example of gunpowder, in this case Hercules Bullseye propellant. (Photograph courtesy of Lucian C. Haag, Forensic Science Services, Inc., Carefree, AZ.)

10.2.2   Ammunition

Small-arms cartridges or rounds are of two general types: rim fire and centre fire. Rimfire ammunition is almost exclusively .22 calibre (plus the recently introduced .17-calibre), whereas larger calibres are centre fire. Some older firearms, other than .22 calibre, did use rim fire ammunition. The terms *rim* and *centre* refer to the position of the primer located in the base of the cartridge. In a rim-fire round, the primer is in the rim in an area around the circumference of the base, while centre fire rounds have the primer in the centre. The primer is a small shock-sensitive explosive charge in the base of the cartridge used to set off the propellant powder when struck by the firing pin. The bullet is the projectile fired from the weapon. Bullets are generally a lead alloy and jacketed with a harder metal such as copper or brass, or they may not be jacketed. The purpose of the jacket is to keep the bullet intact and from breaking up when it strikes a target, to prevent damage while in the weapon, and to control expansion. Gunpowder or smokeless powder consists of tiny cylinders, balls, flakes, or discs of nitrocellulose or nitrocellulose plus nitroglycerine in so-called double-based powder (Figure 10.5). When confined and ignited, the powder rapidly burns, giving off a large quantity of gas. The expanding gas is the means by which the bullet is propelled through the barrel and out of the weapon. Black powder is also used in certain ammunition.

10.3   Firearms Evidence

When a weapon is fired, the firing pin strikes the base of the cartridge, detonating the primer, which in turn ignites the gunpowder. Expansion of gases forces the casing against the breech, which resists the rearward movement and propels the bullet down the barrel. The bullet picks up the tiny imperfections of the rifling as it passes through (Figure 10.6). The scratches or striations are caused by the imperfections in the lands and grooves placed in the barrel at the time of manufacture, as well as through use of the weapon. Characteristic markings from the mechanical action of loading, chambering, and firing the round, as well as from extracting and ejecting the casing, will be present on the bullet, cartridge casing, and cartridge base. If compared against rounds fired from the same weapon, these marks will show similarities that the firearms identification expert can use to determine if the rounds were fired from the same gun.

Figure 10.6 Two bullets viewed under a comparison microscope show characteristic markings imparted by the barrel onto the bullet's surface. (Photograph courtesy of Los Angeles County Sheriff's Department, Los Angeles, CA.)

Beyond determining that two rounds were fired from the same weapon, a great deal of other information can be developed from evidence associated with firearms. The presence of cartridge cases may indicate an automatic, semiautomatic, bolt-action, or slide-action firearm, or a single-shot firearm when more than one round was fired. The relative location of the casings to the shooter may sometimes suggest the type of weapon fired or that a revolver was emptied at the scene. Bullets and even fragments of bullets may be used to determine the type of weapon used from the size and weight of the projectile and an examination of the striations on the outside surface. For example, the number, direction of twist, and measurements of land and groove markings can be useful in determining the type, make, model, and calibre of firearm. Examination of the area that the bullet struck will yield information about the path and distance from which the weapon was fired. This is also possible with shot fired from a shotgun. Tests on the shooter's hands can be made to determine if a weapon was recently fired. Finally, if the firearm is recovered, it can be tested to determine if it is in proper working order and if it could have been accidentally discharged. The owner of the firearm can possibly be determined by serial number examination.

10.3.1 Gunshot Residue Analysis

When the firing pin strikes the base of a cartridge, the shock causes the primer to detonate, in turn causing ignition of the main gunpowder charge. The chemical reaction thus started causes a rapid expansion of gases, which propels the bullet out of the barrel of the gun. The byproducts of the reaction are burned and unburned powder and the components of the primer mixture. When a firearm is discharged, gases from the detonation of the primer and burning gunpowder escape from the barrel (Figure 10.7). These gases, along with burned and unburned particles of gunpowder and primer, can be used to test whether a person recently fired a weapon or was in close proximity to a weapon being fired.

Primers use shock-sensitive compounds containing such materials as lead, barium, and antimony. Barium, antimony, or lead on a shooter's hands may indicate that a gun was recently fired. Recently, some ammunition manufacturers have begun to market non-lead-based primers and bullets to limit the lead exposure of shooting enthusiasts. Upon the discharge of a weapon, microscopic particles of gunshot residue (GSR) are deposited on the

Figure 10.7 Discharge residues escaping from the barrel of a firearm. (Photograph courtesy of Lucian C. Haag, Forensic Science Services, Inc., Carefree, AZ.)

hands of the shooter as an aerosol. These particles adhere to the hands but are removed by washing, wringing, or placing one's hands in pockets. Handcuffing a suspect behind the back will dislodge these particles. Studies show that GSR material will remain on a shooter's hands for up to 6 hours. The particles are in the highest concentration immediately after shooting and are gradually lost over time. Because of this time factor, GSR evidence must be collected as quickly as possible.

Atomic absorption spectrophotometry (AAS), scanning electron microscopy/energy dispersive x-ray analysis (SEM/EDX), and inductively coupled plasma mass spectroscopy (ICP-MS) are methods used to test for GSR. All three are able to identify the lead, barium, or antimony in the primer, but SEM/EDX is particularly valuable because of the microscope function. The particles that condense from the aerosol have a very characteristic size and shape and provide a reliable way to distinguish between environmental contamination and gunshot residues as the source of the metal traces.

The procedure used by a laboratory determines the way in which the evidence is to be collected. GSR evidence is collected in one of two ways: with cotton-tipped applicators and dilute nitric acid solution for AAS and ICP-MS analysis, or with aluminium stubs with double-sided cellophane tape for SEM. The chemical components of the primer present on the shooter's hands are the substances tested for in the GSR procedure. In general, barium, lead, and antimony are characteristic of most ammunition. Certain .22-calibre ammunition (e.g., that made by manufacturers other than the Federal Cartridge Company) contains only lead.

Gunshot residue evidence collection kits are available commercially and through local forensic laboratories. In all cases, the person collecting the evidence should wear plastic gloves to prevent possible contamination of the evidence. Information concerning the subject's occupation and hobbies should be noted. This is important for interpretation of test results. Obtaining GSR results is straightforward, but their interpretation is another matter. Negative GSR results (no GSR detected) do not conclusively mean that a subject did not fire a handgun. Similarly, positive GSR results do not prove someone fired a gun because a person could have handled a gun or been in close proximity to a gun that was fired.

A shooting suspect's hands should be protected until the test is given. Handcuffing behind the back is likely to remove GSR. Hands may be bagged loosely with paper bags but not in plastic bags, which cause perspiration and hence produce a cleansing effect. In the case of a deceased subject, the 6-hour time limit is flexible but the hands should be protected until such time as the evidence can be collected. Because of the ambiguity in conclusions about whether an individual fired a weapon based on finding GSR, a number of forensic laboratories have opted to discontinue this service. Instead, some labs opt to swab the gun, including the trigger, trigger guard, backstrap, slide, grip, and/or unspent ammunition for touch DNA typing instead.

10.3.2   Collecting Firearms Evidence

The crime scene in which a firearm was involved should be processed in much the same way as that discussed earlier in the text. In addition, a number of other considerations must be taken into account in these types of cases. (It goes without saying that in life-or death-situations, when a gun needs to be quickly rendered safe, some of the following may not apply. In these situations, the destruction of evidence should be minimised to the extent possible.) When sketching and measuring the crime scene, it is particularly important to carefully note and measure the location of all cartridge casings, bullet holes, bullets and bullet fragments, and shotgun shot patterns that are found. This information is vital to the reconstruction of the crime and can be used to verify statements by witnesses and suspects. Special care must be taken when walking through the location so that casings or bullets are not stepped on or inadvertently kicked.

If a weapon is found at the scene, it should not be moved until its location is noted through measurement, sketches, and photographs. The investigator should remember that fingerprints or DNA might be present, so when the weapon is moved it must be handled in a way that will not destroy such evidence. The floor below the weapon should be examined for a depression or other marks that would indicate that it was dropped from some height or fell from the shooter's hands. Traces of wood, fibres, paint, building material, blood, and hair should be looked for on the weapon and carefully preserved if found.

If the dead person is holding the weapon, it is important to note the exact grip and position of the weapon in the hand. The murderer may have placed it there. In such a case, the way in which a weapon is held in relation to the injuries on the body may indicate whether or not the dead person could have produced the injuries. In the case of a semi-automatic pistol, the recoil of the slide may have caused a surface graze in the region of the thumb or the web of the hand, and the presence of such an injury is suggestive that the dead person had fired a shot with a semiautomatic pistol. A closer examination of the hand of the dead person may show marks of powder, especially if a revolver had been used. From these marks, the investigator may deduce that both hands were in the vicinity of the muzzle blast or the gap of the revolver. One hand may have been used as a guide while the other pressed the trigger, or both hands may have been held up in defence.

In the case of long-barrelled guns, rifles, and shotguns, special attention should be given to the possibility of the dead person having fired a suicide shot with the weapon. Special arrangements such as string, belts, sticks, and the like may have been used, and these in turn may have left marks in the form of fibres, dirt, soot, or the like on the trigger or trigger guard. One shoe may have been removed to depress the trigger with a toe.

The position of cartridges, cartridge cases, and bullets is just as important as that of weapons. From their position it may be possible to deduce the position of firing, direction of the shot, and in certain cases the path of the bullet. If a bullet has penetrated a tree, piece of furniture, or wall, the shot track gives information regarding the direction of the shot and often also the path of the bullet. There is a much better opportunity of determining the exact course of a bullet when it has passed through a fixed object such as a windowpane

Figure 10.8 Determining the trajectory of a bullet during a shooting reconstruction. (Photograph courtesy of Los Angeles County Sheriff's Department, Los Angeles, CA.)

and then struck a wall (Figure 10.8). With the aid of the path of the bullet and of shot wounds on the dead person, it is possible to determine the deceased's position when shot. In calculating the distance of the shot, the depth to which a bullet has penetrated a wall, for example, may be significant. The penetrating power is dependent on the distance of the shot, but allowance must also be made for the loss of energy in passing through an object, such as a body. A more accurate determination of distance can be made with the aid of gunshot injuries on the clothes and body of the dead person.

The position of a bullet found at the scene of a crime should be recorded in the same way as for weapons; bullets should be collected separately and packed so that there can be no confusion. If two or more weapons have been used, the bullets should not get mixed up; at a later date, it will be important that the place where each one was found has been fixed exactly. Great care should also be taken in collecting and packing bullets so that the microscopic marks from the barrel of the weapon are not injured or destroyed. For this reason, a bullet that has penetrated or lodged in a wall should *not* be probed for and dug out by means of a knife, ice pick, or chisel. Instead, a portion of the wall surrounding the bullet should be carefully removed in one piece and the bullet recovered by breaking away the supporting material. Because it may become important to ascertain other objects that came in contact with the projectile, gloves should always be worn when handling bullets or bullet fragments. Trace evidence should also not be removed or the bullet washed until a microscopic study is performed. Care should be exercised so the investigator's marking of the bullet does not destroy this trace evidence. The firearms examiner should also consult with the forensic biologist when DNA typing is needed in order to determine the best order for the bullet to be examined.

The same considerations with respect to fixing the position and taking possession of weapons and bullets apply to cartridges and cartridge cases found at the scene of a crime. The position of a cartridge that has misfired or of a cartridge case that has been ejected may give an indication of the type of pistol used and form a valuable supplement to determination of the make of pistol from marks left by the weapon on the bullet and casing. Many automatic pistols differ with respect to the ejection of the casings; some throw them out to the left, some to the right, and some straight up. The casing is thrown out with a force that varies for different types of pistols but is generally considerable, so it may rebound against furniture, walls, wall coverings, and so on and change direction. The position may give some indication of the type of weapon; however, there is often variation from weapon to weapon. If a cartridge case has not bounced off any object and has moreover fallen onto an under layer that prevents it from rolling (carpet, lawn, etc.), then its position gives a direct indication of the type of weapon and place or direction of firing. If three of these four factors (position of cartridge case, type of automatic pistol, place of firing, and direction of shooting) are known, then the fourth can be determined. Outdoors, however, it is necessary to take into account the direction and strength of the wind; in all cases, the inclination of the ground must be considered.

The position of wads, which often remain relatively undamaged, from shotgun shells and muzzle-loading weapons, also gives information regarding the direction of shooting. These can generally be found about 5 to 8 metres or more from the place of firing in the approximate direction of fire, but it is necessary to take into consideration the direction and strength of the wind. The overshot card placed in front of the charge of shot shows, if found, a manufacturing mark and also the size of shot given by a number or letters.

As mentioned previously, weapons and also cartridge cases, bullets, shot, and wads may carry marks from the victim or the criminal that may aid in solving the crime. It should always be remembered that DNA, latent fingerprints, and fingerprints in blood, grease, or the like may be found on weapons and must be protected. A weapon that has been used in a case of murder, suicide, or assault may contain clues from the victim in the form of blood, hair, fragments of textiles, cloth fibres, and so on. Such clues may appear to be of little value, but if it is necessary to prove that the weapon was actually used in a particular case, these clues are then of the greatest value. Loose hairs, dried blood, fibres, and the like should be placed into a test tube and the weapon taken and packed in such a way that DNA, fingerprints, or other clues are not destroyed. A cardboard container that suspends the weapon with a minimum of bearing surfaces is preferred. Wrapping an object in cotton, gauze, or tissue will more than likely dislodge trace evidence. If epithelial cells, fingerprints, or bloodstains are present on a weapon, they might be destroyed if the entire weapon is dusted with fingerprint powder. It is therefore appropriate for the latent print examiner to confer with the forensic biologist to determine whether DNA or latent print evidence has the better chance of success. There is no hard and fast rule as to which type of evidence should be collected first; however, examiners should keep in mind that collection of one type of evidence could potentially prevent or inhibit the collection of a subsequent type of evidence.

Contamination in the form of oil, cement, paint, or similar material may also be significant in determining the way in which a criminal acquired a weapon or may give an indication of where a weapon was kept previously. It may possibly have been taken from the criminal's place of work or during an earlier burglary in which the criminal was less careful and left fingerprints or DNA that can be used as incriminating evidence.

If the weapon has been concealed at the scene of the crime or in the vicinity, or taken away by the criminal, it is important to know the type of weapon for which one is searching. The only means of determining this is from a study of the injuries on the victim or by removal of the bullet at autopsy. In practice, it is often difficult to draw the correct conclusions from the appearance of the wounds because they are affected by the elasticity of the skin, underlying bones and muscles, angle of application, and other such factors. In these types of cases, however, the pathologist can give valuable assistance.

10.3.3   Handling of Firearms

In lifting firearms, great care must be taken not to destroy evidence. The best way to lift a pistol or revolver is to hold it with two gloved fingers on the chequered part of the butt, or possibly by the ring on the butt. Shotguns may conveniently be held around the chequered part of the neck of the butt; if necessary, the weapon can be lifted by a steady grip with the fingers on the trigger guard. It is undesirable to lift a weapon by placing a stick or similar object in the trigger guard, even with a light weapon such as a revolver or pistol, because the weapon may be cocked and a shot might be fired if the trigger happens to be touched. It should be taken as a general rule never to lift a weapon found at the scene of a crime before first making sure that no one is in the direction in which the muzzle is pointing; of course, one should not risk being hit if the weapon fires while being lifted. The weapon may actually be cocked so that even the slightest movement could cause a shot to be fired.

The procedure popular in works of fiction for picking up a gun by putting a pencil or stick in the barrel is absolutely wrong. This may destroy valuable clues in the barrel that might possibly have been of use in elucidating the case. In a contact shot (i.e., when the muzzle is in contact with a body) or a close proximity shot, which is common with suicide, it often happens that blood, grease, and textile fibres are forced into the barrel of the gun left by the vacuum from the gas pressure or the splash of tissue and blood in all directions. This phenomenon is known as *backspatter*.

A layer of dust, spider webs, or loose rust particles found in the bore may indicate that no shot has been fired from a weapon for some time. The absence of a powder deposit or the presence of grease in the bore may also indicate that the weapon has not been used, while an examination of the powder layer in the bore may show that the fired cartridge was loaded with black powder or with smokeless powder. It is difficult to decide from the appearance of the powder deposit how much time has elapsed since the last shot was fired from a weapon; therefore, if the bore of a weapon is to be examined for any such clues, introducing any object into it will interfere with its examination or make it impossible. For the same reason, cotton or the like must not be put in the muzzle during transport of the weapon or when it is sent to an expert. In order to protect any deposit in the bore, a twist of paper, rubber cap, or muzzle protector can be placed over the muzzle. The layer of dust in the bore is always thickest near the muzzle and decreases in thickness progressively toward the breech, assuming that it has resulted from a long period of storage. The confirmation of such a distribution of the deposit nearest the muzzle is therefore of great importance. Under no circumstances should an investigating officer put the weapon into his own pocket for safekeeping. After only brief contact with pocket dust, the gun will appear to have been unfired for some time.

Case 1

The victim in this case was shot and killed by the suspect, and the incident reportedly stemmed from a property dispute between neighbouring families. Four firearms were submitted to the lab to be test-fired and examined for blood. One of the firearms submitted was a Mossberg model 500A 12-gauge shotgun. The interior of the muzzle end of the barrel of this shotgun contained apparent dust, cobwebs, and debris, indicating that the shotgun had not been fired recently and that it could not have been discharged during the reported altercation that took place (see Figure 10.9).

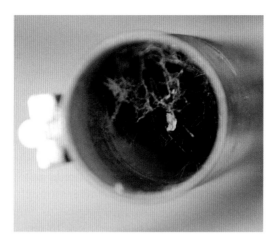

Figure 10.9 Dust, cobwebs, and debris seen in the interior of the muzzle end of the shotgun barrel, which shows that this shotgun had not been fired recently. (Photograph courtesy of Melissa Simons, Central Point Forensic Laboratory, Oregon State Police.)

After the weapon has been picked up, any loose objects or particles such as hair, fibres, dried blood, brain substance, and the like that might fall off in transport are removed and kept. With a near shot against a hair-covered part of the body, sometimes strands of hair or tissue can be found held fast between the slide and barrel of an automatic pistol. Also, any traces on the weapon in the form of fibres of wood, paint, cement, or the like, which might indicate that the weapon had fallen on the floor, should be collected while at the scene of the crime.

When a weapon is taken into possession, it should be subjected to a preliminary examination. Fingerprint impressions in grease or blood can easily be seen. If fingerprints, bloodstains, fibres, and so on are found on the weapon, they all must be preserved. It is important for the firearms examiner to also be mindful of subsequent DNA examinations and the potential for their own DNA to contaminate the evidence. The firearms examination must be conducted with gloves and a mask covering the mouth and nose at a minimum. If latent fingerprints are to be developed by powder, care must be taken to keep the powder from entering the barrel. Likewise, when a revolver is processed by powder dusting, the front of the cylinder must be protected so that the mouth of each chamber can be examined for flaring.

Everything found in the first examination of the weapon should be written down accurately; any objects, particles, or swabs collected should be placed in a test tube or envelope labelled accurately with the exact place of finding. For the sake of identification, any manufacturer's or type markings should also be indicated, as well as the calibre marking and serial number. The investigator's initials should be inscribed on some major part of the weapon such as the barrel or frame, or the weapon may be tagged. It is most important to write down the condition of the weapon when found, whether or not the safety is on (which can be seen from the position of the safety catch), and whether the weapon is cocked and loaded. With some semiautomatic pistols, the latter cannot be observed by a superficial glance, but where it is shown by, for example, an indicating pin, it should be noted. In the most common types of weapon, this condition can easily be confirmed from the position of the rear part of the bolt. It should also be noted whether the bolt (breech block or slide) is closed, partly open, or fully open. A cartridge case jammed in the ejection port should be noted, together with a statement of the exact position of the cartridge, whether the base or neck of the case is turned outward, etc., and whether the magazine is firm or loose (not pushed right home).

After the exterior of the weapon has been processed for fingerprints and swabbed for DNA, the gun may be unloaded and rendered safe. With a semiautomatic pistol the magazine is loosened, after which the slide is moved to remove any cartridge in the chamber. In doing this, it should be remembered that fingerprints might be found in grease on the cartridge in the chamber and on the sides of the magazine, which should therefore be examined first before any further handling. The weapon should not be considered unloaded until an inspection is made by looking into the chamber through the ejection port of the gun and physically checking to confirm that the chamber is empty. A broken extractor, jammed cartridge, or other factor may cause a cartridge to remain in the chamber. It is a poor practice to assume that a weapon is unloaded simply because a cartridge was not ejected. The cartridge is placed into an envelope or container with a label attached; a label can also be tied on by a thread around the groove of the cartridge. Any cartridges in the magazine should not be "stripped" if the weapon is to be sent to an expert for examination. Cartridges may carry DNA, fingerprints, and also marks from the guiding surfaces of the magazine, and it may be of significance to confirm them (e.g., whether the cartridges have been charged into the magazine several times). Furthermore, the order of the cartridges in a magazine may be important in certain cases and should always be noted.

In the case of a revolver, nothing should be done with the cartridges in the cylinder if the weapon is to be examined further. The exact position of the cylinder at the moment when the weapon is found is significant from many points of view and should be noted (e.g., the position of the fired cartridge in relation to the hammer). The position of the cylinder can be marked if desired with a pencil or chalk mark, provided that this does not destroy other clues. The cylinder should not be rolled because irrelevant marks from the recoil plate or firing pin could be formed on the bases of the fired cases and the cartridges.

In the case of weapons of single-shot or repeating types, nothing should be done with the bolt unless the weapon is cocked or has the empty case in the chamber. If, however, the hammer is cocked, an unfired cartridge may be in the chamber and should be removed to prevent an accident. The cartridge is taken out and labelled as described earlier. Semi- or fully automatic weapons generally have a cartridge in the chamber unless the bolt is in the rearward position, so the slide should be moved while making sure that no fresh cartridge is introduced into the chamber. In order to prevent this, a detachable magazine is removed from the weapon; in the case of a fixed magazine, the uppermost cartridges are held back with a piece of wood or some other object that will not injure the cartridges or deposit any fresh marks on them.

All the precautions taken with a firearm must be put down accurately in the report. Later, possibly, the investigating police officer may be required to describe these precautions in connection with legal proceedings. What may appear to be of subordinate importance during investigation of the crime may later be especially significant. In connection with all firearms, when a weapon is to be sent to an expert for examination, the only clues that need to be preserved are those that might be destroyed in transit; the only measures taken are those that cannot be omitted without risk of accident or that are essential in assisting the search for the criminal. Many traces on the weapon or significant facts in connection with the mechanism can be of such a character that special instruments or specially trained personnel are necessary to deal with them properly. Perhaps marks of coloured lacquer from the sealing around the primer are on the breech face or recoil plate; a chemical examination may be required to confirm whether this could have come from a specific fired cartridge. Even in the bore, lacquer pigments from the sealing between the bullet and case or metallic particles from the jacket of the bullet may be found. In grease and dirt on the breech face an impression of the markings may also be on the base of the cartridge case; special arrangements will be required for photographing this impression.

As mentioned earlier, from the point of view of identification, any marks indicating maker, type, and calibre should be recorded, together with the serial number. With many weapons, particularly certain pistols and revolvers, such markings are often lacking. The butt plates, however, are usually marked with the maker's or seller's initials, which can be a good guide. Many weapons also carry *proof marks*. A number of European countries strictly regulate the manufacture of firearms and require a special mark to be stamped on the weapon's barrel to indicate that it has been tested and found safe. Proof marks are also found on some American-made weapons sold in foreign countries. In cases of inexpensive firearms, the proof mark may be the only clue to the manufacturer of the weapon.

Occasionally, firearms are recovered from which serial numbers have been ground off for the purpose of concealing the ownership of the weapon. When numbers are stamped into the frame of the weapon, changes in the metal structure deep below the surface result. If the process that removed the stamp was not sufficiently deep, the serial numbers or markings can be restored. Depending on the nature of the metal, various techniques are possible: magnetic particle testing, chemical etching, electrochemical etching, and heating. An example is shown in Figure 10.10.

10.3.4 Cartridge Cases

If no cartridge cases are found at the scene of a shooting, it may be suspected that a revolver, single-shot pistol, automatic pistol with cartridge case collector, rifle, or shotgun was used. Theoretically, one might expect that criminals would attempt to guard themselves by picking up the cartridge cases thrown out by an auto-loading weapon, but in practice it is hardly ever done because it would waste time and the criminal would run more risk of being discovered, especially if the shooting was heard by persons in the vicinity.

Figure 10.10 An example of serial number restoration. (Photograph courtesy of Los Angeles County Sheriff's Department, Los Angeles, CA.)

Figure 10.11 The difference between a revolver cartridge case (left) and a semiautomatic cartridge case (right) is the extractor groove.

When taking possession of cartridge cases one should not forget the possibility that significant clues may be found on them in the form of loose particles or fingerprints. These may be picked up by means of a clean swab stick or the like, introduced into the case, and then placed into an envelope marked with the place of finding. The internal diameter of a cartridge case corresponds at the neck with the diameter of the bullet. From the size, form, and appearance of a cartridge case, it is possible to obtain an indication of the type of weapon used. Revolver cartridge cases are almost always fully cylindrical, with a rim but without the extractor groove (a groove for the extractor running around the case with the rim) present on a semiautomatic cartridge case (Figure 10.11). They may be made for rim fire (smooth base) or centre fire (with primer cap).

Moon clips allow for chambering semiautomatic ammunition in a revolver (Figure 10.12). Both Colt and Smith & Wesson make revolvers of .45 calibre such that automatic pistol cartridges of .45 calibre can be used in them. Similarly, 7.65-mm automatic pistol cartridges can be fired in .32-calibre revolvers and 6.35-mm automatic pistol cartridges can be fired in .25-calibre revolvers. Automatic pistol cartridges (with the exception of

Figure 10.12 Moon clips allow for chambering of semiautomatic ammunition in a revolver. (Photograph courtesy of Peter Diaczuk, John Jay College of Criminal Justice, New York.)

.45-rimless cartridges, 9-mm Parabellum cartridges, and bottleneck cartridges) have a rim that, although not much larger than the cylindrical surface of the cartridge, is quite sufficient to hold the cartridge fast in the chamber of a revolver cylinder when the internal diameter of the latter corresponds with the diameter of the cartridge. In many revolvers provided with one common extractor for all the cartridges, the rim also functions quite satisfactorily when pistol cartridges are used. Revolver cartridges of .320 calibre can also be fired in certain semiautomatic pistols of 7.65-mm calibre. In some cases, such pistols have also repeated normally and even ejected revolver cartridge cases, but the ejected cases are often ruptured and sometimes jam the pistol.

Smaller calibre projectiles can be fired in larger bore weapons with serious effect. An example of this is the ability of a .38 Special revolver to fire .32-20 cartridges. Desperate persons in need of ammunition wrap cartridges in paper to accommodate a larger chamber, reduce the diameter by filing, or even perform the dangerous act of driving a cartridge into a chamber by means of a hammer. Only an expert can determine with reasonable certainty the type of gun that might have been used in a shooting by an examination of the fired bullets or cartridges. An investigator must be careful not to pass up a weapon because it does not *seem* to correspond to the ammunition at hand.

Calibre and manufacturer's marks generally are found on the base of the cartridge case and sometimes also the year of manufacture. Sometimes the maker's marks are in code consisting of letters and figures or of only letters or figures. Fired cartridge cases are especially valuable for identification because they show marks from the weapon that in most cases make it possible to decide with certainty whether they were fired from a particular weapon or not. It is therefore of special importance in an outdoor shooting that all possible efforts be made to determine the location of the shooting so that any cartridge cases left behind can be found. The most valuable marks on cartridge cases are those made by the firing pin on the primer and by the breech face on the primer and base of the case, but the marks produced by the extractor, ejector, and edge of the breech may also be important, as shown in Figure 10.13.

Flaws or damage in the chamber may also show on the metal case and make identification of the weapon possible. If the criminal has thrown away the weapon where it cannot be recovered (e.g., in water), it is important to attempt to find out whether the criminal or some other person (e.g., the previous or legal owner) ever fired a test shot and, if so, where. It is possible that the cartridge case and the bullet may be found there. With cartridge cases it is not particularly important whether the test shot was fired a long time before. The part of the weapon that leaves marks on the case may not have altered even though there was a long interval of time between the test shot and the crime. It is different in the case of bullets because sometimes the bore of a weapon may undergo such changes in a comparatively

Figure 10.13 Ejector marks on a cartridge casing. (Photograph courtesy of Lucian C. Haag, Forensic Science Services, Inc., Carefree, AZ.)

short time that comparison of a bullet with a test shot fired previously is useless. The nature of the place where the weapon has been kept and the number of shots that have been fired with it are important factors.

From the marks made by the extractor, ejector, and edge of the breech of a semiautomatic pistol on a cartridge case it is also possible to determine the make of semiautomatic pistol from which the case was fired. Semiautomatic pistols of different types and makes are often constructed differently with respect to the position of the extractor and ejector; this in turn affects the formation of the breech. The combination of these factors forms what is known as a system; that is, the characters mentioned allow classification of the type of construction of the pistol. If both cartridge case and bullet are available for determination of the make, the possibilities are increased because the number of land impressions on the bullet, their width, and the angle of twist can also be characteristic of a type of weapon and, in any case, form a valuable contribution to the investigation.

Under no circumstances should a cartridge case that is to be examined be tried in the chamber of a weapon; any marks made by the weapon on the case may be destroyed and other marks may be formed. It happens sometimes that at the scene of a crime in which a firearm has been used a cartridge is found that has misfired and been thrown out by movement of the slide or bolt, or a cartridge may have jammed between the breech lock and the edge of the breech and been removed by hand. Even such an unfired cartridge may carry valuable marks that can make possible an identification or determination of the make of the weapon used.

10.3.5 Bullets

Bullets that penetrate hard objects are often severely mutilated, sometimes to a degree that the weapon from which they were fired cannot be identified; therefore, every effort must be made to preserve what little remains of the rifling impression when a bullet is lodged in a wall, tree, or bone. In the latter case, the method of removal, if at all, will depend on whether the shooting victim is dead. If the victim is dead, the principles for bone, tree, or wall are alike. No projectile should be pried from its position. Instead, the supporting material and the bullet should be cut out as one piece, then the surrounding bone, plaster, or wood can be broken away carefully, leaving the projectile in the best possible condition, considering all circumstances. If the investigator wishes, the bullet as embedded in supporting material may be sent to the laboratory. Bullets removed by probing show ample evidence of the destructive effect of improper technique. Prior to removal, some careful testing will indicate the direction of the bullet's track.

10.3.5.1 Marking Bullets

After removal, the bullet should be initialled on the base. No mark should be placed on the rifling impression or on areas of ricochet. If in doubt as to the proper area to mark, the investigator should place the bullet in an envelope, a plastic vial, or a small box and then seal and mark the container.

10.3.5.2 Types of Bullets

Bullets may be of different sizes and shapes and made in different ways. The most common types are entirely of lead, semijacketed, or fully jacketed, but there are also bullets with a hole in the point (hollow point), with the point covered with softer metal, lead bullets with

Figure 10.14 An example of a hollow-point cartridge.

a copper cone pressed into the point, and the like. (Figure 10.14 shows an example of a hollow-point cartridge.) With fully jacketed (solid nose) bullets, the jacket entirely encloses the point of the bullet but is open at the rear end of it, exposing the lead core. With a semijacketed (soft-nose) bullet, on the other hand, the jacket encloses the whole of the rear end of the bullet while the core is free at the point to a larger or smaller extent. The semijacketed bullet breaks up when it meets a bone or other hard part of the body, but if it passes merely through soft parts it may remain relatively undamaged or it may expand. If it strikes the branch of a tree in its flight it may actually be split or deformed before reaching its objective. On the other hand, a fully jacketed bullet often remains undamaged or only slightly deformed upon striking, for example, a body (Figure 10.15).

Less scrupulous shooters sometimes file the point of a fully jacketed bullet in order to produce the same effect as that of a semijacketed one. This result is obtained if the bullet leaves the barrel whole; however, because the jacket is open at both ends, there is a risk of only the lead core being driven out and the jacket remaining behind in the barrel. If this is not noticed, then when the next shot is fired the weapon will burst or a bulge will be produced in the barrel.

Lead bullets may be of different degrees of hardness. Bullets of soft lead are often greatly deformed and sometimes break up when they strike a body, while those of hard lead may retain their regular shape to the same extent as a fully jacketed bullet. Ammunition intended for automatic pistols usually has fully jacketed bullets, while revolver ammunition usually has lead bullets; however, some automatic pistol cartridges take lead or

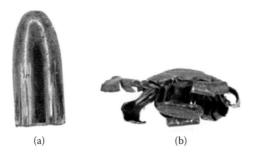

(a)   (b)

Figure 10.15 A fully jacketed bullet (a) is usually not deformed to any extent on striking an object, but a semijacketed bullet breaks up (b). (Photographs courtesy of Los Angeles County Sheriff's Department, Los Angeles, CA.)

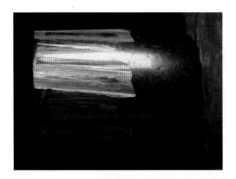

Figure 10.16 The direction and number of lands and grooves on this bullet reveal class characteristics regarding the type of gun that could have fired this bullet. (Photograph courtesy of Los Angeles County Sheriff's Department, Los Angeles, CA.)

semijacketed bullets and some revolver cartridges use fully jacketed bullets. An intermediate position is taken by the previously mentioned .22-calibre cartridges with lead bullets, which can be fired in certain automatic pistols, single-shot pistols, revolvers, and rifles. Also, as mentioned earlier, .320-calibre revolver cartridges with lead bullets can be fired in pistols of 7.65-mm calibre.

The type of jacket, if any; the contour, weight, and composition of the bullet; and the number, size, and design of cannelures may give an indication of the maker of the cartridge. In American cartridges, for example, lead bullets are sometimes copper plated. On a fired bullet the bore of the weapon will have left marks from the lands and sometimes also from the bottom of the grooves. A microscopic examination of these land and groove marks sometimes shows characteristic details that make it possible to identify the weapon. Furthermore, the number, width, and direction of twist of the lands and grooves make possible a determination of the make or makes of weapons from which the bullet may have been fired. The angle or rate of twist can be determined, but doing so is difficult and inaccurate when the projectile is mutilated (Figure 10.16).

The number and width of the land and groove impressions, together with the direction and angle of the twist, vary for different manufacturers and types of weapons. Under no conditions should a bullet be tested in the bore of a weapon by pushing it into the muzzle if the bullet and weapon are to be subjected to further investigation with the goal of identification. The microscopic marks on the bullet might be completely destroyed in this way. If it is necessary to search for a weapon in connection with a bullet that has been found, the police officer can obtain a useful guide from a study of the land impressions on the bullet. The number of marks, their width, and the direction of the twist can be compared with a suspected weapon. A firearms reference collection can be useful for identification exemplars (Figure 10.17).

If it is such a long time after the actual shooting that any deposit of dust or powder in the barrel would no longer be significant or if the barrel has evidently been cleaned or oiled, then a suitable piece of plasticine or, more recently, silicone casting material, moulded to a point, can be introduced into the muzzle of the weapon to obtain an impression of the lands and grooves so that their number and width can be compared with the marks on the bullet. Otherwise, this information must be obtained from inspection of the muzzle of the weapon, possibly with the aid of a flashlight.

Figure 10.17 A firearms reference collection can be used to help narrow down the type of gun that was used based on class characteristics found on test-fired bullets. (Photograph courtesy of Los Angeles County Sheriff's Department, Los Angeles, CA.)

Generally, the number of suspect guns in any investigation is not large, so it is better to let the laboratory sort these weapons by firing test shots. A number of factors affect the width of land impressions so that an exact comparison between a cast of the barrel and the bullet cannot be made. Anything within a reasonable range of tolerance should be submitted for laboratory tests.

10.3.5.3 Projectile Ricochet

Ricochet is the situation when a projectile impacts a surface at a shallow angle and bounces off, either intact or in fragments. The ricochet angle can be equal to but is usually less than the bullet impact angle, but can sometimes be greater. The ricochet bullet path will be influenced by the velocity and the impact angle of the shot, by the type and weight of the bullet, and by the character and the structure of the surface on which the impact is made.

The bullet will often be damaged by the impact either by deformation or fragmentation. In some instances the bullet can be found undamaged—for example, after a ricochet from an impact with the surface of a pool of water. Damage, deformation, or destabilisation of ricochet bullets can cause the bullet to rotate and spin during flight after leaving the point of impact. If such a rotating ricochet bullet then penetrates a surface, the entry hole may be have irregular edges, unlike the circular appearance of a normal bullet hole.

When examining the scene of a shooting incident it can sometimes be very difficult to detect the point of impact of a projectile ricochet. The surface on which the impact was made will not always show any easily visible marks or damage from the ricochet. Surfaces and marks suspected to have been caused by a projectile ricochet should be further examined by the use of chemical testing for lead, copper, or nickel. Following are the most commonly used tests:

- *Dithiooxamide* (DTO) or *rubeanic acid test*, which is chemically specific for the presence of copper-bearing, or cuprous, material (copper-jacketed bullets represent a considerable percentage of ammunition evidence in criminal cases)
- *Dimethylglyoxime*, which is used in the analysis of nickel

Figure 10.18 Ricocheted .357 magnum bullet. (Photograph courtesy of Lucian C. Haag, Forensic Science Services, Inc., Carefree, AZ.)

- *Sodium rhodizonate test*, which is a chemically specific test for the presence of lead in any form, including vaporous lead (smoke), particulate lead, lead in primer residues (e.g., lead azide or lead styphnate), lead bullets, or shot pellet wipe

Although these tests are specific for the metal of interest, they must be regarded as only presumptive evidence for the mark to be an impact point from a bullet, and interpretation should consider all the available information. The result of such a chemical test can also contribute to providing information on the type of bullet; for example, was it jacketed with copper or nickel or was it unjacketed, made of lead?

If there is reason to suspect that a bullet that has been found has ricocheted and it is important to confirm this, it must be remembered that small grains of sand or other foreign matter may have stuck in flaws in the bullet, which should therefore be treated with care so that such particles do not fall off. Damage resulting from a ricochet can often be identified microscopically (Figure 10.18).

10.3.5.4 Muzzle-Loading and Shotgun Charges

If a muzzle-loading weapon has been used it is possible that the bullet may show marks from the ramrod, so these should be looked for. Homemade bullets can possibly be identified with the mould used. In the case of muzzle loaders it is also necessary to search at the scene of the crime for any paper wads or the like that might have been used when loading the gun. These often remain intact, and the paper can perhaps be identified as being torn from a newspaper or from a piece of paper in the possession of a suspect. Although the rifled slugs and single balls of lead sometimes used in shotguns may give an opportunity for identification of the weapon, they can give information only as to the calibre. Homemade balls can possibly be identified with the moulds in which they were made.

10.3.5.4.1 Small Shot   At close range, the charge of shot, which has not yet dispersed, makes a large wound in a body, but at longer range the shot spreads out, more or less depending on the degree of choke of the gun, barrel length and size, and amount of shot. The amount of spread gives an opportunity to estimate the distance of the shot. If scaled photographs of the wound or shot pattern are available, comparison shots can be fired using the suspect weapon and ammunition of the same make and vintage. These are usually fired at heavy poster board or blotting paper. Without scaled photographs or comparison tests, only very broad estimates are possible because the patterns produced by various

Table 10.1 Diameter of Spread in Inches for Distances in Yards

Boring of Barrel	Range						
	10	15	20	25	30	35	40
True cylinder	20	26	32	38	44	51	58
Improved cylinder	15	20	26	32	38	44	51
Half choke	12	16	21	26	32	38	45
Full choke	9	12	16	21	27	33	40

Source: Fisher, B.A.J. and Fisher, D.R., *Techniques of Crime Scene Investigation*,
8th ed., CRC Press, Boca Raton, FL, 2012.

combinations of guns and ammunition vary over a considerable range. Table 10.1 gives an example of the influence of the degree of choke on shot patterns. These figures will not apply to all shotguns or all ammunition. At a distance of 5 to 8 metres or more from the place of firing, in the approximate direction of fire, one can sometimes find wads. The size of shot is sometimes given by a number, sometimes by letters. There is no internationally uniform method of designation of shot; the procedure varies in different countries.

By measuring the diameter of any shot found, it is thus possible to find the size of shot that would be marked on the cartridge (Figure 10.19). In this connection, it should be noted that there might be certain minor variations in size of shot in one and the same cartridge. It is therefore important to collect as many pellets as possible so that the determination is more reliable. Often the shot is deformed to such an extent that it is impossible to measure its diameter with the desired accuracy. In this case, it is convenient to weigh as large a number of shot as possible, calculate the mean weight, weigh the same number of shot from cartridges with the different sizes of shot that may be in question, and finally calculate their mean weight for comparison.

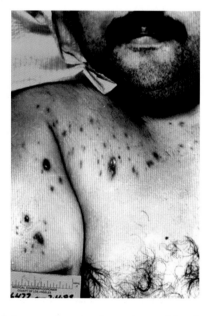

Figure 10.19 The distance of the gunshot can be estimated by the degree of stippling and how spread out it is. This wound pattern is from buckshot to the chest. (Photograph courtesy of Lucian C. Haag, Forensic Science Services, Inc., Carefree, AZ.)

Figure 10.20 Recovering a test shot from a water tank. (Photograph courtesy of Los Angeles County Sheriff's Department, Los Angeles, CA.)

If a weapon is sent to an expert to determine whether a bullet or a cartridge case has been fired from it, a sufficient number of cartridges (five to six or more) of the same type as that used in the actual incident should be sent with it. This is particularly necessary if powder or shot patterns are to be fired. All ammunition in the weapon and any partial boxes of unfired ammunition associated with a victim or suspect should be submitted with the weapon. Sufficient differences may exist between ammunition found in the gun and other ammunition available to the expert so that comparison tests are difficult, doubtful, or impossible.

If a number of tests must be fired for comparison and transmission to various laboratories, inquiries should be made as to the nature and make of test ammunition desired in each investigation. For best results, these test specimens should be obtained by a laboratory and not by the field investigator.

10.3.5.5 Test Firing

Test firings of a weapon must be done so that the bullet can be recovered undamaged. For all jacketed bullets and most types of lead bullets, a cotton wad box or water trap is used to stop the bullet. With a cotton wad box, as a consequence of its rotation, the bullet twists itself up in the waste, which finally forms a ball around the bullet, and the velocity progressively decreases until the bullet is finally held in the cotton waste. Occasionally, long-staple surgical cotton is placed in front of the cotton waste. This forms a ball around the bullet, further protecting the surface. Because of the mild damage to the bullet's surface due to the abrasive action of the cotton, water is frequently used as a collecting medium (Figure 10.20). For the collection of projectiles fired from handguns, 5 to 6 feet of water is ample. Generally, it is undesirable for the police officer to carry out test shots with the weapon personally because the microscopic imperfections in the bore of the weapon may be destroyed in the process. It is particularly important that the expert have an opportunity to examine the weapon before any tests are fired.

10.3.5.6 Powder Pattern Examination

When a weapon is fired at close range (up to several feet), burned and sometimes unburned particles of gunpowder are discharged onto the target. This effect is referred to as *powder pattern deposit*. The appearance of the powder pattern is sometimes helpful in establishing

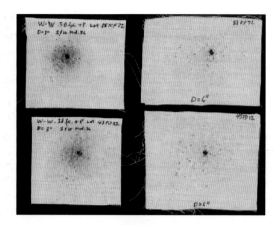

Figure 10.21 The two test firings on the left (distance of 3 inches) show a tighter distribution of particles than the two test firings on the right (distance of 6 inches). (Photograph courtesy of Lucian C. Haag, Forensic Science Services, Inc., Carefree, AZ.)

the distance from the fired weapon to the target. If the weapon was fired perpendicular to the target, the resulting powder pattern distribution will be located in an approximately circular area around the bullet entry hole.

The diameter of the circle and the distribution of particles can be used to establish the distance. The type of firearm, barrel length, and type of ammunition are all factors that affect the size and density of the powder pattern. If the muzzle of the weapon is in contact with the skin or within approximately 1/2 inch, the powder pattern is generally absent. This is due to the lack of space available for expansion of the powder, so that at close range it will penetrate the body through the entrance wound.

To make a distance determination, it is important to use the same firearm and ammunition used in the crime. A series of test firings are made into paper or cardboard at different distances and the test patterns are compared with the evidence. In most instances it is also useful to make the tests on material the same as or similar to the evidence (Figure 10.21).

In certain instances, the powder pattern is not easily visible. Bloodstained or dark-coloured clothing can make visualisation difficult. Infrared photography is helpful in bloodstained clothing cases. Chemical tests that are useful in developing the powder pattern include those for nitrates present in the gunpowder, such as the Walker test or Griess test, or, for lead and barium in the primer, the sodium rhodizonate test (Figure 10.22).

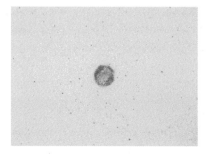

Figure 10.22 The sodium rhodizonate test can be used to test for lead in this bullet wipe. (Photograph courtesy of Peter Diaczuk, John Jay College of Criminal Justice, New York.)

Figure 10.23 An example of an IBIS workstation. (Photograph courtesy of Los Angeles County Sheriff's Department, Los Angeles, CA.)

10.4   Firearms Databases

In the past, comparing firearms evidence from one investigation to that of another was almost impossible unless there was some connection between the cases. Typically, the investigator determined or thought it possible that the same gun was used in two cases and asked the firearms examiner to compare the two recovered bullets or cartridge casings. Today, many countries have a database of fired cartridge casing and bullet images that can be used by investigators and forensic science laboratories. They are mainly based on the Integrated Ballistics Identification System (IBIS) manufactured by Forensic Technologies (Figure 10.23). The system was developed to link firearms evidence and to solve open cases by allowing firearms examiners to compare evidence with fired bullets, cartridge casings, shotgun shells, and firearms recovered in other jurisdictions. By means of a microscope attached to the system, images of bullets and cartridge casings are electronically scanned and stored for later retrieval and comparison with other case images. The system has the ability to compare the new images rapidly with images in regional and national databases. The firearms examiner visually compares the images to determine if there is a hit. The value of these systems is their ability to associate firearms evidence between unrelated crimes. Test firing confiscated firearms that come into the custody of the police becomes even more important because of the possibility of developing more information about cases that have appeared to be unrelated. Firearms evidence occurs in many crimes, such as assault, murder, and the like, and is particularly important because of the large amount of useful information it can provide. Because this type of evidence is encountered so frequently, investigators must be familiar with the proper methods of handling it and its value to the case.

10.5   Summary

The crime scene investigator can encounter guns and their ammunition in several situations, but they will almost always be cases of serious crimes. Identification of the gun, bullets, or cartridge cases can provide good associative evidence, and other evidence recovered from these, such as DNA, may provide information about the identify of the shooter. Firearms evidence therefore addresses mainly WHAT—what weapon, what happened, and, through databases, what other firearms evidence and locations (WHERE) may be linked to the gun. Reconstruction is aided by the collection of gunshot residue for analysis in the laboratory and by distance determinations. Sometimes the object of the investigation is to determine if the weapon is usable or has been altered in any way—which should serve as a reminder to the CSI that handling firearms carries a risk and safety precautions must be observed at all times.

Arson and Explosions

11.1 Introduction

Fires and explosions account for a large number of property crimes but also may be the cause of serious bodily injury and death. In addition to the requisite expertise needed in many other areas of crime scene investigations, fire scene and bomb scene investigators require added skills to properly investigate these types of crimes. This chapter covers some of the basic information, but it should always be kept in mind that when the crime scene investigation unit does not have personnel with the required training and skills, they should call in support from the appropriate specialist unit in their jurisdiction. Arson and explosions are often discussed together, as they both are concerned with the damaging effects of chemical reactions that release large quantities of energy. In contrast, the special skills and knowledge that scene and laboratory investigations require differ between the two. Both share the characteristic that the focus is on the crime, and many investigations will not produce forensic information to identify the criminal. In this chapter, we first deal with arson and then go on to discuss explosives.

Case 1

On 23 December, 1991, a fire destroyed the Corsicana, Texas, home that Cameron Todd Willingham shared with his wife and three daughters, killing the three girls. Willingham, who was asleep when the fire started, survived. His wife was at the Salvation Army buying Christmas presents for the girls. Following investigation, Willingham was charged and tried for intentionally setting fire to his home in order to kill the children. Willingham said he was asleep in the house when the fire started and always maintained his innocence. He was convicted based on the testimony of forensic experts who said they had determined that the fire was intentionally set and a jailhouse informant who said Willingham had confessed to him. He was sentenced to death and subsequently executed. Approximately 15 years after the fire, the case was reviewed by an expert panel set up by the Innocence Project. The panel concluded that advances in knowledge regarding the course of fires had shown that the indicators used at the time to conclude that the fire had been deliberately set using an accelerant were now all known not to be unique to non-accidental fires.

11.2 Arson

Arson is defined as the wilful and malicious burning of another's property or the burning of one's own property for some illegal purpose such as defrauding an insurer or even murder. As a crime, arson ranks only behind traffic-related incidents in the highest losses of life and property. In dollars, property losses due to arson can be placed in the billions of dollars annually. The core issue is that a major fire is a highly destructive event that destroys evidence as well as property and life (Figure 11.1). The investigation is a series of iterations of the elements of the investigative star, as investigators seek to distinguish between cause and effect. Even when it has been extinguished by the fire services, there may be little or nothing left to show what happened in the sense of arson or accident. One specific example from the Willingham case is that of V patterns. If a fire is deliberately set, it will spread outward from the point of origin, leaving a V-shaped burn pattern; however, any source

Figure 11.1 Major property fires. (Top image courtesy of Contra Costa County, CA, Fire District. Bottom image courtesy of Los Angeles County Sheriff's Department, Los Angeles, CA.)

can leave a V pattern, including a new hotspot ignited by debris or electrical failures produced by the fire. Today, investigators place much less emphasis on physical patterns at a fire scene and at best would regard them as corroborative rather than identifying arson.

Arson investigation requires a considerable amount of care, attention to detail, and skill on the part of the investigator. Arson scenes present a host of problems that are uncommon to most other crime scene investigations. In most criminal investigations, once the crime has been committed and the police notified, the scene may be secured in relatively the same condition in which it was found. This is anything but the case in fire investigation. By the time the arson investigator arrives on the scene, numerous individuals, including firefighters, supervisory personnel, onlookers, and possibly the owner of the property, will have visited the crime scene. The firefighters, as with crime scene investigators, must follow the principle of safety first when dealing with the fire, but they should have been trained on how to act when the fire is suspicious and should know how important it is to preserve the scene. The issue of criminal intent is another major difference between arson investigations and other types of investigations. With most other crimes, the investigator frequently knows on arrival or shortly thereafter that a crime has been committed. With arson cases, determining whether a fire was set accidentally or intentionally may require significantly more investigation. Arson and explosion crime scenes are unique in the amount of destruction and devastation present. An item that normally is identifiable as important evidence in an investigation can be totally or partially destroyed by the fire or by firefighters. In spite of the difficulties inherent in arson investigation, a careful and thorough search of the fire scene can produce much useful information.

A number of motives are frequently associated with arson. Probably the most common motives are concealment of other crimes and defrauding an insurance company. A fire investigator frequently finds that the fire was set to cover up another crime such as murder, burglary, embezzlement, or fraud. The attempt in these cases is to destroy records and evidence of the crime that could make identifying the suspect or the victim of a murder impossible. In insurance fraud cases, the suspect may have suffered a business reversal or be heavily in debt. The fire is set to appear accidental with the intent of filing a false insurance claim. Other motives such as malicious mischief caused by juveniles, revenge, extortion, sabotage, terrorist acts, and pyromania all represent potential reasons for setting fires.

The arson investigator should focus the investigation by considering several of the 6Ws:

- *WHERE did the fire originate?* Information can be obtained by questioning firefighters about the location of hot spots, in which direction the fire was moving, how fast, etc. The most information will be gained by going through the scene and noting what areas suffered the most fire damage and exposure to heat. Physical features such as depth of char, degree of destruction, spalling, melting and deformation of glass or metal objects, or burning or discolouration of paint should all be noted. These features, however, provide information only about the severity and course of the burning, not necessarily about whether or not the fire was accidental or arson. For example, an open door or window may assist development of the fire at that point and produce a resulting pattern that is different from another point in the building where the door or window was closed.
- *HOW was the fire started?* The investigator should look for faulty electrical wiring or the presence of igniters, matches, ignitable material, kindling, and other means of starting the fire. Ignitable fluids will run into cracks and under objects on the

floor and cause burning in locations that would not normally burn. They will also char deeper in areas where they were located, sometimes burning through the floor. As with the indicators mentioned above, there may be circumstances such as melting of the material in a synthetic fibre carpet that result in burning in unusual locations. The adage that "water runs downhill but fire rises" is not always a good guide for scene examination.

- *WHAT was the cause of the fire?* Was it an accident or was it intentionally set? This is the key issue in determining whether the fire was arson. Evidence such as breaking into and entering the building, presence of ignitable fluids, and multiple points of origin may indicate a maliciously set fire. What was the course of the fire? How hot did it get? When did it start? (See Figure 11.2.)

Figure 11.2 (Top) Burned-out electrical timer located at a fire scene can give the approximate time of the fire. (Bottom) A melted aluminium awning indicates the approximate fire temperature, as aluminium melts at 660.2°C. (Photographs courtesy of Los Angeles County Sheriff's Department, Los Angeles, CA.)

11.2.1   Forensic Evidence in Arson Cases

Forensic evidence serves two purposes in the investigation of a fire scene: (1) it can provide inceptive evidence and help to determine if the cause was accidental or deliberate, and (2) it can be corroborative and help to reconstruct the course of events by exploring the various hypotheses that are formulated in the attempts to reconstruct the scene. The two purposes overlap, and physical indicators such as the spread of burning from one or more hotspots and the intensity of burning may lead the scene investigator to question whether or not the cause was accidental (Figure 11.3). Detecting the presence of ignitable fluids or incendiary devices provides the best evidence in arson investigation. Even in cases in which fire damage was particularly extensive or the scene was completely wetted down, there is still a good probability of detecting ignitable fluids when evidence is collected properly.

The search for ignitable fluids should be concentrated at the point or points from which the fire has spread (V patterns). If charred carpeting or rugs are noted, these should be collected and sent to the laboratory. Wood flooring, furniture, and carpet padding that may have absorbed ignitable fluid accelerants should also be collected, as well as empty containers or broken glass jars found at the scene. Dogs trained to detect the odour of ignitable fluids have been used with success in some cases (Figure 11.4).

Ignitable fluids are highly volatile and evaporate easily. For this reason, appropriate packaging must be used to preserve these items for laboratory analysis. Packaging evidence in paper or plastic bags or containers will not preserve it. Most jurisdictions now use nylon arson evidence bags to package fire scene debris, but some still use glass jars with metal screw-cap lids or metal paint cans (Figure 11.5). The vapour-proof containers prevent loss of the volatiles, and the laboratory can identify the presence of even minute traces. It is important to also collect controls from surrounding areas, as burned debris from carpets or wood can contain chemicals similar to those used as accelerants.

The quantity of material needed for chemical analysis of an ignitable substance is extremely small. Laboratory instruments are capable of readily identifying ignitable liquids in quantities of less than a fraction of a drop. In fact, if an odour of an ignitable liquid

Figure 11.3 Burn patterns.

Figure 11.4 Explosive detector dog screening an automobile at a checkpoint. (Photograph courtesy of Bureau of Alcohol, Tobacco, Firearms, and Explosives, US Department of Justice, Washington, DC.)

can be detected, there is a good chance that a forensic laboratory can identify the source. It might be thought that the heat of a fire would destroy all traces of any accelerant used, but this is not necessarily the case. Even a fire hot enough to cause the spalling shown in Figure 11.3 (top left) can leave detectable traces. Laboratory analysis can differentiate among the many types of accelerants used in arson cases (Figure 11.6). The common types are gasoline, kerosene, charcoal lighter fluid, paint thinner, and turpentine. In some cases, the dyes contained in gasoline can be used as a means of comparison with known samples.

A careful search of all entrances and windows, if possible, should be made to determine whether the building had been forcefully entered. If toolmarks are observed, the area should be cut out or an impression made and submitted to the laboratory. Also, samples of building materials such as glass, paint, plaster, stucco, wallboard, or cement that may have been deposited on the suspect's clothing should be collected for purposes of control or known samples. All evidence must be properly marked for identification and

Figure 11.5 Metal paint cans containing debris from a fire scene. (Photograph courtesy of Jefferson Parish Sheriff's Office laboratory, New Orleans, LA.)

Figure 11.6 Gas chromatograph–mass spectrometer (GC–MS) used to detect and identify minute traces of accelerant extracted from items recovered from a fire scene. (Photograph courtesy of Los Angeles County Sheriff's Department, Los Angeles, CA.)

packaged properly. In some instances, an apparent forced entry might have been used to cover up arson, so such things as the side from which a window was broken, screen cut, etc., should be checked.

The investigation should include the search for igniting materials; burned matches and matchbooks or match boxes should be collected. Burned matches, in some cases, can be physically fitted into a matchbook found on a suspect, and matchbooks or boxes can be chemically processed for fingerprints or DNA. Occasionally, pieces of a timing device used to delay the ignition of a fire may be discovered. This provides good evidence that the fire was deliberately lit and may yield fingerprint or DNA evidence to identify the arsonist.

Other types of igniters such as candles, black powder, smokeless powder, sodium and water, electrical devices, and similar items should be noted and collected (Figure 11.7). It is important to establish the manner in which the fire started. This determines the modus operandi (MO) of the arsonist.

If the scene of the arson is a business establishment, the investigator may notice that file cabinets have been pulled open and papers strewn about. Burned papers should be carefully collected and placed into cardboard boxes, being sure to handle them as little as possible. Burned paper can be examined at the laboratory and useful information determined; for example, it may be very beneficial to know what files were burned or are missing. If the fire was started outdoors, the area of the origin of the fire should be examined. Soil from that area should be collected and tested for the presence of ignitable materials. Any items left at the scene by the arsonist should be preserved. Traces such as pieces of clothing, hair, blood, tools, broken tools, etc. may prove to be important as a means of establishing the identity of the suspect and reconstruction of the scene (Figure 11.8).

When a suspect is apprehended, a careful search of his property should be made to determine whether anything can be tied to the crime or the crime scene. Any accelerants such as gasoline or kerosene should be packaged and submitted to the laboratory for comparison with solvents detected at the scene of the arson. Similarly, objects such as tools, matches, matchbooks, incendiary devices, and the like should be collected. The suspect's clothing and shoes should be collected, packaged, and sent to the laboratory for examination for the presence of these materials. The suspect's vehicle should be inspected for the

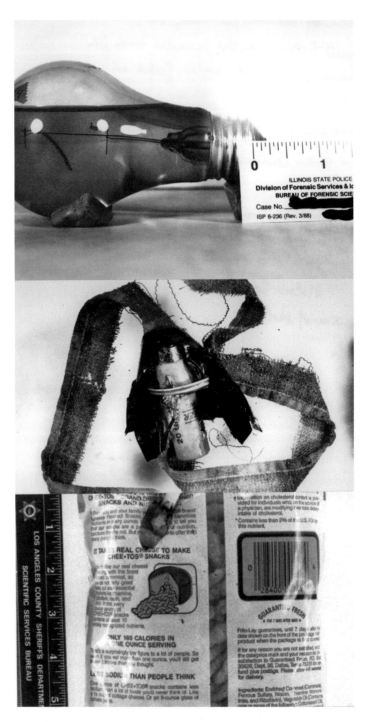

Figure 11.7 Improvised incendiary devices (top to bottom): light bulb with a small hole drilled into the base, filled with medium petroleum distillate, sealed with a putty-like material, and inserted into a socket connected to a timer; portion of a "Molotov cocktail" with a shot shell; and improvised incendiary device consisting of a cigarette and matches that can produce sufficient heat to cause the contents of the bag to burn. (Top and bottom photographs courtesy of Los Angeles County Sheriff's Department, Los Angeles, CA; middle photograph courtesy of Division of Forensic Sciences, Illinois State Police, Springfield, IL.)

Figure 11.8 Melted electrical timer device (top) and a close-up (middle) showing a portion of a label believed to have been used in an arson case. The example of the intact timer (bottom) was used in reconstruction of the device. (Photographs courtesy of Los Angeles County Sheriff's Department, Los Angeles, CA.)

presence of material removed from or transported to the scene of the arson. Any search of the suspect's vehicle or residence may require following the legal rules that apply in the jurisdiction. The local prosecutor should be contacted if there is any question.

In cases in which a dead body is discovered in the investigation, a determination of the cause of death is necessary to ascertain whether the victim died as a result of the fire or the fire was set in order to conceal the killing. The investigators should treat the scene as if it is a murder, until proven otherwise. As in any suspicious death investigation, the pathologist will be required to determine the manner and cause of death and, if possible, the time. There are some indicators associated with fires, such as signs of smoke inhalation.

11.3   Explosions

Explosives are useful tools that have allowed people to accomplish some remarkable engineering feats; however, like many other things, explosives are also used for criminal ends. Murder, burglary, extortion, terrorist activities, and similar activities involving explosives require the attention of the investigator. Bombs can take many forms, including the aircraft used in the 9/11 terrorist attack on the World Trade Center Twin Towers (Figure 11.9). Bomb scene investigation is frequently treated as a specialty within some police agencies and is often associated with arson investigation. Although certain aspects of crime scene investigation of bombings differ from a common crime scene, the basics remain the same.

In broad terms, an explosive is a material capable of rapid conversion from either a solid or a liquid to a gas with resultant heat, pressure, and loud noise (Figure 11.10). Many chemicals, alone or in combination, possess the necessary properties for an explosive. Except for chemical compounds classed as explosives, the rest usually come to the investigator's attention only as the result of some accident. In such cases, consultation with a forensic chemist will provide a satisfactory explanation for the explosion.

Figure 11.9 World Trade Center terrorist attack showing the first tower burning and the aircraft flying toward the second tower.

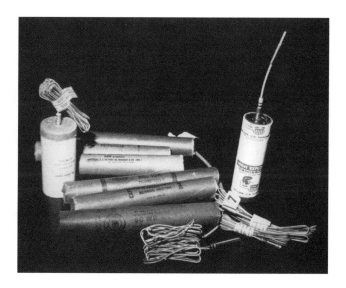

Figure 11.10 Examples of boosters, blasting caps, and dynamite. (Photograph courtesy of Los Angeles County Sheriff's Department, Los Angeles, CA.)

Explosives can be classed into two broad groups: low explosives and high explosives, the difference being in the speed of the shock wave produced in the blast. High explosives produce a detonation resulting in a shock wave that travels faster than the speed of sound; low explosives produce a conflagration with a lower speed shock wave. Damage by low explosives is caused by the force exerted by the rapid expansion of gases formed by burning. These types of explosives must be confined to explode, and can cause considerable damage.

11.3.1 Low Explosives

Black powder is the most common type of low explosive. It is a mixture of potassium or sodium nitrate, sulphur, and charcoal. There has been wide variation in the formulation of this mixture over the years. Black powder is sensitive to heat, impact, friction, and sparks. One of the most common uses of black powder is in the manufacture of safety fuses. When placed into a confined area, such as a pipe bomb, black powder can be a destructive explosive (Figure 11.11). Detonation can easily be accomplished by means of a safety fuse. If an unexploded pipe bomb is encountered, do not attempt to open the device unless you have been trained to do so, because the charge can be set off by friction.

Safety fuses are used to initiate explosives nonelectrically; they are generally composed of black power with a protective covering of cotton yarn or jute followed by an asphalt layer for water resistance. The asphalt covering is then covered with an insulating material such as a polyethylene plastic covering or a wax-impregnated yarn jacket. The colour of the fuse is generally white, black, or orange. Safety fuses should normally burn at a definite rate of speed but may burn faster or slower depending on several factors such as age, handling, altitude, and humidity. Usually, they burn at about 1 second per cm; however, the actual rate should be determined by testing a given length.

Smokeless powder is another low explosive encountered in bomb investigations. It is mainly used for small arms ammunition but is frequently used in pipe bombs. Two types of smokeless powder are marketed: single and double base. Single-base smokeless powder

Figure 11.11 Debris from a pipe bomb packed with a low-order explosive. (Photograph courtesy of Los Angeles County Sheriff's Department, Los Angeles, CA.)

consists of nitrocellulose, while double-base is composed of nitrocellulose and nitroglycerine. Although smokeless powder is not as sensitive to friction as black powder, it should be handled with the same amount of care.

11.3.2   High Explosives

Primary explosives detonate when subjected to heat or shock. They are typically used as initiators of high explosives, to detonate main charges, and in blasting caps and firearm primers. For this type of explosive, the major interest in bomb investigation is in blasting caps. Blasting caps are of two types: electric and nonelectric. They are small explosive devices, about 5 mm in diameter and from 25 to 75 mm in length. The case may be made of aluminium, copper, or bronze (Figure 11.12). The electric blasting caps have coloured wires extending from them. Secondary explosives detonate by shock from a suitable primary explosive. Their detonation velocities range from 1000 metres per second in the case of ammonium nitrate to 9000 metres per second in the case of HMX. Typically, high explosives are used to shatter or destroy objects.

Detonating cord is a cord-like explosive, similar in appearance to a safety fuse. It contains a central core of RDX or PETN covered with cotton or other textile, followed by a waterproof material or plastic covering. The cord detonates at velocities from 5500 to 7000 metres per second. It is very insensitive to shock and heat and presents no special problems in handling. Detonating cord is used to set off charges of high explosives much in the same way as a safety fuse is used to set off multiple pyrotechnic devices. The detonating cord may be inserted, tied, or knotted inside the high explosive to initiate detonation. Detonating cord is used to set off simultaneous charges and is detonated by means of a blasting cap.

Boosters or primer explosives are used to detonate very insensitive high explosives. The booster consists of a secondary explosive such as RDX, PETN, tetryl, or pentolite and is detonated by means of a blasting cap. Boosters are usually cylindrical in shape with a small opening to permit insertion of a blasting cap.

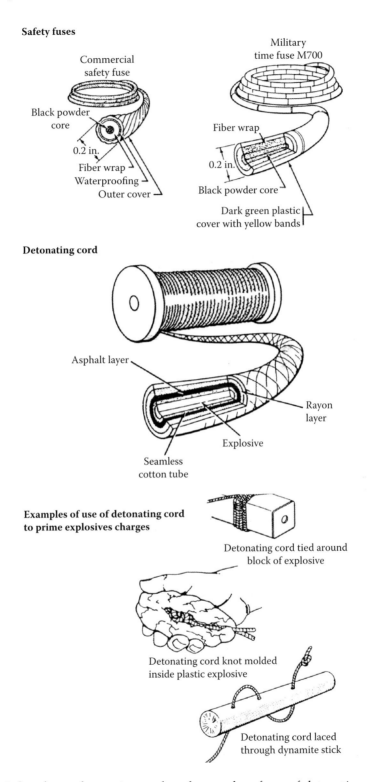

Figure 11.12 Safety fuses, detonating cord, and examples of use of detonating cord to prime explosives charges. (Illlustration courtesy of Bureau of Alcohol, Tobacco, Firearms, and Explosives, US Department of Justice, Washington, DC.)

Numerous high explosives are used commercially and by the military. Some of the more common ones encountered in law enforcement work are detailed next; however, the list is not intended to cover all of the many types. Nitroglycerine was first developed in 1847, but it was not until 1867 that Alfred Nobel developed a method to desensitise this explosive sufficiently so that it could be used commercially. Nobel's invention, dynamite, was a mixture of nitroglycerine and diatomaceous earth. Today, dynamite contains ethyleneglycoldinitrate (EGDN) in addition to other materials used to desensitise the nitroglycerine. Inert materials such as wood pulp or sawdust, cornmeal, sodium nitrate, and many other materials are found in dynamite, which is usually packaged in cylindrical sticks and wrapped in waxed paper. The sticks come in a variety of sizes; the most common is around 3 cm in diameter and 20 cm in length. Other sizes may be as large as 30 cm in diameter and from 10 to 90 cm long. The four basic types of dynamite in use today are straight dynamite, ammonia dynamite, gelatine dynamite, and ammonia–gelatine dynamite:

- *Straight dynamite* is manufactured in strengths of 15 to 60% by weight of nitroglycerine. The nitroglycerine is generally absorbed onto a material such as wood pulp or ground meal (such as cornmeal and corn starch). Dynamite has a sweet, pungent odour and frequently may cause headaches. Straight dynamite has an oily, slightly moist appearance and resembles a mixture of oil, sawdust, and clay. In older sticks of dynamite, the outer wrapper may often look oil-stained from the nitroglycerine seeping out of the mixture. Police should treat such dynamite with extreme caution because it is in a highly unstable form.
- *Ammonia dynamite* has some of the nitroglycerine replaced with ammonium nitrate. Ammonia dynamite is less sensitive to shock than straight dynamite and has less of a shattering effect, but is more suitable for "pushing." The colour of ammonia dynamite is light brown, compared with a slight reddish tint in the case of straight dynamite.
- *Gelatine dynamite* is a water-resistant form of dynamite manufactured by combining nitroglycerine with nitrocellulose. The resulting gel is a thick, viscous liquid useful under wet conditions.
- *Ammonia–gelatine dynamite* is a combination of the last two formulations. The addition of the ammonium nitrate is a cost-saving factor, and the gelatine allows the explosive to be used in wet conditions.

Ammonium nitrate is a readily available material used as an explosive and, in a less pure form, as a fertiliser. In its pure form, it is a white crystalline material but may be a light tan colour in a less pure form. As an explosive it is relatively insensitive and requires a booster charge to be detonated. Because of its easy availability as a fertiliser, although less pure than explosive-grade ammonium nitrate, it is readily available for use in homemade bombs. A modification of ammonium nitrate sometimes used is a mixture of ammonium nitrate and fuel oil, also known as ANFO.

Water gels or slurries are classified as either blasting agents or explosives, depending on what they contain and whether or not they are cap sensitive. Water gels typically have an ammonium nitrate base, a sensitiser, a thickener, and 5 to 40% water. The sensitiser may be an explosive such as trinitrotoluene (TNT), nitrostarch, or smokeless powder, or it may be a nonexplosive such as sugar, fuel oil, carbon, or a powdered metal. These explosives are rapidly gaining in popularity as substitutes for dynamite. Most slurries require a primer or booster for detonation; however, some manufacturers make cap-sensitive gels.

11.3.3 Blasting Agents

Blasting agents, also known as nitrocarbonitrate (NCN), are insensitive chemicals and chemical mixtures that are detonated by means of a high-explosive primer or booster. In order to be classified as a blasting agent, the material must be unable to be detonated by a No. 8 blasting cap and contain no high explosives such as TNT or nitroglycerine. Blasting agents consist largely of ammonium nitrate. ANFO is considered a blasting agent and consists of 94% ammonium nitrate and 6% fuel oil. The advantage of blasting agents is that safety regulations governing shipping and storage are considerably less severe than those applicable to high explosives. Binary explosives are two inert, non-explosive chemicals that, when mixed, form a cap-sensitive high explosive. The materials are either both liquids or a powder and a liquid; in their unmixed states, they are very insensitive to shock or friction. One component is usually ammonium nitrate, while the other is a non-explosive sensitiser.

11.3.4 Military Explosives

Sheet explosives are flexible, rubberlike sheets approximately 1/4-inch thick that can be cut with a knife. These explosives are used in commercial and military circumstances. The high explosive used is either RDX or PETN. Sheet explosives are known as Flex-X, Datasheet®, or M118 demolition blocks (the latter being a military sheet explosive). The most common type of military explosive is TNT. Military explosives differ somewhat from commercial explosives in that they must be used in combat conditions. Typically, they must be relatively insensitive to heat, shock, friction, and bullet impact; have high destruction power (brisance); be lightweight and convenient to use; be usable under water; etc. TNT is generally encountered in military explosives in 100-, 200-, and 400-g blocks. The blocks have metal ends with a threaded well at one end for a blasting cap. The container is cardboard, and the TNT is a light yellow to brown colour, although some newer formulations of TNT may be grey due to the addition of graphite.

So-called plastic explosives contain RDX. Plastic explosives contain plasticiser in addition to RDX and are easy to mould in warm temperatures. Composition C3, containing 77% RDX, is a yellow putty-like material that has a distinctive heavy, sweet odour. When moulded, it will stain the hands and clothing. The 1-kg M3 block is enclosed in glazed paper that is perforated around the middle for ease in breaking it open. The block does not have a cap well. Composition C4 is replacing C3 in military use. C4 contains 91% RDX, is white to light brown in colour, has no odour, and does not stain the hands. The 1-kg M5A1 block demolition charge contains C4 in a clear white plastic container with a threaded cap recess at each end. Composition C4 also comes in a M112 block demolition charge, an improvement over the M5A1 that replaces it as a standard issue. The M112 contains approximately 500 g of composition C4 and has a pressure-sensitive adhesive tape on one surface, protected by a peelable paper cover. The C4 in some blocks is coloured dull grey and packed in a clear Mylar®-film bag. In blocks of more recent manufacture, the C4 is white and packed in an olive-drab Mylar bag.

Military dynamite is not really dynamite but a mixture of 75% RDX, 15% TNT, 5% SAE 10 motor oil, and 5% guar flour. It is packaged in waxed manila paper and marked M1, M2, or M3. Military dynamite is buff-coloured granular material that crumbles easily and is slightly oily to the touch. It does not have the characteristic odour usually associated with dynamite because it contains no nitroglycerine.

The explosives discussed to this point are some of the more common ones encountered and represent explosives available through commercial and military sources. The explosives industry, however, is a rapidly changing one and the reader should understand this when studying the subject. It is suggested that the investigator consult explosive manufacturers, law enforcement agencies that routinely deal with explosive cases, and forensic science laboratories for the latest information on the subject.

11.3.5   Homemade Explosives

If commercial or military explosives are not available, it is not particularly difficult for an individual to improvise from a large number of chemicals that, when mixed together, can produce highly destructive explosive devices (Figure 11.13). The investigator should recognise at least some of the more common materials that often find their way into homemade explosive devices. Materials such as starch, flour, sugar, or cellulose can be treated to become effective explosives. Powder from small-arms ammunition and from firecrackers, match heads, and ammonium nitrate from fertilisers can be used in explosive devices. Several methods are used to detonate an improvised explosive device, including those listed below:

- *Blasting caps*—Caps, especially electrical blasting caps, lend themselves to homemade bombs. Such devices may be set off by a timing mechanism, by movement, by wiring into an automobile ignition system, etc.
- *Percussion primers*—Primers from shotgun, rifle, or pistol ammunition are sometimes used to detonate explosives that are heat sensitive.
- *Flashbulbs*—Flashbulbs may be used to ignite heat-sensitive explosives such as black powder. If the bulb is placed in contact with the explosive, the resulting heat from the flashbulb will ignite materials such as black powder, smokeless powder, or incendiary mixtures. As mentioned earlier, because of its relative ease to manufacture, black powder is frequently used in homemade bombs.
- *Match heads*—Match heads are frequently found confined inside pipe bombs. They are sensitive to heat, friction, and shock and when confined in this type of device can produce an effective explosion.
- *Smokeless powder*—Powder from ammunition or for reloading purposes is frequently used as the main charge in pipe bombs.
- *Ammonium nitrate fertiliser*—Ammonium nitrate mixed with fuel oil and an appropriate booster makes an extremely effective homemade explosives device.
- *Potassium or sodium chlorate*—These compounds and sugar are used as incendiary and explosive materials.

It is wrong to assume that "homemade" means that the explosive device is lacking in explosive power. The 1993 World Trade Center bomb was made from urea nitrate and caused major damage.

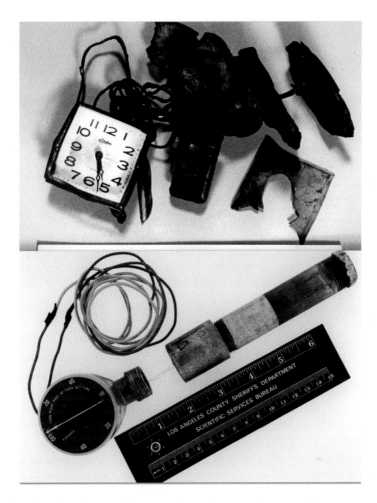

Figure 11.13 (Top) Debris from a homemade explosives device with a timing mechanism. (Bottom) Example of an unexploded homemade device with a timer. (Photographs courtesy of Los Angeles County Sheriff's Department, Los Angeles, CA.)

Case 2

On 26 February, 1993, at 12:18 p.m., an improvised explosive device located in a van exploded in the underground garage of the World Trade Center. Six people were killed and more than a 1000 were injured. The crater formed by the explosion was approximately 45 metres in diameter and more than five stories deep (Figure 11.14). This, together with the damage done to the surrounding building and automobiles, suggested to investigators that the explosive had a detonation velocity of between 4250 and 4750 metres per second, and that the explosive was probably 550 to 680 kg. Due to the estimated size of the explosive and height restrictions on the parking garage, it was suspected that the explosive had been transported in a pickup truck or van.

Two days after the attack, explosive residues were collected and taken for analysis. At this time, the explosives experts examining the crime scene found a large fragment from a vehicle, from which they were able to obtain a vehicle identification number. This identified the vehicle as being a van that had been reported as stolen the previous day.

Figure 11.14 Some of the damage produced by the World Trade Center bomb.

The rental records and other documentation led investigators to an apartment in Jersey City where acids and other chemicals had been used in the manufacture of explosives. Agents determined that there were traces of nitroglycerine and urea nitrate present on the carpet of the apartment. A nearby storage shed was searched and items found there included 135 kg of urea, 110 lb of sulphuric acid, empty and full 4-litre containers of nitric acid and sodium cyanide, fuses, and a trash can in which were found traces of urea nitrate. On March 3, a letter was received by *The New York Times* from someone claiming responsibility for the attack in the name of Allah. DNA tests of saliva revealed that the envelope of this communication had been licked by one of the suspects.

In the past few years, the peroxide-based explosive triacatone triperoxide (TATP) and urea nitrate have been used by terrorist organizations, including the so-called "shoe bomber," Richard Reid in 2001 and, more significantly, in the London transport attacks in 2005.

The list of possible chemicals for improvised explosives is endless. Officers who come upon locations with large numbers of chemicals such as nitrates, chlorates, perchlorates, nitric acid, aluminum powder, magnesium, sodium, sulphur, charcoal, sugar, and sulphuric acid, to name just a few, should be aware that the location may be one where homemade explosives are made.

Case 3

On 7 July, 2007, at about 8:50 a.m., three bombs exploded on three separate trains in the London underground system. Approximately an hour later, a bomb exploded on a London Transport bus. The force of the blasts initially led the investigators to suspect that military-grade high explosives had been used, but investigations showed that they were homemade devices based on TATP. Figure 11.15 shows police beginning the process of cordoning off access to the Russell Square underground station. The photograph reinforces how chaotic a bomb scene can become.

Figure 11.15 Police cordon off one of the underground stations associated with the London transport terrorist bombings on 7 July, 2007.

11.3.6 Bomb Scene Examination

Forensic evidence in bombing cases is useful in answering many questions, by now familiar to us from the 6W or investigative star approach to scene investigation. Some of the questions that the investigator will be interested in answering include the following:

- What materials were used to make the explosive device?
- What was the level of skill or expertise of the suspect?
- What was the target of the bomb?
- Was the explosion accidental or was there criminal intent?
- Where was the bomb made?
- Where was the bomb placed?
- Where did the suspect obtain the material to construct the device?
- How was the bomb detonated?
- Who was the victim or intended victim?
- Who made the bomb and who placed it?

The nature of the target, whether or not the bomb exploded, the extent of damage, the location of the incident, and weather conditions are some of the factors that influence the action to be taken by the investigator. If a bomb is found that has not exploded, it is necessary to call in a bomb disposal expert, variously described in different parts of the word as "bomb technician" or "ordnance disposal unit personnel," to render the device safe. The first priority of the technician is to disarm the bomb safely. The crime scene investigator should under no circumstances move the suspect device, but instead should take extensive photographs of its location and physical dimensions. If the bomb must be exploded to be disarmed, it should be done in such a way as to avoid total destruction of the device if possible and, of course, in a manner that does not threaten the safety of people (Figure 11.16). The scene should be thoroughly searched for evidence that may have been left by the

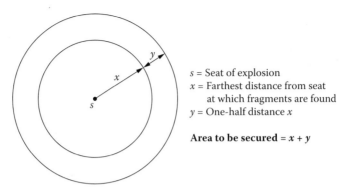

s = Seat of explosion
x = Farthest distance from seat
   at which fragments are found
y = One-half distance x

Area to be secured = $x + y$

If the explosion takes place in an open space, the area in which the
fragments are found and a surrounding buffer zone should be secured.

Figure 11.16 If an explosion takes place in an open space, the area in which the fragments are found and a surrounding buffer zone should be secured. (Illustration courtesy of Bureau of Alcohol, Tobacco, Firearms, and Explosives, US Department of Justice, Washington, DC.)

suspect. Collection of evidence should include a search for a forced entry and accompanying toolmarks, fingerprints, footprints, and any other traces that may help link a suspect to the crime scene (Figure 11.17).

In cases where the explosive device detonated, the work of the investigator is complicated considerably. The duties of the crime scene investigator are basically the same as outlined in Chapter 3, but safety will be an even greater area of concern than normal because the scene of a bombing is generally very unsafe. The structure of the building where the bomb exploded may be seriously weakened and can collapse. Other unexploded devices may still be in the area. Hazards such as broken gas mains and downed electrical lines are potential safety problems.

Securing the crime scene is another problem. Unlike most crime scenes, bomb scenes frequently attract a large number of people such as police, fire department personnel, medical and ambulance personnel, utility company personnel, property owners, the press, and sightseers. One of the first priorities must be to coordinate the activities of the large number of people likely to be present and to remove individuals who are not needed.

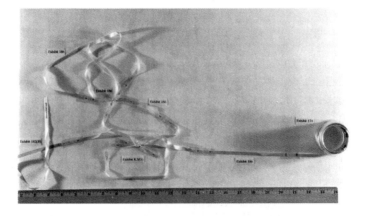

Figure 11.17 A parcel with an explosive wrapped as a gift was shipped through the US mail. The ribbon used to wrap the package (left) was matched to ribbon found in the suspect's home (right). (Photograph courtesy of the US Postal Service.)

Bomb scenes frequently contain a considerable amount of confusion. It is necessary to restore order and control to the situation quickly to enable the investigator to accomplish the task of processing the scene. The first officers to arrive at the scene of a bombing will be concerned with emergency and safety-related activities such as rescue, evacuation, and assisting fire department personnel if required. Once the emergency phase is complete, efforts should be made to secure the crime scene and begin developing information on the circumstances of the case. Witnesses and victims should be interviewed and as much information as possible about what happened should be gathered.

Because of the number of persons present at the scene and the likelihood of several different investigative agencies being involved in the investigation, it is useful to set up a team to coordinate and control the investigation. Such a unit can act as a clearinghouse of information so that all of the information gathered can be integrated and studied. Investigation of the actual scene of the bombing is a time-consuming task requiring a considerable amount of physical effort and attention to minute pieces of physical evidence. It is also dirty work requiring the investigator to sift through large quantities of debris to locate items of evidence. It is useful to have proper equipment to go through the scene. Coveralls, gloves, safety helmets, goggles, work shoes, and other such items are useful for the investigator. Hand tools such as shovels, rakes, brooms, a heavy-duty magnet, and cutting tools are useful. Sifting screens of various sizes are necessary for going through the debris. Wheelbarrows, trash cans to collect debris, portable lighting, ladders, and so on may be required, as well.

As with any scene, the scene coordinator will be responsible for processing and directing the bomb scene investigation and for coordination with the tactical investigation. The extent of the crime scene must be identified; a useful plan is to use the seat of the explosion as the centre, or focal point, and the location farthest from the seat where fragments from the explosion are located will define the outer perimeter of the scene. A buffer area equal to approximately half the distance from the seat to the farthest point should then be added. This represents the total area that should be secured and searched. The bomb scene should be recorded. This may be accomplished in the standard way by means of photography and sketches. If the capabilities exist, the scene may be videotaped. If needed, aerial photographs should be taken. Photographing, measuring, and sketching the crime scene may be done while the scene is searched.

The scene examination strategy will cover the search for and recovery of items that may lead to information about the nature and type of explosive and the identity of the suspect. A search for the fusing mechanism of the bomb should be conducted. Items such as timing mechanisms, batteries, pieces of wire, safety fuses, and blasting cap debris may yield information about how the bomb was set to detonate. The scene should be searched for evidence to determine the type of explosive used. The seat of the explosion should be carefully examined for unexploded material and packaging material that may indicate the type of explosive used. If a portion of the container that held the device is found, laboratory tests may indicate the type of explosive. Similarly, the extent of damage to the container (e.g., a pipe bomb) can indicate whether the explosive was a low or high explosive. In general, large fragments of a pipe bomb indicate a low explosive such as black powder, while small fragments indicate a high explosive. The package that contained the explosive device may contain evidence to lead the investigator to a suspect. Fingerprints, names, addresses, and postmarks may be important information in the investigation. The investigator should not forget to search for other evidence besides the bomb debris. Items such as tyre tracks and toolmarks and any object that may be a source of DNA must not be overlooked.

If a suspect is apprehended shortly after the explosion, the clothing should be collected and submitted to the laboratory for examination for trace evidence and explosive debris. The suspect's hands should be swabbed with cotton applicators moistened with acetone to test them for certain explosives. If the suspect's vehicle is located, it too should be carefully searched for tools, trace evidence, explosive residue, and materials that may have been used in the crime. All evidence should be photographed where it was found, measured, and located on a crime scene sketch prior to being moved. The investigator should also remember to search high areas such as trees, roofs, ledges of buildings, and other places that may contain pieces of the exploded device.

Because of the large number of persons involved with the bomb scene search and the amount of evidence collected, it is helpful to keep an evidence log to detail each item of evidence collected, including the date, time, and name of the person collecting the material. The use of a log facilitates establishing a chain of evidence and makes inventory of all the evidence somewhat easier.

Caution: Terrorists sometimes employ secondary explosive devices. Extreme care should be exercised when searching the crime scene, and consideration should be given to the possibility of other explosive devices.

The forensic laboratory plays an important role in bomb scene investigation. Often the nature of the explosive used and information about the type of mechanism used to detonate it cannot be determined in the field. The laboratory will carefully and systematically examine all the items of evidence and attempt to answer some of the questions required by the investigator to assist in the solution of the case. Bomb and arson scene investigations require much time and patience, as well as crime scene investigators' extreme attention to detail. An officer's willingness to carefully and painstakingly go through large amounts of debris and rubble in an attempt to locate pertinent physical evidence may result in a successful conclusion to the case.

11.4   Summary

Fires and explosions are complex and dangerous scenes to examine. They are first of all about WHERE: Where is or are the origin(s) of the fire or explosion? This is followed by an investigation of HOW: How was the fire started? How was any device that might have been used constructed and deployed? This in turn leads us to seek answers for WHAT: What caused the damage? Was it accident or crime? If it was a crime, reconstructions and the application of modern techniques of DNA and fingerprint identification can provide excellent evidence of WHO. The technical aspects relating to inceptive evidence, such as the cause of the fire and the construction of the explosive device, are best dealt with by subject area specialists; however, the first officer attending may well be a crime scene investigator or the initial scene may not be immediately recognised as requiring specialist units to attend. It is important therefore for the crime scene investigator to have a basic understanding of how these scenes are to be investigated. Conversely, much of the associative evidence is the same as crime scene investigators will encounter in their daily duties, and it is equally important for specialists to be aware of these evidence sources or to include a more generalist crime scene investigator on the team.

Illicit Drugs and Toxicology

12

12.1 Drugs

Drugs in bulk form or in blood or urine specimens are encountered in a wide variety of criminal cases, such as traffic accidents and fatalities, driving under the influence of alcohol or drugs, public intoxication, possession or sale of controlled substances, and illicit manufacture of controlled substances. The purpose of this chapter is to describe the various types of drugs commonly encountered by police and to examine some of the crime scene investigation issues with regard to this class of evidence. To simplify the topic, a distinction is made between bulk drugs (i.e., drugs in their usual solid or liquid form) and toxicological specimens (i.e., blood or urine samples that are to be tested to determine whether a drug is present in a person's body). Some of the information is provided for general interest, as it is unlikely that the situation will be encountered by a general crime scene investigation unit. Investigations of suspicious deaths possibly involving drugs are often dealt with by special units attached to a pathology or coroner's department, and breath testing for alcohol is likewise usually conducted by specially trained personnel.

12.2 Illicit Psychoactive Drugs

Drugs that find their way into police investigations are typically *psychoactive drugs*. These are drugs that affect the user's psychological processes and change his or her mood, thinking, perception, and behaviour. Psychoactive drugs may be illicit (e.g., LSD) or ethical (e.g., barbiturates). They may be controlled and require a prescription, or they may be uncontrolled and do not require a prescription (e.g., alcohol, certain over-the-counter preparations). Psychoactive drugs can be divided into several types based on their effect on the user. The seven major categories are central nervous system depressants, central nervous system stimulants, hallucinogens, cannabis, designer drugs, nonprescription drugs, and inhalants.

12.2.1 Central Nervous System Depressants

Originally meaning a drug that induces sleep or stupor, the term *narcotics* has become synonymous with illegal mood-altering drugs, particularly in the United States, and opiates are the classic example of both definitions. They are central nervous system depressants used medically for their analgesic or pain-killing properties and have a high potential for abuse. There are two categories of narcotics: natural opiate alkaloids and synthetics or semisynthetics. Natural opiate alkaloids are derived from the opium poppy, *Papaver somniferum* (Figure 12.1). The most frequently encountered examples are raw opium, morphine, and codeine. Common synthetic and semisynthetic narcotics are pethidine, methadone, heroin, hydromorphone, and oxycodone.

Figure 12.1 Opium poppies (left) and heroin made from them (right). (Photograph courtesy of US Drug Enforcement Administration, Washington, DC.)

The second category of central nervous system depressants is sedative–hypnotics. These are generally prescribed for treatment of insomnia and tension and have a high potential for abuse and addiction. Drugs in this category include barbituric acid derivatives such as secobarbitone, amobarbitone, and phenobarbitone, and nonbarbiturates such as glutethimide, methaqualone, and chloral hydrate. Another drug classified as a sedative–hypnotic is the illicit drug phencyclidine, or PCP. Persons taking PCP report feelings of weightlessness, unreality, and hallucination.

The third category of central nervous system depressants is comprised of tranquillisers and energisers. Tranquillisers are grouped into major and minor tranquilliser groups. Major tranquillisers such as chlorpromazine, prochlorperazine, and trifluoperazine are prescribed for treatment of neurosis, psychosis, and other psychological disorders and are considered addictive. Minor tranquillisers can produce psychological dependence with prolonged use. Drugs in this category include meprobamate, chlordiazepoxide, diazepam, oxazepam, and chlorazepate dipotassium. These drugs are generally prescribed for the treatment of tension and anxiety. Energisers or antidepressants are used for the treatment of moderate to severe depression. Drugs in this group include imipramine and amitriptyline.

Perhaps the most widely used and best known central nervous system depressant today is ethyl alcohol, or ethanol. Its usual short-term effects are sedation, euphoria, impaired judgement, slowed reaction time, decreased coordination, and decreased emotional control.

12.2.2   Central Nervous System Stimulants

One of the few types of psychoactive drugs that have not become a law enforcement problem is the xanthine alkaloids, which contain such drugs as theophylline, theobromine, and caffeine. Cocaine is another class of central nervous system stimulant. It is derived from the leaves of the erythroxylon coca tree native to South America. The drug in its pure state is a white crystalline substance (Figure 12.2) and is not generally used medicinally except as a local anaesthetic in certain eye, nose, and throat surgical procedures. In recent years, illicit use of cocaine has been on the rise, both the white powder, which is snorted, and the solid form known as "crack," which is smoked (Figure 12.3). The third class of stimulants is amphetamines. Drugs in this group include amphetamine, dextroamphetamine,

Figure 12.2 Cocaine white powder. (Photograph courtesy of US Drug Enforcement Administration, Washington, DC.)

methamphetamine, and non-amphetamine stimulants such as methyl phenidate and phenmetrazine. These drugs are often prescribed for fatigue, narcolepsy, and hyperkinesis in children and in combination with barbiturates for treating obesity.

12.2.3 Hallucinogens

Hallucinogens are a group of drugs that currently have no accepted medical use. The drugs produce perceptual alterations, intense and varying emotional changes, ego distortions, and thought disruption. Drugs in this group include mescaline, which is derived from the *Lophophora* cactus; psilocybin, which occurs in several species of mushrooms (e.g., *Psilocybe mexicana*); lysergic acid diethylamide (LSD); dimethyltryptamine (DMT); diethyltryptamine (DET); phencyclidine (PCP), a central nervous system depressant; and methyldimethoxymethyl–phenethylamine (STP). LSD is often presented as a single dose applied to absorbent paper, perforated into stamp-size sections having a colourful cartoon picture printed on them, as shown in Figure 12.4.

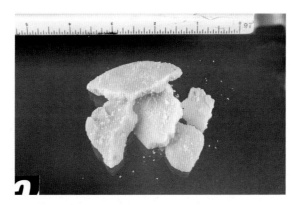

Figure 12.3 Crack cocaine. (Photograph courtesy of US Drug Enforcement Administration, Washington, DC.)

Figure 12.4 A sheet of LSD blotters. Each "stamp" is one dose, and the cartoon character on the sheet is a typical presentation. (Photograph courtesy of US Drug Enforcement Administration, Washington, DC.)

12.2.4 *Cannabis*

Marijuana consists of derivatives from the plant *Cannabis sativa* L. and is most often consumed by smoking the dried, crushed tops and leaves (Figure 12.5) or resinous material known as hashish. Pharmacologically, marijuana is not classed in any of the preceding drug categories. Its usual short-term effects include relaxation, increased appetite, some alteration of time perception, and impairment of judgement and coordination.

12.2.5 Designer Drugs

Every few years, new types of drugs become popular, the so-called *designer drugs*. Designer drugs are a class of synthetic drugs synthesised by chemists working in clandestine drug laboratories. The motive is profit. Clandestine drugs present a serious problem for law enforcement and a danger to those who use them. Illicit chemists do what pharmaceutical researchers do to develop new active drugs. They synthesise drugs with structural features similar to those of known psychoactive substances; however, with designer drugs, neither quality control nor testing of the substances is undertaken to determine if there are any

Figure 12.5 *Cannabis* plant. (Photograph courtesy of US Fish and Wildlife Service, Washington, DC.)

Figure 12.6 MDMA tablets. (Photograph courtesy of US Drug Enforcement Administration, Washington, DC.)

harmful side effects. Designer drugs include fentanyl analogues, pethidine analogues, and 3,4-methylenedioxymethamphetamine (MDMA), which is known on the street by several names, such as MDM, Adam, Ecstasy, and XTC (Figure 12.6).

Synthetic cannabis is a psychoactive herbal and chemical product that mimics the effects of cannabis. It is best known by the street names K2 and Spice, both of which have largely become generic trademarks used to refer to any synthetic cannabis product. These drugs are chemically similar to cannabinoids but are not uniformly controlled. These drugs are often marketed as "herbal incense"; however, some brands market their products as "herbal smoking blends" and are usually smoked by users. Although synthetic cannabis does not produce positive results in drug tests for cannabis, it is possible to detect its metabolites in human urine.

12.2.6 Steroids

Steroid abuse has long been a factor in professional sports and amateur athletic competition and bodybuilding. Anabolic steroids build muscle mass and thereby enhance performance. They are reported to cause liver and adrenal gland damage, infertility and impotency in men, and masculine characteristics in women. Steroids are scheduled, controlled substances. They have become a law enforcement problem as illicit sales of anabolic steroids have been noted. Many of the steroids sold to athletes through illicit channels are not manufactured for use in human beings but rather are veterinary drugs. Sometimes packaging and labelling claiming the drugs to be specific steroids are misleading and incorrect (Figure 12.7). The drugs are available in a wide variety of forms and may be injectable solutions, capsules, or pills.

12.2.7 Medicines

Medicines used as prescribed and over-the-counter remedies rarely present law enforcement with major difficulties. They are included here as a reminder for officers investigating traffic accidents, fatalities, and cases of driving while under the influence. There is also the opposite, where someone causes an accident because of the effects of *not* taking prescribed medications—perhaps a rare example where absence of evidence could be evidence! Many

Figure 12.7 Steroids seized by DEA agents. (Photograph courtesy of US Drug Enforcement Administration, Washington, DC.)

over-the-counter drugs, particularly sleep aids, sedatives, and antihistamines, contain materials that make the user drowsy. The investigator who finds a subject who has taken these drugs alone or in combination with alcohol and is exhibiting unusual behaviour can reasonably assume that the individual is likely to be under the influence.

12.2.8 Inhalants

The last group of psychoactive substances is chemicals that are inhaled. Such materials include glue, gasoline, paint, solvents, and the like. Juveniles frequently use these chemicals. The most common method involves placing the material into a plastic bag or onto a piece of cloth such as a sock and sniffing the material to obtain the intended result, intoxication. Another class of inhalants contains amyl nitrite, a vasodilator, used to relieve symptoms associated with angina pectoris. Amyl nitrite is also sometimes used recreationally and is sold under various trade names.

12.2.9 Date-Rape Drugs

Although not conventionally included in the narcotics category, the so-called date-rape or drug-facilitated-rape drugs, gamma-hydroxybutyrate (GHB) and Rohypnol®, can be encountered by the crime scene investigator. These are used to spike the drink of the victim; in addition to reducing the person's awareness and control, they also induce an amnesia that can make reconstructions difficult. The crime scene investigator should collect any drink containers, even if empty, from the scene (Figure 12.8).

12.2.10 Crime Scene Search

Searching a crime scene for contraband drugs is somewhat different from other types of cases. In the contraband drug investigation, the officer is looking for evidence that has been hidden on the person, in a dwelling, or in a vehicle. The various rules of evidence, including search and seizure and requirements for establishing a chain of evidence, hold in these cases as in others, and the investigator must be aware of current laws regulating search activities. Some drug squads use specially trained sniffer dogs, with some success.

Figure 12.8 White powder GHB ready to be dissolved in water for date-rape abuse. (Photograph courtesy of US Drug Enforcement Administration, Washington, DC.)

12.2.10.1 Searching a Suspect

Concerning personal search, the officer must be aware of unusual hiding places in which contraband may be hidden. Clothing and personal property should be carefully examined. Places such as cigarette packages, small cases, film cans, hollowed-out compartments in canes or umbrellas, lining of clothing, luggage, shoes, wallets, and similar items may conceal evidence. Suspects have been known to swallow contraband or hide it in a body cavity such as the mouth, nose, rectum, or vagina. Thoroughness and experience will aid the officer in the search. Some useful equipment to aid personal searches include endoscopes for searching internal body cavities and x-ray or ultrasound scanners.

12.2.10.2 Searching a Dwelling

When searching a dwelling, the investigation should be done in a thorough, systematic manner. In addition to contraband, investigators should be alert for intelligence information such as telephone and address books, names and telephone numbers on loose pieces of paper, and so on. Sums of money and possibly stolen property should be documented and collected. Additionally, any damage to personal property or to the residence should be carefully noted and, if possible, photographed; the owner should be notified. One officer should be assigned to record the location and the name of the finder of each item of evidence.

To assist in the recording, a crime scene sketch should be made so that each piece of evidence can be charted. The officer should also make certain that each item of evidence is correctly marked for identification and properly preserved. If possible, two investigators should be assigned to a room. The search should begin at one wall and everything hanging on that wall or resting against it should be carefully examined. Light switches and outlet boxes should be examined to determine whether paint on the screws or around the plate is chipped. The plates should be removed and searched. Moulding around door frames should be examined for signs of stress to determine whether they conceal a hollow area. The tops of doors and door-frames should be examined for indentations. A plug on top of a door or hinges may conceal a hiding place. Walls should be checked to determine whether they were replastered. Wall pictures and the backs of television sets and radios should be examined. Curtain rods, the tops and bottoms of window blinds, and shades should be searched.

After the walls have been searched, furniture should be inspected. Items should be turned upside down and their undersides examined. Throw pillows and cushions should be unzipped and the contents searched. Rugs should be rolled up. When searching the bathroom, the officer should look for waterproof containers inside flush tanks, containers under sinks, or containers in laundry hampers. Prescription medicine bottles should be examined to determine whether they contain the drug listed on the container and for whom the prescription was intended. When evidence is located, it should be brought to the officer maintaining the evidence log and the search should be continued. It is a good practice to search each room a second time. Occasionally, evidence overlooked the first time will be noticed in the subsequent search.

12.2.10.3 *Searching a Vehicle*

Automobiles are often used to hide contraband drugs. Searches involving motor vehicles should be conducted in a systematic and thorough manner. The vehicle can be divided into three areas for the search: the front end, interior, and rear. The front end of the vehicle offers many areas in which to hide contraband. A careful search should include the grill, bumper, radiator, inside surfaces of the fenders, air filter, and body frame. Using a hydraulic lift helps in the examination of the undercarriage of the vehicle. The interior of the vehicle is frequently used to conceal drugs. The seats should be removed from the car and carefully searched. The area behind the dashboard, the door side panels, headliner, and floor are possible areas where drugs may be hidden. Finally, the trunk and rear of the vehicle should be examined. Areas such as the spare tyre well, spare tyre, rear fender, and bumper area and undercarriage of the vehicle are all potential hiding places.

12.2.11 Clandestine Drug Laboratories

An important source of illicit drugs today is the clandestine laboratory (Figure 12.9). Illicit drugs such as LSD, PCP, methamphetamine, and some ethical pharmaceuticals are manufactured in illicit laboratories. Police become involved in crime scene investigations

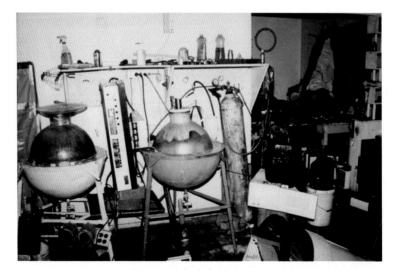

Figure 12.9 Equipment at a clandestine drug laboratory. (Photograph courtesy of US Drug Enforcement Administration, Washington, DC.)

involving illicit laboratories through intelligence gathering, complaints from neighbours, fires and explosions, and often from detection of chemical odours while on routine patrol. Whatever the means of detection, the investigator must have an understanding of how such crime scenes are processed. The trained forensic chemist must be an integral part of any such investigation. His or her training and experience in dealing with chemicals is extremely important from the standpoint of identifying drugs as finished and intermediate products and also from a safety consideration. In larger police agencies, specialised hazardous chemical response teams have been developed who handle chemical spills and disposal of toxic substances. These teams are especially helpful and should most certainly be included in any clandestine laboratory investigation.

The clandestine laboratory scene is a potentially dangerous and hazardous location. Chemicals present are often flammable, explosive, toxic, and corrosive. Proper precautions must be taken to ensure the safety of personnel at the scene. Scenes should be approached with extreme caution. It is not uncommon for chemicals to be unlabelled, and there are even reports of laboratories that have been booby-trapped. As soon as the location has been secured, all windows and doors should be opened to ensure adequate ventilation and minimise the risk of fire. Light switches should not be turned on until the area is adequately ventilated; sparks can easily ignite highly flammable chemicals. Under no circumstances should anyone be allowed to smoke. The fire department should be notified and asked to stand by. Certain chemicals are especially dangerous if mixed with others. Chemicals such as lithium aluminium hydride are extremely explosive when combined with water, as is the combination of sodium and water. Cyanide salts will liberate hydrogen cyanide gas when in contact with acid. Most chemical solvents, such as ether, benzene, and the like, are highly flammable. Acids and alkaline materials are dangerous and can cause severe burns; others such as piperidine may cause headaches. Prolonged exposure to many volatile organic chemicals may be injurious.

Extreme caution must be exercised in clandestine laboratory investigations! Before any evidence is collected, the laboratory should be photographed. Photographs should be taken of individual pieces of equipment, chemicals, laboratory glassware, finished products, and intermediates. The location should be searched for fingerprints and for laboratory notes, recipes, records, sales receipts from chemical supply companies, and other related items. Samples of chemicals from the final products, chemical precursors or intermediate products, and basic raw materials should be collected for forensic laboratory analysis (Figure 12.10). A complete inventory of all chemicals, equipment, packaging material, and the like should be made. Such evidence will be very important if no final product is found. Laboratory notes, recipes, chemical precursors, and glassware will be important evidence at trial to prove conspiracy to manufacture controlled substances. A further caution to be considered is that clandestine chemical labs may be homemade explosives laboratories rather then drug manufacturing labs. It is not unreasonable that chemicals are unlabelled; therefore, care should be taken when examining and collecting products.

Case 1

Not all drug laboratories are efficient factories set up to manufacture drugs to sell, as the following case illustrates. One of us was called out by the drug squad to attend a suspected drug factory. It was 3:00 a.m. on a cold, wet, winter night, and the scene was an isolated farm cottage. The cottage was rented by a man and his partner, both known heroin addicts. The police believed that they were making their own heroin. A search of the property showed this to be correct, but the process used was one known as "home bake," where codeine in over-the-counter cold medicines is converted first to morphine and then the morphine converted to heroin. The evidence seized included more than 50 20-kilogram-capacity sacks filled with foil packs that had contained the cold medicine tablets, as well as photocopied pages from a chemical textbook describing the two chemical reactions used. The whole process is cumbersome, inefficient, and costly; however, rather than risk being caught purchasing heroin, they preferred to go through the laborious process of making it.

12.2.12   Collection and Preservation of Evidence

As with all forensic evidence, the ultimate aim of collecting drug evidence is to provide legally admissible evidence in court. To ensure this end, as with all items collected from any scene, the crime scene investigator must be concerned with maintaining the integrity of the evidence from the time of seizure until its presentation to the court. In addition to the usual requirements to maintain a chain of possession of the evidence, some other procedures are important. All drugs should be accurately weighed. The gross weight of the package, including the drug and packaging material, should be determined and recorded. Individual pills, tablets, packets, balloons, etc. should be counted and the number written on the outer package and in the report. (In cases involving a large number of units, 100 capsules can be weighed and the total number of units can be estimated by determining the total weight and dividing that weight by the unit weight.) Liquids should be measured in metric units such as litres or millilitres. The packing material seized with the contraband should be kept with the evidence and properly marked for identification. Items should be placed in an appropriate evidence envelope and sealed and marked. Liquids should be placed in a clean, stoppered container to minimise evaporation and then sealed and labelled. If the original container can be tightly sealed, it may be used to preserve the liquid.

Figure 12.10 Equipment and chemicals from a methamphetamine clandestine drug laboratory. (Photograph courtesy of US Drug Enforcement Administration, Washington, DC.)

12.2.13   Statutory Classification of Controlled Substances

All major countries have laws that define the controls on medicinal and nonmedicinal drugs. Although they vary in detail, they generally are graded from substances with no generally accepted medical use but with a high potential for abuse down to drugs or other substances that have a low potential for abuse and are accepted as being useful medicines in the treatment of illnesses. Drugs such as heroin and LSD would be in the top category, and drugs such as over-the-counter cough medicines containing low concentrations of codeine would be in the bottom category.

12.3   Toxicology

Toxicology is usually defined as the study of poisons, but in forensic science a distinction is made between antemortem and postmortem toxicology. Antemortem ("before death") toxicology is concerned with the detection of drugs, including alcohol, in blood and urine samples collected from living persons in certain types of criminal investigations. The question being addressed is whether or not the person was under the influence of a drug, and it is important in traffic investigations, driving under the influence cases, the legal defence of diminished capacity, and public intoxication cases. Postmortem ("after death") toxicology is concerned with examination of blood and tissues from the deceased to ascertain whether drugs were the cause of death.

In both cases, the drugs are not necessarily poisons but may be medicines or recreational drugs taken for their psychological calming or exciting effects. Postmortem toxicology involves the same types of drugs, but consumed or administered at doses greater than those associated with the desired therapeutic or social effect. True poisons, such as arsenic or strychnine, may also be encountered in postmortem toxicology.

Finally, there is a very specialised area of toxicology, concerned with detection of the use of substances prohibited by regulations concerning sporting events and horse racing. This last area of toxicology will not be considered here.

There are important differences between all the branches of toxicology and the investigation of drugs offences at the point of forensic laboratory testing. The levels of drug found in blood are typically 1000 times less than in the drug formulation consumed, their identity is more difficult because of the presence of metabolites (related chemical compounds that are created in the body as part of the natural process of eliminating foreign compounds), and the analysis will almost always require that the amount of drug present is measured in addition to establishing its identity. The reason for measuring the amount of drug is that the biological effects are usually proportional to the amount in the blood, and of course the amount in the blood reflects the amount of drug consumed.

Case 2

Mrs. S lived alone in her house in a small Scottish city, her husband having left her several years earlier. One day early in 1972, she reported a smell of gas to the supply company, who sent an engineer to investigate. When the engineer lifted the access hatch to the underfloor space in the kitchen where the gas supply entered the house, he found the partially mummified body of a man. Police were called, and the body was identified as the husband of Mrs. S. When interviewed by the police she gave the following account of how the body came to be there. Her husband was a known alcoholic and drug addict. He had come home very late and very drunk one night and took some Tuinal capsules and drank some beer. Mrs. S went to bed and left him sleeping. When she got up in the morning, she found him dead. It was generally accepted in the community that Mr. S had left her, and she had enjoyed rebuilding her life in the subsequent years. She thought she was done with him and wanted it to remain that way, so she disposed of the body by pushing him through the access way.

The question for the police came down to whether or not Mr. S was dead when she disposed of the body, or was he in an unconscious drug-induced state from which he would recover in time? If the former, Mrs. S had committed the minor offence of concealing a body, but if it was the latter, then she was guilty of murder.

Tuinal is a mixture of equal parts of two barbiturates, secobarbitone (or secobarbital) and amylobarbitone (or amobarbital), formerly prescribed as a sleeping pill or sedative and a popular recreational drug in the 1970s. Although both components are chemically similar, they are not identical, and the differences are reflected in the speed with which the body removes them from the blood, with amylobarbitone being eliminated approximately twice as rapidly as secobarbitone.

The ratio of the levels of the two drugs in blood will therefore change with time, changing from approximately equal proportions soon after taking the capsules to about 2:1 in favour of amylobarbitone after about 24 hours. The conditions in the underfloor area were warm and dry and the organs in the partially mummified body had not undergone significant putrefaction. Samples of liver were taken and the barbiturate level measured. Although circumstances meant that no absolute conclusion could be drawn, the data favoured the story of Mrs. S, and the charges were dropped.

12.3.1 Alcohol

The most common substance tested for in most forensic laboratories is alcohol in blood and urine specimens submitted in drunk-driving cases. Cases of driving under the influence of alcohol represent a large percentage of all traffic fatalities and traffic accidents. Implied-consent laws require a driver suspected of being under the influence of alcohol to submit to testing (blood or breath) to determine the blood alcohol level. Different countries, and in some cases different jurisdictions within a country, have different laws regarding the maximum blood alcohol levels permitted in the blood of a driver. They also express the results differently, usually as mass of alcohol per volume or mass of blood but with the mass expressed in different ways:

- Percent (1/100 g) alcohol per mL of blood, which is used in the United States, Canada, Spain, France, and Australia
- Milligrams alcohol per mL blood, which is used in the Netherlands, Switzerland, and some other European countries
- Milligrams alcohol per 100 mL blood, which is used in the United Kingdom
- Milligrams alcohol per g of blood, which is used in Scandinavian countries and Germany

Table 12.1   Drunk Driving Limits in Different Countries

Country	Level	Comment
Australia	0.05% for full licence holders, zero for learner and probationary licence holders	Some aspects vary by state.
Canada and United States	0.08%	Some aspects vary by state; for example, Florida has a zero tolerance law under which drivers younger than 21 are not permitted to drive with detectable amounts of alcohol in their blood.
European Union	Varies between zero (Germany for drivers with less than 2 years of experience) to 0.08% (United Kingdom, Ireland, Malta); most countries have 0.05%	Some countries have sliding penalty scales; for example, Sweden has a limit of 0.02% with a penalty of up to 6 months of imprisonment but mandatory imprisonment of up to 2 years if over 0.10%.
Asia	Muslim countries, zero limit; India, an unusual limit of 0.03% and Sri Lanka, 0.06%; Philippines and Vietnam, no limit	—

The rationale for drunk-driving legislation is now well established and dates back to the 1964 Grand Rapids study which measured the relative risk of causing an accident at different blood alcohol levels. The risk is about five times greater at a blood alcohol of 0.08% or 80 mg/mL and increases exponentially as the blood alcohol rises—for example, to over 30-fold at a blood alcohol of 0.2% or 200 mg/mL. Some examples of maximum permitted levels are shown in Table 12.1. As can be seen, the average value is about 0.05%, which equates to around two to three standard alcoholic drinks.

Blood and breath testing are routine procedures used to measure the blood alcohol level. Breath testing relies on the relationship between the concentration of alcohol in the blood and that in expired air, due to diffusion in the lungs. Some jurisdictions, including Australia and the United States, use breath testing equipment that has an output that converts the breath level to the equivalent blood concentration; others, including the United Kingdom, have legislation that sets a proscribed limit for alcohol in breath directly of 35 µg of alcohol per 100 mL of breath.

Blood that is taken should be collected in a medically approved manner. The syringe used should not have been cleaned with alcohol, and nonalcoholic cleansing agents should be used to clean the area of skin from which the blood is to be taken. The blood will be collected in a container with an appropriate preservative and anticoagulant and a unique identification. If urine is collected, the subject should first be requested to void the bladder, wait approximately 20 minutes, and then urinate into a container into which an appropriate preservative has been placed. Approximately 25 mL of sample should be collected. The officer should be present in each case to observe the collection procedure and to mark the evidence properly. The specimen should then be submitted to the laboratory for analysis (Figure 12.11).

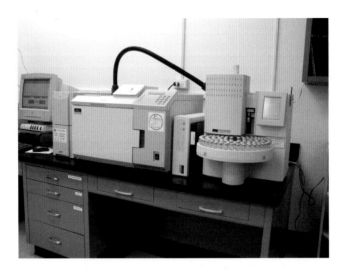

Figure 12.11 Blood alcohol analysis by head space gas chromatography. (Photograph courtesy of Los Angeles County Sheriff's Laboratory, Los Angeles, CA.)

12.3.2 Drug-Impaired Driving

Officers will find that some subjects, although exhibiting alcohol-like intoxication symptoms, have no or only a small amount of alcohol in their blood. The reason for this may be that the suspect has taken some other central nervous system depressants with similar physiological effects. When questioning the suspect, the officer should try to determine whether the suspect has taken any other medication; when searching the individual during the booking process, it should be noted whether any solid-dose drugs are found. This information is helpful to the forensic toxicologist when running tests on blood and urine specimens. A large number of depressant-type drugs are routinely encountered in traffic-related incidents today. Barbituric acid derivatives, Valium®, Quaalude, PCP, cocaine, and marijuana are among the more common substances encountered. The type and quantity of sample required for analysis may vary from one jurisdiction to another, and the local crime laboratory should be contacted to determine the best sample for a specific drug analysis. In homicide cases in which a suspect is arrested shortly after the killing, it is sometimes a useful practice to obtain blood and urine specimens from the suspect to be screened for the presence of drugs and alcohol. This strategy is particularly useful in those cases in which the suspect may raise the issue of diminished capacity at the time of trial.

12.4 Summary

Drugs, whether in the materials involved in the investigation of drug abuse or in biological tissues in death investigations, are essentially examples of WHAT. The first issue is always that of identification of the drug or drugs involved. In drug abuse cases, the scene may yield evidence of WHERE and HOW: Where did the drug come from? How was it manufactured? Death investigations are one of the few occasions where the investigative star goes directly to the question of WHY—Why did the person die?—rather than inferring why from the multiple possible relationships linking the 6Ws. Drug abuse cases account for a high proportion of the workload of a forensic laboratory but are relatively uncommon in the cases encountered by a crime scene investigator. On the other hand, specialist crime scene investigators attached to a coroner's unit will be familiar with the requirement for examination of scenes for drugs that may have been involved in an unexplained death. Drugs are encountered in many types of criminal cases, however, from the specific instance of impaired driving to the investigation of rape and questions of drug-induced violent behaviour.

Scene Investigation and Type of Crime

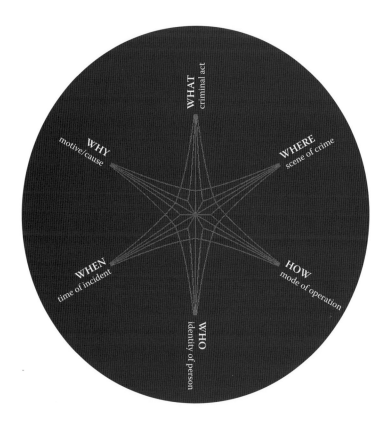

The more outré and grotesque an incident is, the more carefully it deserves to be examined, and the very point which appears to complicate the case is, when duly considered and scientifically handled, the one which is most likely to elucidate it.

—A. Conan Doyle (*The Hound of the Baskervilles*)

Investigating Sexual Assault ✳13

13.1 Rape

Forensic science and the crime scene examiner play an important part in the investigation of an alleged rape. Superficially, it may be regarded as simply a matter of identifying semen stains found at the scene and assisting in the collection of intimate body samples, in order to identify the assailant; however, the offence of rape has a quite specific legal definition, with some variation from jurisdiction to jurisdiction, that requires some form of sexual activity without consent and usually involving penetration. The penetration need not be vaginal; indeed, the victim does not have to be female, and ejaculation does not have to occur.

Generally, we have seen that the role of forensic science is to add objective evidence to an investigation and assist resolution of the elements of the investigative star, including eliminating hypotheses that may have seemed highly plausible and developing new lines of inquiry. The core question of consent in a rape case can be very subjective, can be difficult to prove, and can dominate the investigation and trial. If we add to the subjectivity the very considerable emotional (and often physical) trauma suffered by the victim, we soon see that the work of the scene examiner has to be conducted with sensitivity and an awareness of the significance of physical evidence in all areas of the investigative star, not only the question of who was the source of any semen.

Case 1

After more than two years of validations, a forensic laboratory introduced its DNA testing service. The first case seemed simple enough—an anal swab submitted from an investigation into the rape of a man in a public park. The results were greeted with great excitement that turned to despair when the semen in the swab turned out to match that of the victim and not the suspect. The tests were rerun with the same result. A fresh sample was requested and received from the victim, with the same result. Eventually the laboratory and the crime scene investigators accepted that the results were correct and revisited the hypothesis of rape. The victim was questioned by the investigators about his relationship with the suspect and admitted that they had been partners for some time but had fallen out. He had decided to take his revenge by introducing some of his own semen into his rectum and falsely reporting that he had been raped. An unexpected but successful first case for the forensic laboratory!

Today, many of the issues surrounding forensic investigations have been resolved or at least ameliorated by using specially trained medical and nursing personnel, often working from specialist centres. Because this is where the clinical examination of the victim takes place, they become an extension of the crime scene; therefore, it is as necessary for these care professionals to know about the principles and practices of forensic investigations as it is for crime scene unit personnel to understand the care needs of the victim. A good example is where forensic personnel are able to give care personnel rapid information about whether or not there is semen in a vaginal sample and so corroborate or contradict the victim's account. Counselling can then be more effectively directed. We have tried to write this chapter in a way that will assist this mutual understanding.

Consideration of all these factors explains why few crimes rely so heavily upon physical evidence as does the crime of sexual assault. In hardly any other type of case is the testimony of the victim viewed with as much mistrust by juries, courts, and sometimes even prosecutors and police. It is for this very reason that physical evidence is so important to the investigation and prosecution of this crime.

Rape investigation can present the crime scene investigator with many challenges. The offence is one that has a major impact on the emotional well-being of the victim, whom dealing with can require great skill and understanding of interpersonal communication on the part of the investigator. On the other hand, the task of identifying, collecting, and preserving evidence must be carried out thoroughly, as the intimate contact involved in the crime can provide a rich source of associative evidence.

In recent years, there has been a move to provide coordinated police and victim support service responses to sexual assault to encourage a more victim-centred approach to the investigation of sexual assault. In Australia, for example, the Victoria Police embraced this coordinated service approach by creating integrated sexual offence criminal investigation teams. The Victoria Police also successfully implemented multidisciplinary units that bring together police, counsellors, forensic management teams, and Department of Health Services.

Finally, although the manner in which medical, investigative, and judicial systems deal with rape is complex, the focus of this chapter is on the crime scene aspects.

13.2   First Officer Attending and Clinical Examinations

The response to the notification of a rape may be made by ambulance, regular police (that is, not from a special sexual assault or crime scene investigation unit), or special sexual assault investigation personnel. As with any scene, the first priority is to attend to any physical injuries to the victim but without compromising the subsequent identification, preservation, and collection of evidence. The initial approach of the first officer attending (FOA) will reflect that person's background: Ambulance personnel should have procedures and training directed to preserving evidence when caring for acute injuries and treating victims with sensitivity. Regular police officers should be able to reassure the victim and call out the appropriate support services, but they will also begin the interview process without adding to the distress of the victim. Specially trained sexual assault investigation teams are best prepared to deal with the matrix of requirements but not all jurisdictions will have these. In jurisdictions that do have sexual assault response teams, they are usually involved from the earliest stages of the response. Many of the functions of the FOA will therefore be performed by clinical or other specialists, some of whom may be specially trained police.

13.2.1   The Initial Interview

Maintaining scene integrity and developing a scene investigation strategy often begin with information obtained in interviews conducted by the FOA. Interviews of rape victims require special skills. Intimate questions about the attack are best left to trained personnel, but questions that can shed light on the broader events should be asked to determine what evidence may be available and to produce a scene examination strategy. Training in crisis counselling will help the FOA assist the victim in dealing with the trauma, but even where such training is not provided officers need to be aware that the victim should be treated nonjudgmentally and with sensitivity. Observations about the victim noted in the police report will be important at a later time. The psychological state of the victim may be significant, but it is important to emphasise that people in serious emotional crises might not immediately exhibit states of anguish and grief. Victims might appear perfectly calm and in control, and no inference should be drawn from this. After a rape, the victim may feel psychologically dirty and may have an urge to wash, bathe, douche, urinate, throw away her clothing, and clean up the scene of the rape. During the interview, the officer should determine which, if any, of these actions occurred. If any did, an attempt to collect evidence should still be made. A tissue or washcloth used by the victim to clean herself might still have semen present. Underwear, clothing, or condoms worn at the time of the crime, even if discarded or cleaned, should be collected for examination.

13.2.2   The Medical Examination and Interview

The medical examination of the victim is the core activity in the investigation of a rape. In rape cases, the body of the victim should be addressed as a crime scene in and of itself and with the same care and thoroughness. In the case of rape and violent crimes against the person such as assault and homicides, scene investigation of the body of the victim is best conducted by medically trained personnel and generally will not involve crime scene investigators other than in a liaison role. An exception may be photography of injuries when crime scene photographers may be used rather than those from the hospital medical photography unit. However, as discussed earlier, teamwork across the forensic process and among the different roles within it is essential, which is why we will treat the medical examination in the same detail as the physical scene investigation of the location where the crime transpired.

Following the immediate response to the reported incident, the examination of the victim will proceed according to the protocols in the jurisdiction where the event took place. Most often, the examination will be conducted by specialists in a hospital or sexual assault referral centre. In some instances, the first action of the victim may be to go to a hospital emergency unit or to a sexual assault centre.

Many hospitals have protocols established to deal with rape victims in which they are ranked in medical priority immediately after life-threatening cases. Hospitals are responsible for the victim's medical and psychological well-being, as well as the collection of physical evidence. Upon arriving at the hospital, the officer should briefly go over the case with the attending physician or registered nurse. Pertinent information gleaned from the interview should be communicated to the examiner because it may facilitate the examination for physical evidence. The healthcare provider first takes a medical history from the victim and again goes over the details of the assault. Doctors and nurses should be encouraged to

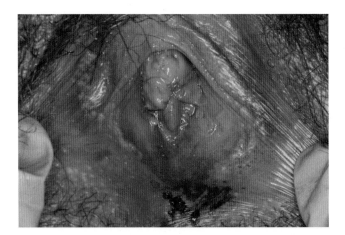

Figure 13.1 Toluidine blue dye used to highlight recent injuries. (Photograph courtesy of Diana Faugno, MSN, RN, Sexual Assault Nurse Examiner.)

take detailed notes and later couple the notes with medical findings during the examination phase. Details such as the date of the last menstruation, time of last consensual intercourse, presence of bruises not related to the assault, presence of bruises from the assault, and other related factors are all pertinent information. A change of clothes should be obtained so the clothing worn during the rape may be collected and submitted as evidence.

The victim must still be asked several very important questions of an intimate nature. It may be best that these are dealt with in the more clinical and supportive environment of the medical unit in cases where the initial response to the scene does not include multi-disciplinary sexual assault investigation teams. Questions about oral and anal intercourse should be asked. The interviewer should ascertain whether the victim is sexually experienced and hence able to testify whether penetration or ejaculation took place. Another question that should be asked is whether the victim had consensual sex recently. When asking these types of questions, the investigator should be aware that many rape victims do not volunteer particularly sensitive details of the assault.

Following the medical history, the examiner should conduct a thorough physical examination. It is important to ensure that whoever carries out the medical examination does not focus solely on the genital area, thus missing important evidence that might have aided in establishing other important aspects of the investigation. Toluidine blue dye highlights fresh injuries, because it adheres to the nuclei of the white blood cells that have been disrupted (Figure 13.1).

If the victim is wearing clothes from the assault, these should be collected and packaged in a paper bag (Figure 13.2). The location of any cuts, bruises, lacerations, or contusions should be noted in the medical report. A helpful practice is the use of an anatomical diagram on which the locations of cuts, bruises, and the like can be indicated. Photographs of bruises or wounds should also be taken with an appropriate scale being included in the photograph. Wounds on the body that are difficult to see can be enhanced with the help of ultraviolet photography. If the hospital does not have this capability, the police officer or crime scene investigator may provide a suitable camera. In some instances, the officer may wish to wait a day or so until the bruises become black and blue and better show the location and extent of the assault.

Figure 13.2 Underwear from the victim is examined for the presence of semen. (Photograph courtesy of Office of Chief Medical Examiner, New York City.)

Many hospitals, police departments, and commercial hospital or law enforcement supply firms have sexual assault evidence kits. These kits greatly facilitate the collection and preservation of rape evidence. They also direct the examiner to look for certain evidence commonly found in rape cases. Figure 13.3 shows the content of a typical rape kit.

The victim should next be carefully examined for trace evidence adhering to the body. The location of any items such as debris, grass, soil, vegetation, loose hair, and fibres should be noted and the items collected. The presence of dried secretions such as semen, blood, and saliva (from bite marks, licking, "hickies," etc.) is especially useful because such evidence may be typed using DNA testing. Some facilities use an ultraviolet lamp or alternative light source to examine for the presence of seminal fluid, as semen fluoresces under

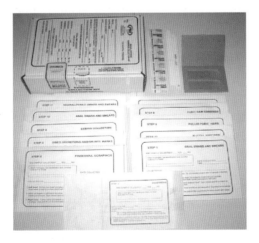

Figure 13.3 A typical rape kit. (Photograph courtesy of Office of Chief Medical Examiner, New York City.)

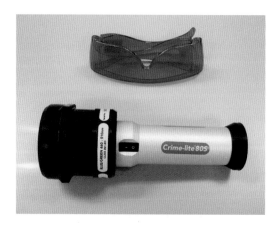

Figure 13.4 Crime-lite® by Foster + Freeman is an example of an alternative light source used for trace evidence detection and bodily fluids. Also shown are the viewing glasses.

ultraviolet light. Many types of these are available, and one is shown in Figure 13.4. Note that the light from these can damage the eyes, and the figure shows the safety glasses that should always be used. Dried secretions can easily be collected and preserved using slightly moistened cotton swabs.

Following examination of the extremities and torso, the genitalia are examined. Pubic hair combings are taken in an attempt to find foreign hairs and fibres or other debris. The hairs, any debris, and the comb are all submitted for examination. As with all other evidence, these items should be appropriately documented in the medical report and labelled. A vaginal specimen is collected with cotton-tipped applicators and a portion is smeared onto microscope slides. Figure 13.5 shows the results of such an examination, with sperm detected in a smear circled in red. The slides should be air-dried and *not* stained when prepared. The slides should be stored in a slide protector, *not* in alcohol. Some centres also collect specimens from the cervix and vulva.

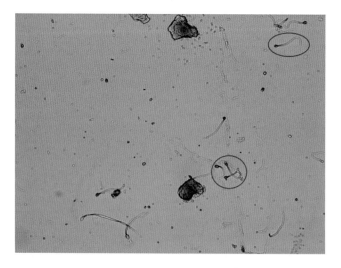

Figure 13.5 Microscope examination of a vaginal smear can show the presence of spermatozoa. Sperm cells circled in red were dyed with "Christmas Tree" stain. (Photograph courtesy of Office of Chief Medical Examiner, New York City.)

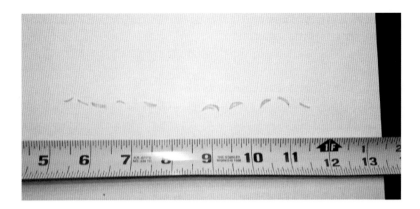

Figure 13.6 Clipped fingernails from a rape victim can be sent for DNA typing to determine the identity of a scratched suspect. (Photograph courtesy of Office of Chief Medical Examiner, New York City.)

There are separate sexual assault kits for suspects, acquaintances, and estranged partners. The collection of evidence from a suspect may require a court order. If a court order can be obtained expeditiously (these kits must be used within a shorter period of time than the kit for a victim), then penile swabs can be collected to determine if the victim's DNA is present. If anal or oral contact occurred, appropriate rectal and oral swabs should be collected.

Anal intercourse or sodomy is not limited to female victims (see earlier case). Male sexual assaults occur with some frequency in prison environments and elsewhere. Of particular importance in these cases is the physician's examination of the rectum as well as swab evidence taken for the examination of semen. Medical examination will indicate if anal penetration has occurred and whether the person was accustomed to anal intercourse. Beyond the medical examination and search for semen, other evidence is sometimes uncovered in such cases. Faeces may be found on clothing or other articles. A lubricant such as petroleum jelly may have been used and should be looked for. Lubricant containers can be examined for fingerprints or touch DNA. Additionally, any condoms or condom wrappers found at the scene should be collected. If oral sodomy is suspected, the oral cavity should be rinsed after the swab is taken prior to collection of a known buccal (cheek) swab from the victim.

Fingernails may also be examined, and if sufficient debris is present nail scrapings can be collected for trace evidence examination. The fingernails can also be clipped and submitted for DNA analysis if the victim scratched the perpetrator (see Figure 13.6). Toxicology samples should be collected if the victim appears to be under the influence of some substance.

13.3 Investigation of the Scene

13.3.1 General Examination

Examination of the crime scene will proceed generally on the basis of the principles and practices outlined elsewhere in this book, but several other aspects will require attention either immediately or as follow-up as information becomes available. These include questions about the following:

- Did the assailant practice any unusual acts, such as urination or defecation?
- Did he do or say anything unusual?
- Is there any physical evidence to substantiate these acts?
- Did he bite or lick the victim?
- Was the victim or suspect scratched or bruised?
- Does the victim recall drinking something that may have contained a date-rape or drug-facilitated rape substance?

The purpose of the general examination is to identify, preserve, and collect evidence that can address the questions at issue, which is aided by utilizing the 6Ws. In a number of ways, then, the investigation of a scene of rape is no different from any other scene examination and requires the same approaches to scene and evidence management. Issues to be addressed include evidence of real or simulated forcible access, evidence of violence, evidence of personal contact including fingerprints and footwear marks, and, where the suspected assailant is known to the victim and not a stranger to the scene, evidence of any unusual activity. Given the particular formulation of the offence of rape, however, there are some important aspects of such cases that need to be established in order for the case to be processed in a criminal court. In relation to rape, forensic evidence is generally collected and made use of to answer three major questions:

- WHAT happened?—Establish that sexual contact occurred.
- HOW did it happen?—Establish that nonconsensual intercourse occurred.
- WHO was involved?—Establish the identity of the assailant.

The presence of seminal fluid and spermatozoa in the vaginal cavity is suggestive of vaginal penetration. The presence or absence of this evidence can be explained in any number of ways. The absence of seminal fluid in a case in which it was expected could be caused by the following:

- The time period between the rape and medical examination was too long.
- The suspect wore a condom.
- The suspect penetrated but did not ejaculate in the vagina.
- The doctor or nurse examiner did not take an adequate sample.
- Seminal fluid and spermatozoa may be present from a consensual intercourse and not from an alleged rape. In this instance, seminal fluid typing is indicated.
- Seminal fluid, without spermatozoa, could be present from a male who underwent a vasectomy procedure or is azospermic.

Forensic evidence may also help substantiate that the victim did not consent to the intercourse. Evidence such as torn or soiled clothing, bruises, pulled-out hair, cuts, and other indications assist in proving that a struggle occurred during the time of the intercourse. Evidence as to the sexual act or acts that took place as well as evidence of lack of consent may be obtained from the following:

- Examination of discarded clothing, bedding, tissues, washcloths, and condoms for semen, blood, saliva, or faeces
- Examination for weapons, restraints, or drugs that may have been used during the assault
- Examination of the scene for bloodstains, semen stains, saliva, faecal stains, or hair, particularly tufts of hair that may have been pulled out in an attack

Saliva traces from bite marks or from regions of contact during oral sex can yield DNA profiles. Condom wrappers may have been opened by tearing them between the teeth, resulting in deposition of saliva. Identification of faecal traces can corroborate allegations of anal rape and may yield confirmatory DNA profiles. Any physical violence that results in bloodshed can result in valuable evidence, not only regarding identity but also regarding non-consensual activity, from DNA profiling of stains on clothing or at the scene.

Often in rape cases the question of identity comes down to whether or not the assailant was known to the victim. Unknown assailants, or stranger rapes, have become much easier to deal with since the establishment of DNA databases. Rape is an offence with a high recidivism rate, and many assailants have a history of other crimes, which means that there is a high likelihood that their DNA will be on the database. Where the assailant is known to the victim, such as date rapes, rape by a work colleague, or rape by a spouse or family member, the scene investigation is much more difficult. Unless the accused denies intercourse, the investigation will centre on evidence related to consent. DNA will still be of value in corroborating that sexual intercourse did take place. If there is an identified suspect, the identity of the assailant may be directly established by DNA typing of semen in vaginal samples or samples from stains and comparison with the profile from the suspect. Condoms are becoming more common evidence in rapes, partly because rapists believe that by not ejaculating into the victim that will prevent establishing a direct association between the rapist, the victim, and the sexual activity. DNA typing is so sensitive, however, that the traces of material from the vagina of the victim on the outside of the condom will provide a profile and so indicate contact.

As in any major crime, the suspect's identity may be established by a variety of means: eyewitness testimony, fingerprints, hair, fibres, or bloodstains left behind at the scene. Additionally, it may be possible to determine the assailant's DNA type through semen typing or typing of cellular material at the hair root (especially prevalent with freshly pulled hairs) (see Figure 13.7). The suspect may have left an article of clothing at the crime scene or unknowingly picked up some trace material such as fibres from a rug, clothing, or bedding. A cigarette butt, beer can, or piece of paper may yield fingerprint and DNA evidence. All of these are possible from a carefully and thoroughly conducted crime scene investigation.

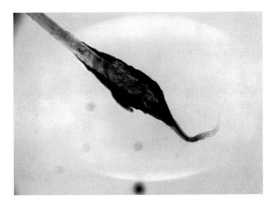

Figure 13.7 A pulled head hair with root. The abundance of epithelial cells from the scalp makes it ripe for DNA testing. In the absence of a root, a hair shaft can be typed with mitochondrial DNA testing. (Photograph courtesy of Los Angeles County Sheriff's Department, Los Angeles, CA.)

Forensic science laboratory tests involving comparative analysis such as hair examination require known pubic and scalp specimens. This can be a painful procedure, as the hairs must be pulled, and many victims refuse to submit to collection of these samples. Not being able to submit pulled hair samples to the lab should be carefully weighed against the pain it causes the victim and the limited value of the microscopic examination; for example, cut hair sample are adequate controls for mtDNA testing. Semen and saliva specimens require known DNA samples from the parties involved in the investigation, including consensual partners. Rape investigation presents unusual challenges to the investigator. Issues such as myths about rape, psychological trauma of the victim, and, in some cases, the investigator's feelings of discomfort in dealing with the victim must be addressed when investigating this crime of violence.

13.3.2 Outdoor Scenes

Outdoor crime scenes in general are more difficult to examine than indoor ones. This is especially so in the investigation of a sexual assault because the type of biological evidence important in the investigation of a rape, such as semen, saliva, and blood, can be difficult to detect in an outdoor environment. Rapes and other sexual assaults can occur in many different outdoor locations, including a parking lot, a beach, in a park, or in the bushes near a forest trail. Environmental factors can have a considerable negative influence on the integrity of evidence here, as rain may dilute or wash away most types of biological evidence and wind can cause evidence to be lost or moved away from the scene. This can affect various kinds of evidence, such as fibres and pubic hair, and the environment in itself could cause damage to biological evidence. Cold, heat, and moisture can degrade biological evidence, and soil can absorb and chemically interact with blood and semen.

An outdoor environment can also contribute positive evidence. A struggle can result in disturbance of vegetation and the surface of the ground. Grass and other bottom-growth plants could be found pressed down in a few or several directions, and branches of trees and vegetation could have been broken off. Scrapes, marks or impressions from body parts or moving limbs, clothing, or shoes could be present. Blood or other biological evidence from the involved persons could be present on the surface of broken branches, along with fibres from their clothing. Evidence relating to objects that may have been used in committing the crime (e.g., rope, bags, other belongings) may be present.

Taken together, all of the evidence left at the scene may contribute information and knowledge that can be used to reconstruct what has happened. The way that vegetation has been disturbed and to what extent may suggest whether there was a minor or major degree of struggle. As pointed out earlier, however, the investigator must always be aware of and consider alternative explanations, and passionate sexual activities with consent are very often presented at trial as possible explanations for evidence that is being used to suggest force and therefore lack of consent.

Where the ground is sufficiently soft, impressions from vehicle tyres or footwear worn by the victim or imprints and marks left by the assailant could be collected for further examination and relevant comparison. Imprints or impressions made by the victim's clothing or body (e.g., torso, buttocks, knees, arms, hands) may be present. Although less specific than footwear marks, these can be used in reconstructing the events that may have taken place at the scene. In addition to securing evidence relating to the presence of the assailant and victim, it will also often be appropriate to take samples of plants, bushes, trees, and the surface of the ground for possible comparison with findings from the victim's and suspect's person and clothing.

Searching for biological evidence at an outdoor crime scene with vegetation should be undertaken with extreme caution and care. The biological evidence and the possible substrates on which it may have been deposited are very fragile and the conditions can make it extremely difficult to detect. Basically, it should not be expected that these types of biological evidence will be readily apparent to the naked eye because they could be absorbed, diluted, or dried out before the scene examination starts; therefore, the use of special lamps, test fluids, or other methods of crime scene investigation should be considered.

A different approach that has been successful in Denmark is the use of police dogs that have been specially trained to search for and detect the presence of semen. Areas marked by the police dog should be examined thoroughly using special light sources or semen detection kits such as those used to screen for acid phosphatase or prostate-specific antigen. The procedures to be followed when the scene examination has indicated that semen is present will vary from jurisdiction to jurisdiction and may depend on the environment. Options available include the crime scene examiner collecting the items, such as leaves or twigs. In some cases, the examiner may consider digging up the upper layer of the ground to bring to the laboratory. The upper layer of the ground can be dug up by cutting edges around the finding with a trowel, spade, or similar tool and then lifting the piece of intact substrate from the ground by using a spade, shovel, or similar tool. After placing the intact piece of substrate in a rigid evidence box, it can be taken to the laboratory for closer examination (see Figure 13.8).

In addition to being aware of these types of evidence typically involved with sexual crime scenes—and the possible complexities involved with them—the crime scene examiner should also remember that the persons involved might have lost personal property at the crime scene. This could include jewellery, such as necklaces or earrings, torn off during the struggle and fight, as well as mobile phones, wallets, or buttons from clothing.

Finally, in considering the overall outdoor scene, the crime scene examiner should also consider other possible circumstances regarding "where from" and "where to." Was the victim attacked at the crime scene or had the victim been transported by the assailant to the location where the sexual crime was committed? By what route did the assailant enter and leave the scene? Had the assailant been hiding, observing, and watching the victim before the attack? If any of these scenarios turns out to be likely, then another crime scene has to be located and examined in relation to the case.

13.4   Date-Rape Drugs

Drugs may play a significant part in rape cases and can be valuable evidence in relation to establishing issues of lack of consent. If, during the course of an investigation, the victim makes a statement such as, "I was at a party, and this man gave me a drink. Next thing I know, its morning and I'm in someone's bed. I have no idea what happened in between," consider the possibility that the victim was drugged with Rohypnol® or gamma-hydroxybutyrate (GHB). The collection of blood and urine specimens as part of the medical examination of the victim, to be sent to the laboratory for analysis, is key to the effective investigation of drug-induced sexual assault cases.

Figure 13.8 Sample of top surface of ground removed from the scene in a box; it is being screened in the laboratory for semen by pressing paper impregnated with acid phosphatase reagent onto the surface (top). The results are shown at the bottom, where the box with vegetation is on the left and the purple acid phosphatase results are on the right.

Rohypnol is the brand name of a sleeping pill (flunitrazepam) marketed by Roche Pharmaceuticals in Mexico, South America, Europe, and Asia; it is known by various street names: Roachies, La Roche, Rope, Rib, Roche, Rophies, Roofies, and Ruffies. Rohypnol first entered the commercial market in Europe in 1975 and was introduced in the United States in the early 1990s. Rohypnol belongs to a family of medications known as nitrobenzodiazepines that includes Valium® (diazepam) and Librium® (chlorodiazepoxide). It is a potent sedative used clinically as a hypnotic (sleeping pill). Its main recreational abuse is to combine it with alcohol to produce intoxication. The combination of intoxication with possible amnesia makes it a candidate date-rape drug although the actual frequency of abuse for this purpose may be less than imagined.

The street names "grievous bodily harm," "liquid ecstasy," and "easy lay," plus a host of other names depending on the region of the country, are all used to refer to GHB (or gamma-hydroxybutyrate). GHB is a depressant affecting the central nervous system, and its effects are rapidly felt. Like Rohypnol, it can cause amnesia, unconsciousness, coma, and sometimes (when combined with alcohol) death. GHB generally comes in pure powder form or mixed with water. Body builders sometimes use it. Its availability is controlled in most countries, and it is either a prohibited substance or a prescription-only medication. GHB is a liquid that can render a victim unconscious when as little as a teaspoonful is mixed into a drink. The onset of symptoms appears within approximately 5 to 20 minutes. The victim has a feeling of extreme intoxication and impaired judgment. GHB does not produce the muscle paralysis and memory loss associated with Rohypnol but can cause unconsciousness and strong memory impairment.

Victims who experience being drugged or are suspicious that they may have been drugged should refrain from voiding their bladders. If voiding is necessary, any clean container is suitable for a urine collection. GHB is eliminated rapidly from the blood (less than 6 hours), but it may be detected in urine. Samples collected from 12 to 24 hours after consumption of the drug will yield negative results. These samples should be submitted in a drug-facilitated sexual assault kit to the toxicology laboratory.

Investigators should collect any portion of the drink, if it is available, for laboratory examination. Also, if any powdery or crystalline material or pills are found, they too should be sent to the forensic science laboratory. It should also be mentioned that alcohol by itself is involved in many sexual assaults. Additionally, victims sometimes state that they have been drugged, when in reality they have had way too much to drink. Finally, for any and all evidence that is collected during a sexual assault investigation, a chain of custody must be started.

13.5   Other Sexual Assaults

13.5.1   Child Sexual Molestation and Incest

Child molestation and incest investigations have two related problem areas: difficulty in interviewing the victim and possible problems regarding the child's competency to testify in court. These difficulties, coupled with the family's reluctance to pursue or cooperate in the matter, make these cases a challenge. The key person in a sexual assault case involving children is the physician. The physician's ability to examine the victim and document findings of sexual assault is of major importance in this type of case. Because of the usual inability of the victim to testify, the forensic evidence and medical testimony are particularly important. Child psychologists are also playing an increasing role in child abuse and child molestation cases. They help investigators by pointing out specific child behaviour patterns generally associated with this type of crime; however, investigators should be aware that child psychologists might inadvertently cause young victims to colour their story so as to tell the psychologists what they "want to hear."

Forensic evidence is often minimal in child molestation cases. The child's parents are often unaware of the crime. Tell-tale signs of child molestation such as nightmares, bed-wetting, urinary tract infections, and strange stories eventually lead parents or authorities to a suspicion of the cause. If molestation is suspected, the police are brought into the investigation. If clothing or bedding is available from a recent assault, they should be collected for DNA typing. In cases where pregnancy results from a case of incest and the pregnancy is terminated, the foetus or products of conception can be used in DNA paternity testing to determine the identity of the father. If the product of conception is

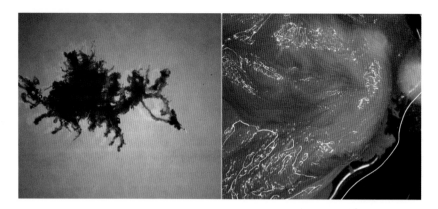

Figure 13.9 The foetal (chorionic villi, left) and maternal (decidua, right) parts of the placental tissue can be differentiated under the microscope to be used in DNA paternity testing. (Photographs courtesy of Office of Chief Medical Examiner, New York City.)

not morphologically well defined, the differences between the foetal (chorionic villi) and maternal (decidua) parts of the placental tissue can be differentiated under the microscope, and the former used in DNA paternity testing (Figure 13.9). Beyond this, the police will need to rely heavily on medical findings.

Child abuse cases also rely upon the findings of the paediatrician. Here, unexplained bruises, x-rays showing broken bones, and so forth will be important in the investigation. In addition to physical abuse, instances of malnutrition and poor hygienic conditions may occur. These types of cases are almost always emotionally charged and are difficult to prosecute and take to trial. To be sure, these crimes certainly do occur; however, investigators must be especially careful in these cases. Innocent people's names can be tarnished irrevocably if a careful investigation is not made. On occasion, children have been known to fabricate allegations of sexual abuse.

13.5.2 Public Lewdness and Forcible Touching

There are several types of relatively minor sexually related crimes, including groping, masturbating in public, or rubbing up against someone on a crowded public transport and ejaculating on them. DNA testing may assist resolution of these cases if required.

13.6 A Final Word on Consent

We have mentioned in several places that the investigation of a rape is a complex matter. It requires cooperation among many different groups, including police investigators, nursing and medical specialists, trained counsellors, forensic science laboratories, and crime scene examiners. Much of the complexity surrounds the issue of consent, which will hardly ever have unquestionable objective evidence to confirm or remove it from consideration. Even with objective data, the borderline between acceptable and not acceptable can be a fine one. Establishing the context of a rape case by providing answers to the 6Ws can be a complex task. Often the identities of the victim and perpetrator are intermingled with modus, motive, and sequence of events, along a continuum of possible events—from contact between partners that began as consensual and ended otherwise to a brutal attack from a stranger forcing his way into the home of the victim.

The cycle of hypothesis formulation and reformulation as evidence is obtained, which we presented earlier in this chapter, is possibly even more important in the investigation of rape than in any other crime. It is essential to understand the limits of factual information and its evidential value, as well as the limits to what can objectively be established on the basis of forensic evidence. The reason for this is that the question of consent involves matters that are less objective and therefore less easily answered than many situations involving scene examination; for example, partners may have a history of sexual experimentation, and the scene may include items such as restraints or drugs used during earlier consensual activities. The presence of these is a matter of fact and does not in itself absolutely prove that there was or was not consent in the encounter under investigation.

13.7 Summary

Sexual assaults are a particularly serious subset of the crime of assault because of the vulnerability of the victims. They present the crime scene investigator with a number of challenges, many of which are being resolved by teamwork involving medical and paramedical personnel in the investigation. The most direct question addressed is that of WHO: From whom did the biological or trace material originate? Applying the investigative star to the reconstruction of events assists the investigator in answering the WHAT and WHERE questions also. Of these, "where" is relatively simple and is mainly based on searching for semen. "What" is perhaps the most difficult but important of the 6Ws in a rape investigation, as it addresses the core question of consent, the significance of which is discussed in the chapter. The power of DNA typing, coupled with the high recidivism rate and effective use of DNA databases, has made the identification of suspects in stranger rapes much more likely. On the other hand, the issue of consent remains a core issue that forensic evidence is limited in its ability to address, and there are also limitations as to what forensic evidence can contribute to child molestation cases.

Burglary Investigation

14.1 Volume Crime

Burglary is one of the most commonly encountered crimes investigated by police. Because the nature of the crime is so varied it is difficult to set down specific guidelines for its investigation. Many of the techniques and procedures outlined in earlier chapters of the text are pertinent to the burglary investigation, but this chapter discusses some of the aspects of crime scene investigation that deal more specifically with the crime of burglary.

Burglary is generally classed as a volume crime, and many jurisdictions have policies in place that assign lesser resources to these offences than to major crimes. Some countries go further, and have policies that volume crime scenes are investigated with the view of finding evidence to identify the perpetrator by DNA typing or from fingerprints. In addition to being more cost effective, this approach has produced positive results with regard to DNA database hits, as many serious crimes are committed by persons who have a record in volume crime.

The investigator must always keep in mind, however, that other types of evidence may exist, such as footwear marks, fibres, and toolmarks, and that there will be occasions when burglaries are given a more serious rating. Examples include when there is a series of high-value burglaries or where the method employed is more dangerous, such as the use of explosives to open safes.

Case 1

The complainant's home was burgled. She smelled cigarette smoke upon entering the home and found a cigarette end in the toilet (Figure 14.1). A mixture of DNA including a predominantly male profile was obtained from the cigarette end and matched an entry in the DNA database.

Figure 14.1 The complainant's home was burgled. She smelled cigarette smoke upon entering the home and found this cigarette end in the toilet. (Photograph courtesy of Harris County, Texas, Medical Examiner's Office DNA Laboratory.)

14.2   Scene Investigation

14.2.1   The First Officer Attending

The first officer attending (FOA) at the burglary scene must be concerned with the suspect's location. In cases where the burglary is in progress and the officer was called because of the presence of a prowler, silent alarm, or ringing burglar alarm, the first considerations must be to apprehend the suspect and protect the safety of the occupants of the home. When the suspect has been located or a determination has been made that the suspect is not at the scene, the location must be secured. Witnesses should next be located and arrangements made for interviewing at a later time. The officer should be aware of the agency policy on volume crime and may have to decide how far to proceed with identification and collection of the wide range of potential forensic evidence or whether to call for crime scene investigation support. In some cases, no decision will be required as policy will dictate what has to be done—usually fingerprinting and DNA only.

14.2.2   Scene Investigation Strategy

The officer conducting the crime scene investigation of a burglary should understand that most experienced burglars attempt to leave only a minimum amount of evidence at the location. Frequently, a suspect may be responsible for a large number of burglaries in an area, and similarities in the cases may enable the investigator to concentrate on one rather than a number of suspects. Thus, in some instances, it may be useful to include consideration of this in the strategy; for example, it may be desirable to examine footwear and toolmarks left at different crime scenes in order to determine whether there are any links between the burglaries (Figure 14.2).

The point or points of entry are an important feature of the investigation of a burglary scene; however, the investigator should not ignore the general approach to a scene and should perform an initial assessment and overview, develop a plan, and identify and prioritise the types of evidence that will be searched for. The strategy should not overlook the possibility that this is not a simple burglary (Figure 14.3). If the initial assessment indicates that it is best to treat the scene as a straightforward burglary, then the initial focus will be

Figure 14.2 A sliver of wood with multiple layers of paint can be compared to known samples at the point of entry and matched. (Photograph courtesy of Royal Canadian Mounted Police Forensic Laboratory Services.)

Figure 14.3 Two apparent burglary scenes. The point of entry shown on the left turned out to lead to a homicide and not a burglary, but the similar jemmied screen on the right was a point of entry at a routine breaking and entry. (Left photograph courtesy of Washoe County Sheriff's Department Crime Laboratory; right photograph courtesy of Los Angeles County Sheriff's Department, Los Angeles, CA.)

to identify and examine the points of entry. These will usually have been chosen by the burglar as providing the easiest access to the property along with the greatest cover for the burglar to avoid detection.

The strategy developed will identify the best approach to examination of the scene and include consideration of the boundaries. Generally, the detailed examination of the crime scene proper should begin only after the perimeter has been identified and secured and will begin with a search of the surrounding areas when the strategy considers this advisable. Failure to do this may result in the inadvertent destruction of evidence by sightseers as well as officers at the location. The location of the perimeter will depend on the circumstances; for example, in the case of a home burglary with little or nothing of value stolen, it may be reasonable to set the perimeter no further out than the doors and windows of the property.

14.2.2.1 *Entry through Windows*

Window entry is usually accomplished by breaking a hole through a pane and removing the broken glass to reach the latch. In order to minimise the noise from falling glass, the burglar may press a rag against the window, or sometimes adhesive tape may be used. In some cases, the burglar may remove the entire windowpane by removing the putty holding the glass in place. It has even happened that the burglar has replaced the glass intact and put in new putty. Where a screen covers a window, a careful examination of the edges for any cuts may show fibres from the sleeve left when the suspect's arm was inserted to open or break the window. Glass is one type of evidence often found on the suspect when a window was broken to gain entrance. When the window is broken, it is almost unavoidable that some pieces of the flying glass will adhere to the suspect's clothing. If the protocols allow for it, the investigator can collect specimens of the broken window for use as reference materials for comparison with glass that may be found on the burglar's clothes. The investigator should search for any fingerprints present on the windowpane, as well as prints present in the window putty. It is also possible for the suspect to have cut or scraped himself on the broken glass. Any blood found on glass should be sent for DNA typing. The ground in front of the window may provide valuable evidence in the form of footwear marks.

Similarly, fingerprints should be looked for in dust that may be present on the window or ledge. Entry may also be gained by forcing in a tool to push back a window latch. In such cases, toolmarks should be looked for, and samples of wood and paint may be taken for comparison if a tool is later found; again, reference has to be made to the agency protocols for investigation of volume crimes. A pry bar, screwdriver, or other tool is also sometimes used in forcing a window. In these cases, toolmarks and specimens of building debris should be collected. Sometimes the burglar may try to force several different windows in order to enter the building. The investigator should therefore examine all windows to determine if any toolmarks are present and collect the evidence appropriately. Paint chips frequently are dislodged during the course of breaking in, and the investigator may collect samples for later comparison, but many volume crime protocols do not encourage this. Later, examination of the suspect's clothing and tools may uncover paint that matches paint recovered at the crime scene.

14.2.2.2   Entry through Doors

A burglar usually opens a door by using a pry bar to attack the door and jamb around the lock until the bolt can be pushed back or is actually freed from the striker plate. A door jamb is sometimes so weak that it may be spread apart far enough to free the bolt. This can be done by mere pressure from the body or by inserting a jack horizontally across the door frame. The lock might also be made accessible through a hole that is drilled, sawed, or broken in a door panel. Far too many doors are fitted with glass that is simple to break so that the lock may be reached. Other weak points are mail slots, the frame of which may be removed, and transoms that may have been left open. At one time, spring-loaded locks were commonly used to secure the doors of houses and other buildings. These are seldom found today because of the ease with which they can be opened. Today, a door is almost always secured with some form of deadbolt or padlock, and burglary requires the forceful application of a tool to break it open, providing a potential source of valuable impression mark evidence (Figure 14.4).

Figure 14.4 Evidence in a burglary case. A cut lock hasp (left) and close-up of the hasp shown pieced together (right). (Photographs courtesy of Los Angeles County Sheriff's Department, Los Angeles, CA.)

If there is reason to suspect that the lock has been picked, great care should be taken to avoid contaminating the potential evidence by marks made during disassembly of the mechanism. It may be better to remove the intact lock for examination in the laboratory or workshop. If a pick has been used, it may have left marks in the coating of dust and oil usually found inside locks. Broken knife points, metal fragments from lock picks, and the like may also be found inside the lock. Cases have been recorded in which mechanics who installed the lock made certain alterations in order to facilitate a later burglary.

Entry can also be gained by cutting the hinge pins off by means of a bolt cutter. More commonly, however, the pins are simply knocked out with hammer and chisel or screwdriver. With the pins out, the door can be lifted off the hinges. The door may then be replaced and the pins reinserted. This method of entry is readily revealed by damage to the hinges and chips of paint or metal on the floor below the hinges. Cylinder (pin-tumbler) locks may be picked by special picks, but usually the whole door is forced or the cylinder is removed. The cylinder may be pulled out by means of a special puller shaped from a pair of large nippers. To avoid detection of the removal, the lock cylinder is sometimes replaced or a similar cylinder put in its place. Sometimes the retaining screw is removed surreptitiously during an earlier visit to the premises, which facilitates removing the cylinder.

Still another means of gaining access through a door is by means of a wrench placed on the doorknob. The twisting motion exerted on the doorknob is sufficient to defeat the locking mechanism of inexpensive locking devices. Examination of the doorknob would reveal characteristic markings caused by the tool (Figure 14.5). The doorknob should be removed and submitted to the laboratory for comparison with toolmarks made by the wrench and also for comparison of any metal shavings found in the teeth of the tool. In instances in which a padlock was used on a hinged hasp to lock a door, the padlock and cut shackle should be collected and sent to the laboratory. If a pair of bolt cutters or similar cutting device is found, test cuts can be made and compared with toolmarks left on the lock shackle.

Figure 14.5 An exterior doorknob showing toolmarks where a pair of adjustable grips was used to force it open.

14.2.2.3 Entry through Basement Windows and Skylights

These types of windows are forced in the same manner as other windows, and investigators should be aware that the burglar's clothes may have become torn and cloth fragments or fibres left behind. Samples of dust and dirt usually found in such places should be taken.

14.2.2.4 Entry through Roofs

The presence of convenient utility poles, ladders, or other aids, plus concealment offered by the edge parapet, makes entry through flat roofs a favourite modus operandi. Many otherwise well-protected stores have "tissue-paper" roofs, and most stores are equipped with roof ventilators and exhaust fans. Entry through the ventilating system may result in toolmarks, DNA, fingerprints, and dust contamination of clothing. A careful search of the roof may also show signs of ropes for entry and exit. Building materials may contaminate the clothing of any burglar using the roof to gain access.

14.2.2.5 Entry through Walls

Walls can be broken by tools, by explosives, or by ramming with a stolen vehicle; sometime two vehicles will be stolen for this purpose, with the second one being used for the getaway. A brick wall is easily broken by a hammer and chisel or a sledgehammer. Burglars can be expected to become covered with dust during such an operation, and samples of mortar and brick may be collected for comparisons if protocols permit. For blasting, a hole is usually chiselled between two bricks and a charge inserted. Several small charges are normally used to avoid severe detonations and the possibility of the entire wall collapsing. When a small hydraulic jack is used to force holes into a wall, a narrow passageway is usually chosen where the base force can be distributed over a wide area by padding. After the initial hole is made, repeated thrusts are used to enlarge the hole sufficiently to gain an entry. When an empty or infrequently occupied store is adjacent to the target, plaster walls may be cut to a thin supporting layer and the entire section removed at once. Entry into vaults is usually accomplished through the walls, which are easier to force than the door. The walls are often constructed of reinforced concrete that can be broken by repeated blasting or with a hammer and chisel and oxyacetylene torch. These kinds of entry will usually result in a layer of dust being formed on the floor, providing a source of evidence from footwear marks.

14.2.2.6 Entry through Floors

This method of entry is sometimes used in the case of warehouses or other buildings that have a crawl space underneath. The burglar usually drills or saws a hole in the floorboards large enough to crawl through; however, the burglar will need to find a different egress route if the stolen items are bulky. Entry through walls and floors is also made when the criminal suspects or knows that the premises are protected by burglar alarms on doors and windows. Because many burglaries occur when the premises are unoccupied, which often means at night, the investigator should also check any outdoor lights to see if the bulbs were unscrewed by the burglar to darken the area near the point of entry. These bulbs might contain fingerprints or DNA.

14.2.3 Simulated Burglaries

Simulated burglaries are often attempts at insurance fraud. To create a successful imitation of a burglary that will deceive the police, the simulator must strive to carry it out as naturally as possible; otherwise, there will be gaps in the sequence of events. When windows are entered, the officer should always check whether the windowpanes were in fact broken from the outside, whether footprints are outside the window or inside on the window sill, whether broken glass has been trampled in these prints, whether the burglar really could have reached the window, whether there are traces of actual entry (sand, dirt, etc.), whether objects inside the window are so placed that the window could be opened to permit entry, and so on. If the outside of the window glass is very dirty, there should be marks from the object used to break it. If the glass is relatively clean, the side on which the force was applied might be revealed by dusting with fingerprint powder. The physical nature of the radiating cracks in the glass from the window should be examined to determine from which side it was broken (see Chapter 7). In cases of forced doors, the damage should be examined to see whether it is only on the outside portions. Marks of prying should be present on the door as well as on the door jamb. If the toolmarks are located so high up that the burglar must have stood on a box or a ladder, the support should be examined.

Whenever a burglary is suspected of being simulated, all relevant tools belonging to the victim should be compared with the toolmarks present and, if necessary, recovered for further examination. Holes in floors, walls, and ceilings should be examined to determine the side from which the attack was started. The holes should also be examined to determine any evidence of a person having crawled through. There may be footwear marks leading to or from the possible entry point that would indicate whether or not it was made from inside. The officer should further make an estimate of how long the burglar spent on the premises. The officer should follow the burglar's actions in searching for valuables—were doors first opened and drawers emptied or did the burglar go directly to the location of the valuables?

14.2.4   Detailed Examination of the Scene

As has been mentioned several times, the degree to which the detailed examination is conducted will depend on the agency policy on volume crime and whether or not there was anything of particular importance in the specific case being investigated. Most of what follows in the next paragraph will not be carried out in a routine volume crime situation.

Approaches leading to and away from the scene should be examined for footprints, tyre impressions, drag marks (caused by dragging a heavy object such as a safe), and abandoned items such as tools, clothing, and opened cash boxes. Obstacles leading to the building such as fences and gates should be examined for traces of blood, fabric and fibres, and toolmarks. The number of suspects involved should be estimated from footprints when possible. Areas where a suspect had to crawl or climb should be examined for traces of fibres and clothing. Samples of building material and soil can be collected for comparative purposes.

The location from which the burglar may have reconnoitred the location or where a lookout could have been standing should be examined for footprints, cigarette butts, cigarette package wrappers, matches, food items, and other such evidence. The point of entry should be examined for broken tools, toolmarks, broken window glass, fibres, hair, blood, fingerprints, footprints, paint chips, wood, and other building materials. Known samples of materials should be collected. Photographs, measurements, and sketches should, as always, be made before any items are moved or collected. The examination of the interior of the burgled premises must sometimes be carried out while taking into account the wishes of the owner and in keeping with the seriousness of the burglary.

The investigator should carry out the inside crime scene investigation in the normal detailed and systematic way and according to protocol. Attention should be given to evidence such as fingerprints, touch DNA and DNA from bloodstains, and possibly to footprints, broken tools, toolmarks, and any other evidence that could aid in solution of the case (see Figure 14.5). When the examination of various areas of the location has been completed, the proprietor should be notified. If evidence is found that requires time-consuming recovery, the owner and other personnel should be asked to stay out of the area until the examination is complete. A complete inventory of all items missing should be obtained from the owner, as well as a complete description of the items, including brand names, labels, markings, serial numbers, size, shape, colour, and value. This facilitates identification of the stolen property in the event the items are recovered.

The investigator should attempt to form a picture of the entire crime scene in order to estimate whether or not the burglar was familiar with the premises. If the burglar removed valuables from a rather unlikely location without disturbing the rest of the scene or if keys that were hidden were used, then the officer might infer that the suspect was familiar with the location. The investigator should try to make a determination about the type of person being sought. Was the burglary the work of a professional burglar? Was the crime simply a case of vandalism involving juveniles? Was anything unusual left at the scene? Answers to these questions, information obtained from interviews, and physical evidence examination will prove useful in the overall investigation.

An apprehended suspect should be thoroughly searched. Cuts and scratches should be noted and photographed, possibly with the participation of a forensic clinical medical officer. The clothing may be collected for examination for tears and building material that can place the suspect at the crime scene. The suspect's vehicle should be searched for stolen property, burglary tools, and any other items of physical evidence. The investigator should remember that in some instances a search warrant might be necessary before the vehicle may be completely searched.

14.2.5   Safe Burglaries

Safes may be classified into two basic types: fire-resistant and burglar-resistant. Although providing a minimum resistance to attack by a professional burglar, fire-resistant safes are designed to withstand, resist, and retard the penetration of heat and to protect documents from destruction by fire. Such safes are constructed of metal and insulation consisting of a variety of materials such as vermiculite, cement, diatomaceous earth, sawdust, and the like. Burglar-resistant safes are specifically designed to resist the efforts of safe burglars and are constructed of steel that is resistant to forced entry by tools or torch. Burglar-resistant safes are not burglar proof but are designed to resist attack for a certain period of time.

Safes can be opened by a number of methods such as manipulation, punching, peeling, prying, ripping, chopping, drilling, burning, or explosives. Manipulation is essentially a lost art that involves opening a safe by means of listening to and feeling the combination lock mechanism. Most safes today have manipulation-proof locks; the investigator should therefore assume that the suspect had knowledge of the combination if a safe is found in which the lock has been opened.

The punching method involves knocking off the dial and punching the dial spindle into the safe. Newer safes have punch-proof spindles and relocking devices that automatically relock the safe when such an attempt is made. Peeling involves prying or peeling the faceplate from the safe door in such a way as to expose the locking mechanism. This is sometimes accomplished by first pounding the door with a sledgehammer until the door buckles and then inserting a pry bar. Entry by ripping or chopping is achieved by tearing a hole through a part of the safe other than the door such as the top, side, or bottom.

Drilling is usually effective but is a time-consuming method and therefore only rarely used in safe burglaries. It is commonly done by perforating the doorplate around the keyhole by drilling a series of holes close together. A large portion of the lock mechanism is thereby laid bare so the bolts can be manipulated. The front plate of some safes can also be peeled back if some of the screws or rivets in the edge are first removed. The paint covering the rivets is first scraped off to reveal the rivets. The rivets are then drilled deeply enough for the plate to be separated. After a few rivets have been removed, the front plate is then forced up sufficiently to insert a chisel, which is used to break the remaining rivets without drilling. On some safes, the locking bolts can be reached by drilling through the side of the safe, directly against the face of the bolt. The bolt can then be driven back with a punch. The exact location of the bolts can be determined by the marks in the door frame that occur in daily use when the safe door is shut while the bolts are protruding. In cases of drilling, the burglar can be expected to have used some kind of lubricating oil for the bit. Samples of such oil and samples of metal shavings should be collected because the burglar's body or clothing may contain these materials. Simpler types of safes with combination locks may be opened by means of a thick, square steel plate provided with an opening at the centre to be slipped over the dial knob. The corners of the plate are equipped with threaded bolts, the points of which touch the safe door. By tightening the bolts with a wrench, the knob and spindle are torn out. It also happens that safes can be opened using a special bridge device screwed to the safe with bolts. The portion of the bridge over the door frame contains a threaded hole. A strong bolt is fitted into this hole and tightened far enough to force the door open.

Another method employs a circular cutter. Such devices are made in several different forms. Some are affixed to one or more holes that have been drilled into the safe, while others are strapped to the safe by long bolts and nuts or steel cable. Common to all types, however, is one or more hardened steel cutters held against the safe under tension and turned by means of a handle. The result is a round hole in the safe wall. These devices are normally not used on the safe door because the locking bars would interfere; instead, they are used on the side or back of the safe. Cutting by oxyacetylene torch is a very effective method against which only specially designed steel chests are completely resistant. A considerable disadvantage of this method lies in the fact that the apparatus required is heavy and difficult to transport. For this reason, this approach is usually used only where complete welding equipment is available on the premises. Some burglars have used compact equipment that is large enough to do the job but light enough to be carried easily.

Burning is another method used by safe burglars and involves the use of a so-called burning bar. The bar, a metal pipe, is packed with a mixture of powdered aluminium and iron oxide. The mixture is known as thermite and when ignited gives off a very intense heat that can be directed to the safe. Burning is usually started around the dial hole. A sufficiently large hole is cut in the front plate of the door so the lock mechanism is accessible. The operator may cut this hole in the form of a tongue that is folded back. Where the cutting is done on the sides or back of the safe, the inside plate must also be cut through. This method often ignites the contents of the safe, whereupon the burglar may use a soda pop bottle as a fire extinguisher. Sometimes the burglar cuts off the safe door hinges, which reveals an ignorance of the construction of the safe. The manner of opening the safe by burning reveals the skill of the burglar. When the investigator is unable to estimate this skill, a specialist should be consulted. Samples to be collected at the scene include molten particles of metal (beads), slag, molten safe insulation, and the like. Such particles may be found on the clothing of a suspect.

The investigator should also keep in mind the possibility of minor burns in the burglar's clothes from flying particles. When the contents of the safe caught fire, the burglar may have been able to recover paper currency, some of which may be charred. Safe burglaries are often carried out by transporting the safe to an isolated location where it is opened by tools or explosives. In such cases, the burglars are usually less careful in their movements at the place of opening. Valuable footprints or tyre tracks may be found at such places. The investigation should be carried out as soon as possible because inclement weather conditions may destroy the most valuable evidence.

Case 2

A safe was hauled out during a burglary and transported in a car to a wooded area, where it was opened with explosives. During examination of the outdoor scene, a door handle from an automobile was recovered. The car of a suspect who was later arrested for the burglary was found to have a broken handle. The handle from the scene matched the remains of the handle on the car. It had apparently broken off when the safe was taken out of the car. The suspect confessed.

It is sometimes very difficult to gather sufficient associative evidence to link a safe burglar specialising in explosives to a scene. As a rule, the burglar is skilled at this method and takes pride in sweeping the crime scene clean of all traces that may be used as incriminating evidence. When examining such burglary scenes, the investigator should therefore proceed very thoroughly and take advantage of the mistakes sometimes made even by this type of burglar.

Experience has shown that these burglars usually make mistakes when disturbed or when fleeing the premises. The burglar may then leave behind or drop objects that have potential value as evidence. One weakness of these specialists is that they usually stick to one method in all their burglaries. The investigator thereby gets an opportunity to tie certain burglaries to a given criminal or to others whom they have trained. This fact may be valuable even when the burglars are not known. Explosives operators usually do not pick locks or make their way into the premises by other light-fingered methods. Their work is carried out with a great deal of noise and this is also characteristic of their method of entry. They generally use great force on doors and windows and may even use a charge on a door that could much more easily have been opened the usual way. On the other hand, they are very careful to protect themselves from surprise. They very rarely work alone and may have several helpers whose only duty is to act as lookouts.

Regarding placement of the safe for blowing it, three approaches are normally found: The safe is left in place, it is pulled out from the wall, or it is laid on the floor. The first method is the most common. The second is used by burglars who do not want to have the safe blown against the wall, thus setting off vibrations in the building that may be more noticeable than the detonation. It has happened that a safe was thrown so violently against the wall that it broke the wall and started cracks that ran into an apartment above. The third method is seldom used; its advantage is that it facilitates placing the charge.

When examining safes that have been moved or laid down, the investigator should be very careful in searching for latent finger and palm prints. Although explosives specialists will be sure to use gloves or other covering, it is still possible that they may leave identifiable fragments of palm prints on a safe that they have moved. The glove may slip during the heavy work, exposing a small piece of the palm, enough to produce a valuable print. In developing prints deposited under such conditions, great care must be exercised because they easily become smeared or even completely filled in because of the great pressure.

The charge is usually placed in the dial spindle hole after the dial is knocked off; it may be dynamite in powder or paste or other explosives. The hazard and the refined technique associated with the use of nitroglycerine usually limit its use to only the elite of safe burglars. Round door safes have discouraged the use of explosives, however. Wrappers from explosives should be searched for and recovered, even though latent fingerprints are usually not found on waxed wrappers. In a favourable case, the wrapper may still be valuable as evidence. In general, the adhesive material used to affix the detonator that is found on the scene, such as clay, putty, plasticine, or soap, is brought in by the burglar. These substances must be soft and well kneaded in order to serve their purpose. Because the burglar may have kneaded these materials without wearing gloves before going to the scene, plastic fingerprints or DNA may be present. Such evidence should be searched for not only on the surface but also on inside layers of the kneaded material.

Plastic prints or DNA may also be found on strips of tape, but these are usually difficult to detect. The amount of safety fuse, when it is used, may vary in length. Explosives specialists usually cut these lengths before going to the scene and have widely varying ideas of the proper length—a fact that may have some value. Those using the longer fuses usually prefer to light the fuse and then retire to a safe place from which they can observe the effect of the explosion and whether it was noticed. Safe burglars vary as to whether they use a dam or sound-absorbing blanket to contain the explosion. Those who do use a dam probably do so to muffle the detonation and to keep windows from bursting. Because the charge is mostly inside the door, the effect of the explosion is not enhanced by the use of a dam. When the burglar intends to demolish the door completely, the dam does have some effect but it is usually an effect that he wants to avoid. The burglar runs the risk that the inside door plate is blown into the safe with such force that new charges must be placed to dislodge it. Many explosives specialists make a habit of not using a dam at all. Instead, they open windows in the room in which the safe is located so the shock wave will dissipate without breaking windows or attracting unwanted attention. Some burglars soak the dam with water, partly to make it denser and heavier and partly to prevent the possibility of fire. The materials used in dams are brought to or collected at the scene. The damage to the material gives an indication of how many separate charges were used. Whenever an unexploded charge is found in the safe it should be neutralised with great care.

Material that has been brought to the scene may sometimes provide good leads for the investigation and the search for the criminal. The ideal explosion occurs when the charge is so well balanced that the locking bolts are pulled back and the door flies open. In such cases, the external damage to the safe may be limited to a slight bulge in the front plate around the dial hole. It does happen, however, that the locking bolts remain more or less closed, so new charges must be set off. In order to avoid this snag, some burglars put weight on the door handle in the direction in which the handle opens. A heavy cord is commonly tied to the handle and a heavy object is attached to the other end. Another method is to tie a heavy metal bar to the handle to act as a lever. At the detonation, the handle is turned by the weight of the heavy object so that the locking bolts are turned back. Locked drawers and compartments inside the safe are either forced open or blown. The investigator should keep in mind the possibility of finding parts of broken tools as well as toolmarks at these places.

Fragments of tools should be searched for with a magnet because they are very difficult to find in the powdered insulation that usually pours from the broken safe. The search for fingerprints at safe blowing scenes is usually complicated by the fine layer of safe insulation that settles on everything in the room. This dust should be removed, preferably by careful blowing, before developing with powder. Do not brush off the dust, because the dust usually consists of gritty particles that will destroy any fingerprints. Visible prints that have been deposited by a dusty finger must be treated very carefully. Footwear marks may also be present.

An apprehended suspect's clothes should be thoroughly searched for the presence of safe insulation or paint. Anyone who has been present in a room where a safe has been blown can hardly avoid getting dust and safe insulation on his or her clothing. The dust may also adhere to the burglar's skin or in the hair, ears, and nostrils and under the fingernails. Such dust may be found on any part of the clothing, but particularly in pant cuffs and on shoes, mainly in the seams and lace holes and on the soles.

In addition, paint chips are usually loosened in the explosion, and the burglars run the risk of picking them up on their clothing when examining the safe after the detonation. When searching the scene, the investigator should therefore collect samples of the safe insulation and paint on the outside and inside of the safe for use in possible comparisons and should also evaluate the possibility of wall paint loosened by the explosion falling on the burglar. The investigator should note the manufacturer of the safe so the company may later be contacted for information on the composition of insulation and paint. If safe insulation or paint is not found on the suspect's clothes, the investigator should remember that the suspect might have done everything possible to eliminate such traces. The suspect's hands and clothing should also be examined for the presence of trace explosives. If the hands were not immediately washed, traces may be found under the suspect's fingernails. In clothing, such traces should primarily be searched for in pockets; even gloves may contain traces. If the burglar carried safety fuses in his pockets, there may be characteristic stains on the pocket lining.

When a safe is blown, the burglar may be injured by the sharp metal edges, or his nose may bleed due to the shock of the detonation. Nose bleeds are more common when electric detonators are used because the burglar may be forced to stay rather close to the safe, although extension cords can be used. If blood is found at the scene, it should be recovered for later examination. The burglar may possibly be so severely injured that immediate aid must be sought. Burglary is such a common crime that frequently a less than thorough investigation is conducted; however, a careful and detailed examination of the crime scene may result in developing evidence useful in ultimate solution of the case.

14.2.6   Burglary Investigation and Intelligence

Today all investigators have access to DNA typing. Work in volume crimes makes use of DNA databases and is an important source of profiles found in them. This has resulted in a complete reversal of the situation a few year ago, when DNA testing in burglaries was regarded as an expensive waste of time. Although blood shed from an injury incurred during the crime is the most obvious source, crime scene investigators should not forget that profiles can be developed from touch DNA and should consider any potential source where the burglar may have been in contact with an item and not protected by gloves or other barriers.

14.3 Summary

Burglary investigations, unless involving high-value thefts, serious assaults, or murder, once were the poor relations of crime scene investigations. The time and effort required for a thorough examination were not deemed worthwhile; however, serious burglaries do occur. Some are associated with violence, and some display a modus operandi that can link various burglary scenes, representing a very substantial total monetary value. This chapter has described the elements of the scene investigation that are most appropriate to a burglary and places them in the context of the processes described in Chapter 3. The most significant change in attitude with regard to the investigation of burglary scenes arose from the discovery that DNA from a burglary scene produced a high probability of associating different scenes that at first were believed to be separate events and linking the burglar to other more serious crimes. The application of the investigative star here, therefore, involves not only addressing WHO and WHERE to identify the perpetrator and to link scenes, but also WHAT happened and HOW; for example, was it a simulated burglary to cover another crime?

Motor Vehicle Investigation

15.1 Introduction

The widespread use of motor vehicles in today's society has resulted in automobiles being associated with many different types of police investigations. Motor vehicles may be the instrument of crimes such as hit-and-run cases or traffic fatalities. A vehicle may also be a crime scene—for example, in cases when a crime was committed in an automobile or in cases of auto theft. This chapter deals with evidence commonly associated with crimes in which a motor vehicle is involved.

Case 1

One night a young lady left a nightclub in order to use the pay phone across the street. During her trip back across the four-lane highway, a vehicle that was travelling at a high speed struck her. Found at the scene was a piece of a white body moulding kit known to be associated with high-end Corvettes. The company that produced this product was contacted and reported that only two of these white body moulding kits had been sold on Long Island in New York. A witness reported that he observed a white Corvette at a stoplight take off at a high speed and strike the victim. He believed that the driver might have been racing. After receiving the addresses of the kit purchasers, the detectives started their investigation with the closer address. Upon arrival, they discovered a white Corvette in the process of being disassembled. After searching dumpsters in the adjacent industrial area, they found the majority of the pieces. The deconstruction of the hood had been achieved through the use of a chain saw, reciprocating saw, and pick axe. When it was reassembled, blood was discovered. A laboratory investigation was initiated, but before work was completed the owner confessed to the hit and run that killed the young lady (see Figure 15.1).

15.2 Vehicle Theft and Recovery for Examination

A vehicle may be stolen by juveniles for joyriding, in connection with another crime as a means of fleeing, or for the purpose of stripping the vehicle of parts to be sold for profit. Stolen vehicles may be found in a variety of circumstances. Uniformed officers on patrol often observe them. Officers may refer to a "hot sheet" that lists stolen vehicle licences, use a description from a police bulletin or broadcast, or notice some furtive movement on the part of the driver that results in a routine traffic stop and subsequent check for a stolen vehicle. With so many occurrences of theft that are not related to other crimes or to an organised vehicle theft ring, decisions are inevitably made at times to pursue the investigation only to a limited extent.

Figure 15.1 (a) Vehicle part found at scene. (b) Reassembled bonnet from vehicle. (c) Front view of disassembled suspect vehicle. (Photographs courtesy of Suffolk County Crime Lab, New York.)

When a vehicle has been identified as stolen, the examination for forensic evidence begins. A short preliminary investigation will determine whether a full search is needed. When the police stop a vehicle reported as having been stolen, there is no need to pursue physical evidence to identify the thief, as it was the driver (unless the unfortunate individual driving the car had bought the car from the thief). Some care should be exercised and the details of the car recorded to confirm its identity. It is also a good idea to look for evidence of other crimes. In one case, an automobile was recovered and at the officer's request towed to an impound yard. Some days later, much to the officer's chagrin, a dead body was discovered in the boot.

It is possible that the theft may be only one of other, more serious crimes; with this in mind, the first officer to locate the stolen vehicle should take appropriate precautions. As with other crime scenes, the most fragile and discriminating evidence should be collected first. This usually means DNA and fingerprints. Where detailed examination of the vehicle is required, it should be taken to a secure and appropriately equipped garage. Depending on the size and organisation of the crime scene investigation unit, this may be a dedicated workshop with ramps, power tools, and complete lock-down security, or access to such an area may have to be arranged with the assistance of another agency. If a fully secure facility is not available, the vehicle itself should be sealed off with notices not to touch.

The removal is best carried out by means of a transporter truck. The vehicle should not be driven and towing is not advisable because either could lead to the loss or contamination of valuable physical evidence. Furthermore, before any extensive search is undertaken, the need for a search warrant should be considered.

If the vehicle is wet from rain or dew it should first be allowed to dry. In cold weather, the vehicle should be placed indoors and allowed to warm up to room temperature prior to taking fingerprints. The examination for fingerprints should be conducted in a systematic manner and should concentrate first of all on areas most likely to have been handled by the suspect. These include the rearview mirror, steering wheel, gear shift, door handles, glove compartment, and windows. After prints have been lifted, the location, date, time, and other identifying information should be noted on the record. Swabs of the vehicle should also be taken for touch DNA. Note that care will be required in the interpretation of touch DNA; for example, a swab from an area with a partial but indistinct fingerprint may give a DNA profile from material underneath the print, not from the outer surface. Signs of forced entry or forced access to the ignition system should be noted. Known specimens of broken glass, chipped paint, and similar items if present can be collected for future comparison.

If the vehicle had been fitted with electronic systems, such as radio, tape deck, CD player, mobile phone, navigation system, or MP3 player hook-up, and these have been removed by cutting the connections, the electrical wires should be collected for possible comparison against recovered property, based on comparison of toolmarks. The wires should be marked in a way that clearly shows which ends were originally connected to the unit.

15.3   Abandoned Vehicles

An officer who finds or investigates an ownerless vehicle not reported as stolen should *not* drive it away or subject it to more detailed examination until informed by the driver or owner of the car why the vehicle was standing at that place. What follows is based on the premise that it is suspected that the vehicle was involved in a serious crime. The vehicle and its surroundings now constitute a crime scene, the examination of which should follow the principles described in Chapter 3. There may not be sufficient information to develop a scene examination strategy and hypotheses as fully as the crime scene investigation coordinator would wish, but, in the absence of anything to the contrary, an initial focus on the vehicle and its immediate surroundings is reasonable. The basic search for evidence in and on the vehicle should be carried out in a well-sheltered place, preferably in a garage or other suitable building, because rain or snow or even strong sunlight can destroy certain evidence. The vehicle should not be driven but should be removed from the place at which it was found as soon as possible, as described earlier in this chapter.

The place where the vehicle is found should be photographed and can be sketched in the usual way. Photography is done while the vehicle is still on the spot, but sketching can wait until later if sketches are required. The distance to the nearest occupied dwelling and to the nearest town or city should be indicated on the sketches. If necessary, a sketch plan may be made of the immediate surroundings and another of neighbouring districts, but suitable maps may replace the latter. The recording of the odometer or taxi meter should be noted; it is best to ask an expert whether anything of special significance can be observed. Also, the supply of fuel should be checked.

Addresses in any satellite navigation system should be checked to determine where the car might have come from and where it was headed. The account information from automatic toll collection devices, such as the E-ZPass® in the Northeastern region of the United States, should be checked to establish where a vehicle might have been and when (see Figure 15.2).

Figure 15.2 (a) Digital tachograph (http://en.wikipedia.org/wiki/File:Tachograph.jpg). (b) Car fitted with electronic toll payment system (white box near the rearview mirror) and satellite navigation unit.

If the vehicle in question is a commercial vehicle in the European Union, it will be fitted with a tachograph (also shown in Figure 15.2), which automatically records its speed and distance travelled. An attempt is also made to determine whether the vehicle stopped at that particular point for some reason unforeseen by the driver, such as engine trouble, depleted fuel supply, or an inability to drive it further. The floor in front of the driving seat should be examined carefully. Preferably all dust and dirt found there should be kept. The exterior should be examined for the presence of any evidence that might fall off when the vehicle is moved.

Furthermore, a preliminary examination of the entire vehicle should be made to look for any evidence that is easy to collect or that for any reason might be damaged or destroyed when the vehicle is moved. The detailed investigation of a vehicle should *not* be carried out at the place where it is found, but the site chosen should be as near as possible to where the vehicle was found. A long tow can cause a deposit of dust or dirt that may completely destroy any possibility of finding evidence in the form of fingerprints.

After the vehicle has been moved to a sheltered place, a thorough investigation can be made of the location where the vehicle was found and the surrounding area, including footwear and tyre marks. It is possible that the driver unconsciously dropped or threw away objects that could indicate the route taken or could supply valuable evidence. The investigation must be done quickly, especially if snow, strong winds, or heavy rains are expected. If larger areas or stretches of road must be searched, it may be advisable to call for a search team; however, they must first be instructed on how to proceed if they find any evidence.

The detailed investigation of the vehicle is done only after it is completely dry. In general, the floor of the vehicle and seats are examined first; only after this is done are any fingerprints developed and DNA swabs collected. It may be best to treat the vehicle like any other scene and work from the outside to the inner or at least create the equivalent of a common approach path to the main area of interest (most likely the driver's seat, but could be the boot). This will avoid the risk of anyone unthinkingly destroying evidence or leaving prints.

If the search begins at the area of the driver's seat, then contents of ashtrays should be examined and kept, with the various objects being noted in the order in which they occur from the top. The contents of the glove compartment and any other storage spaces are examined and noted in a similar way. Objects that have been dropped may be found in and under the seats.

Any bloodstains in and on the vehicle are examined for direction of fall, height of fall, direction of movement, etc., after which they are preserved. Marks of swinging a weapon, damage from gunshot, and the like are preserved. The engine and boot are examined. In the investigation of a vehicle in which a crime of violence has been committed, it is advisable, after collecting the evidence, to take measurements of the amount of room in the vehicle. A question may arise about the possibility of a criminal swinging an instrument, handling a firearm, and other such acts. Any evidence of the vehicle's being used in any crime should be noted; safe paint and insulation in the trunk, outlines of boxes or tools, even bullet holes should be sought. All normal vehicle identification numbers (VINs) should be checked to detect alterations in the identity of the vehicle. Damage to the vehicle may indicate that the abandonment and report of theft were intended to hide an accident. The exact damage should be carefully noted and photographed.

Figure 15.3 The colour of the seat of this car made it difficult to visualise any blood using the naked eye. Luminol was sprayed on the seat to determine if the victim was shot in this car. Blood from the victim was found on the seat lever, and the owner of the car was subsequently arrested. In order to capture the chemiluminescence of the luminol in a digital photograph (shown in purple), a 30-second exposure was used in a darkened room with a rear curtain flash. (Photograph courtesy of Office of Chief Medical Examiner, New York City.)

Under suspicious circumstances, the temperature of the water in the radiator and the surrounding air temperature should be recorded. From these data, it may be possible to estimate the duration of time since abandonment. A careful search of the vehicle interior and boot is required in those cases in which it carried a hostage or dead body. If the victim was killed in one location, transported in the vehicle, and dropped at another site, only a very small amount of blood or other evidence may be present. Touch DNA, DNA from residues of blood or semen if there was physical injury or a sexual assault, and the whole range of trace evidence previously discussed would be screened for and collected if present. In some cases, the interior may have been cleaned, in which case it may be worthwhile to remove and dismantle the seats. As with the examples in previous chapters, where it is suspected that blood may have been washed away the application of luminol can be very useful. The photograph in Figure 15.3 was taken with a long exposure time to capture the weak light emitted from the luminol.

Electronic noses can also be used to detect odours of decomposition inside the vehicle. Weapons, tools, and sometimes trace evidence that can link the victim to the vehicle may be uncovered.

15.4   Murder in a Vehicle

Taxicab drivers are sometimes the victims of robberies, sometimes in combination with assaults that may be fatal. For a criminal who is desperate enough, it is a relatively simple matter to order the driver to a desolate area; assault the driver from behind, risking little personal danger; and then rob him. Because it would be dangerous to attack the driver while the cab is moving, the driver is asked to stop under some pretext or other. After the robbery is completed, it is not uncommon for the attacker to hide the victim and then drive the car far away from the scene.

When the robbery victim dies, one can expect to find the vehicle and the victim in different locations; sometimes the vehicle is found first. For this reason, every officer who finds an abandoned vehicle should suspect the worst and exercise extreme care, rather than assume that the simplest case of joyriding applies. After a licence check has revealed that the vehicle may have been the scene of a crime, the procedure suggested in the earlier discussion on abandoned vehicles should be followed, as well as the procedure for the specific type of crime. The search of a vehicle in which a homicide was committed must be conducted with the same degree of care as would be used in conducting the search of an indoor or outdoor crime scene involving a murder. Because of the cramped working area, it is especially important to exercise care so as not to destroy any physical evidence in the vehicle. The procedures discussed in Chapter 3 for processing the crime scene are generally the same for vehicles.

Cases involving sabotage or acts of terrorism in which the vehicle was blown up by an explosive charge require a thorough investigation to recover as many parts of the device as possible. The debris from the explosion may cover a wide area, and a careful and systematic search is necessary to locate, chart, and recover as many pieces of the damaged vehicle and bomb as possible. Pieces of a timing mechanism, electrical devices, wires, and batteries, as well as explosives residue, may prove to be valuable evidence in the investigation.

Caution: Investigators should be extremely careful, as secondary devices can be placed to cause maximum casualties to first responders and investigators!

15.5 Hit-and-Run Investigations

Hit-and-run cases include two types: damage to other vehicles or property and death or injury to individuals. In both cases, forensic evidence can assist in identifying the hit-and-run vehicle, establishing a connection between the vehicle and the victim or crime scene, and reconstructing the scene in general to determine the events surrounding the crime. Cases involving damage to other vehicles are often the result of driving under the influence or driving in a careless or reckless manner.

The usual evidence items found at the scene are paint chips or scrapings, glass, pieces of headlamps or plastic reflectors, and pieces from the grillwork of the vehicle (Figure 15.4). Most of these are very small and therefore easily overlooked during crime scene searches.

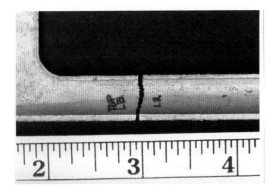

Figure 15.4 This close-up of a physical match of broken pieces of a license plate holder proved a vehicle was associated with a hit-and-run accident. (Photograph courtesy of Los Angeles County Sheriff's Department, Los Angeles, CA.)

Also, the impact from the crash may throw certain items some distance from the vehicle, and loose or broken parts still attached to the hit-and-run vehicle may subsequently fall off at considerable distance from the scene. These considerations make a search of a greater area important in these cases.

The hit-and-run crime scene often has a factor not present at other scenes: traffic. If the fatality occurred in a busy intersection or on a well-travelled street, the officer may feel pressured to complete the investigation more quickly. Although time may be a consideration, it should not deter the investigator from doing a thorough and complete job of processing the scene. Overall crime scene photographs should be taken, as well as photographs from different views. Close-up photographs of the victim as well as of items of physical evidence must be taken. If the crime occurred at night, portable lighting should be brought in so the area is adequately lit. The area should be examined for tyre impressions and particularly for skid marks, which can be used to determine the direction and speed of the suspect vehicle and therefore are important in the case.

Care must be taken when moving the deceased so as not to lose valuable items of trace evidence. When the deceased is brought to the mortuary, clothing should be carefully searched for paint, glass, and other parts from the suspect's vehicle. These items should be packaged, tagged, and submitted to the forensic laboratory for examination. Figure 15.5 shows smears of paint transferred from the hit-and-run vehicle to the clothing of a victim by the force of the impact. If the victim was on a bicycle or motorcycle, it should be carefully examined for items such as paint that could provide associative evidence to link the cycle to the suspect vehicle. Lights from a struck vehicle should be recovered and submitted to the laboratory to determine if they were operational and whether they were on or off. Clumps of soil or dirt found at the scene should be documented and collected. These can be compared with dirt found on the underneath of the suspect's vehicle when it is found and may demonstrate a connection.

The scene should be examined for specific damage to the unknown vehicle. Broken parts of the vehicle should be collected for possible physical matching. In certain cases, the make and sometimes the model of the vehicle can be determined by these parts. This information may be helpful when an investigator contacts automobile repair body shops or parts stores to determine if anyone recently came in to have a vehicle repaired. Occasionally, the force of impact is so great that impressions from the vehicle are made on the victim's body or clothing. Such evidence should be photographed and preserved for later comparison. Airbags, if they have been deployed, should be cut out and sent to the lab for DNA typing. This can help determine who was driving the vehicle and the time of impact.

Paint chips are especially important items of physical evidence. If they are sufficiently large, it may be possible to fit them physically into the vehicle in jigsaw puzzle fashion. Paint will, at a minimum, be useful to determine the colour of the hit-and-run vehicle, and in some instances the make of the vehicle can be determined through laboratory examination. Further, physical and chemical comparisons of paint recovered at the scene can sometimes be made with that from the suspect's vehicle.

When the vehicle suspected to be responsible for the hit-and-run is found, it should be treated as described earlier in Section 15.2. If the owner of the vehicle claims that the car had been stolen, examination of the door locks and ignition lock for touch DNA and fingerprints may provide valuable information to help prove or disprove this contention.

Examination of the underneath of the vehicle could be important with regard to collecting evidence such as hair, blood, skin, fabric, and fibres. Specimens of grease and dirt should be collected for comparison with debris found on the victim (Figure 15.6). The front

Figure 15.5 A careful examination of victim's clothing collected in a hit-and-run investigation clearly showed paint transfer from the red car suspected of striking the victim. (Photograph courtesy of Illinois State Police.)

Figure 15.6 Various imprints and impressions, including round and hexagonal marks found on a victim's coat from a traffic accident (top). The suspected bus driver denied hitting the victim; however, examination of the underside of the bus (bottom) determined that part of the oil sump could have made the marks. Because the bolt orientations were shown to be unique, the conclusion was made that the suspect bus caused the imprints. (Photographs courtesy of Israel National Police.)

area of the vehicle and the bonnet should be thoroughly examined. Occasionally, fabric impressions from the impact appear in the dust on the bumper. These should be carefully photographed with a scale, and if possible the bumper should be removed and submitted to the laboratory. All broken parts and damage to the vehicle are important items of evidence. Any damage to the front end, such as broken grills, headlamps, scratched paint, or other scratches, should be carefully noted and, if possible, removed and submitted to the laboratory. In some instances, evidence from a motorcycle or bicycle that a vehicle hit may be present; these items should be preserved.

Known specimens from the hit-and-run vehicle should be collected. These especially include paint that should be collected in the area of any damage to the vehicle. If scrapes containing other paint material are noted, these too should be collected to be compared with the victim's vehicle. In some cases the victim may have been hit and thrown onto the vehicle hood or windshield. Fingerprints belonging to the victim as well as hairs, fibres, and blood should be searched for with this in mind. If the windshield is broken, glass should be collected and a search made for hairs and blood. Headlamps and tail lights should be examined to determine whether they work; if possible, they should be sent to the laboratory, as examination of the filament can determine if the lights were on or off at the time of impact. Broken headlamp lenses and signal light reflectors should be removed for comparison with evidence collected at the scene. Sometimes it is possible to make a physical match with these items.

If tyre impressions were made at the scene, photographs containing a scale should be made of each tyre. Inked tyre impressions on paper can be made for comparison with tyre impressions located at the crime scene. If the suspect driver is apprehended soon after the hit-and-run incident, a blood sample should be obtained. The sample should be submitted to the laboratory for testing for alcohol or other drugs to determine if the suspect was under the influence.

Case 2

During a sailboat race on Lake Ontario, one of the boats was struck by lightning. The crew radioed to the race organiser that they were dropping out of the race and heading for Rochester, New York; this was the last contact with them. There was no SOS call, and no search for the boat was undertaken. Three days later, an American fisherman found two bodies tied together and floating with a beacon light attached to one of them. The beacon was lit at the time of the discovery. When the beacon later came into possession of Canadian authorities, the bulb was burned out. At the inquest, there was apparently conflicting evidence: The type of light bulb (no. 13) used in the beacon can only last for approximately 2 hours with a set of new batteries. Thus, if the fisherman found the beacon lit, then the boat must have capsized only hours before the bodies were discovered. The pathologist had determined, however, that the bodies had been dead approximately 70 hours. Scanning electron microscopic (SEM) examination of the filament discovered two breaks, both while the bulb was hot (on)—an indication that the bulb had a second life. The conflicting evidence could be explained with the bulb's apparent two lives (although it was not proof). In the case of the very fine filament in the lamp, the SEM has a considerable advantage over conventional microscopes in demonstrating the breaks and reestablished contact by providing a clear photograph with good depth of focus and a reflection-free image (Figure 15.7).

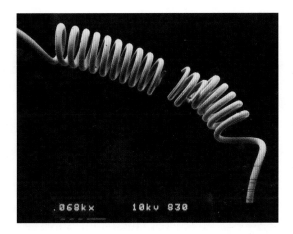

Figure 15.7 A scanning electron photomicrograph of a lamp filament showing that there had been a break that reconnected and then a second break. (Photograph courtesy of Centre of Forensic Science, Toronto, Canada.)

Case 3

Sometimes what initially appears to be a motor vehicle investigation turns out to be very different, as this case demonstrated (see Figures 15.8 to 15.12). D. Cotton, a 23-year-old male, died as a result of a motor vehicle accident. He was the sole occupant of a car that had overshot an intersection and slammed into a solid stone wall. The car was, in fact, registered to a Mr. Caffrey, who lived on the same street as Cotton. When the police went to question Mr. Caffrey at his home about why Cotton had been driving his car, they found that he had been murdered. His body had numerous knife wounds. The crime scene investigation suggested a sole assailant. When the car was examined, a bloodstained knife was found in a plastic bag in the rear compartment. The tip of the knife had been snapped off. Postmortem examination of Mr. Caffrey's body revealed stab wounds to the head. The possibility of the knife having left a piece

Figure 15.8 Damaged car. (Photograph courtesy of South Australia Police Department.)

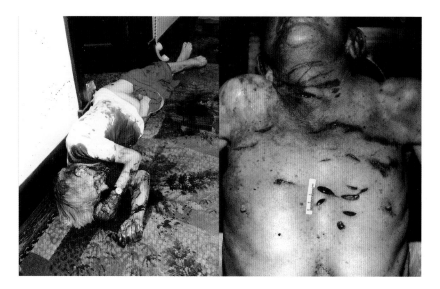

Figure 15.9 The body of Mr. Caffrey at the scene (left) and at autopsy (right). (Photographs courtesy of South Australia Police Department.)

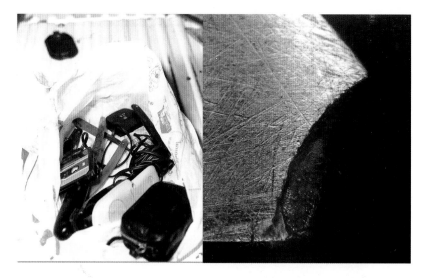

Figure 15.10 Tools found in the car (left) including the bloody knife (right) with its tip missing. (Photographs courtesy of South Australia Police Department.)

of blade in the skull was confirmed when an x-ray revealed a small metal fragment lodged in the skull behind the left ear. A physical match between the piece of metal and the knife confirmed it as the murder weapon. Combined with the blood evidence (on the knife and a glove worn by Cotton), and the location of bloodied shoe sole impressions at the scene, which were similar in size and pattern to Cotton's shoes, the state coroner was satisfied that Cotton had been responsible for the death of Caffrey and had stolen his car.

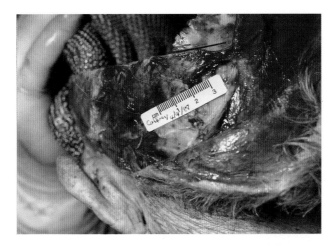

Figure 15.11 Recovery of the knife tip from behind the left ear. (Photograph courtesy of South Australia Police Department.)

Figure 15.12 Physical fit of the recovered fragment into the broken end of the knife. (Photograph courtesy of South Australia Police Department.)

15.6 Vehicles Found under Water

Sometimes vehicles involved in a crime will be recovered in or under water. A joy-rider, for example, may abandon the car by driving it into a river, or the perpetrator may attempt to conceal a car involved in a crime by driving over a cliff into the sea. These locations require extra precautions during examination to avoid loss and degradation of evidence. The underwater location is now part of a crime scene, and consideration has to be given to what must be recorded and how. It may be necessary to engage an experienced underwater photographer to photograph the general location of the vehicle and any specific details such as damage or items near it. Ultimately, the vehicle will have to be lifted out, but before that takes place the seabed (or whatever surface on which the vehicle came to rest) should be searched for items such as weapons, papers, or clothing.

Because of the risk that the conditions of the vehicle may be changed while raising it from the water, the following should be noted before raising: How is the vehicle positioned (e.g., upside down, lying on its side, in what direction, at what distance from the land, quay, or bridge)? Are the doors, windows, bonnet, and boot lid open or closed? Are the windows intact or broken? Are there any dents in the car? Are there any persons in the car? If so, where are they placed? What is the gear shift position? Raising the vehicle can be done in various ways depending on the circumstances. Raising can sometimes be done just by towing it up onto the beach bank or a boat ramp. There is always a risk that evidence and items can fall or be left behind when the vehicle is being raised. When the vehicle is free of the water, the inside water will drain from the car, which can lead to evidence being lost. If necessary, this loss of evidence can be avoided by sinking a container onto which the vehicle can be lifted by a crane or by attaching inflatable balloons. When a crane is used to raise a vehicle, it can dent the vehicle when it is pulled free from the seabed, when it is raised through the water, and, in particular, when the vehicle breaks free of the water and loses its buoyancy.

Divers involved in the search and recovery operation must be competent divers and familiar with crime scene investigation. Not all crime scene investigation units will have such personnel within the unit, but those that do not should have made arrangements with specialist emergency services or similar agencies to provide such services as needed.

15.7   Wheel Marks

15.7.1   Tyre Marks

With the aid of wheel marks, direction of movement can be determined. When the ground is damp, the surface on which the wheel rolls forward is compressed and the bottom of the mark is formed as a series of steps. The compressed clods of earth in the mark are lifted in the same direction as the wheel is rolling. To assist the memory in this respect, it is easy to remember this rule: For the mark to become level again, the wheel must roll in the opposite direction. A vehicle that travels in a straight line actually leaves only the track of the rear wheels; to observe marks of the front wheels, it is necessary to find some place where the vehicle has turned sharply or reversed. When examining wheel marks, it is necessary to look for places showing defects or repairs in the tyres. With the aid of successive marks of this type, the circumference of the tyre can be determined. The track is measured between the centre points of the two wheel marks. Preservation is achieved by photography and casting selected points showing characteristic marks or wear. For photographs, a scale is placed across the track and another along one side of it. Casting is done in the same way as for foot impressions (discussed in Chapter 9). In examining vehicle marks, it should be noted whether wheels that follow one another go in the same track or whether there is any deviation. If dual wheels are found, both tread marks should be recorded simultaneously because the relationship of one tread pattern to the other provides additional characteristics for identification of the vehicle (Figure 15.13).

15.7.2   Skid Marks

The speed of the suspect vehicle at the time of impact is sometimes at issue. Some crime scene investigation units utilize accident reconstruction experts to investigate evidence from skid marks; these experts may be full-time employees of the CSI unit or they may

Figure 15.13 (Right) Kirkland tyre with unique defects. (Left) Tyre cast with unique marks. (Photographs courtesy of Los Angeles County Sheriff's Department, Los Angeles, CA.)

Figure 15.14 An investigator submitted a speedometer head to determine the speed of a vehicle at the time of impact. The speedometer dial was examined under ultraviolet light, and a "speed mark" was detected in the area of 20 mph. This speed mark is an imprint of the speedometer pointer (needle) on the dial caused by the force of inertia at the time of impact. (Photograph courtesy of Forensic Laboratory, Office of Attorney General, Pierre, SD.)

be contract workers called in as needed. Based on such factors as the length of the mark and the coefficient of friction of the road surface, an approximation of the speed at which the suspect vehicle was travelling may be calculated. Figure 15.14 shows a different way of determining the speed of a vehicle at impact. The impact can cause the needle of an analogue speedometer to be deformed and leave an impact mark (or "speed mark") on the dial. For newer vehicles with digital instrumentation, a record may be found on the engine management system computer.

15.8 Summary

The crime scene investigator can encounter scenes requiring the examination of vehicles in many situations, but mostly related to the question of WHAT in the investigative star. The crime may relate to the vehicle itself, such as in a theft or hit-and-run, or it may have been used in another crime, such as to transport a dead body or hostage (what vehicle, what happened, what was it used for). The investigation can also address WHO (who was driving, who was in the vehicle) and WHERE (where has the vehicle been, including associative evidence in hit-run cases). Some questions, such as the vehicle functionality or speed at impact are of a specialised nature, but most of the time the general principles of scene examination and location, collection, and preservation of forensic evidence already described will apply.

Homicide Investigation* ✦ 16

16.1 The Initial Scene

Society regards the taking of human life as the ultimate crime and therefore demands the greatest thoroughness in the investigation of deaths that are not due to natural causes, whether murder, suicide, or accident. Some cases are relatively simple, such as a homicide–suicide where the killer leaves a note explaining his actions and the evidence at the scene is clear cut. Others can require collecting a vast amount of evidence, including information and statements from witnesses and suspects, as well as physical evidence obtained from the primary scene and from secondary scenes identified during the course of investigations. More than with most crimes, death investigation requires a team effort. Identifying the time, manner, and cause of death can involve specialists in addition to the pathologist, such as an entomologist, a toxicologist, a radiologist, and a firearms expert. When the investigation moves to reconstructing events at the scene and identifying the killer, the full battery of crime scene investigation and forensic laboratory personnel could also be involved in gathering and analyzing fingerprint and DNA evidence, hair and fibre evidence, impression evidence such as footwear and toolmarks, and digital evidence, in addition to creating animations to describe the scene.

The circumstances surrounding the investigation can easily appear chaotic at first, but careful consideration of investigative strategies and adherence to protocols will bring logic to bear and help achieve a successful outcome. This chapter brings together many of the concepts discussed previously in the text and examines areas unique to the investigation of death. Notification of the finding of a dead body is the usual starting point of a death investigation. Occasionally, a death must be investigated even when a body has not been found, although this is usually more difficult. The preliminary determination of time and cause of death—and, most importantly, whether there are reasons to believe that the manner of death was anything other than from natural causes—will be made by a medical doctor who attends either directly on request of relatives or friends of the deceased or as part of the immediate response to a notification to the police. The doctor may have sufficient information, such as recent medical history and condition of the body, to declare death by natural causes, in which case a death certificate will be issued and there will be no investigation. In other cases, the doctor may have sufficient information to declare that the death was *not* from natural causes (e.g., obvious gunshot or knife injuries), or the doctor may not have sufficient information to certify a cause of death. The second of these alternatives will result in some form of investigation, but we shall restrict what follows to the situation

---

* English-speaking countries outside of the United States generally refer to the offence of wilfully killing someone as *murder*; however, the term *homicide* has a long history of usage meaning death other than from natural causes. Indeed, Scots law, the roots of which are embedded in Roman law, contains an offence of "culpable homicide." This chapter is intended to help those investigating any suspicious death and so uses the term *homicide* in the broader sense.

where the determination is "not from natural causes." Although not considered further, the case where the doctor cannot sign a death certificate of natural causes but there are no obvious signs of suspicious death can result in a long and complex investigation.

If the initial call was made to the police, the rules for the first officer to arrive at the crime scene are the same as outlined in earlier chapters. The first step should always be to treat the scene as a potential homicide. The officer will secure the scene, administer life-saving measures, and summon emergency services if needed. When it has been determined that a suspicious death has occurred, the first officer attending (FOA) will notify homicide investigators and crime scene investigators, and the investigation will begin.

The investigation will usually focus on the very important matter of identifying the victim or victims. This will provide some direction as to places and persons that may have some relationship with the deceased and provide a starting point for the case. In the majority of cases, it is not difficult to determine that the suspicious death was the result of a murder rather than a suicide or accident. Some deaths, by their nature, are difficult to differentiate—for example, an accidental fall compared to a homicidal pushing down the stairs. Common sense, experience, and careful analysis of the situation by the FOA and crime scene and murder investigators are important. Those involved should keep in mind that if a supposed suicide is judged to be a murder then a serious error has not been committed, even though the investigation may become more extensive than is necessary. If, on the other hand, a murder is initially judged to be a suicide, then the officer has not only failed in the investigation but may also have made the solution of the crime and the apprehension of the killer more difficult, if not impossible.

16.2   Suicide, Murder, or Accident?

When evaluating whether the deceased died from an accident or suicide, or if death was caused by another person, it is generally best to suspect the worst—murder. Even if circumstances give the overwhelming appearance of suicide or accident, the investigation should be conducted in as much detail as possible. Murderers have been known to intentionally stage deaths to appear to be accidents or suicide. The investigating officer must be aware of this possibility. Only through systematic and accurate investigation can such a deception be revealed. The FOA, the officer in charge of the tactical investigation, and the crime scene coordinator will communicate with each other to address questions regarding the circumstances as they initially appear: What was the cause of death? Could the deceased have produced the injuries or brought about the circumstances that caused the death? Are there any signs of a struggle? Are there defensive wounds on the victim? Where is the weapon, instrument, or object that caused the injuries or traces of the medium that caused death? These questions will form the basis of discussions regarding development of a scene investigation strategy.

16.2.1   Cause of Death

The FOA may or may not be from a specialist homicide unit, depending on the information given to the police during the initial notification. Irrespective of that, the first question the FOA has to deal with is whether there are any signs that the death was not from natural causes. Obvious information such as a body suspended from a ligature around the neck or lying in a pool of blood with severe injuries should be passed along with the request for assistance from the homicide unit, or equivalent, in the jurisdiction where the investigation is taking place (if the FOA was not a murder squad specialist), in addition to medical and crime scene investigation specialists. FOAs not from a homicide unit should restrict their actions to preserving the scene and making factual observations of obvious signs of foul play. Trained and experienced homicide or crime scene investigators will have sufficient expertise to probe further, even in advance of the examination by the pathologist, and set the investigation off on the correct direction. The specific team response will vary from country to country, but probably the best start will come from the team approach described earlier where the scene examination of the body is conducted by the pathologist working together with the crime scene investigation unit and other investigators.

16.2.2   Suicide

Could the deceased have produced the injuries or brought about the effect that caused death? A determination of whether death was the result of suicide or murder is extremely important in the initial phase of the investigation. Usually the decision is based on an evaluation of the injuries that resulted in the death and other factors regarding the deceased's mental and emotional state prior to the death. The common modes of death by suicide are drowning, hanging, shooting, poisoning or overdosing, jumping from heights, cutting arteries, stabbing, and jumping in front of a train. These factors must be considered along with the physical and psychological ability of the deceased to accomplish the act. A detailed examination of the crime scene should be undertaken to determine if the facts are consistent with the theory of suicide. For example, it is reasonable to expect to find the means of death, such as a weapon or poison, to be close at hand and in close proximity to the body. Failure to discover a weapon in the case of a suspected suicide makes that possibility unrealistic.

The nature and position of the injuries are useful considerations in drawing a conclusion. Hesitation marks are quite common in suicide cases and can often be seen near the fatal cut or stab wound (Figure 16.1). Gunpowder tattooing located around a gunshot wound is consistent with the firing of a weapon at close range, which would be consistent with suicide. Defence wounds, however, are not expected to be found on the hands or arms of a suspected suicide.

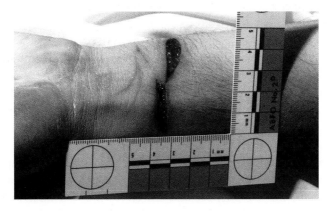

Figure 16.1 Investigators need to be able to distinguish between defence wounds and hesitation marks. This is an example of the latter. (Photograph courtesy of County of Los Angeles—Department of Coroner, Los Angeles, CA.)

Wound location should be considered. The wound location should be within reach of the deceased—in the case of stabbing or cutting, generally on the wrists, neck, abdomen, or chest. A wound to the back of the torso would therefore raise suspicion. Also, wounds are generally grouped in one area, as in the case of hesitation marks on the wrist. It is not uncommon for persons committing suicide to open their clothing before stabbing or cutting their throat, chest, or abdomen. It is believed that this is done to ensure that the injury occurs where intended and that the suicide weapon is not, for example, deflected by the ribs.

In suicides involving handguns, the victim usually drops the weapon or throws it several feet away when the arms are flung outward. In such cases, the floor or ground should be examined for dents or scratches resulting from the impact. Occasionally, the weapon is found in the victim's hand, but this is usually due to the gun or hand having been supported in some way at the moment of discharge.

No blood on the insides of the hands or on the corresponding parts of the gun grip is usually a good indication that the victim fired the shot if the rest of the hand is bloody. The same condition applies to knife handles when the victim causes the slashes. Bloodstains on the palm of the hand and the grip of the gun do not necessarily indicate murder; however, there is reason to be suspicious if the blood marks on the hand and grip do not match. In some cases, a murderer has placed a gun in the victim's hand after rigor mortis has set in.

Someone found dead in a room in which the door is locked from the inside is usually considered to be a case of suicide or natural death. The crime scene investigator should not, however, be satisfied with this simple conclusion. Because there are methods by which doors, windows, or other openings can be locked from the outside, the investigator should pay particular attention to unusual traces and marks on doors, locks, latches, windows, etc.

Suicide by jumping from buildings or bridges is not uncommon in large cities. The body may land at some considerable distance from the perpendicular; for example, after a jump from a 25-metre vertical cliff, the body was found 12 metres from the base. This circumstance may seem suspicious, but it is explained by the fact that the force of an outward jump continues to act on the falling body. Conversely, finding a body close to the wall of a building could be due to an already dead or unconscious body being tipped from a higher floor of a building.

A determination of suicide should also be based on interviews with the deceased's relatives and friends and on information from a physician or psychologist under whose care the victim may have been. Instances in which the individual had a history of suicide threats or suicidal tendencies are, of course, significant to the investigation. A careful and thorough search for a suicide note at the crime scene, as well as at the victim's residence and workplace, is particularly important. Although such notes are frequently found in plain view, usually near the body, the note may have been written earlier and left in another location. In some instances, several notes have been written and placed around the house or even mailed to friends or relatives. It may be considered necessary to verify the authenticity of a suicide note. Specialist resources available include document examiners, who can examine the writing (if the note is handwritten) and possibly a forensic linguist, who can compare the content with other compositions of the deceased. Both approaches may be restricted unless there is a lot of writing on the note. The investigator should collect known handwriting exemplars for this purpose and search for the writing instrument and paper used. The document and envelope should also be examined for latent fingerprints and DNA. In most jurisdictions, the police investigators will retain custody of the suicide note.

Motives for suicide should be considered. A terminal illness may prompt an individual to take his life, so the investigator should gather information from the deceased's physician, prescriptions, medical records, etc. Poor financial situations may also be a cause, so an investigation of the person's finances and debts should be undertaken. Other motives such as marital or family problems, high stress, and psychological problems must also be investigated. Bullying has also driven young people to commit suicide in recent years. Investigating a young person's social standing at their school and interviewing teachers and classmates should be done if the suicide victim is a student.

In cases of mental disorder, it is not uncommon that killing family members precedes the suicide. These cases must be investigated as thoroughly as other homicides. If the killer in such an instance survives an attempted suicide, it will be necessary to produce evidence about the mental state of the defendant. Psychiatric evaluation of the defendant may be considerably influenced by the findings at the crime scene. Even if the suicide victim does not survive, the investigation must be conducted with care. Inheritance and insurance matters will be influenced by the order in which the victims died.

Cases of suicide in which none of the commonly accepted motivations is apparent (even after some investigation) do occur. The opinions of relatives or friends of the deceased who are reluctant to accept the fact of suicide should not unduly influence the investigator. In many cases, the motivations for suicide are so deeply hidden that they may remain a mystery forever.

16.2.3 Murder

16.2.3.1 Signs of a Struggle

If obvious signs of a struggle are found at the scene of a death, the case may be considered from the start to be one of death by violence by the action of another person. In a room, the signs of a struggle generally consist of bloodstains, pulled-out hair, overturned or displaced articles of furniture, rumpled rugs, marks of weapons, and injuries caused by the deceased in self-defence. Signs of a struggle show most clearly when an injured victim retreated or when an attempt was made to avoid the attack. From the visible signs, the course of events can usually be reconstructed accurately. If the struggle involved stabbing, beating, or shooting, there should be blood at the scene. Bloodstains can therefore be considered the best clues for reconstructing the course of events in these cases. Generally, no bloodstains are produced during the first stage of the attack, before any bleeding has commenced. If victims do not immediately become unconscious at the first blow, stab, cut, or shot, it can nearly always be assumed that their hands will become covered with blood from touching the injured parts of their body. If victims attempt to escape or resist, their blood-covered hands leave marks that often indicate their position in certain situations. After a struggle in a furnished room, a surprisingly large number of marks of bloodstained hands may be found on the legs of tables and chairs. A frequently occurring bloodstain is the typical one that comes from bloody hair. Bloody hair imprints are often found on the underside of tables and chairs.

Pulled-out hair found in a case of death from violence is a certain indication that a struggle has occurred. When found, such hairs should be collected immediately because they can easily disappear or their position can be altered (e.g., due to a draught).

Those who examine the scene of a crime should look very carefully for bloody prints on doors (and especially keys, door handles, and knobs), telephones, hung-up clothes, draperies, curtains, and the like. If blood has spattered on a door, it is not sufficient to state on which side; it is necessary to consider the position of the door when the blood was spattered against it, and from what direction it came. Drops of spattered blood can indicate how far a drawer was pulled out or whether the door of a closet, kitchen cupboard, or other piece of furniture was open during a struggle. An especially important clue is a footprint in blood. Sometimes such a print is blurred and hardly suitable for identification, but it may be possible to determine whether it was made by the victim or the criminal. One should not forget to pull down any window shades to look for marks on them. The parts of the legs of tables and chairs that touch the floor should also be examined. Any voids or areas that show an absence of blood can be important clues.

Overturned and displaced furniture gives a good idea of the direction in which a struggle moved or the route by which the victim attempted to escape. Chairs, pedestals, lamps, and other light pieces of furniture fall in the direction in which the struggling persons are moving. If there is reason to suspect that a criminal has righted overturned furniture, the articles should be examined for possible fingerprints or touch DNA. When a print is found on a light piece of furniture, its position should be examined carefully; for example, a firm grip on a chair may give rise to the suspicion that the chair was used as a weapon. When heavy furniture has been displaced, the amount of force required and the way in which this force acted should be determined. Furniture placed irregularly often gives the impression that it has been displaced from its position. Marks of scraping indicate displacement, and the floor generally shows clearly whether furniture has stood in the same place previously. Rumpled rugs often provide signs of a struggle, and sliding marks on the floor can sometimes serve as a useful guide (Figure 16.2).

Murder victims lying in a position of self-defence may kick against a wall, the floor, or furniture, and their shoes will leave marks of shoe polish, dirt, or rubber scraping. Such marks should also be looked for on the undersides of furniture. Marks of weapons may also be found, such as when an axe or similar weapon is swung and scrapes the ceiling or slips along a piece of furniture, or when the victim avoids a blow and the weapon hits the wall,

Figure 16.2 Bloodstain pattern caused by dragging a body through blood. (Photograph courtesy of Bloodstain Pattern Analysis Workshop, Cedar Crest College Forensic Science Training Institute, Allentown, PA.)

Figure 16.3 Footwear impression in mud found in the woods far from the road at this outdoor crime scene. A good-quality photograph using oblique lighting, as seen here, can help the examiner compare imperfections seen in the impression to the questioned shoe. (Photograph courtesy of Los Angeles County Sheriff's Department, Los Angeles, CA.)

floor, or furniture instead. A bloodstained weapon may also leave cast-off stain patterns on the ceiling or walls or passive blood drops on the floor where blood dripped off the weapon. It could also produce a transfer stain where it was laid down or dropped.

Defence injuries are a fairly certain indication that a fight has taken place. In cases of suicide and accidental death, marks are often found that at first sight appear to be marks of a struggle. Persons weary of life may have taken a number of measures at various places to shorten their life. In a state of confusion, the individual may overturn or move furniture and also leave blood and other marks that at first raise suspicion. A careful investigation of the scene, however, can give a more clear picture of the true course of events.

In cases of death by violence outdoors, signs of a struggle are in general not as distinct as those indoors. If a fight preceded the murder, the ground will be trampled (Figure 16.3). When footmarks made with shoes of different sizes and appearances are found or if the marks have the form that results from feet set down obliquely against the ground, these marks must be considered to be evidence of a fight.

At the scene of a suicide, especially in a case of hanging, the ground may be trampled, but as a rule the marks have the normal appearance of those of a person walking. Other signs of a struggle outdoors may be bloodstains, pulled-out tufts of hair, marks of weapons, and resistance injuries. Broken twigs, trampled leaves, torn-up moss and grass, footprints in places that a person would normally avoid, and other such indications can also be considered signs of a struggle.

16.2.3.2 Location of Weapon

In cases of violent death, the cause of death must be decided as soon as possible so a search for the weapon, tool, instrument, or other lethal object can be conducted. The absence of a weapon or instrument at the scene sometimes indicates murder. If the weapon or instrument has been found, then the analysis of the situation must give a preliminary decision as to whether it is a case of murder or suicide. When searching for a weapon, nothing should be moved or altered at the scene of the incident; if evidence may be destroyed in the search, the search must be postponed. If the weapon is found, it should be photographed and the position in which it was found described. The pathologist who was present at the scene and who conducted the postmortem examination should be consulted when it is necessary to determine would kind of object or weapon could have caused the injuries found on the victim.

16.2.3.3 *Examination of a Dead Body at the Crime Scene*

16.2.3.3.1 Preliminary Examination by the First Office Attending and the Crime Scene Investigator Before any preliminary or detailed examination is conducted, a common approach path should be identified, cleared, and marked, and the preliminary scene perimeter should be identified and protected. The FOA should now consider all the precautions to be taken during the course of the examination. A careless move—even one so slight as undoing a button or lifting a flap of a garment—may subsequently prove to be a great mistake. An example is on record of a police officer who, in misdirected zeal, proceeded so far with the examination of a dead body that an attempt was made to determine the track of a bullet and depth it had penetrated into the body by probing the wound with a pencil. Such measures are entirely misguided.

The overall condition of clothing worn by the deceased should be described in the report, including, among other matters, how clothes are buttoned, attached, creased or wrinkled, marked by injuries and stains, and so on. More detailed examination of the clothing should be conducted only after it has been removed at the postmortem examination. Any marks, cuts, or tears made by paramedics during lifesaving measures should also be noted. Discarded gloves, gauze, bandages, and other medical equipment left at the scene by paramedics should not be confused with actual evidence. When necessary, paramedics should be asked to provide fingerprint or DNA samples for elimination purposes. Discarded medical paraphernalia should be collected for further examination, as it may hold evidence, such as blood or DNA from the perpetrator, that has been transferred from the dead body.

The position of the clothes may be of great importance, such as how far the pants are pulled up or whether garments are twisted sideways, pulled down, backward, or even inside-out. Any displacement from the normal position should be measured. Buttons and other fastenings (e.g., zippers, safety pins, casings) should be described, including unbuttoned or torn-off buttons and buttonholes. Shirts should be checked to determine if they button right to left or left to right. Sometimes men wear women's clothes and vice versa.

Folds in the clothes should be examined, especially on the lower parts of the body. The report should indicate whether the folds go horizontally or vertically and if they have resulted from crumpling of the garment. When a body is dragged, horizontal creases occur that are dirty on the outside but clean in the folds. When a body is lifted or moved by a grip on the clothing, characteristic formations are produced. If the raised part of a fold is bloodstained but the inner part is free from blood, then the position of a part of the body when violence was exerted can be determined. If a garment is bloodstained and sharply delineated clean areas are on the inside of the bloodstain, then the fold formation can be reconstructed.

Damage to the clothes occurs from tearing, crushing, cutting, or penetration by edged weapons, axe blows, etc. The damage should be measured, and the report should contain statements of the type, position, size, and manner of occurrence of the damage. In some cases, damage to the clothes should be compared during the autopsy with the position of corresponding wounds on the body. In this way, important information can be obtained regarding a particular body position when the injury was inflicted. Mannequins can also be used for this purpose to examine trajectory and other reconstruction scenarios.

Stains may consist of blood, semen, saliva, phlegm, vomit, faeces, urine, or other liquid, as well as dust, dirt, or other contamination. Stains are described with reference to type, location, size, degree of wetness, and, when relevant, direction of flow. If liquid stains go through clothing material, it is necessary to determine from which side the liquid has penetrated. Important information can be obtained from blood, saliva, phlegm, vomit, urine, or other liquid stains on a dead body if the direction of flow is observed. Especially, streams of blood can contribute to the reconstruction of events in a case of death by violence. All marks of blood flowing "in the wrong direction" or against gravity are examined and photographed. These suggest that the position of the body was moved.

When describing blood marks on a dead body or crime scene, some of the terms generally used are *bloodstain*, *swipe*, *wipe*, *spatter*, *drip stain*, *expired blood* (that is, blood that has been coughed up), *parent stain*, *satellite stain*, and *insect stain*, among others. Here, again, a team approach is vital, and everyone involved in the case should have the same understanding of the meaning of the terms used.

A special form of bloodstain is expired blood. When a person continues to breathe or cough after blood has entered the air passages, expiration patterns can be found. These sometimes contain air bubbles in them and look similar to other spatter patterns. The presence of air bubbles does not always indicate that the blood has been expired, as air bubbles can also result from a transfer stain. Investigators should be very careful about not overstating opinions resulting from bloodstain pattern analysis.

Occasionally, a case of murder occurs in which the criminal wipes or washes the blood away from the victim. Such cleaning is generally easy to detect, especially when the skin is clean around the wound. Washing or wiping the hands generally leaves a thin rim of blood on the nails near the cuticles. When the blood has coagulated, small rolls of blood and dirt are often formed that penetrate cracks and hollows of the skin. If blood has been washed from the head, this fact is often easily detected by the traces of blood that remain in ears, nostrils, and hair. Moisture around the body may also reveal washing.

In connection with the occurrence of blood at the scene of a crime, some attempt should always be made to estimate the amount. If blood has flowed out onto an absorbing layer, the depth of penetration should be determined. Floorboards should be lifted, carpet rolled back, etc. (Figure 16.4).

Figure 16.4 Blood revealed under the linoleum floor at a crime scene. (Photograph courtesy of Wendy van Hilst, Forensische Opsporing Amsterdam–Amstelland, Amsterdam, Holland.)

Case 1

A woman was found lying dead outdoors, with her head partly shattered by a number of axe blows, and it could be assumed that most of the blood had been lost from the body. Under the head of the dead woman only a small amount of blood, possibly 250 mL, was found. From this it was apparent that the woman had not been murdered at the place where she was discovered. On further investigation, the majority of the woman's lost blood was found about a quarter of a mile away from the body. The woman had been murdered there, at the primary crime scene, and her body had then been transported to the secondary scene, where it was found. If the small amount of blood at the place where the body was found had not been noticed, it is possible that that place would have been considered the scene of the crime and investigated as such, while the actual primary scene of the crime would never have been known. Investigation of the latter produced evidence against a local suspect who later confessed to the crime.

16.2.3.3.2 Preliminary Examination by the Pathologist and the Crime Scene Investigator   When examining a dead body, it is generally possible to take the necessary steps in a certain order, which is a guarantee that nothing will be forgotten or neglected. The various steps in an investigation when a pathologist is present are described next. If the pathologist or medicolegal investigator does not arrive in time, the investigation is carried out in the same way, but the crime scene investigator's moves must be recorded so that evidence that only a medical expert is capable of judging and investigating is protected as much as possible. The first measure that should be taken without delay is to confirm the appearance of signs of certain death, of which the type and development and the time of their confirmation should be noted in the report. This is sometimes performed by paramedics if they are on the scene when they fail to revive the victim. The body is then photographed. Preferably, all photography should be completed before the position of the body is altered. If for some reason a change has been made after the body was discovered, such as when relatives cover the body or emergency personnel perform lifesaving measures, the actual position should be photographed first, and then the original position should be reconstructed and photographed. The camera should be held in readiness for additional pictures during the course of the examination. In addition to digital photographs, various types of digital panoramic imagery should also be utilized to accurately document, measure, and map the crime scene. These types of systems can be beneficial to quickly and accurately document the crime scene and create a permanent record that can be referred to days, months, or years after the incident. The scans also serve as excellent courtroom exhibits for juries to show how the crime scene appeared.

A preliminary investigation of the pockets of the dead person may precede the more detailed investigation only when it is considered absolutely necessary. This is to be avoided if possible, but it may be necessary to confirm quickly whether there are any identification documents, wallet, purse, watch, or other valuable articles in the pockets. This examination must be done so carefully that the original position of the clothes can easily be restored later. It should be noted whether the pockets are turned inside out, as this may reveal that they have been previously gone through, possibly by the perpetrator. A sketch of the position of the body is then made. The body's position in relation to the nearest article of furniture, object, or fixed point is measured and noted, and then the visible clothing is described. The next step is the detailed examination, during which only visible details are examined and described. The original position must not be changed. It is preferable to describe the head, then the trunk, arms, and finally the legs.

The head is described and examined in relation to its position with respect to the body, whether the eyes and mouth are open, colour of the skin, injuries, presence of blood, state of the hair, and presence of saliva, phlegm, vomit, or foreign bodies (e.g., soil, sand, vegetable matter, hair). The direction of flow of liquids is easily determined on the skin of the face and should be noted. In examining the trunk, notes should be made of its position, any bending or twisting, the position of visible clothing and condition, folds, injuries to the body and clothes, and presence of blood, saliva, semen, phlegm, vomit, or foreign bodies (especially hair). The arms and, finally, the legs are then examined in the same way as the trunk. The hands should be given special attention. The presence of rings, jewellery, or a wristwatch or marks left by these objects should be noted. Foreign objects are examined, especially fragments of hair or skin under the nails. The hands should be enclosed in clean paper bags tied securely at the wrists. Collection of fingernail scrapings or clippings should be taken during autopsy. When examining the legs, the distance between the knees and the distance between the heels should be measured. Special attention should be given to the soles of the feet or shoes with respect to the presence of blood or other material in which the person may have stepped. After reviewing these preliminary findings, it may be necessary to reconsider the hypothesis of what happened and review not only the perimeter placement but perhaps also whether there are any indications that another scene may be involved.

The underside of the body and those portions covered by clothes should not be examined at the scene, unless it is done in the presence and at the request of the pathologist. Normally, the body will not be turned over or undressed until the time of the autopsy; however, after the body has been photographed and described in all pertinent detail and has been lifted onto a stretcher, the area under the body should be examined. A critical piece of evidence may have been hidden under the body, perhaps in a large pool of blood. Bullets, or fragments of bullets, sometimes penetrate a body completely but are stopped by clothing. The projectile may thus roll out of the clothing of the victim and may even be overlooked, unless great care is exercised in lifting and transporting. The relationship between the location of injuries and bloodstains on the floor should also be established.

The body should be transported in the position in which it was found, if possible. If necessary, the clothing can be fixed in its original position by means of pins. In some cases, the body should be moved on a clean sheet of cotton or plastic, body bag, or on an undertaker's impregnated paper sheet. This is partly to protect the body from contamination and partly to prevent minute evidence from being lost. An officer should accompany the body to the place where the autopsy is to take place.

16.2.4   Accident

Any death that cannot be ascribed to natural causes has to be treated as suspicious. So far, we have discussed the two main circumstances that would be investigated by a crime scene investigator: suicide and murder. Many deaths are dues to accidents, though, and the crime scene investigator must be able to recognise these and differentiate them from murder or suicide. There are occasions where this is difficult to do—for example, a murder or suicide carefully staged to appear accidental. On the other hand, occasionally an accidental death raises suspicion. The position of the body, injuries, and appearance of the crime scene can

Figure 16.5 The unusual position of the body at this scene resulted from the woman experiencing a heart attack after stepping from her bathtub. (Photograph courtesy of Western Maryland Regional Crime Lab, Hagerstown, MD.)

all lead investigators into thinking that the accidental death was a homicide. It is always better for an accidental death to be investigated as a homicide than the reverse. Figure 16.5 illustrates such a case, where investigation showed that the unusual position of the body at the scene resulted from the deceased experiencing a heart attack after stepping from her bathtub. Accidental death from sexual asphyxiation is another example.

Some of the more straightforward examples of accidental deaths are those arising from shooting and from drowning. Someone can be shot fatally by accident or through personal fault. During hunting, it is possible to slip or stumble on awkward ground, fall when climbing over a gate or other obstacle, or drop the weapon, whereupon a fatal shot may be fired. In such cases, marks at the scene of the accident or marks on the weapon usually give a clear indication of what has happened. A fatal shot may also be fired accidentally when handling a firearm, such as when cleaning it. In such cases, the investigating officer should observe the greatest caution and not assume from the start that it was an accident. The victim may very well have committed suicide while giving the incident the appearance of an accident or a murderer may have simulated an accident.

Careful attention must be given to those cases that appear to be hiking, mountain climbing, or camping accidents. These may be the result of an attempt to cover up criminal assault or robbery. Lone hikers or naturalists can be easy prey for criminal attacks. Special attention must be paid to the absence of valuables, minor bruises from subduing blows, and evidence of soil or vegetation not found in the immediate vicinity.

16.3   Detailed Examination of the Scene

16.3.1   General Approach

This discussion will proceed in general terms as described in Chapter 3 and for the specific case in Chapter 4. What follows here is more detailed guidance for the crime scene investigator covering the wider range of circumstances that may be met in death investigation scenes. When the preliminary examination of the body at the scene has been concluded, including all photography, it can generally be removed for the autopsy. Care must be taken that the team responsible for transport of the body use the cleared approach path, and that no evidence is lost or compromised during the removal. Even if the body is wrapped up well, drops of blood may fall from it as a result of unforeseen circumstances. Such marks can cause much unnecessary work for the investigators later. Those who carry away the body should be warned not to step in any blood.

After removal of the body and completion of the preliminary review by the crime scene coordinator, the strategy for the detailed scene investigation will be developed. How thoroughly this is to be done must be decided for each particular case; for example, it may be determined that the scene should be locked off until the autopsy is completed. In suicide or accidental death, it can be limited simply to those matters that appear to be directly related to events. If the death is caused by the intent or action of another person, every-thing should be investigated, even in cases where the criminal has been arrested immediately after the crime and has confessed, because there have been cases where confessions have been retracted or disallowed in court. In such cases, the investigation should decide whether the statements of the criminal are consistent. In a first statement, a criminal often makes consciously incorrect statements about personal actions in order to create extenuating circumstances. Those who investigate the scene of a crime have an opportunity to produce such an accurate reconstruction of the actual course of events that such an attempt by the criminal cannot succeed.

Case 2

Near midnight one summer's evening in Malta, police were called by a man to report that he had been held up in his car on a remote country road by an armed robber, who had shot his wife and himself. Police and ambulance arrived to find the wife dead from a gunshot wound to the right temple, and the husband weak and bleeding from a wound to his upper left arm. The police took a statement from the man and then he was rushed to the hospital. The investigators were curious about how the woman had come to be shot in the right temple (cars in Malta are right-hand drive), as the husband had stated that the gunman had shot her from the passenger door. They went to the hospital the next day to interview him again. This time his story was a little different and provided a possible explanation, but the suspicion of the investigators was aroused. They made inquiries and discovered that a few months earlier the brakes on the car had apparently failed when it was parked on a hill, and it had run down the hill into the sea with the wife held inside by her seatbelt.

The car was now a crime scene of a different sort, with the husband as the prime suspect. Crime scene investigators scrutinised the interior for any evidence that would falsify the husband's version of events. Fine blood spatters were found in the interior, with two separate points of origin. One set, that typed the same as the wife, originated just above the gear shift, and the other, that typed the same as the husband, originated from a point at about the position of the left shoulder of someone sitting in the driver's seat. The reconstruction included consideration of cartridge cases found in the folds of the wife's skirt and the floor of the car and resulted in a report that the husband had pulled his wife down and toward himself and then shot her in the head. He then shot himself in the arm and discarded the gun. He was found guilty of murder.

An interesting aspect of this case is the way in which trials are conducted in Malta. After cross-examination is complete, the judge invites the jury to question the witness. Several members asked about the reconstruction, and it was obvious that this provided them with the opportunity to clarify in their own minds how it had been conducted and interpreted.

The strategy for investigation identifies places within the overall scene where it is most likely that anything of significance might be expected to be found. These areas are examined first, following a methodically planned examination using one of the search patterns described in Chapter 3. If the body is found in a house, for example, it may be convenient to examine and describe the entrance, doors, and lock arrangements using a wheel pattern, followed by a description of the room as a whole, perhaps using lanes. Window and door dimensions, height of the ceiling, floor coverings, paint on walls and ceilings, colour of wallpaper, lighting conditions, and other features should be noted. Next, the room is described in detail and investigated in a certain order beginning from the entrance or from the place of death. Everything must be examined and described as a coherent whole. If a writing desk is examined, for example, then nearby parts of the floor and walls as well as the surface of the floor under the piece of furniture should be described. As a rule, it is best for the ceiling to be described and examined last and as a whole. If for some reason, a place has been examined in detail and described earlier, then a reference to it is put in the notes to facilitate writing of the final report.

In the investigation everything is noted, even if it appears to have no significance in the case. Such unessential details are sorted out when the report is written, as are details that appeared to be important at first but were later found to be immaterial. The notes made at the scene of a crime must not under any circumstances be thrown away but should be placed in the file and kept with the records. Experience shows that such rough notes may be of great importance at some future date if the investigator is required to prove that the examination of certain details was not omitted. It is convenient to develop and preserve fingerprints and palm prints at the same time as the final detailed investigation.

The positions of items should be recorded before they are moved or collected. If something is moved for any reason, that reason should be recorded and the item returned to its original position. When furniture is moved, it should be replaced with the greatest accuracy because the scene must be in its original state in case the suspect or witnesses are returned to the scene for questioning. Before any furniture is moved, a mark should be made around the legs or other suitable parts. Objects placed on furniture can be treated similarly.

A final important step after sketching the scene of the crime is measurement. It is desirable to do this earlier, but this may not have been possible because of a risk that those doing the measuring might destroy evidence not yet discovered or produce fresh and misleading clues. One approach is to make a preliminary sketch as early as possible. Gradually, as the investigation proceeds and before each object is moved, measurements can be made and recorded on the sketch. This method is somewhat inconvenient, however, because the measuring cannot be done as systematically as is desirable. Under such conditions, even experienced sketchers can easily forget important measurements. Laser scanners and software programs are excellent tools that can record measurements quickly and accurately. The scanners rotate 360 degrees, capturing thousands of laser data points that can be easily fashioned into a three-dimensional model (see Figure 16.6 for an example).

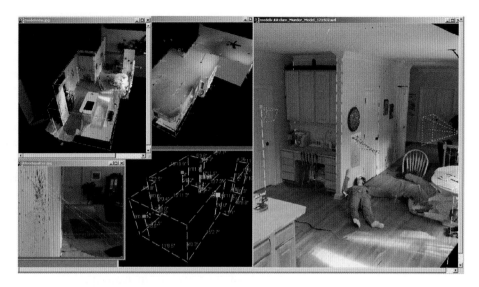

Figure 16.6 Three-dimensional models and measurements of a mock crime scene. (Photographs courtesy of DeltaSphere, Durham, NC; http://www.deltasphere.com/.)

When there has been a shooting at the scene of the crime, it is necessary to look for weapons, cartridges, cartridge cases, and bullets. If a weapon is found, it is photographed at that spot, and a chalk line is drawn around it before it is moved. The weapon should always be made safe before sending it to the lab. In cases of presumed suicide, it is necessary to check whether the weapon lies in a place to which it might have dropped or slid. The base on which the weapon lies should always be examined. A dropped or thrown weapon generally leaves a mark, such as a scratch or dent in the furniture or floor, and the absence of such marks should be considered suspicious.

When cartridge cases are found, their position should be noted in the report, on the sketch, and on the envelope into which they are then placed. Bullets and bullet holes are examined. The direction from which the shot was fired can be determined quite accurately from the direction of the bullet penetration, and a string can be stretched along the calculated path of the bullet (see Chapter 4). Lasers and dowels can also be used. The reconstruction is then photographed. Figure 16.7 illustrates the use of sequential image burning

Figure 16.7 Using sequential image burning to demonstrate the path of a laser in a mock trajectory reconstruction (with appreciation to Brian Gestring for demonstrating this technique).

to demonstrate the path of a laser in a mock trajectory reconstruction. A bullet that has buried itself in a wall must be cut out, but great care should be taken to prevent the tool from touching the bullet. In cases of suicide, the shooter may fire one or more trial shots before firing the actual suicide shot. Chemical tests can also be performed to see if the suicide victim was actually the one holding the gun.

Case 3

During a search for a young successful model and her boyfriend, the police arrived at a Jerusalem apartment where they had been living. The door was locked and the telephone went unanswered. The boyfriend's brother forced entry through a porch door and let the police in. Inside they found the dead bodies of the couple. A loaded gun was found next to the girl's right hand. Her index finger was clutching the hammer of the gun (Figure 16.8(a)). The man had two bullet holes in his chest, both fired from close range. The girl had one bullet entry wound in the lower section of her left breast and an exit wound on the right side of her back. In his preliminary assessment, the medical examiner assumed that before committing suicide the woman killed her

Figure 16.8 Photographs of the scene. (Photographs courtesy of Division of Identification and Forensic Science, Israel National Police.)

boyfriend, since he had been shot twice with heavy-calibre bullets, and the gun was found next to her. This was also the message released to the media. After the medical team completed their examinations, Ferrotrace (manufactured by Ezra Technology, Jerusalem, Israel) was applied to the hands of the two bodies. The appearance of a violet–magenta stain on the hand indicates a chemical reaction between the reagent and iron found on the gun.

The reaction on the woman's index finger was exceptionally strong, and its shape matched the upper back of the gun's hammer. There was one puzzling question, however, which had to be answered. The reaction on the finger that touched the gun was very intense, but there was no reaction on the palm of the hand (Figure 16.8(b)–(d)). The absence of a palm reaction raised the suspicion that the woman never really held the gun, and that it had been placed near her hand only after her death. Ferrotrace examination of the boyfriend's right hand indicated that he held the gun both in the regular position (typical of shooting) and in reverse position (typical of suicide, with the thumb on the trigger, and the index and middle fingers on the safety) (Figure 16.8(e)). The fact that there were two bullet holes in the man's chest and only one in his girlfriend's did not change the police's conclusion that it was he who shot the girl, then committed suicide. Multiple shots as part of suicide are a known phenomenon when the first shot is not immediately fatal. The primary suspect in moving the gun was the boyfriend's brother, who had helped the police enter the apartment.

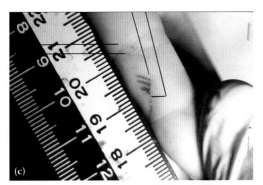

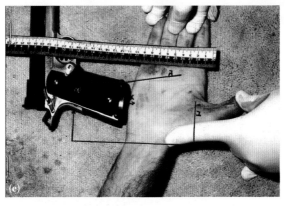

Figure 16.8 (cont.) Photographs of the scene. (Photographs courtesy of Division of Identification and Forensic Science, Israel National Police.)

16.3.2   Specific Areas and Items

The following is a list of certain details that should be included in the detailed examination of the scene where appropriate:

- *Stairs, passages, and entries to the scene, together with streets, passages, and yards in the immediate vicinity*—Are there bloodstains, footwear marks, or fingerprints on railings? Mirrors can be used to help locate these on the underside of railings. Are objects present that the criminal has dropped or thrown away? Is there illumination? Do trash cans contain evidence? Is there an elevator? If so, the elevator shaft should be examined. Is video surveillance footage available? If so, it should be reviewed to determine possible probative pieces of evidence the suspect might have handled.
- *Outer doors*—Are they bolted and/or locked? Are there marks of breaking in? Does the doorbell work?
- *Windows*—Are they bolted? What is the position of the window catch? Are there marks of breaking in or a possibility of seeing in? What are the positions of curtains and blinds? Are there indications of marks outside the windows?
- *Unopened mail*—What is the date on mail or papers? Are the pieces of mail in the right order of time?
- *Other documents, newspapers, etc. at the scene of the crime*—Are there date marks? Have letters been opened? Do papers give the impression of having been read?
- *Inside doors*—Are they bolted or locked? On which side is the key?
- *Hall, entrance*—Are clothing and objects present that do not belong to the place and residents there, especially outer garments, headgear, scarves, gloves, galoshes, umbrellas?
- *Lighting*—Which lamps were on when the crime was discovered? What are the electric meter readings?
- *Television, stereos, MP3 players*—Have they been left on or off? Where are they?
- *Heating conditions*—Is there a fire or any embers in fireplaces or any remaining heat? Do not forget to examine ash and burned residues and the setting on the thermostat.
- *Cooking conditions*—Is the oven or stove on or is there any remaining heat? Was food or drink preparation in progress? In what condition is the food in the refrigerator?
- *Odours*—Gas? Gunpowder? Strong tobacco fumes? Alcohol? Perfume? Decomposition?
- *Clocks and watches*—Are they running and showing the right time? When did they stop? Is there a time set on the alarm clock? What are the time stamps of e-mails sent or received?
- *Signs of a party*—How many bottles are present? Are there labels on them? What are their actual contents? Are seals or corks on or in the bottles? How many glasses or cups of different kinds are present? What are their contents? Is there a residue or odour in them? Has liquor been spilled or objects overturned? Have cigarette butts and match sticks been thrown on the table or floor? How many persons was the table set for and with what dishes? Are there any fingerprints? Are the beverage containers suitable for DNA testing?

- *Contents of ashtrays*—Are there remains of smoked tobacco or brand marks on cigarette butts? How were they extinguished? Are there lipstick marks? Burned matches? Are there signs that more than one person had smoked (e.g., different makes of cigarettes)? Remember that DNA and fingerprints may be present on cigarette butts.
- *Drawers and compartments in writing desks, cabinets, or other furniture*—Are they shut and locked? In which drawer is the key? Have drawers been pulled out or taken away or have objects been taken out of them? Are there signs of disorder such as might result from a hurried search? Are cash, bank books, and objects of value exposed in a conspicuous or easily detected place?
- *Wastepaper baskets, trash cans*—Has any object been thrown there by the criminal or anyone else that may provide evidence? Are there torn letters? Did the perpetrator throw out any latex gloves he might have been wearing?
- *Kitchen, bathroom, toilet*—Are towels, rags, or like objects dry or damp? Do they show bloodstains? Are there bloodstains on a counter, bath, sink, toilet, or bucket? Are there objects or suspicious liquids in the water trap or toilet? Are there fingerprints on used paper? Is there evidence that the perpetrator tried to clean up? Is there any other material that may produce evidence, such as soil on the floor?
- *Damage to ceiling, walls, and furniture*—How could the damage have occurred, particularly in connection with the crime? Marks of plaster or paint soon disappear from the floor due to trampling.
- *Garments taken off*—At what places and in what order, beginning from the top, were they taken off? Are they turned right side out or inside out? Are they properly hung up or in disorder? Are there clothes in the washing machine? Hamper?
- *General disorder*—Is this disorder typical of a violent act or a struggle? Could it be the result of a lack of cleaning up over a long period? Could it simply be the result of carrying out some ordinary household activities?
- *Shooting*—The investigating officer should be able to account for the actual number of bullets fired, as well as the corresponding number of cartridge cases, or should be able to give a good explanation of why they are not found or cannot be found in the correct number. Consider the possibility of a cartridge case getting caught up in the clothes of the dead person and not being found before the autopsy. Also, the absence of a cartridge case could indicate that a revolver was used. Cartridge cases may also be moved or removed by being stepped on and could be present in the soles of shoes worn by the notifier, witnesses, or police and emergency service personnel.
- *Hanging and strangling*—Was the cord used taken from the scene or locality?
- *Suicide note*—Is it in the handwriting of the victim? Has the writing instrument been found? Has indented writing come through onto the paper underneath? Is there more than one note? Are there fingerprints or DNA of persons other than the deceased on the note?
- *Hiding places for weapons or objects that the criminal wished to conceal quickly*—Some of the places most often overlooked by investigating police officers are locations above appliances and high furniture or between these and the wall, behind books in a bookcase, among bedclothes in a bed, behind heating elements, and on high shelves in wardrobes, pantries, or kitchen cupboards. Ordinary items with false bottoms (e.g., cans, books) are sold in spy shops and should also be considered.
- *Compost heaps, manure heaps*—These are very convenient for concealing objects without distinct signs of digging.

In cases of serious crime, when the crime scene investigation has been concluded, the scene of the crime should be kept intact until the final report has been written and read through by the superior officer and the prosecutor, until recovered evidence has been examined, and until the postmortem examination has been completed. It is not uncommon for a second or third visit to the crime scene to be made in order to collect additional evidence. When material recovered for examination has value as evidence, it should be preserved even after the criminal has been tried. There may be a review of the case, perhaps several years or decades later, and the evidence may then have to be produced.

16.3.3 Outdoor Crime Scenes

The examination of a crime scene located outdoors was discussed in Chapter 3 and illustrated in Chapter 4. The basic principles of planning and protection must be observed at all times, no matter how apparently simple or complex the scene. Changes in weather conditions have to be considered, as they can jeopardise the chances of finding evidence that is there (see Chapter 4). A number of different clues that may be easily detected at first could disappear in a very short time due to, for example, precipitation, drying, vegetation, flood conditions, and animals. It is even more difficult to examine such a scene at night. Identification of decomposed remains requires techniques such as forensic odontology, forensic anthropology, and DNA typing. The victim shown in Figure 16.9 was murdered and dumped in Los Angeles County's high desert, where animals consumed facial tissue and hands.

Because bloodstains on grass change colour rapidly, they are difficult to detect. A brief shower may completely wash away smaller stains. Other biological evidence, such as hair, seminal fluid, urine, faeces, vomit, saliva, nasal secretions, skin fragments, brain substance, and so on, is quickly changed by drying or may be washed away. (See also Chapter 13 for advice on how to deal with these situations, particularly Figure 13.8.) During the

Figure 16.9 This victim was murdered and dumped in Los Angeles County's high desert, where animals consumed facial tissue and hands. (Photograph courtesy of Los Angeles County Sheriff's Department, Los Angeles, CA.)

time of year when insects are especially plentiful, biological evidence may be destroyed by their action. The path of a person through dewy grass may be discernible to the naked eye, but after an hour or so of direct sunlight the dew has dried and the grass has recovered its original shape. It may subsequently take hours to follow the track. Footprints and tyre marks should be protected and recorded as soon as possible.

When a shooting has taken place outdoors, the direction of firing must be determined quickly. Fresh twigs and leaves that have fallen to the ground usually mark a bullet's path through foliage, bushes, or hedges. After a few hours, these traces may take on the appearance of the surroundings. Evidence of a bullet striking the ground is usually found in the form of dirt or sand thrown over the surrounding vegetation. A passing shower may wash off these traces and make the location of the impact impossible to determine. Cartridge cases may be trampled into the ground. Detector dogs can be used to conduct the first search, after which a metal detector might then be the only way to find such evidence.

In cases of suspicious death, the crime scene coordinator can anticipate that the person, or persons, who discovered the body did not enter the scene with caution—which is to be expected. One of the first duties of the crime scene investigator is therefore to find out where those persons walked. The record of many cases indicates that clues created by these citizens have caused a tremendous amount of unnecessary work that could have been avoided if the person had been properly interviewed.

Case 4*

On a winter day, a man called the police to report the discovery of an apparently deceased female behind his neighbour's residence. He informed the emergency services operator that after noticing the body he had proceeded behind the house to confirm his observation. When the officer arrived at the scene, he was met by the notifier at the front of his house. The neighbour repeated that he had walked around the right side of the home (as viewed from the front) to view the body and returned by the same route. The officer and the caller then proceeded around the right side of the home to view the body together.

When other police officers arrived at the scene, the responding officer had secured the entire scene for protection. He had observed that fresh, undisturbed snow was located to the left and right prior to them walking around the home. The scene was processed with one key piece of evidence in mind: There were only four sets of tracks when there should have been six. The caller had already locked himself multiple times into his story of proceeding around the residence to double check on the status of the body, thus arousing suspicion.

During the processing of the scene, CSI personnel discovered additional tracks leading away from the decedent. These tracks did not lead to the front of the house but to the neighbour's backyard through an opening in the fence. Because the caller was now the main suspect he was placed under surveillance. Soon after, he was observed dumping several trash bags in a nearby dumpster. The forensic lab personnel were called and the bags were retrieved and determined to contain bloody clothing. There was then significant evidence to obtain an arrest warrant for the suspect.

---

* Case information provided by Suffolk County Crime Laboratory, New York.

Examining outdoor crime scenes at night should be avoided. This rule should be followed even when suitable illumination is available. Most clues at outdoor scenes consist of minor changes in the ground cover, such as matted grass, torn moss, broken twigs, and indistinct footprints. Such tracks may be visible from several yards away in daylight but are almost impossible to detect at night even with powerful illumination. When a scene is viewed at night and an estimate made of the topography, it might be found in daylight that the actual picture is quite different. Because it is difficult enough to survey the scene and correctly interpret even gross evidence, it follows that it is even more difficult to find evidence as small as bloodstains, fragments of cloth, and fibres at night. Such evidence may be overlooked or destroyed if a thorough examination is attempted in inadequately lit settings. In such cases, an officer should be placed at the scene to guard the scene overnight until a proper search can be conducted in the morning.

Before the arrival of daylight, certain precautions should be taken. Some flash exposures should be taken of the body. The body should then be covered with a clean sheet over which is laid a tarpaulin to keep out dust, leaves, and other debris. If the body is suspended, the noose may break, so it is advisable to secure the body with a rope tied loosely around the chest. If the body is on a shoreline, it should be lifted far enough onto the beach so that swells will not make changes on the body. When taking photographs and precautionary measures, officers should not walk around aimlessly. As described earlier, a path should be selected and marked with stakes. The investigator should, of course, make note of changes that may take place on the body, such as signs of death, moisture on the clothing and under the body, and so on.

16.3.4 Discovering a Body Hidden at Another Location

When a murder victim has been moved from the actual crime scene and hidden at another location, conditions are somewhat different. The examination of these secondary scenes must be as thorough as that of the primary scene, even though these scenes may not yield as much evidence as the place of attack. The question often arises as to how long the body has been lying at the place where it was found. The vegetation and other surrounding conditions may give some indications. The path over which the body was transported should be established at the outset. This detail should be attended to immediately, especially when there is risk of precipitation. If the criminal's footprints are not clear enough, the path should be estimated as being that most easily traversed if someone were carrying a body. Even when there are no footprints, other signs may be present, such as trampled grass, stains of dripping blood, marks from dragging, broken twigs, etc. If the criminal left the scene by another route, that path should also be examined at this time.

The body should be examined as described earlier in this chapter in Section 16.2.3.3, Examination of a Dead Body at the Crime Scene. Dust, dirt, and other traces on the skin and clothing that might fall off during transport should be recovered. A preliminary evaluation of such traces may suggest leads for the search for the actual scene. When removing the dead body from the place where it was found, it should be placed in a new body bag, clean plastic sheet, or bed sheet that is then wrapped around the body. Blankets and tarpaulins should not be used because one can never be sure that they are absolutely clean. Because it is difficult to properly examine and recover trace evidence on the body under such conditions, it should be transported intact to the place of autopsy where the detailed examination can take place.

16.3.5 Investigation of a Greatly Altered Body or Skeleton

Difficulties may arise in the identification of a dead body that has undergone such a great amount of alteration that only the skeletal parts remain. Important information can be obtained from a skeleton found whole or dismembered after a very long time or even after burning or other destruction of the body. Clothing or other objects found near the remains can also be used to help identify the deceased. Skeletal remains found in remote areas offer a special challenge to the investigator. In the case illustrated in Figure 16.10, absent anything more than part of the pelvis, leg bones, and shoes, a forensic anthropologist may only be able to provide the gender, height, and race of the victim. DNA typing can also help identify the remains through national DNA databases, particularly those that include a missing persons sub-database. Missing person reports and debris scattered in the vicinity of the remains can offer additional information.

Such bodies or their remains are most frequently discovered outdoors; occasionally, they are found indoors in a cellar, attic, basement, heating furnace, or other places. The remains may be those of a person who was murdered, was run over by a vehicle, committed suicide, was lost and became the victim of exhaustion or exposure, or was suddenly overcome by sickness and death.

If dismembered body parts are discovered, the investigation of the scene must be extended to cover a large area. In this case, it is quite normal for the parts of the body to be scattered over a number of places at some distance from one another. The same applies, however, to bodies that have not been dismembered because various animals and birds can drag the parts for a distance of up to several hundred yards from the original site.

From what has been said, it follows that the nature of the place where the discovery is made can vary considerably. Remains may be found under the ground or under a floor; they may be lying in the open, covered with brushwood, moss, sacks, and so forth, or

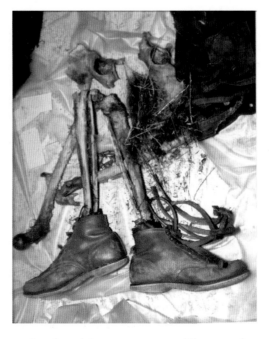

Figure 16.10 Skeletal remains found in remote area. (Photograph courtesy of Los Angeles County Sheriff's Department, Los Angeles, CA.)

Figure 16.11 A body was dumped in a wooded area. By the time it was discovered about 24 hours after the killing, animals had already attacked and eaten a significant amount of it. (Photograph courtesy of Los Angeles County Sheriff's Department, Los Angeles, CA.)

overgrown by vegetation. If the body was originally in the open outdoors, then the remains (both bones and clothing) will often be dispersed over a large area due to animals dragging them away. It is not uncommon for remains and objects with some connection to them to be found several hundred yards away from the main site. This also applies to parts of a dismembered or burned body that have been buried or left on the ground, because different parts may have been concealed or buried at different places, often far apart. Figure 16.11 shows a body that was dumped in a wooded area. By the time it was discovered about 24 hours after the killing, animals had already attacked and eaten a significant amount of it.

Foreign objects connected with the body or with transport of the body to the site (bags, sacks, cords, etc.), which possibly form the sole proof of a crime and may even indicate how to trace the criminal, may also be found near the remains. A number of cases have occurred in which a correctly performed and accurate investigation of the place of discovery, combined with careful technical and pathological investigation of the remains of the body and other related objects, has led to identification of the body. In order for the best result to be obtained, the investigating officer needs to have a good knowledge of the proper methods of investigation and preservation of the remains and objects and of the factors that affect distribution of the objects within a larger area.

The crime scene coordinator also needs to know the special methods used for further investigation of the discovery and how these methods can assist in determination of gender, age, and race of the deceased and of the time elapsed since the objects were first placed there. This knowledge is absolutely essential in order to pay the necessary attention to the possibly small and apparently insignificant objects that are especially significant in these respects. Precise determination of the characteristics necessary for establishing age, gender, stature, and so forth must be left to the forensic anthropologist. Likewise, the investigation will benefit from seeking the expert advice of entomologists with regard to the life cycles of insects; of botanists, for growth rates of roots, grasses, and other plants; of meteorologists, for weather conditions that might suggest the time of repose of the body; as well as any other experts with special knowledge pertinent to the case.

16.4   Special Considerations Regarding
the Discovery of Old Remains

Sometimes the specific place that a body is found will bring with it certain requirements for its correct examination.

16.4.1   Outdoors

A discovery outdoors may be one of three different types according to whether the remains are found buried, lying exposed on the ground, or in water. Remains that have been buried usually come to light during digging, construction, or even by a family walking their dog when the animal digs up the remains. The remains may have a purely historical origin, such as old burial sites and the like, or they may be the result of much more recent acts used to hide or dispose of a body. The police officer called to such a scene should first photograph it in the state in which it was found and then expose the body with great care. During this work, preferably done with assistants and in the presence of a forensic anthropologist or forensic archaeologist, detailed photographs should be taken as necessary to show the position of the body, noteworthy details or conditions, etc.

In exposing the body, special attention should be given to the occurrence of any filling material above it that differs from the surrounding earth, to any objects used as covering near it, and to any foreign material or bodies in the ground or near the body. It has happened that quicklime has been placed on bodies to accelerate the decomposition and make the identification difficult. If anything of this kind is suspected, a sample of the earth should be taken for further examination. Attention should also be given to the properties of the earth (e.g., type of soil, dampness, pH) because this is very important in deciding the length of time the body has been buried.

The colour of bones can vary from light greyish-white to dark brownish-black, depending on the age of the find, kind and properties of the soil, whether the parts are or were enclosed or covered in some way, or the measures that may have been taken with the body before burial (e.g., burning). It is often difficult to distinguish between small bones and stones, twigs, or other debris; therefore, the search should be carried out with great care, and all remains, even if very small, should be kept and examined by an anthropologist. Certain very small bones and the teeth are very important for determining the identity of the deceased. If the skeleton is much disintegrated, the earth should be sifted through a small mesh sieve.

The scene investigation that followed the attack on the World Trade Center in New York City on 11 September, 2001, required distinguishing between small bones and other debris on a scale never performed before. A special piece of equipment, seen in Figure 16.12, was custom built for the purpose of sifting through large amounts of debris in order to identify and collect human remains. The work continues at the New York City Office of Chief Medical Examiner as of this writing, 11 years later, to identify the remains of the victims.

Items associated with the discovery of remains are of great importance for investigation and identification and include all remains of clothing and other objects that may be connected with the find, such as contents of pockets, buttons, ornaments, rings, and coins, as well as objects that may be connected directly with the death or transport of the body to the scene of discovery, such as ropes, cords, sacks, bullets, duct tape, garbage bags, duffel bags, or objects pushed into the mouth of the victim. Such loose objects should be sought

Figure 16.12 Sifting through the large amounts of debris from the World Trade Center attack in order to identify and collect human remains. (Photograph courtesy of Office of Chief Medical Examiner, New York City.)

and handled with great care because the risk of them breaking into pieces may be great if they have been there for a very long time. Objects on or attached to the remains are not to be moved from their position before the discovery has been fully revealed or unearthed. The position of loose objects in relation to the remains of the body should be accurately marked, sketched, and photographed.

When taking possession of bones and associated objects, attention should be given to their relationship with any vegetation. Roots of trees or shrubs that have grown through them are a valuable aid in determining the length of time the object has been there. A determination of the age of a root of a tree that has grown through clothing gives a minimum value for the time the object has lain in the ground; this can be used as a starting point for further investigations and calculations. As far as possible such roots should be cut off and allowed to remain with the object; otherwise, they must be kept and labelled with the necessary information on their origin.

Attention should also be given to the occurrence of insect larvae and pupae or remains of them on the body. They should be placed in a conical tube or other suitable container for examination by an expert forensic entomologist. Remains of fly larvae found on a buried body, for example, indicate that it was above ground for a certain period of time before being buried; the stage of development of the insect, larva, or pupa can give further valuable information. The amount and type of insect activity can also yield other clues about such things as the time of death.

If only a part of a body is found, then dismemberment may have been carried out before burial. In such a case, a large area of the surroundings must be investigated carefully, with attention being directed especially to all changes in the surface of the ground that give the impression of having been produced by human agency. The character of the ground, the possibility of burial at different places, etc. must then be used to guide the search. In some cases, police cadaver dogs can be used to help with the search. Ground-penetrating radar (GPR) is a tool that can be used to search for anomalies in the earth that could reveal evidence of a clandestine grave. Additional manpower should be brought in when large areas need to be searched. A sketch should be made of the terrain that indicates where each object was found, and photographs should be taken. Commercial or public digital maps can be helpful in this process, but they may be several years old and not entirely accurate. Each site is marked with a number or letter that is visible on photographs, and these are also indicated on the sketches. The objects found at the different sites are placed in cartons or boxes marked with the number or letter given to the discovery location in the photographs and sketches.

The place of discovery should be cleared and any remains and objects found kept. Earth that has been sifted may be preserved for further examination or soil analysis. The character of the ground (e.g., type of soil, dampness) should be noted. Samples should be taken of any apparent foreign matter such as lime. When exposing the body, attention should be given to any indications of its having been covered with stones, leaves, brushwood, sacks, and the like. If there is evidence that the body was relatively recently placed in a grave that was dug into the ground, the physical condition of the burial site should be closely scrutinised for any toolmarks that could be associated with the digging tool used. Again, whenever necessary, detailed photographs should be taken.

If the remains of a body are found in water, it is generally much more difficult to investigate the place of discovery accurately, unless it is merely a small pool that can be drained. It must be remembered that currents, ice, floating timber, and other items may have carried parts of the body to places far away from the place of discovery. Alternatively, any body parts found may have been carried to the place of discovery in the same manner, possibly from a considerable distance.

If the discovery has been made in a harbour or river navigated by steamers or motorboats, propellers may have caused some of the injuries on the body. A propeller can cut off a leg or arm in such a way that it appears as if the body has been dismembered intentionally. Injuries to tissues and organs produced in this way often show clean cuts, as from an edged tool. Feeding by aquatic life can also be mistaken for injuries. In addition to having crime scene experience, investigators of underwater crime scenes need to be expert divers. The Professional Association of Diving Instructors (PADI) offers courses in investigating underwater crime scenes. PADI is a global organisation but headquartered in the United States, so it may be better to seek assistance from a regional equivalent. Water immersion itself causes damage to the body. Figure 16.13 shows an adult male who was missing for 2 weeks and was eventually recovered on a beach after drowning in the ocean. The condition of the facial tissue from being in the water so long obviously prevented visual identification so the victim was identified using dental records.

16.4.2 Indoors

It is very rare for remains of a body found indoors to undergo as extensive a degree of change due to decay or other causes as in the preceding cases. There have been cases where a body has been buried in a cellar or cut up and burned in the furnace, and the remains of a dismembered or burned body have been placed in a suitcase in an attic or garage. The procedures for investigating such cases are the same as that described above.

If a body has been buried or if remains have been found in a suitcase, sack, or the like, then all objects that have been used to conceal the body or for wrapping are of special interest. Figure 16.14 shows a body that was discovered in a suitcase. With such discoveries, the

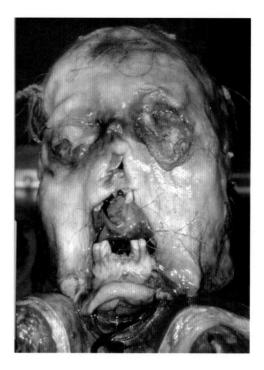

Figure 16.13 This adult male was missing for 2 weeks; his body was eventually recovered on a beach after he drowned in the ocean. The condition of the facial tissue from being in the water so long obviously prevented visual identification so the victim was identified using dental records. (Photograph courtesy of C.M. Bowers, DDS, JD, Ventura, CA.)

Figure 16.14 This body was discovered in a suitcase. (Photograph courtesy of Los Angeles County Sheriff's Department, Los Angeles, CA.)

floor, walls, and ceiling of the place of discovery should be examined for bloodstains, and objects should be looked for that might be supposed to have been used in connection with the crime. For example, a furnace that has been used to burn a body should be examined very carefully. After a cremation, the volume of the bones of an adult amounts to 2 to 3.5 litres. In a freshly burnt state, the bones have a white to yellowish or greyish-white shade, which quickly changes to brown or brownish black in the ground. At a certain state of burning, the bones are soft and may assume peculiar twisted forms that depend to some extent on the underlayer. The contents of the firebox and of the ash pit should be sifted; every fragment of bone must be kept. Certain very small bones have been found to be very resistant to fire and may therefore be valuable for determining the age and gender of the deceased. Teeth are especially valuable. The crowns of teeth generally break up and split under the action of heat, but the roots often remain whole. On the other hand, teeth that have not erupted (such as is found in children) rarely break up and do not change in form or shrink to any appreciable extent; after burning, they have a whitish colour and a chalky consistency. It is even possible to recover DNA from the pulp of a whole tooth because of the hard enamel that protects it.

In searching for and taking possession of burnt skeletal remains, great care should be observed due to their fragile nature. Remains that are especially brittle or liable to fall to pieces should be packed separately in test tubes, containers, or cartons according to size, with cotton, tissue paper, or the like as an underlayer and filling for the container.

16.4.3 Packing and Transporting

Packing the remains of a body with any associated objects to be moved or sent to an expert should be done so in such a way as to eliminate any danger of destruction or falling apart of the associated objects as the result of shaking or other movement. A skeleton with the long bones still hanging together, with or without remains of soft tissues or organs, should be packed in such a way that it will remain in that state during transport. Styrofoam, rags, tissue paper, or similar materials can be used as filling in the container and to support the parts so they do not rest on the bottom. Well-burnt remains should be transported in the custody of a police officer who keeps the package under control at all times and ensures that it is not exposed to shocks or jarring (see Figure 16.15). Suitable

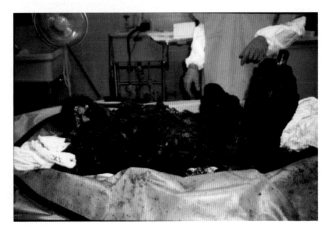

Figure 16.15 Charred human remains being carefully transported in a body bag to the mortuary. (Photograph courtesy of Office of Chief Medical Examiner, New York City.)

packing materials are thin, soft paper; soft and flexible cloth; tissue paper; cotton; and the like. They should be packed in the container to provide soft support to the object and to support it in a definite position.

16.4.4   Examining Remains of Clothing and Other Objects

The investigation of any remains of clothing and other objects in these cases has the same objective as any other case of personal identification, but it may be more difficult because of degradation that has occurred over time. It does, of course, have the additional objective of determining the original appearance of the garments (e.g., kind of cloth, colour). Everything that arises from this investigation is combined to form, if possible, a description of the deceased and an explanation of the cause of death, time of death, and so on; this information can subsequently be used to determine if the body is that of a missing person, to trace the perpetrator, to check statements of a suspect, and other such objectives.

16.4.4.1   *Clothing*

Roots or other parts of plants that have penetrated portions of clothing should be kept and given a label indicating the type of garment and vegetation; the material will be given to a botanist for determination of age. From tree and shrub roots that have penetrated the remains it is possible to determine the minimum period of time that the object has lain at the site. In the case of unburied remains, this estimate must be increased by 1 or 2 years because the material must first be consolidated into the soil before it can be penetrated by roots. Ideally, the type and colour of cloth, the type of garment, and whether it was ready-made or tailor-made can be determined, possibly with the assistance of an expert. An expert should preferably also be called in to decide the length of time the material has been lying based on any changes in the garments resulting from climatic effects. Manufacturer's and laundry marks are looked for, using an ultraviolet lamp in the latter case. Buttons and the manner in which they are sewn on (by machine or by hand) may be significant, as are any repairs in the garments. The remains of clothes are also examined for damage caused by edged tools, firearms, vehicles, and similar objects that may possibly correspond to marks and injuries on the body. The assistance of the pathologist is required for this procedure. Damage caused by animals may also occur on clothing, but this can generally be distinguished from other damage, although this was a source of considerable criticism in the Lindy Chamberlain, or "Dingo Baby," case. The remains of underclothing and stockings or socks are also examined for colour, textile material, manufacturer's marks, other marks, repairs, etc. Depending on their condition, clothes may give DNA profiles that can be searched in databases.

16.4.4.2   *Boots and Shoes*

The original colour of boots and shoes may be difficult to determine because of changes to the leather by the action of earth, dampness, etc. The name of the maker, which is sometimes embossed, may be found inside or at the back of the heel; stamped marks may sometimes be a guide for identification. Any rubber soles or heels and their make, size, and type are also significant. The size of shoes can be determined from the length. Sometimes, a distinct impression of the sole of the foot and the toes can be observed on the inner sole of a shoe, and this may be of value for comparison with shoes that may possibly be found in the house of a missing person. Shoe repairs may also help in identification.

16.4.4.3 Other Objects

Objects found in the pockets of clothing or at the scene of the discovery that may be suspected of having belonged to the deceased can provide valuable information. These objects are examined for name, initials, trademarks, and other markings. The description of a missing person may mention such objects or possibly relatives may be able to identify them as belonging to the deceased. It may also be important to determine the application of a particular object, which may be characteristic of a particular trade. A particular collection of objects may be typical of a hiker or a person interested in sports, fishing, photography, or hunting, for example.

16.5 Estimating the Time of Death

In cases of murder, suicide, or suspicious death, determination of the time of death is a very important piece of information in the reconstruction; indeed, WHEN is one of the legs of the investigative star. The most reliable estimate of the time of death is obtained from a variety of sources, including postmortem changes such as body temperature, rigor mortis, lividity, and decomposition, as well as information developed during the investigation such as the last time the victim was seen alive. The correct estimate of the time of death is important when interviewing suspects in a homicide investigation. It can serve to eliminate a suspect who was elsewhere at the time of death or establish opportunity (i.e., the suspect could have been with the victim at the time of death). The investigator should realise that the estimate of the time of death is just that, an estimate and not a rigorous scientific fact. In some cases, a more precise determination can be made if the death occurred at or near the time of another known event.

16.5.1 Postmortem Changes in the Body

After death, a number of postmortem changes occur that are useful in determining, within limits, the approximate time of death. The various methods available are useful to make estimates—that is, ranges of times. Unless there is testimony from a reliable witness, the precise moment of death will not be possible to determine. The amount of time between the death and discovery of the body also has a bearing on the estimate of time of death. Generally, the shorter the time interval between death and the discovery of the body, the better is the estimate of the time of death.

16.5.1.1 Changes in the Eyes

After death, changes become noticeable in the eyes. The cornea becomes dull and a film may appear over the eye. This may appear within several minutes to a few hours depending on whether the eyelid is open or closed, temperature, humidity, and air current. Because of these factors, clouding of the cornea is not considered a reliable indicator of the time of death.

16.5.1.2 Temperature of the Body

Cooling of the body, or algor mortis, occurs after death. The rate of cooling depends on several factors, including body temperature at the time of death, temperature of the environment, whether or not there is any exposure to wind, body covering and clothing, and the relationship of surface area to body weight. The body temperature will continue to fall or rise until it reaches ambient temperature, which usually occurs in about 18 to 20 hours. Core body temperature is generally considered one of the more reliable indicators of the time of death up to approximately 18 hours. The usual way to determine core body temperature at the scene is to insert a thermometer into the rectum. Liver temperature is a better indicator of core internal body temperature but should not be taken at the scene so as not to introduce external injuries. A comparison between core or liver temperature and ambient temperature is used to determine the approximate time of death.

16.5.1.3 Rigidity of the Body

Immediately after death, the body becomes flaccid. Biochemical changes in body muscles produce stiffening, known as rigor mortis, which usually appears within 2 to 6 hours after death. Rigor mortis is most notable first in the small muscles, such as the eyelids, neck, and jaw, and is complete within 6 to 12 hours. The rigidity remains for 2 to 3 days and disappears gradually. An examination of the body for rigor mortis can help indicate the time of death. If the rigidity is broken, it will generally not reappear unless the body is in the very early stages of rigor mortis. The victim's muscular development will affect the intensity of the rigidity. The very young and very old will likely develop less rigidity than adults with well-developed musculature.

16.5.1.4 Lividity

After blood circulation stops, blood settles to the lowest portions of the body because of gravity. This is known as livor mortis and is noted by the appearance of blue or reddish-violet marks on the skin; in cases of cold or poisoning by carbon monoxide or cyanide, the marks are cherry red, and for potassium chlorate poisoning they are light brown. The first indications of lividity occur in approximately 1 hour, with full development after 3 to 4 hours. Lividity can sometimes be confused with bruising or black-and-blue marks. The pathologist can differentiate between the two during the autopsy.

Under certain conditions lividity can move or change if the body is moved or the position of the body is changed. Postmortem lividity does not form on parts of the body exposed to pressure (e.g., parts that lie against the floor). If the position of the body or the position of articles of clothing pressing on the body is changed within 3 to 4 hours, the original lividity discolouration may partially disappear and a new pattern form. After this time, at least some of the original discolouration will remain. Even 9 to 12 hours after death, and sometimes later, new but successively weaker patterns are produced when the position of the body is changed, although the discolouration that was first formed is usually fixed by this time and does not change. If there was a large blood loss, livid stains will be weak. As a rule, fresh livid stains are not produced by a change in position more than 12 hours after death. Lividity discolouration may provide a limited indication of the time of death but can demonstrate a change of position or movement of the body several hours after death.

16.5.1.5 Decomposition of the Body

The most certain sign of death, one that cannot be misinterpreted by anyone, is the beginning of putrefaction. Decomposition, or putrefaction, is a combination of two processes: autolysis and bacterial action. Autolysis, the softening and liquefaction of tissue, occurs when body cell membranes lose their integrity and their contents leak out. Bacterial action results in the conversion of soft tissues in the body to liquids and gases.

Putrefaction begins immediately upon death and generally first becomes noticeable within 24 hours as a discolouration of the skin in the lower abdomen and groin. The discolouration has been described as greenish-red, blue-green, and even black and is quite pronounced within 36 hours. Bacterial action produces gases that cause the body to swell up, while an unpleasant odour becomes quite apparent. The swelling is particularly noticeable in the penis, scrotum, breasts, and other areas of loose skin attachment.

Blisters filled with watery fluid and gas appear on the skin, which gradually darkens in colour. Material from tissue breakdown (purge) may exude through the mouth, nose, and anus. Within 3 days, the entire body shows signs of decomposition. The environment affects the rate of decomposition of the body. Colder temperatures tend to impede putrefaction, while warmer temperatures increase it. Similarly, if the body is in water containing a large amount of bacteria, such as that from sewage effluent, decomposition is accelerated. A body in water generally decomposes more slowly because of colder temperatures and lack of oxygen. Because the body has a greater specific gravity than water, it sinks initially. Prolonged submersion in water causes a wrinkling effect around the skin of the hands and feet. The body orients itself in a head-down position that sometimes results in the forehead being scraped when it comes into contact with the rough bottom. After a period of 3 to 4 days in warmer water and about a week in cold, the body will surface due to the formation of gas (Figure 16.16). Sometimes the skin and tissues burst and the body sinks again to the bottom. The process may repeat itself, so the body floats back to the surface again.

When a body is buried in a shallow grave with loose earth, it is destroyed fairly quickly; in 1 to 3 years all of the soft tissue will disappear. The skeleton remains much longer. These time periods will vary greatly according to the type of soil, amount of water, acidity, drainage, and other such factors. In peat bogs, for example, the body will remain relatively well preserved for many years. Bodies buried in clay soil decompose at a slower rate than in other soils. In certain cases, bodies are relatively well preserved through mummification or the formation of adipocere, a wax-like substance caused by hydrolysis of body fat.

In very dry conditions, putrefaction is retarded and mummification may begin. It can become complete in warm, dry air or when a body is buried in dry, porous earth. Formation of adipocere occurs in bodies located in damp environments such as a swamp, wet soil, or

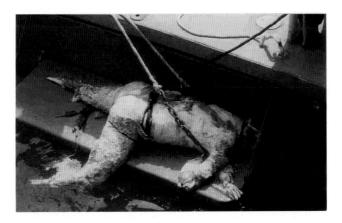

Figure 16.16 A body found floating in the Hudson River just to the west of Manhattan. The missing hands and feet were due to the actions of marine animals. (Photograph courtesy of Office of Chief Medical Examiner, New York City.)

even water. Adipocere is characterised by reasonably well-preserved external contours of the body; its formation is noticeable in about 6 to 8 weeks, with complete formation in 18 months to 2 years. When a body lies in a cellar or other damp place it may become completely covered with mould, leaving black marks on the body. Buried embalmed bodies may also have mould present.

16.5.2   Action of Insects and Other Animals on a Dead Body

A dead body above ground is generally quickly invaded by insects and their larvae. Various kinds of insects lay their eggs on the body, and these rapidly develop into larvae (maggots). When weather conditions are favourable, they can appear in such numbers that the dead body positively teems with life. The body of an adult can be completely destroyed in less than 2 months, with only the skeleton remaining; that of a child in less than a month. The insects that appear on a body, either to feed on it or to lay their eggs in it, always arrive in a certain order based on the state of decomposition of the body. This relationship between insects and a dead body has attained great importance in medicolegal practice because, by examining the insects found on a body at a particular time, it is possible to obtain a good idea of how long it has lain at a particular place (Figure 16.17).

As a rule, the first insects that attack the body are flies. Even before death actually occurs, the flies may begin to lay their eggs in the body, usually in the mucous membranes (e.g., eyes, nose, mouth) but also in wounds and bloody parts of the body. The eggs are white and about 1.5 mm long, and they are laid in clumps. On a body lying indoors, they come especially from common houseflies (*Musca domestica*). This may be a significant point in the investigation because if eggs, larvae, or pupae of houseflies are found in a body lying outdoors or buried, it must be concluded that it had previously lain indoors. On bodies lying outdoors, the main sources of infestation are common bluebottles (*Calliphora erythrocephala*), greenbottles (*Lucilia caesar*), and sheep maggot flies (*Lucilia sericata*). Flies can also lay their eggs in bodies buried in shallow graves. After only 1 to 2 days, the larvae of the fly emerge from the eggs and immediately commence their work of destruction. They change into pupae after 10 to 14 days, and after another 12 to 14 days they develop into flies, to multiply again in their turn after a couple of weeks.

Figure 16.17 The lifecycle of maggots found on the body can be used to help estimate the time of death. This is a photograph of a member of the flesh fly family, *Sarcophaga nodosa*, feeding on meat (http://en.wikipedia.org/wiki/File:Sarcophaga_nodosa.jpg).

Among the beetles that live or multiply on a body, burying beetles and other kinds of carrion beetles appear on a dead body. Carrion beetles, as their name implies, are an important part of a vast host of scavengers responsible for recycling decaying materials. When a body is buried immediately after death, insects are not able to lay their eggs. Certain types of boring worms accelerate the decomposition process into the body. Some fly species can live and multiply for long time periods in a buried body.

When larvae, pupae, or insect eggs are found on a body or in clothing, it is possible to estimate the shortest time that the body has been at the scene. This applies also to fully developed insects that, in their natural course, must have gone through all the stages of development in the body. A forensic entomologist should perform these examinations. If insects are to be sent for expert examination to an entomologist, they are first killed by placing them in a killing jar that contains a few cotton balls soaked in fresh ethyl acetate. After immobilisation they are then preserved in 75% ethyl alcohol. Insect eggs, larvae, and pupae are killed and preserved by placing in 70% to 80% alcohol.

Animals often attack unburied bodies. Rats attack projecting parts of bodies, such as the nose, ears, and fingers. When they attack the hands, the injuries may give the impression of being defence injuries. When such injuries are discovered, the pathologist should examine them immediately because they dry comparatively quickly, making it difficult to decide on their origin. Other animals may also produce injuries to a body and sometimes eat it. Gulls, ravens, and crows may eat the loose tissues (e.g., in the eye sockets). Bodies in water are exposed to injury from lampreys, crabs, lobsters, water beetles, and mackerel. Eels use the hollows of the body as hiding places but do not eat it to any extent. Starfish cause injuries by firmly attaching themselves.

16.5.3   Other Indications of Time of Death

In certain cases, the pathologist can draw conclusions from the stomach contents and intestines about the time of the last meal, its quantity, and composition. The investigator can assist the pathologist by relaying any information found relevant to the composition of the last meal. Watches and clocks may be guides in determining the time of death. Watches of older construction generally stop immediately upon contact with water, but a watch equipped with a tightfitting case and crystal can run longer before stopping. Watertight watches run for a long time underwater. If a pocket or wristwatch is found on a body, the police officer should not carry out any further examination of it or perform any tests but instead should consult a watchmaker. Digital watches and clocks do not lend themselves to these techniques.

When a dead body is found outdoors, the growth of vegetation under and around it can be a good guide to how long it has been there. Flowering plants may be buried and thus may indicate closely the time of burial. The coloured matter of plant leaves under the body undergoes certain changes; for example, chlorophyll generally disappears after a week. A good indication can also be obtained from a comparison between the stage of growth of plants under the body and of similar plants in the vicinity. When a body has laid in one place for a considerable time, in favourable cases the decaying vegetation underneath can indicate the time of year when the body was placed there. If the weather has changed, the amount of moisture under the body, compared with that in the surrounding area, may give some information. When a dead body is found in snow, its position in relation to layers produced by successive snowfalls should be determined accurately.

Some guidance may also be obtained from the extent of decay of clothing. Cotton fabrics decompose after 4 to 5 years; wool after 8 to 10 years; leather and silk only after 20 years or even longer.

16.6   The Autopsy

The forensic autopsy is a very specialised activity and only those elements appropriate to the work of the crime scene investigator are described here. The investigator present at the crime scene should also be present at the autopsy so the forensic pathologist can be briefed about pertinent finds at the crime scene, as well as other information that will be of value during the examination. Additionally, information uncovered at the autopsy and communicated verbally by the pathologist to the homicide investigator will be helpful in the criminal investigation.

Besides photographs taken at the crime scene, the victim should be photographed at the mortuary clothed and unclothed. The pathologist and investigator should be present and carefully examine the victim prior to undressing the body. Colour photographs should be taken of all pertinent details, such as the overall appearance of the body and close-ups of the face, injuries, ligatures, and marks. A scale should be included in the photographs, as well as an indicator of the case number or autopsy number.

Care should be taken in undressing the body. It should be undressed in the usual way, with photographs taken at each stage; the clothing should not be cut, if possible. If cutting is required, care should be taken not to cut through bullet holes, knife cuts, tears, or stains. The garments should be packaged separately. If they are wet or blood soaked, they should be allowed to air-dry at room temperature and away from direct sunlight. The clothes should be hung up to dry, preferably in a ventilated drying cabinet, with paper draped loosely around the article of clothing to catch any trace material that might fall, or they should be carefully spread out on clean paper. It is important to properly preserve blood-stained articles in order to obtain the most information from forensic biology testing (see Chapter 8 to review preservation procedures for bloody evidence).

After the clothes have been dried, they may be packaged for submission to the forensic laboratory. The investigator and pathologist should be careful to establish a chain of custody of the evidence so it will be admissible in court. Trace evidence present on the victim and the clothing should not be overlooked. Body bags used to carry the body from the scene to the mortuary should be inspected for debris and trace material. Any trace evidence found on the body should be removed and properly packaged. Traces noted on the clothing should be removed and packaged only if the evidence might be lost in transit to the laboratory; otherwise, the traces should remain and be packaged with the clothing.

Following photography, initial examination, and undressing, the body should be examined for physical evidence, such as bloody fingerprint marks, bruises, or ligature marks. The techniques described earlier to obtain latent fingerprints from skin may be attempted on promising areas. An alternative light source can also be used to look for biological fluids on the body. Ultraviolet light can also be used to look for ligature and strangulation marks or other bruises that may not be visible to the naked eye. Fingernail scrapings and hair samples should routinely be taken from all murder victims. If the body has not been identified, a forensic dentist may be consulted at this stage to take dental records. A blood specimen should be collected during the actual postmortem examination. This phase of the examination is completed by taking fingerprints of the deceased. The body should next be washed and photographed again. Identity photographs of the victim's face should be made at this time. The entire body, including injuries, should again be photographed. Photographs taken during the remainder of the autopsy may be of value in the subsequent investigation and should be encouraged. If the victim died as a result of a shooting, x-rays or MRI scans should be taken prior to the autopsy to identify and locate the bullet fragments, jacket, etc.

The purpose of the autopsy is to establish the cause and manner of death as well as the circumstances immediately surrounding the time of death. The homicide investigator uses this information together with information gathered from other sources in the solution of the crime. Two factors will have a significant bearing on the outcome of the case: (1) the degree of care and skill with which the postmortem examination is conducted, and (2) the level of cooperation between the investigator and forensic pathologist. The pathologist will describe and interpret the various types of injuries encountered on the body. Some examples of potential significance to the crime scene investigator are discussed below.

16.6.1 Cutting Wounds

Cutting wounds have even, sharp edges. When the direction of cutting is across the direction of the fibres of elastic tissue, the wound gapes; when the direction of cut is parallel to the fibres, the edges of the wound generally lie against one another. Often it is difficult to decide whether a cutting wound occurred during life or after death because contusion injuries, which may serve as a guide in such cases, are not found around the wound. As a rule, a cutting wound is deepest at the place where the cutting object was first applied. A cutting wound in soft tissue leaves hardly any detailed information about the instrument that caused it, but a wound that cuts into cartilage or bone may leave toolmark impression evidence as shown in Chapter 9 (Figures 9.21 to 9.24).

In cases of suicide, the cutting force is generally directed against the throat or insides of the wrists and, sometimes, against other parts of the body. The intent of the suicide is usually to produce bleeding by cutting the arteries. Occasionally, there may be one or several cuts, generally not of a dangerous type, either parallel or running into one another, which are known as *hesitation cuts*. If it is established that such surface cuts were produced before the final fatal cut, it is quite certain that the case is one of suicide; the surface cuts were made because the suicide did not know how much force was required to produce the fatal cut or feared the pain anticipated from the act. The police officer should not, however, draw hasty conclusions from superficial cuts that give the impression of having been made before the fatal cut.

In cases of death from cutting the throat, there is reason to suspect murder when the position of the wound does not correspond with a natural hold on the weapon, or the direction of the wound does not correspond with the right- or left-handedness of the victim. Murder may be suspected if the wound is very deep or if it is irregular. Special attention should be given to the possible occurrence of fingernail marks and scratch injuries that would be produced if the murderer held the head of the victim, and also to the presence of defence injuries on the hands and arms. If cuts are on the clothing, it may be murder because suicides generally lay bare the part of the body that they intend to cut.

16.6.2   Stab Wounds

Stab wounds are generally produced by a knife, dagger, or scissors but may also result from other weapons, such as an ice pick, awl, or pointed stick. If a stab wound has been produced by a sharp knife or dagger, it is not possible to determine the width of the blade from the size of the surface wound because the wound channel is generally wider than the weapon, especially if it is two-edged. When the weapon is stuck into the body, the edge has a cutting action, so the surface wound is considerably wider than the width of the blade; when the weapon is withdrawn, it usually assumes a different position, so the wound is enlarged still further. The weapon may also be turned when withdrawn, so the surface wound becomes curved or angular. A knife with a thick back produces a wedge-shaped wound.

When stab wounds are produced by a weapon with a blunt point, the outer wound is smaller than the cross-sectional width of the instrument. In such cases, when the weapon is driven into the body, the elastic skin is actually pressed inward and stretched until it breaks. When the weapon is withdrawn, the skin returns to its normal position and the external wound contracts. If the weapon is cone shaped and rough, the skin around the wound may break in radial cracks. With a stab wound in the heart, death may not occur immediately. In some cases, people have survived a wound in the heart.

A suicide attempt by stabbing is generally in the region of the heart or, in some cases, in the stomach or other parts of the body. In suicide, the stab is generally directed into the body at right angles. In cases of murder, the stab wounds are usually not concentrated in one place but scattered, especially when the victim has attempted self-defence. Knife stabs are, as a rule, directed in an oblique direction against the body, with the exception of cases in which the victim was lying down. A number of deep wounds and wounds in the back indicate murder. If the victim attempted self-defence, the wound channel may be curved due to the body being in a certain position when stabbed. At the autopsy it may be found that a wound channel does not go right through because the position of the body was such that the muscles were displaced from their normal position when they were penetrated. In such a case, the position of the dead person when he or she was stabbed can be reconstructed.

Case 5

The body of a dead woman was found by police in a house in Amsterdam. When the police arrived there were three people in the living room. Two of them pointed to the third and said that he stabbed the woman to death. The man was taken into custody. The job of the crime scene investigators was to determine whether the findings confirmed the alleged accusation. The entire house was covered with bloodstains, varying from swipes, altered stains, flow patterns, and footprints made with and in blood. In the living room five knives were found, of which two were bloody. After removal of all the clothing that had been placed over the body, the victim was found lying naked on her stomach (Figure 16.18(a)). Female clothing that most probably belonged to the victim was found in a closet in the living room. The clothing was examined and perforations were found in several places. Considering the damage to the clothing it was very likely that the victim was wearing it during the stabbing. The Dutch Forensic Institute (NFI) in The Hague examined it for the blood of the victim and compared the damages in the clothing to the knives. Large amounts of blood on the mattress and bedding in the first and second bedrooms on the first floor were also found (Figure 16.18(b)). In the first bedroom, a rope was found tied to the central heating pipes.

Figure 16.18 Investigation of the death of a woman in an Amsterdam apartment. (Case submitted by Wendy van Hilst, Forensische Opsporing Amsterdam–Amstelland, Amsterdam, Holland.)

Similar pieces of rope were found next to the body, and there was a roll of similar rope in the bathroom. It was surmised that the victim was tied to the central heating pipes next to the mattress. Several bloody sponges, a cleaning mop, and a bucket filled with bloody water were also recovered. Several bloody swipes and efforts taken to clean up the floor were also observed (Figure 16.18(c)).

Several blood transfers on the seat of a stair elevator normally used by the deceased, who was handicapped, indicated that there had been more than one instance of blood transfer made by a bloody person or bloody object. Looking at the blood pattern on the seat, the guard underneath the seat, and on the footboard of the chair elevator it is probable that a bloody person was seated on the chair. This hypothesis is supported by the fact that several bloodstained tissues were found on the chair of the elevator and underneath the bare feet of the victim (Figure 16.18(d)). Further investigation led to the discovery of a partial bloody shoeprint on the floor next to the bed in bedroom number two and in the living room next to the victim. The shoeprint was of the same kind as the shoes the suspect was wearing during his arrest.

The story according to the suspect and witnesses was that the man and woman had a relationship based on friendship and drugs. They lived together in the house. She asked him to give her some drugs but he did not want to. She kept on asking and he got tired of it. When they were sitting on the sofa he stabbed her in the waist and they got into a fight. Blood was shed. He put her on the stair elevator and moved her up to the bedroom, where he tied her with a rope to the central heating pipes. He left her and went downstairs. After a while she managed to get herself loose and went downstairs. There they continued the fight, which eventually led to her death. She was stabbed several times, her throat was cut, and she bled to death. The suspect did not really know what to do with the situation and covered her with clothing and made an effort to clean up the house.

16.6.3 Postmortem Wounds

Postmortem wounds caused by cutting, stabbing, or chopping can be found on bodies. Such wounds are significantly different in appearance from attacks on a living person. Postmortem wounds do not show a vital reaction on the cutting edge, meaning blood will not be present in the edges of the wounded tissue because of the lack of circulating blood. Postmortem wounds are commonly found when a body has been dismembered or when a perpetrator has tried to make a homicide look like a suicide by cutting the victim's wrists.

16.6.4 Defence Injuries

Self-defence wounds are often found on the hands and arms of the murder victim. If a knife was used, the insides of the hands may be badly gashed from gripping the blade of the knife. Stab and cut wounds may be produced on the arms and hands when a victim attempts to parry an attack. When a crushing weapon is used in a murder, the hands of the victim may be badly injured from putting them on the head to reduce the violence of the blow. Among defence injuries are also included those that occur when victims attempt to defend themselves from their attackers; knuckles may be injured when a victim hits his assailant with his fists, or nails may be broken from scratching the assailant.

16.6.5   Firearm and Bullet Injuries

Because firearm injuries are frequently covered with blood, it is often impossible for a crime scene investigator to distinguish between a gunshot injury and one produced by other external mechanical violence. Under these circumstances it is necessary to wait patiently for the arrival of the pathologist; this holds even when it is important that the type of injury be determined at an early stage. The officer should never probe in or around a gunshot wound because that may destroy or reduce the chances of the expert being able to determine the type of injury and reconstruct the course of events.

When a bullet strikes the body, the skin is first pushed in and then perforated while in the stretched state. After the bullet has passed, the skin partially returns to its original position; the entry opening is drawn together and is smaller than the diameter of the bullet. Slower bullet velocities result in smaller entry openings. The bullet passing through the stretched skin forms an *abrasion ring* around the entrance opening because the bullet slips against the skin that is pressed inward and scrapes the external epithelial layers. The skin in the abrasion ring becomes conspicuous by drying after some hours. In a favourable case, rifling marks on the bullet leave such a distinct mark in the abrasion ring that the number of grooves in the rifling can be counted. The combined section of the abrasion ring and entrance opening corresponds to or slightly exceeds the calibre of the bullet. When a bullet strikes the body squarely, the abrasion ring is round, and when it strikes at an angle it is oval.

Along with the abrasion ring, another black-coloured ring, the *smudge ring*, often entirely covers the abrasion ring. This does not contain any powder residues or contamination from the bore of the firearm but consists wholly of small particles originating from the surface of the bullet. The smudge ring, or bullet wipe, may be absent in the case of clean-jacketed bullets or when the bullet has passed through clothing.

It is often difficult to distinguish the exit wound from the entrance wound, especially at long range with a metal-jacketed bullet, assuming that the bullet passed through the body intact. In a favourable case, the exit wound may have a ragged appearance with flaps directed outward. To determine the direction of the shot with certainty in such a case, an autopsy is necessary. If the bullet has been damaged by its passage through the body or if there has been a bursting effect, then it is generally easy to determine the exit wound. This wound is often considerably larger than the entrance wound and displays a star-shaped, ragged character, with flaps directed outward. Note, however, that in contact shots the entrance wound also may be ragged and star-shaped. A bullet that ricochets may strike with its side or obliquely and produce a large and uncharacteristic entrance wound.

It can be important to be able to estimate the distance from which a shot was fired. In some cases, this fact is the only evidence available that can distinguish among suicide, a self-defence killing, manslaughter, or murder. In practice, a distinction is made among contact, close, and distant shots. A contact shot is one in which the muzzle of the weapon is pressed against the body when the shot is fired. In a close shot, the distance of the muzzle is less than about 50 cm from the body, while a distant shot is one fired at a distance greater than 50 cm.

In the case of a contact shot against an exposed part of the body, soot, metallic particles, and powder residues are driven into the body and can be found there during the autopsy. Blackening, caused by soot and powder, is often absent around the entry opening. A contact shot against a part of the body protected by clothing often produces a powder zone on the skin or in the clothes, while soot, powder residue, and fragments of clothing are driven into the track. With a contact discharge, the entrance wound differs considerably from an entrance wound in a close shot or distant shot. When the shot is fired, the gases from the explosion are driven into the track; however, they are forced out again and produce a bursting effect on the skin and clothes. The entrance wound is often star shaped, with flaps directed outward. It is also possible, in a contact shot, for the muzzle of the weapon to mark the skin, causing an impression that reproduces the shape of the muzzle of the weapon.

A close shot produces a zone of blackening around the entrance wound of the track, on the skin or also on the clothes. Sometimes, the flame from the muzzle singes the area around this opening, and the hair and textile fibres curl up. The zone of blackening is formed of substances carried along with the explosion gases.

When a cartridge is fired, the bullet is forced through the barrel of the weapon by the explosion gases. Only a small amount of this gas passes in front of the bullet. The combustion of the powder is never complete, even with smokeless powder, still less with black powder, and the explosion gases therefore carry with them incompletely burned powder residues, the amount of which decreases as the distance increases. Thus, in a close shot, a considerable amount of incompletely burned powder residue is found on the target. Together with this residue, the gases also carry along impurities from the inside of the barrel consisting of rust (iron), oil, and particles rubbed off the bullet. Metallic residues from the percussion cap and cartridge case also occur in the gases of the explosion. If the shot is fired at right angles to the body, the zone of blackening is practically circular; if it is fired obliquely, the zone is oval. The extent of the zone of blackening is often difficult to determine by direct observation, so it is often better to photograph it using infrared-sensitive material, which intensifies the zone so that its extent is more easily determined. The zone of blackening gives valuable information for determining the distance from which a shot has been fired, which may be an important factor in deciding between murder and suicide. It is important that comparative test shots be fired with the same weapon and same type of ammunition as those used in the actual crime. Close shots with black powder show marks of burning up to a distance of 10 to 15 cm and a distinct deposit of powder smoke up to 25 to 30 cm. Dispersed grains of powder embedded in the target may be detected even at a distance of 90 cm.

For a distant shot (over about 50 cm), none of the characteristics of a close shot can be detected. Powder residues occur on the object fired at in the form of incompletely and completely burned particles. A careful microscopic examination should precede any chemical examination because it is often possible to establish in this way the shape and colour of unburned powder particles and to distinguish many kinds of powder.

Black powder, which consists of potassium nitrate, sulphur, and charcoal, is identified by the presence of potassium and nitrate in the entrance wound. Smokeless powder consists chiefly of nitrocellulose or of nitrocellulose with nitroglycerine and is identified by the presence of nitrite, which can be detected by various microchemical reactions. The grains of smokeless powder are generally coated with graphite and occur in many forms (e.g., round or angular discs, pellets, and cylinders).

At one time, a primer generally contained a percussion composition of fulminate of mercury, stibnite (antimony sulphide), and potassium chlorate with a varying amount of powdered glass. In primers today, fulminate of mercury and rust-forming potassium chlorate have been eliminated. Fulminate of mercury has been replaced by lead compounds, such as lead azide and lead styphnate (lead trinitroresorcinate), and potassium chlorate has been replaced by barium nitrate. Stibnite is still used, however, to a limited extent. Thus, in a chemical examination of a gunshot injury, the metals that first come into question are barium, lead, and antimony. Determining the lead content of a bullet wound and comparing it with that obtained from a test discharge against a similar object with the same ammunition from various distances can provide quite reliable information regarding the distance from which the actual shot was fired.

With injuries from plain lead bullets, such as those usually used in ordinary revolver ammunition, there is always a considerable amount of lead in the zone of blackening and in the smudge ring; in the latter, it is even possible to detect lead from a distant shot. Lead traces from the surface of the bullet can also be found frequently in the exit hole. In some types of ammunition, the bullet is greased; residues from these substances may be carried along with the bullet and found around the entrance opening. Metal-jacketed bullets, which are used chiefly for automatic weapons, consist of an inner lead core with an outer shell of some hard metal or alloy, the so-called jacket. The usual materials are copper, cupronickel, or brass. Traces of all of these metals may be found in gunshot injuries.

It is often possible to detect copper in the track and in perforated clothing up to a range of 15 to 20 cm. This copper comes from the cartridge case when the expansion pressure wears off small particles of metal. Large amounts of copper found in the smudge ring are considered a characteristic indication of a close shot. If, however, a copper-coated bullet has been used, then naturally no conclusion can be drawn regarding the possibility of a close shot because, in this case, even a distant shot shows a distinct amount of copper.

Iron can be found in and around the entrance wound in a case of shooting with a weapon that has not been used for a long time because the barrel may be rusty. With automatic hand weapons, traces of iron can be detected up to a distance of 20 to 30 cm.

With shotguns, the shot column can have a very concentrated effect at distances up to 1 metre. With a distance of up to 10 to 20 cm, the wound is practically circular. The greater the distance is, the more irregular the wound is. At a distance of up to 2 to 3 metres, there is generally a central entrance opening, and around it are single small holes from individual scattered shot. At a greater distance, the shot spreads out more into small groups; at 10 metres, the scattering can amount to 30 to 40 cm.

16.7   Serial Murders

Serial murders are distinguished from multiple murders in that the latter are committed at about the same time and the victims are in some way connected with one another (e.g., family ties, socially, neighbours). Serial murders occur over a period of time, sometimes years, and often over large geographic areas. Probably the most celebrated serial murderer in history was the infamous and unidentified Jack the Ripper, who terrorised London in the 1880s. The name was resurrected by the media in the 1970s for the so-called "Yorkshire Ripper" cases. Like many others, the case was solved by accident due to carelessness on the part of the perpetrator, Peter Sutcliffe, although it appears that the police may have caught him not long after, thanks to an early example of crime mapping. The specialist team assembled to solve the case had concluded that the murderer was probably a truck driver, and they reviewed all the information available for someone of that description who lived near the centre of gravity of the murders. Peter Sutcliffe was on file and the best fit to the data.

Serial murders are among the most difficult types of homicides to investigate because of their complexity and a component unique to this type of crime: public alarm. They follow an almost predictable course. Investigators discover that the modus operandi of a case they are working on has similarities to other cases. As the investigation progresses, investigators from a variety of agencies may become involved in the investigation, including criminalists, pathologists, and psychologists. Once it becomes clear that the case involves a serial murder, communication with all others in the total investigation is imperative. Principal investigators, forensic scientists, and others who must take an active role in the case should be identified and should coordinate the investigation from this point on. All suspected future cases should be reviewed and, if possible, the crime scenes visited. Because of the delicate balance between the public's right to know and the possibility of public hysteria, all press contacts should be handled from a centralised source and specific details about the case should be withheld from the public so as not to hamper the investigation.

When the news story breaks, enormous demands will be placed upon those responsible for the investigation. Here cool heads must reign. Doubtless, there will be tremendous public pressure to solve the case, and the investigation may be complicated by copycat cases, those with certain similarities to the serial murders.

16.8   Summary

At first glance, to address WHAT (what happened) and WHO (who is the deceased and who might be the perpetrator), a thorough homicide investigation requires consideration of all the elements of the investigative star. WHERE was the body found? Are there linked or secondary scenes that will yield significant evidence? HOW was death caused? WHEN did the incident occur? WHY did it occur? Was it willful murder, culpable homicide, or accident? Homicide investigation brings together nearly all the skills and principles discussed throughout this text. It requires the coordination and cooperation of many disciplines and the capability of the investigator to assimilate large amounts of information. The skills needed to process the crime scene and the ability to recognise, collect, and preserve physical evidence are crucial. A mastery of the techniques of crime scene investigation is essential to modern law enforcement.

Appendix: Digital Evidence

A.1 Digital Evidence

Digital evidence is information and data of value to an investigation that is stored on, received, or transmitted by an electronic device. The recovery of evidence from these items is a highly specialised activity and in almost all jurisdictions will be performed by specialist examiners having the required technical competencies. In some, the specialists will be involved right from the point of identifying and seizing the devices, but in most this will fall to the crime scene unit or groups within it. It is perhaps appropriate to regard the crime scene investigator (CSI) in digital evidence cases as a first responder, whose actions are critical to the timely identification and preservation of the devices that may contain potential evidence.

This chapter is therefore written from that perspective and is *not* to be taken as a guide for the actual recovery of digital evidence. Under no circumstances should the untrained CSI attempt to explore the contents of, or to recover information from, a computer or other electronic device, other than to record what is visible on its display screen. The following sections on potential evidence are included to inform the CSI as to what kind of evidential information may be obtained from their examination; they are not exhaustive and must *not* be taken as an invitation to crime scene investigators not trained in the examination of digital devices to try to extract it from any device identified in the scene search. Finally, this appendix is written for overall guidance, and any instructions in the standard operating procedures in the CSI's department take precedence.

A.2 Digital Devices

Digital devices include the following:

- Computer systems
- Storage devices
- Peripheral devices
- Mobile phones
- Handheld devices
- Audio and video recording, storage, and playback devices, including closed-circuit television (CCTV) surveillance equipment
- Video game consoles
- Global positioning system receivers, including satellite navigation units

Any scene investigation should also include conventional paper documents such as instruction manuals and any paper printouts.

A.3   Crime and Digital Evidence

There are two sets of circumstances where the CSI may have to recognise and secure digital evidence. The most straightforward, in the sense that it is known from the start and can be included in the scene examination strategy and subsequent examination, is where the crime itself involves digital devices. Examples include child pornography, abuse, and exploitation; computer intrusion; e-mail threats and harassment; identity theft; online fraud; and software piracy. In nearly all of these, the need for a digital evidence specialist will be identified during the initial strategy discussions, and the CSI role will be limited to support and possibly scene security until the arrival of the specialist. A subset of known digital evidence is investigators making use of surveillance recordings, including digital enhancement of quality.

The more complex circumstance is where a conventional crime involves the use of a digital device for communication, record storage, or as an agent in carrying out the crime. Examples include e-mail and mobile phone records, Internet pages with instructions on how to make bombs or drugs, and digital "snooping" in domestic violence cases where a spouse may covertly record his or her partner's activities and use such recordings to initiate a confrontation. These are all situations where digital devices have replaced traditional analogue media such as landline telephones, letter writing, handwritten or typed instructions, and books.

A.4   Protecting the Overall Scene

All of the procedures and precautions described in Chapter 3 apply equally to scenes where digital evidence is to be identified and seized. Two additional protective precautions are to have antistatic bags for collection of small devices or parts of larger ones, as well as nonmagnetic tools for when it is necessary to disassemble a larger item. Having access to these must *not* entice the CSI to make any unnecessary intrusions into digital devices. Protecting individual devices is discussed under the heading for each, in the sections below. When securing and evaluating any scene where it is suspected that digital evidence may be involved and in the absence of a digital evidence expert, the CSI should do the following:

- Document and photograph the scene, paying attention to the electronic devices and any obvious network or wireless access points that may be present and capable of linking computers and other devices to each other and the Internet. The existence of network and wireless access points may indicate that additional evidence exists beyond the initial scene; however, it is not uncommon for wireless devices to be hidden, and their detection requires trained personnel with equipment that can search the frequency spectrum. This is an example of where absence of evidence, in the sense of no visible object, is not evidence of absence.
- Secure all electronic devices, including personal or portable ones such as mobile phones and MP3 players (the drives in portable digital music players can be configured as general digital data storage units, so do not assume that devices associated with entertainment will not contain evidence).

- Ensure that no unauthorised person has access to any electronic devices at the scene.
- Refuse all offers of help or technical assistance from any person not identified and authorised at the strategy meeting.
- Leave all devices that are not switched on in the OFF condition; do *not* switch a device on to see if it may contain anything of interest.
- Remember that the devices may yield other forensic evidence such as DNA and fingerprints and make sure that they are handled appropriately

A.5 Computer Systems

In this discussion, *computer systems* refers to entities that can be moved, including networked desktop personal computers; they do not include installations conventionally referred to as *mainframe*, which are physically large and fixed. Mainframe computers should be examined only by digital evidence examination experts, and the role of the CSI should be restricted to physical security of the room or rooms in which the computer and peripherals is located. Computer systems encompass laptops (see Figure A.1), desktops, smaller minicomputers, and peripheral devices. They may be self-contained units manufactured by companies such as HP®, Dell®, or Apple®, or they may be constructed from individual components assembled into cases or racks. They may use Microsoft® Windows®, Apple, or Linux operating systems.

Peripherals include printers, modems and routers, scanners, and external storage devices. Two or more computers may be linked together to create a network over which data and resources can be shared. The parts of the network will be connected by cables (e.g., Ethernet) or wirelessly or a combination of the two. Physical devices that should be searched for and secured in regard to a network are hubs, modems, wireless access points, network cards, and Ethernet cabling.

Figure A.1 (a) AT&T™ modem–router (left) and HP® desktop PC (right). (b) Apple® MacBook® laptop.

A.5.1   Potential Evidence

Word processor documents, spreadsheets, charts and diagrams, still photographs and video recordings, e-mails, databases, browsing histories, chat logs and buddy lists, event logs, and data stored on external devices can all yield valuable evidence for just about any kind of crime investigation. The device functions and capabilities, including Internet Protocol (IP) and local area network (LAN) addresses, may provided useful evidence as to the history of its usage.

A.5.2   Examining and Securing Computers at the Scene

After identifying a computer at the scene, a CSI acting as first responder should document its condition by means of photographs and notes. The record should record the power state of the device, determined by checking for fixed or flashing lights, listening for running fans or spinning hard drives, and looking at the monitor or display. If the screen is ON and displays such activity as a photograph, diagram, e-mail, word processing document or spreadsheet, or website, the CSI should photograph the screen. If the screen is blank or shows a screensaver, move the mouse slightly or swipe the trackpad on a laptop but do *not* click the mouse or tap the trackpad. If there is a change in the display, photograph the screen.

If there is no change in the display, what to do next depends on whether it is a desktop computer monitor or the screen of a laptop. In the former case, check to see if the ON/OFF switch of the monitor is in the OFF position; if so, switch it ON, then follow the actions in the preceding paragraph. If the unit is a laptop display with no indicator lights for ON and no sounds of disc or fan activity, then disconnect the unit at the power source. Check any local procedure for this step, as some agencies prefer to leave the unit untouched until a digital examination expert is available.

If the above steps indicate that the computer is OFF, continue to record and protect the item. Photograph and document any visible identity marks and serial numbers, and place evidence tape over any optical disk drive trays or slots. As with all evidence, be aware that your actions should preserve and not destroy evidence such as latent prints and DNA. If the above steps indicate that the computer is ON, the first step should be to seek advice. A flashing hard-drive indicator light may mean that data is being deleted, in which case the correct step would be to disconnect the power. Unfortunately, it could also mean that data is in the process of being written to a document, in which case the system should be left running so that the information can be recovered.

A.6   External Storage Devices

External storage devices include external hard drives connected by USB or other cable, or wirelessly, and removable media such as thumb drives, floppy disc drives, and flash memory cards such as SmartMedia™ (SM) or Secure Digital (SD™). The 1-TB drive shown in Figure A.2 is not much larger than a smartphone and can store 1 million million bytes of data. Just 55 of these could store the contents of the entire US Library of Congress.

Figure A.2 A 1-TB external hard drive with USB connector and a 4-GB thumb drive on top of it. A £1 coin is shown for size comparisons.

A.6.1 Potential Evidence

External storage devices such as hard drives, external hard drives, removable media, thumb drives, and memory cards may contain information such as e-mail messages, Internet browsing history, Internet chat logs and buddy lists, photographs, image files, databases, financial records, and event logs that can be valuable evidence in an investigation or prosecution.

A.6.2 Examining and Securing External Storage Devices at the Scene

External storage drives not connected to a computer can be photographed, documented, and packaged. Drives connected to a computer that is ON must not be disconnected—this is especially important if the computer is an Apple®, such as an iMac® or MacBook®, as the data can be lost or corrupted unless the device is properly disconnected; although less critical, this is good advice for PCs as well. Drives connected to a computer that is OFF can be left attached until the digital evidence expert arrives. If the CSI is instructed to collect them, they can be disconnected and packaged.

A.7 Peripheral Devices

Peripheral devices include those associated directly with a computer, such as printers, scanners, and web cameras. A combination printer/scanner is shown in Figure A.3.

A.7.1 Potential Evidence

The physical objects are potential sources of fingerprint and DNA evidence, just like any other. A fax or device that incorporates a faxing capability can yield evidence of the suspect's activity in the form of incoming and outgoing phone numbers.

A.7.2 Examining and Securing Peripheral Devices at the Scene

These can be treated as conventional physical objects and be documented *in situ* by photography and made available for fingerprint and DNA evidence.

Figure A.3 A Kodak® combination printer/scanner with built-in wireless connectivity (blue status light indicates that wireless link is ON).

A.8 Mobile Phones

Mobile phones range from simple devices used to place and receive calls, usually with built-in contact lists and associated numbers, to units such as the iPhone® (see Figure A.4), a range of devices running Android™, and some models running a mobile version of Microsoft® Windows®, which are essentially mobile computers capable of also acting as phones. These are described as *smartphones*. Apart from the most very basic units, mobile phones will incorporate some form of camera. The quality can be very good and the output on the more advanced models of smartphones can include high-definition (HD) video. Most phones incorporate a global positioning system (GPS) function.

Figure A.4 An Apple® iPhone® smartphone and an iPod touch®. The phone screen shows some of the computer functions that they can perform, including web browsing and e-mail, and the iPod screen shows its ability to take and store still and video images.

A.8.1 Potential Evidence

Mobile phones contain data on their usage, such as calls made and received; in the case of smartphones, they contain the same kinds of evidence that can be extracted from computers, as well as voice recorders for making audio notes. There may be a database of images taken by the built-in camera that can provide evidence, including geopositioning, which automatically tags the location where the photographic was taken.

A.8.2 Examining and Securing Mobile Phones at the Scene

Caution: Many mobile phones, especially smartphones, incorporate software that permits them to be locked or even have their data erased remotely. For this reason, after it has been photographed and its status recorded, any mobile phone to be seized for examination should be switched off completely. Different makes and even different models of the same brand have different ways to switch them to sleep mode or to turn them off, so it is probably better to contact support, identify the make and model from the information on the case, and receive instructions on how to proceed. In some cases, data can be lost if the phone battery runs out; again, it is important to seek advice or at least not delay in transferring the phone to the digital examiner.

A.9 Other Handheld Devices

Personal data assistants (PDAs), digital multimedia players and recorders (e.g., iPod®), pagers, digital cameras, and GPS receivers may contain data similar to that found on smartphones. For example, the iPod touch® shown in Figure A.4 is not just a device to store and play back audio and video media, as it can also take still and video photographs, send and receive e-mails, download and open e-mail attachments, and text message and video chat with people on the contacts list.

A.9.1 Potential Evidence

The potential evidence available from handheld devices includes data such as documents, e-mail messages, Internet browsing history, Internet chat logs and buddy lists, photographs, image files, databases, and financial records.

A.9.2 Examining and Securing Handheld Devices at the Scene

These devices should be handled in the same way as mobile phones.

A.10 Audio and Video Recording, Storage, and Playback Devices, Including CCTV Surveillance Equipment and Digital Cameras

Examples of audio–video (AV) devices that could be encountered are more or less obvious, including webcams, tape and optical disc recording and playback machines, audio dictation recorders, and still and video cameras (Figure A.5). Note that some of these are

Figure A.5 Examples of video (JVC®) and still (Nikon® Coolpix®) cameras.

actually analogue devices but the recovery of evidence from them is the responsibility of digital evidence units, as is enhancement of the data. Also remember that smartphones and some other handheld devices can take good-quality still and video images (see Figure A.4). Surveillance units will range from domestic webcams to commercial security recordings in retail shops, fuel stations, and hotels to government monitoring of airports, train stations, major roads, and city centre business environments. As with the AV recording devices mentioned above, some surveillance units may still use tape and be in analogue form, but modern units record digitally to a hard drive. The data storage units for tapes and discs should be included in any scene search.

A.10.1 Potential Evidence

The most obvious evidential application is images in cases of child pornography or exploitation; however, any audio or video record may provide evidence as to who is involved in the crime under investigation and could include instructions, for example, for making drugs or bombs.

A.10.2 Examining and Securing AV Devices at the Scene

Proceed as for Section A.7, Peripheral Devices.

A.11 Video Game Consoles

These include the Sony PlayStation® (Figure A.6) and Microsoft® XBox®.

A.11.1 Potential Evidence

Videogame consoles may contain media relevant to pornography or the theft of digital materials. These units can also be configured to access the Internet legitimately to allow remote game playing, but the connections can also be used for identity theft or electronic fraud.

Figure A.6 Sony PlayStation® 2 (PS2™) system.

A.11.2   Examining and Securing Gaming Consoles at the Scene

Videogame consoles should be treated as computers.

A.12   Global Positioning Systems, Including Satellite Navigation Units

Global positioning system (GPS) units range from low-cost, hand-held devices that can be used by hikers, cyclists, and motorists to identify where they are and to navigate to specified destinations, to very expensive units installed in boats. Figure A.7 shows a popular, low-cost, portable, satellite navigation unit.

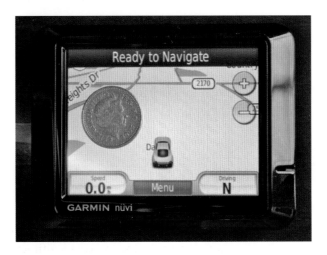

Figure A.7 Garmin™ satellite navigation unit.

A.12.1   Potential Evidence

Global positioning system units can show where an individual or vehicle has been, and they can be valuable in establishing movements in smuggling and trafficking cases or any other situation in which the questions of WHERE and WHEN are raised.

A.13   Summary

The digital era offers many advantages to the criminal; for example, it has made fraud, forgery, and child pornography so much easier. Fortunately, the same advances can be used to control the same criminal due to the records that they leave behind. Recovery of data from digital device is a specialised activity, and the main role of the conventional CSI is to identify and protect digital device at a scene, where these may contain useful information. In doing so, the CSI should be cautious and aware of the limits of his or her expertise; for example, wireless access points are not necessarily large and connected to something by cable, and wireless units may well be hidden and require specialist scanners to detect. The role of the CSI, therefore, is mainly to address WHAT (what items are present that may yield evidence when examined by digital recovery experts) and a special aspect of HOW (how do I best handle these items to preserve and protect the potential evidence).

Bibliography

The following list suggests further reading relevant to many of the areas covered in the text. Because this book is written primarily for police officers and crime scene investigators, material of a highly technical nature has been intentionally omitted. Thus, certain areas requiring a greater level of scientific knowledge may be limited in this bibliography. The references below serve as a starting point from which the reader wishing additional information may begin, but they by no means represent an exhaustive bibliography on forensic science. The Internet is an additional resource for persons interested in the subject, and readers are also encouraged to consider membership in the fine professional organizations noted in the text.

Chapter 1

Innocence Project. (2011). *Fact Sheet*. The Innocence Project, New York (http://www.innocenceproject.org/Content/Facts_on_PostConviction_DNA_Exonerations.php#).

Kirk, P. L. (1974). *Crime Investigation*, 2nd ed. John Wiley & Sons, New York.

Kuhn, T. S. (1966). *The Structure of Scientific Revolutions*, 3rd ed. University of Chicago Press, Chicago, IL.

Lakatos, I. and Musgrave, A., Eds. (1970). *Criticism and the Growth of Knowledge*, Cambridge University Press, Cambridge, UK.

Nickell, J. and Fischer, J. F. (1999). *Crime Science: Methods of Forensic Detection*. The University Press of Kentucky, Lexington.

NRC. (2009). *Strengthening Forensic Science in the United States: A Path Forward*, Report of the Committee on Identifying the Needs of the Forensic Sciences Community, National Research Council. National Academies Press, New York.

Peirce, C. S. (1934). *Collected Papers of Charles Sanders Peirce*, Vol. 5, Hartshorne, C. and Weiss, P., Eds. Harvard University Press, Cambridge, MA.

Chapter 2

Aristotle. (1991). *The Art of Rhetoric*, Lawson-Tancred, H., Ed. Penguin Books, London.

Kennedy, G. A. (1994). *A New History of Classical Rhetoric*. Princeton University Press, Princeton, NJ.

Petherick, W. A., Turvey, B. E., and Ferguson, C. E. (2010). *Forensic Criminology*. Elsevier, Amsterdam.

Chapter 3

ENFSI. (2002). *Performance-Based Standards for Forensic Science Practitioners*. European Network of Forensic Science Institutes, The Hague, The Netherlands (http://www.enfsi.eu/page.php?uid=108).

ILAC. (2002). *Guidelines for Forensic Science Laboratories*. International Laboratory Accreditation Cooperation, Silverwater, NSW.

Jackson, A. R. W. and Jackson, J. M. (2008). *Forensic Science*, 2nd ed. Pearson Education, London.

Chapter 5

Barnett, P. (2001). *Ethics in Forensic Science: Professional Standards for the Practice of Criminalistics.* CRC Press, Boca Raton, FL.

EA. (2008). *Guidance for the Implementation of ISO/IEC 17020 in the Field of Crime Scene Investigation,* EA-5/03. European Co-operation for Accreditation, Utrecht, The Netherlands (www.european-accreditation.org/n1/doc/EA-5_03.pdf).

ENFSI. (2002). *Performance-Based Standards for Forensic Science Practitioners.* European Network of Forensic Science Institutes, The Hague, The Netherlands (http://www.enfsi.eu/page.php?uid=108).

ENFSI. (2003). *Guidance on the Production of Best Practice Manuals within ENFSI.* European Network of Forensic Science Institutes, The Hague, The Netherlands (www.enfsi.eu/get_doc.php?uid=72).

ENFSI. (2005). *Code of Conduct.* European Network of Forensic Science Institutes, The Hague, The Netherlands (http://www.enfsi.eu/search_results.php?chk_all=on&fnd=code+of+conduct).

Knight, B. (1989). Ethics and discipline in forensic science. *Journal of the Forensic Science Society,* 29:53–59.

NRC. (2009). *Strengthening Forensic Science in the United States: A Path Forward,* Report of the Committee on Identifying the Needs of the Forensic Sciences Community, National Research Council. National Academies Press, New York.

Peterson, J. L. and Murdock, J. E. (1989). Forensic science ethics: Developing an integrated system of support and enforcement. *Journal of Forensic Sciences,* 34(3):749–762.

Rosner, R. (1996). Ethical practice in the forensic sciences and justification of ethical codes. *Journal of Forensic Sciences,* 41(6):913–915.

Chapter 6

Abalos, A. (1989). Regenerating finger pads on burnt, putrefied or mummified corpses. *International Criminal Police Review,* 44:16–19.

Allen, M. J. and Rimmer, P. A. (1988). The dating of a will. *Journal of the Forensic Science Society,* 28:199–203.

Allison, H. C. (1973). *Personal Identification.* Holbrook Press, Boston.

Arbouine, M. W. and Day, S. P. (1994). The use of drum defects to link laser-printed documents to individual laser printers. *Journal of the Forensic Science Society,* 34(2):99–104.

Arensburg, B. (1989). Methods for age identification on living individuals of uncertain age. *Canadian Society of Forensic Science Journal Journal,* 22(2):147–157.

Austin-Smith, D. and Maples, W. R. (1994). The reliability of skull/photograph superimposition in individual identification. *Journal of Forensic Sciences,* 39:446–455.

Barton, B. C. (1989). The use of an electrostatic detection apparatus to demonstrate the matching of torn paper edges. *Journal of the Forensic Science Society,* 29(1):35–38.

Beck, J. (1995). Sources of error in handwriting evaluation. *Journal of Forensic Sciences,* 40(1):78–82.

Bentsen, R. K., Brown, J. K., Dinsmore, A., Harvey, K. K., and Kee, T. G. (1996). Post-firing visualization of fingerprints on spent cartridge cases. *Science & Justice,* 36(1):3–8.

Berg, E. (1996). Digital enhancement and transmission of latent prints. *Journal of Forensic Identification,* 46(5):573–580.

Bettencourt, D. S. (1991). A compilation of techniques for processing deceased human skin for latent prints. *Journal of Forensic Identification,* 41(2):111–120.

Black, J. (1990). The interaction of visualization fluids and fingerprints. *Journal of Forensic Identification,* 40(1):28–30.

Bobev, K. (1995). Fingerprints and factors affecting their condition. *Journal of Forensic Identification*, 45(2):176–183.

Brandt-Casadevall, C., Krompecher, T., and Gujer, H.-R. (1989). Identification based on medical data. *Canadian Society of Forensic Science Journal Journal*, 22(1):35–42.

Breedlove, C. H. (1989). The analysis of ballpoint inks for forensic purposes. *Journal of Chemical Education*, 68:170.

Brunelle, R. L. (1992). Ink dating—the state of the art. *Journal of Forensic Sciences*, 37(1):113–124.

Brunelle, R. L. and Cantu, A. A. (1987). A critical evaluation of current ink dating techniques. *Journal of Forensic Sciences*, 32(6):1522–1536.

Brunelle, R. L., Breedlove, C. H., and Midkill, C. R. (1987). Determining the relative age of ballpoint inks using a single-solvent extraction technique. *Journal of Forensic Sciences*, 32(6):1511–1521.

Buquet, A. et al. (1989). The application of statistical methods to the analysis of typewritten documents: Regression and covariance. *International Criminal Police Review*, 44:10–16.

Burnes, K. R. and Maples, W. R. (1976). Estimation of age from individual adult teeth. *Journal of Forensic Sciences*, 21(2):343–356.

Caldwell, J. P. and Kim, N. D. (2002). Extension of the color suite available for chemical enhancement of fingerprints in blood. *Journal of Forensic Sciences*, 47(2):332–340.

Campbell, B. M. (1991). Separation of adhesive tapes. *Journal of Forensic Identification*, 41:102–106.

Camps, F. E. (1953). *Medical and Scientific Investigations in the Cristie Case*. Medical Publications, London.

Cantu, A. A. and Prough, R. S. (1987). On the relative aging of ink—the solvent extraction technique. *Journal of Forensic Sciences*, 32:1151–1174.

Choudhry, M. Y. and Whritenour, R. D. (1990). A new approach to unraveling tangled adhesive tape for potential detection of latent fingerprints and recovery of trace evidence. *Journal of Forensic Sciences*, 35:1373–1383.

Cole, S. A. (2001). *Suspect Identities: A History of Fingerprinting and Criminal Identification*. Harvard University Press, Cambridge, MA.

Conway, J. V. P. (1959). *Evidential Documents*. Charles C Thomas, Springfield, IL.

Cook, S. (1996). The use of embalming fluids in the restoration of mummified fingers. *Journal of Forensic Identification*, 46(5):529–541.

Cowger, J. F. (1979). Moving towards professionalization of latent print examiners. *Journal of Forensic Sciences*, 24(3):591–595.

Cowger, J. F. (1983). *Friction Ridge Skin*. CRC Press, Boca Raton, FL.

Creighton, J. (1997). Visualization of latent impressions after incidental or direct contact with human blood. *Journal of Forensic Identification*, 47:534–541.

Crown, D. A. (1989). The differentiation of electrostatic photocopy machines. *Journal of Forensic Sciences*, 34(1):142–155.

Dalrymple, B. E. (1979). Case analysis of fingerprint detection by laser. *Journal of Forensic Sciences*, 24(3):586–590.

Dalrymple, B. E. and Menzies, T. (1994). Computer enhancement of evidence through background noise suppression. *Journal of Forensic Sciences*, 39(2):537–546.

Dalrymple, B. E., Duff, J. M., and Menzel, E. R. (1977). Inherent fingerprint luminescence detection by laser. *Journal of Forensic Sciences*, 22:106–115.

Day, S. P. (1985). Evaluation of the application of the argon-ion laser to document examination: A review of casework and experimental data. *Journal of the Forensic Science Society*, 25:285–296.

Doherty, P. E. and Mooney, D. J. (1990). Deciphering bloody imprints through chemical enhancement. *Journal of Forensic Sciences*, 35(2):457–465.

Drake, W. and Lukash, L. (1978). Reconstruction of mutilated victims for identification. *Journal of Forensic Sciences*, 23(1):218–230.

El-Najjar, M. Y. and McWilliams, K. R. (1977). *Forensic Anthropology: The Structure, Morphology and Variation of Bones and Dentition*. Charles C Thomas, Springfield, IL.

Ellen, D. (2006). *The Scientific Examination of Questioned Documents Methods and Techniques*. CRC Press, Boca Raton, FL.

FBI. (1973). *The Science of Fingerprints: Classification and Use*. US Federal Bureau of Investigation, Washington, DC.

Gamboe, T. E. (1989). Small particle: Developing latent prints on water-soaked firearms and effect on firearms analysis. *Journal of Forensic Sciences*, 34(2):312–320.

Geng, Q. (1998). Recovery of super glue over-fumed fingerprints. *Journal of Forensic Identification*, 48(1):17–23.

Gilmour, C. and Bradford, J. (1987). The effect of medication on handwriting. *Canadian Society of Forensic Science Journal*, 20:119–138.

Glaister, J. and Brash, J. C. (1937). *Medico-Legal Aspects of the Ruxton Case*. E & S Livingstone, Edinburgh.

Goetz, M. (1996). Cyanoacrylate fuming precautions. *Journal of Forensic Identification*, 46(4):409–411.

Golden, G. S. (1994). Use of alternative light source illumination in bite mark photography. *Journal of Forensic Science*, 39(3):815–823.

Gupta, A. K., Lai, A., and Misra, G. J. (1989). Electrostatic detection of secret writings. *Forensic Science International, Ireland*, 41(1–2):17–23.

Haglund, W. D. (1987). A technique to enhance fingerprinting of mummified fingers. *Journal of Forensic Sciences*, 33(5):1244–1248.

Haglund, W. D. and Sperry, K. (1993). The use of hydrogen peroxide to visualize tattoos obscured by decomposition and mummification. *Journal of Forensic Sciences*, 38(1):147–150.

Hall, R. F. (1979). Latent skin print identification solves homicide. *FBI Law Enforcement Bulletin*, 48:9–11.

Haque, F., Westland, A. D., Milligan, J., and Kerr, F. M. (1989). A small particle (iron oxide) suspension for detection of latent fingerprints on smooth surfaces. *Forensic Science International*, 41(1–2):73–82.

Harada, H. (1988). A rapid identification of black color materials with specific reference to ballpoint ink and Indian ink. *Journal of the Forensic Science Society*, 28:167–177.

Harris, J. (1992). Developments in the analysis of writing inks on questioned documents. *Journal of Forensic Sciences*, 37(2):612–619.

Harris, J. et al. (1989). Characterization and dating of correction fluids on questioned documents using FTIR. *Canadian Society of Forensic Science Journal*, 22:349.

Harrison, W. R. (1958). *Suspect Documents: Their Scientific Examination*. Praeger, New York.

Hart, L. J. and Hart, R. P. (1989). Photographically subtracting interfering images from ESDA. *Journal of Forensic Sciences*, 34(6):1405–1407.

Hart, L. J. and Carney, B. B. (1989). Typewriting versus writing instrument: A line intersection problem. *Journal of Forensic Sciences*, 34(6):1329–1335.

Harvey, W. (1976). *Dental Identification and Forensic Odontology*. Henry Kimpton Publishers, London.

Herod, D. W. and Menzel, E. R. (1982). Laser detection of latent fingerprints: Ninhydrin followed by zinc chloride. *Journal of Forensic Sciences*, 27(3):513–518.

Hewlett, D. and Sears, V. (1997). Replacements for CFC113 in the ninhydrin process: Part 1. *Journal of Forensic Identification*, 47(3):287–300.

Hewlett, D., Sears, V., and Suzuki, S. (1997). Replacements for CFC113 in the Ninhydrin process: Part 2. *Journal of Forensic Identification*, 47(3), 300–306.

Hicks, A. F. (1995a). Computer imaging for questioned document examiners I: The benefits. *Journal of Forensic Sciences*, 40(6):1045–1051.

Hicks, A. F. (1995b). Computer imaging for questioned document examiners II: The potential for abuse. *Journal of Forensic Sciences*, 40(6):1052–1054.

Hilton, O. (1979). History of questioned documents examination in the United States. *Journal of Forensic Sciences*, 24:890.

Hilton, O. (1981). *Scientific Examination of Questioned Documents*. Elsevier, New York.

Hilton, O. (1992). Signatures—review and a new view. *Journal of Forensic Sciences*, 37(1):125–129.

Hooft, P. J., Noji, E. K., and Van de Voorde, H. P. (1989). Fatality management in mass casualty incidents. *Forensic Science International*, 40(1):3–14.

Horan, G. J. and Horan, J. J. (1988). How long after writing can an ESDA image be developed? *Forensic Science International*, 39(2):119–125.

INTERPOL. (2009). *Disaster Victim Identification Guide*. INTERPOL, Lyon, France.

Jackson, G. R. (1994). A high-resolution electronic imaging system for crime scene use. *Journal of Forensic Sciences*, 39(4):912–918.

James, J. D., Pounds, C. A., and Wilshire, B. (1991). Obliteration of latent fingerprints. *Journal of Forensic Sciences*, 36(5):1376–1386.

Jaret, Y., Meriau, M., and Donche, A. (1997). Transfer of bloody fingerprints. *Journal of Forensic Identification*, 47(1):38–41.

Jones, N. (1990). Arson-for-profit investigations, success or failure? Recovering water-damaged business records. *Fire and Arson Investigator*, 40(3):50–52.

Kahana, T., Grande, A., Tancredi, D. M., Penalver, J., and Hiss, J. (2001). Fingerprinting the deceased: Traditional and new techniques. *Journal of Forensic Sciences*, 46(4):908–912.

Kam, M., Fielding, G., and Conn, R. (1997). Writer identification by professional document examiners. *Journal of Forensic Sciences*, 42(5):778–786.

Kam, M., Weststein, J., and Conn, R. (1994). Proficiency of professional document examiners in writer identification. *Journal of Forensic Sciences*, 39(1):5–14.

Katz , J. O. and Cottone, J. A. (1988). The present direction of research in forensic odontology. *Journal of Forensic Sciences*, 33(6):1319–1327.

Kaymaz, E. and Mitra, S. (1993). A novel approach to Fourier spectral enhancement of laser-luminescent fingerprint images. *Journal of Forensic Sciences*, 38(3):530–541.

Keating, D. M. and Miller, J. J. (1993). A technique for developing and photographing ridge impressions on decomposed water-soaked fingers. *Journal of Forensic Sciences*, 38(1):197–202.

Kempton, J. B., Sirignano, A., DeGaetano, D. H., Yates, P. J., and Rowe, W. F. (1992). Comparison of fingernail striation patterns in identical twins. *Journal of Forensic Sciences*, 37(6):1534–1540.

Kerley, E. R. (1973). Forensic anthropology. In *Legal Medicine Annual*, Wecht, C. H., Ed. Appleton-Century-Crofts, New York, pp. 163–198.

Killam, E. W. (1989). Is it human? Differentiating between human and animal bones. *Crime Laboratory Digest*, 16:9.

Kopainsky, B. (1989). Document examination: Applications of image processing systems. *Forensic Science Review*, 1:85.

Krauss, T. C. (1976). Forensic odontology in missing person cases. *Journal of Forensic Sciences*, 21(4):959–962.

Kremer, R. D. and Tabb, D. L. (1989). Paper, its material and macro-structural characteristics relevant to analytical and diagnostic test development. *American Laboratory*, 21:16.

Larson, C. P. (1974). Unusual methods of human identification used in three cases. *Journal of Forensic Sciences*, 19(2):402–405.

Lee, H. C. and Gaensslen, R. E. (2001). *Advances in Fingerprint Technology*, 2nd ed. CRC Press, Boca Raton, FL.

Lee, H. C., Gaensslen, R., Pagliaro, E., Guman, M., Berka, K., Keith, T., and Phipps, P. (1989). The effect of presumptive test, latent fingerprint and some other reagents and materials on subsequent serological identification, genetic marker and DNA testing in bloodstains. *Journal of Forensic Identification*, 39(6):339–358.

Lennard, C. J. and Margot, P. A. (1988). Sequencing of reagents for the improved visualization of latent fingerprints. *Journal of Forensic Identification*, 38(5):197–210.

Lifschultz, B. D. and Donoghue, E. R. (1993). Deaths caused by lightning. *Journal of Forensic Sciences*, 38:353–358.

Lunt, D. A. (1974). Identification and tooth morphology. *Journal of the Forensic Science Society*, 14(3):203–207.

Luntz, L. L. and Luntz, P. (1972). Dental identification of disaster victims by a dental disaster squad. *Journal of Forensic Sciences*, 17(1):63–69.

MacFarlane, T. W., MacDonald, D. G., and Sutherland, D. A. (1974). Statistical problems in dental identification. *Journal of the Forensic Science Society*, 14(3):247–252.

Marchand, P. (1989). A nondestructive method for determining the grain direction of paper. *Canadian Society of Forensic Science Journal*, 22:69.

Margot, P. and Lennard, C. (1990). *Manual of Fingerprint Detection Techniques*. Institute de Police Scientifique et de Criminologie, Universite de Lausanne, Lausanne.

Marks, M. K., Bennett, J. L., and Wilson, O. L. (1997). Digital video image capture in establishing positive identification. *Journal of Forensic Sciences*, 42(3):492–495.

Masters, N. and De Haan, J. (1996). Vacuum metal deposition and cyanoacrylate detection of older latent prints. *Journal of Forensic Identification*, 46(1):32–42.

McCarthy, M. M. (1990). Evaluation of Ardrox as a luminescent stain for cyanoacrylate processed latent impressions. *Journal of Forensic Identification*, 40(2):75–80.

McCarthy M. M. and Grieve, D. L. (1989). Preprocessing with cyanoacrylate ester fuming for finger-print impressions in blood. *Journal of Forensic Identification*, 39(1):23–32.

Menzel, E. R. (1979). Laser detection of latent fingerprints with phosphorescers. *Journal of Forensic Sciences*, 24:582–585.

Menzel, E. R. (1985). Comparison of argon-ion, copper-vapor and frequency-doubled neodymium:yttrium aluminum garnet (ND:YAG) laser for latent fingerprint development. *Journal of Forensic Sciences*, 30(2):383–397.

Menzel, E. R. (1989a). Detection of latent fingerprints by laser-excited luminescence. *Analytical Chemisty*, 61:557A.

Menzel, E. R. (1989b). Pretreatment of latent prints for laser development. *Forensic Science Review*, 1(1):43–66.

Menzel, E. R. and Fox, K. E. (1980). Laser detection of latent fingerprints: Preparation of fluorescent dust-ing powders and the feasibility of a portable system. *Journal of Forensic Sciences*, 25(1):150–153.

Menzel, E. R., Burt, J. A., Sinor, T. W., Tubach-Ley, W. B., and Jordon, K. J. (1983). Laser detection of latent fingerprints: Treatment with glue containing cyanoacrylate ester. *Journal of Forensic Sciences*, 28:307–317.

Menzel, E. R., Bartsch, R. A., and Hallman, J. L. (1990). Fluorescent metal-Ruhemann's purple coor-dination compounds: Application to latent fingerprint detection. *Journal of Forensic Sciences*, 35(1):25–34.

Mittal, S. et al. (1989). The forensic examination of unfamiliar scripts. *International Criminal Police Review*, 44:11.

Morse, D., Duncan, J., and Stoutamire, J. (1983). *Handbook of Forensic Archaeology and Anthropology*. Rose Printing, Tallahassee, FL.

Munson, T. O. (1989). A simple method for sampling photocopy toners for examination by pyrolysis gas chromatography. *Crime Laboratory Digest*, 16(1):6–8.

Noble, H. W. (1974). The estimation of age from dentition. *Journal of the Forensic Science Society*, 14:215–221.

Olenik, J. H. (1989). Cyanoacrylate fuming: An alternative non-heat method. *Journal of Forensic Identification*, 39(5):302–304.

Osborn, A. S. (1929). *Questioned Documents*, 2nd ed. Sweet & Maxwell, London.

Owen, T. (1989). An introduction to forensic examination of audio and videotapes. *Journal of Forensic Identification*, 39(2):75.

Parkinson, G. (1996). Certification programs of the International Association for Identification. *Journal of Forensic Identification*, 46:169.

Penalver, J., Kahana, T., and Hiss, J. (1997). Prosthetic devices in positive identification of human remains. *Journal of Forensic Identification*, 47:400–405.

Phillips, C. E., Cole, D. O., and Jones, G. W. (1990). Physical developer: A practical and productive latent print developer. *Journal of Forensic Identification*, 40(3):135–147.

Pierce, D. S. (1989). Tonally reversed friction ridge prints on plastics. *Journal of Forensic Identification*, 39(1):11–22.

Plamondon, R. and Lorette, G. (1989). Automatic signature verification and writer identification: The state of the art. *Pattern Recognition*, 22(2):107–131.

Reichardt, G. J., Carr, J. C., and Stone, E. G. (1978). A conventional method for lifting latent fingerprints from human skin surfaces. *Journal of Forensic Sciences*, 23(1):135–141.

Richardson, L. and Kade, H. (1972). Readable fingerprints from mummified or putrefied specimens. *Journal of Forensic Sciences*, 17(2):325–328.

Ruprecht, A. (1989). Use of direct positive photographic paper in the preparation of fingerprint exhibits. *Journal of Forensic Identification*, 39(4):244–246.

Ruslander, H. (1997). Super glue fuming of vegetation at crime scenes. *Journal of Forensic Identification*, 47(1):42–46.

Sams, C. (1970). The role of the fingerprint officer. *Journal of the Forensic Science Society*, 10(4):219–225.

Saunders, J. (1993). Macroscopic examination of overlapping latent prints on non-porous items. *Journal of Forensic Identification*, 43(2):138–143.

Sauvarin, A. (1993). Latent fingerprints on a fingernail. *Journal of Forensic Identification*, 43:35.

Scheuer, J. L. and Elkington, N. M. (1993). Sex determination from metacarpals and the first proximal phalanx. *Journal of Forensic Sciences*, 38:769–778.

Sedeyn, M. J. (1988). Handwriting examination: A practical approach. *Forensic Science International*, 36:169–171.

Seguss, R. K. (1988). Altered and counterfeit travel documents: A Canadian perspective. *International Criminal Police Review*, 43:11.

Sekharan, P. C. (1989). Personal identification from skull suture pattern. *Canadian Society of Forensic Science Journal*, 22(1):27–34.

Sharf, S., Gabbay, R., and Brown, S. (1997). Infrared luminescence of indented writing as evidence of document alteration. *Journal of Forensic Sciences*, 42(4):729–732.

Shelef, R., Levy, A., Rhima, I., Tsaroom, S., and Elkayam, R. (1996a). Development of latent fingerprints from unignited incendiary bottles. *Journal of Forensic Identification*, 46(5):556–560.

Shelef, R., Levy, A., Rhima, I., and Elkayam, R. (1996b). Development of latent fingerprints from glass surfaces washed in accelerant fluids. *Journal of Forensic Identification*, 46(5):561–565.

Shelef, R., Levy, A., Rhima, I., Tsaroom, S., and Elkayam, R. (1996c). Recovery of latent fingerprints from soot-covered incendiarized glass surfaces. *Journal of Forensic Identification*, 46(5):565–569.

Shonberger, M. (1997). A variation of super glue processing of small, immovable, or difficult to move items. *Journal of Forensic Identification*, 47(1):47–48.

Skinner, M. F. (1988). Method and theory in deciding identity of skeletonized human remains. *Canadian Society of Forensic Science Journal*, 21(3):114–134.

Skinner, M. F. (1989). Applied archaeology and physical anthropology in a forensic context: A review of 12 years of forensic anthropology in British Columbia. *Canadian Society of Forensic Science Journal*, 22:83–88.

Sognnaes, R. F. (1977a). Progress in forensic dentistry I. *New England Journal of Medicine*, 296:79.

Sognnaes, R. F. (1977b). Progress in forensic dentistry II. *New England Journal of Medicine*, 296:149.

Song, H.-W. and Jia, J.-T. (1989). The estimation of tooth age from attrition of the occlusal surface. *Medicince, Science, & the Law*, 29:69–73.

Sopher, I. M. (1973). Dental identification of aircraft-accident fatalities. *Journal of Forensic Sciences*, 18(4):356–363.

Stewart, T. D., Ed. (1970). *Personal Identification in Mass Disasters*. National Museum of Natural History, Washington, DC.

Stewart, T. D. (1972). What the bones tell—today. *FBI Law Enforcement Bulletin*, 41(2):16–20.

Stewart, T. D. (1979). *Essentials of Forensic Anthropology*. Charles C Thomas, Springfield, IL.

Taylor, L. R. (1986). The restoration of water-soaked documents: A case study. *Journal of Forensic Sciences*, 31(3):113–118.

Tolliver, D. K. (1990). The electrostatic detection apparatus (ESDA): Is it really nondestructive to documents? *Forensic Science International*, 44(1):7–21.

Trowell, F. (1975). A method for fixing latent fingerprints developed with iodine. *Journal of the Forensic Science Society*, 15(3):189–195.

Tucker, G. (1990). A modified crystal violet application technique for black electrical tape. *Journal of Forensic Identification*, 40(3):148–150.

Twibell, J. D., Home, J. M., Smallson, K. W., and Higgs, D. G. (1984). Transfer of nitroglycerine to hands during contact with commercial explosives. *Journal of Forensic Sciences*, 27(4):783–791.

Twibell, J. D., Home, J. M., Smallson, K. W., Higgs, D. G., and Hayes, T. S. (1984). Assessment of solvents for the recovery of nitroglycerine from hands using cotton swabs. *Journal of Forensic Sciences*, 27(4):792–800.

Walton, A. N. (1989). Laser photography using laser beam painted light technique on curved surfaces. *Journal of Forensic Identification*, 39(3):177–180.

Wanxiang, L. U. O. and Xiaoling, C. I. A. (1988). A study of the principle of the electrostatic imaging technique. *Journal of the Forensic Science Society*, 28(4):237–242.

Warren, C. P. (1979). Verifying identification of military remains: A case study. *Journal of Forensic Sciences*, 24(1):182–188.

Weaver, D. E. (1988). Photographic enhancement of latent prints. *Journal of Forensic Identification*, 38(5):189–196.

Weaver, D. E. and Fullerton, D. C. (1993). Large scale cyanoacrylate fuming. *Journal of Forensic Identification*, 43:135–137.

Weisner, S. and Springer, E. (1997). Improved technique for recovering fingerprints on aluminum foil. *Journal of Forensic Identification*, 47:138.

Wilkinson, D. and Watkin, J. (1994). A comparison of forensic light sources: Polilight, Luma-light, and Spectrum 9000. *Journal of Forensic Identification*, 44(6):632–651.

Zugibe, F. T. and Costello, J. T. (1986). A new method for softening mummified fingers. *Journal of Forensic Sciences*, 31(2):726–731.

Chapter 7

Aginsky, V. N. (1993). Some new ideas for dating ballpoint inks—a feasibility study. *Journal of Forensic Sciences*, 38(5):1134–1150.

Antoci, P. R. and Petraco, N. (1993). A technique for comparing soil colors in the forensic laboratory. *Journal of Forensic Sciences*, 38(2):437–441.

Blackledge, R. D. (1987). Tapes with adhesive backings: Their characterization in the forensic science laboratory. In *Applied Polymer Analysis and Characterization*, Mitchell, J., Ed. Macmillan, New York, pp. 413–421.

Bock, J. H. and Norris, D. O. (1997). Forensic botany: An underutilized resource. *Journal of Forensic Sciences*, 42(3):364–367.

Bresee, R. R. (1987). Evaluation of textile fiber evidence: A review. *Journal of Forensic Sciences*, 32(2):510–521.

Brunelle, R. L. and Reed, R. W. (1984). *Forensic Examination of Ink and Paper*, Charles C Thomas, Springfield, IL.

Brunner, H. and Coman, B. J. (1974). *The Identification of Mammalian Hair*, Inkata Press, Melbourne.

Budworth, G. (1982). Identification of knots. *Journal of the Forensic Science Society*, 22(4):327–331.

Burd, D. Q. and Kirk, P. L. (1942). Clothing fibers as evidence. *Journal of Criminal Law and Criminology*, 32(3):353–357.

Chable, J., Roux, C., and Lennard, C., Collection of fiber evidence using water-soluble cellophane tape. *Journal of Forensic Sciences*, 39:1520.

Cole, M. D. and Thorpe, J. W. (1992). The analysis of black shoe polish marks on clothing. *Journal of the Forensic Science Society*, 32(3):237–244.

Crown, D. A. (1968). *The Forensic Examination of Paints and Pigments*, Charles C Thomas, Springfield, IL.

Dixon, K. C. (1983). Positive identification of torn burned matches with emphasis on cross-cut and torn fiber comparisons. *Journal of Forensic Sciences*, 28(2):351–359.

Flinn, L. L. (1992). Collection of fiber evidence using a roller device and adhesive lifts. *Journal of Forensic Sciences*, 37(1):106–112.

Gerhart, F. J. (1992). Identification of photocopiers from fusing roller defects. *Journal of Forensic Sciences*, 37(1):130–139.

Grieve, M. C. (1983). The role of fibers in forensic science examinations. *Journal of Forensic Sciences*, 28(4):877–887.

Hashimoto, T., Deki, S., and Kanaji, Y. (1994). Discrimination of ceramics—study on the microstructures of ceramics. *Journal of Forensic Sciences*, 39(3):824–838.

Innocence Project. (2011). *Fact Sheet*. The Innocence Project, New York (http://www.innocenceproject.org/Content/Facts_on_PostConviction_DNA_Exonerations.php#).

Junger, E. P. (1996). Assessing the unique characteristics of close-proximity soil samples: Just how useful is soil evidence? *Journal of Forensic Sciences*, 41(1):27–34.

Kirk, P. L. (1974). *Crime Investigation*, 2nd ed. John Wiley & Sons, New York.

Koons, R. D., Peters, C. A., and Merrill, R. A. (1993). Forensic comparison of household aluminum foils using elemental composition by inductively coupled plasma—atomic emission spectrometry. *Journal of Forensic Sciences*, 38(2):302–315.

Laska, P. (1996). Forensic search of a landfill. *Journal of Forensic Identification*, 46(1):7–12.

Longhetti, A. and Roche, G. (1958). Microscopic identification of man-made fibers from the criminalistics point of view. *Journal of Forensic Sciences*, 3(3):303–329.

McQuillan, J. and Edgar, K. (1992). A survey of the distribution of glass on clothing. *Journal of the Forensic Science Society*, 32(4):333–348.

Merrill, R. A., Bartick, E. G., and Mazzella, W. D. (1996). Studies of techniques for analysis of photocopy toners by IR. *Journal of Forensic Sciences*, 41(2):264–271.

Murray, R. C. and Tedrow, J. C. F. (1975). *Forensic Geology*. Rutgers University Press, New Brunswick, NJ.

Nickolls, L. C. (1962). The identification of stains of nonbiological origin. In *Methods of Forensic Science*, Vol. I, Lundquist, F., Ed. John Wiley & Sons, New York, pp. 335–371.

Petraco, N. (1986). Trace evidence: The invisible witness. *Journal of Forensic Sciences*, 31(1):321–328.

Petraco, N. (1987). A simple trace evidence trap for the collection of vacuum sweepings. *Journal of Forensic Sciences*, 32(5):1422–1425.

Pounds, C. A. (1975). The recovery of fibers from the surface of clothing for forensic examination. *Journal of the Forensic Science Society*, 15(2):127–132.

Robertson, J. (1999). *The Forensic Examination of Hair*. CRC Press, Boca Raton, FL.

Robertson, J., Harkin, C., and Govan, J. (1984). The identification of bird feathers: Scheme for feather examination. *Journal of the Forensic Science Society*, 24(2):85–98.

Roux, C., Chable, J., and Margot, P. (1996). Fiber transfer experiments onto car seats. *Science and Justice*, 36:143–151.

Spencer, R. (1994). Significant fiber evidence recovered from the clothing of a homicide victim after exposure to the elements for twenty-nine days. *Journal of Forensic Sciences*, 39(3):854–859.

Stratmann, M. (1987). Identification of textile fibers. In *Applied Polymer Analysis and Characterization*, Mitchell, J., Ed. Macmillan, New York, pp. 387–411.

Strelis, I. and Kennedy, R. W. (1967). *Identification of North American Commercial Pulpwoods and Pulp Fibers*. University of Toronto Press, Toronto.

Suzanski, T. W. (1988). Dog hair comparison: A preliminary study. *Canadian Society of Forensic Science Journal*, 21(1–2):19–28.

Suzanski, T. W. (1989). Dog hair comparison: Purebreds, mixed breeds, multiple questioned hairs. *Canadian Society of Forensic Science Journal*, 22:299–309.

Taupin, J. M. (1996). Hair and fiber transfer in an abduction case—evidence from different levels of trace evidence transfer. *Journal of Forensic Sciences*, 41(4):697–699.

Vanderkolk, J. (1995). Identifying consecutively made garbage bags through manufactured characteristics. *Journal of Forensic Identification*, 45(1):38–50.

Walsh, K. A. J., Buckleton, J. S., and Triggs, C. M. (1996). A practical example of the interpretation of glass evidence. *Science and Justice*, 36(4):213–218.

Chapter 8

Anderson, A. (1989). Forensic science: DNA fingerprinting on trial. *Nature*, 342(6252):844.

Becker, P. B. and Schütz, G. (1988). Genomic footprinting. In *Genetics Engineering Principles and Methods*, Vol. 10, Setlow, J. K., Ed. Plenum Press, New York, pp. 1–19.

Bevel, T. and Gardner, R. (2002). *Bloodstain Pattern Analysis*, 2nd ed. CRC Press, Boca Raton, FL.

Bigbee, P. D., Sarin, P. S., Humphreys, J. C., Eubanks, W. G., Sun, D., Hocken, D. G., Thornton, A., Adams, D. E., and Simic, M. G. (1989). Inactivation of human immunodeficiency virus (HIV), ionizing radiation in body fluids and serological evidence. *Journal of Forensic Sciences*, 34(6):1303–1310.

Boles, T. C., Snow, C. C., and Stover, E. (1995). Forensic DNA testing on skeletal remains from mass graves: A pilot project in Guatemala. *Journal of Forensic Sciences*, 40(3):349–355.

Butler, J. (2005). *Forensic DNA Typing*, 2nd ed. Academic Press, San Diego, CA.

Cawood, A. H. (1989). DNA fingerprinting. *Clinical Chemistry*, 35(9):1832–1837.

CDC. (1995). Recommended childhood immunization schedule: United States 1995. *Morbidity and Mortality Weekly Report*, 44:1–9.

CDC. (1996). A case-control study of HIV seroconversion in health care workers after percutaneous exposure to HIV-infected blood—France, United Kingdom, and United States, January 1988–August 1994. *Morbidity and Mortality Weekly Report*, 44(50):929–933.

Cherfas, J. (1990). Genes unlimited. *New Scientist*, 126(1712):29–33.

Cohen, J. E. (1990). DNA fingerprinting for forensic identification: Potential effects on data interpretation of subpopulation heterogeneity and band number variability. *American Journal of Human Genetics*, 46:358–368.

Culliford, B. J. (1971). *The Examination and Typing of Bloodstains in the Crime Laboratory*. US Government Printing Office, Washington, DC.

Evett, I. W. (1992). Evaluating DNA profiles in a case where the defense is "it was my brother," *Journal of the Forensic Science Society*, 32(1):5–14.

Evett, I. W., Werrett, D. J., Gill, P., and Buckleton, J. S. (1989). DNA fingerprinting on trial [comment]. *Nature*, 340(6233):435.

Gaensslen, R. E. (1983). *Sourcebook in Forensic Serology, Immunology and Biochemistry*. US Department of Justice, National Institute of Justice, Washington, DC.

Gardner, R. and Bevel, T. (2009). *Practical Crime Scene Analysis and Reconstruction*. CRC Press, Boca Raton, FL.

Gerberding, J., Lewis, F. R., and Schecter, W. P. (1995). Are universal precautions realistic? *Surgery Clinics of North America*, 75(6):1091–1104.

Gimeno, F. E. (1989). Fill flash photo luminescence to photograph luminol bloodstain patterns. *Journal of Forensic Identification*, 39(3):149–156.

Graham, M. G. and Kochanski, J. (1983). *Move over Quincy: Forensic Science Beyond the Microscope*. National Institute of Justice, Washington, DC, 5 pp.

Grispino, R. R. J. (1990). Effect of luminol on the serological analysis of dried human bloodstains. *Crime Laboratory Digest*, 17(1):13–23.

Grubb, A. (1993). Legal aspects of DNA profiling. *Journal of the Forensic Science Society*, 33(4):228–233.

Healing, T. A., Hoffman, P. N., and Young, S. E. (1995). Infection hazards of human cadavers. *Communicable Disease Report/CDR Review*, 5:R61–R68.

Heller, E. T. and Greer, R. (1995). Glove safety: Summary of recent findings and recommendations from health care regulators. *Southern Medical Journal*, 88(11):1093–1098.

Henderson, D. K. (1995). Postexposure prophylaxis for occupational exposures to hepatitis B, hepatitis C, and human immunodeficiency virus. *Surgical Clinics of North America*, 75(6):1175–1187.

Holland, M. M., Fisher, D. L., Mitchell, L. G., Rodriquez, W. C., Canik, J. J., Merril, C. R., and Weedn, V. W. (1993). Mitochondrial DNA sequence analysis of human skeletal remains: Identification of remains from the Vietnam War. *Journal of Forensic Sciences*, 38(3):542–553.

INTERPOL. (2009). *INTERPOL Handbook on DNA Data Exchange and Practice: Recommendations from the INTERPOL DNA Monitoring Expert Group*, 2nd ed. OIPC-INTERPOL, Lyon, France.

James, S., Kish, P. E., and Sutton, T. P. (2005). *Principles of Bloodstain Pattern Analysis*. CRC Press, Boca Raton, FL.

Jeffreys, A. J. (1993). DNA typing: Approaches and applications. *Journal of the Forensic Science Society*, 33(4):204–211.

Karhunen, P. J., Brummer, H., Leinikki, P., and Nyberg, M. (1994). Stability of human immunodeficiency virus (HIV) antibodies in postmortem samples. *Journal of Forensic Sciences*, 39(1):129–135.

Klatt, E. C. and Noguchi, T. T. (1990). AIDS and infection control in forensic investigation. *American Journal of Forensic Medicine and Pathology*, 11(1):44–49.

Lander, E. S. (1989). DNA fingerprinting on trial. *Nature*, 339(6225):501–505.

Lee, H. E., Gaensslen, R., Pagliaro, E., Guman, M., Berka, K., Keith, T., and Phipps, P. (1989). The effect of presumptive test, latent fingerprints and some other reagents and materials on subsequent serological identification, genetic marker and DNA testing in bloodstains. *Journal of Forensic Identification*, 39(6):339–358.

Lind, W. and Carlson, D. (1995). Recovery of semen from chewing gum in an oral sexual assault. *Journal of Forensic Identification*, 45(3):280–282.

MacDonell, H. L. (1971). *Flight Characteristics and Stain Patterns of Human Blood*. US Department of Justice, Washington, DC.

MacDonell, H. L. (1982). *Bloodstain Pattern Interpretation*. Laboratory of Forensic Science, Corning, NY.

Montagna, C. P. (1996). The recovery of seminal components and DNA from the vagina of a homicide victim 34 days postmortem. *Journal of Forensic Sciences*, 41(4):700–702.

Neufeld P. J. and Colman, N. (1990). When science takes the witness stand. *Scientific American*, 262(5):46–53.

Nicas, M. (1996). Refining a risk model for occupational tuberculosis transmission. *American Industrial Hygiene Association Journal*, 57(1):16–22.

Owen, G. W. (1973). *A Comparison of Some Presumptive Tests for Blood*, HOCRE Report No. 84. Home Office Central Research Establishment, Aldermaston, UK.

Petrosillo, N., Puro, V., Ippolito, G., Di Nardo, V., Albertoni, F., Chiaretti, B., Rava, L., Sommella, L., Ricci, C., Zullo, G. et al. (1995). Hepatitis B, hepatitis C, and HIV virus infection in health care workers: A multiple regression analysis of risk factors. *Journal of Hospital Infection*, 30(4):273–281.

Pitt, M. J. (1994). Safety myths in chemical laboratories. *Journal of Chemical Health and Safety*, 1(3):8–11.

Pizzola, P. A., Roth, S., and DeForest, P. R. (1986a). Blood droplet dynamics—I. *Journal of Forensic Sciences*, 31:36–49.

Pizzola, P. A., Roth, S., and DeForest, P. R. (1986b). Blood droplet dynamics—II. *Journal of Forensic Sciences*, 31:50–64.

Plog, B., Ed. (1988). *Fundamentals of Industrial Hygiene*. National Safety Council, Itasca, IL.

Puro, V., Petrosillo, N., and Ippolito, G. (1995). Risk of hepatitis C seroconversion after occupational exposures in health care workers. *American Journal of Infection Control*, 23(5):273–277.

Raymond, M. A., Smith, E. R., and Liesegang, J. (1996). The physical properties of blood—forensic considerations. *Science & Justice*, 36(3):153–160.

Ross, A. M. and Harding, H. W. (1989). DNA typing and forensic science. *Forensic Science International*, 41(3):197–203.

Saferstein, R., Ed. (1982). *Forensic Science Handbook*. Prentice Hall, Englewood Cliffs, NJ.

Schiro, G. (1997). Collection and preservation of blood evidence from crime scenes. *Journal of Forensic Identification*, 47:557.

Sepkowitz, K. A. (1996). Occupational acquired infections in health care workers, part I. *Annals of Internal Medicine*, 125(1):826–834.

Stewart, G. D. (1990). Sexual assault evidence collection procedures. *Journal of Forensic Identification*, 40(2):69–74.

Sweet, D. J. and Sweet, C. H. W. (1994). DNA analysis of dental pulp to link incinerated remains of homicide victim to crime scene. *Journal of Forensic Sciences*, 40(2):310–314.

Thornton, J. (1989). DNA profiling: New tool links evidence to suspects with high certainty. *Chemical Engeering News*, 67(47):18–30.

Tokars, J. I., Chamberland, M. E., Schable, C. A., Culver, D. H., Jones, M., McKibbens, P. S., and Bell, D. M. (1992). A survey of occupational blood contact and HIV infection among orthopedic surgeons. *Journal of the American Medical Association*, 268(4):489–494.

USDOJ. (2002). *Using DNA to Solve Cold Cases*. US Department of Justice, Washington, DC, 32 pp.

USDOJ. (2005). *Identifying Victims Using DNA: A Guide for Families*. US Department of Justice, Washington, DC, 13 pp.

Van Buren, J., Simpson, R. A., Jacobs, P., and Cookson, B. D. (1994). Survival of HIV virus in suspension and dried-onto surfaces. *Journal of Clinical Microbiology*, 32(2):571–574.

Wegel, Jr., J. G. and Herrin, Jr., G. (1994). Deduction of the order of sexual assault by DNA analysis of two condoms. *Journal of Forensic Sciences*, 39(3):844–846.

Zweidinger, R. A., Lytle, L. T., and Pitt, C. G. (1973). Photography of blood-stains visualized by luminol. *Journal of Forensic Sciences*, 18(4):296–302.

Chapter 9

Apolinar, E. and Rowe, W. F. (1980). Examination of human fingernail ridges by means of polarized light. *Journal of Forensic Sciences*, 25(1):154–161.

Beckstead, J. W., Rawson, R. D., and Giles, W. S. (1979). Review of bite mark evidence. *Journal of the American Dental Association*, 99(7):69–74.

Benson, B. W., Cottone, J. A., Bomberg, T. J., and Sperber, N. D. (1987). Bite mark impressions: A review of techniques and materials. *Journal of Forensic Sciences*, 33(5):1238–1243.

Bodziak, W. J. (1986). Manufacturing processes for athletic shoe outsoles and their significance in the examination of footwear impression evidence. *Journal of Forensic Sciences*, 31(1):153–176.

Bonte, W. (1975). Tool marks in bones and cartilage. *Journal of Forensic Sciences*, 20(2):315–325.

Cassidy, F. H. (1980). Examination of tool marks from sequentially manufactured tongue-and-groove pliers. *Journal of Forensic Sciences*, 25(4):796–809.

Cassidy, M. J. (1980). *Footwear Identification*. Royal Canadian Mounted Police, Ontario.

Davis, R. J. (1988). Systematic approach to the enhancement of footwear marks. *Canadian Society of Forensic Science Journal*, 21(3):98–105.

Denton, S. (1981). Extrusion marks in polyethene film. *Journal of the Forensic Science Society*, 21(3):259–262.

Diaz, A. A., Boehm, A. F., and Rowe, W. F. (1990). Comparison of fingernail ridge patterns of monozygotic twins. *Journal of Forensic Sciences*, 35(1):97–102.

Dinkel, Jr., E. H. (1974). The use of bite mark evidence as an investigative aid. *Journal of Forensic Sciences*, 19(3):535–547.

Ellen, D. M., Foster, D. J., and Morantz, D. J. (1980). The use of electrostatic imaging in the detection of indented impressions. *Forensic Science International*, 15(1):53–60.

Facey, O. E., Hannah, I. D., and Rosen, D. (1992). Shoe wear patterns and pressure distribution under feet and shoes, determined by image analysis. *Journal of the Forensic Science Society*, 32(1):15–25.

Fairgrieve, S. I. (1994). SEM analysis of incinerated teeth as an aid to positive investigation. *Journal of Forensic Sciences*, 39(2):557–565.

Fawcett, A. S. (1970). The role of the footmark examiner. *Journal of the Forensic Science Society*, 10(4):227–244.

FBI. (1975). FBI laboratory makes toolmark examinations. *FBI Law Enforcement Bulletin*.

Giles, E. and Vallandigham, P. H. (1991). Height estimation from foot and shoeprint length. *Journal of Forensic Sciences*, 36(4):1134–1151.

Glass, R. T., Jordan, F. B., and Andrews, E. E. (1975). Multiple animal bite wounds: A case report. *Journal of Forensic Sciences*, 20(2):305–314.

Gordon, C. C. and Buikstra, J. E. (1992). Linear models for the prediction of stature from foot and boot dimensions. *Journal of Forensic Sciences*, 37(3):771–782.

Hamm, E. D. (1989). Individuality of class characteristics in Converse All-Star footwear. *Journal of Forensic Identification*, 39(5):277–292.

Hebrard, J. and Donche, A. (1994). Fingerprint detection methods on skin: Experimental study on 16 live subjects and 23 cadavers. *Journal of Forensic Identification*, 44(6):623–631.

Hilderbrand, D. (1994). Using manufacturing companies to assist in footwear cases. *Journal of Forensic Identification*, 44(2):130–132.

Hilderbrand, D. and Miller, M. (1995). Casting materials—which one to use! *Journal of Forensic Identification*, 45(6):618–630.

Hodge, E. E. (1988). Guarding against error. *AFTE Journal*, 20(3):290–293.

Houde, J. (1993). Image enhancement for document examination using the personal computer. *Journal of Forensic Sciences*, 38(1):143–146.

Hueske, E. E. (1991). Photographing and casting footwear/tiretrack impressions. *Journal of Forensic Identification*, 41:92.

Jungbluth, W. O. (1989). Knuckle print identification. *Journal of Forensic Identification*, 39(6):375–380.

Lennard, C. J. and Margot, P. A. (1989). The analysis of synthetic shoe soles, FTIR microspectrometry and pyrolysis–GC: A case example. *Journal of Forensic Identification*, 39(4):239–243.

Leslie, A. G. (1977). Identification of single element typewriter and type elements. Part I. Type elements. *Canadian Society of Forensic Science Journal*, 10(3):87–101.

Levinson, J. (1979). Single element typewriters. *Forensic Science International*, 13:15–24.

MacDonald, D. G. (1974). Bite mark recognition and interpretation. *Journal of the Forensic Science Society*, 14(3):229–233.

Mankevich, A. (1990). Determination of shoe size in out-of-scale photographs. *Journal of Forensic Identification*, 40(1):1–13.

Nielson, J. P. (1989). Laser enhancement of footwear marks on brown paper. *Journal of Forensic Identification*, 39(1):42–51.

Novoselsky, Y., Glattstein, B., Volkov, N., and Zeichner, A. (1995). Microchemical spot tests in toolmark examination. *Journal of Forensic Sciences*, 40(5):865–866.

Ojena, S. M. (1984). A new improved technique for casting impressions in snow. *Journal of Forensic Sciences*, 29(1):322–325.

Petraco, N. (2010). *Color Atlas of Forensic Toolmark Identification*. CRC Press, Boca Raton, FL.

Pierce, D. S. (1990). Identifiable markings on plastics. *Journal of Forensic Identification*, 40(2):51–59.

Rao, V. J. and Souviron, R. R. (1984). Dusting and lifting the bite print: A new technique. *Journal of Forensic Sciences*, 29(1):326–330.

Sahs, P. (1993). Interesting case involving automotive pedal control/shoe imprinting. *Journal of Forensic Identification*, 43(1):20–26.

Sampson, W. (1996). Latent fingerprint evidence on human skin, part 1. *Journal of Forensic Identification*, 46(2):96–100.

Sperber, N. D. (1978). Chewing gum—an unusual clue in a recent homicide investigation. *Journal of Forensic Sciences*, 23(4):792–796.

Springer, E. (1995). Toolmark examinations—a review of its development in the literature. *Journal of Forensic Sciences*, 40(6):964–968.

Stone, I. C. (1988). Fingernail striations: An unusual toolmark. *AFTE Journal*, 20:391.

Vale, G. L., Sognnaes, R. F., Felando, G. N., and Noguchi, T. T. (1976). Unusual three-dimensional bite mark evidence in a homicide case. *Journal of Forensic Sciences*, 21(3):642–652.

VanHoven, H. (1985). A correlation between shoeprint measurements and actual sneaker size. *Journal of Forensic Sciences*, 30(4):1233–1237.

Von Bremen, A. (1990). The comparison of brake and accelerator pedals with marks on shoe soles. *Journal of Forensic Sciences*, 35(1):14–24.

Von Bremen, U. G. and Blunt, L. K. R. (1983). Physical comparison of plastic garbage bags and sandwich bags. *Journal of Forensic Sciences*, 28(3):644–654.

Wilkinson, D., Watkin, J., and Misner, A. (1996). A comparison of techniques for the visualization of fingerprints on human skin including the application of iodine and α-napthoflavone. *Journal of Forensic Identification*, 46(4):432–453.

Yaron, S. M., Kennedy, R. B., Tsach, T., Volkov, N., Novoselsky, Y., and Vinokurov, A. (2003). Physical match: Insole and shoe. *Journal of Forensic Sciences*, 48(4):808–810.

Zugibe, F. T., Costello, J., and Breithaupt, M. (1996). Identification of a killer by a definitive sneaker pattern and his beating instruments by their distinctive patterns. *Journal of Forensic Sciences*, 41(2):310–313.

Chapter 10

AFTE. (1980). *Glossary of the Association of Firearms and Toolmark Examiners*, Fonville Printing, Augusta, GA.

Andrasko, J. (1992). Characterization of smokeless powder flakes from fired cartridge cases and from discharge patterns on clothing. *Journal of Forensic Sciences*, 37(4):1030–1047.

Andrasko, J. and Maehly, A. C. (1977). Detection of gunshot residues on hands by scanning electron microscopy. *Journal of Forensic Sciences*, 22(2):279–287.

Andrasko, J. and Pettersson, S. (1991). A simple method for collection of gun shot residues from clothing. *Journal of the Forensic Science Society*, 31(3):321–330.

Barnes, F. C. and Helson, R. A. (1974). An empirical study of gunpowder residue patterns. *Journal of Forensic Sciences*, 19(3):448–462.

Barnum, C. and Klasey, D. (1997). Factors affecting the recovery of latent prints on firearms. *Journal of Forensic Identification*, 47(2):141–149.

Basu, S. (1982). Formation of gunshot residues. *Journal of Forensic Sciences*, 27(1):72–91.

Basu, S., Boone, C. E., Denio, D. J., and Miazga, R. A. (1997). Fundamental studies of gunshot residue deposition by glue-lift. *Journal of Forensic Sciences*, 42(4):571–581.

Biasotti, A. A. (1964). The principles of evidence evaluation as applied to firearms and tool mark identification. *Journal of Forensic Sciences*, 9(4):428–433.

Brazeau, J. and Wong, R. K. (1997). Analysis of gunshot residues on human tissues and clothing by x-ray microfluorescence. *Journal of Forensic Sciences*, 42(3):424–428.

Burke, T. W. and Rowe, W. F. (1992). Bullet ricochet: A comprehensive review. *Journal of Forensic Sciences*, 37(5):1254–1260.

Burnett, B. (1989). The form of gunshot residue is modified by target impact. *Journal of Forensic Sciences*, 34(4):808–822.

Burnett, B. (1991). Detection of bone and bone-plus-bullet particles in backspatter from close-range shots to heads. *Journal of Forensic Sciences*, 36(6):1745–1752.

Collins, K. A. and Lantz, P. E. (1994). Interpretation of fatal, multiple, and exiting gunshot wounds by trauma specialists. *Journal of Forensic Sciences*, 39(1):94–99.

Dahl, D. B. and Lott, P. F. (1987). Determination of black and smokeless powder residues in firearms and improvised explosive devices, *Microchemical Journal*, 35(1):40–50.

Davis, J. E. (1958). *An Introduction to Toolmarks, Firearms and the Striagraph*. Charles C Thomas, Springfield, IL.

DeGaetano, D. and Siegel, J. A. (1990). Survey of gunshot residue analysis in forensic science laboratories. *Journal of Forensic Sciences*, 35(5):1087–1095.

Di Maio, V. J. M., Petty, C. S., and Stone, Jr., I. C. (1976). An experimental study of powder tattooing of the skin. *Journal of Forensic Sciences*, 21(2):367–372.

Fackler, M. L. (1986). Ballistic injury. *Annals of Emergency Medicine*, 15(12):1451–1455.

Fackler, M. L. (1988). Wound ballistics: A review of common misconceptions. *Journal of the American Medical Association*, 259(18):2730–2736.

Garrison, Jr., D. (1995). Reconstructing drive-by shootings from ejected cartridge case location. *Journal of Forensic Identification*, 45(4):427–433.

Goleb, J. A. and Midkiff, Jr., C. R. (1975). Firearms discharge residue sample collection techniques. *Journal of Forensic Sciences*, 20(4):701–707.

Harruff, R. C. (1995). Comparison of contact shotgun wounds of the head produced by different gauge shotguns. *Journal of Forensic Sciences*, 40(5):801–804.

Havekost, D. G., Peters, C. A., and Koons, R. D. (1990). Barium and antimony distributions on the hands of nonshooters. *Journal of Forensic Sciences*, 35(5):1096–1114.

Hoffman, C. M. and Byall, E. B. (1974). Peculiarities of certain .22 caliber revolvers (Saturday night specials). *Journal of Forensic Sciences*, 19(1):48–53.

Josserand, M. H. and Stevenson, J. A. (1972). *Pistols, Revolvers and Ammunition*. Bonanza Books, New York.

Kilty, J. W. (1975). Activity after shooting and its effects on the retention of primer residues. *Journal of Forensic Sciences*, 20(2):219–230.

Tschirhart, D. L., Klatt, E. C., and Noguchi, T. T. (1989). Wounding characteristics of .38 caliber revolver cartridges. *Journal of Forensic Sciences*, 34(6):1387–1394.

Krishnan, S. S. (1977). Detection of gunshot residues on the hands by trace element analysis. *Journal of Forensic Sciences*, 22(2):304–324.

Madea, B. (1988). Determination of the sequence of gunshot wounds of the skull. *Journal of the Forensic Science Society*, 28(5–6):321–328.

Matricardi, V. R. and Kilty, J. W. (1977). Detection of gunshot residue particles from the hands of a shooter. *Journal of Forensic Sciences*, 22(4):725–738.

McGuire, P. J. and Boehm, A. (1990). Analysis of gunshot residue test results in 112 suicides. *Journal of Forensic Sciences*, 35(1):62–68.

Medich, M. G. et al. (1990). Single wound produced by simultaneous discharge of both shells from a double-barrel shotgun. *Journal of Forensic Sciences*, 35(2):473–476.

Meng, H. and Caddy, B. (1997). Gunshot residue analysis—a review. *Journal of Forensic Sciences*, 42(4):553–570.

Miller, J. (1993). The value of a firearms open-case file. *Journal of Forensic Identification*, 43(3):245.

Missliwetz, J., Denk, W., and Wieser, I. (1991). Shots fired with silencers—a report on four cases and experimental testing. *Journal of Forensic Sciences*, 36(5):1387–1394.

Nesbitt, R. S., Wessel, J. E., and Jones, P. F. (1976). Detection of gunshot residue by use of the scanning electron microscope. *Journal of Forensic Sciences*, 21(3):595–610.

Nichols, C. A. and Sens, M. A. (1990). Recovery and evaluation, cytologic techniques of trace material retained on bullets. *American Journal of Forensic Medicine and Pathology*, 11(1):17–34.

Nichols, R. G. (1997). Firearm and toolmark identification criteria: A review of the literature. *Journal of Forensic Sciences*, 42(3):466–474.

Nichols, R. G. (2003). Firearm and toolmark identification criteria: A review of the literature, part II. *Journal of Forensic Sciences*, 48(2):318–327.

Oliver, W. R., Chancellor, A. S., Soltys, M., Symon, J., Cullip, T., Rosenman, J., Hellman, R., Boxwala, A., and Gormley, W. (1994). Three-dimensional reconstruction of a bullet path: Validation by computer radiography. *Journal of Forensic Sciences*, 40(2):321–324.

Petraco, N. and De Forest, P. R. (1990). Trajectory reconstruction. I. Trace evidence in flight. *Journal of Forensic Sciences*, 35(6):1284–1296.

Rouge, D., Telmon, N., Alengrin, D., Marril, G., Bras, P. M., and Arbus, L. (1994). Fatal injuries caused by guns using shotshell: Case reports and ballistic studies. *Journal of Forensic Sciences*, 39(3):650–656.

Seamster, A., Mead, T., Gislason, J., Jackson, K., Ruddy, F., and Pate, B. D. (1976). Studies of the spatial distribution of firearms discharge residues. *Journal of Forensic Sciences*, 21(4):868–882.

Simpson, K. (1989). Identification of a firearm in murder without the weapon. *AFTE Journal*, 21:62.

Singer, R. L., Davis, D., and Houck, M. M. (1996). A survey of gunshot residue analysis methods. *Journal of Forensic Sciences*, 41(2):195–198.

Smith, O. C., Symes, S. A., Berryman, H. E., and LeVaughn, M. M. (1993). Characteristic features of entrance wounds from hollow-point bullets. *Journal of Forensic Sciences*, 38(2):323–326.

Stone, I. C., Di Maio, V. J. M., and Petty, C. S. (1978). Gunshot wounds: Visual and analytical procedures. *Journal of Forensic Sciences*, 23(2):361–367.

Stone, I. C. and Petty, C. S. (1991). Interpretation of unusual wounds caused by firearms. *Journal of Forensic Sciences*, 36(3):736–740.

Wolten, G. M., Nesbitt, R. S., Calloway, A. R., Loper, G. L., and Jones, P. F. (1979a). Particle analysis for the detection of gunshot residue. I. Scanning electron microscopy/energy dispersive x-ray characterization of hand deposits from firing. *Journal of Forensic Sciences*, 24:409–422.

Wolten, G. M., Nesbitt, R. S., Calloway, A. R., and Loper, G. L. (1979b). Particle analysis for the detection of gunshot residue. II. Occupational and environmental particles. *Journal of Forensic Sciences*, 24:423–430.

Wolten, G. M., Nesbitt, R. S., and Calloway, A. R. (1979c). Particle analysis for the detection of gunshot residue. III. The case record. *Journal of Forensic Sciences*, 24:864–869.

Zeichner, A. and Glattstein, B. (1986). Improved reagents for firing distance determination. *Journal of Energetic Materials*, 4:187–197.

Zeichner, A. and Levin, N. (1993). Collection efficiency of gunshot residue (GSR) particles from hair and hands using double-side adhesive tape. *Journal of Forensic Sciences*, 38(3):571–584.

Chapter 11

Beveridge, A. D., Payton, S. F., Audette, R. J., Lambertus, A. J., and Shaddick, R. C. (1975). Systematic analysis of explosive residues. *Journal of Forensic Sciences*, 20(3):431–454.

Blackledge, R. D. (1991). Methenamine—an unusual component in an improved incendiary device. *Journal of Forensic Sciences*, 36(1):261–263.

Brauer, K. O. (1974). *Handbook of Pyrotechnics*. Chemical Publishing, New York.

Brodie, T. G. and Gleason, A. W. (1973). *Bombs and Bombings: A Handbook to Detection, Disposal and Investigation for Police and Fire Departments*. Charles C Thomas, Springfield, IL.

Carroll, J. R. (1979). *Physical and Technical Aspects of Fire and Arson Investigation*. Charles C Thomas, Springfield, IL.

Davis, T. L. (1941). *The Chemistry of Powder and Explosives*. John Wiley & Sons, New York.

DeHaan, J. D. (2002). *Kirk's Fire Investigation*, 5th ed. Prentice Hall, Englewood Cliffs, NJ.

Dhole, V. R., Kurhekar, M. P., and Ambade, K. A. (1995). Detection of petroleum accelerant residues on partly burnt objects in burning/arson offences. *Science & Justice*, 35(3):217–221.

Dietz, W. R. (1991). Improved charcoal packaging for accelerant recovery by passive diffusion. *Journal of Forensic Sciences*, 36(1):111–121.

Ellern, H. (1968). *Military and Civilian Pyrotechnics*. Chemical Publishing, New York.

Evans, H. K. (1986). An unusual explosive, triacetonetriperoxide (TATP). *Journal of Forensic Sciences*, 31(3):1119–1125.

FBI. (1973). *Introduction to Explosives*. Picatinny Arsenal, Dover, NJ.

Fisco, W. (1975). A portable explosives identification kit for field use. *Journal of Forensic Sciences*, 20(1):141–148.

Fitch, R. D. and Porter, E. A. (1968). *Accidental or Incendiary*. Charles C Thomas, Springfield, IL.

Furton, K. G., Almirall, J. R., and Bruna, J. C. (1996). A novel method for the analysis of gasoline from fire debris using headspace solid-phase microextraction. *Journal of Forensic Sciences*, 41(1):12–22.

Garner, D. D. and Fultz, M. L. (1986). The ATF approach to postblast explosives detection and identification. *Journal of Energetic Materials*, 4(1–4):133–148.

Glattstein, B., Landau, E., and Zeichner, A. (1991). Identification of match head residues in postexplosion debris. *Journal of Forensic Sciences*, 36(5):1360–1367.

Henderson, R. W. (1988). Fire investigation from the consultant's point of view. *Fire & Arson Investigator*, 39(2):23–28.

Hermann, S. L. (1977). *Explosives Data Guide*. Explosives Research Institute, Scottsdale, AZ.

Hoffman, C. M. and Byall, E. B. (1974). Identification of explosive residues in bomb scene investigations. *Journal of Forensic Sciences*, 19(1):54–63.

International Association of Chiefs of Police. (1974). *Bomb Investigations*. National Bomb Data Center, Dover, NJ, 92 pp.

Jones, B. R. (1988). Putting the fire scene in perspective. *Fire & Arson Investigator*, 38:59–60.

Jones, N. (1990). Arson-for-profit investigations: Success or failure? Recovering water-damaged business records. *Fire & Arson Investigator*, 40(3):50–52.

Kempe, C. R. and Tannert, W. T. (1972). Detection of dynamite residues on the hands of bombing suspects. *Journal of Forensic Sciences*, 17(2):323–324.

Keto, R. O. (1986). Improved method for the analysis of the military explosive composition C-4. *Journal of Forensic Sciences*, 31(1):241–249.

Kolla, P. (1991). Trace analysis of explosives from complex mixtures with sample pretreatment and selective detection. *Journal of Forensic Sciences*, 36(5):1342–1359.

Lenz, R. R. (1965). *Explosives and Bomb Disposal Guide*. Charles C Thomas, Springfield, IL.

Loscalzo, P. J., DeForest, P. R., and Chao, J. M. (1980). Study to determine the limit of detectability of gasoline vapor from simulated arson residues. *Journal of Forensic Sciences*, 25(1):162–167.

Meyers, R. (1977). *Explosives*. Verlag Chemie, Weinheim, Germany.

O'Donnell, J. J. (1989). Interferences from backgrounds in accelerant residue analysis. *Fire & Arson Investigator*, 39(4):25–27.

Perr, I. N. (1979). Comments on arson. *Journal of Forensic Sciences*, 24(4):885–889.

Phillips, S. A. (1988). How wood chars and what it means to the fire investigator. *Fire & Arson Investigator*, 38(4):28–30.

Pinorini, M. T., Lennard, C. J., Margot, P., Dustin, I., and Furrer, P. (1994). Soot as an indicator in fire investigations: Physical and chemical analysis. *Journal of Forensic Sciences*, 39(4):933–973.

Posey, E. P. and Posey, J. E. (1988). Outline for fire scene documentation. *Fire & Arson Investigator*, 38(3):55–58.

Powell, G. L. F. and Spanswick, K. R. (1979). A case of arson? *Journal of Forensic Sciences*, 24(3):627–630.

Price, T. A. (1989). Appliances as a fire cause. *Fire & Arson Investigator*, 39(3):30–34.

Smith, F. P. (1991). Concrete spalling: Controlled fire tests and review. *Journal of the Forensic Science Society*, 31(1):67–75.

Stoffel, J. F. (1962). *Explosives and Homemade Bombs*. Charles C Thomas, Springfield, IL.

Stone, I. C., Lomonte, J. N., Fletcher, L. A., and Lowry, W. T. (1978). Accelerant detection in fire residues. *Journal of Forensic Sciences*, 23(1):78–83.

Tindall, R. and Lothridge, K. (1995). An evaluation of 42 accelerant detection canine teams. *Journal of Forensic Sciences*, 40(4):561–564.

Townshend, D. G. (1973). Identification of electric blasting caps by manufacture. *Journal of Forensic Sciences*, 18(4):405–407.

Tsaroom, S. (1996). Investigation of a murder case involving arson. *Journal of Forensic Sciences*, 41(6):1064–1067.

Twibell, J. D. and Lomas, S. C. (1995). The examination of fire-damaged electrical switches. *Science & Justice*, 35(2):113–116.

Yallop, H. J. (1980). *Explosion Investigation*. Forensic Science Society Press, Harrogate, UK.

Chapter 12

AMA. (1970). *Alcohol and the Impaired Driver: A Manual on the Medicolegal Aspects of Chemical Tests for Intoxication*. Committee on American Medical Association, Chicago, IL.

Baum, R. M. (1985). New variety of street drugs poses growing problem. *Chemical & Engineering News*, 63(36):7–16.

Chung, B., Choo, H. Y., Kim, T. W. et al. (1990). Analysis of anabolic steroids using GC/MS with selected ion monitoring. *Journal of Analytical Toxicology*, 14(2):91–95.

Cone, E. J. (1988). Marijuana-laced brownies: Behavioral effects, physiologic effects, and urinalysis in humans following ingestion. *Journal of Analytical Toxicology*, 12(4):169–175.

Cone, E. J. (1990). Testing human hair for drugs of abuse. I. Individual dose and time profiles of morphine and codeine in plasma, saliva, urine and beard compared to drug-induced effects on pupils and behavior. *Journal of Analytical Toxicology*, 14(1):1–7.

Cravey, R. H. and Baselt, R. C. (1981). *Introduction to Forensic Toxicology*. Biomedical Publications, Davis, CA.

Daigle, R. D. (1990). Anabolic steroids. *Journal of Psychoactive Drugs*, 22(1):77–80.

DOT. (1981). *Hazardous Materials Emergency Response Guidebook*. US Department of Transportation, Washington, DC.

ElSohly, M. A. and Jones, A. B. (1989). Morphine and codeine in biological fluids: Approaches to source differentiation. *Forensic Science Review*, 1(1):13–22.

Fasanello, J. A. and Henderson, R. A. (1974). Vacuum searches in narcotics cases. *Journal of Forensic Sciences*, 19(2):379–383.

Garriott, J. C. and Latman, N. (1976). Drug detection in cases of "driving under the influence." *Journal of Forensic Sciences*, 21(2):398–415.

Garriott, J. C., Di Maio, V. J. M., Zumwalt, R. E., and Petty, C. S. (1977). Incidence of drugs and alcohol in fatally injured motor vehicle drivers. *Journal of Forensic Sciences*, 22(2):383–389.

Graham, K., Koren, G., Klein, J., Schneiderman, J., and Greenwald, M. (1989). Determination of gestational cocaine exposure, hair analysis, *Journal of the American Medical Association*, 262(23):3328–3330.

Harkey, M. R. and Henderson, G. L. (1989). Hair analysis for drugs of abuse. In *Advances in Analytical Toxicology*, Baselt, R. C., Ed. Year Book Medical Publishers, Chicago, IL, pp. 298–329.

Hill, V. A., Baumgartner, W. A., and Blahd, W. H. (1989). Hair analysis for drugs of abuse. *Journal of Forensic Sciences*, 34(6):1433–1453.

Hudson, J. D. (1989). Analysis of currency for cocaine contamination. *Canadian Society of Forensic Science Journal*, 22(2):203–218.

James, R. D. (1989). Hazards of clandestine drug laboratories. *FBI Law Enforcement Bulletin*, 58(4):16–21.

Jones, A. W. and Pounder, D. J. (2007). Update on clinical and forensic analysis of alcohol. In *Drug Abuse Handbook*, 2nd ed., Karch, S., Ed. Taylor & Francis, Boca Raton, FL, pp. 21–64.

Kram, T. C., Cooper, D. A., and Allen, A. C. (1981). Behind the identification of china white. *Analytical Chemistry*, 53(12):1379A–1386A.

LeBeau, M. A. and Mozyani, A., Eds. (2001). *Drug Facilitated Sexual Assault: A Forensic Handbook*. Academic Press, San Diego, CA.

Le, S. D., Taylor, R. W., Vidal, D., Lovas, J. J., and Ting, E. (1992). Occupational exposure to cocaine involving crime lab personnel. *Journal of Forensic Sciences*, 37(4):959–968.

Lundberg, G. D., White, J. M., and Hoffman, K. I. (1979). Drugs (other than or in addition to ethyl alcohol) and driving behavior: A collaborative study of the California Association of Toxicologists. *Journal of Forensic Sciences*, 24(1):207–215.

Mason, M. F. and Dubowski, K. M. (1974). Alcohol, traffic and chemical testing in the United States: A résumé and some remaining problems. *Clinical Chemistry*, 20:126.

McBay, A. J. and Mason, A. P. (1989). Forensic science identification of drugs of abuse. *Journal of Forensic Sciences*, 34(6):1471–1476.

Mulé, S. J. and Casella, G. A. (1988). Rendering the "poppy-seed defense" defenseless: Identification of 6-monoacetylmorphine in urine, gas chromatography/mass spectroscopy. *Clinical Chemistry*, 34(7):1427–1430.

O'Conner, D. L. (1988). Developing a standard operating procedure for crime scene and identification processing of illicit methamphetamine labs. *Journal of Forensic Identification*, 38(6):299–302.

Turk, R. F., McBay, A. J., and Hudson, P. (1974). Drug involvement in automobile driver and pedestrian fatalities. *Journal of Forensic Sciences*, 19(1):90–97.

Walls, H. and Brownlie, A. (1985). *Drink, Drugs and Driving*. Sweet & Maxwell, London.

Willette, R. E., Ed. (1977). *Drugs and Driving*, NIDA Research Monograph 11. National Institute on Drug Abuse, Washington, DC.

Chapter 13

Albi, F. J. and Schram, D. D. (1978). *Forcible Rape: A Manual for Sex Crime Investigators*, Police Vol. III. US Department of Justice, Washington, DC.

Brauner, P. and Gallili, N. (1993). A condom—the critical link in a rape. *Journal of Forensic Sciences*, 38(5):1233–1236.

Duenhoelter, J. H., Stone, I. C., Santos-Ramos, R., and Scott, D. E. (1978). Detection of seminal fluid constituents after alleged sexual assault. *Journal of Forensic Sciences*, 23(4):824–829.

Enos, W. F., Beyer, J. C., and Mann, G. T. (1972). The medical examination of cases of rape. *Journal of Forensic Sciences*, 17(1):50–56.

Fraysier, H. D. (1987). A rapid screening technique for the detection of spermatozoa. *Journal of Forensic Sciences*, 32(2):527–530.

Hazelwood, R. R. and Warren, J. (1989a). The serial rapist: His characteristics and victims (part I). *FBI Law Enforcement Bulletin*, 58(1):11–17.

Hazelwood, R. R. and Warren, J. (1989b). The serial rapist: His characteristics and victims (conclusion). *FBI Law Enforcement Bulletin*, 58(2):18–25.

Schiff, A. F. (1978). Rape in the United States. *Journal of Forensic Sciences*, 23(4):845–851.

Chapter 14

Anon. (1973). Building material evidence in burglary cases. *FBI Law Enforcement Bulletin*.

Fong, W. (1973). Value of glass as evidence. *Journal of Forensic Sciences*, 18(4):398–404.

Plumtree, W. G. (1975). The examination of disc and pin tumbler locks for tool marks made by lock picks. *Journal of Forensic Sciences*, 20(4):656–667.

Chapter 15

Anon. (1976). Don't overlook evidentiary value of glass fragments. *FBI Law Enforcement Bulletin*.

Baker, J. S. and Lindquist, T. (1977). *Lamp Examination for On or Off in Traffic Accidents*. Traffic Institute, Northwestern University, Evanston, IL.

Basham, D. J. (1979). *Traffic Accident Management*. Charles C Thomas, Springfield, IL.

Clark, W. E. (1982). *Traffic Management and Collision Investigation*. Prentice Hall, Englewood Cliffs, NJ.

Cousins, R., Holding, R., Locke, J., and Wilkinson, J. (1989). A data collection of vehicle top-coat colours. IV. A trial to assess the effectiveness of colour identification. *Forensic Science International*, 43:183–197.

Dabdoub, G. and Severin, P. (1989). The identification of domestic and foreign automobile manufacturers through body primer characterization. *Journal of Forensic Sciences*, 34(6):1395–1404.

Dolan, D. N. (1971). Vehicle lights and their use as evidence. *Journal of the Forensic Science Society*, 11(2):69–82.

Drummond, F. C. and Pizzola, P. A. (1990). An unusual case involving the individualization of a clothing impression on a motor vehicle. *Journal of Forensic Sciences*, 35(3):746–852.

Eastman Kodak. (1981). *Photography in Traffic Investigation*, Kodak Publ. No. M-21. Eastman Kodak Co., Rochester, NY, 12 pp.

Hamm, E. D. (1988). Locating an area on a suspect tire for comparative examination to a questioned track. *Journal of Forensic Identification*, 38(4):143–151.

Lambourn, R. F. (1989). The calculation of motor car speeds from curved tyre marks. *Journal of the Forensic Science Society*, 29(6):371–386.

Mackay, G. M. (1970). The role of the accident investigator. *Journal of the Forensic Science Society*, 10(4):245–254.

Monahan, D. L. and Harding, H. W. J. (1990). Damage to clothing—cuts and tears. *Journal of Forensic Sciences*, 35(4):901–912.

Russo, R. E., Pelkey, G. E., Grant, P., Whipple, R. E., and Andresen, B. D. (1994). Laser interrogation of latent vehicle registration number. *Journal of Forensic Sciences*, 39(5):1331–1333.

Ryland, S. G. and Kopec, R. J. (1979). The evidential value of automobile paint chips. *Journal of Forensic Sciences*, 24(1):140–147.

Shkrum, M. J., Green, R. N., McClafferty, K. J., and Nowak, E. S. (1994). Skull fractures in fatalities due to motor vehicle collisions. *Journal of Forensic Sciences*, 39(1):107–122.

Zeldes, I. (1980). Speedometer examination: An aid in accident investigation. *FBI Law Enforcement Bulletin*, 49(3):11–15.

Chapter 16

Adelson, L. (1974). *The Pathology of Homicide*. Charles C Thomas, Springfield, IL.

Anderson, G. S. (1997). The use of insects to determine time of decapitation: A case study from British Columbia. *Journal of Forensic Sciences*, 42(5):947–950.

Anon. (1985). Classifying sexual homicide crime scenes: Interrater reliability. *FBI Law Enforcement Bulletin*, 54(8):2–5.

Blanke, R. V. (1974). Role of toxicology in suicide evaluation. *Journal of Forensic Sciences*, 19(2):284–291.

Burnharn, J. T., Preston-Burnharn, J., and Fontan, C. R. (1976). The state of the art of bone identification by chemical and microscopic methods. *Journal of Forensic Sciences*, 21(2):340–342.

Burton, J. F. (1974). Fallacies in the signs of death. *Journal of Forensic Sciences*, 19(3):529–534.

Byrd, J. H. and Castner, J. L., Eds. (2001). *Forensic Entomology: The Utility of Arthropods in Legal Investigations*. CRC Press, Boca Raton, FL.

Chai, D. S. (1989). A study on the standard for forensic anthropologic identification of skull-image superimposition. *Journal of Forensic Sciences*, 34(6):1343–1356.

Copeland, A. R. (1989a). Multiple homicides. *American Journal of Forensic Medicine and Pathology*, 10(3):206–208.

Copeland, A. R. (1989b). Suicide among non-whites: The Metro Dade County experience, 1982–1986. *American Journal of Forensic Medicine and Pathology*, 10(1):10–13.

Costello, J. and Zugibe, F. T. (1994). Identification of a homicide victim by a Casio data bank watch. *Journal of Forensic Sciences*, 39(4):1117–1119.

Danto, B. L. and Streed, T. (1994). Death investigation after the destruction of evidence. *Journal of Forensic Sciences*, 39(3):863–870.

Di Maio, V. J. M. (1985). *Gunshot Wounds: Practical Aspects of Firearms, Ballistics and Forensic Techniques*. Elsevier, New York.

Di Maio, V. J. M. and Zumwalt, R. E. (1977). Rifle wounds from high velocity, center-fire hunting ammunition. *Journal of Forensic Sciences*, 22(1):132–140.

Eckert, W. G. (1977). The pathology of self-mutilation and destructive acts: A forensic study and review. *Journal of Forensic Sciences*, 22(1):242–250.

Eisele, J. W., Reay, D. T., and Cook, A. (1981). Sites of suicidal gunshot wounds. *Journal of Forensic Sciences*, 26(3):480–485.

Emson, H. E. (1978). Problems in the identification of burn victims. *Canadian Society of Forensic Science Journal*, 11(3):229–232.

Felthous, A. R. and Hempel, A. (1995). Combined homicide–suicides: A review. *Journal of Forensic Sciences*, 40(5):846–857.

Fossum, R. M. and Descheneau, K. A. (1991). Blunt trauma of the abdomen in children. *Journal of Forensic Sciences*, 36(1):47–50.

Gee, D. J. (1988). A pathologist's view of multiple murder. *Forensic Science International*, 38(1–2):53–65.

Gilliland, M. G. F. and Folberg, R. (1996). Shaken babies—some have no impact injuries. *Journal of Forensic Sciences*, 41(5):729–730.

Glassman, D. M. and Crow, R. M. (1996). Standardization model for describing the extent of burn injuries to human remains. *Journal of Forensic Sciences*, 41(1):152–154.

Goff, M. L. (1991). Comparison of insect species associated with decomposing remains recovered inside dwellings and outdoors on the island of Oahu, Hawaii. *Journal of Forensic Sciences*, 36(3):748–753.

Haglund, W. D., Reay, D. T., and Tepper, S. L. (1990). Identification of decomposed human remains by deoxyribonucleic acid (DNA) profiling. *Journal of Forensic Sciences*, 35(3):724–729.

Haglund, W. D., Reichert, D. G., and Reay, D. T. (1990). Recovery of decomposed and skeletal human remains in the "Green River Murder" investigation. *American Journal of Forensic Medicine and Pathology*, 11(1):35–43.

Henssage, C. (1988). Death time estimation in case work. I. The rectal temperature time of death nomogram. *Forensic Science International*, 38(3–4):209–236.

Henssage, C., Madea, B., and Gallenkemper, E. (1988). Death time estimation in case work. II. Integration of different methods. *Forensic Science International*, 39(1):77–87.

Hirsch, C. S. and Adelson, L. (1976). A suicidal gunshot wound of the back. *Journal of Forensic Sciences*, 21(3):659–666.

Houck, M. M., Ubelaker, D., Owsley, D., Craig, E., Grant, W., Fram, R., Woltanski, T., and Sandness, K. (1996). The role of forensic anthropology in the recovery and analysis of Branch Davidian compound victims: Assessing the accuracy of age estimations. *Journal of Forensic Sciences*, 41(5):796–801.

Howard, J. D., Reay, D. T., Haglund, W. D., and Fligner, C. L. (1988). Processing of skeletal remains: A medical examiner's perspective. *American Journal of Forensic Medicine and Pathology*, 9(3):258–264.

Keppel, R. D. (1995). Signature murders: A report of several related cases. *Journal of Forensic Sciences*, 40(4):670–674.

Kerley, E. R. (1972). Special observations in skeletal identification. *Journal of Forensic Sciences*, 17(3):349–357.

Kerley, E. R. (1976). Forensic anthropology and crimes involving children. *Journal of Forensic Sciences*, 21(2):333–339.

Kerley, E. R. (1978). The identification of battered-infant skeletons. *Journal of Forensic Sciences*, 23(1):163–168.

Kintz, P., Godelar, B., Tracqui, A., Mangin, P., Lugnier A. A., and Chaumont A. L. (1990). Fly larvae: A new toxicological method of investigation of forensic medicine. *Journal of Forensic Sciences*, 35(1):204–207.

Lord, W. D., Goff, M. L., Adkins, T. R., and Haskell, N. H. (1994). The black soldier fly *Hermetia illucens* (Diptera: Stratiomyidae) as a potential measure of human postmortem interval: Observations and case histories. *Journal of Forensic Sciences*, 39(1):215–222.

Mack, Jr., H. (1995). Identification of victims: The beginning of a homicide investigation. *Journal of Forensic Identification*, 45(5):510–512.

Malik, M. O. A. (1971). Problems in the diagnosis of the causes of death in burned bodies. *Journal of the Forensic Science Society*, 11(1):21–28.

Mann, R. W., Bass, W. M., and Meadows, L. (1990). Time since death and decomposition of the human body: Variables and observations in case and experimental field studies. *Journal of Forensic Sciences*, 35(1):103–111.

Masters, N., Morgan, R., and Shipp, E. (1991). DFO, its usage and results. *Journal of Forensic Identification*, 41(1):3–10.

Muramatsu, Y. and Parr, R. M. (1988). Concentrations of some trace elements in hair, liver and kidney from autopsy subjects—relationship between hair and internal organs. *Science of the Total Environment*, 76(1):29–40.

Murphy, G. E., Gantner, G. E., Wetzel, R. D., Katz, S., and Ernst, M. F. (1974). On the improvement of suicide determination. *Journal of Forensic Sciences*, 19(2):276–283.

Owsley, D. W. (1995). Techniques for locating burials, with emphasis on the probe. *Journal of Forensic Sciences*, 40(5):735–740.

Palmer, C. H. and Weston, J. F. (1976). Several unusual cases of child abuse. *Journal of Forensic Sciences*, 21(4):851–855.

Pfau, R. O. and Sciulli, P. W. (1994). A method for establishing the age of subadults. *Journal of Forensic Sciences*, 39(1):165–176.

Pollanen, M. S. and Chiasson, D. A. (1996). Fracture of the hyoid bone in strangulation: Comparison of fractured and unfractured hyoids in victims of strangulation. *Journal of Forensic Sciences*, 41(1):110–113.

Prahlow, J. A. and Lantz, P. E. (1995). Medical examiner/death investigator training requirements in state medical examiner systems. *Journal of Forensic Sciences*, 40(1):55–58.

Prouty, R. E. (1989). The zodiac: An unsolved serial murder. *Journal of Forensic Identification*, 39(3):165–174.

Randall, B. and Jaqua, R. (1991). Gunshot entrance wound abrasion ring width as a function of projectile diameter and velocity. *Journal of Forensic Sciences*, 36(1):138–144.

Rentoul, E. and Smith, H., Eds. (1973). *Glaister's Medical Jurisprudence and Toxicology*, 13th ed. Churchill Livingston, London.

Ressler, R. K. and Douglas, J. E. (1985). Crime scene and profile characteristics of organized and disorganized murderers. *FBI Law Enforcement Bulletin*, 54(8):18–25.

Rhine, J. S. and Curran, B. K. (1990). Multiple gunshot wounds of the head: An anthropological view. *Journal of Forensic Sciences*, 35(5):1236–1245.

Rodriguez, A. (1977). *Handbook of Child Abuse and Neglect*. Medical Examination Publishing, New York.

Rodriquez, W. C. and Bass, W. M. (1983). Insect activity and its relationship to decay rates of human cadavers in East Tennessee. *Journal of Forensic Sciences*, 28(2):423–432.

Rodriquez, W. C. and Bass, W. M. (1985). Decomposition of buried bodies and methods that may aid in their location. *Journal of Forensic Sciences*, 30(3):836–852.

Rumsch, B. J. (1977). Medical examiner report of a Boeing 727-95 aircraft accident. *Journal of Forensic Sciences*, 22(4):835–844.

Simpson, K. (1989). Identification of a firearm in murder without the weapon (a case study). *AFTE Journal*, 21:62.

Skinner, M. F. (1988). Case report in forensic anthropology: Animal and insect factors in decomposition of homicide victim. *Canadian Society of Forensic Science Journal*, 21(1–2):71–81.

Snyder, L. (1977). *Homicide Investigation*, 3rd ed. Charles C Thomas, Springfield, IL.

Spitz, W. U. and Fisher, R. S. (1973). *Medicolegal Investigation of Death: Guidelines for the Application of Pathology to Crime Investigation*. Charles C Thomas, Springfield, IL.

Stephens, B. G. (1979). A simple method for preparing human skeletal material for forensic examination. *Journal of Forensic Sciences*, 24(3):660–662.

Sundick, R. I. (1977). Age and sex determination of subadult skeletons. *Journal of Forensic Sciences*, 22(1):141–144.

Thali, M., Dirnhofer, R., and Vock, P. (2008). *The Virtopsy Approach*. CRC Press, Boca Raton, FL.

Tschirhart, D. L., Klattet, E. C., and Noguchi, T. T. (1989). Wounding characteristics of .38 caliber revolver cartridges. *Journal of Forensic Sciences*, 34(6):1387–1394.

Ubelaker, D. H. (1992). Hyoid fracture and strangulation. *Journal of Forensic Sciences*, 37(5):1216–1222.

Usher, A. (1970). The role of the pathologist at the scene of the crime. *Journal of the Forensic Science Society*, 10(4):213–218.

Vass, A. A., Bass, W. M., Wolt, J. D., Foss, J. E., and Ammons, J. T. (1992). Time since death determinations of human cadavers using soil solution. *Journal of Forensic Sciences*, 37(5):1236–1253.

Vieira, D. N. (1988). Homicidal hanging. *American Journal of Forensic Medicine and Pathology*, 9(4):287–289.

Walker, P. L., Cook, D. C., and Lambert, P. M. (1997). Skeletal evidence for child abuse: A physical anthropological perspective. *Journal of Forensic Sciences*, 42(2):196–206.

Warren, C. P. (1978). Personal identification of human remains: An overview. *Journal of Forensic Sciences*, 23(2):388–395.

Watanabe, T. (1972). *Atlas of Legal Medicine*, 2nd ed. Lippincott, Philadelphia, PA.

Watson, A. A. (1974). Estimation of age from skeletal remains. *Journal of the Forensic Science Society*, 14(3):209–213.

Wertheim, P. A. (1989). Investigation of ritualistic crime scenes. *Journal of Forensic Identification*, 39(2):97–106.

Wright, R. K. and Davis, J. (1976). Homicidal hanging masquerading as sexual asphyxia. *Journal of Forensic Sciences*, 21(2):387–389.

Appendix

ENFSI. (2010). *Guidelines for Best Practise in the Forensic Examination of Digital Technology*. European Network of Forensic Science Institutes, The Hague, The Netherlands (www.enfsi.eu/get_doc.php?uid=326).

USDOJ. (2008). *Electronic Crime Scene Investigation: A Guide for First Responders*, 2nd ed. US Department of Justice, Washington, DC.

Index